Guide to
TEXAS
TAXES

Eric L. Stein

G. Brint Ryan

John R. Ferrell

Sandi Farquharson

Lester C. Rhodes

William M. Samuels

Adina Christian

John P. Skidmore

Contributing Editors

CCH
a Wolters Kluwer business

CCH Editorial Staff

Editors .... Edward Bryant, Robert Wilson, Victor Woo

Production Coordinator .... Zuhriati Tahir

Production .... Roshaini Rashid

This publication is designed to provide accurate and authoritative information in regard to the subject matter covered. It is sold with the understanding that the publisher is not engaged in rendering legal, accounting, or other professional service and that the author is not offering such advice in this publication. If legal advice or other expert assistance is required, the services of a competent professional person should be sought.

ISBN 978-0-8080-2758-4

©2011 CCH. All Rights Reserved.

4025 W. Peterson Ave.
Chicago, IL 60646-6085
800 248 3248

CCHGroup.com

No claim is made to original government works; however, within this Product or Publication, the following are subject to CCH's copyright: (1) the gathering, compilation, and arrangement of such government materials; (2) the magnetic translation and digital conversion of data, if applicable; (3) the historical, statutory, and other notes and references; and (4) the commentary and other materials.

Printed in the United States of America

SUSTAINABLE FORESTRY INITIATIVE   Certified Sourcing
www.sfiprogram.org
SFI-00453

PREFACE

This *Guidebook* gives a general picture of the taxes imposed by the state of Texas and the general property tax levied by the local governments. All references to Texas and federal laws are to the laws as of the date of publication of this book.

The emphasis is on the law applicable to the filing of franchise (margin) tax returns in 2012 for the 2011 report year. However, if legislation has made changes effective after 2011, we have tried to note this also, with an indication of the effective date to avoid confusion.

The taxes of major interest—franchise and sales and use—are discussed in detail. Other Texas taxes, including inheritance taxes, are summarized, with particular emphasis on application, exemptions, returns, and payment.

Throughout the *Guidebook,* tax tips are highlighted to help practitioners avoid pitfalls and use the tax laws to their best advantage.

The *Guidebook* is designed as a quick reference work, describing the general provisions of the various tax laws, rules or regulations, and administrative practices. It is useful to tax practitioners, businesspersons, and others who prepare or file Texas returns or who are required to deal with Texas taxes.

The *Guidebook* is not designed to eliminate the necessity of referring to the law and rules for answers to complicated problems, nor is it intended to take the place of detailed reference works such as the CCH TEXAS TAX REPORTS. With this in mind, specific references to the publisher's Texas and federal tax products are inserted in most paragraphs. By assuming some knowledge of federal taxes, the *Guidebook* is able to provide a concise, readable treatment of Texas taxes that will supply a complete answer to most questions and will serve as a time-saving aid where it does not provide the complete answer.

SCOPE OF THE BOOK

This *Guidebook* is designed to do three things:

1. Give a general picture of the impact and pattern of all taxes levied by the state of Texas and the general property tax levied by local governmental units.

2. Provide a readable quick-reference work for the corporation franchise tax. As such, it explains briefly what the Texas law provides and indicates whether the Texas provision is the same as federal law.

3. Analyze and explain the differences, in most cases, between Texas and federal law.

HIGHLIGHTS OF 2011 TEXAS TAX CHANGES

The most important Texas tax changes that take effect in the 2011 tax year or thereafter that were received by press time are noted in the "Highlights of 2011 Texas Tax Changes" section of the *Guidebook,* beginning on page 11. This useful reference gives the practitioner up-to-the-minute information on changes in tax legislation.

FINDERS

The practitioner may find the information wanted by consulting the general Table of Contents at the beginning of the *Guidebook,* the Table of Contents at the beginning of each chapter, the Topical Index, or the Law and Rule Locator.

The Topical Index is a useful tool. Specific taxes and information on rates, allocation, credits, exemptions, returns, payments, collection, penalties, and remedies are thoroughly indexed and cross-referenced to paragraph numbers in the *Guidebook*.

The Law and Rule Locator is an equally useful finders tool. Beginning on page 385, this finding list shows where sections of Texas statutory law and administrative rules referred to in the *Guidebook* are discussed.

November 2011

ABOUT THE EDITORS

Eric L. Stein, Coordinating Editor

Eric L. Stein is the managing principal of the Austin office of Ryan, a national state and local tax consulting firm. Mr. Stein is the practice leader for the firm's Texas franchise tax consulting practice, and frequently advises and practices on matters of administrative litigation, transactional analysis, and unclaimed property. He has spoken regularly on various state and local tax topics throughout the year, including as guest lecturer at the MPA program at the University of Texas at Austin, and has also authored the BNA Portfolio No. 2400—Texas Franchise Tax.

Early in his career, Mr. Stein served as an administrative law judge and supervising hearings attorney over the franchise tax section for the Comptroller of Public Accounts of the State of Texas. More recently, he advised the Comptroller on state tax matters as a Member to the Industry/Practitioner Liaison Group to the Comptroller. Mr. Stein served as a member of the State & Local Taxation Committee, Nexus Tax Force, and Liaison to NAUPA for the American Institute of Public Accountants, and Chair of the State Taxation Committee, member of the State Taxation Conference Committee, and member of the Regulation and Legislation Council Steering for the Texas Society of Public Accountants.

Mr. Stein obtained his BBA in Accounting from the University of Texas at Austin, his JD from Texas Tech University School of Law, and his LLM from Boston University School of Law. He is licensed as a CPA in Texas and as an attorney in Texas and in Massachusetts.

G. Brint Ryan, Contributing Editor

G. Brint Ryan, M.S., C.P.A., is the Founder and Managing Principal of Ryan, a national state and local tax consulting firm. Mr. Ryan is the practice leader for the firm's transaction tax consulting practice. Mr. Ryan is a graduate of the University of North Texas ("UNT") where he received his Bachelor of Science Degree in Accounting and Master of Science Degree in Accounting with an emphasis in taxation. He was honored as the UNT Department of Accounting's Alumnus of the Year, April 1997, and was named Distinguished Alumnus by the Beta Pi Chapter of Beta Alpha Psi. He formerly served as Chairman of the UNT Accounting Advisory Board.

Mr. Ryan is a member of the American Institute of Certified Public Accountants, the Texas Society of Certified Public Accountants, the Institute for Professionals in Taxation ("IPT"), and the Dallas/Fort Worth State Tax Association. Mr. Ryan serves on the Board of Directors of the Texas Taxpayers and Research Association (TTARA) and previously served as the Executive Director of the Dallas/Fort Worth State Tax Association. He is currently an appointee to the Texas Comptroller's Tax Advisory Group, an advisory committee appointed by Texas Comptroller Carole Keeton Strayhorn to assist with various tax policy matters.

Mr. Ryan is a frequent speaker on state and local tax topics. He regularly appears as a speaker for the IPT, the National Business Institute, the Tax Executives Institute, and the Texas Society of Certified Public Accountants. Mr. Ryan is the recipient of the TSCPA Houston Chapter's "Salute to Excellence Award" for continuing professional education presentations.

John R. Ferrell

John R. Ferrell is a principal with the state and local tax consulting firm of Ryan. With over thirty years of experience in the property tax consulting industry, Mr. Ferrell was one of only six property tax consultants appointed to the first State of Texas Property Tax Consultants Advisory Council where he co-authored the Code of Ethics and Standards of Professional Conduct currently used to regulate licensed property tax consultants in the State of Texas. He was the only property tax consultant directly involved in the successful legislative and constitutional amendment effort that established the Texas Freeport Property Tax Exemption.

Mr. Ferrell is a past President of the Texas Association of Property Tax Professionals where he also served as Vice President and Secretary/Treasurer. He is also a member of the Institute for Professionals in Taxation, International Association of Assessing Officers, Texas Association of Assessing Officers and Texas Taxpayers and Research Association.

Mr. Ferrell received his BBA degree from the University of Texas at El Paso. He also holds a State of Texas Senior Property Tax Consultant's License.

Sandi Farquharson

Sandi Farquharson is a Senior Taxpayer Advocate in Ryan's Controversies and Appeals Group in Austin, Texas. She concentrates her tax controversy practice on sales and use tax, franchise tax, independently procured insurance tax, and unclaimed property. In particular, Ms. Farquharson has had experience in the administrative appeals process of Arizona, California, Florida, Ohio, and Texas. She has also contributed to published materials addressing the Texas franchise tax.

Ms. Farquharson is a member of the Austin Bar Association, Texas Society of Certified Public Accountants, and Institute for Professionals in Taxation. She is a certified public accountant in Texas and is licensed to practice law in both Texas the District of Columbia.

Ms. Farquharson received her BBA degree in accounting, *summa cum laude*, from Baylor University and her JD from the University of Texas at Austin School of Law.

Lester C. Rhodes

Lester C. Rhodes, ASA, is a Principal in the Dallas office of Ryan. Mr. Rhodes has over twenty-five years experience in the appraisal and property tax industry, having served clients in both private industry and government. He served on the American Society of Appraisers USPAP task force from 1998 to 2000 and as the El Paso Area Chapter President of ASA in 1997-98. Mr. Rhodes is a Senior Member of the American Society of Appraisers and an Accredited Senior Appraiser (ASA) in both the Real Property – Ad Valorem, and the Machinery and Technical Specialties – Machinery and Equipment appraisal disciplines. He is a State Certified General Real Estate Appraiser currently licensed in Texas. He is also a licensed Senior Property Tax Consultant in Texas. Mr. Rhodes is a frequent speaker and writer on appraisal and property tax valuation. In addition to the American Society of Appraisers, he is member of the Institute for Professionals in Taxation (IPT) and the Dallas/Fort Worth State Tax Association.

William M. Samuels

William M. Samuels is a Principal in the Houston office of Ryan, a state and local tax consulting practice with a national scope. Mr. Samuels is the firm's oil and gas severance tax practice leader. Mr. Samuels' practice concentrates primarily on multistate production incentives, deductions, and exemptions. In addition to assisting clients with identifying, quantifying, and certifying potential incentives, Mr. Samuels also assists clients with severance tax controversies at the administrative level.

Prior to joining Ryan, Mr. Samuels was employed as a senior manager in a national accounting firm, specializing in state and local tax issues for energy clientele. Mr. Samuels is a member of both the Texas Oil & Gas Association and the Louisiana Mid-Continent Oil & Gas Association.

Mr. Samuels graduated with a BBA degree from the University of Texas at Austin and is a Certified Public Accountant licensed in Texas.

About the Editors

Adina Christian

Ms. Christian is a Director in Ryan's Client Support Services Group, which assists Ryan clients with prompt and accurate responses to their state and local tax questions. During her 29-year career at the Comptroller's Office, Ms. Christian provided advice and guidance to taxpayers, tax practitioners, members of the Legislature and agency employees on state and local sales taxes, motor vehicle taxes, hotel occupancy taxes, motor fuels taxes, oil and gas severance taxes and insurance taxes. She wrote, edited and approved administrative rules, and Tax Policy News and Sales Tax Update publications. In addition, Adina participated in and provided assistance and background to the Comptroller's Tax Policy Committee, the Comptroller's Taxpayer Advisory Group, the Texas Internet Tax Policy Working Group and the Texas E-Commerce and Technology Advisory Group. As Area Manager for Tax Policy, Ms. Christian supervised 45-50 tax professionals responsible for Texas state and local taxes, including sales and use, franchise, insurance, severance, motor fuels, hotel, mixed beverage, and utility receipts.

Ms. Christian represented Texas in the Border States Caucus, the Executive Committee of Multi-State Tax Commission, and the Uniformity Committee of the Multi-State Tax Commission and chaired the Border States Caucus and Sales and Use Tax Subcommittee of the Uniformity Committee.

John P. Skidmore

John P. Skidmore is the Director of Property Tax for Ryan's office in El Paso, Texas. Mr. Skidmore is a licensed Senior Property Tax Consultant and a licensed Real Estate Broker in the State of Texas. He has worked for over fifteen years in the property tax industry with experience in consulting, appraisal and management of a property tax department in a national Real Estate Investment Trust. Mr. Skidmore specializes in larger commercial and industrial properties in Texas and throughout the nation.

Mr. Skidmore received both his BBA and Master of Business Administration degrees from the University of Texas at El Paso. He is a member of the Institute for Professionals in Taxation, the Texas Association of Property Tax Professionals, and the Texas Association of Assessing Officers for which he is currently serving as president of Far West Texas Chapter.

CONTENTS

Chapter		Page
	Highlights of 2011 Texas Tax Changes	11
	Tax Calendar	15

PART I—TABLES

	Tax Rates	19
	Federal/State Key Feature Comparisons	20
	Business Incentives and Credits	26

PART II—FRANCHISE TAX

1.	Rates, Taxpayers Subject, Exemptions	29
2.	Basis of Tax	41
3.	Allocation and Apportionment	59
4.	Credits and Other Tax Incentives	69
5.	Returns and Payment	81
6.	Collection of Tax	95
7.	Taxpayer Remedies	101

PART III—SALES AND USE TAXES

8.	Persons and Transactions Subject to Tax	103
9.	Basis and Rate of Tax	117
10.	Exemptions	191
11.	Returns, Payments, Records, Administration	239
12.	Credits	251
13.	Collection of Tax	253

PART IV—INHERITANCE TAXES

14.	Estate and Generation-Skipping Taxes	259

PART V—PROPERTY TAXES

15.	Property Taxes	265

PART VI—MISCELLANEOUS TAXES

16.	Unemployment Compensation	297
17.	Other State Taxes	307
	Alcoholic Beverages Taxes	307
	Cigarette and Tobacco Products Taxes	308
	Insurance Taxes	310
	Motor Fuel Taxes	314
	Motor Vehicle Registration Fees	324
	Hotel Occupancy Tax	325
	Utilities Taxes	329
	Severance Taxes	330
	Environmental Taxes and Fees	334
	Sexually Oriented Business Admission Fee	335

Chapter		Page
	PART VII—ADMINISTRATION AND PROCEDURE	
18.	Administration, Reports, and Payment	337
19.	Collection of Tax	343
20.	Taxpayer Remedies	353
21.	Texas Resources	363
	PART VIII—DOING BUSINESS IN TEXAS	
22.	Fees and Taxes	379
	PART IX—UNCLAIMED PROPERTY	
23.	Unclaimed Property	381
	Law and Rule Locator	385
	Topical Index	391

HIGHLIGHTS OF 2011 TEXAS TAX CHANGES

The most important 2011 tax changes received by press time are noted below.

Franchise Tax

- *Small business exemption threshold increased*

The small business exemption from the franchise tax for businesses with total revenues less than or equal to $1 million is extended until December 31, 2013. The exemption was scheduled to decrease to $600,000 for 2012. See ¶102. (Sec. 171.002(d), Tax Code)

- *Cost of goods sold deduction for service entities clarified*

Legislation changes the latest date that a corporation can carry forward unused franchise tax credits under the former tax for job creation activities or capital investments from the earlier of the date the credit would have expired under former state law had it continued in existence or December 31, 2012, to the earlier of the date the credit would have expired under former state law had it continued in existence or December 31, 2016. See ¶406. (Uncodified Sec. 31.01, S.B. 1, Laws 2011)

Sales and Use

- *Sales and use tax nexus expanded*

Effective January 1, 2012, a retailer will be considered to be engaged in business in Texas for use tax collection purposes if the retailer holds a substantial ownership interest in, or is owned in whole or substantial part by, a person who maintains a business location in Texas and either (1) the retailer sells the same or a substantially similar line of products under the same or a substantially similar business name as the person with the location in Texas or (2) the facilities or employees of the person with the location in Texas are used to advertise, promote, or facilitate sales by the retailer to consumers or to perform any other activity on behalf of the retailer that is intended to establish or maintain a marketplace for the retailer in Texas, including receiving or exchanging returned merchandise. In addition, a retailer will be considered to be engaged in business in Texas if the retailer holds a substantial ownership interest in, or is owned in whole or substantial part by, a person that (1) maintains a distribution center, warehouse, or similar location in Texas and (2) delivers property sold by the retailer to consumers. Finally, the definition of a "seller" or "retailer" is expanded to include a person who has been entrusted with the possession of tangible personal property and has the power to sell, lease, or rent the property without further action by the owner of the property. See ¶803. (S.B. 1, Laws 2011, 1st Sp. Session)

- *Registration number required for agricultural and timber exemptions*

Beginning January 1, 2012, a registration number issued by the Texas Comptroller must be included on an exemption certificate for claiming certain sales and use tax and motor vehicle sales and use tax exemptions relating to a timber, farm, ranch, or agricultural aircraft operation. The comptroller must develop a procedure for persons to electronically apply for a registration number and an online system for sellers to verify the validity of a registration number. Registration numbers must be renewed every four years. A person is entitled to notice and hearing requirements if the comptroller proposes to revoke the person's registration number. See ¶1002, ¶1003. (Ch. 225 (H.B. 268), Laws 2011)

- *Sales tax holiday dates changed*

Beginning in 2012, the annual Texas sales tax holiday for eligible clothing, footwear, backpacks, and school supplies will take place in July (formerly held in

August). The sales tax holiday dates are now established by first determining the earliest possible date a school district may begin instruction (the first Monday in August), then counting back eight days and finding the Friday before that date. In 2012, the first Monday in August falls on August 6. The eighth day preceding August 6 is Sunday, July 29. The Friday before is July 27. Thus, the sales tax holiday for 2012 will begin at 12:01 a.m. on Friday, July 27, and end at 12 a.m. (midnight) Sunday, July 29, 2012. See ¶1002. (S.B. 1, Laws 2011, 1st Sp. Session)

- *Definition of "sale for resale" amended*

Effective October 1, 2011, a sale for resale includes a sale of tangible personal property to a purchaser who acquires the property for the purpose of transferring it as an integral part of performing a contract or subcontract with the federal government, but only if the purchaser (1) allocates and bills to the contract the cost of the property as a direct or indirect cost and (2) transfers title to the property to the federal government under the contract and applicable federal acquisition regulations. On the other hand, a sale for resale does not include the sale of tangible personal property or a taxable service to a purchaser who acquires the property or service for the purpose of performing a service that is not taxed, unless the tangible personal property or taxable service is purchased for the purpose of reselling it to the United States in a contract or subcontract with any branch of the Department of Defense, Department of Homeland Security, Department of Energy, National Aeronautics and Space Administration, Central Intelligence Agency, National Security Agency, National Oceanic and Atmospheric Administration, or National Reconnaissance Office to the extent allocated and billed to the contract with the federal government. See ¶1003. (S.B. 1, Laws 2011, 1st Sp. Session)

- *Use of Internet hosting services in Texas does not create nexus*

A person whose only activity in Texas is using the Internet hosting services of a Texas provider is not engaged in business in the state for sales and use tax nexus purposes. In addition, a person that provides Internet hosting services in Texas is not required to (1) examine a user's data to determine the applicability of Texas sales and use tax to the user, (2) report a user's activities to the Texas Comptroller, or (3) advise a user as to the applicability of Texas sales and use tax. "Internet hosting" means providing to an unrelated user access over the Internet to computer services using property that is owned or leased and managed by the provider and on which the user may store or process the user's own data or use software that is owned, licensed, or leased by the user or provider. The term does not include telecommunications services. See ¶803. (Ch. 1144 (H.B. 1841), Laws 2011)

- *Purchasing office not a "place of business" for sourcing local tax*

Beginning September 1, 2011, the Texas Comptroller will not recognize a purchasing office as a "place of business of a retailer" for purposes of sourcing local sales tax if (1) the office receives a rebate of local sales and use taxes or (2) a related entity (parent, subsidiary, or affiliate) is able to avoid or reduce its local tax liabilities by establishing or operating the purchasing office in a location with a lower sales tax rate than the former location where the purchasing functions were performed. See ¶904. (Ch. 942 (H.B. 590), Laws 2011)

- *Property attached to dairy farm structures exempt*

A sales and use tax exemption is enacted for tangible personal property incorporated into or attached to a structure that is located on a commercial dairy farm, is used or employed exclusively for the production of milk, and is either a free-stall dairy barn or a dairy structure used solely for maternity purposes, effective September 1, 2011. See ¶1002. (Ch. 225 (H.B. 268) and Ch. 1144 (H.B. 1841), Laws 2011)

Highlights of Tax Changes **13**

- *Taxation of oilfield portable units clarified*

    Oilfield portable units are exempt from motor vehicle sales and use tax and hotel occupancy tax but continue to be subject to sales tax, effective September 1, 2011. An oilfield portable unit is a bunkhouse, manufactured home, trailer, or semitrailer that does not require attachment to a foundation or real property to be functional and is designed and used at an oil, gas, water disposal, or injection well site as temporary lodging or office space by employees, contractors, or other workers. See ¶1002. (Ch. 566 (H.B. 3182), Laws 2011)

- *Sales tax prepayment required in August 2013*

    In August 2013, a taxpayer who reports sales and use taxes on a monthly basis and who pays taxes by electronic funds transfer must remit a tax prepayment by August 20th (for the July 2013 reporting period) that is equal to 25% of the amount the taxpayer owes for the July reporting period. This one-time tax prepayment is in addition to the amount the taxpayer is otherwise required to remit during August. The taxpayer may then take a credit in the amount of the tax prepayment on the tax report due in September 2013. Taxpayers who normally prepay taxes based on a reasonable estimate of tax liability under Sec. 151.424 are not subject to this special tax prepayment. See ¶1104. (S.B. 1, Laws 2011, 1st Sp. Session)

- *Joint statement required on gift of motor vehicle*

    The reduced motor vehicle sales tax on a qualified gift of a motor vehicle from a related person or an estate is available only if a joint statement is filed in person by the recipient of the gift or, as applicable, the person from whom the gift is received or a person authorized to act on behalf of an estate. A motor vehicle title service may not be used to file the statement. The person who files the statement must present to the tax assessor-collector an identification document that bears the person's photograph and meets other requirements. See ¶903. (Ch. 884 (S.B. 267), Laws 2011)

- *Alcoholic beverage sales reports required*

    By the 25th day of each month, each brewer, manufacturer, wholesaler, distributor, or package store local distributor of alcoholic beverages must electronically file with the Texas Comptroller a report regarding the preceding calendar month's net sales made to retailers for each outlet or location covered by a separate retail permit or license number, effective September 11, 2011. See ¶1102. (Ch. 145 (H.B. 11), Laws 2011)

- *Additional $50 penalty imposed on late filing of tax report*

    A $50 penalty will be assessed for the late filing of certain tax reports due on or after October 1, 2011. The penalty is in addition to any other applicable penalty and will be assessed regardless of whether the taxpayer subsequently files the report or whether any taxes or fees were due for the reporting period. The taxes and fees affected by this additional penalty include sales and use tax, hotel occupancy tax, mixed beverage gross receipts tax, motor vehicle gross rental receipts tax, motor vehicle seller finance sales tax, the off-road, heavy-duty diesel equipment surcharge tax, and the 911 prepaid wireless emergency service fee. See ¶1306. (S.B. 1, Laws 2011, 1st Sp. Session)

- *Criminal penalty imposed for failing to pay collected taxes to Comptroller*

    If a person intentionally or knowingly fails to pay collected taxes to the Texas Comptroller, the person commits (1) a Class C misdemeanor if the unpaid tax is less than $50 (formerly, $10,000); (2) a Class B misdemeanor if the unpaid tax is from $50 to $499; (3) a Class A misdemeanor if the unpaid tax is from $500 to $1,499; and (4) a state jail felony if the unpaid tax is $1,500 (formerly, $10,000) or more but less than $20,000. The offense is a felony of the first degree if the unpaid tax is $200,000 or more. See ¶1306. (Ch. 68 (S.B. 934), Laws 2011)

- *Penalty imposed for failing to provide resale records to Comptroller*

If a person intentionally fails to provide the Texas Comptroller with records that document a taxpayer's sale of items that had been obtained using a resale certificate, the person commits (1) a Class C misdemeanor if the tax avoided by the use of the resale certificate is less than $20; (2) a Class B misdemeanor if the tax is from $20 to $199; (3) a Class A misdemeanor if the tax is from $200 to $749; (4) a felony of the third degree if the tax is from $750 to $19,999; or (5) a felony of the second degree if the tax is $20,000 or more. See ¶1306. (Ch. 68 (S.B. 934), Laws 2011)

- *Price of export stamps for customs brokers increased*

The Comptroller's charge to a customs broker for export stamps increased from $1.65 per stamp to $2.10 per stamp, effective September 1, 2011. See ¶1003. (Ch. 904 (S.B. 776), Laws 2011)

Miscellaneous Taxes

- *Hotel occupancy tax provisions amended*

If a taxpayer fails to file a county or municipal hotel occupancy tax report, the county or municipality may determine the amount of tax due by conducting an audit and may perform the audit itself or contract with another person to perform the audit on an hourly rate or fixed-fee basis. If the audit information results in the collection of a concurrent state tax delinquency, the comptroller will distribute a percentage of the amount collected to the municipality or county to defray the cost of the local audit. A 15% penalty shall be imposed only if the tax has been delinquent for at least one complete municipal fiscal quarter. See ¶1707. (Ch. 1152 (H.B. 2048), Laws 2011)

- *Online travel companies' hotel tax liability based on discounted room rate*

Local hotel occupancy taxes were imposed on the discounted room rates that hotels charged online travel companies (OTCs) rather than on the marked-up room rates that consumers paid to the OTCs. Hotels charged the OTC a discounted room rate, to which the OTC added a "markup" to arrive at the online rate displayed on the OTC's website. The OTC charged the consumer's credit card for the marked-up rate. The hotel later invoiced the OTC for the room charge at the discounted rate plus local hotel occupancy taxes based on that amount. The local taxes at issue were imposed on the "cost of occupancy," a term that was not defined. The court held that this phrase could be reasonably interpreted as the amount paid by an OTC to a hotel on the occupant's behalf for the right to use a room. See ¶1707. (*City of Houston v. Hotels.Com, L.P.*, Texas Court of Appeals, Fourteenth District, Houston, No. 14-10-00349-CV, October 25, 2011)

- *Nude entertainment business fee upheld*

A Texas fee on businesses that offered live nude entertainment in combination with alcohol consumption on the premises did not violate the right to free speech under the First Amendment. Reversing a decision by the state court of appeals, the Texas Supreme Court held that the fee was content-neutral and satisfied the constitutional test for content-neutral restrictions on symbolic speech. The fee was not directed at any expressive content in nude dancing, but, rather, at the negative secondary effects of nude dancing when alcohol was consumed (e.g., sexual assault and abuse, prostitution, and disorderly conduct). Because the fee was not content-based, it was not subject to a constitutional strict scrutiny test. The $5 fee per customer was a minimal restriction that could be avoided if a business offered nude entertainment without allowing alcohol to be consumed. See ¶1711. (*Combs v. Texas Entertainment Association, Inc., and Karpod, Inc.*, Texas Supreme Court, No. 09-0481, August 26, 2011)

TAX CALENDAR

The following table lists significant dates of interest to Texas taxpayers and tax practitioners.

Annual Requirements*

Note: For surplus lines agents, prepayment is due by the 15th of the month after the month in which the agent accrues $70,000 or more.

January

1st—Valuation of property fixed for tax purposes

Date that taxable values and qualification for certain property tax exemptions are determined (except for inventories appraised Sept. 1)

Property tax lien attaches to property to secure tax payment, starting point for penalties and interest that will be imposed for the year

10th—If the prior year's property tax bill is not mailed on or before this date, the delinquency date is postponed

20th—Annual state and local sales and use taxes returns due

February

1st—Delinquency date for property taxes imposed the preceding year if split payment and open-date discounts inapplicable

Last day for chief appraiser to deliver applications for special property tax appraisal and exemptions requiring annual applications

Last day for taxpayers, who are eligible to make installment payments due to a disaster declaration, to pay one quarter installment of homestead property taxes

Last day for motor vehicle, boat and outboard motors, heavy equipment and manufactured housing dealers to file dealer's inventory declarations

Last day for appraisal district to give public notice of 2010 capitalization rate used to appraise property with low- and moderate-income housing exemption

2nd—Date that taxes become delinquent if a bill was mailed on or before Jan. 10. Rollback tax for change of use of 1-d-1 land becomes delinquent if taxing unit delivered a bill to the owner on or before Jan. 10

March

1st—Insurance companies' premiums reports and insurance companies' other than life, health, and accident, payments due

Last day to request cooperative housing appraisal

31st—Last day for taxpayers, who are eligible to make installment payments due to a disaster declaration, to pay second quarter installment of homestead property taxes

Last day for qualified community housing development corporations to file listing of property acquired or sold during the past year with the chief appraiser

April

15th—Last day for property owners to file property tax renditions and property information reports unless they request a filing extension in writing

30th—Last day for property owners to file most applications or reports with the county appraisal districts, including: certain exemption applications; notices that property is no longer entitled to an exemption not requiring annual application; applications for special appraisal or notices that property no longer qualifies for 1-d and 1-d-1 agricultural land, timberland, restricted-use timberland, recreational-park-scenic land and public access airport property; railroad rolling stock reports; requests for separate listing of separately owned land and improvements; requests for proportionate taxing of a planned unit development property; requests for separate listing of separately-owned standing timber and land; requests for separate listing of undivided interests; and requests for joint taxation of separately owned mineral interest.

May

1st—Deadline for filing single-family homeowner protests before appraisal review boards
    Deadline for filing single-family homeowner protests before appraisal review boards
15th—Regular annual franchise tax report and payment due
    Independently procured insurance tax due
17th—Last day for property owners to file renditions and property information reports if they requested an extension in writing. For good cause, chief appraiser may extend this deadline another 15 days

June

1st—Last day for property owners to file protest with appraisal review board (or by 30th day after notice of appraised value is delivered, whichever is later) and last day for taxing units to file challenges with appraisal review board (or within 15 days after review board receives appraisal records, whichever is later)
    Last day for taxpayers, who are eligible to make installment payments due to a disaster declaration, to pay third quarter installment of homestead property taxes
    Last day for religious organizations to amend charters and file new applications for property tax exemption (or within 60 days of exemption denial, whichever is later)
30th—Last day to pay Second half of preceding year's property taxes, if split payment option was adopted
    Last day for private schools to amend charters and file new applications for property tax exemption (or within 60 days of exemption denial, whichever is later)

August

1st—Insurance premiums semiannual payment due
2nd—Last day for property owners to apply for September 1 inventory appraisal
    Last day for taxpayers, who are eligible to make installment payments due to a disaster declaration, to pay fourth quarter installment of homestead property taxes
15th—Public utility administrative expense assessment due, if election to report and pay tax quarterly not made
31st—Last day for property owner to give, in writing, correct address to county appraisal district for tax bill; penalties and interest waived if the bill is not sent to the correct address 21 days before delinquency date

October

1st—Tax assessor required to mail property tax bills on this date (or soon after)

December

1st—First half of current year's property taxes due if split payment option adopted

Monthly Requirements

15th—Alcoholic beverage tax and reports due
20th—Mixed beverage tax and reports due
    Gas producer's tax and reports due, second month following production
    Gas first purchasers' reports and tax due, second month after purchases
    Monthly state and local sales and use taxes returns due
    Monthly hotel occupancy tax report and tax due
25th—Gasoline distributors' reports and tax due
    Diesel fuel suppliers' reports and tax due
    Oil producers' report and tax due
    Oil first purchasers' report and tax due
    Petroleum product delivery reports and fees due
Last day—Manufactured housing sales and use taxes payments due
    Coastal protection fee due
    Cigarette distributors' reports due

Cigarette manufacturers' reports due
Distributors' cigar and tobacco products tax payments and reports due
Manufacturers' cigar and tobacco products tax payments and reports due

Quarterly (Jan., April, July, Oct.) Requirements

20th—Quarterly hotel occupancy tax reports and tax due
Quarterly state and local sales and use taxes returns due

25th—Gasoline tax—Interstate truckers' reports and tax due
Diesel fuel tax—Users' and interstate truckers' reports and tax due
Liquefied gas tax—Permitted dealers' and permitted interstate truckers' reports and tax due

Last day—Sulphur production reports and tax due
Report and payment of gross receipts tax of utilities due

Quarterly (Feb., May, Aug., Nov.) Requirements

15th—Public utility administrative expenses assessment due

PART I

TABLES

Tax Rates
¶1	Introduction
¶5	Franchise Tax
¶10	Sales and Use Taxes
¶15	Death Taxes

Federal/State Key Feature Comparisons
¶45	Corporate Income Tax Comparison of Federal/State Key Features

Business Incentives and Credits
¶50	Introduction
¶55	Franchise Tax
¶60	Sales and Use Taxes
¶65	Insurance Taxes

TAX RATES

¶1 Introduction

The tax rates for the major tax types are discussed below.

¶5 Franchise Tax

The franchise (margin) tax rate is generally 1% of the taxpayer's taxable margin. However, a reduced rate of 0.5% of taxable margin applies to taxable entities primarily engaged in retail or wholesale trade. (Sec. 171.002, Tax Code) An "exit" tax is imposed at equivalent rates upon a taxable entity, other than a passive entity, that ceases to be subject to the business margin tax. (Sec. 171.0011) (See ¶102)

A taxable entity with total revenue of $10 million or less may elect to pay the franchise tax by multiplying its apportioned total revenue by 0.575%. (Sec. 171.1016, Tax Code) Tax discounts are also available for small businesses with total revenue of between $300,000 ($600,000 effective January 1, 2012) and $900,000. (Sec. 171.0021, Tax Code) (See ¶102)

Taxable entities with total revenues of $300,000 (increased to $1 million for reports originally due after 2009 and decreased to $600,000 for reports originally due after 2011) or less or whose total tax liability is $1,000 or less, owe no tax, but are required to file returns (¶104).

- *Prior law*

Applicable to reports originally due to be filed prior to January 1, 2008, the franchise tax rates were 0.25% per year of privilege period of net taxable capital and 4.5% of net taxable earned surplus (¶102).

¶10 Sales and Use Taxes

The state sales and use tax rate is 6.25% (¶903). Special state sales and use taxes apply to motor vehicles (6.25%), manufactured housing (5%, on 65% of the sales price), and boats and boat motors (6.25%).

A municipality that has adopted the sales and use taxes authorized by the Municipal Sales and Use Tax Act must impose the tax at the rate of 1% (¶904). A qualified municipality may vote to adopt an additional tax of up to ¹/₂%. A county that has adopted the sales and use taxes authorized by the County Sales and Use Tax Act must impose the tax at the rate of ¹/₂%, unless the county does not include territory within the limits of a municipality, in which case it must impose the tax at the rate of 1% (¶904). Certain counties and municipalities may also impose a tax for crime prevention and control purposes at a rate not to exceed ¹/₂% (¶904). Additional taxes may be imposed by transit authorities, hospital districts, and venue districts (¶904).

¶15 Death Taxes

Texas imposes an estate tax (¶1402) and a generation-skipping transfer tax (¶1408). Both taxes are "pickup" taxes, *i.e.*, the tax is designed to absorb the credit allowed for state death taxes under the federal estate tax and generation-skipping transfer tax laws. However, these taxes are not currently being imposed.

FEDERAL/STATE KEY FEATURE COMPARISONS

¶45 Corporate Income Tax Comparison of Federal/State Key Features

The following is a comparison of key features of the franchise (margin) tax and federal law. Texas franchise (margin) tax is based on total revenues with deductions for either compensation or cost of goods sold (see ¶202). Although federal taxable income is not used as a starting point for computing the franchise (margin) tax, many Internal Revenue Code (IRC) deductions, exclusions, and adjustments are incorporated by reference. Texas incorporates these Internal Revenue Code provisions as in effect for the federal tax year beginning on January 1, 2007, not including any changes made by federal law after that date (see ¶202). Exclusions from total revenues are discussed at ¶203. Details of the expenses includible in deductions for compensation and cost of goods sold may be found at ¶204 and ¶205, respectively.

- *IRC Sec. 27 foreign tax credit*

   Texas has no equivalent to the federal foreign tax credit (IRC Sec. 27).

- *IRC Sec. 40 alcohol fuel credit*

   Texas has no equivalent to the federal alcohol fuel credit (IRC Sec. 40).

- *IRC Sec. 41 incremental research expenditures credit*

   Although Texas does not allow taxpayers to claim a new research credit against the franchise (margin) tax, taxpayers who qualified for the research credit against the former franchise tax, which was based, in part, on the federal research credit, may continue to claim any credit carryovers (see ¶409).

- *IRC Sec. 42 low-income housing credit*

   Texas has no equivalent to the federal low-income housing credit (IRC Sec. 42).

- *IRC Sec. 44 disabled access credit*

   Texas has no equivalent to the federal disabled access credit (IRC Sec. 44).

- *IRC Sec. 45A Indian employment credit*

   Texas has no equivalent to the federal Indian employment credit (IRC Sec. 45A).

- *IRC Sec. 45B employer social security credit*

   Texas has no equivalent to the federal employer social security credit (IRC Sec. 45B).

Part I—Tables

- *IRC Sec. 45C orphan drug credit*

    Texas has no equivalent to the federal orphan drug credit (IRC Sec. 45C).

- *IRC Sec. 45D new markets credit*

    Texas has no equivalent to the federal new markets credit (IRC Sec. 45D).

- *IRC Sec. 45E small business pension start-up costs credit*

    Texas has no equivalent to the federal small business pension start-up costs credit (IRC Sec. 45E).

- *IRC Sec. 45F employer-provided child care credit*

    Texas has no equivalent to the federal employer-provided child care credit (IRC Sec. 45F).

- *IRC Sec. 45K fuel from nonconventional source credit*

    Texas has no equivalent to the federal fuel from nonconventional source credit (IRC Sec. 45K).

- *IRC Sec. 46—Sec. 49 investment credit*

    Texas has no equivalent to the former federal investment credit (repealed effective for property placed in service after 1985) or to the current federal investment credits (IRC Sec. 47, IRC Sec. 48, IRC Sec. 48A, and IRC Sec. 48B). However, with regard to the enterprise zone credits, if the corporation is allowed to carry forward unused credits prior to the repeal, the corporation may continue to apply those credits on or with each consecutive report until the earlier of the date the credit would have expired had it continued in existence, or December 31, 2012 (see ¶403). Under the revised franchise tax, taxable entities are allowed a deduction for the cost of a solar energy device from margin apportioned to Texas (see ¶206).

- *IRC Sec. 51—Sec. 52 (and IRC Sec. 1396, IRC Sec. 1400R) wage credits*

    Texas has no equivalent to the federal work opportunity or welfare-to-work tax credits (IRC Sec. 51 and IRC Sec. 51A), the empowerment zone employment credit (IRC Sec. 1396), or the employee retention credit applicable to employees hired in specific hurricane and tornado disaster areas (IRC Sec. 1400R). However, taxpayers that elect to deduct compensation from total revenues, may deduct wages for which the federal credit was claimed (see ¶204). Taxpayers that elect to claim the cost of goods sold deduction may also deduct the wages for which the federal credit was claimed if the employee for whom the credit was claimed worked on producing the good sold (see ¶205). Additionally, if the corporation is allowed to carry forward unused credits, the corporation may continue to apply credits on or with each consecutive report until the earlier of: the date the credit would have expired prior to the repeal, or December 31, 2012 (see ¶406).

- *IRC Sec. 55—Sec. 59 tax preferences*

    There is no Texas equivalent to the federal alternative minimum tax on tax preference items (IRC Sec. 55—IRC Sec. 59).

- *IRC Sec. 78 deemed dividends*

    Texas excludes from total revenues amounts included in federal taxable income as dividend gross-up under IRC Sec. 78 when the federal foreign tax credit is claimed (see ¶203).

- *Interest on federal obligations*

    Interest received on obligations of the United States is not included in total revenues subject to the franchise (margin) tax (see ¶203).

¶45

- **IRC Sec. 103 interest on state obligations**

The same as federal (IRC Sec. 103) because Texas utilizes line 5, Interest, of federal Form 1120, which excludes interest on tax-exempt state obligations, for purposes of determining a taxpayer's total revenues (see ¶202).

- **IRC Sec. 108 discharge of indebtedness**

Texas does not follow federal IRC Sec. 108 exclusion of discharge of indebtedness income.

- **IRC Sec. 164 income and franchise tax deductions**

Texas does not follow federal law concerning income and franchise tax deductions (IRC Sec. 164). Income taxes, including local state, federal, and foreign income taxes, and franchise taxes that are assessed on the taxable entity based on income may not be included in the cost of goods sold deduction (see ¶205).

- **IRC Sec. 165 losses**

Generally, the same as federal (IRC Sec. 165) because taxable entities subtract bad debt expensed for federal income tax purposes that corresponds to items of gross receipts included in income for the current reporting period or a past reporting period (see ¶203).

- **IRC Sec. 166 bad debts**

The same as federal (IRC Sec. 166) because Texas allows a subtraction from total revenues of bad debt expensed for federal income tax purposes (see ¶203).

- **IRC Sec. 167 and Sec. 168 depreciation**

Taxpayers claiming the costs of goods sold deduction may include the federal deprecation deduction allowed on the 2006 federal return in determining the costs of goods sold. The Texas depreciation deduction does not incorporate post-2006 amendments to IRC Sec. 168 (see ¶205).

- **IRC Sec. 168(f) safe harbor leasing (pre-1984 leases)**

Texas neither references nor contains a provision similar to federal provision governing safe harbor leases (IRC Sec. 168(f)).

- **IRC Sec. 169 pollution control facilities amortization**

Taxpayers claiming the cost of goods sold deduction may include the same amortization expenses deducted on the federal return that are associated with producing the goods for which the cost of goods sold deduction is claimed. In addition, the cost of renting or leasing pollution control equipment used for the production of the goods may be included in the cost of goods sold deduction (see ¶205). Finally, Texas allows deductions for a percentage of the amortized cost of qualified solar energy devices and equipment used in a clean coal project (see ¶206).

- **IRC Sec. 170 charitable contributions**

There is no charitable contributions deduction for purposes of the franchise (margin) tax.

- **IRC Sec. 171 amortizable bond premium**

Texas has no provisions similar to federal law (IRC Sec. 171) concerning the amortization of bond premiums.

- **IRC Sec. 172 net operating loss**

Texas does not follow the federal NOL provisions (IRC Sec. 172). Instead, Texas allows a credit for business loss carryovers incurred by corporations and limited

Part I—Tables

liability companies that were doing business in Texas on May 1, 2006, if the losses were not exhausted on a report filed prior to January 1, 2008 (see ¶402).

- *IRC Sec. 174 research and experimental expenditures*

For taxpayers that claim the cost of goods sold deduction, Texas allows an expanded version of the federal deduction for research and experimental expenditures (IRC Sec. 174) (see ¶205).

- *IRC Sec. 179 asset expense election*

Taxpayers claiming the cost of goods sold deduction may include the same depreciation expenses on their federal return associated with producing the goods for which the cost of goods sold (COGS) deduction is claimed. However, because Texas only incorporates the IRC as in effect on January 1, 2007, Texas does not incorporate the increases to the allowable federal deduction enacted after that date (see ¶205). The limit for the Sec. 179 expense that can be included in COGS for the 2008 franchise tax report is $112,000. The limit for the Sec. 179 expense that can be included in COGS for the 2009 franchise tax report is $115,000. The limit for the Sec. 179 expense that can be included in COGS for the 2010 franchise tax report is $120,000.

- *IRC Sec. 179D energy efficient commercial buildings deduction*

Texas neither incorporated nor has a provision similar to the federal deduction for energy efficient commercial buildings (IRC Sec. 179D).

- *IRC Sec. 190 deduction for barriers removal*

Texas neither incorporates nor has a provision similar to the federal deduction for barriers removal (IRC Sec. 190).

- *IRC Sec. 195 start-up expenditures*

Texas neither incorporates nor has a provision similar to the federal deduction for start-up expenditures (IRC Sec. 195).

- *IRC Sec. 197 amortization of intangibles*

An amortization deduction is available equal to the amount reported on the federal income tax return to the extent associated with and necessary for the production of goods, including recovery described by IRC Sec. 197 (see ¶205).

- *IRC Sec. 198 environmental remediation costs*

Texas has no equivalent to the federal environmental remediation costs deduction (IRC Sec. 198).

- *IRC Sec. 198A disaster costs*

Texas does not incorporate the federal provision that allows taxpayers to currently expense qualified disaster expenses (IRC Sec. 198A).

- *IRC Sec. 199 domestic production activities*

Texas has no equivalent to the federal domestic production activities deduction (IRC Sec. 199).

- *IRC Sec. 243—Sec. 245 dividends received deduction*

Texas excludes from total revenues the federal dividends received deduction to the extend the dividends are included in the total revenues subject to the franchise (margin) tax (see ¶203).

- *IRC Sec. 248 organizational expenditures*

Texas has no equivalent to the federal deduction for organizational expenditures (IRC Sec. 248).

¶45

- **IRC Sec. 301—Sec. 385 corporate distributions and adjustments**

  Generally items of revenue, including gains and losses, are treated for purposes of the revised Texas franchise tax in the same manner as they are treated for federal income tax. Thus, any gains or losses recognized for federal purposes from the deemed sale of assets will be part of total revenue. (IRC Sec. 301—IRC Sec. 385).

- **IRC Sec. 401—Sec. 424 deferred compensation plans**

  Taxpayers that elect to claim the compensation deduction from total revenues may deduct employer contributions made to retirement plans to the extent deductible for federal income tax purposes (see ¶204). In addition, benefits may also be included in the cost of goods sold deduction to the extent the benefits are part of the direct costs of acquiring or producing the goods (see ¶205).

- **IRC Sec. 441—Sec. 483 accounting periods and methods**

  Unless permission is granted by the Comptroller, a taxable entity must use the same accounting methods used in computing federal taxable income to determine its cost of goods sold deduction and to apportion margin (see ¶205, ¶303). Texas franchise (margin) tax reports are based on privilege periods (see ¶501).

- **IRC Sec. 501—Sec. 530 exempt organizations**

  Certain corporations that are tax-exempt for federal income tax purposes under IRC Sec. 501(c) are exempt from Texas franchise (margin) tax. In addition, an entity that is not a corporation, but whose activities would qualify it for an exemption if it were a corporation, may also qualify for an exemption from the tax (see ¶104).

- **IRC Sec. 531—Sec. 547 corporations used to avoid shareholder taxation**

  Texas has no provisions regarding corporations used to avoid shareholder taxation (IRC Sec. 531—IRC Sec. 547). Texas does not impose a tax on accumulated earnings or an additional tax on the undistributed income of personal holding companies (IRC Sec. 541).

- **IRC Sec. 581—Sec. 597 banking institutions**

  Banking corporations and savings and loan associations are treated as taxable entities for the franchise (margin) tax and are subject to the same tax treatment as other taxable entities, except that (1) proceeds received by lending institutions from the principal repayment of loans are excluded from total revenues; (2) the federal tax basis of loans and securities sold is excluded from total revenues; and (3) lending institutions that claim the cost of goods sold deduction may also include interest expense as a cost of goods sold (see ¶103, ¶203, ¶205).

- **IRC Sec. 611—Sec. 638 natural resources**

  Taxpayers claiming the cost of goods sold deduction may deduct the depletion expenses deducted on the federal return associated with producing the goods for which the cost of goods sold deduction is claimed (see ¶205).

- **IRC Sec. 801—Sec. 848 insurance companies**

  There is no Texas equivalent to the federal provisions relating to insurance companies (IRC Sec. 801—IRC Sec. 848). A gross premiums tax is imposed on insurers in lieu of the franchise (margin) tax (see ¶104, ¶1704).

- **IRC Sec. 851—Sec. 860L RICs, REITs, REMICs, and FASITs**

  REMICs and qualified REITs are exempt from the franchise tax. Texas has no special provisions governing RICs, however, it does exempt passive entities from the franchise (margin) tax (see ¶104).

Part I—Tables

- *IRC Sec. 861—Sec. 865 foreign source income*

Texas does not follow the federal foreign sourcing rules (IRC Sec. 861—IRC Sec. 865). Multistate and international businesses that conduct business both inside and outside Texas utilize the state's apportionment rules (see ¶303) for determining whether income is attributable to state sources.

- *IRC Sec. 901—Sec. 908 foreign tax credit*

Texas has no provisions comparable to those relating to the foreign tax credit (IRC Sec. 901—IRC Sec. 908).

- *IRC Sec. 1001—Sec. 1092 gain or loss on disposition of property*

Generally, the same as federal (IRC Sec. 1001—IRC Sec. 1092) because Texas includes income reported on federal Form 1120, line 9, net gain or loss, in total revenues for purposes of calculating the franchise (margin) tax (see ¶202). However, because Texas regulations refer to the 2006 version of Form 1120, differences may arise due to post-2006 federal amendments that relate to basis adjustments related to straddles; like-kind exchange treatment for certain mutual ditch, reservoir or irrigation company stock; and involuntary conversion treatment extended to the May 2007 Kansas tornado victims. Texas also does not follow federal amendments that require the determination of the basis of securities to be done on an account by account basis, effective January 1, 2011.

- *IRC Sec. 1201 alternative capital gains tax*

Texas does not provide for an alternative tax rate on capital gains.

- *IRC Sec. 1211 and Sec. 1212 capital losses*

The same as federal because Texas includes income reported on federal Form 1120, line 8, capital net income, in total revenues for purposes of calculating the franchise (margin) tax (see ¶202).

- *IRC Sec. 1221—Sec. 1260 determining capital gains and losses*

The same as federal because Texas includes income reported on federal Form 1120, line 8, capital net income, in total revenues for purposes of calculating the franchise margin tax (see ¶202).

- *IRC Sec. 1361—Sec. 1379 S corporations*

Texas does not generally follow federal treatment of S corporations (IRC Sec. 1361—Sec. 1379). S corporations are treated as taxable entities subject to the franchise (margin) tax with no special pass-through treatment because Texas has no personal income tax (see ¶104, ¶202).

- *IRC Sec. 1391—Sec. 1397F and IRC 1400E—Sec. 1400J empowerment zones and renewal communities*

Texas has no equivalent to the federal provisions regarding empowerment zones and renewal communities (IRC Sec. 1391—IRC Sec. 1397F and IRC 1400E—IRC Sec. 1400J).

- *IRC Sec. 1400M—Sec. 1400T disaster relief*

Texas does not incorporate federal provisions that, among other things: allow a current deduction for 50% of any qualified Gulf Opportunity Zone clean-up costs and allow Gulf Opportunity Zone public utility disaster losses resulting from Katrina to be deducted in the fifth tax year preceding the loss. However with the exception of the increased IRC Sec. 179 asset expense election for Gulf Opportunity Zone property discussed above, to the extent these provisions impact the amount of depreciation claimed on the federal return, a taxpayer that claims the cost of goods sold deduction may claim the same amount of depreciation claimed on the federal return (see ¶202).

¶45

Because of Texas's current federal conformity date of January 1, 2007, Texas does not follow the recent federal amendments that extend these relief provisions to victims of the tornadoes that hit Kansas in May of 2007.

- *IRC Sec. 1501—Sec. 1504 consolidated returns*

Any corporation that joins in filing a federal consolidated return (IRC Sec. 1501—IRC Sec. 1504) must compute its franchise (margin) as if separate federal returns had been filed (see ¶202). Texas does require combined reporting (see ¶507).

BUSINESS INCENTIVES AND CREDITS

¶50 Introduction

Texas has created a number of tax incentives designed to attract business to the state, stimulate expansion, and/or encourage certain economic activity. These incentives are listed below, by tax, with a brief description and a cross-reference to the paragraph at which they are discussed in greater detail. Exemptions and deductions, which are too numerous to be included below, are discussed under the taxes to which they apply (see the Table of Contents or the Topical Index).

Practice Tip: On-Line Search Service Available

An online research service called Economic Data for Growth and Expansion (EDGE) is available on the Texas Comptroller's website that provides data and analysis, including tax information, to local governments, economic development organizations, and businesses. The expanded research service is designed to provide data and analysis useful in revenue planning, financial analysis, economic forecasting, and site location decisions. The services is available at: http://www.window.state.tx.us/texasedge.html.

¶55 Franchise Tax

Under the franchise (margin) tax, applicable to reports originally due after 2007, with the exception of credits for qualified enterprise projects and the temporary credit for business loss carryforwards, all franchise tax credits are repealed and carryovers of credits accrued may not be claimed on reports filed after 2007, other than carryovers of the research and development, job creation, and capital investment credits (see below).

- *Refund of wages paid to employees receiving financial assistance*

A refund of franchise tax is available for wages paid by a taxpayer to employees who receive state financial assistance and for whom the taxpayer provides or pays for a portion of the cost of qualifying health benefit coverage. The amount of the refund is 20% of total wages, up to $10,000 per employee, paid during the employee's first year of employment (¶2002).

- *Temporary credit for business loss carryovers*

Corporations and limited liability companies that were doing business on May 1, 2006, may claim a credit against the franchise (margin) tax based on business loss carryforwards that were not exhausted on a report originally due prior to 2008 (see ¶402).

- *Enterprise zone project investment credit*

A qualified business may claim a credit against franchise (margin) tax for a capital investment made after 2004 and before 2007, in a qualified enterprise project that was designated as an enterprise project after August 31, 2001, and before 2005. The credit is equal to 7.5% of the qualified capital investment made after 2004 and before 2007 (see ¶403).

- *Research and development credit*

    Corporations may claim unused research and development credits accrued under the former franchise tax, until the credit is exhausted or until December 31, 2027, whichever is earlier (¶405).

- *Economic development credits*

    Corporations operating in a strategic investment area (SIA) or an agricultural processing business operating in a low-population county may claim job creation or qualified capital investment credits established under the franchise tax in effect prior to 2008, until the credits are exhausted or until December 31, 2016, whichever is earlier (¶406).

- *Refund for certain property taxes on property located in reinvestment zone*

    A refund of franchise tax is allowed for franchise taxes paid in a calendar year on property:

    — for which the taxpayer has also paid property taxes to a school district on property that is located in a reinvestment zone;

    — that is wholly or partially exempt from county or municipal property taxes under a tax abatement agreement; and

    — that is not subject to a tax abatement agreement with the school district.

    A taxpayer must make specified investments in the zone in order to qualify (¶407).

- *Refund for job creation in enterprise zone*

    A refund of up to the lesser of 25% of franchise tax paid or $5,000 is available to qualified enterprise zone businesses that create at least 10 new jobs for qualified employees (¶408).

¶60 Sales and Use Taxes

- *Refunds for enterprise zone projects*

    An enterprise project designated by the Texas Department of Economic Development qualifies for a refund of state sales and use taxes. The refund is equal to $2,000 for each new permanent job or retained job that the enterprise project provides for an employee that performs at least 50% of his or her services in the enterprise zone during the designation period. In addition, qualified businesses operating in a zone for at least three consecutive years that retain at least 10 jobs held by qualified employees may claim a one-time refund of sales and use taxes paid on purchases of equipment and machinery for use in the zone (¶1005).

- *Qualified hotel projects*

    During the first 10 years after a qualified hotel project is open for occupancy, the hotel owner is entitled to receive a rebate, refund, or payment of 100% of sales and use taxes paid or collected by the qualified hotel project or businesses located in the project. The hotel project must be owned by a municipality or a nonprofit municipally sponsored local government corporation created under the Texas Transportation Corporation Act and must be within 1,000 feet of a convention center owned by a municipality having a population of 1.5 million or more (¶1005).

- *Cooperative research and development ventures*

    Items that are sold by a joint research and development venture to an entity that participated in the venture are exempt from sales and use taxes if the items were created, developed, or substantially modified by or for the venture. In addition, any items that are *purchased* by the venture for its stated purpose are exempt if certain conditions are satisfied (¶1005).

- *Carbon dioxide capture and sequestration project*

    A sales and use tax exemption is enacted for qualified components used in connection with an advanced clean energy project under the Health and Safety Code or a clean energy project under the Natural Resources Code. The components must be installed to capture carbon dioxide from an anthropogenic emission source, transport or inject carbon dioxide from such a source, or prepare carbon dioxide from such a source for transportation or injection. In addition, the carbon dioxide must be sequestered in Texas either (1) as part of an enhanced oil recovery project that qualifies for a severance tax rate reduction; or (2) in a manner that creates a reasonable expectation that at least 99% of the carbon dioxide will remain sequestered from the atmosphere for at least 1,000 years (¶1005).

- *Media production facility*

    A sale, lease, or rental of a taxable item to a qualified person is exempt from sales and use tax for a maximum of two years if the item is used (1) for the construction, maintenance, expansion, improvement, or renovation of a media production facility at a qualified media production location; (2) to equip a media production facility at a qualified media production location; or (3) for the renovation of a building or facility at a qualified media production location that is to be used exclusively as a media production facility (¶1002).

- *Defense readjustment projects*

    A business designated as a defense readjustment project by the Texas Department of Economic Development is eligible for a refund of state sales and use taxes paid on qualified purchases of equipment or machinery, building materials, labor costs, and electricity and natural gas for use in the zone. The amount is limited to $2,500 for each new permanent or retained job in the readjustment zone (¶1005).

- *Temporary credit for real property contributed to institution of higher education*

    A credit against sales and use taxes is available for 50% of the fair market value of real estate transferred by the taxpayer to an institution of higher education by August 31, 1996. The credit is claimed over a 20-year period (¶1205).

- *Refund of wages paid to employees receiving financial assistance*

    A refund of sales and use taxes is available for wages paid by a taxpayer to employees who receive state financial assistance and for whom the taxpayer provides or pays for a portion of the cost of qualifying health benefit coverage. The amount of the refund is 20% of total wages, up to $10,000 per employee, paid during the employee's first year of employment (¶2002).

¶65 Insurance Taxes

- *Credit for examination and valuation fees*

    A credit against insurance gross premiums tax may be taken for most examination and valuation fees paid by an insurance company during the tax year to or for the use of the State of Texas (¶1704).

- *Credit for qualified capital investments*

    Insurance companies that invest in certified capital companies that provide venture capital to small, early-stage businesses engaged in specified activities and/or low-income community businesses, may claim a nonrefundable credit against insurance gross premiums tax equal to the amount of qualified investment made, but only 10% of the credit may be claimed in any taxable year (¶1704).

PART II

FRANCHISE TAX

CHAPTER 1
RATES, TAXPAYERS SUBJECT, EXEMPTIONS

¶101	Overview of Texas Franchise Tax
¶102	Tax Rates
¶103	Entities Subject to Tax
¶104	Exempt Entities
¶105	S Corporations
¶106	Limited Liability Companies

¶101 Overview of Texas Franchise Tax

In 2006, the 79th Texas legislature enacted major tax reform that made substantial reductions in the Texas property tax rates and substituted a portion of the lost revenue by repealing portions of the franchise tax based on net earned surplus and/or taxable capital and replacing it with a revised franchise (margin) tax. The franchise (margin) tax is applicable to reports originally due after 2007, and is based on a taxable entity's activities undertaken in 2007.

The franchise (margin) tax is levied on taxable entities, including pass-through entities, that are doing business in Texas or that are chartered in Texas. It is imposed on a unitary group basis (¶507). The tax is based on total revenues after certain deductions (¶202).

The franchise (margin) tax is imposed on a much broader class of taxpayers than those subject to the former franchise tax, and includes many limited liability entities exempt from the prior franchise tax (¶103). Sole proprietorships, general partners, real estate investment trusts (REITs), and real estate mortgage investment conduits (REMICs), and other specified entities are exempt from the tax (¶104). In addition, unlike the former franchise tax, a taxable entity includes a combined group for franchise (margin) tax purposes (¶507).

Chapter 1 discusses rates, entities subject to tax, and exempt entities. The basis of tax, including total revenues, and the deduction of compensation and/or cost of goods sold, as well as the computation of net taxable capital and net taxable surplus that applied under the former franchise tax provisions, is discussed in Chapter 2. Allocation and apportionment are discussed in Chapter 3. Credits are the subject of Chapter 4, while returns and payment requirements, including due dates, are discussed in Chapter 5. Collection provisions, with information on penalties and interest, are discussed in Chapter 6. Taxpayer remedies may be found in Chapter 7.

For information concerning the franchise tax in effect for returns due prior to 2008, consult prior issues of the Guidebook to Texas Taxes.

¶102 Tax Rates

Law: Secs. 171.001, 171.0011, 171.002, 171.0021, 171.005, 171.1016, Tax Code; 34 TAC Sec. 3.592 (CCH TEXAS TAX REPORTS, ¶10-380).

The rate of the franchise (margin) tax is generally 1% of the taxpayer's taxable margin. However, a reduced rate of 0.5% of taxable margin applies to taxable entities primarily engaged in retail or wholesale trade. (Sec. 171.002, Tax Code) Retail trade and wholesale trade are defined in reference to Division F and G of the federal Office of Management and Budget's 1987 Standard Industrial Classification Manual.

An entity is primarily engaged in a retail or wholesale trade if:

—more than half of its revenues come from retail or wholesale trade activities;

—for an entity not engaged in restaurant or bar activities, less than half of its total wholesale or retail trade activity revenues comes from sales of products produced by the entity or its affiliates; and

—the entity does not provide retail or wholesale utilities, such as telecommunications services or electricity or gas. (Sec. 171.002(c), Tax Code)

Effective January 1, 2012, apparel rental companies will also qualify for the 0.5% rate as retail trade.

CCH Practice Tip: Annualized revenue requirements

The discounts on tax due based on total revenue amounts less than $900,000 or less than or equal to $1 million effective January 1, 2010 and through December 31, 2013 (discussed below) and qualification for the E-Z computation are typically based on a 12-month (365 day) accounting period. Note, however, that when the accounting period upon which the report is based is more or less than 12 months, a taxable entity must annualize its total revenue calculation to determine its eligibility for these provisions. To annualize total revenue, a taxable entity must divide total revenue by the number of days in the period upon which the report is based, and then multiply the result by 365. (*Tax Policy News, Vol. XVIII, Issue 3*, Texas Comptroller of Public Accounts, March 2008).

- *E-Z computation and tax rate*

A taxable entity whose total revenue from its entire business is not more than $10 million may elect to pay the tax as calculated under the E-Z computation method. The amount of tax is computed by:

(1) determining the taxable entity's total revenue from its entire business;

(2) apportioning the total revenue amount to determine the entity's apportioned total revenue; and

(3) multiplying the apportioned total revenue by 0.575%.

Taxpayers that elect to use the E-Z computation method may not take a credit, deduction, or other adjustment, other than the discount for small businesses discussed immediately below. (Sec. 171.1016, Tax Code) A deduction for cost of goods sold or compensation is not allowed.

- *Discounts for small businesses*

There is a discount of the tax imposed for small businesses with total revenues of between $300,000 and $900,000. The discount is applied after calculating the tax using the appropriate tax rate and applying any allowable tax credits. The amount of the discount is determined on the basis of the taxpayer's total revenue. For tax years 2008 and 2009 the small business tax discount was applied as follows:

— 80% for entities with total revenues of more than $300,000 but less than $400,000;

— 60% for entities with total revenues of $400,000 or more and less than $500,000;

— 40% for entities with total revenues of $500,000 or more and less than $700,000; and

— 20% for entities with total revenues of $700,000 or more but less than $900,000.

¶102

Part II—Franchise Tax

> **CCH Practice Tip: Discounts for 2010 and 2011**
>
> The small business exemption from the revised franchise tax increased from business with total revenues less than or equal to $300,000 to less than or equal to $1 million for the years 2010 through 2013 and will then decrease to $600,000 effective January 1, 2014. (Sec. 171.002(d), Tax Code)

The amounts above will be indexed for inflation every other year, beginning January 1, 2010.

Effective January 1, 2014, the discount will be determined as follows:

— 40% for entities with total revenues of greater than $600,000 and less than $700,000; and

— 20% for entities with total revenues of $700,000 or more but less than $900,000.

(Sec. 171.0021, Tax Code)

- *Additional tax*

An additional tax is imposed on a taxable entity, other than a passive entity (see ¶104), that ceases to be subject to the business margin tax. Although the statute refers to this tax as an "additional tax", a better name might be an "exit" tax.

The additional tax is equal to 1% (0.5% for wholesalers or retailers) of the taxable entity's taxable margin computed on the period beginning on the day after the last day for which the tax was computed and ending on the date the taxable entity is no longer subject to the tax. The additional tax and any required report are due on the 60th day after the date the taxable entity ceases to be subject to the margin tax. (Sec. 171.0011, Tax Code; 34 TAC Sec. 3.592)

¶103 Entities Subject to Tax

Law: Secs. 171.001, 171.002, 171.101, 171.1015, 171.109, 171.110, Tax Code; 34 TAC Sec. 3.581 (CCH Texas Tax Reports, ¶¶ 10-075, 10-210, 10-240).

Except as discussed at ¶104, a taxable entity includes a partnership (other than general partnership comprised solely of partners who are natural persons), limited liability partnership, corporation, banking corporation (other than a bank holding company), savings and loan association, limited liability company, business trust, professional association, business association, joint venture, joint stock company, holding company, or other legal entity. (Sec. 171.002, Tax Code; 34 TAC Sec. 3.581)

The term also includes a combined group, see ¶507 for details.

A joint venture does not include qualified joint operating or co-ownership arrangements that elect out of federal partnership treatment under IRC 761(a). (Sec. 17.002, Tax Code)

- *Tiered partnership arrangements*

A tiered partnership arrangement is an ownership structure in which any of the interests in one taxable entity treated as a partnership or S corporation (a "lower-tier" entity) are owned by one or more other taxable entities (an "upper-tier" entity). A tiered partnership arrangement may have two or more tiers.

An upper-tier taxable entity may pay the tax on the taxable margin of a lower-tier entity if the lower-tier entity submits a report to the Comptroller showing the amount of taxable margin that each upper-tier entity that owns it should include within the upper-tier entity's own taxable margin, according to the profits interest of the lower tier entity. A lower-tier entity is not required to pay a franchise (margin) tax on any taxable margin so reported. However, the upper-tier entity must pay tax on its and the lower-tier entity's taxable margin. (Sec. 171.1015, Tax. Code)

This tiered entity reporting arrangement is not available to a lower-tier entity that is included in a combined group. A lower tier entity that is not part of a combined group may choose to report total revenue to any or all of its upper tier entities. The lower tier entity must submit a franchise tax report for the total revenue that remains with the lower tier entity. The lower tier entity does not reduce its cost of goods sold or compensation deduction based on the amount of total revenue reported to the upper tier entities. (*Tax Policy News, Vol. XVIII, Issue 1*, Texas Comptroller of Public Accounts, January 2008)

Practice Note: Compliance Tips

The requirements for filing under the tiered partnership provision are:

— all taxable entities involved in the tiered partnership election must file a franchise tax report, a Public Information Report (Form 05-102) or Ownership Information Report (Form 05-167), and the Tiered Partnership Report (Form 05-175);

— both the lower and the upper tier entities must blacken the tiered partnership election circle on their tax reports;

— total revenue may be passed only to upper tier entities that are subject to the Texas franchise tax;

— deductions (cost of goods sold or compensation) may not be passed to upper tier entities;

— total revenue must be passed to taxable entities based on ownership percentage;

— upper tier entities may file a No Tax Due Report (Form 05-163) only if the lower tier entity has less than $300,000 ($1 million for reports due after 2009) in annualized total revenue before total revenue is passed to the upper tier entities;

— upper tier entities may use the E-Z Computation (Form 05-169) only if the lower tier entity has $10 million or less in annualized total revenue before total revenue is passed to the upper tier entities; and

— upper tier entities may not take a discount greater than the discount that is allowed for the lower tier entity before total revenue is passed to the upper tier entities. (*Press Release*, Office of the Texas Comptroller, May 6, 2009)

- *Nexus and P.L. 86-272*

The franchise tax extends to the limits of the U.S. Constitution and federal law. An entity is "doing business" in Texas for the purpose of the franchise (margin) tax if it has sufficient contact with Texas to be taxed without violating the U.S. Constitution. Consistent with this doctrine, the Texas Comptroller has held that an out-of-state retailer can have "physical presence" with a state if the seller's activities, whether conducted by an employee or agent, or by an independent contractor, are significantly associated with the seller's ability to establish and maintain a market in the state. (*Comptroller's Decision No. 46,540*, Texas Comptroller of Public Accounts, May 10, 2006, received July 2006, CCH Texas Tax Reports, ¶ 403-121)

In addition to the standard nexus-creating activities of having employees or owned or leased property located within Texas or performing services in Texas, the following list of activities, although not all inclusive, establish nexus for purposes of the franchise (margin) tax (34 TAC Sec. 3.586):

— *contracting:* performance of a contract in Texas regardless of whether the taxable entity brings its own employees into the state, hires local labor, or subcontracts with another;

— *delivering:* delivering into Texas items it has sold;

¶ 103

Part II—Franchise Tax

— *franchisors:* entering into one or more franchise contracts with persons, corporations, or other business entities located in Texas;

— *holding companies:* maintaining a place of business in Texas or managing, directing, and/or performing services in Texas for subsidiaries or investee entities;

— *inventory:* having an inventory in Texas or having spot inventory for the convenient delivery to customers, even if the bulk of orders are filled from out of state;

— *loan production activities:* soliciting sales contracts or loans, gathering financial data, making credit checks, collecting accounts, repossessing property or performing other financial activities in Texas through employees, independent contractors, or agents, regardless of whether they reside in Texas;

— *partners:* acting as a general partner in a general or a limited partnership that is doing business in Texas;

— *services,* including, but not limited to maintaining or repairing property located in Texas whether under warranty or by separate contract; conducting training classes, seminars or lectures in Texas; and investigating, handling or otherwise assisting in resolving customer complaints in Texas;

— *shipment:* sending materials to Texas to be stored awaiting orders for their shipment;

— *solicitation:* having employees, independent contractors, agents, or other representatives in Texas, regardless of whether they reside in Texas, to promote or induce sales of the foreign taxable entity's goods or services; or

— *telephone listing:* having a telephone number that is answered in Texas.

In the franchise (margin) tax enacting legislation, the Texas Legislature stated that the franchise (margin) tax is not an income tax and P.L. 86-272 does not apply to the tax. (Uncodified Section 21, H.B. 3, Laws 2006) However, the classification of the franchise (margin) tax as an income or franchise tax is not at all clear. Many people feel that the margin tax is indeed an income tax and it is quite likely that this issue will have to be resolved by the courts. It is questionable how much of an impact the legislature's statement would have in the judicial forum as P.L. 86-272 is a federal standard and a federal standard cannot be overridden by state law.

Texas follows the *Joyce* rule, not the *Finnigan* rule, for non-nexus unitary entities.

CCH Advisory: COA Does Not Establish Nexus

The Comptroller of Public Accounts cannot constitutionally impose Texas franchise tax against a company whose only contact with Texas is the possession of a certificate of authority to do business in the state. This sole contact, with no physical presence in the state, is insufficient under the Due Process and Commerce Clauses of the U.S. Constitution to establish substantial nexus with Texas (*Bandag Licensing Corp.*, 18 S.W.3d 296 (Tex. CtApp 2000), *cert. denied* 2001, CCH TEXAS TAX REPORTS, ¶402-114). As a result of this decision, Texas law was amended by 2003 legislation (H.B. 2424) to repeal the tax on foreign businesses that held a certificate of authority in Texas but were not conducting business in Texas.

The Texas Tax Commission took the position that a corporation hiring legal counsel to defend itself in litigation in Texas did not create nexus for the former Texas franchise tax purposes. (*Letter*, Texas Comptroller of Public Accounts, No. 200311234L, November 21, 2003, CCH TEXAS TAX REPORTS, ¶402-614)

In addition, the mere holding of a membership interest in an LLC that is doing business in Texas does not create nexus for a non-Texas multi-member LLC. Thus, the Texas Comptroller ruled that if a multi-member LLC was not organized in Texas and

¶103

its only contact with the state was its ownership interest in the single-member LLC, it was not subject to franchise tax. (*Letter*, Texas Comptroller of Public Accounts, No. 200606695L, June 1, 2006, CCH TEXAS TAX REPORTS, ¶403-149) However, it should be noted that this letter was issued prior to the enactment of the franchise (margin) tax combined reporting requirements (see ¶507).

¶104 Exempt Entities

Law: Secs. 171.001, 171.002, 171.003, 171.051—171.088, 171.107, Tax Code; 34 TAC Secs. 3.541, 3.566 (CCH TEXAS TAX REPORTS, ¶10-245).

Comparable Federal: Sec. 501(c) (CCH U.S. MASTER TAX GUIDE ¶602).

The same organizations exempt under the former franchise tax law are also exempt from the franchise (margin) tax (see discussion below). In addition, the following entities are also exempt from the franchise (margin) tax:

— sole proprietorships, other than entities that are sole proprietorships whose liability is limited by any state's law or other country's statutes (e.g., single member limited liability companies) (*Letter*, Texas Comptroller of Public Accounts, No. 200609763L, September 8, 2006, CCH TEXAS TAX REPORTS, ¶403-182);

— nonbusiness trusts;

— estates of natural persons;

— an escrow;

— general partnerships comprised solely of partners who are natural persons. Similarly, a joint venture that is wholly and directly owned by natural persons is not a taxable entity (*Letter No. 200810206L*, Texas Comptroller of Public Accounts, October 20, 2008, CCH TEXAS TAX REPORTS, ¶403-512);

— a noncorporate entity who's activities would qualify for a specific exemption if it were a corporation (Sec. 171.088, Tax Code);

— real estate mortgage investment conduits (REMICs);

— insurance companies subject to the Texas gross premiums tax, regardless of whether any gross premiums taxes are actually paid in any given year (Sec. 171.002, Tax Code; 34 TAC Sec. 3.583). Note: surplus line insurers are subject to franchise tax (*Tax Policy News*, Texas Comptroller of Public Accounts, August 2009);

— a nonprofit self-insurance trust;

— a qualified trust under IRC Sec. 401(a); and

— a voluntary employee's beneficiary association trust or other entity that is exempt under IRC Sec. Section 501(c)(9).

Real estate investment trusts (REITs) and qualified REIT subsidiaries are also exempt. However, a REIT is only exempt if it holds interests in a limited partnership or other entities that are taxable entities and that directly hold real estate; and the REIT does not directly hold real estate, other than real estate it occupies for business purposes.

Effective for franchise (margin) tax reports due on or after January 1, 2012, qualified live event promotion companies may exclude from total revenue payments made to an artist in connection with the provision of a live entertainment event or live event promotion services and qualified courier and logistics companies may exclude from total revenue payments made by the taxable entity to nonemployee agents for the performance of delivery services on behalf of the taxable entity.

Part II—Franchise Tax   **35**

> **CCH Caution: Insurance Companies May Lose Exemption**
>
> Effective January 1, 2008, an insurance company that violates an order issued by the Texas Department of Insurance because of excessive or unfairly discriminatory rates becomes subject to the Texas franchise tax. Such an order may be issued if the Commissioner of Insurance determines that an insurance company has used an excessive or unfairly discriminatory rate to determine premiums for personal automobile or residential property insurance. (*Letter*, Texas Comptroller of Public Accounts, No. 200606639L, June 1, 2006, CCH Texas Tax Reports, ¶ 403-109)

- *Small business exemption*

Texas offers a small business exemption for qualifying taxpayers. Currently the exemption applies to qualified taxpayers with total revenues less than or equal to $1 million. For tax years 2008 and 2009 taxpayers with less than $300,000 of revenue were exempt from the revised franchise tax. (Sec. 171.002(d), Tax Code; 34 TAC Sec. 3.584)

The small business exemption increased effective January 1, 2010 and through December 31, 2013 (previously, through December 31, 2011). The exemption from the revised franchise tax increased from business with total revenues less than or equal to $300,000 to less than or equal to $1 million for the years 2010 through 2013 and will then decrease to $600,000 effective January 1, 2014. (Sec. 171.002(d), Tax Code as amended by S.B. 1, § 37.01, Laws 2011, effective September 28, 2011)

- *Passive entities*

An entity is not subject to the franchise (margin) tax, if during the period on which the report is based, the entity qualifies as a "passive entity." (Sec. 171.001(c), Tax Code) A passive entity is a general or limited partnership or trust (other than a business trust), that receives less than 10% of its federal gross income from conducting an active trade or business. In addition, the entity's federal gross income must consist of at least 90% of the following:

— dividends, interest, foreign currency exchange gain, periodic and nonperiodic payments with respect to notional principal contracts, option premiums, cash settlement or termination payments with respect to a financial instrument, and income from a limited liability company;

— distributive shares of partnership income to the extent that those distributive shares of income are greater than zero;

— capital gains from the sale of real property, or gain from the sale of commodities traded on a commodities exchange or from the sale of securities; and

— royalties, bonuses, or delay rental income from mineral properties and income from other nonoperating mineral interests.

(Sec. 171.0003, Tax Code)

Passive entities that are registered or are required to be registered with either the Texas Secretary of State (SOS) or the Comptroller's office will be required to file an annual report affirming that the entity qualifies as a passive entity for the period upon which the tax is based. Previously, an entity that filed as passive on a prior report was not required to file a subsequent franchise tax report, so long as the entity continued to qualify as passive. A passive entity that is registered or is required to be registered with the SOS or the Comptroller's office must now annually file Form 05-163, No Tax Due Information Report, as a passive entity. Passive entities are not required to file Form 05-167, Ownership Information Report. (2011 Texas Franchise Tax Report Information and Instructions)

¶104

> **CCH Comment: Active Trade or Business**
>
> A regulation specifies that activities performed by the entity include activities performed by persons outside the entity, including independent contractors, to the extent that the persons perform services on behalf of the entity and those services constitute all or part of the entity's trade or business. (34 TAC Sec. 3.582)

Compliance tips—A partnership or trust that is registered with the Comptroller's office or with the Texas Secretary of State's office must establish its passive status by filing a No Tax Due Information Report (Form 05-163) for the period upon which the tax is based and must blacken the circle in Item 1, enter the accounting period in Items 5a and 5b and sign the report. Passive entities are not required to file an Ownership Information Report (Form 05-167). A partnership or trust that qualifies as a passive entity for the period upon which the franchise tax report is based, and is not registered with the Comptroller's office or with the Texas Secretary of State's office, does not have to register with or file a franchise tax report with the Comptroller's office.

An entity that filed as passive on the 2008 report is not required to file a subsequent franchise tax report, as long as the entity continues to qualify as passive.

Any passive entity, whether or not it is registered with the Comptroller's office or with the Secretary of State's office, that subsequently loses its status as passive, must file a Nexus Questionnaire (Form AP-114) or a Business Questionnaire (Form AP-224) to register with the Comptroller's office and file a franchise tax report for the period in which the passive status is lost and any subsequent periods until the entity establishes itself once again with the Comptroller's office as a passive entity. (*Tax Policy News*, Texas Comptroller of Public Accounts, April 2009)

- *Corporations exempt from federal income tax*

A corporation exempt from federal income tax under IRC Sec. 501(c)(2), (3), (4), (5), (6), (7), (8), (10), (16), (19), or (25) is exempt from Texas franchise tax. Such a corporation may establish its exempt status for franchise tax purposes by furnishing the Comptroller with a copy of the federal exemption letter or evidence that the corporation has applied in good faith for a federal tax exemption. A copy of the federal exemption letter must be filed within 15 months after the last day of the calendar month that is nearest to the date of the corporation's charter or certificate of authority.

A corporation may establish its exemption from franchise tax by filing evidence that it applied in good faith for the federal exemption within the past 15-month period and the IRS has not yet issued the federal exemption letter. No penalty is imposed on the corporation from the date of the corporation's charter or certificate of authority until the date of the final federal denial if the application for the exemption is finally denied by the IRS.

> **CCH Caution: Political Organizations Not Exempt**
>
> A political organization (PAC) exempt from federal income tax under IRC Sec. 527 is not exempt from Texas franchise tax because it is not among the entities specified as exempt under the franchise tax law (*Comptroller of Public Accounts Letter*, No. 200503036L, March 9, 2005, CCH TEXAS TAX REPORTS, ¶402-888).

- *Other exempt corporations*

Insurance companies required to pay an annual gross receipts tax, including nonadmitted captive insurance companies that are required to pay a gross premium receipts tax are exempt from the franchise tax (¶1704). The exemption is available

¶104

Part II—Franchise Tax

regardless of whether the gross premium tax is actually paid. (Proposed 34 TAC Sec. 3.583) However, an insurance company that violates an order issued by the Texas Department of Insurance because of excessive or unfairly discriminatory rates is subject to the franchise tax, effective January 1, 2008. (*Letter No. 200606639L*, Texas Comptroller of Public Accounts, June 1, 2006).

The following corporations are specifically exempted from franchise tax under Texas law (Sec. 171.051, Tax Code, et seq.):

— railway terminal corporations having no annual net income from business (Sec. 171.053, Tax Code);

— open-end investment companies;

— corporations engaged solely in the business of manufacturing, selling, or installing solar energy devices;

— corporations organized solely to promote the public interest of a county, city, town, or another area in the state (an entity will not be considered to be promoting the public interest if it engages in activities to promote or protect the private, business, or professional interests of its members or patronage (34 TAC Sec. 3.583));

— nonprofit corporations organized for the purpose of religious worship, or solely for educational purposes, or purely for public charity (Secs. 171.058, 171.061, 171.062, Tax Code), corporations organized for the purpose of nontheistic belief systems qualify as well (*Ethical Society of Austin v. Rylander*, 110 S.W.3d 458 (Tex. CtApp 2003), denial of petition for review, Texas Supreme Court, No. 03-0479, April 23, 2004; CCH Texas Tax Reports, ¶402-484);

— nonprofit corporations organized to: (1) provide places of burial; (2) hold agricultural fairs and encourage agricultural pursuits; (3) educate the public about the protection and conservation of fish, game, other wildlife, grasslands, or forests; (4) construct, acquire, own, lease, or operate a natural gas facility on behalf and for the benefit of a city or residents of a city; or (5) provide a convalescent home or other housing for persons who are at least 62 years old or who are handicapped or disabled;

— nonprofit corporations engaged solely in the business of owning residential property for the purpose of providing cooperative housing for persons;

— cooperative associations incorporated under the Cooperative Association Act or under Chapter 301, Subchapter B, Health and Safety Code;

— marketing associations, lodges, farmers' cooperative societies, housing finance corporations, hospital laundry cooperative associations, cooperative credit associations, credit unions, electric cooperative corporations, and telephone cooperative corporations incorporated under Texas law;

— nonprofit corporations organized under the Development Corporation Act of 1979;

— nonprofit corporations organized and operated primarily to obtain, manage, construct, and maintain the property in or of a residential condominium or residential real estate development, if the owners of individual lots, residences, or residential units (other than a single individual or family, or one or more developers, declarants, banks, or similar parties) control at least 51% of the corporation's votes;

— nonprofit corporations organized for the sole purpose of and engaging exclusively in providing emergency medical services, including rescue and ambulance services;

¶104

— corporations whose only business activity in the state is the occasional solicitation of orders at trade shows (less than five solicitation periods of 120 hours or less per business period (34 TAC Sec. 3.583(j));

— corporations engaged solely in the business of recycling sludge, as defined in the Solid Waste Disposal Act;

— corporations formed by the Texas National Research Laboratory Commission under Government Code Sec. 465.008(g);

— nonprofit corporations organized for student loan funds or student scholarship purposes;

— state cooperative credit associations, federal production credit associations, and agricultural credit associations; and

— farm mutual, local mutual aid, and burial associations under Article 4.10, Sec. 14, Insurance Code.

CCH Comment: Exemptions Clarified

Regulation 34 TAC Sec. 3.583(d) clarifies the exemption eligibility for the religious, charitable, and educational organizations. The regulation makes it clear that eligibility for these exemptions is fairly restrictive and provides listings of the types of organizations that are ineligible for the exemption.

- *Application procedures*

Organizations must submit a written application to the Comptroller's office specifying the particular provision of the Tax Code under which the exemption is claimed and detailing the organization's past, current, and proposed activities that substantiate its eligibility for the exemption. If the application is approved, the exemption is granted retroactively back to the first date the entity was eligible for the exemption, and the entity may claim a refund of any franchise taxes paid prior to the approval of the exemption. If the effective date of the exemption occurs after the beginning of a privilege period, the entity must pay through the end of such privilege period. An entity that has been subject to the tax and becomes eligible for exemption is liable for the "additional tax" discussed at ¶102. Organizations that are denied an exemption may pay any tax, penalties, and interest due and appeal the denial or request a redetermination hearing if the Comptroller issues a deficiency determination. (34 TAC Sec. 3.583)

A nonprofit organization that has been exempted from the federal income tax under specified provisions of IRC Sec. 501(c) is automatically exempt from the franchise (margin) tax upon furnishing to the Comptroller a copy of a IRS's current exemption letter. Provisional state tax exemptions are available to taxpayers applying for a federal exemption. An entity denied the federal exemption must file reports and pay all franchise taxes due since its beginning date. However, late filing and payment penalties will be waived for any reports and payments postmarked within 90 days after the date of the final denial of the federal exemption if a written request for penalty waiver and a copy of the letter denying the federal exemption is filed when the entity files it franchise reports and pays its outstanding taxes.

The loss of an organization's federal exemption automatically terminates its state exemption and the entity is responsible for reporting the loss of the federal exemption to the Comptroller within 30 days of its change of status. (34 TAC Sec. 3.583)

¶105 S Corporations

Law: Sec. 171.0002, Tax Code (CCH Texas Tax Reports, ¶10-215).

S corporations are treated like any other taxable entity with no special pass-through treatment because Texas has no personal income tax. (see ¶103 and ¶202).

Part II—Franchise Tax

¶106 Limited Liability Companies

Law: Sec. 171.0002 (CCH Texas Tax Reports, ¶10-225).

Comparable Federal: (CCH U.S. Master Tax Guide ¶402B).

Limited liability companies (LLCs) are subject to the franchise tax and are generally treated in the same manner as C corporations under the current franchise (margin) tax (see ¶103).

FRANCHISE TAX

CHAPTER 2

BASIS OF TAX

¶201	In General
¶202	Starting Point for Computation of Franchise (Margin) Tax
¶203	Exclusions From Total Revenues
¶204	Compensation Deduction
¶205	Cost of Goods Sold Deduction
¶206	Other Deductions
¶207	Special Taxpayers

¶201 In General

The franchise (margin) tax is imposed on a taxpayer's apportioned taxable margin after specified deductions are claimed. The tax base is based on a taxpayer's total revenues (¶202) and is much broader than the former franchise tax based on earned surplus and/or taxable capital. Special rules for calculating an entity's taxable revenues apply to lending institutions, legal service providers, health care providers, health care institutions, and entities filing a combined report (see ¶207, ¶507). Taxpayers may then elect to deduct either 30% of the gross revenues, or deductions for compensation or costs of goods sold (¶202, ¶204, ¶205).

Allocation and apportionment of the franchise tax is discussed in Chapter 3.

¶202 Starting Point for Computation of Franchise (Margin) Tax

Law: Secs. 171.002, 171.101, 171.1011, Tax Code; 34 TAC Sec. 3.584 (CCH TEXAS TAX REPORTS, ¶10-510, 10-515).

A taxable entity's taxable margin is computed by determining the lesser of:

—70% of the taxable entity's total revenue from its entire business; or

—the entity's total revenues less cost of goods sold (COGs) or compensation.

Staff leasing companies are prohibited from deducting cost of goods sold. (Sec. 171.101(b), Tax. Code)

CCH Practice Tip: Making the Election

Taxpayers must elect to utilize the COGs or compensation deduction by the latest of the due date, the extended due date, or the date the report is filed. (*Letter No. 200803059L*, Texas Comptroller of Public Accounts, March 20, 2008, CCH TEXAS TAX REPORTS, ¶403-384) If no election is made or if an election is later determined to be invalid, the taxable entity's margin will be 70% of total revenue. An election may not be changed on an amended report.

Taxpayers filing the long form report make the election simply by filing the report using one method or the other. No other action is required. Taxpayers filing the "No Tax Due" report must make an election by checking the appropriate box on the form. The election is required even though taxpayers filing the "No Tax Due" report do not actually calculate tax due. The election protects taxpayers who might later have to amend their report, by ensuring they can take the deduction most advantageous to them.

No election is required for taxpayers using the E-Z Computation, because the E-Z Computation Report is not based on taxable margin. Therefore, neither COGS nor compensation may be deducted when using the E-Z Computation Report. (*Frequently Asked Questions—Account and Report Information,* Texas Comptroller's Office, updated April 29, 2008)

After the due date of the report, a taxable entity may not amend its report to change its election to cost of goods sold or compensation. However, a taxable entity may amend its report to change its method of computing margin from cost of goods sold or compensation to 70% of total revenue or, if eligible, the E-Z Computation. (34 TAC Sec. 3.584)

Once the election is made, the entity may subtract compensation paid to a resident individual during the period the individual is serving on active duty as a member of the U.S. Armed Forces and the cost of training a replacement for the individual.

The resultant margin figure is then apportioned using a single receipts factor (see ¶303) to determine the entity's apportioned margin. The entity may then subtract any allowable deductions discussed at ¶206. (Sec. 171.101, Tax Code)

Practice Pointer: References to Lines on Federal Forms

In determining the revenues to include, references are made to the amounts entered on a taxpayer's federal return. A reference to an amount reportable as income entered on a line number on an IRS form is the amount entered to the extent the amount entered complies with federal income tax law and includes the corresponding amount entered on a variant of the form, or a subsequent form, with a different line number to the extent the amount entered complies with federal income tax law. (Sec. 171.1011(b), Tax Code) The line items refer to line items on the 2006 Internal Revenue Service forms. (34 TAC Sec. 3.587(d))

In determining the revenues to include, references are made to the amounts entered on a taxpayer's federal return.

CCH Practice Tip: Allocated Revenue

Revenue that Texas cannot tax because the activities generating that item of revenue do not have sufficient unitary connection with the entity's other activities conducted in Texas under the U.S. Constitution is not included in total revenue. (34 TAC Sec. 3.587(c)(9))

- *Total revenue of corporations*

The total revenue of a taxable entity treated as a corporation for federal income tax purposes is an amount computed by adding the following:

— the amount reportable as income on IRS Form 1120 line 1c;

— the amounts reportable as income on IRS Form 1120 lines 4 through 10, which includes the costs of goods sold (less returns and allowances), dividends, interest, gross rents and royalties, capital gain, net gain, and other income; and

— any total revenue reported by a lower tier entity required to be included in the taxable entity's total revenue (see ¶103).

From this amount, taxpayers may subtract to the extent included in the computation above:

— bad debts deducted for federal income tax purposes that corresponds to items of gross receipts included for the current reporting period or a past reporting period;

— foreign royalties and dividends, including amounts under IRC Sec. 78 or IRC Secs. 951—964;

Part II—Franchise Tax

— net distributive income from an entity treated as a partnership or S corporation for federal income tax purposes, other than a passive entity (see ¶104);

— federal dividends received deductions reported on Schedule C to the extent the relating dividend income is included in total revenue;

— to the extent included in the entity's revenues above, income attributable to an entity that is disregarded for federal income tax purposes; and

— other authorized amounts.

(Sec. 171.1011, Tax Code)

CCH Advisory: Consolidated Groups

A taxable entity that is included in a federal consolidated group, but not required to participate in a Texas combined group return (see ¶507), must compute its total revenue as if it had filed a separate federal return. (Sec. 171.1011(d), Tax Code)

- *Total revenues of partnerships*

A partnership's total revenues are determined by adding:

— the amount reportable as income on line 1c, IRS Form 1065;

— the amounts reportable as income on lines 4, 6, and 7, IRS Form 1065;

— the amounts reportable as income on lines 3a, and 5 through 11, IRS Form 1065, Schedule K;

— the amounts reportable as income on line 17, IRS Form 8825;

— the amounts reportable as income on line 11, plus line 2 or line 45, Internal Revenue Service Form 1040, Schedule F; plus

— any total revenue reported by a lower tier entity as includable in the taxable entity's total revenue (see ¶103).

With the exception of the dividends received deductions, the subtractions listed above for corporations also apply to partnerships.

- *Total revenues of other taxable entities*

The discussion immediately below outlines the income that must be added to determine total revenues of S corporations, trusts, and single member LLCs. With the exception of the dividends received deductions, the subtractions listed above for corporations also apply to S corporations and trusts. (34 TAC Sec. 3.587)

S corporations.—An S corporation's total revenues are determined by adding:

— the amount reportable as income on line 1c, IRS Form 1120S;

— the amounts reportable as income on lines 4 and 5, IRS Form 1120S;

— the amounts reportable as income on lines 3a and 4 through 10, IRS Form 1120S, Schedule K;

— the amounts reportable as income on line 17, IRS Form 8825;

— any total revenue reported by a lower tier entity as includable in the taxable entity's total revenue (see ¶103).

As noted below, because Texas only incorporates the IRC as in effect on January 1, 2007, Texas does not incorporate any amendments made to the federal S corporation provisions by the Small Business and Work Opportunity Tax Act of 2007, the Emergency Economic Stabilization Act of 2008, or the American Recovery and Reinvestment Tax Act of 2009. Taxpayers should use the line amounts from the 2006 IRS Form 1120S to ensure that they are not inadvertently incorporating these federal amendments when computing their franchise (margin) tax liability.

¶202

The federal amendments specify that:

— capital gain from the sale or exchange of stock or securities is no longer characterized as passive investment income, effective May 25, 2007;

— an S corporation's sale of a QSub's stock is treated as a sale of an undivided interest in the QSub's assets followed by a deemed creation of the subsidiary in an IRC Sec. 351 transaction, effective for tax years after 2006;

— a bank changing from the reserve method of accounting for bad debts for its first tax year for which it is an S corporation may elect to take into account all IRC Sec. 481 adjustments in the last tax year it was a C corporation, effective for tax years after 2006;

— restricted bank director stock is not treated as a disqualifying second class of stock for tax years beginning after 1996, a director is not treated as an S corporation shareholder, and the stock is disregarded in allocating items of income and loss among the shareholders. In addition, the stock is not treated as outstanding for purposes of determining whether an S corporation holds 100% of the stock of a qualified subchapter S subsidiary, generally, effective for tax years after 2006; and

— the modified basis reduction in stock of an S corporation making a charitable property donation is extended to apply to the 2008 and 2009 tax years.

Trusts.—A trust's total revenues are determined by adding:

— the amount reportable as income on lines 1, 2a, 3, 4, 7, and 8, IRS Form 1041;

— the amounts reportable as income on lines 3, 4, 32, and 37, IRS Form 1040, Schedule E;

— the amounts reportable as income on line 11, plus line 2 or line 45, Internal Revenue Service Form 1040, Schedule F; plus

— any total revenue reported by a lower tier entity as includable in the taxable entity's total revenue (see ¶103).

Single member limited liability company filing as a sole proprietorship.—The total revenues for a single member LLC (SMLLC) filing as a sole proprietorship for federal income tax purposes are determined by adding:

— the amount reportable as income on line 3, IRS Form 1040, Schedule C;

— the amounts reportable as income on line 17, IRS Form 4797, to the extent that it relates to the LLC;

— ordinary income or loss from partnerships, S corporations, estates and trusts, IRS Form 1040, Schedule E, to the extent that it relates to the LLC;

— the amounts reportable as income on line 16, IRS Form 1040, Schedule D, to the extent that it relates to the LLC;

— the amounts reportable as income on lines 3 and 4, IRS Form 1040, Schedule E, to the extent it relates to the LLC;

— the amounts reportable as income on line 11, plus line 2 or line 45, IRS Form 1040, Schedule F, to the extent it relates to the LLC;

— the amounts reportable as income on line 6, IRS Form 1040, Schedule C, that has not already been included; plus

— any total revenue reported by a lower tier entity as includable in the taxable entity's total revenue (see ¶103).

¶202

Other entities.—For a taxable entity other than a taxable entity treated for federal income tax purposes as a corporation, S corporation, partnership, trust, or SMLLC filing as a sole proprietorship, the total revenue is an amount determined in a manner substantially equivalent to the amount calculated for the entities listed above.

> **CCH Advisory: Treatment of Income From Pass-Through Entity**
>
> A taxable entity that owns an interest in a passive entity must exclude from the taxable entity's total revenue the taxable entity's share of the net income of the passive entity, but only to the extent the net income of the passive entity was generated by the margin of any other taxable entity. (Sec. 171.1011(e), Tax Code)

- *Federal conformity*

Effective January 1, 2008, references to the Internal Revenue Code in the franchise (margin) tax provisions refer to the IRC of 1986 in effect for the federal tax year beginning on January 1, 2007, not including any changes made by federal law after that date, and any regulations adopted under that Code applicable to that period. (Sec. 171.0001(9), Tax Code) Consequently, Texas does not incorporate any amendments made by the following federal Acts:

— the Small Business and Work Opportunity Tax Act (Small Business Tax Act) (P.L. 110-28);

— the U.S. Troop Readiness, Veterans' Care, Katrina Recovery, and Iraq Accountability Appropriations Act of 2007 (U.S. Troop Readiness Act) (P.L. 110-28);

— the Energy Independence & Security Act of 2007 (Energy Act) (P.L. 110-140);

— the Mortgage Forgiveness Debt Relief Act of 2007 (Mortgage Relief Act) (P.L. 110-142);

— the Tax Increase Prevention Act of 2007 (TIPA) (P.L. 110-166);

— the Tax Technical Corrections Act of 2007 (TTCA) (P.L. 110-172);

— the Economic Stimulus Act of 2008 (ESA) (P.L. 110-185);

— the Heartland, Habitat, Harvest, and Horticulture Act of 2008 (Farm Act) (P.L. 110-246);

— the Heroes Earnings Assistance and Relief Tax Act of 2008 (HEART) (P.L. 110-245);

— the Housing Assistance Tax Act of 2008 (HATA) (P.L. 110-289);

— the Emergency Economic Stabilization Act of 2008 (P.L. 110-343);

— the Worker, Retiree, and Employer Recovery Act of 2008 (P.L. 110-458); and

— the American Recovery and Reinvestment Tax Act of 2009 (P.L. 111-5).

- *Accounting periods and methods*

A taxpayer must use the same accounting methods to apportion margin as is used in computing its reportable federal taxable income. A taxpayer may not change its accounting methods used to calculate gross receipts more often than once every four years without the express written consent of the Comptroller. A change in accounting methods is not justified solely because it results in a reduction of tax liability. (Sec. 171.1121, Tax Code)

Texas law does not provide for the filing of short period franchise tax reports. A change in a federal accounting period or the loss of a federal filing election does not change the beginning and ending date of an accounting period for franchise tax reporting purposes. The keys to the period upon which the tax is based are the

¶202

beginning and ending dates. The beginning date will be the day after the ending date on the prior franchise tax report, and the ending date will be the last federal tax accounting period end date in the year prior to the year in which the report is originally due. (Instructions, 2008 Texas Franchise Tax Report)

The accounting period for a combined reporting group comprised of two or more members that file a federal consolidated return is the federal tax period of the federal consolidated group. For all other combined groups, the accounting period is the federal tax period of the reporting entity. (Instructions, 2008 Texas Franchise Tax Report)

¶203 Exclusions From Total Revenues

Law: Secs. 171.002, 171.1011, Tax Code (CCH Texas Tax Reports, ¶10-510, 10-515).

The following items may be excluded from total revenues to the extent included in the items discussed at (¶202):

—flow-through funds that must be legally distributed to other entities, such as taxes collected from a third party and remitted by the taxable entity to a taxing authority;

—flow-through funds that are mandated by contract to be distributed to other entities, such as commissions to nonemployees, the tax basis of securities underwritten, or subcontracting payments handled by the taxable entity to provide labor or materials for real property improvements or the location of real property boundaries [CCH Note: 34 TAC Sec. 3.587 limits this exclusion to these enumerated items.];

—proceeds received by lending institutions from the principal repayment of loans;

—the federal tax basis of loans and securities sold (Sec. 171.1011(f), (g), (g-1), (g-2), Tax Code);

—dividends and interest from federal obligations (34 TAC Sec.3.587(e)(8));

—amounts received that are directly derived from the operation of a facility that is located on property owned or leased by the federal government and managed or operated primarily to house members of the U.S. armed forces members (34 TAC Sec. 3.587(e)(12));

—specified oil and gas revenues received from small oil and gas wells but only during the dates certified by the Comptroller in which the monthly average closing price of West Texas Intermediate crude oil falls below specified levels (34 TAC Sec. 3.587(e)(13)); and

—payments made by qualified destination management companies to persons providing services, labor, or materials in connection with the provision of destination management services, see ¶207. (Sec. 171.1011(g-6), Tax Code)

CCH Practice Tip: Commissions

Any form of compensation paid to nonemployees, including compensation paid to corporations, may be excluded from total revenue, to the extent included, if paid to a person or entity for engaging in an act for which a real estate license is required. All other sales commissions that are paid to corporations are not allowed as exclusions from total revenue. (*Tax Policy News*, Texas Comptroller of Public Accounts, March 2009)

CCH Practice Tip: Landlord reimbursements

Property tax and insurance expense reimbursements received by landlords from lessees are not excludable from total revenue for Texas franchise tax purposes even if landlords have reduced their property tax and insurance expenses by these reimbursements for

Part II—Franchise Tax

Internal Revenue Service (IRS) reporting purposes. Under the governing federal regulation the reimbursement of landlord expenses should be reported for federal tax purposes in gross rental income and should not be reported as an offset expense. (*Tax Policy News, Vol. XVIII, Issue 4*, Texas Comptroller of Public Accounts, April 2008)

These exclusions may not be claimed for items paid to members of the entity's affiliated group. (Sec. 171.1011(h), Tax Code)

Amounts excluded above, may not also be used in determining the deductible amount of costs of goods sold (¶205) or compensation (¶204). The Comptroller originally interpreted this treatment to apply to all exclusions from total revenue. However, the Comptroller has now stated that this provision only applies to expenses that have been excluded from total revenue. Consequently, items such as flow-through funds and the costs of uncompensated care that have been excluded from total revenue may now be subtracted as compensation or a cost of goods sold. (*Tax Policy News, Vol. XVIII, Issue 2*, Texas Comptroller of Public Accounts, February 2008)

Other deductions.—Dividends and interest from federal obligations may also be deducted.

A number of specific exclusions from total revenue are provided for legal service providers, staff leasing services, management companies, and health care providers and institutions (see ¶207).

¶204 Compensation Deduction

Law: Secs. 171.101, 171.1013, Tax Code (CCH Texas Tax Reports, ¶10-913).

As discussed at ¶201, taxpayers may elect to deduct either employee compensation or cost of goods sold from their total revenues. (Sec. 171.101, Tax Code)

Compensation includes all wages and cash compensation paid to an officer, director, owner, partner, or employee by an entity up to a $300,000 maximum per 12-month period on which margin is based and, to the extent deductible on the entity's federal income tax return, benefits paid to the entity's officers, directors, owners, partners, and employees. The $300,000 figure is indexed for inflation beginning in 2010 and is determined on a combined group basis. The compensation deduction limit for reports due in 2010 and 2011 is $320,000. Benefits include workers' compensation benefits, health care, employer contributions made to employees' health savings accounts, and retirement to the extent deductible for federal income tax purposes. Payroll taxes are not included. (Sec. 171.1013, Tax Code)

Planning Point: Deduction for Small Employers Providing New Health Care Coverage

A small employer who did not provide health care benefits during the prior calendar year preceding the beginning date of its reporting period may subtract a portion of the health care benefits provided in the first two years the employer provides health care benefits to all of its employees. The deduction is equal to 50% of the benefits provided for the first 12-month period on which margin is based and 25% of the benefits for the second 12-month period on which margin is based. Employers with more than 50 employees are ineligible. Amounts paid by the employee may not be deducted. (Sec. 171.1013(b), Tax Code; 34 TAC Sec. 3.589)

CCH Comment: Employees vs. Independent Contractors

Payments to independent contractors or temporary leasing companies are not included in deductible compensation. Consequently, the benefits received from being able to deduct employee wages should be considered when choosing whether to hire additional employees or to use independent contractors or temporary workers.

For purposes of the compensation deduction, "wages and cash compensation" means the amount entered in the Medicare wages and tips box of IRS Form W-2. The term also includes, to the extent not included in the W-2 Medicare wages and tips box:

— net distributive income distributed to natural persons from pass-through entities; and

— stock awards and stock options deducted for federal income tax purposes.

Wages and cash compensation paid to an undocumented worker may not be deducted. Nor may wages or cash compensation paid to an employee whose primary employment is directly associated with the operation of a federal government facility used to house U.S. armed forces personnel. (Sec. 171.1013, Tax Code)

Practice Note: Amounts Excluded From Compensation

The following items are not includible in deductible compensation:

— an employer's share of payroll taxes;

— discounts on the price of the taxable entity's merchandise or services sold to the taxpayer's employees, officers, directors, partners, or owners that are not available to the customers;

— working condition amounts provided so employees can perform their jobs, such as use of a company car, job-related education, and travel reimbursement; and

— an employee's contribution toward his or her own benefits.

In addition, amounts included in the definition of wages and cash compensation that are excluded because of the $300,000 limitation may not be included in deductible benefits. (34 TAC Sec. 3.589)

- *Staff leasing companies and management companies*

A staff leasing company may not deduct payments received from its client companies' wages, payroll taxes on those wages, employee benefits, and workers' compensation benefits for the assigned employees of the client company. These payments may, however, be deducted by the client company. Only wages and compensation paid for the staff leasing company's actual employees that are not assigned employees may be deducted by the staff leasing company. The client company may not deduct any administrative fees paid to the staff leasing company or any other amount paid in relation to the leased employees, including payroll taxes.

Similarly, a management company may not include reimbursements received from a managed entity as wages or cash compensation. Such amounts may only be deducted by the managed entity.

A "management company" generally is an entity retained by owners to manage properties such as hotels and resorts. Providing services in the regular course of business and services performed under a cost-plus contract, or providing shipping or accounting services to another company would not qualify under the management company provisions.

¶204

Part II—Franchise Tax

To qualify as a management company, an entity must:

— perform active and substantial management and operational functions;

— control and direct the daily operations; and

— provide accounting, general administration, legal, financial and other similar services.

If the entity does not conduct all of the active trade or business of the managed business, the entity must conduct all operations for a distinct, revenue-producing component of the managed business. (*Tax Policy News*, Texas Comptroller of Public Accounts, August 2009)

¶205 Cost of Goods Sold Deduction

Law: Secs. 171.0001, 171.101, 171.1012, Tax Code; 34. TAC Sec. 3.588 (CCH Texas Tax Reports, ¶10-914).

As discussed at ¶201, taxpayers may elect to deduct from their total revenues, either 30% of their total revenues, employee compensation (¶204) or cost of goods sold. (Sec. 171.102, Tax Code) Except as discussed below, the cost of goods sold (COGS) deduction must be determined in accordance with the methods used on the federal income tax return on which the Texas franchise tax report is based. However, this federal treatment does not affect the type or category of cost of goods sold. (Sec. 171.1012(h), Tax Code)

CCH Comment: Federal vs. state cost of goods sold deduction

According to the Comptroller's Office, it is very unlikely that the COGS reported on Schedule A of IRS Form 1065 or 1120 will equal COGS for franchise tax reporting purposes. (*Letter No. 200810209L*, Texas Comptroller of Public Accounts, October 23, 2008, CCH Texas Tax Reports, ¶403-520).

A "good" is limited to real and tangible property, including the husbandry of animals, the growing and harvesting of crops, and the severance of timber. (34 TAC Sec. 3.588). The definition of tangible property is also broad in that it includes any personal property perceptible to the senses in any manner and includes computer programs, films, sound recordings, videotapes, live and prerecorded television and radio programs, books, and other similar property, regardless of the means in which the property is stored or distributed. (Sec. 171.1012(a), Tax Code)

The good must be owned by the taxpayer. For purposes of this deduction, a federal contractor or subcontractor is considered the owner of goods being produced or manufactured for the federal government. (Sec. 171.1012(i), Tax Code) Similarly, a taxable entity furnishing labor or materials to a project for the construction, improvement, remodeling, repair, or industrial maintenance of real property is considered to be an owner of the labor or materials. (34 TAC Sec. 3.588(c)(7))

The cost of goods sold includes all direct costs of acquiring or producing the goods including:

— labor costs, such as W-2 wages, IRS Form 1099 wages, temporary labor, payroll taxes and benefits (34 TAC Sec. 3.588(d));

— cost of materials that are an integral part of specific property produced;

— cost of materials that are consumed in the ordinary course of performing production activities;

— handling costs, including costs attributable to processing, assembling, repackaging, and inbound transportation costs;

— storage costs, including the costs of carrying, storing, or warehousing property, subject to the exclusions listed below;

— depreciation, depletion, and amortization, reported on the federal income tax return on which the report under this chapter is based, to the extent associated with and necessary for the production of goods, including recovery described by IRC Sec. 197, and property described in IRC Sec. 179;

— the cost of renting or leasing equipment, facilities, or real property directly used for the production of the goods, including pollution control equipment and intangible drilling and dry hole costs;

— the cost of repairing and maintaining equipment, facilities, or real property directly used for the production of the goods, including pollution control devices;

— costs attributable to research, experimental, engineering, and design activities directly related to the production of the goods, including all research or experimental expenditures described by IRC Sec. 174;

— geological and geophysical costs incurred to identify and locate property that has the potential to produce minerals;

— taxes paid in relation to acquiring or producing any material, or taxes paid in relation to services that are a direct cost of production;

— the cost of producing or acquiring electricity sold; and

— a contribution to a partnership in which the taxable entity owns an interest that is used to fund activities, the costs of which would otherwise be treated as cost of goods sold of the partnership, but only to the extent that those costs are related to goods distributed to the taxable entity as goods-in-kind in the ordinary course of production activities rather than being sold by the partnership (if this subtraction is taken, the partnership may not also claim a deduction for the costs of goods sold). (Sec. 171.1012(c), Tax Code; 34 TAC Sec. 3.588(d)(13))

Practitioner Comment: Change from COGS deduction to Compensation deduction

In Taylor & Hill, Inc. v. Combs, et al. (Cause No. D-1-GN-10-004429), July 7, 2011, the taxpayer originally filed its 2009 report electing the COGS deduction in computing its Texas revised franchise tax ("Margin Tax"). The Comptroller audited the taxpayer, determined that it did not qualify for the COGS deduction, and applied the 30% default deduction to derive taxable margin. The taxpayer sued the Comptroller for the right to use the Compensation deduction, which was greater than the default deduction. The district court ruled that the taxpayer qualified as a Staff Leasing Company, and could elect the Compensation deduction.

The Comptroller, by rule, does not allow a taxpayer to amend a report to switch from one elected deduction to another. While a district court case is not precedential under Texas law, this case raises the question of whether there is an exception from the agency's rule that would enable a taxpayer to change elections under audit. A further question arises as to whether the agency's rule that bars a different election is valid.

Eric L. Stein, Ryan

CCH Comment: Service Industry Entities

Texas Tax Code Sec. 171.1012 specifically provides that, in determining the cost of goods sold, the term "goods" means real or tangible personal property sold in the ordinary course of business and does not include services. The Tax Code does not allow a cost of goods sold deduction for entities that provide services such as dry cleaners, law firms, parking facilities, rental services, towing companies, etc. Franchise tax rule 3.588(c)(8) does allow a cost of goods deduction for transactions that contain elements of both a sale of tangible personal property and a service; however, an entity may only subtract

Part II—Franchise Tax   51

as cost of goods sold the costs otherwise allowed in relation to the tangible personal property sold. (*Tax Policy News*, Texas Comptroller of Public Accounts, July 2010)

Practice Tip: Difference in Federal/State Depreciation, IRC Sec. 179 Asset Expense Election, and Depletion Deductions

Because Texas only incorporates the Internal Revenue Code as in effect on January 1, 2007 (see ¶202), Texas does not incorporate the federal amendments that increased the IRC Sec. 179 dollar limitation to $250,000 for 2008 and 2009 ($125,000 for 2007 and 2010) and the investment limitation to $800,000 for 2008 and 2009 ($500,000 for 2007 and 2010) for property placed in service after 2006 and before 2011. The limit for the Section 179 expense that can be included in COGS for the 2009 franchise tax report is $115,000 ($112,000 for 2008). (*Letter No. 200810200L*, Texas Comptroller of Public Accounts, October 17, 2008, CCH Texas Tax Reports, ¶403-509) Nor does Texas incorporate the extension of the Gulf Opportunity Zone Act (GOZA) provisions through 2008 (previously through 2007) that increased the limitation by the lesser of $100,000 and the investment limit by the lesser of $600,000 or the cost of qualified section 179 GO Zone property placed in service during the tax year, but only for property in specific GO Zone areas. The increased IRC Sec. 179 expense allowance and investment limitation for qualified section 179 disaster assistance property placed in service after 2007 is also inapplicable for Texas franchise margin tax purposes. Consequently, taxpayers that claim these increased deductions on their federal return must adjust their depreciation deductions claimed on their Texas reports.

Following are the limits for IRC § 179 expense that can be included in the cost of goods sold deduction for Texas franchise tax reports: $112,000 for franchise tax report year 2008 (for accounting years ending in 2007); $115,000 for franchise tax report year 2009 (for accounting years ending in 2008); $120,000 for franchise tax report year 2010 (for accounting years ending in 2009); $25,000 for franchise tax report year 2011 (for accounting years ending in 2010). (*Tax Policy News*, Texas Comptroller of Public Accounts, February 2010)

Texas also limits the amount of depreciation that may be taken to the amount that could be claimed on the 2006 federal return. Consequently, Texas does not incorporate the post-2006 amendments to federal depreciation provisions including amendments that:

— allow bonus depreciation for property placed in service in 2008 and 2009;

— shorten the amortization period of geological and geophysical expenditures for certain major integrated oil companies;

— reduce the recovery period for young racehorses placed in service after 2008 and before 2014;

— extend the 15-year recovery period for qualified leasehold improvements and restaurant property to apply to property placed in service in 2008 and 2009 and allow a 15-year recovery period for retail improvement property placed in service during the 2009 calendar year;

— allow accelerated depreciation for qualified smart electric meters and qualified smart grid systems placed in service after October 3, 2008;

— treat certain farming business machinery and equipment as five-year property for property placed in service in 2009;

— extend the 7-year MACRS recovery period for motorsports entertainment complexes to property placed in service in 2008 and 2009;

— allow an additional 50% first year depreciation deduction for the cost of facilities that produce cellulosic biofuel that are placed in service after October 3, 2008, and before January 1, 2013;

— extend the accelerated recovery periods for qualified Indian reservation property to apply to property placed in service in 2008 and 2009;

— allow a 50% additional depreciation allowance for the adjusted basis of qualified reuse and recycling property acquired and placed in service after August 31, 2008; and

¶205

— allow a 50% depreciation allowance for qualified disaster assistance property placed in service after 2007, with respect to disasters declared after 2007 and before 2010.

In addition, Texas does not follow the federal amendment that extended the suspension of the percentage depletion limitation for oil and gas produced from marginal properties to include tax years beginning in 2009.

Lending institutions, including qualified motor vehicle sales finance companies (see *Letter No. 200809207L*, Texas Comptroller of Public Accounts, September 24, 2008, CCH TEXAS TAX REPORTS, ¶ 403-556) that claim the cost of goods sold deduction, may also include interest expense as a cost of goods sold. However, the exclusion may not be claimed by entities primarily engaged in used merchandise stores, including pawnshops. (Sec. 171.1012(k), Tax Code)

Film or television producers, broadcasters, or distributors of films, sound recordings, videotapes, live and prerecorded television and radio programs, books, and other similar property may depreciate, amortize, and subtract other expenses directly related to the acquisition, production, or use of the property, including expenses for the right to broadcast or use the property.

In addition to the items above, cost of goods sold includes the following costs in relation to the taxable entity's goods:

— deterioration of the goods;

— obsolescence of the goods;

— spoilage and abandonment, including the costs of rework labor, reclamation, and scrap;

— if the property is held for future production, preproduction direct costs allocable to the property, including costs of purchasing the goods and of storage and handling the goods;

— postproduction direct costs allocable to the property, including storage and handling costs;

— the cost of insurance on a plant or a facility, machinery, equipment, or materials directly used in the production of the goods;

— the cost of insurance on the produced goods;

— the cost of utilities directly used in the production of the goods;

— the costs of quality control, including replacement of defective components pursuant to standard warranty policies, inspection directly allocable to the production of the goods, and repairs and maintenance of goods; and

— licensing or franchise costs, including fees incurred in securing the contractual right to use a trademark, corporate plan, manufacturing procedure, special recipe, or other similar right directly associated with the goods produced. (Sec. 171.1012(d), Tax Code)

CCH Pointer: Mixed transactions

If a transaction contains elements of both a sale of tangible personal property and a service, a taxable entity may only subtract as cost of goods sold the costs otherwise allowed by this section in relation to the tangible personal property sold. (34 TAC Sec. 3.588(c)(6))

- *Exclusions*

Excluded from the cost of goods sold are the following:

— the cost of renting or leasing equipment, facilities, or real property that is not used for the production of the goods;

Part II—Franchise Tax

- selling costs, including employee expenses related to sales;
- distribution costs, including outbound transportation costs;
- advertising costs;
- idle facility expense;
- rehandling costs;
- bidding costs, including costs associated with unsuccessful bids;
- interest, including interest on debt incurred or continued during the production period to finance the production of the goods;
- income taxes, including local state, federal, and foreign income taxes, and franchise taxes that are assessed on the taxable entity based on income;
- strike expenses, including costs associated with hiring employees to replace striking personnel, but not including the wages of the replacement personnel, costs of security, and legal fees associated with settling strikes;
- officers' compensation;
- costs of operation of a federal government facility that is used to house U.S. Armed Forces personnel; and
- any compensation paid to an undocumented worker used for the production of goods. (Sec. 171.1012(e), Tax Code)

• *Indirect and administrative overhead expenses*

Up to 4% of a taxpayer's indirect or administrative overhead costs may be deducted if it can demonstrate that the costs are allocable to the acquisition or production of goods. Indirect or administrative overhead costs include all mixed service costs, such as security services, legal services, data processing services, accounting services, personnel operations, and general financial planning and financial management costs. However, costs listed in the exclusions above may not be subtracted as indirect or administrative overhead expenses. (Sec. 171.1012(f), Tax Code)

CCH Practice Tip: Restaurants

Restaurants may deduct for cost of goods sold only those expenses allowed above that relate to the production of food. Any costs related to both the production of food and to other activities must be allocated to production on a reasonable basis. (34 TAC Sec. 3.588(c)(10))

• *Capitalized expenses*

Except as otherwise excluded or discussed above, expenses that are required to be capitalized for federal income tax purposes under IRC Sections 263A, 460, or 471 may also be capitalized or expensed for Texas margin tax purposes in the same manner and to the same extent that the taxable entity capitalized or expensed that cost on its federal income tax return. (Sec. 171.1012(g), Tax Code) The election to capitalize or expense allowable costs is made by filing the franchise tax report using one method or the other. The election is for the entire period on which the report is based and may not be changed after the due date or the date the report is filed, whichever is later. (34 TAC Sec. 3.588)

The Comptroller has taken the position that taxpayers electing to capitalize cost of goods sold are allowed a beginning inventory. (*Letter No. 200801034L*, Texas Comptroller of Public Accounts, January 11, 2008, CCH TEXAS TAX REPORTS, ¶403-363)

¶205

Practice Tip: Expensing Costs

A taxable entity that elects to begin expensing a cost after it previously capitalized such cost, may not deduct any cost in ending inventory from a previous report. A taxable entity that elects to expense a cost of goods sold may not subtract a cost incurred before the first day of the period on which the report is based. Finally, a taxable entity that elects to expense a cost of goods sold and later elects to capitalize that cost of goods sold may not capitalize a cost that was previously expensed. (Sec. 171.1012(g), Tax Code)

- *Rental and leasing companies*

Notwithstanding the "production or acquisition" requirements discussed above, the following taxable entities may subtract as a cost of goods sold the otherwise allowable costs associated with the following tangible personal property that the entity rents or leases in the ordinary course of business of the entity:

— a motor vehicle rental or leasing company that remits a motor vehicle sales, rental, or use tax (see ¶ 903);

— a heavy construction equipment rental or leasing company; and

— a railcar rolling stock rental or leasing company. (Sec. 171.1012(l), Tax Code)

- *Affiliated group members*

A payment made by one member of an affiliated group to another member of that affiliated group that is not included in the combined group (¶ 507) may be subtracted as a cost of goods sold only if it is a transaction made at arm's length. (Sec. 171.1012(m), Tax Code) An affiliated group means a group of one or more entities in which a controlling interest (80%) is owned by a common owner or owners, or by one or more of the member entities. (Sec. 171.0001(1), Tax Code)

- *Items not included in cost of goods sold*

The following items are not included in the cost of goods sold:

— the cost of renting or leasing equipment, facilities, or real property that is not used for the production of the goods;

— selling costs, including employee expenses related to sales;

— distribution costs, including outbound transportation costs;

— advertising costs;

— bidding costs, whether the contract is awarded or not;

— interest, including interest on debt incurred or continued during the production period to finance the production of the goods;

— income taxes, including local, state, federal, and foreign income taxes, and franchise taxes that are assessed on the taxable entity based on income;

— strike expenses, including costs associated with hiring employees to replace striking personnel, but not including the wages of the replacement personnel, costs of security, and legal fees associated with settling strikes;

— officers' compensation;

— facility operation costs of federal property used to house members of the U.S. armed forces;

— compensation paid to an undocumented worker; and

— costs funded by a partnership contribution, to the extent that the contributing taxable entity made claimed the cost of goods sold deduction. (34 TAC Sec. 3.588(g))

¶205

Part II—Franchise Tax

¶206 Other Deductions

Law: Secs. 171.107, Tax Code (CCH Texas Tax Reports, ¶10-905).

The following items may be deducted from the apportioned margin (see ¶201):

— 10% of the amortized cost of a solar energy device used in Texas for heating, cooling, or power production (Sec. 171.107, Tax Code); and

— 10% of the cost of equipment used in a clean coal project for use in Texas in the generation of electricity, production of process steam, or industrial production. (Sec. 171.108, Tax. Code)

To qualify for the deduction, the amortization of the cost of the device or equipment must:

— be for a period of at least 60 months;

— provide for equal monthly amounts;

— begin on the month in which the device or equipment is placed in service in Texas; and

— cover only a period in which the device or equipment is in use in this state. (Sec. 171.107, Tax. Code, Sec. 171.108, Tax Code)

Amortization of a solar energy device does not have to be in equal monthly installments if the amortization conforms to federal depreciation schedules. (Sec. 171.107, Tax Code)

¶207 Special Taxpayers

Law: Secs. 171.1011, Tax Code (CCH Texas Tax Reports, ¶10-525).

Special provisions apply for purposes of calculating total revenues for the following industries and entities.

• *Destination management companies*

A qualified destination management company may exclude from its total revenues, to the extent previously included, payments made to persons providing services labor, or materials in connection with the provision of destination management services. (Sec. 171.1011(g)-6, Tax Code)

A "qualified destination management company" is a business entity that is incorporated or is a limited liability company, receives at least 80% of its annual total revenue from providing destination management services, and meets other conditions specified in Sec. 151.0565, Tax Code.

"Destination management services" are defined as the following services when provided under a qualified destination management services contract:

— transportation management;

— booking and managing entertainers;

— coordination of tours or recreational activities;

— meeting, conference, or event registration;

— meeting, conference, or event staffing;

— event management; and

— meal coordination.

A "qualified destination management services contract" is a contract under which a management company provides at least three destination management services in Texas to a business entity and the management company pays or accrues tax liability on purchases of taxable items that will be consumed or used by the company in performing the contract. The definition also contains other requirements as specified in Sec. 151.0565, Tax Code.

- *Lending institutions*

A taxable entity that is a lending institution will exclude from its total revenue, to the extent previously included, proceeds from the principal repayment of loans. (Sec. 171.1011(g)-1, Tax Code)

- *Legal service providers*

A taxable entity that provides legal services may exclude from total revenue, to the extent previously included, the following flow-through funds that must be distributed to the claimant or to other entities on behalf of the claimant by the claimant's attorney:

— damages due the claimant;

— funds subject to a lien or other contractual obligation arising out of the representation, other than fees owed to the attorney;

— funds subject to a subrogation interest or other third-party contractual claim; and

— fees paid an attorney in the matter who is not a member, partner, shareholder, or employee of the taxable entity.

Reimbursement of the taxable entity's expenses incurred in prosecuting a claimant's matter that are specific to the matter and that are not general operating expenses may also be excluded. In addition, $500 per pro bono service case handled by an attorney may be excluded if specified records are maintained. (Sec. 171.1011(g-3), Tax Code)

- *Health care providers*

A taxable entity that is a health care provider may exclude from total revenue, to the extent previously included, the total amount of payments the health care provider received:

— under the Medicaid program, Medicare program, Indigent Health Care and Treatment Act, and Children's Health Insurance Program (CHIP), including copayments and deductibles received from patients or from supplemental insurance;

— for professional services provided in relation to a workers' compensation claim; and

— for professional services provided to a beneficiary rendered under the TRICARE military health system.

In addition, the actual cost to the health care provider for any uncompensated care provided, may also be excluded provided that the provider maintains records of the uncompensated care for auditing purposes. The cost of uncompensated care is calculated by taking uncompensated care charges less partial payments and dividing them by total charges and then multiplying that result by operating expenses (see 34 TAC Sec. 3.587(b)(1) for details). If the provider later receives payment for all or part of that care, the provider must adjust the amount excluded for the tax year in which the payment is received. (Sec. 171.1011(n), Tax Code)

Health care providers must maintain records for all uncompensated care that clearly identify each patient, the procedure performed, and the standard charge for such service, as well as payments received from each patient. Additionally, a corresponding adjustment must be made to reduce the compensation deduction by multiplying the compensation amounts (salaries, wages, guaranteed payments, officer compensation capped at $300,000 per person per 12-month period, and benefits)

¶207

included in operating expenses by the uncompensated care ratio. (*Release*, Texas Comptroller Susan Combs, May 13, 2008)

CCH Pointer: Treatment of excluded amounts

Expenses that have been excluded from total revenue may not be included in the determination of compensation or cost of goods sold. However, the exclusion from amounts used to determine costs of goods sold or compensation, does not apply to revenue exclusions such as receipts received from the Medicaid, Medicare and other programs specified in Tax Code Section 171.1011(n). (*Tax Policy News, Vol. XVIII, Issue 5*, Texas Comptroller of Public Accounts, May 2008)

- *Health care institutions*

A health care institution may exclude from total revenue 50% of the amounts excluded by health care providers, listed above. Some of the listed health care institutions are: ambulatory surgical center, licensed assisted living facility, emergency medical services provider, home and community support services agency, hospice, hospital, birthing center, nursing home, and a pharmacy. (Sec. 171.1011(o), Tax Code)

- *Pharmacy cooperatives*

A pharmacy cooperative must exclude from its total revenue the flow-through funds from rebates from pharmacy wholesalers that are distributed to the pharmacy cooperative's shareholders. However, the revenues may not be excluded if the taxable entity is in an affiliated group and the payments are made to affiliated members. (Sec. 171.1011(g)(4) and (h), Tax Code)

- *Staff leasing services*

A taxable entity that is a staff leasing services company will exclude from total revenue payments received from a client company for wages, payroll taxes on those wages, employee benefits, and workers' compensation benefits for the assigned employees of the client company. (Sec. 171.1011(k), Tax Code)

- *Transportation companies*

The exclusion of flow through funds described at ¶203 does not generally apply to a transportation company. A transportation company will not be allowed to use the cost of goods sold in computing its margin because it generally provides a service, rather than goods. Finally, transportation companies must report Texas receipts from transportation services in intrastate commerce by:

— the inclusion of revenues that are derived from the transportation of goods or passengers in intrastate commerce within Texas; or

— the multiplication of total transportation receipts by total mileage in the transportation of goods and passengers that move in intrastate commerce within Texas divided by total mileage everywhere.

(*Letter No. 200810208L*, Texas Comptroller of Public Accounts, October 21, 2008, CCH Texas Tax Reports, ¶403-522)

¶207

FRANCHISE TAX

CHAPTER 3

ALLOCATION AND APPORTIONMENT

¶ 301	Allocation and Apportionment—In General
¶ 302	UDITPA
¶ 303	Apportionment Formula

¶301 Allocation and Apportionment—In General

A single-factor apportionment formula is applied to apportion a taxpayer's margin (see ¶ 303).

Texas has adopted the Multistate Tax Compact (MTC). However, the MTC's Uniform Division of Income for Tax Purposes Act (UDITPA) provisions do not apply to Texas franchise tax (¶ 302).

> *Practitioner Comment: Chapter 141 Applicability*
>
> Many years ago, the Legislature adopted the provisions of the Multistate Tax Compact under Chapter 141 of the Tax Code. Article IV of Chapter 141 is that portion of the Compact that applies to the Division of Income. Under § 171.112(d) of the pre-margin tax statutes, Chapter 141 of the Tax Code did not apply to the franchise tax. However, when HB3 was passed, § 171.112 was repealed and the language barring the applicability of Chapter 141 to the franchise tax was not reinstated.
>
> The question now appears whether Article IV of Chapter 141 applies to the revised franchise tax. Article III of Chapter 141 allows a taxpayer to elect to apportion and allocate its net income pursuant Article IV of Chapter 141, with the requirement that the tax in question qualifies as an income tax.
>
> Is the revised franchise tax an income tax or a gross receipts tax? The answer turns, perhaps, on the definitions of each type of tax in Article II. If a taxpayer may deduct expenses that are not specifically and directly related to a particular transaction, then Article II declares the tax to be an income tax. For example, if a taxpayer deducts salary expenses, which are not related to a particular transaction, then the tax is an income tax. And if the election is made, will all the provisions under Article IV apply, or just the specific provision elected?
>
> The Comptroller is bound to argue that Chapter 141 does not apply to the revised franchise tax because of the specific Legislative declaration in HB3 that the new tax is not an income tax. As a result of this argument, Chapter 141 would not apply to Chapter 171 of the Tax Code. It is likely that this issue will be resolved in court.
>
> In July 2011, Allcat Claims Service, L.P., filed a petition with the Texas Supreme Court ("Court") challenging the constitutionality of the Texas franchise tax or the "Margins Tax." The petition claims that the Margins Tax, in effect since 2006, constitutes a tax on a natural person's partnership income. The Texas Constitution provides that the state may not impose a net income tax on natural persons without the approval of a majority of registered voters. Under Texas law, the Court must rule on the constitutionally of the tax within 120 days of the petition or by late November 2011. The Court will hear oral arguments in October.

> Although the Court has been asked to decide whether the Margins Tax is a tax on the income of a natural person, corporations and limited liability companies may be able to amend their Texas franchise tax returns to obtain tax refunds if the Court finds that the Margins Tax is an income tax.
>
> *Eric L. Stein, Ryan*

The Texas Comptroller stated in the July issue of *Tax Policy News* that the apportionment provision in Texas Tax Code Chapter 141, related to the Multistate Tax Compact (MTC), does not apply to the revised Texas franchise tax and entities may not elect to use the MTC's three-factor apportionment formula in lieu of the formula specified in Texas Tax Code Chapter 171. (*Tax Policy News*, Texas Comptroller of Public Accounts, July 2010)

¶302 UDITPA

Law: Secs. 141.001, 171.112(g), Tax Code (CCH TEXAS TAX REPORTS, ¶ 11-505).

The statute governing the apportionment of a taxpayer's margin makes no reference to UDITPA and refers to the apportionment of gross receipts, rather than business and nonbusiness income. Consequently it appears that UDITPA is not incorporated for purposes of the franchise (margin) tax. A regulation provides detailed guidance as to how certain items of gross receipts are to be allocated or apportioned (see ¶ 303).

¶303 Apportionment Formula

Law: Secs. 171.103, 171.105, 171.1055, 171.106, 171.1121, Tax Code; 34 TAC Secs. 3.581, 3.591 (CCH TEXAS TAX REPORTS, ¶ 11-520).

Texas has a single-factor apportionment formula; the single factor is gross receipts. A taxable entity's margin is apportioned to Texas by multiplying the margin by a fraction, the numerator of which is the taxable entity's gross receipts from business done in Texas, and the denominator of which is the taxable entity's gross receipts from its entire business. (Sec. 171.106, Tax Code)

Unlike the former franchise tax, there is no "throwback" rule for purposes of apportioning the margins tax.

"Gross receipts" means all revenues reportable on a taxpayer's federal tax return, without deduction for the cost of property sold, materials used, labor performed, or other costs incurred, unless otherwise specifically provided. (Sec. 171.1121, Tax Code) However, any item of revenue that is excluded from total revenue under Texas law (see ¶ 203) or federal law is excluded from the gross receipts numerator and denominator. (34 TAC Sec. 3.591(d)(5))

A taxpayer must use the same accounting methods to apportion margin as used in computing margin. A taxpayer may not change its accounting methods used to calculate gross receipts more often than once every four years without the express written consent of the Comptroller. A change in accounting methods is not justified solely because it results in a reduction of tax liability. (Sec. 171.1121, Tax Code)

- *Receipts factor numerator*

In apportioning margin a taxpayer's gross receipts from its business done in Texas is the sum of the taxable entity's receipts from:

¶302

Part II—Franchise Tax

— sales of tangible personal property delivered or shipped to buyers in Texas regardless of the FOB point or another condition of sale;

— services performed in Texas, except that receipts derived from servicing loans secured by real property are in Texas if the real property is located in Texas;

— rentals of property situated in Texas;

— the use of a patent, copyright, trademark, franchise, or license in Texas;

— sales of real property located in Texas, including royalties from oil, gas, or other mineral interests; and

— other business done in Texas. (Sec. 171.103, Tax Code)

CCH Advisory: Adoption of Joyce Rule

Texas has adopted the *Joyce* rule for purposes of apportioning the franchise (margin) tax. Consequently, a combined group assigns an entity's gross receipts to a destination state (the state where the sale is made) only if the entity has nexus with the destination state. (Sec. 171.103, Tax. Code)

A combined group must include in its gross receipts the gross receipts of each taxable entity that is a member of the combined group and that has nexus with Texas for the purpose of taxation. A combined group must also provide information regarding the above-listed items on its initial and annual reports for members of the group that do not have nexus with Texas. (Sec. 171.103(b), Tax Code). See ¶507 for a discussion of combined reporting.

Practitioner Comment: Will P.L. 86-272 Reduce A Taxpayer's Revised Franchise Tax?

The apportionment methodology adopted by the Legislature for the revised franchise tax is the *Joyce* rule. That is, only Texas sales of entities with Texas nexus are included in the numerator for purposes of determining the Texas apportionment factor. If the revised franchise tax is determined to be an income tax, then out-of-state entities that are protected under P.L. 86-272 would be able to exclude their Texas sales from the numerator. The applicability of P.L 86-272 will be resolved in court.

In July 2011, Allcat Claims Service, L.P., filed a petition with the Texas Supreme Court ("Court") challenging the constitutionality of the Texas franchise tax or the "Margins Tax." The petition claims that the Margins Tax, in effect since 2006, constitutes a tax on a natural person's partnership income. The Texas Constitution provides that the state may not impose a net income tax on natural persons without the approval of a majority of registered voters. Under Texas law, the Court must rule on the constitutionally of the tax within 120 days of the petition or by late November 2011. The Court will hear oral arguments in October.

Although the Court has been asked to decide whether the Margins Tax is a tax on the income of a natural person, corporations and limited liability companies may be able to amend their Texas franchise tax returns to obtain tax refunds if the Court finds that the Margins Tax is an income tax.

Eric L. Stein, Ryan

¶303

- *Receipts factor denominator*

The gross receipts of a taxable entity from its entire business are the sum of the taxable entity's receipts from:

— each sale of the taxable entity's tangible personal property;

— each service, rental, or royalty; and

— other business.

If a taxable entity sells an investment or capital asset, the taxable entity's gross receipts from its entire business for taxable margin will include only the net gain from the sale. (Sec. 171.105, Tax Code)

CCH Advisory: Gross Receipts Everywhere Not the Same as Total Revenues

"Gross receipts everywhere" does not always equal "total revenue." For instance, the amounts differ in the following situations:

— an entity that treats a loan or security as inventory for federal tax purposes reports the *gain* on the sale of these items as total revenue, but reports the *gross proceeds* on the sale of these items as gross receipts everywhere; or

— an entity subtracts from total revenue expenses that have no related revenue (i.e., expenses that are not flow-through funds). For example, gross receipts everywhere are not reduced by the amount a health care provider subtracts from total revenue for the cost of uncompensated care or the amount a law firm subtracts from total revenue for pro bono work.

(*Tax Policy News*, Texas Comptroller of Public Accounts, June 2009)

- *Exclusion of certain receipts*

Receipts excluded from total revenues (discussed at ¶203), are not included in either the receipts factor numerator or denominator. (Sec. 171.1055(a), Tax Code)

Receipts from transactions between individual members of a combined group that are excluded from total revenues for purposes of calculating the combined group's margin (see ¶507) are also excluded from the apportionment receipts factor numerator and denominator. However, such receipts may be included in the receipts factor numerator if one of the members does not have nexus with Texas and that member resells the property without substantial modification to a third-party purchaser in Texas. (Sec. 171.1055, Tax Code)

Notwithstanding the above, if a loan or security is treated as inventory of the seller for federal income tax purposes, the gross proceeds of the sale of that loan or security are considered gross receipts. (Sec. 171.106(f), Tax Code; *Letter No. 200809240L*, Texas Comptroller of Public Accounts, September 1, 2008, CCH TEXAS TAX REPORTS, ¶403-534) Additionally, effective January 1, 2010, if a lending institution categorizes a loan or security as "securities available for sale" or "trading securities" under Financial Accounting Standard No. 115, (as in effect as of January 1, 2009) the gross proceeds of the sale of that loan or security are also considered gross receipts. (Sec. 171.106(f-1), Tax Code)

¶303

Part II—Franchise Tax 63

> **CCH Comment: Apportionment of Proceeds From Certain Sales of Loans or Securities**
>
> The Texas Comptroller issued a policy letter ruling clarifying that a lending institution may use the gross proceeds from the sale of securities or loans that are categorized under Financial Accounting Standard No. 115 as "available for sale" or "trading securities" for all franchise tax reports originally due on or after January 1, 2008. The Comptroller notes that its position that the classification of a security under financial accounting principles, including FASB Statement No. 115, is not dispositive of the treatment of a security for federal income tax purposes has not changed. For example, for purposes of Sec. 475, a security may in certain cases qualify for the held-for-investment exception to the mark-to-market rules even though, under applicable financial accounting principles, the security is classified as available for sale. (Texas Policy Letter Ruling 201005671L, Texas Comptroller, May 28, 2010)

A banking corporation may exclude from its gross receipts numerator, but not the denominator, interest that is earned on federal funds and interest that is earned on securities that are sold under an agreement to repurchase and that are held in a correspondent bank that is domiciled in Texas. (34 TAC Sec. 3.581(e)(8))

- *Allocation and apportionment rules*

Regulation 34 TAC Sec. 3.591 provides detailed guidance on how to allocate and apportion specified items of income and revenues. Listed below is the treatment outlined in these regulations:

— *Bad Debt:* Bad debt recoveries are gross receipts.

— *Capital assets:* Net gain on sales of intangibles held as capital assets or investments is apportioned to the location of the payor.

— *Computer software services and programs:* Gross receipts from the sale of computer software services are apportioned to the location where the services are performed. Gross receipts from the sale of a computer program are receipts from the sale of an intangible asset and are apportioned to the legal domicile of the payor.

— *Condemnation:* Revenues from condemnation that result from the taking of property are apportioned based on the location of the property condemned.

— *Debt forgiveness:* The amount of a debt that is forgiven is apportioned to the legal domicile of the creditor.

— *Debt retirement:* Revenues from the retirement of a taxable entity's own indebtedness, such as through the taxable entity's purchase of its own bonds at a discount, are gross receipts that are apportioned to the taxable entity's legal domicile. The indebtedness is treated as an investment in the determination of the amount of gross receipts.

— *Deemed sales of assets under Internal Revenue Code § 338:* Amounts that are deemed to have been received by the target taxable entity are treated as sales of assets by the target taxable entity, and are apportioned according to rules that otherwise apply to sales of such assets. The purchaser of the target's stock is considered the purchaser of the assets.

— *Dividends and/or interest:* Dividends that are recognized as a reduction of the taxpayer's basis in stock of a taxable entity for federal income tax purposes are not gross receipts. Dividends that exceed the taxpayer's basis for federal

¶303

income tax purposes that are recognized as a capital gain are treated as dividends for apportionment purposes. Dividends and/or interest that are received from a corporation or other sources and that are includible in a taxpayer's total revenues for purposes of computing an entity's margin are apportioned to the legal domicile of the payor.

Dividends and/or interest that are received from a national bank are apportioned to Texas if the bank's principal place of business is located in Texas. Dividends and/or interest that are received from a bank that is organized under the Texas Banking Code are apportioned to Texas.

— *Exchanges of property:* Exchanges of property are included in gross receipts to the extent that the exchange is recognized as a taxable transaction for federal income tax purposes. Unless otherwise specified, the exchange must be included in receipts based on the gross exchange value.

— *Federal enclave:* All revenues from a taxable entity's sales, services, leases, or other business activities that are transacted on a federal enclave that is located in Texas are Texas receipts, unless otherwise specified.

— *Insurance proceeds:* Business interruption insurance proceeds intended to replace lost profits are apportioned to the legal domicile of the payor of the proceeds. Revenues from fire and casualty insurance proceeds are apportioned to the location of the damaged or destroyed property.

— *Internet access fee:* A fee that is charged to obtain internet access in Texas is a Texas gross receipt.

— *Leases and subleases:* Revenues are apportioned based on the location of the property. Rental receipts for property used both inside and outside Texas, including vessels engaged in commerce, are apportioned using a ratio of the number of days the property is used or engaged in commerce in Texas to total number of days the property is used or engaged in commerce everywhere. If the rental revenues are determined based on miles, the revenues are apportioned using a ratio based on miles used in Texas to total miles everywhere. Receipts from lump sum contracts for leased property that is located both inside and outside Texas are allocated based on the rental value of each item of property.

If a lease, sublease, rental, or subrental of real property or tangible personal property is treated as a sale for federal income tax purposes, then the receipts from the transaction are apportioned in the same manner as a sale. Any portion of the payments that the contracting parties designate as interest is interest receipts.

— *Litigation awards:* Revenues that are realized from litigation awards are gross receipts that are apportioned to the legal domicile of the payor of the proceeds, unless another rule applies.

— *Loan servicing of real property:* Receipts from the servicing of loans secured by real property are apportioned to the location of the real property that secures the loan being serviced.

— *Loans and securities:* If a loan or security is treated as inventory of the seller for federal income tax purposes, the gross proceeds of the sale of that loan or security are considered gross receipts.

— *Membership or enrollment fees paid for access to benefits:* Membership or enrollment fees paid for access to benefits are gross receipts from the sale of an intangible asset and are apportioned to the legal domicile of the payor.

¶303

Part II—Franchise Tax

— *Net distributive income:* The net distributive income from a passive entity that is included in total revenue is apportioned to the principal place of business of the passive entity.

— *Newspapers or magazines:* All advertising revenues of a newspaper or magazine are apportioned to Texas based on the number of newspapers or magazines distributed in Texas. All other receipts must be apportioned in accordance with the other apportionment rules otherwise set out.

— *Patents, copyrights, and other intangible rights:* Revenues from a patent royalty, copyright royalty, trademark, franchise or license are included in Texas receipts to the extent that the patent, copyright, etc. is utilized in Texas. Royalties from an affiliated taxable entity that does not transact a substantial portion of its business or regularly maintain a substantial portion of its assets in the United States are excluded from Texas receipts and receipts everywhere. Sales of intangibles are apportioned based on the location of payor.

— *Radio/television:* All advertising revenues of a radio or television station that broadcasts or transmits from a Texas location constitute Texas receipts. All other receipts must be apportioned in accordance with the other apportionment rules otherwise outlined.

— *Real property:* Revenues from the sale, lease, rental, sublease, or subrental of real property, including mineral interests, are apportioned to the location of the property. Royalties from mineral interests are considered revenue from real property.

— *Sales taxes:* State or local sales taxes that are imposed on the customer, but are collected by a seller are not gross receipts of the seller. However, discounts that a seller are allowed to take in remittance of the collected sales tax are gross receipts to the seller.

— *Securities:* Receipts from the sale of securities are apportioned based on the location of the payor. If securities are sold through an exchange, and the buyer cannot be identified, then 7.9% of the revenue is a Texas receipt.

— *Services:* Receipts from a service are apportioned to the location where the service is performed. If services are performed both inside and outside Texas, then such receipts are Texas receipts on the basis of the fair value of the services that are rendered in Texas. Receipts from services that a defense readjustment project performs in a defense economic readjustment zone are not Texas receipts.

— *Services procurement:* Revenues for the procurement of services are apportioned to the place where the service procurement is performed.

— *Subsidies or grants:* Proceeds of subsidies or grants that a taxable entity receives from a governmental agency are gross receipts, except when the funds are required to be expended dollar-for-dollar (i.e., passed through) to third parties on behalf of the agency. Receipts from a governmental subsidy or grant are apportioned in the same manner as the item to which the subsidy or grant was attributed. For example, if a taxable entity qualifies for a grant to conduct research for the government, then the receipts from that grant are receipts from a service and are apportioned to the location where the research is performed.

— *Tangible personal property:* Numerous examples regarding how to determine if a sale of an item is assignable to Texas are provided in the regulation.

— *Telephone companies:* Revenues from telephone calls that both originate and terminate in Texas are Texas receipts. Revenues from telephone calls that

¶303

originate in Texas but terminate outside of Texas or that originate outside of Texas but terminate in Texas are excluded from Texas receipts. Other revenues from telecommunication services are Texas receipts if the services are performed in Texas. A fee that is charged to obtain access to a local exchange network in Texas and that is based on the duration of an interstate telephone call may be excluded from Texas receipts.

— *Texas waters:* Revenues from transactions that occur in Texas waters are Texas receipts. Texas waters are considered to extend to 10.359 statute miles, or nine nautical miles, from the Texas coastline.

— *Transportation companies:* Transportation companies must report Texas receipts from transportation services in intrastate commerce by: (1) the inclusion of revenues that are derived from the transportation of goods or passengers in intrastate commerce within Texas; or (2) the multiplication of total transportation receipts by total mileage in the transportation of goods and passengers that move in intrastate commerce within Texas divided by total mileage everywhere.

Special rules also apply to the revenues from natural gas production. Taxpayers should consult the regulation for details, see 34 TAC Sec. 3.591(f).

- *Special apportionment rules*

The following paragraphs discuss special apportionment formulas applied to specified taxpayers.

Employee retirement plans.—A taxable entity's margin derived from the sale of management, administration, or investment services to an employee retirement plan is apportioned by multiplying the taxable entity's total margin from the sale of services to an employee retirement plan company by a fraction. The fraction numerator is the average of the sum of beneficiaries domiciled in Texas at the beginning of the year and the sum of beneficiaries domiciled in Texas at the end of the year, and the fraction denominator is the average of the sum of all beneficiaries at the beginning of the year and the sum of all beneficiaries at the end of the year. (Sec. 171.106(c), Tax Code)

Regulated investment companies (RICs).—A taxpayer's margin derived from the sale of management, distribution, or administration services to or on behalf of a RIC, including a taxpayer that includes trustees or sponsors of employee benefit plans that have accounts in a regulated investment company, is apportioned by multiplying the taxpayer's total margin from the sale of services to or on behalf of a RIC by a fraction. The fraction numerator is the average of the sum of shares owned at the beginning of the year and the sum of shares owned at the end of the year by the investment company Texas shareholders, and the fraction denominator is the average of the sum of shares owned at the beginning of the year and the sum of shares owned at the end of the year by all investment company shareholders. (Sec. 171.106(b), Tax Code)

Banking corporations.—A banking corporation excludes from the numerator of the bank's apportionment factor interest earned on federal funds and interest earned on securities sold under a repurchase agreement that are held in this state in a correspondent bank that is domiciled in Texas. (Sec. 171.106(d), Tax Code)

Defense readjustment projects.—Receipts from services that a defense readjustment project performs in a defense economic readjustment zone are not receipts from business done in this state. (Sec. 171.106(e), Tax Code)

Lending institutions.—A lending institution that categorizes a loan or security as "securities available for sale" or "trading securities" under Financial Accounting Standard No. 115, (as in effect as of January 1, 2009) the gross proceeds of the sale of that loan or security are considered gross receipts for purposes of the revised franchise tax. (Sec. 171.106(f-1), Tax Code)

FRANCHISE TAX

CHAPTER 4

CREDITS AND OTHER TAX INCENTIVES

¶401	Credits and Other Tax Incentives
¶402	Temporary Credit for Business Loss Carryovers
¶403	Enterprise Zone Project Investment Credit
¶404	Refund of Wages Paid to Employees Receiving Financial Assistance
¶405	Research and Development Credit
¶406	Economic Development Credits
¶407	Refund for Certain Property Taxes on Property Located in Reinvestment Zone
¶408	Refund for Job Creation in Enterprise Zone
¶409	Clean Energy Project Credit

¶401 Credits and Other Tax Incentives

Law: Sec. 171.111, Tax Code (CCH TEXAS TAX REPORTS, ¶12-001, 12-127, 12-129, 12-150).

Under the franchise (margin) tax all credits that were available against the former franchise tax are repealed. A corporation or limited liability company that had any unused credits established prior to the repeal could claim those unused credits on or with the tax report for the period in which the credits were established. However, special carryover provisions apply to the research and development (¶405), job creation (¶406), and capital investment credits (¶406).

The following chapters outline the temporary credit for business loss carryforwards (¶402) and enterprise zone project investment credits (¶403) that may be claimed against the franchise (margin) tax. In addition, Texas also provides three incentives in the form of tax refunds, which are discussed at ¶404, ¶407, and ¶408.

• *Priority of credits*

Texas currently has no statutory or regulatory provisions governing the prioritization of credits.

¶402 Temporary Credit for Business Loss Carryovers

Law: Sec. 171.111, Tax Code; 34 TAC Sec. 3.594 (CCH TEXAS TAX REPORTS, ¶12-127).

Taxpayers may elect to claim a temporary nonrefundable credit against taxable margin that is based on business loss carryforwards that were created on the 2003 and subsequent franchise tax reports that were not exhausted or expired on a report due before January 1, 2008. To do so, a taxpayer had to notify the Comptroller in writing of its intent to take a credit on a form prescribed by the Comptroller on or before May 15, 2008. The taxpayer may thereafter elect to claim the credit for the current year and future years by the original due date of any report due after 2007 until the taxable entity revokes the election or the credit expires, whichever is earlier. (Sec. 171.111, Tax Code)

> *CCH Practice Tip: Effect of E-Z computation*
>
> For any report year in which the E-Z Computation is used, the business loss carryforward credit for that year is lost and may not be carried over to subsequent years. (34 TAC Sec. 3.594(e))

A taxable entity, other than a combined group, may not claim the credit unless the taxable entity was, on May 1, 2006, subject to the franchise tax as it existed on that date. (Sec. 171.111(d), Tax Code)

A combined group may claim the credit for each member entity that was, on May 1, 2006, subject to the franchise tax as it existed on that date. If a member of a combined group changes combined groups after June 30, 2007, the member's business loss carryforward may no longer be included in the group's temporary credit calculation and the related share of any temporary credit carried over from a previous year is lost to the group. There is no proration for a partial year. In addition, the business loss carryforward does not follow the member to a separately filed report or another combined group. If a member merges into another member of the group, that member's business loss carryforward will remain with the group. If the member dissolves, terminates, or otherwise leaves the group, the business loss carryover of that member is no longer eligible for use. If the combined group adds a new member or members, the credit of the existing members will remain intact, but no credit is allowed for the new member(s). (34 TAC Sec. 3.594(c)(3))

> *Practitioner Comment: Mini-Audit by the Comptroller*
>
> Under Texas Tax Code § 171.111, an entity is entitled to take a credit based on its business loss carryforward as of January 1, 2008. To do so, the entity was required to file a Preservation of Temporary Credit form on or before the original or extended due date of the 2008 report. The temporary credit may then be taken on a tax report, which treated as the election.
>
> At the end of September 2011, the Comptroller sent letters to the reporting entity of every combined report that claimed a temporary credit on a 2008, 2009, or 2010 franchise tax report. The reporting entity is asked to provide the name of the entity or individual that owned, directly or indirectly, more than 50% of all of the entities included on said combined report. Furthermore, the reporting entity is required to report the temporary credit for each affiliate that filed a preservation form or claimed the credit in the 2008 report.
>
> The requested information must be provided by October 31, 2011, or the reporting entity will forfeit all of its temporary credit for prior years and for future years. On a go-forward basis, the reporting entity of a combined group with a temporary credit preserved will need to submit common owner information each year by the due date of the report, regardless of whether the credit is claimed on said report.
>
> Issuing a letter that declares the complete forfeiture of temporary credit for missing a non-statutory deadline may be challengeable as an unlawfully promulgated rule. See Combs v. Entertainment Publications, Inc., 292 S.W.3d 712 (Tex.App.Austin 2009). However, to avoid having to fight that battle with the State, taxpayers may wish to comply timely with the agency's request.
>
> Eric L. Stein, Ryan

Part II—Franchise Tax

- *Credit amount*

The credit is computed by multiplying the amount of the taxpayer's business loss carryforwards determined under the prior net earned surplus provisions by 2.25% for reports originally due after 2007 and before 2018 and by 7.75% for reports originally due after 2017 and before September 1, 2027. This figure is then multiplied by 4.5%. (Sec. 171.111, Tax Code)

CCH Practice Tip: Change in carryforward amount

Once the original notification is made, a taxpayer may change the amount of carryforward preserved only as the result of an Internal Revenue Service (IRS) audit. The taxpayer must notify the Comptroller in writing of the change within 120 days after the IRS audit is final. The taxable entity will be liable for any additional tax, penalty, and interest due for years in which the credit was improperly claimed. (34 TAC Sec. 3.594(d))

- *Planning considerations*

A taxable entity may claim the credit for not more than 20 consecutive privilege periods beginning with the first report originally due after 2007. A taxable entity may make only one credit election, which may not be conveyed, assigned, or transferred to another entity. (Sec. 171.111, Tax Code)

The credit is nonrefundable and may only be claimed if the tax due exceeds $1,000. Unused credit may be carried over to subsequent years. (34 TAC Sec. 3.594(g))

Expiration.—The credit is scheduled to expire on September 1, 2027. Unused credits may not be claimed on reports filed after August 31, 2026.

¶403 Enterprise Zone Project Investment Credit

Law: Secs. 171.815-171.817, Tax Code; 34 TAC Sec. 3.593 (CCH TEXAS TAX REPORTS, ¶12-150).

A qualified business may claim a credit against Texas franchise (margin) tax for a capital investment made after 2004 and before 2007, in a qualified enterprise project. The project must have been designated as an enterprise project after August 31, 2001, and before 2005. An enterprise project is not eligible for this credit if a credit was claimed for the project under the enterprise zone capital investment credit provision that was in effect until January 1, 2008 (see ¶410). (Sec. 171.817, Tax Code; 34 TAC Sec. 3.593)

A taxable entity, other than a combined group, may only claim the credit if it was subject to the franchise tax as it existed on May 1, 2006. A combined group may claim this credit for each member entity that was subject to the franchise tax as it existed on May 1, 2006. (Sec. 171.817, Tax Code)

A "qualified business" must be certified by the Texas Development Bank as a person engaged in or who has provided substantial commitment to initiate the active conduct of a trade or business:

— in an enterprise zone and at least 25% of the person's new employees in the enterprise zone are residents of any Texas enterprise zone or economically-disadvantaged individuals; or

— in Texas and at least 35% of the person's new employees at the qualified business site are residents of a Texas enterprise zone or are economically-disadvantaged individuals. (Sec. 2303.402(c), Gov't Code)

¶403

The capital must be invested in IRC Sec. 1245(a) tangible personal property that is first placed in service in an enterprise zone by an enterprise project. Property that is leased under a capitalized lease qualifies for the credit, but property that is leased under an operating lease is not. In addition, the credit may not be claimed for property expensed under IRC Sec. 179. (Sec. 171.815, Tax Code, Sec. 171.816, Tax. Code)

- *Credit amount*

The credit is equal to 7.5% of the qualified capital investment made after 2004 and before 2007. (Sec. 171.818, Tax Code) The total credit, including any carryforward, may not exceed 50% of the amount of franchise tax due for the report before any other applicable credits. (Sec. 171.819, Tax Code)

- *Planning considerations*

Claiming the credit: Subject to the limitation discussed above, the enterprise project may claim the entire credit earned on a report originally due during 2008. (Sec. 171.818, Tax Code)

Credit carryover: Unused credit may be carried over for five years. (Sec. 171.820, Tax Code)

Fee: At the time the tax credit is received, 3% of the tax benefit must be transferred to the Texas Economic Development Bank Fund. (Sec. 2303.540, Gov't Code)

Assignment of credit: The credit may not be conveyed, assigned, or transferred unless all of the enterprise project's assets are conveyed, assigned, or transferred in the same transaction. (Sec. 171.822)

¶404 Refund of Wages Paid to Employees Receiving Financial Assistance

Law: Sec. 111.109, Tax Code; Secs. 301.101—301.107, Labor Code (CCH Texas Tax Reports, ¶89-224).

Texas Form: 1098 (Employer Application for Refunding Taxes Paid to the State of Texas).

A refund of franchise taxes (and other taxes) is authorized for wages paid by a taxpayer to employees who receive state financial assistance and for whom the taxpayer provides or pays for a portion of the cost of qualifying health benefit coverage; see ¶2002 for details.

¶405 Research and Development Credit

Law: Secs. 171.721—171.731, Tax Code, 34 TAC Sec. 3.593 (CCH Texas Tax Reports, ¶12-150).

Comparable Federal: Sec. 41 (CCH U.S. Master Tax Guide ¶1330).

Texas Forms: Schedule D, Schedule F, Schedule G, Schedule K.

Applicable to franchise tax reports originally due prior to January 1, 2008, corporations could claim a credit for certain incremental qualified research expenses and basic research payments made for research conducted in Texas. The credit was based on the federal credit governed by IRC Sec. 41.

However, if the corporation was unable to exhaust the credit carryover prior to the credit's repeal, the corporation may continue to apply the credit carryover on or with each consecutive report until the earlier of the date the credit would have expired had it continued in existence, or December 31, 2027. (Uncodified Sec. 18, H.B. 3, Laws 2006, as amended by Sec. 33, Ch. 1282, (H.B. 3928), Laws 2007)

The total research and development credit carryforward that a taxable entity may claim for a report may not exceed 50% of the amount of franchise tax that is due for the report before any other tax credits are applied. (34 TAC Sec. 3.593(e))

- *Credit amount*

The credit equaled 5% of qualifying expenses and payments.

Alternative incremental credit: A taxpayer could use the alternative incremental method authorized under IRC Sec. 41(c)(4) for computing the credit if:

— for the corresponding federal tax period, a taxpayer made a federal election to use the alternative method;

— the corporation was a member of a consolidated group that made the alternative election; or

— the corporation did not claim the federal credit.

For purposes of computing the credit under the alternative method for Texas franchise tax purposes, the credit percentages listed in IRC Sec. 41(c)(4)(A) were replaced with 0.41%, 0.55%, and 0.69%, respectively.

Bonus credit: Corporations that made qualified expenditures in a strategic investment area (SIA) were eligible for an increased credit; see ¶410 for a definition of "strategic investment area." For reports due after 2001, a corporation could double the amount of expenditures made in an SIA.

- *Planning considerations*

Carryovers: Unused credit could be carried forward for up to 20 consecutive reports, however, see above for current carryover provisions. A credit carryforward from a previous report was considered to be utilized before the current year's credit.

¶406 Economic Development Credits

Law: Secs. 171.723, 171.751—171.761, 171.801—171.811, Tax Code; 34 TAC Sec. 3.593 (CCH Texas Tax Reports, ¶12-150).

Texas Forms: Schedule D, Schedule H, Schedule J, Schedule K.

Applicable to franchise tax reports originally due prior to 2008 (see ¶401), corporations that made specific investments within a strategic investment area (SIA) could qualify to claim a credit for jobs creation and a credit for capital investment. In addition, a corporation that claimed the credit for research and development, discussed at ¶405, could claim a bonus credit for research and development expenditures within an SIA. However, if the corporation was unable to exhaust the credit carryovers prior to the credit's repeal, the corporation may continue to apply the credit carryover(s) on or with each consecutive report until the earlier of the date the credit(s) would have expired had they continued in existence, or December 31, 2016. (Uncodified Sec. 31.01, S.B. 1, Laws 2011)

The credit for job creation was similar in some ways to the refund of franchise tax authorized for creation of jobs in enterprise zones (¶408).

¶406

Corporations primarily engaged in agricultural processing in a Texas county with a population of less than 50,000 population could qualify for the jobs creation and capital investment credits.

"Strategic investment area" defined: An SIA is either:

— a Texas county with above average unemployment and below state average per capita income;

— an area within Texas that is a federally designated urban enterprise community or an urban enhanced enterprise community; or

— a defense economic readjustment zone.

Loss of designation: A corporation may claim any of the economic development credits or take a carryforward credit for qualified investments made in an SIA even if the area subsequently loses its designation as such.

- *Jobs creation credit*

A qualified business operating in an SIA or an agricultural processing business operating in a low-population county could claim a jobs creation credit if it created at least 10 new qualifying jobs and paid an average weekly wage, for the year in which credits were claimed, of at least 110% of the county average weekly wage for the county where the qualifying jobs are located.

CCH Comment: Wage Requirement Applied Expansively

In a letter ruling issued to a taxpayer, the Texas Comptroller took the position that the county average weekly wage requirement had to be applied to all the jobs in the county, not just the jobs for which the credit was claimed. Thus, the Comptroller determined that the taxpayer was ineligible to claim the credit even though the jobs for which the taxpayer wanted to claim the credit satisfied the 110% of the county average weekly wage requirement.

For example, if a qualified business created 85 new jobs, 27 of which met all of the requirements for the credit and 58 of which did not meet the wage requirement, the corporation could take the tax credit for the 27 qualifying jobs so long as the wages for all of the jobs for that corporation in the county where the new jobs are created average to 110% or more of the county average weekly wage (*Letter,* Texas Comptroller of Public Accounts, No. 200307010L, July 17, 2003, CCH TEXAS TAX REPORTS, ¶402-549).

Qualification criteria: For purposes of this credit, a qualified business was an establishment primarily engaged in agricultural processing, central administrative offices, distribution, data processing, manufacturing, research and development, or warehousing.

A "qualifying job" for purposes of this credit, was one that:

— required at least 1,600 hours of work a year;

— paid at least 110% of the county average weekly wage for the county where the job was located;

— was covered by a group health benefit plan for which the business paid at least 80% of the premiums or other charges assessed under the plan for the employee;

— was not transferred from one area in this state to another area in this state; and

— was not created to replace a previous employee.

¶406

Part II—Franchise Tax

Credit amount: The credit was equal to 5% of the total wages paid for qualifying jobs. The credit was established on five consecutive reports beginning with the report based upon the period during which the qualifying jobs were created.

Planning considerations: The total credit, including any amount carried forward, could not exceed 50% of the amount of tax due for the report period before any other applicable tax credits were claimed. In addition, the amount claimed for this credit plus any amounts claimed for the research and development credit (¶405) and the capital investment credit (see below) could not exceed a taxpayer's franchise tax due for the report period after any other applicable credits. The amount claimed for the jobs creation credit, research and development credit (¶405), the capital investment credit (discussed below), the former child care credit, and the former before or after school child care credit (¶412), including any carryforwards, could not exceed a taxpayer's franchise tax due for the report period.

For reports originally due after 2007, the jobs creation credit carryforward that a taxable entity may claim for a report may not exceed 50% of the amount of franchise tax that is due for the report before any other tax credits are applied. (34 TAC Sec. 3.593(e))

CCH Caution: Interplay with R&D Credit

A corporation could not claim a research and development credit and a jobs creation credit for the same period. However, a corporation with a jobs creation credit carryover could establish a research and development credit in a period to which a jobs creation credit was carried forward (*Franchise Tax Credits for Economic Development*, Comptroller of Public Accounts, February 2001).

Forms: Taxpayers must file Schedules D and H along with their franchise tax report for each year the credit is claimed.

- *Capital investment credit*

A corporation that makes a qualified capital investment in an SIA or that was primarily engaged in agricultural processing in a Texas county with less than 50,000 population was eligible to claim a capital investment credit if the corporation did the following:

— paid an average weekly wage that was at least equal to 110% of the county average weekly wage;

— paid at least 80% of its employees' health care coverage; and

— made a minimum qualified capital investment of $500,000 in the SIA or low-population county.

"Qualified capital investment" defined: A "qualified capital investment" meant tangible personal property first placed in service in an SIA or low-population county, which was described in IRC Sec. 1245(a) (such as engines, machinery, tools, and implements used in a trade or business), and held for investment and subject to an allowance for depreciation, cost recovery under the accelerated cost recovery system (ACRS), or amortization. The term did not include investments in:

— real property or buildings or their structural components;

— property leased under an operating lease; or

— property currently expensed under IRC Sec. 179.

¶406

CCH Comment: Capital Investment Clarified

The Texas Comptroller determined that transportation costs and direct labor costs necessary to fabricate, install, or place tangible personal property in service were included in the qualified capital investment amount eligible for the capital investment credit. However, a qualified capital investment amount did not necessarily include all costs incorporated in the depreciable basis of IRC Sec. 1245(a) property for federal income tax purposes. A qualified capital investment did not include indirect labor costs, interest, intangibles, or overhead. (*Letter*, Texas Comptroller of Public Accounts, No. 200608709L, August 31, 2006, CCH TEXAS TAX REPORTS, ¶403-151)

Credit amount: The credit was equal to 7.5% of the qualified capital investment and was claimed in five equal installments over five years. However, a corporation that was designated as an enterprise project or as a defense readjustment project could claim the entire credit earned on a report originally due after August 31, 2003, and before January 1, 2006.

Planning considerations: The total credit, including any amount carried forward, could not exceed 50% of the amount of tax due for the report period before any other applicable tax credits were claimed. In addition, the amount claimed for this credit plus any amounts claimed for the research and development credit (¶409) and the jobs creation credit (see above) could not exceed a taxpayer's franchise tax due for the report period after any other applicable credits. In addition, the amount claimed for the capital investment credit, jobs creation credit, research and development credit (¶409), the child care credit (¶411), and the before or after school child care credit (¶412), including any carryforwards, could not exceed a taxpayer's franchise tax due for the report period.

A corporation could claim a credit or take a carryforward credit for a qualified capital investment made after 2002, even if the county in which it made the investment lost its designation as a strategic investment area if:

— the corporation committed to the investment in that county before 2003;

— at the time the corporation made the commitment, the county was designated as a strategic investment area;

— the total investment was at least $100 million;

— the county had a population of less than 15,700; and

— the corporation made a qualified capital investment in the county in each of the two years preceding the year in which the corporation made the qualified capital investment.

For reports originally due after 2007, the total qualified capital investment credit carryforward that a taxable entity may claim for a report may not exceed 50% of the amount of franchise tax that is due for the report before any other tax credits are applied. (34 TAC Sec. 3.593(g))

A taxable entity may not take any remaining unaccrued installments of the credit if the taxable entity:

— disposes of the qualified capital investment, unless a replacement of equal or greater value is purchased within 90 days;

— takes the qualified capital investment out of service;

— moves the qualified capital investment out of the strategic investment area; or

¶406

— fails to pay an average weekly wage, at the location for which the credit is claimed, that amounts to at least 110% of the county average weekly wage. (34 TAC Sec. 3.593(g))

Carryovers: Unused credit could be carried forward for up to five consecutive reports. A credit carryforward from a previous report was considered to be utilized before the current credit. However, see the discussion above for the carryover provisions effective January 1, 2008.

¶407 Refund for Certain Property Taxes on Property Located in Reinvestment Zone

Law: Secs. 111.301, 111.302, Tax Code; 34 TAC Sec. 9.105 (CCH Texas Tax Reports, ¶89-224).

Texas Form: AP-186 (Application for Refund of State Taxes Paid by Person Owning Certain Abated Property).

A refund of franchise tax is allowed for taxes paid in a calendar year for which the taxpayer has also paid property taxes to a school district on property that is:

— located in a reinvestment zone established under Chapter 312 of the Tax Code;

— wholly or partly exempt from municipal or county property taxes under a tax abatement agreement with the municipality or county entered into after January 1, 1996; and

— not subject to a tax abatement agreement with the school district.

Limitations: The refund may not exceed the amount of property taxes paid to the school district for the applicable tax year that the taxpayer would not have had to pay if the school district had entered a tax abatement agreement with the taxpayer covering the property on the same terms as the applicable municipal or county tax abatement agreement. The refund is available only if:

— the taxpayer establishes a new business in the reinvestment zone;

— expands an existing business located in the reinvestment zone; or

— modernizes an existing business located in the reinvestment zone to retain jobs of employees of the business.

In addition, the business must:

— increase its payroll by at least $3 million, specific to property located in Texas, after the taxpayer enters into the tax abatement agreement with the municipality or county; or

— experience an increase of at least $4 million in the appraised value of its property subject to the tax abatement agreement after an initial comparison year beginning after 1995.

A taxpayer that makes certain payments in lieu of property taxes or makes certain other payments such as gifts, grants, or donations to a municipality or county during the period of the tax abatement agreement may be ineligible for the refund.

Procedures: A taxpayer's refund for a calendar year may not exceed the taxpayer's net state franchise tax and state sales and use taxes paid, after any applicable tax credit, in that year. A taxpayer is eligible for refunds only for the lesser of five years or the duration of the tax abatement agreement.

An application for refund must be filed with the Comptroller before August 1 of the year after the tax year for which the taxpayer has paid the property taxes on which the refund is based. Within 90 days of receiving an application for refund, the Comptroller will compute the total amount of eligible refunds and grant them in full if the total amount allowed is less than $10 million or, if the total amount exceeds $10 million, reduce the amount of each refund to allow all claimants to share proportionally $10 million in total refunds. No interest is paid on the refunds.

The amount of the refund for those taxpayers with an abatement agreement that exempts different portions of property value is computed based on the greater of the portions exempted. The amount by which any taxpayer's refund is reduced may not be included in a taxpayer's refund claim for a subsequent year. If the tax abatement agreement is canceled or the taxpayer relocates the taxpayer's business outside the reinvestment zone, no refund may be applied for after the date of the cancellation or relocation.

¶408 Refund for Job Creation in Enterprise Zone

Law: Sec. 171.501, Tax Code (CCH Texas Tax Reports, ¶89-224).

Texas Form: 00-105.

Texas authorizes a partial refund of franchise taxes to enterprise zone businesses that create new jobs. A qualified enterprise zone business that creates 10 or more new jobs for qualified employees during the calendar year containing the end of the accounting period on which its franchise tax report is based is entitled to a refund equal to the lesser of (1) 25% of the franchise tax due for that privilege period before any other applicable credits or (2) $5,000. For purposes of the refund, the initial and second reporting periods are considered to be the same privilege period.

A "qualified business" is one certified by the Department of Economic Development as a qualified business pursuant to the requirements of the Government Code.

Procedures: For a qualified business to receive the refund, the governing body or bodies of an enterprise zone must certify the eligibility of the business to the Department of Economic Development, which must in turn certify the business's eligibility to the Comptroller. No more than three qualified businesses may be certified from any one enterprise zone during one calendar year.

A municipality or county may certify no more than a total of three qualified businesses from all enterprise zones for which it is a governing body, and must allocate certifications as evenly as possible among zones. The Department of Economic Development may require multiple governing bodies to make joint certifications and to follow uniform procedures or selection criteria in selecting businesses for certification.

¶409 Clean Energy Project Credit

Law: Secs. 490.352, Gov't Code, (CCH Texas Tax Reports, ¶12-129).

Entities implementing clean energy projects may be eligible for a franchise tax credit, beginning September 1, 2013, equal to the lesser of 10% of the total capital cost of the project or $100 million, provided that:

— the Railroad Commission has issued a certificate of compliance for the project;

— the facility is completed and fully operational;

¶408

— the Bureau of Economic Geology of the University of Texas at Austin has verified that the facility is sequestering at least 70% of the carbon dioxide resulting from the generation of electricity by the facility; and

— the project's owners have signed an interconnection agreement with the Electric Reliability Commission of Texas. (Sec. 490.352, Gov't Code)

- *Credit amount*

The credit is equal to 10% of the total capital cost of the project, up to a $100 million maximum.

The amount of the franchise tax credit for each report year is calculated by determining the amount of franchise tax that is due based on the taxable margin generated by a clean energy project from the generation and sale of power and the sale of any products that are produced by the electric generation facility. The amount of the franchise tax credit claimed under this section for a report year may not exceed the amount of franchise tax attributable to the clean energy project for that report year.

Capital costs include the cost of designing, engineering, permitting, constructing, and commissioning the project, the cost of procuring land, water, and equipment for the project, and all fees, taxes, and commissions paid and other payments made in connection with the project, but exclude the cost of financing the capital cost of the project. (Sec. 490.352, Gov't Code)

FRANCHISE TAX

CHAPTER 5

RETURNS AND PAYMENT

¶ 501	Privilege Periods
¶ 502	Payment Due Dates
¶ 503	Payment Upon Withdrawal, Merger, Consolidation, or Conversion
¶ 504	Reports
¶ 505	Extensions
¶ 506	Confidentiality
¶ 507	Combined Reports

¶ 501 Privilege Periods

Law: Secs. 171.001, 171.151—171.154, Tax Code; 34 TAC Secs. 3.544, 3.595 (CCH Texas Tax Reports, ¶ 89-102).

Taxable entities that become subject to the franchise tax **on or after October 4, 2009,** will file a first annual report in lieu of an initial franchise tax report. If a taxable entity became subject to the franchise tax from October 4, 2009, through December 31, 2009, the entity will have a first annual report due on May 17, 2010. Entities that become subject to the tax during calendar year 2010 will have a first annual report due on May 16, 2011. The first annual report will be based on the accounting period beginning on the date the entity became subject to the tax and ending on the last accounting period ending date for federal income tax reporting purposes in the calendar year before the year the report is originally due. (2010 Texas Franchise Tax Report Information and Instructions, Texas Comptroller of Public Accounts, October 2009)

For reports due prior to October 4, 2009, There were three periods covered by franchise tax payments—an initial period, a second period, and regular annual periods. These periods were also referred to as "privilege periods."

- *Initial period*

The initial period for tax payment commenced on a taxable entity's "beginning date," which for a taxable entity chartered or organized in this state was the date a taxable entity's charter or organization took effect. For a foreign taxable entity the beginning date was the date it begins doing business in the state. The initial period ended on the day before the first anniversary of the beginning date.

The franchise (margin) tax covering the privilege periods included on the initial report wa based on the business done by the taxable entity during the period beginning on the taxable entity's beginning date and ending on: (1) the last accounting period ending date that is at least 60 days before the original due date of the initial report; or (2) if there is no such period ending date, then ending on the day that is the last day of a calendar month and that is nearest to the end of the taxable entity's first year of business.

Example:

A Texas taxable entity that is chartered on June 1, 2008, must pay tax with the initial report for the privilege periods from June 1, 2008—December 31, 2009. In addition, when the first anniversary occurs during the period from October 4 through December 31, there must also be computed and paid with the initial report an additional year's tax for the privilege period beginning on January 1 following the first anniversary and ending on the following December 31.

For example, if a Texas taxable entity is chartered on November 1, 2008, the payment due with the initial report will be for the privilege periods from November 1, 2008—December 31, 2010. The taxable margin computed on the initial report is based on the business done during the period beginning on the beginning date and ending on the last accounting period ending date for federal income tax purposes that is at least 60 days before the original due date of the initial report, or, if there is no such ending date, then ending on the day that is the last day of the calendar month nearest to the end of the taxable entity's first year of business. (34 TAC Sec. 3.584)

- *Second report period*

The second period covered by the franchise tax commences on the first anniversary of the beginning date and ends on the following December 31. The tax is based on the same business as the tax covering the initial period, and is prorated based on the length of the second period. (Sec. 171.151, Sec. 171.152, Tax Code)

- *Regular annual periods*

The first regular annual period begins the January 1 after the end of the second period and ends the following December 31. Thereafter, a regular annual period begins each year on January 1 and ends on the following December 31.

The tax covering the regular annual period, other than a regular annual period included on the initial report, is based on the business done by the taxable entity during the period beginning with the day after the last date upon which taxable margin on a previous report was based and ending with its last accounting period ending date for federal income tax purposes in the year before the year in which the report is originally due, or if there is no such ending date, then ending on December 31 of the calendar year prior to the reporting calendar year.

CCH Planning Note: Change of Accounting Period

Notification or approval of a change in accounting year end was not required for franchise tax reporting purposes under the former franchise tax provisions. Additionally, a corporation is not required to file any short period franchise tax reports because of the change in accounting year end. Generally a corporation's change in accounting year end will be reflected on its next annual franchise tax report. (*Letter,* Texas Comptroller of Public Accounts, No. 200606694L, June 1, 2006, CCH TEXAS TAX REPORTS, ¶403-148) Presumably, the same reasoning would be applied to the franchise (margin) tax.

¶502 Payment Due Dates

Law: Sec. 171.152, Tax Code; 34 TAC Secs. 3.544, 3.567, 3.584 (CCH TEXAS TAX REPORTS, ¶89-102).

The initial report (¶504) and payment for the initial period (¶501) are due no later than 89 days after the first anniversary date of a taxable entity's beginning date.

The franchise tax covering the regular annual period (¶501) is due May 15 of each year after the beginning of the regular annual period. However, if the first anniversary of the beginning date is after October 3 and before January 1, the

Part II—Franchise Tax

payment of the tax covering the first regular annual period is due on the same date as the tax covering the initial period.

> ### Practitioner Comment: Loss of Nexus
>
> An entity that files its initial franchise tax report remits tax for the initial, second, and sometimes the first regular annual privilege periods. However, if that entity leaves the state prior to the expiration of the privilege periods included on the initial report, it will be liable for franchise tax for only those privilege periods in which it had nexus for one day. In other words, if the entity leaves the state within the initial privilege period, it should request a refund for franchise tax paid for the second and any regular annual privilege periods included in the initial franchise tax report.
>
> Eric L. Stein, Ryan

The additional tax imposed on certain entities that cease to do business in Texas (¶102) is due, along with a final report, within 60 days after the entities no longer have sufficient nexus with Texas to be subject to the franchise (margin) tax. An estimated return and payment may need to be filed and paid before a corporation will receive clearance from the Comptroller to dissolve, merge, or withdraw (see ¶503).

¶503 Payment Upon Withdrawal, Merger, Consolidation, or Conversion

Law: Secs. 171.1531, 171.158, Tax Code; 34 TAC Secs. 3.565, 3.568.

Texas Form: 05-139 (Texas Final Corporation Franchise Tax Report).

Withdrawal: A foreign taxable entity may not withdraw from doing business in Texas unless it has first paid any franchise tax or penalty due. Once such payments are made, the withdrawal is accomplished by filing a certificate of withdrawal with the Secretary of State. (Sec. 171.158, Tax Code)

Conversion: An entity that was subject to franchise tax prior to conversion and that continues to be subject to franchise tax after conversion will not have a new beginning date for franchise tax purposes because of the conversion. However, for an entity that becomes subject to the franchise tax as a result of a conversion, the date of the conversion is the beginning date for franchise tax purposes. The Texas Secretary of State may not issue a certificate of conversion unless all franchise taxes have been paid or the articles of conversion provide that the converted entity will be liable for the payment of such franchise taxes. (34 TAC Sec. 3.568)

Termination: If a foreign corporation or foreign LLC doing business in Texas is dissolved, merged out of existence, or otherwise terminated under the laws of its state of incorporation or organization, it may close its Texas franchise tax account only by paying all franchise tax, penalties, and interest owed through the end of the privilege period in which the entity is dissolved. No refund or credit is available for the period from the date of the dissolution, merger, or withdrawal through the end of the privilege period. (34 TAC Sec. 3.568)

Corporations and limited liability companies (LLCs) that dissolve, merge, withdraw, or gain reinstatement must pay all franchise tax, penalty, and interest owed through the end of the privilege period containing the effective date of the dissolution, merger, withdrawal, or reinstatement. No refund or credit is given for the period from the date of the organizational change through the end of the privilege period. In addition, domestic corporations and LLCs seeking to dissolve must obtain a certificate from the Comptroller stating that all taxes administered by the Comptroller, including franchise taxes, have been paid through the effective date of the dissolution. (34 TAC Sec. 3.568)

¶503

¶504 Reports

Law: Secs. 171.109, 171.110, 171.112, 171.1121, 171.201, 171.202, 171.2022, 171.203, 171.204, 171.212, Tax Code; 34 TAC Secs. 3.544, 3.547, 3.584 (CCH Texas Tax Reports, ¶89-102).

Texas Forms: 05-141 (Franchise No Tax Due Information Report), 05-142 (Texas Corporation Franchise Tax Report), 05-143 (Texas Corporation Franchise Tax Report), 05-158-A Franchise (Margin) Tax Report, page 1, 05-158-B Franchise (Margin) Tax Report, page 2, 05-163 (No Tax Due Information Report).

Each taxable entity subject to franchise tax must mail an initial franchise tax report and an annual franchise tax report thereafter, unless the entity owes no franchise tax. However, an information report must be filed even if no tax is due. The filing of a consolidated return is prohibited. However, combined reporting is required (see ¶507).

Forms may be obtained by writing to the Comptroller of Public Accounts, P.O. Box 13528, Austin, TX 78711-3528, or by calling 1-800-252-1381. Forms may also be downloaded from the Comptroller's Internet website at http://window.state.tx.us/taxinfo/taxforms/05-forms.html.

Initial report: A taxable entity subject to franchise tax must file an initial report with the Comptroller no later than 89 days after the first anniversary date of the taxable entity's "beginning date." The "beginning date" for a taxable entity chartered or organized in Texas is the date the taxable entity's charter or organization takes effect, and the "beginning date" for a foreign taxable entity is the date on which the entity begins doing business in Texas.

CCH Practice Tip: Initial Report Filing Requirements Revised

The annual report for entities that become subject to the Texas franchise tax after October 3, 2009 is the first franchise tax report that a taxable entity must file and it is due May 15 in the year following the calendar year the entity became subject to the tax. The first annual report will be based on the accounting period beginning on the date the entity became subject to the franchise tax and ending on the last accounting period ending date used for federal income tax reporting purposes in the calendar year before the year the report is originally due. A taxable entity that has a federal tax year end date that is prior to the franchise tax responsibility begin date for the first franchise tax report filed will file a one-day No Tax Due Information Report with zero revenue. A Public Information Report, Ownership Information Report, Affiliate Schedule, etc., must also be filed as applicable.

A taxable entity that ends its franchise tax responsibility in the same year that it became subject to the tax will not owe an annual report the following year; instead, the entity will owe a final report for the year it ends its responsibility, due 60 days after its ending date. (*Tax Policy News*, Texas Comptroller of Public Accounts, October 2009)

The initial report must contain the following:

— financial information of the taxable entity necessary to compute the franchise (margin) tax;

— the name and address of each officer, director, and manager of the taxable entity, or if a limited partnership, each general partner; for each general partnership or limited liability partnership, each managing partner or, if there is not a managing partner, each partner; or for a trust, each trustee;

— the name and address of the entity's resident agent designated for service of process; and

— other information required by the Comptroller. (Sec. 171.201, Tax Code)

Part II—Franchise Tax

CCH Practice Tip: Combined Groups

Generally, an entity that is part of a combined group would not report its data on a separate initial report, but would include its data with the combined group's report for the corresponding accounting period. However, if the entity was not part of the combined group for any portion of the accounting period that would be covered by its initial report or has an accounting year begin date that is before the accounting year begin date that will be used by the combined group, the entity is required to file a separate initial report for the period that will not be included in the combined report. (*Tax Policy News*, Vol. XIX, Issue 2, Texas Comptroller of Public Accounts, February 2009)

Annual report: The annual franchise tax report, required of all taxable entities unless they owe no tax, is due May 15 of each year after the beginning of the regular annual period (¶ 501).

The annual report must be filed on forms supplied by the Comptroller and must contain the following:

— financial information of the taxable entity necessary to compute the franchise tax;

— the name and address of each officer and director of the taxable entity;

— the name and address of the entity's resident agent designated for service of process; and

— other information required by the Comptroller. (Sec. 171.202, Tax Code)

Annual abbreviated report: Taxable entities may file an abbreviated report for the reporting period at issue if the entity had:

— no Texas gross receipts;

— total revenue of less than $300,000; or

— total tax due of less than $1,000.

Public information report: Corporations or LLCs subject to franchise tax must file an annual public information report with the Comptroller on Form 5-102. The public information report must be signed by a corporate or LLC officer, director, or another authorized person, unless it is filed electronically. A copy of the public information report must be sent to each person who is a corporate or LLC officer or director on the date the report is filed and who is not currently employed by the corporation or LLC filing the report or by a related corporation or LLC.

Ownership information reports.—Ownership Information Reports (OIR), Form 05-167, must be filed annually for each taxable entity other than a legally formed corporation, limited liability company, or financial institution. This includes professional associations, partnerships, and trusts.

The OIR is due on the date the franchise tax report is due and must be completed and signed by a partner, member, owner, or other authorized person of the taxable entity. A separate OIR is to be filed by each taxable entity that files a separate franchise tax report or that is part of a combined group (unless the taxable entity does not have physical presence in Texas).

Even if the franchise tax report is filed and all taxes paid, the entity's right to transact business may be forfeited for failure to file the completed, signed OIR. The effects of forfeiture may include the denial of the taxable entity's right to sue or defend in a Texas court, and each partner, member, or owner may become personally liable for certain debts of the entity. (Secs. 171.251, 171.252, and 171.255, Tax Code)

Amended reports: Amended reports may be filed by a taxpayer:

— to correct a mathematical or other error in a report;

¶504

— to support a claim for a refund; or

— to change its method of computing margin to 70% of total revenue or, if qualified, to the E-Z Computation.

A taxable entity *must* file an amended franchise tax report if:

(1) there are changes to the entity's taxable margin as a result of a final Revenue Agent's Report (RAR) issued after an Internal Revenue Service (IRS) audit;

(2) the entity files an amended federal income tax return or other return that changes the entity's taxable margin;

(3) there are changes to an entity's taxable margin as a result of an audit or other adjustment by a competent authority other than the IRS;

(4) a final determination resulting from an IRS administrative proceeding or a judicial proceeding arising from an administrative proceeding that affects the amount of franchise tax liability.

The amended report must be filed by the 120th day after the RAR or other adjustment is final if situation (1), (3), or (4) occurs. The RAR or other adjustment is final on the date on which all administrative appeals with the IRS or other competent authority have been exhausted or waived. An administrative appeal with the IRS does not include an action or proceeding in the U.S. Tax Court or any other federal court. The amended report must be filed by the 120th day after the entity files its amended federal income tax return or other return if situation (2) occurs.

Practitioner Comment: Report Years Barred from Amendment

Although the statutes require a corporation that receives an RAR to timely amend the affected franchise tax reports, the Comptroller bars a corporation from amending its franchise tax reports for any RAR adjustment that is not within the statute of limitations as of September 1, 1997. In other words, if a corporation receives an adjustment in an RAR for its 1991 accounting year, which would affect the 1992 franchise tax report, it would be barred from amending its 1992 franchise tax report because it would not be open under the four-year statute of limitations as of September 1, 1997. See *Comptroller's Hearing No. 42,310* (2003), CCH TEXAS TAX REPORTS, ¶ 402-586.

Eric L. Stein, Ryan

An entity *may* file an amended report to correct a mathematical or other error in the report or to support a claim for refund. However, changes in accounting estimates, such as changes in estimates of service lives and salvage values of depreciable assets, do not qualify as accounting errors that would allow an amended report to be filed. Changes in accounting estimates may be made only prospectively and must be based on facts that substantiate that the newly proposed estimate is correct while the original estimate was erroneous. (*Decision of the Texas Comptroller of Public Accounts, Hearing* No. 42,492, June 30, 2003, CCH TEXAS TAX REPORTS, ¶ 402-574) Nor may an amended report be filed to change between a cost of goods sold deduction and a compensation deduction.

Practitioner Comment: Final Report

An entity that is seeking to receive clearance from the Comptroller to dissolve, merge, or withdraw, must file a final report in order to obtain the necessary certificate from the Comptroller. If the requisite financial information is not available at the time the entity must exit the state, it is permissible to file a zero tax due final report in order to secure the necessary certificate from the Comptroller to present to the Secretary of State. Provided the estimated final report is amended to reflect the correct liability within the 60-day filing period, the Comptroller will not assess any penalty or interest.

¶504

Part II—Franchise Tax

Under the revised Texas franchise tax, when an affiliate is sold from one unitary group to another unitary group, a final report is filed but no tax is due. The financial information of the affiliate is split between the two reporting groups based on the effective date of the sale.

Eric L. Stein, Ryan

CCH Practice Tip: Final Report for Members of a Combined Group

Generally, if an entity that ceases doing business in Texas is part of a combined group, the data that should be reported on the final report would be included in the combined group's report for the corresponding accounting period. The entity should use Form 05-359 (Request for Certificate of Account Status) to identify the reporting entity of the combined group. If an entity was not part of the combined group for any portion of the accounting period that would be covered by its final report, the entity is required to file a final report for the period that will not be included in the combined report. However, if every member of a combined group ceases doing business in Texas, the reporting entity must file a final report for the combined group. (*Tax Policy News*, Vol. XIX, Issue 2, Texas Comptroller of Public Accounts, February 2009)

- *No tax due entities*

A taxable entity will owe no tax if its tax due is less than $1,000, it has zero Texas receipts, or its annualized total revenue is less than or equal to $1 million ($600,000 for reports due after 2011). A taxable entity that does not owe any tax must still file a report as follows:

— a taxable entity, other than a combined group, that has zero Texas receipts or has annualized total revenue of $1 million or less may file a No Tax Due Information Report;

— a taxable entity that has tax due of less than $1,000 cannot file a No Tax Due Information Report and must file either a regular annual report or, if qualified, the E-Z Computation Report; and/or

— a combined group cannot file a No Tax Due Information Report and must file either a regular annual report or, if qualified, the E-Z Computation Report.

(34 TAC Sec. 3.584(d)(5)(C))

¶505 Extensions

Law: Secs. 171.202, 171.362, Tax Code; 34 TAC Secs. 3.545, 3.585 (CCH Texas Tax Reports, ¶89-102).

Texas Form: 05-164 (Texas Franchise Tax Extension Request), Form 05-165 (Texas Franchise Tax Extension Affiliate List).

Texas allows extensions for filing franchise tax reports, but the rules differ for taxable entities required to make payments by electronic funds transfer (EFT) and those who are not required to make payments by EFT. Requirements for making payments by EFT are discussed at ¶1805. In addition, a taxpayer may telefile its extension request if the taxpayer owed no tax for the previous year or will owe no tax on the current year's franchise tax report by calling 1-888-434-5464 on or before the due date of the report. In addition, filing extensions may be made electronically on the Comptroller's WebFile site at: http://www.window.state.tx.us/taxinfo/franchise/webfile_franchise.html.

- *Corporations not required to make payments by EFT*

The Comptroller must grant an extension for the filing of an annual franchise tax report by an entity not required to make its tax payments by EFT, until any date on or before the next November 15 if the entity requests the extension on 05-164, Texas Franchise Tax Extension Request, by May 15.

To receive the extension the entity must remit with the request at least (1) 90% of the amount of tax reported as due on the report filed by November 15, or (2) 100% of the tax reported as due on the prior year's timely filed report (without extensions). The option to pay 100% of the tax paid in the previous year is not available to newly taxable entities, entities that failed to file the prior year's report on or before May 14, or entities that were included in a combined report originally due in the previous calendar. (34 TAC Sec. 3.585) (Form 05-165 Instructions) However, it is available to entities that filed a previous year report but had zero tax liability. (*Letter No. 200809204L*, Texas Comptroller of Public Accounts, September 30, 2008, CCH TEXAS TAX REPORTS, ¶ 403-510)

A taxpayer whose previous return was its initial report must pay an amount produced by multiplying the corporation's taxable margin, as reported on its initial report filed by May 14 (of the year for which the extension is requested), by the applicable rate of tax imposed on taxable margin that is effective January 1 of the year in which the report is due. (Sec. 171.202, Tax Code)

A special rule applies to a taxable entity that is not required to make franchise tax payments by EFT that elects to obtain an extension for filing its report by paying 90% of the tax due for the year at the time it requests the extension. If the payment made by the entity at the time it requested the extension turns out to be less than 90% of the tax due for the year, penalty and interest will be imposed on the difference between the amount so paid and the 90% required to have been paid. If, however, the amount paid is at least 90% of the tax due for the year or the entity obtains the extension by paying 100% of the tax paid in the previous year, no penalties will be imposed on any further amounts of the tax due for the year if remitted on or before November 15. (Sec. 171.362, Tax Code; 34 TAC Sec. 3.585)

CCH Practice Tip: Combined groups

A reporting entity filing an extension request on behalf of a combined group must file a Form 05-165, Texas Franchise Tax Extension Affiliate List, with the extension request Form 05-164. However, a combined group required to pay electronically using TEXNET is only required to file an Extension Affiliate List. The Affiliate List will be submitted only once: when the extension request is originally filed. It does not need to be submitted again, either with the second extension request or when the report and Affiliate Schedule are filed.

NOTE: If an entity was included on the Affiliate List but not on the Affiliate Schedule, the combined group will not be in good standing. If an entity was included on the Affiliate List in error, the taxpayer should notify the Comptroller's office in writing explaining the error and whether the entity will be reporting separately, or as a part of another combined group.

Combined groups must have paid at least 90% of the tax that will be due on the current year's report unless all members of the combined group were previously subject to the franchise tax. (*Tax Policy News, Vol. XVIII, Issue 7*, Texas Comptroller of Public Accounts, July 2008; *Tax Policy News*, Texas Comptroller of Public Accounts, April 2009)

- *Corporations required to make payments by EFT*

The Comptroller is required to extend the filing deadline from May 15 to any date on or before August 15 for a taxable entity that is required to pay franchise taxes by EFT if the entity files form 05-164, Texas Franchise Tax Extension Request, by May 15. To qualify for the extension the entity must remit with the request either (1) 90% or more of the tax ultimately reported as due in the current year by August 15, or (2) 100% of the tax reported as due for the previous calendar year on the report due in the previous calendar year and filed by May 14. The option to pay 100% of the tax paid in the previous year is not available to newly taxable entities, entities that failed to file the prior year's report on or before May 14, or entities that were included in a

Part II—Franchise Tax

combined report originally due in the previous calendar. (34 TAC Sec. 3.585) (Form 05-165 Instructions) An additional 3-month extension is also available to an entity that files an extension request (Form 05-164), by August 15 and remits with the request the difference between the amount remitted under the first extension and 100% of the amount of tax reported as due on the report filed by November 15.

Practitioner Comment: Interest-Free Deferral Payments

Because an extension effectively changes the due date of the franchise tax payment, a taxpayer filing a regular annual report in the current year that faces a higher franchise tax liability than in its regular annual report filed last year may remit 100% of the tax paid on its regular annual report filed last year and defer the payment on the balance of the franchise tax owed in the current year interest-free until November 15 for non-EFT filers and until August 15 for EFT filers.

Under the revised Texas franchise tax, if any member of the unitary combined group has been notified of its responsibility to file its taxes under EFT, the EFT obligation binds the entire group.

Eric L. Stein, Ryan

Practitioner Comment: Statute of Limitations for EFT Filers

For EFT filers that are required to remit 100% of the tax owed in the current report year in order to qualify to extend the filing date of the report from August 15 to November 15, any franchise tax due with the November 15 report means that the August 15 extension was not valid. As a result, the statute of limitations for the current year runs from August 15, not November 15.

For most taxpayers, the filing status changes under the new margin tax from a single entity to a combined entity. Therefore, a combined group of taxpayers cannot rely upon the 100% paid of the prior year's franchise tax report extension provision under the **Tax Code for purposes of the 2008 report year.**

Because the Comptroller granted a universal extension for the 2008 report from May 15, 2008, to June 16, 2008, it is unclear whether all the extensions filed by a taxpayer in 2008 will extend the statute of limitations four-years hence. In other words, if a taxpayer extended through November 15, 2008, but relied on the Comptroller's universal extension, and not the statute, to qualify for that extension, will that taxpayer have to file a refund for report year 2008 by May 15, 2012, or November 15, 2012. A similar issue applies for assessment purposes. Our recommendation is to file 2008 report year refunds in this situation by May 15, 2012, and protest any assessment issued after that date.

Eric L. Stein, Ryan

¶506 Confidentiality

Law: Secs. 171.206—171.210, 171.361, Tax Code (CCH Texas Tax Reports, ¶ 89-136).

With the exceptions discussed below, information obtained from documents filed with the Comptroller and from examinations connected with the franchise tax is confidential. No person who has access to confidential information may make known in a manner not permitted by law, the amount or source of the taxable entity's income, profits, losses, expenditures, cost of goods sold, compensation, or other information relating to the entity's financial condition. (Sec. 171.208, Tax Code) To do so is an offense punishable by a fine of not more than $1,000, confinement in jail for not more than one year, or both. (Sec. 171.361, Tax Code)

¶506

• *Exceptions*

Information contained in a document filed with a county clerk as notice of a tax lien is open to public inspection. The information contained in the public information report (¶ 504) is also open to public inspection.

The Comptroller or Attorney General may use confidential information to enforce the franchise tax provisions, and may authorize the use of the information in a judicial proceeding in which the state is a party. They may also authorize examination of the information by other Texas state officers or law enforcement officials, or by tax officials of another state or of the federal government, provided the other state or the federal government has a reciprocal arrangement with Texas. (Sec. 171.210, Tax Code)

Owners of a taxable entity are entitled to examine or receive a copy of initial or annual reports. (Sec. 171.209, Tax Code)

¶ 507 Combined Reports

Law: Secs. 171.0001, 171.1014, Tax Code; 34 TAC Sec. 3.584 (CCH TEXAS TAX REPORTS, ¶ 11-550).

Taxable entities that are part of an affiliated group engaged in a unitary business must file a combined group report based on the combined group's business. The combined report is in lieu of individual reports for the group members, except that a public information report or ownership information report must be filed for each member of the combined group with nexus, see ¶ 501. (34 TAC Sec. 3.584(c)(1)(H))

Caution Note: Joint and Several Liability

Each member of a combined group is jointly and severally liable for the tax of the combined group. (Sec. 171.1014(i), Tax Code)

Reporting is done on a water's-edge basis. Consequently the combined group may not include a taxable entity that conducts business outside the United States if 80% or more of the taxable entity's property and payroll are assigned to locations outside the U.S utilizing the Multistate Tax Compact apportionment formula (Property + Payroll + Sales divided by 3). However, if the property or payroll factor is zero, the denominator is one.

Also excluded from the combined group is a taxable entity that conducts business outside the United States and has no property or payroll if 80% or more of the taxable entity's gross receipts (see ¶ 303) are assigned to locations outside the United States. Exempt entities are also excluded from a combined group. However, eligible entities are required to be included, even if they do not have nexus with Texas. (Sec. 171.1014, Tax Code; Reg. 34 TAC Sec. 3.590)

• *"Affiliated group" defined*

An "affiliated group" is a group of one or more entities in which a controlling interest is owned by a common owner or owners, either corporate or noncorporate, or by one or more of the member entities. (Sec. 171.0001(1), Tax Code)

• *"Controlling interest" defined*

"Controlling interest" means a 50% common ownership interest. (Sec. 171.0001(8), Tax Code) For purposes of determining whether the 50% ownership test is satisfied, an individual constructively owns stock that is owned by his or her spouse, but not stock that is owned by his/her spouse's estate. (34 TAC Sec. 3.590(b)(4)(E); *Letter No. 200810220L*, Texas Comptroller of Public Accounts, October 29, 2008, CCH TEXAS TAX REPORTS, ¶ 403-517)

¶507

Part II—Franchise Tax

CCH Advisory: Affiliation Termination
A membership in an affiliated group will be treated as terminated in any year, or fraction thereof, in which the ownership interest test is not met, except when (1) an affiliated is sold, exchanged or otherwise disposed of and the ownership test is again immediately satisfied after the sale, exchange, or disposition or (2) at the option of the Comptroller, if the ownership test is met again within a period not to exceed two years. (Reg. 34 TAC Sec. 3.590)

- *"Unitary business" defined*

A unitary business is a single economic enterprise that is made up of separate parts of a single entity or a commonly controlled group of entities that are sufficiently interdependent, integrated, and interrelated through their activities so as to provide a synergy and mutual benefit that produces a sharing or exchange of value among them and a significant flow of value to the separate parts. In determining whether a unitary business exists, the Comptroller will consider any relevant factor, including, but not limited to, whether:

— the activities of the group members are in the same general line, such as manufacturing, wholesaling, retailing of tangible personal property, insurance, transportation, or finance;

— the activities of the group members are steps in a vertically structured enterprise or process, such as the steps involved in the production of natural resources, including exploration, mining, refining, and marketing; or

— the members are functionally integrated through the exercise of strong centralized management, such as authority over purchasing, financing, product line, personnel, and marketing. (Sec. 171.0001(17), Tax Code)

All affiliated entities are presumed to be engaged in a unitary business. When a taxable entity acquires another entity, a rebuttable presumption exists for finding a unitary relationship during the first reporting period. Furthermore, a unitary relationship exists when a taxable entity forms another taxable entity at the date of formation unless the business is not unitary on a longer term basis. (34 TAC Sec. 3.590)

Other factors that the Comptroller will evaluate is whether there are any non-arm's-length prices paid for goods or services between members; whether the members enjoy benefits from joint, shared or common activity; and the relationships of joint, shared, or common activity to income-producing operations. (34 TAC Sec. 3.590)

CCH Practice Tip: Affiliated Schedules and Nexus
The reporting entity should only include on the Affiliate List and Affiliate Schedule those entities that are part of the affiliated group (ownership interest of more than 50%) and are unitary. An affiliate that meets both criteria should be included regardless of whether the entity has nexus in Texas. If an affiliate does not meet both criteria, the affiliate should not be included on the Affiliate List or Affiliate Schedule. Taxpayers should blacken the circle on the Affiliate Schedule indicating that the affiliate does not have nexus in Texas regardless of whether the entity is treated as disregarded for federal or franchise tax reporting purposes. If the nexus circle is left blank, the Comptroller will assume the entity has nexus and will expect the applicable information report. (*Tax Policy News*, Texas Comptroller of Public Accounts, April 2009)

- *Calculation of margin*

A combined group determines its total revenues by adding all the revenues of each member together and, to the extent included in such revenues, subtracting any

¶507

revenues received by a member of the group from another group member. Similar procedures are followed for purposes of determining the amount of the compensation deduction or cost of goods sold deduction. Consequently, each member's compensation and or cost of goods sold is added together, and then any inter-group payments must be subtracted. However, a member of a combined group may claim as cost of goods sold those costs that qualify if the goods for which the costs are incurred are owned by another member of the combined group. (Sec. 171.1014(d), Tax Code)

A combined group's election to subtract from the group's total revenues either compensation or cost of goods sold is binding on all members of the group. Regardless of the election, the taxable margin of the combined group may not exceed 70% of the combined group's total revenue from its entire business. (Sec. 171.1014(d), Tax Code)

- *Combined apportionment*

The combined margin is generally apportioned utilizing the apportionment formula and methods applied to other taxable entities. However, gross receipts from business done in Texas by taxable entities without nexus in Texas are excluded from the combined group's numerator. However, receipts from sales of tangible personal property made to third party purchasers will be included in the numerator if the property is ultimately delivered to a purchaser in Texas without substantial modification. For example, drop shipments made from a Texas location to a Texas purchaser would be included in Texas receipts based on the amount billed to the third party purchaser if the seller is a member of the combined group and the seller does not have nexus. When a disregarded entity's revenue, cost of goods sold, compensation, and gross receipts is reported with its parent; both entities are presumed to have nexus. (34 TAC Sec. 3.590).

An information report must be filed for each member of the combined group that does not have nexus with Texas that provides information concerning all gross receipts excluded from the numerator, and the gross receipts excluded from the numerator that are subject to taxation in another state under a throwback law or regulation.

- *Reporting entity*

A reporting entity for the combined group is responsible for filing the combined group report and remitting payments on behalf of the group, along with all other required reports and schedules. Any elections required by the combined group are binding on all members of the group. The reporting entity must provide access to all the members tax, financial and nonfinancial records of the individual members, even those that do not have nexus with Texas. In addition, the entity may file refund claims, give wavers, and execute agreements on behalf of the combined group, all of which are binding on the individual members as well. Notices mailed to the reporting entity are deemed to have been mailed to each of the taxable entities in the combined group.

The reporting entity is usually the parent entity, unless it is not part of the unitary business. If not the parent entity, the reporting entity must (1) be a member of the combined group; (2) have nexus with Texas; and (3) have the greatest Texas business activity during the first year that a combined report is required to be filed, as measured by the Texas receipts after eliminations for that period. A change of reporting entity is only allowed if the entity (other than the parent) is no longer subject to Texas' jurisdiction to tax or the reporting entity is no longer a member of the combined group. (34 TAC Sec. 3.590)

¶507

Part II—Franchise Tax

- *Credits*

Unless otherwise provided by law, credits generally may be applied against the combined tax liability of the combined group. (34 TAC Sec. 3.590)

- *Accounting period*

All members of the combined group must use the same accounting period for purposes of determining margin and apportionment. (Sec. 171.1014(d), Tax Code) Members of a combined group with different accounting periods must prepare a separate income statement based on federal income tax reporting methods. (34.TAC Sec. 3.590)

If two or more members of a combined group file a federal consolidated return, the group's accounting period is the federal taxable period of the federal consolidated group. In all other instances, the accounting period is the federal taxable period of the reporting entity. If the federal taxable period of a member differs from the federal taxable period of the combined group, the reporting entity will determine the portion of that member's revenue, cost of goods sold, compensation, etc. to be included by preparing a separate income statement prepared from the books and records for the months included in the group's accounting period. (34 TAC Sec. 3.590)

A combined group's election to subtract from the group's total revenues either compensation or cost of goods sold is binding on all members of the group. Regardless of the election, the taxable margin of the combined group may not exceed 70% of the combined group's total revenue from its entire business. (Sec. 171.1014(h), Tax Code)

¶507

FRANCHISE TAX

CHAPTER 6

COLLECTION OF TAX

	¶601	In General
	¶602	Penalties and Interest
	¶603	Suit to Enforce the Tax
	¶604	Forfeiture of Corporate or Taxable Entity Privileges
	¶605	Forfeiture of Charter, Certificate of Authority, or Registration—Generally
	¶606	Forfeiture of Charter, Certificate of Authority, or Registration—Nonjudicial
	¶607	Forfeiture of Charter, Certificate of Authority, or Registration—Judicial
	¶608	Revocation of Charter of Banking Corporation or Savings and Loan Association

¶601 In General

Law: Secs. 171.204, 171.205, 171.211, Tax Code.

The Tax Code provides for centralized administration and collection of all taxes, including the franchise tax. These provisions are discussed in detail in Chapters 18—20 of Part VII, "Administration and Procedure," beginning at ¶1801.

Penalties and interest are discussed at ¶602.

If the franchise tax is not paid when due, a suit may be brought (¶603), or the Comptroller may revoke the corporation's privileges or a taxable entity's right to transact business in Texas (¶604) and cause the charter or certificate of authority to be revoked (¶605—607). The provisions concerning the suspension of corporate privileges or an entity's right to transact business and the forfeiture of a corporate charter or certificate of authority do not apply to banking corporations. A provision allowing the revocation of a bank's corporate charter because of the delinquent payment of franchise tax is discussed at ¶608.

The Comptroller may require a taxable entity to furnish information from its books and records necessary for the determination of the amount of the franchise tax or any other information the Comptroller may request. The Comptroller may investigate or examine the entity's records to determine franchise tax liability. (Secs. 171.204, 171.205, 171.211, Tax Code)

¶602 Penalties and Interest

Law: Secs. 111.103, 171.212, 171.362, 171.363, Tax Code; 34 TAC Sec. 3.544, 3.584 (CCH Texas Tax Reports, ¶89-202—89-210).

The following penalties and interest apply as noted.

- *Penalties*

The penalty for failure to file a report or pay the franchise tax when due is 5% of the tax due. An additional 5% penalty is imposed if the tax is not paid or the report is not filed within 30 days after the due date. (Sec. 171.362, Tax Code) The failure to file a report or pay the tax could also result in the forfeiture of corporate privileges or an entity's right to transact business (¶ 604), or the forfeiture a corporation's charter certificate of authority (¶ 605).

A taxable entity that fails to file an amended franchise tax report (¶ 504) is liable for a penalty of 10% of the tax that should have been reported under the amended report requirements and that had not previously been reported to the Comptroller. The penalty is in addition to any other penalty provided by law. (Sec. 171.212, Tax Code)

Criminal penalties: A taxable entity subject to franchise tax commits a criminal offense if it willfully:

— fails to file a franchise tax report;

— fails to keep books and records as required by the statute;

— files a fraudulent report;

— violates a rule of the Comptroller for the administration and enforcement of the tax; or

— attempts to evade or defeat the franchise tax.

Furthermore, it is a criminal offense for a person who is an accountant or agent for, or an officer or employee of, a taxable entity to knowingly enter or provide false information on any franchise report, return, or other required document. An offense under this provision is a felony of the third degree. A person who commits an offense under this provision may also be liable for a penalty under the other franchise tax provisions. (Sec. 171.363, Tax Code)

- *Interest*

Delinquent taxes accrue interest beginning 60 days after the due date. Interest on delinquent state taxes is imposed at the rate of the prime rate plus 1%. For the 2010 calendar year, the interest rate is 4.25%. For the 2009 calendar year, the interest rate was 4.25%. For the 2008 calendar year, the interest rate was 8.25%. For the 2007 calendar year the interest rate was 9.25%, or 0.02534% per day. The rate was 8.25% for 2006, 6.25% for 2005, and 5.0% for 2004.

For a discussion of general provisions on penalties and interest, see ¶ 1909.

- *Waiver of penalties and/or interest*

Generally, the Comptroller will waive penalties and/or interest if the taxpayer exercised reasonable diligence to comply with the tax law.

¶603 Suit to Enforce the Tax

Law: Secs. 171.351, 171.352, 171.354, 171.355, Tax Code.

A court may enjoin or restrain a violation of the franchise tax provisions. A suit to enforce the tax against a taxable entity may be brought in the county where the entity's principal office is located according to its charter or certificate of authority, or in Travis County.

- *Service of process*

Service of process for a suit to enforce the tax may be had on the entity's registered agent. (Sec. 171.354, Tax Code) Service on a domestic corporation may also be had on the Secretary of State in an action relating to the forfeiture of the charter or the collection of tax or penalty if: (1) the local agent or officers named in the charter or annual report do not reside in or cannot be located in the county of the principal office of the corporation; or (2) the principal office of the corporation is not maintained or cannot be located in the county specified in the charter. (Sec. 171.355, Tax Code)

Part II—Franchise Tax

¶604 Forfeiture of Corporate or Taxable Entity Privileges

Law: Secs. 171.251—171.258, 171.308, Tax Code; 34 TAC Sec. 3.570 (CCH Texas Tax Reports, ¶89-206).

A corporation's or taxable entity's privileges will be forfeited if it does not pay the franchise tax within 45 days of the due date. The corporate charter, certificate of authority, or registration will also be forfeited if the tax remains unpaid for 120 days after corporate or entity privileges are forfeited (¶605). This provision does not apply to banking corporations and savings and loan associations.

- *Grounds for forfeiture of privileges*

There are three grounds for forfeiture of corporate or entity privileges, as follows:

(1) failure to file a report (¶504) within 45 days after the due date;

(2) failure to pay any franchise tax (¶502) or a penalty within 45 days after the due date; or

(3) failure to permit the Comptroller to examine the corporate or entity records in order to determine the franchise tax liability (¶601).

- *Forfeiture procedure*

The forfeiture of corporate or entity privileges is effected by the Comptroller without a judicial proceeding. The Comptroller must send the corporation or entity a written or printed notice, verified by the seal of the Comptroller's office. The notice must inform the corporation or entity that the forfeiture will occur unless the corporation or entity files the required report or pays the required tax or penalty within the 45-day period after its due date.

The Comptroller must mail the notice at least 45 days before the forfeiture of corporate or entity privileges. It must be addressed to the corporation or entity and mailed to the address named in the charter as its principal place of business or to another known place of business of the corporation or entity. A record of the mailing date of the notice is kept at the Comptroller's office. The notice and record of mailing is legal notice of the forfeiture.

- *Effect of forfeiture*

A corporation or entity that has forfeited its privileges may not sue or defend in a Texas court. Each director and officer is personally liable for each debt of the corporation or entity created or incurred in the state after the due date of the delinquent report or payment unless incurred over the director's objection, or without the director's knowledge, if reasonable diligence would have revealed to the director the intention to create the debt.

A Texas Court of Appeal has also held that individuals who had been corporate officers when a corporation's Texas franchise tax report was due, but who resigned before the corporate debt was incurred after the report was not filed, were not personally liable for the corporation's debts. (*Paccar Financial Corp. v. Potter*, Texas Court of Appeals, Fifth District, No. 05-05-00403-CV, October 31, 2007, CCH Texas Tax Reports, ¶403-338)

The forfeiture of the corporate or entity privileges does not prohibit a corporation or entity from defending itself in a suit to forfeit the corporate or entity charter, certificate of authority, or registration. It does deny the corporation or entity affirmative relief on a cause of action arising before the forfeiture unless the privileges are revived.

¶604

> **CCH Comment: Liability for Tax During Forfeiture**
> The Texas Supreme Court has long held that a corporation remains liable for franchise tax for the period of forfeiture of its corporate privileges (*State v. Dyer* (TexSCt, 1947), 145 Tex 586, 200 SW2d 813; CCH TEXAS TAX REPORTS [1960—1982 Transfer Binder], ¶ 200-155), even if the corporation is not doing business during that period (*Federal Crude Oil Co. v. State* (TexCtCivApp, 1943), 169 SW2d 283, error refused, pet for cert den, 320 US 758, 64 SCt 66).

- *Tax liens*

In addition to the general provisions on tax liens (¶ 1904), a rule provides that a delinquent corporation must file all delinquent reports and pay all taxes, penalties, and interest owed, not just the amount of the lien, in order to have its franchise tax lien released. (34 TAC Sec. 3.570)

- *Revival of privileges*

The corporate or entity privileges will be revived if the corporation or entity, before the forfeiture of its charter, certificate of authority, or registration (¶ 605), pays the tax, penalty, or interest due. The privileges will also be revived if a court sets aside the forfeiture of its charter, certificate of authority, or registration.

¶ 605 Forfeiture of Charter, Certificate of Authority, or Registration—Generally

Law: Secs. 171.301, 171.3015, 171.302, 171.310, Tax Code.

A corporate or taxable-entity charter, certificate of authority, or registration is subject to forfeiture if the corporate or taxable-entity privileges are forfeited (¶ 604) and the corporation or taxable entity does not pay, within 120 days after the forfeiture, the amount necessary to revive its privileges. The charter, certificate of authority, or registration is also subject to forfeiture if the corporation or taxable entity does not permit the Comptroller to examine the corporate or entity records (¶ 601).

If the corporation or taxable entity has not complied within the 120-day period following the forfeiture of corporate or taxable entity privileges, the Comptroller must certify the corporation or taxable entity to the Attorney General, who may bring suit for judicial forfeiture of the charter, certificate of authority, or registration (¶ 607), and to the Secretary of State. The Secretary of State may forfeit the charter, certificate, or registration without judicial proceeding (¶ 606).

¶ 606 Forfeiture of Charter, Certificate of Authority, or Registration—Nonjudicial

Law: Secs. 171.309, 171.311—171.315, Tax Code.

The Secretary of State may effect a forfeiture of a taxable entity's charter, certificate of authority, or registration with an entry on the taxable entity record in the Secretary's office. This is done if:

— the Secretary receives the Comptroller's certification; and

— the taxable entity does not revive its forfeited entity privileges before January 1 following the date of the forfeiture of the privileges.

- *Revival of charter, certificate of authority, or registration*

A corporation or taxable entity whose charter, certificate, or registration has been forfeited by the Secretary of State may have it revived if:

— the corporation or entity files each report required;

— the corporation or entity pays all tax, penalty, and interest due; and

— the forfeiture is set aside in a proceeding of the Secretary of State, requested by a stockholder, director, or officer of the corporation of entity.

The Comptroller will revive the corporate entity privileges if the Secretary of State sets aside the forfeiture of a corporation's or entity's certificate, charter, or registration.

Upon revival of its charter, certificate, or registration, a corporation or entity must determine from the Secretary of State whether the corporate or entity name is still available for use. The corporation or entity must amend its charter, certificate, or registration to change its name if its former name is no longer available.

¶607 Forfeiture of Charter, Certificate of Authority, or Registration—Judicial

Law: Secs. 171.303—171.308, 171.353, Tax Code.

The Attorney General will bring suit for forfeiture if, on certification of the Comptroller, grounds exist for the forfeiture of a corporate or taxable entity charter, certificate, or registration, on certification by the Comptroller. Once a district court forfeits a corporate or entity's charter, certificate, or registration the Secretary of State will record the forfeiture on the corporation's or entity's record at the Secretary's office.

The court, upon forfeiting a corporation's or entity's charter, certificate of authority, or registration, may appoint a receiver for the corporation or entity, and may administer the receivership.

- *Appeal of judgment of forfeiture*

If an appeal of a judgment of forfeiture is perfected, the Secretary of State will record the appeal on the corporation's or entity's record at the Secretary's office. The Secretary will also record the final disposition of the appeal.

- *Suit to set aside judicial forfeiture*

A corporation or taxable entity may have its charter, certificate of authority, or registration revived if:

— the corporation or entity files each delinquent report required;

— the corporation or entity pays all taxes, interest and penalty due; and

— the forfeiture is set aside in a suit brought by a corporate or entity stockholder, director, or officer.

A suit to set aside the forfeiture of a charter, certificate, or registration must be brought in the corporate or entity name in a district court of Travis County. The suit must be in the nature of a bill of review with the Secretary of State and the Attorney General as defendants. If the court sets aside the forfeiture, the Secretary of State must record the decision on the corporate or entity record in the Secretary's office.

- *Revival of corporate privileges*

Upon the setting aside of the forfeiture of a corporation's or entity's charter, certificate of authority, or registration, the Comptroller will revive the corporate privileges (¶604).

¶608

¶608 Revocation of Charter of Banking Corporation or Savings and Loan Association

Law: Secs. 171.259, 171.260, 171.316, 171.317, Tax Code.

Banking corporations or taxable entities or savings and loan associations that are organized under federal or Texas law and have their main offices in Texas may not have their corporate or entity privileges, corporate charter, certificate of authority, or registration forfeited under the provisions of subchapters F and G of the Tax Code for failing to pay franchise tax or timely file franchise tax returns (¶604, 606, 607). A conservator must be appointed by the banking commissioner to pay the franchise tax of a delinquent banking corporation/entity or savings and loan association organized under Texas law.

FRANCHISE TAX

CHAPTER 7

TAXPAYER REMEDIES

¶701 In General

Texas has uniform administrative provisions that apply to all taxes administered by the Comptroller of Public Accounts, including the franchise tax. Remedies available to taxpayers who are subject to the franchise tax are discussed in detail in Chapter 20, "Taxpayer Remedies," beginning at ¶2001.

PART III

SALES AND USE TAXES

CHAPTER 8

PERSONS AND TRANSACTIONS SUBJECT TO TAX

¶ 801	Overview of Texas Sales and Use Taxes
¶ 802	Application of Sales Tax
¶ 803	Nexus—Out-of-State Vendors
¶ 804	Taxable Services
¶ 805	Use Tax

¶ 801 Overview of Texas Sales and Use Taxes

Law: Secs. 141.001, 142.001—142.011, Tax Code (CCH Texas Tax Reports, ¶¶ 60-080, 60-096).

The Texas Constitution does not grant specific authority to the legislature to levy sales and use taxes. However, Art. VIII, Sec. 17, of the Texas Constitution provides that the specification of objects and subjects of taxation does not deprive the legislature of the power to tax subjects or objects not specified. The Texas Court of Civil Appeals rejected a challenge to the legislature's authority to enact the Limited Sales, Excise and Use Tax Act. (*American Transfer and Storage Co. v. Bullock* (TexCtCivApp, 1975), 525 SW2d 918; CCH Texas Tax Reports, ¶ 200-537)

The state tax rate is 6.25% of the sales price of the item sold (¶ 903). A chart of local tax rates may be found at ¶ 905.

Texas is a member of the Multistate Tax Compact.

- *Streamlined Sales and Use Tax Agreement*

The purpose of the Streamlined Sales and Use Tax (SST) Agreement is to simplify and modernize sales and use tax administration in the member states to substantially reduce the burden of tax compliance. The Agreement was developed by representatives of state governments, with input from local governments and the private sector. The Agreement is in effect as of October 1, 2005, with a Governing Board made up of member states.

Texas is not a member of the Agreement because, although it has enacted legislation authorizing it to enter into the Agreement (Sec. 142.005, Tax Code), it has not yet enacted all of the changes to its laws necessary to comply with the Agreement's requirements. However, as an Advisor State to the Governing Board it will serve in an ex officio capacity on the Board, with non-voting status, and may speak to any matter presented to the Board for its consideration. It will also have input through its representation on the State and Local Advisory Council, which advises the Board on matters pertaining to the administration of the Agreement.

Texas had enacted numerous provisions to conform Texas law to the Agreement, as summarized below. Additional discussion may be found at the indicated paragraphs.

Rate changes: A tax rate change must take effect on the first day of a calendar quarter (¶ 903).

Exemptions: The conforming amendments include modifications to existing exemptions as well as the enactment of new exemptions and the repeal of several exemptions. Localities are no longer given the option to repeal state exemptions for local sales and use tax purposes (¶1002).

Bundled transactions: Taxable telecommunications services that are bundled with nontaxable telecommunications services and sold as a single package for one price, are subject to tax on the entire amount, unless the taxpayer's records substantiate separate treatment (¶1002).

Practitioner Comment: No Obligation to Collect Local Use Tax Without Representation

In 2003, Texas amended Tax Code § 151.103 to require sellers to collect all local use taxes statewide without regard to whether they maintained a place of business or other physical presence in such local taxing jurisdictions. The change was intended to prepare Texas for participation in the Streamlined Sales Tax Project. Because Texas has more than 1,300 jurisdictions imposing local sales and use taxes, the requirement imposed an unreasonable burden on Texas retailers, and the state delayed implementation. In the 80th regular session of the Texas Legislature, House Bill 3319 repealed § 151.103(d), meaning that Texas sellers are not required to collect local use tax for jurisdictions in which they do not maintain a physical presence.

Adina Christian, Ryan

- *Scope of chapter*

Basic application of the sales tax, including key definitions, is discussed below at ¶802. A similar discussion of the use tax is at ¶805. Principles concerning the taxability of out-of-state vendors are at ¶803. Services subject to tax are listed at ¶804.

The tax base and rates of taxes are discussed in Chapter 9.

Under Art. XI, Secs. 4 and 5, of the Texas Constitution, cities and towns may levy such taxes as may be authorized by law or (in the case of cities having more than 5000 inhabitants) by their charter. Local taxes are discussed at ¶904.

Exemptions from tax are discussed in detail in Chapter 10, and information on credits may be found in Chapter 12. Administrative requirements, including information on returns, payment of tax, vendor registration, and recordkeeping are set forth in Chapter 11. Provisions on collection of tax, including assessments, penalties and interest, and limitation periods are discussed in Chapter 13.

The Texas limited sales, excise, and use tax is administered by the Comptroller of Public Accounts and is therefore administered according the uniform administration provisions discussed in Chapters 18—20 of Part VII, "Administration and Procedure," beginning at ¶1801.

See ¶1707 for a discussion of the hotel occupancy tax.

¶802 Application of Sales Tax

Law: Secs. 151.005, 151.006, 151.008, 151.009, 151.010, 151.024, 151.051, 151.052, 151.302, Tax Code; 34 TAC Sec. 3.294 (CCH TEXAS TAX REPORTS, ¶60-020).

The Texas sales tax is imposed on sales, except sales for resale, within the state of "taxable items." "Taxable items" include both tangible personal property and specified services (¶804), but excludes sales of intangibles. The term "tangible personal property" is defined as something that can be seen, weighed, measured, felt, or touched or that is otherwise perceptible to the senses.

Part III—Sales and Use Taxes

> **CCH Advisory: Electronic Mediums**
> Except as otherwise specified by statute, the sale or the use of a taxable item by electronic form instead of on a physical medium does not alter the item's taxable status.

See ¶804 for a discussion of services. The use tax is discussed at ¶805.

- *Incidence of sales tax*

Either the purchaser or the seller are liable for unpaid sales tax. Although sellers are responsible for collecting and remitting the tax to the state, the tax is intended to fall on the purchaser and a seller's failure to collect the tax from the purchaser does not relieve the purchaser of its own tax liability.

- *"Seller" or "retailer" defined*

The term "seller or retailer" means a person engaged in the business of making sales of taxable items, the receipts from which are included in the measure of sales or use tax. The definition includes, but is not limited to:

— a person who makes more than two sales of taxable items during a 12-month period, including sales made in the capacity of an assignee for the benefit of creditors or a receiver or trustee in bankruptcy (see ¶1003 for exempt occasional sales);

— persons who are deemed to be retailers under Tax Code Sec. 151.024; and

— persons who regularly or systematically solicit orders for sales of taxable items in Texas through the distribution of catalogs, periodicals, advertising flyers, or other advertising, whether by means of print, radio, or television media, or by mail, telegraph, telephone, computer database, cable, optic, microwave, or other communication system (see ¶803 for nexus issues).

A corporation that was established by its parent company for the sole purpose of selling four airplanes that were secured by loans was liable for Texas sales tax on its sale of an aircraft in Texas. The Comptroller found that the taxpayer was a "seller" for purposes of the Texas sales tax and that the transaction did not qualify as an exempt occasional sale (see ¶802). (*Decision, Hearing No. 49,270,* Texas Comptroller of Public Accounts, May 6, 2008, CCH TEXAS TAX REPORTS, ¶403-479)

The Comptroller of Public Accounts may regard any salesperson, representative, peddler, or canvasser as the agent of a dealer, distributor, supervisor, or employer for whom he or she operates and may regard the dealer, distributor, supervisor, or employer as a retailer or seller for purposes of sales and use taxes. This was the basis of a court of appeals decision that found an out-of-state manufacturer with a network of 20,000 independent sales persons in Texas to be a direct sales organization and required the manufacturer to collect and remit sales tax on behalf of its independent salespersons. (*Alpine Industries, Inc. v. Strayhorn,* Texas Court of Appeals, Third District, No. 03-03-00643-CV, July 15, 2004; CCH TEXAS TAX REPORTS, ¶402-727)

- *"Sale" or "purchase" defined*

A taxable "sale or purchase" is defined to mean any of the following transactions when supported by consideration:

— a transfer of title or possession of tangible personal property;

— the exchange, barter, lease, or rental of tangible personal property;

— the performance of a taxable service (¶804), a charge for an extended warranty or service contract for the performance of a taxable service, or, in the case of an amusement service, either (a) the transfer of admission tickets or (b) the collection of an admission fee, whether by individual performance, subscription series, membership privilege, or the use of a coin-operated machine;

¶802

— the production, fabrication, processing, printing, or imprinting of tangible personal property for consumers who furnish the materials;

— the furnishing and distribution of tangible personal property by a social club or fraternal organization;

— the furnishing, preparation, or service of food, meals, or drinks;

— a transfer of the possession of tangible personal property if the title to the property is retained by the seller as security for the payment of the price; or

— a transfer of title or possession of tangible personal property that has been produced, fabricated, or printed to a customer's special order.

- *Leases*

Generally, the lease or rental of an item of tangible personal property for consideration is a "sale" or "purchase" of the item for sales tax purposes. The lease or rental of particular items is discussed at the paragraph where the subject is treated. See ¶902 for a discussion of the tax base applicable to leases.

Financing leases. A financing lease that is executed while the property is within the state is subject to sales tax if the lessee takes delivery of the property in Texas. Tax is due on the total amount of the contract regardless of where the property that was received in Texas is used during the lease.

A financing lease is a written lease contract containing either of the following:

— a provision that title to the property must be transferred at the end of the lease; or

— an option to purchase the property at a nominal price at the end of the lease (a price is considered nominal if it is estimated, at the time the contract is executed, to be less than 10% of the property's fair market value when the option is exercised).

A written lease is presumed to be a financing lease if:

— it has no provision for the return of the property to the lessor; and

— either the lease term is equal to 75% or more of the estimated economic life of the property or the residual value of the leased property is less than 10% of the property's fair market value at the inception of the lease.

However, the presumption may be rebutted by showing that the contract is not merely a security device, that the property will be usable for its intended purpose at the end of the lease term, and that the lessor in good faith intends to reclaim possession of the property at the end of the lease term or to sell or re-lease it at that time for its fair market or fair rental value.

Operating leases. An operating lease that is executed while the property is in Texas is subject to sales tax. Tax is imposed on the total lease amount for the entire term of the lease regardless of where the property is used if the lessee takes delivery of the property in the state. No tax is imposed on lease contract renewals, extensions, or options that are exercised while the property is outside the state, unless the property reenters the state. All written leases that do not qualify as financing leases and all oral leases are treated as operating leases.

¶803 Nexus—Out-of-State Vendors

Law: Secs. 151.008, 151.059, 151.107, 151.108, Tax Code; 34 TAC Sec. 3.286 (CCH TEXAS TAX REPORTS, ¶60-020, 60-025).

For sales or use tax purposes, a retailer who performs any of the following activities is deemed to be engaged in business in Texas and thus has sufficient nexus with Texas to be subject to its sales and use tax requirements:

Part III—Sales and Use Taxes

(A) maintains, occupies, or uses in Texas permanently, temporarily, directly, or indirectly or through a subsidiary or agent, an office, distribution center, sales or sample room or place, warehouse, storage place, or any other physical location where business is conducted;

(B) has a representative, agent, salesman, canvasser, or solicitor operating in Texas under the authority of the retailer or its subsidiary for the purpose of selling or delivering or the taking of orders for a taxable item;

(C) derives receipts from the sale, lease, or rental of tangible personal property situated in Texas;

(D) engages in regular or systematic solicitation of sales of taxable items in Texas by the distribution of catalogs, periodicals, advertising flyers, or other advertising, by means of print, radio, or television media, or by mail, telegraphy, telephone, computer data base, cable, optic, microwave, or other communication system for the purpose of effecting sales of taxable items;

(E) solicits orders for taxable items by mail or through other media and under federal law is subject to or permitted to be made subject to the jurisdiction of Texas for purposes of collecting Texas sales and use taxes;

(F) has a franchisee or licensee operating under its trade name if the franchisee or licensee is required to collect Texas sales or use tax;

(G) [effective January 1, 2012] holds a substantial ownership interest in, or is owned in whole or substantial part by, a person who maintains a location in Texas from which business is conducted either:

(1) the retailer sells the same or a substantially similar line of products under the same or a substantially similar business name as the person with the location in Texas; or

(2) the facilities or employees of the person with the location in Texas are used to advertise, promote, or facilitate sales by the retailer to consumers or to perform any other activity on behalf of the retailer that is intended to establish or maintain a marketplace for the retailer in Texas, including receiving or exchanging returned merchandise;

(H) [effective January 1, 2012] holds a substantial ownership interest in, or is owned in whole or substantial part by, a person that (1) maintains a distribution center, warehouse, or similar location in Texas and (2) delivers property sold by the retailer to consumers; or

(I) otherwise does business in Texas.

Place of business of the seller. The term "place of business of the seller" means an established outlet, office, or location that the seller, his agent, or employee operates for the purpose of receipt of orders for taxable items. A warehouse, storage yard, or manufacturing plant is not a place of business of the seller unless the seller receives three or more orders in a calendar year at the warehouse, storage yard, or manufacturing plant. A kiosk is not considered a place of business for purposes of collecting local sales and use taxes.

Solicitation of sales in Texas. In addition, a retailer is engaged in business in Texas if the retailer either:

—engages in regular or systematic solicitation of sales of taxable items in Texas by the distribution of catalogs, periodicals, advertising flyers, or other advertising, by means of print, radio, or television media, or by mail, telegraphy, telephone, computer data base, cable, optic, microwave, or other communication system for the purpose of effecting sales of taxable items; or

¶803

—solicits orders for taxable items by mail or through other media and under federal law is or may be made subject to the jurisdiction of Texas for purposes of collecting tax.

Agents hired to advertise in Texas. A broadcaster, printer, outdoor advertising firm, advertising distributor, or publisher that broadcasts, publishes, displays, or distributes paid commercial advertising in Texas that is (1) intended to be disseminated primarily to consumers located in Texas and (2) is only secondarily disseminated to bordering jurisdictions, including advertising appearing exclusively in a Texas edition or section of a national publication, is considered to be the agent of the person placing the advertisement and that person placing the advertisement is considered a retailer engaged in business in Texas for tax purposes. The agent is not required to report or pay tax for the out-of-state advertiser or seller.

Trade shows. A retailer is engaged in business in Texas if the retailer permanently or temporarily uses any place of business in the state or has representatives operating in the state for the purpose of selling, delivering, or taking orders for taxable items. The Comptroller has held that a taxpayer's presence at trade shows for the purpose of demonstrating its wares and soliciting orders was sufficient to establish nexus. (*Decision, Hearing No. 46,628*, Texas Comptroller of Public Accounts, August 28, 2006, CCH TEXAS TAX REPORTS, ¶ 403-228) The possession of a certificate of authority or the holding of a sales tax permit, in and of itself, is not sufficient to establish taxable nexus for sales and use tax purposes. (*Decision of Comptroller of Public Accounts*, Hearing No. 38,829, February 24, 2004; CCH TEXAS TAX REPORTS, ¶ 402-678)

Internet hosting. A person whose only activity in Texas is using the Internet hosting services of a Texas provider is not engaged in business in Texas for sales and use tax nexus purposes." Internet hosting" means providing to an unrelated user access over the Internet to computer services using property that is owned or leased and managed by the provider and on which the user may store or process the user's own data or use software that is owned, licensed, or leased by the user or provider. The term does not include telecommunications services.

A person providing Internet hosting in Texas is not required to (1) examine a user's data to determine the applicability of Texas sales and use tax to the user, (2) report a user's activities to the Texas Comptroller of Public Accounts, or (3) advise a user as to the applicability of Texas sales and use tax.

Department of Revenue Comment: Internet Hosting Services

No nexus is created if an out-of-state purchaser's only contact with Texas is using Internet hosting services purchased from an unrelated third-party provider who provides those services by use of servers and software located in Texas. If a purchaser of Internet hosting does nothing else that meets the definition of "doing business in Texas," it is not required to collect tax on its sales to purchasers in Texas. On the other hand, a person who owns or leases servers in Texas has nexus and must collect and remit tax on sales of taxable items. Internet hosting services are taxable under the definition of data processing. Therefore, sellers of these services with nexus in Texas must collect sales or use tax on the charges for these services, subject to a 20% exemption allowed for services sold to Texas purchasers. (*Letter No. 201107220L*, Texas Comptroller of Public Accounts, July 2011; CCH TEXAS TAX REPORTS, ¶ 403-766)

CCH Advisory: Provision of Third-Party Warranty Services

The Comptroller has taken the position that on-site warranty services for a corporation's computer hardware products that was provided by third-party contractors was sufficient to establish nexus for sales and use tax purposes. (*Decision of Comptroller of Public Accounts*, Hearing No. 41,140, September 19, 2002; CCH TEXAS TAX REPORTS, ¶ 402-495)

¶803

Part III—Sales and Use Taxes

• *Federal limitations*

The U.S. Supreme Court in the 1967 *National Bellas Hess* case (386 US 753) ruled that an out-of-state vendor cannot be compelled to collect the state's use tax on sales made to the state's residents unless the vendor has retail outlets, solicitors, or property within the state. In *Quill Corp. v. North Dakota*, 504 US 298 (1992), the U.S. Supreme Court held that physical presence in the state is required for creating nexus under the Commerce Clause, but not under the Due Process Clause.

CCH Comment: Texas Business May Challenge Other State's Nexus Determination in Texas Court

A Texas business that has been sued by another state over collection of that state's sales or use taxes may seek declaratory relief in a Texas district court on the issue of whether requiring the business to collect and remit tax to that state constitutes an undue burden on interstate commerce, applicable to causes of action that accrue after August 31, 2007. (Sec. 37.0055, Civ. Prac. & Rem. Code) Previously, the business would have to seek relief in the other state's courts.

CCH Caution: MTC Communique Applies to Texas

A joint communique by the Multistate Tax Commission and 26 states, including Texas (*Nexus Program Bulletin*, Multistate Tax Commission, December 20, 1995; CCH TEXAS TAX REPORTS, ¶ 401-884), puts out-of-state computer companies on notice that their in-state repair services open the door to use tax on revenues from mail order sales in these states. The repair services establish the critical tax "nexus" to a state that is required of a company before the state may impose its taxes.

¶ 804 Taxable Services

Law: Secs. 151.0028, 151.0033, 151.0034, 151.0035, 151.0036, 151.0038, 151.0039, 151.0045, 151.0047, 151.0048, 151.0101, 151.0103, 151.061, Tax Code; 34 TAC Sec. 3.310(b)(1), 34 TAC Sec. 3.333 (CCH TEXAS TAX REPORTS, ¶ 60-020, 60-665).

Only those services specifically enumerated by statute are subject to tax. It is important to determine whether the transaction is a purchase of a service or the purchase of tangible personal property. A taxpayer was held liable for sales tax on its purchases of pre-employment psychological tests used for evaluating job applicants because the Texas Comptroller determined that the transactions involved tangible personal property (i.e., tests) rather than nontaxable pre-employment testing services. (*Decision, Hearing No. 47,913*, Texas Comptroller of Public Accounts, January 16, 2009, CCH TEXAS TAX REPORTS, ¶ 403-544) Also, transactions between a refinery owner and independent contractors for the installation of temporary scaffolding at a refinery were held to be taxable rentals of tangible personal property rather than purchases of nontaxable services because possession (operational control) of the scaffolding was transferred to the taxpayer. Although the contractors performed some nontaxable services, including erecting and disassembling the scaffolding, the essence of the transactions was the rental of the scaffolding for use by the taxpayer's maintenance employees. (*Combs v. Chevron USA, Inc.*, Texas Court of Appeals, Third District, No. 03-07-00127-CV, April 9, 2010; CCH TEXAS TAX REPORTS, ¶ 403-597)

CCH Comment: True Object

Generally, the law defines the taxable "sales price" of a purchase to include any services that are a part of the sale. Therefore, for example, sales tax is applicable to fees charged by an interior designer for services rendered in connection with the sale of furnishings to a customer. However, if the true object of a sale is the provision of a nontaxable service rather than the transfer of tangible personal property, the transaction is not subject to tax. For example, in the *Direct Resources for Print*, 910 SW2d 535 (TexCtApp 1995), CCH TEXAS TAX REPORTS, ¶ 401-873, a Texas appellate court held that a direct mail service was not liable for sales tax on the portion of its service related to ink-jet addressing of envelopes because the essence of the transaction was a nontaxable mailing service rather than the taxable printing of envelopes.

In addition, in *Rylander v. San Antonio SMSA Limited Partnership,* 11 S.W.3d 484 (2000), CCH TEXAS TAX REPORTS, ¶ 402-098, a Texas appellate court held that a retailer may provide a nontaxable service and sell tangible personal property to one customer in two transactions billed on a single invoice. The existence of a single invoice does not make the nontaxable service part of the taxable sale of tangible personal property, so long as each item is provided by the seller on a stand-alone basis and the price of each item is separately stated. Furthermore, the price of the service should not be affected if the purchaser acquires the supplies from a different vendor, or vice versa.

Generally, taxable services include the following:

— amusement services, including the rental of an athletic facility's volleyball and basketball courts, batting cages, and weight room (*Letter*, Texas Comptroller of Public Accounts, No. 200404506L, April 8, 2004; CCH TEXAS TAX REPORTS, ¶ 402-684) and cover charges, door charges, entry fees, or admission fees collected by mixed beverage license holders (*Notice to Mixed Beverage License Holders*, Texas Comptroller of Public Accounts, October 2007);

— cable television services, defined as the distribution of video programming, with or without the use of wires, to subscribing or paying customers;

— credit reporting services, defined as the assembling or furnishing of credit history or credit information;

— data processing services, including all forms of computerized data storage (other than classified advertisements, advertising through toll-free numbers (*Decision of the Texas Comptroller of Public Accounts*, Hearing No. 39,557, March 10, 2004, CCH TEXAS TAX REPORTS, ¶ 402-695), banner advertisements, vertical advertisements, or links displayed on an Internet website owned by another person) and manipulation, such as word processing, data entry and retrieval, data search, information compilation, web-hosting services (*Letter No. 200701906L*, Texas Comptroller of Public Accounts, January 30, 2007, CCH TEXAS TAX REPORTS, ¶ 403-247), web-based application services (*Letter No. 200805095L*, Texas Comptroller of Public Accounts, May 28, 2008, CCH TEXAS TAX REPORTS, ¶ 403-424) and the rental of computer time for data processing, no matter who performs the processing service. Data processing services do not include transcription of medical dictation by a medical receptionist but do include medical transcription using voice recognition software (*Decision of Texas Comptroller of Public Accounts, Hearing* No. 201004665L, April 29, 2010; CCH TEXAS TAX REPORTS, ¶ 403-606);

— debt collection services, including commissions paid an employee for collecting accounts (*Decision of Texas Comptroller of Public Accounts, Hearing* No. 38,963, February 8, 2002; CCH TEXAS TAX REPORTS, ¶ 402-278), but excluding the collection of (a) a judgment by the attorney that represented the judgment creditor in the action from which the judgment arose, (b) court-ordered child support or medical child support, and (c) a trustee's real property foreclosure services;

— information services, including electronic data retrieval and research, and the furnishing of news or other current information except (a) to newspapers and federally licensed radio and television stations, and (b) information furnished by or on behalf of a homeowners association to one of its members. Also included are pre-employment screening services (*Position Letter*, Texas Comptroller of Public Accounts, No. 39,952, January 6, 2004, CCH TEXAS TAX REPORTS, ¶ 402-651);

— insurance services, including loss or damage appraisal, inspection, investigation, actuarial work, claims adjustment and processing, loss prevention, and premium audits (*Decision of the Texas Comptroller of Public Accounts*, Hearing No.

¶ 804

Part III—Sales and Use Taxes 111

40,123, February 22, 2001, CCH TEXAS TAX REPORTS, ¶402-198), claims adjustment services performed by a medical service billing company on behalf of physicians (*Letter*, Texas Comptroller of Public Accounts, No. 200602595L, February 21, 2006, CCH TEXAS TAX REPORTS, ¶403-087), and issuance of a Federal Emergency Management Agency (FEMA) Elevation Certificate that is used to determine the correct insurance premium, or to determine the eligibility or qualifications for insurance coverage (*Tax Policy News, Vol. XVIII, Issue 12,* Texas Comptroller of Public Accounts, December 2008). Insurance coverage is exempt from tax;

— internet access services;

— motor vehicle parking and storage services. Charges for valet parking services are taxable. Leases of parking spaces, whether or not the spaces are actually guaranteed are considered taxable parking services. (*Letter No. 200805091L*, Texas Comptroller of Public Accounts, May 27, 2008, CCH TEXAS TAX REPORTS, ¶403-421) Charges to store empty boat trailers, golf trailers, and motorcycle trailers are subject to sales tax as the provision of motor vehicle parking and storage. However, charges to store boats on boat trailers, golf carts on golf trailers, and unlicensed off-road motorcycles on motorcycle trailers are not subject to sales tax. The item contained on the specialized trailer and not the trailer itself is considered to be the item stored in such situations (*Letter*, Texas Comptroller of Public Accounts, March 22, 2004; CCH TEXAS TAX REPORTS, ¶402-696);

— real property repair and remodeling services, such as work done on improvements to realty, other than (a) certain residential realty, (b) improvements adjacent to such realty, including improvements located in apartment complex common areas such as parking lots, hallways, swimming pools, and laundry rooms. (Letter No. 200711067L, Texas Comptroller of Public Accounts, November 12, 2007, CCH TEXAS TAX REPORTS, ¶403-397), and (c) improvements to manufacturing or processing production units in a petrochemical refinery or chemical plant that provides increased capacity in the production unit. Scheduled and periodic maintenance services are not taxable (*Decision of the Texas Comptroller of Public Accounts*, Hearing No. 42,981, December 22, 2003, CCH TEXAS TAX REPORTS, ¶402-647);

— real property services, such as landscaping, yard work, garbage removal or collection (other than the removal or collection of certain hazardous and industrial solid waste, but not recycled waste materials (*Decision of the Texas Comptroller of Public Accounts*, Hearing No. 41,876, January 14, 2004, CCH TEXAS TAX REPORTS, ¶402-664)), janitorial and custodial services, certain structural pest control services, duct cleaning, and surveying real property; however, these services are not considered "real property services" if they are purchased by a contractor as part of the improvement of real property while building a new residential structure or an improvement to be used for residential purposes that is adjacent to that structure. Real property services do not include a service performed by a landman if the service is necessary to negotiate or secure land or mineral rights for acquisition or trade (Ch. 1266 (H.B. 3199), Laws 2007);

— repair, remodeling, maintenance, and restoration of tangible personal property other than aircraft, motor vehicles, certain ships, boats, and vessels, and certain computer programs;

— specified personal services: laundry, cleaning, carpet cleaning, and garment services, massage parlors, escort services, and Turkish baths (34 TAC Sec. 3.310(b)(1));

— private security services, including computer security services (*Letter No. 200712008L*, Texas Comptroller of Public Accounts, December 20, 2007, CCH TEXAS TAX REPORTS, ¶403-359), bounty hunter services (*Letter*, Texas Comptroller of Public Accounts, No. 200407011L, July 21, 2004, CCH TEXAS TAX REPORTS,

¶804

¶402-733), and locksmiths and security service consultants (*Special Tax Mailing to Locksmiths and Security Consultants*, Texas Comptroller of Public Accounts, October 24, 2007) for which a license is required under Texas law. The sale and installation of security systems in new residences under construction are taxable security services and not exempt residential improvement services (*Decision of the Texas Comptroller of Public Accounts*, Hearing No. 42,502, September 18, 2003, CCH TEXAS TAX REPORTS, ¶402-626);

— telecommunications services. A telephone company's provision of telephone line service and rerouting of 800-prefix calls originating in designated counties to the taxpayer's business telephone number were taxable telecommunications services. (*Decision of Texas Comptroller of Public Accounts*, No. 39,916, March 22, 2004, CCH TEXAS TAX REPORTS, ¶402-696.) Telephone calls from a pay telephone are exempt from tax if paid by coin but are taxable if paid by other means. (Sec. 151.0103, Tax Code) The state's prepaid wireless 911 emergency fee is discussed at ¶1708; and

— telephone answering services.

Practitioner Comment: Health and Wellness Screenings Are Not Insurance Services

Insurance services include insurance investigation services, which are defined in 34 TAC Sec. 3.355(a)(3) as activities to evaluate an individual's eligibility or qualifications for insurance coverage or the payment of benefits. Since 1995, the Comptroller has imposed sales and use tax on health and wellness screenings when performed pursuant to a policy of insurance.

In October 2008, the Comptroller reversed its previous interpretation and determined that health and wellness screenings, i.e., the analysis of blood and electrocardiograms, are non-taxable medical services even when performed for an insurance carrier. (*Comptroller Letter No. 200810293L* (2008)).

Adina Christian, Ryan

Practitioner Comment: Transmission and Distribution Services Purchased by End Users Are Taxable Services

In Texas' deregulated electricity market, an electric generation company, a transmission and distribution (transportation) utilities, and a company selling electricity directly to consumers (a retail electric provider) must be separate entities.

Transmission and distribution utilities sell their service to retail electric providers who resell the service to their customers along with electricity. The delivery is part of the price of the electricity and subject to tax if the electricity sold is subject to tax. As a general rule, transmission and distribution utilities do not sell their transportation services to end users.

When a purchaser buys transmission or distribution services directly from a transmission and distribution utility, the delivery is a taxable service under Texas Tax Code § 151.0101, which includes electricity transmission and/or distribution services sold to end-users in the definition of taxable services.

A retail electric provider sold security lighting to its customers. It purchased poles, fixtures, bulbs, wires, electricity, and transmission and distribution services to provide its service.

The Comptroller determined that security lighting was a non-taxable service, and that the retail electric provider owed tax on all taxable items purchased to provide the service.

The retail electric provider argued that its purchase of electricity was exempt from sales and use tax under Tax Code § 151.317(a)(9), and the transmission and distribution service it purchased was not a taxable service. The Comptroller denied the exemption because § 151.317(a)(9) provides an exemption for electricity purchased by an electric

¶804

Part III—Sales and Use Taxes 113

utility. A retail electric provider is specifically excluded from the definition of electric utility in Utilities Code § 31.002(6)(H). Because retail electric provider was the end user of electricity subject to tax, the transmission and distribution service purchased was also taxable under Tax Code § 151.0101. (*Comptroller Letter No. 200902284L*)

Adina Christian, Ryan

Early termination fees: Early termination fees exercised as part of a service agreement are treated as part of the taxable service. (*Decision of the Texas Comptroller of Public Accounts,* Hearing No. 43,052, March 8, 2006, CCH TEXAS TAX REPORTS, ¶ 403-077)

Practitioner Comment: Services Benefiting Non-Texas Locations

Taxable services that are purchased to support a separate, identifiable segment of a business (other than general administration or operation of the business) are not taxable to the extent such services benefit locations outside Texas. See the Multi-State Service Benefit Allocation provisions of Comptroller's Rules §§ 3.330(f), Data Processing Services, 3.333(o), Security Services, 3.342(g), Information Services, 3.343(f), Credit Reporting Services, 3.354(g), Debt Collection Services, 3.355(j), Insurance Services, and 3.366(f), Internet Access Services. Any reasonable method of allocation may be used, provided that business records support such method. There is no requirement that the method used be the "best" method or the method that results in the largest tax liability.

G. Brint Ryan, Ryan

CCH Comment: Sourcing of Mobile Telecommunications

Texas law conforms to the federal Mobile Telecommunications Sourcing Act (4 U.S.C. Sections 116—126). Under the Act, mobile telecommunications services are taxable only in the state and locality where the customer resides or maintains its primary business address and any other state or locality is prohibited from taxing the services, regardless of where the services originate, terminate, or pass through. The Act does not apply to prepaid telephone calling services or air-ground service.

Furthermore, the Act provides that a state or a company designated by the political subdivisions of a state may provide an electronic database identifying the proper taxing jurisdiction for each street address in that state. A provider of mobile telecommunications services that uses such a database will be held harmless from any tax otherwise due solely as a result of an error in the database. If no such database exists, then a provider employing an enhanced zip code and exercising due diligence in assigning a street address to a taxing jurisdiction will be held harmless for any incorrect assignment.

Sourcing of Wireless Calls Made in Mexico: A telecommunications services retailer's itemized charges for "roaming" service when its Texas customers traveled to Mexico and used a wireless device to place or receive a call that originated and terminated in Mexico were not subject to Texas sales tax because the services were provided in Mexico. The Mobile Telecommunications Sourcing Act's place-of-primary-use rule, under which a mobile telecommunications service will be deemed to have been provided at a subscriber's place of primary use only applies to a mobile telecommunications service provided in the United States. When a subscriber travels to a foreign country and uses a wireless device to place or receive calls that originate and terminate in the foreign country, the subscriber is not using facilities located in the United States and the MTSA's place-of-primary-use rule does not apply. Therefore, the wireless telecommunications services in this case could not be deemed to have been provided in Texas for purposes of assessing tax. (*Decision of the Texas Comptroller of Public Accounts,* Hearing No. 100,587, June 4, 2010, CCH TEXAS TAX REPORTS, ¶ 403-615)

¶804

¶805 Use Tax

Law: Secs. 151.011, 151.101—151.105, 151.330, Tax Code; 34 TAC Sec. 3.346 (CCH Texas Tax Reports, ¶60-020).

The Texas use tax is a complementary tax imposed on the storage, use, or other consumption in the state of a taxable item purchased from a retailer. With respect to a taxable service, the term "use" means the derivation in Texas of a direct or indirect benefit from the service. See ¶1003 for the discussion of exempt transactions.

- *Incidence of use tax*

The incidence of the use tax is on the person consuming, using, or storing the taxable item in the state. The consumer's liability continues until the tax is paid to the state unless the consumer pays the tax to, and obtains a receipt from, the retailer or other person authorized to collect the tax. Upon the purchase of goods, the use tax becomes part of the sales price and is a debt owed by the purchaser to the retailer. If the tax is unpaid, the retailer may file a lawsuit to recover it.

- *Collection of local use taxes*

Generally, the sale of a taxable item, both tangible personal property and taxable services, occurs within the local taxing jurisdiction in which the seller's business is located. However, under specified circumstances, the sale will be sourced to the location of the purchaser, see ¶905 for details.

- *One-year presumptions*

A sale of a taxable item for delivery in Texas is presumed to be a sale for storage, use, or consumption in Texas unless the seller accepts a resale or exemption certificate. Similarly, a taxable service that is used in Texas is presumed to have been purchased for use in Texas. The presumption continues for one year after purchase.

A contrary presumption applies to items purchased outside Texas and used outside Texas for more than one year before the date of entry into Texas; such items will be presumed not to have been purchased for use in Texas. This presumption applies to an item shipped by the seller to a point outside Texas when the purchaser returns the item to Texas. The purchase of the item must be primarily for use outside Texas and its use outside the state must be substantial.

- *Shipments from out of state*

Use tax is also due on taxable items that are purchased outside Texas by a person engaged in business in Texas for delivery, at the direction of the purchaser, to recipients in Texas who are designated by the purchaser. Thus, a Texas court of appeal held that the out-of-state printing of advertising materials for a Texas department store was subject to Texas use tax because the store exercised a right or power incidental to the ownership of tangible personal property over the advertising materials that were the result of the printing. The store made the purchase from a retailer printer, directed the advertising materials to prospective customers in Texas, used the advertising to promote sales in Texas, and took physical possession of some of the advertising materials in the form of coupons returned by customers to its stores in Texas. (*The May Department Stores Co. v. Strayhorn*, Texas Court of Appeals, Third District, No. 03-03-00729-CV, August 26, 2004, CCH Texas Tax Reports, ¶402-749)

Similarly, a publisher was liable for Texas use tax on printing charges for telephone directories that were printed by out-of-state printers and delivered to users in Texas because directing the delivery of tangible personal property to Texas recipients constituted the exercise of a power or right incident to ownership of the property. (*Decision, Hearing No. 48,135*, Texas Comptroller of Public Accounts, August 23, 2006, CCH Texas Tax Reports, ¶403-224)

¶805

Part III—Sales and Use Taxes

A person is deemed to be engaged in business in Texas if the person is required by law to collect sales or use tax, or if the person has some physical presence in Texas in connection with a commercial enterprise.

> **CCH Practice Tip: Use Tax Due on Software Used in State**
>
> A taxpayer was liable for Texas use tax on the purchase price of software that was shipped into Texas for testing and acceptance prior to shipment and installation outside the state because the taxpayer made a taxable use of the software in Texas. Upon initiating the testing and acceptance activities, the taxpayer paid significant amounts of consideration and worked with the software in Texas, which was sufficient to constitute use of the software in Texas. (*Decision of Comptroller of Public Accounts*, Hearing No. 36,957, December 20, 1999; CCH TEXAS TAX REPORTS, ¶402-112)

- *Exceptions*

Use tax is not applicable to any of the following activities:

— the sale, lease, or rental of tangible personal property or a taxable service in the regular course of business;

— the holding of property for subsequent use outside Texas; or

— the processing, fabricating, or manufacturing of tangible personal property, other than printed material, into other property, or attaching property or incorporating property into other property for use outside Texas.

No use tax is due if the purchaser paid sales tax to a Texas retailer or owes sales tax to a Texas retailer who fails to collect it.

In addition, there are instances in which property that is brought into Texas is not subject to use tax. First, tangible personal property acquired outside Texas and stored temporarily in Texas is exempt from use tax, provided the property is used solely outside Texas or is attached to other property used solely outside Texas. Second, tangible personal property acquired outside Texas is exempt from use tax if the property would be exempt from sales or use tax had it been sold, leased, or rented in Texas. Finally, the storage or use of repair or replacement parts that are acquired outside of Texas and used in the vehicles of licensed or certificated common carriers that transport persons or property is exempt.

- *Storage tax*

In 1978, the Texas Supreme Court held that there exists a tax on the storage of items that is separate from the use tax (*Bullock v. Lone Star Gas Co.* (TexSCt, 1978), 567 SW2d 493, cert den 439 US 985, 99 SCt 577; CCH TEXAS TAX REPORTS, ¶200-778). It noted that the storage tax is most commonly imposed on property that is purchased in another jurisdiction (and therefore not subject to Texas sales tax), stored in Texas, and thereafter used as part of an interstate commerce activity (thus exempting it from the use tax).

SALES AND USE TAXES

CHAPTER 9

BASIS AND RATE OF TAX

¶901	In General
¶902	Tax Base
¶903	Rate of Tax
¶904	Local Taxes and Rates
¶905	Local Tax Rate Chart
¶906	Bracket Schedule

¶901 In General

Texas sales and use taxes are measured by the sales price of the taxable tangible personal property or taxable service (¶902). Generally, the sales price is the total amount for which a taxable item is sold, leased, or rented, valued in money. Specified, separately stated charges are excluded from the sales price of a taxable item or service.

The state tax rate is 6.25% of the sales price of the item sold (¶903). In lieu of the standard rate, special sales and use tax rates apply to motor vehicles, manufactured housing, and boats and boat motors.

Municipalities and counties are authorized to impose additional sales and use taxes (¶904). Local sales and use taxes are authorized for certain districts or for specified purposes.

A chart of current local tax rates is located at ¶905.

The current bracket schedule is located at ¶906.

¶902 Tax Base

Law: Secs. 151.007, 151.010, 151.051, 151.101, 151.154, 151.411, 151.426, 151.428, 152.0412, Tax Code; 34 TAC Secs. 3.79, 3.286, 3.301, 3.302, 3.303, 3.346 (CCH Texas Tax Reports, ¶61-110, 61-120, 61-130, 61-140, 61-150, 61-160, 61-180, 61-190).

Sales and use taxes are measured by the sales price of the taxable item (tangible personal property or taxable service).

- *"Sales price" or "receipts" defined*

"Sales price" or "receipts" is the total amount for which a taxable item is sold, leased, or rented, valued in money, without a deduction for the cost of any of the following:

— the taxable item sold, leased, or rented;

— the materials used, labor or service employed, interest, losses, or other expenses; or

— the transportation or installation of tangible personal property or transportation incident to a taxable service.

Compliance Pointer: Tax Base Includes Service That Is Part of Sale

The total amount for which a taxable item is sold includes a service that is a part of the sale. A printer was liable for sales tax on separate monthly fees it charged customers for storing excess printed materials not currently needed by the customers. The taxpayer charged and collected sales tax on the production and sale of the printed items to customers, but did not charge tax for storing the excess printed products in a warehouse. When customers later placed an order for the stored products, the taxpayer pulled and shipped the products from the warehouse. The storage, packaging, and shipping of the excess printed materials related back to, and were part of, the original sale of the printed materials and thus were taxable, even if separately stated. They were not part of a nontaxable, stand-alone fulfillment service. (*Decision, Hearing No. 102,191* , Texas Comptroller of Public Accounts, February 16, 2011; CCH TEXAS TAX REPORTS, ¶ 403-708)

The tax base for food sold through vending machines is 50% of the total gross receipts from such sales, excluding soft drinks and candy. The tax base for vending machine sales of soft drinks and candy is 100%.

The sales price of membership in a private club or organization consists of the dues, fees, and other charges and assessments, including initiation fees, required for membership or a special privilege, status, or membership classification in the club or organization.

CCH Advisory: Taxes Must Be Separately Stated

The amount of the Texas sales tax must be separately stated on the bill, contract, or invoice to the customer or there must be a written statement to the customer that the stated price includes sales or use taxes. Contracts, bills, or invoices that merely state that "all taxes" are included are not specific enough to relieve either party to the transaction of its sales and use tax responsibilities. In such instances, the total amount that is shown on such documents is presumed to be the taxable item's sales price, without tax included.

- *Exclusions from "sales price"*

"Sales price" does not include any of the following if separately stated:

— cash discounts (including government-issued coupons such as the U.S. Department of Commerce's digital-to-analog convertor box coupons) (*Letter No. 200712092L*, Texas Comptroller of Public Accounts, December 27, 2007, CCH TEXAS TAX REPORTS, ¶ 403-422; *Notice to Retailers*, Texas Comptroller of Public Accounts, September 12, 2008);

— refund of the amount charged for a returned item or the refund of charges for performance of a taxable service;

— finance, carrying, and service charges and interest under a conditional sales contract or other contract providing for the deferred payment of the purchase price;

— trade-ins;

— receipts from the sale of U.S. coins and currency equal to the face value of the coins or currency;

— voluntary tips and gratuities and reasonable mandatory gratuity charges for the service of meals or food products, including soft drinks and candy for immediate consumption; or

— receipts from transactions totaling less than 8¢, provided the retailer can establish that 50% or more of the retailer's total receipts arise from such transactions and the retailer has obtained written approval from the Comptroller. Such approval may be obtained in advance if the retailer can maintain adequate records to prove conclusively that at least 50% of the receipts are from sales of less than the taxable amount.

¶ 902

Part III—Sales and Use Taxes 119

> **CCH Caution: Tax Refund on Returned Item**
> A buyer who receives less than the original purchase price upon returning an item to the seller is not entitled to a refund of the sales tax paid on the original purchase. A return of an item is considered a cancellation of the sale only if there is a full cash or credit refund to the customer. (*Decision of Comptroller of Public Accounts*, Hearing No. 103,306, May 17, 2010; CCH TEXAS TAX REPORTS, ¶403-635).

- *Used motor vehicles*

The sales price of a used motor vehicle, for purposes of determining the tax due, can be no less than 80% of the used motor vehicle's standard presumptive value, or an appraised value as established by a certified appraisal. "Standard presumptive value" means the private-party transaction value of a motor vehicle based on a nationally recognized motor vehicle value guide service or other vehicle guide publication. The Texas Department of Transportation is required to maintain and publish information on the standard presumptive values of motor vehicles. The standard presumptive value does not apply to even exchanges or gifts, or to vehicles sold by a federal, state, or local governmental entity at public auction. If a used motor vehicle is purchased from a dealer, the sales price on the title application or dealer's invoice must be used to calculate the tax due. (Sec. 152.0412, Tax Code; 34 TAC Sec. 3.79)

Classic motor vehicles: A sale or gift of a motor vehicle 25 years old or older is excluded from Standard Presumptive Value (SPV) procedure for determining the amount of motor vehicle sales tax due in a private-party sale. Instead, tax is calculated on the actual sales price. The purchaser and seller must complete a joint statement as to the sales price. (*Tax Policy News*, Texas Comptroller of Public Accounts, September 2010)

The sales price on the title application or dealer's invoice must be used to calculate the tax due when a motor vehicle is purchased from a dealer. (Sec. 152.0412, Tax Code; 34 TAC Sec. 3.79)

- *Leases*

The total amount for which a taxable item is leased or rented is included in the definition of "sales price" or "receipts." Operating and financing lease agreements and related billings may contain charges in addition to the basic payment terms, including charges that occur subsequent to the rental. All charges related to a lease agreement are taxable unless specifically excluded. The following are examples of such charges and their tax treatment:

— Separately stated charges for labor or services rendered in installing, applying, remodeling, servicing, maintaining, or repairing the leased property are subject to tax;

— Damage waiver fees and charges after the rental for repair of a damaged rental item are taxable, but charges for items lost or destroyed by the lessee are not taxable unless the lessee is required to purchase the damaged item;

— All transportation charges that relate to leased property and are billed by the lessor to the lessee are taxable, but transportation charges billed directly to the lessee by third-party carriers are not taxable;

— Charges in the lease agreement for labor, such as charges for supervision, set-up, hook-up, assembly, disassembly, erection, and dismantling, are included in the lease price and are taxable;

— A charge for the early termination of the lease is included in the lease price and is taxable;

¶902

— Interest charges under an operating lease are taxable whether separately stated or not, unless the interest charge is clearly imposed for late payments or other defaults under the lease; and

— Interest charges under a financing lease are taxable unless the rate of interest or actual interest charged is separately stated in the contract.

Separately stated charges for property tax reimbursement is not taxable. However, a prorated reimbursement of all the property taxes paid on all the rental equipment owned by the lessor becomes part of the selling price of the lease and is subject to tax. (*Letter*, Texas Comptroller of Public Accounts, No. 200403425L, March 4, 2004; CCH TEXAS TAX REPORTS, ¶ 402-666)

An equipment lessor that assigned its rights to lease payments to third parties was required to accelerate and pay sales tax on all remaining lease payments at the time of assignment. (*Decision, Hearing No. 45,095*, Texas Comptroller of Public Accounts, July 12, 2006; CCH TEXAS TAX REPORTS, ¶ 403-165).

- *Bad debts*

A seller or any person who extends credit to a purchaser under a retailer's private label credit agreement, or an assignee or affiliate of either may exclude from tax any amount that is entered in its books as a bad debt during the reporting period in which the underlying item was sold, leased, or rented and that is claimed as a deduction for federal income tax purposes during the same or subsequent reporting period. No deduction may be taken for expenses incurred in collecting the debt. (Sec. 151.426(c), Tax Code)

A seller that has paid taxes on an account that is later determined to be a bad debt and that is actually charged off for federal income tax purposes is entitled to a credit or reimbursement of the corresponding portion of the taxes represented by the bad debt. Tax paid on an account that later becomes a bad debt is not considered to be tax paid in error and does not accrue interest.

The assignee of a tax refund must directly submit the refund assignment form before any refund or credit can be claimed. (*Letter*, Texas Comptroller of Public Accounts, No. 200203888L, March 2, 2002;). However, the assignee may only claim a refund if the original retailer was eligible to claim the bad debt deduction. (*MFC Finance Company of Texas v. Strayhorn*, Texas Court of Appeals, Third District, No. 03-06-00328-CV, May 1, 2008, CCH TEXAS TAX REPORTS, ¶ 403-405)

The term "bad debt" is defined as any portion of the sales price of a taxable item that the seller cannot collect. The seller must pay tax on a bad debt that is subsequently paid during the reporting period in which the payment is made.

CCH Advisory: Bad Debt Requirements

According to the Comptroller, in order for a transaction to be considered a bad debt for sales and use tax purposes, the taxpayer must show:

— the date of the original sale;

— the name and address of the purchaser;

— the amount on which the taxpayer paid tax;

— the taxable and nontaxable charges;

— the amount on which the taxpayer paid tax;

— all payments or other credits applied to the account of the purchaser; and

— evidence that the uncollected amount has been designated as a bad debt in the taxpayer's books and records and has been or will be claimed as a bad debt deduction for income tax purposes. (*Decision of Comptroller of Public Accounts*, Hearing No. 20,132, October 8, 1987; CCH TEXAS TAX REPORTS, ¶ 400-690)

¶902

Part III—Sales and Use Taxes

Taxpayers who receive prior approval from the Comptroller and whose volume and character of uncollected accounts warrant an alternative method, may use other records that fairly and equitably apportion taxable and nontaxable elements of a bad debt and substantiate the amount of tax paid with respect to the taxable charges that remain unpaid. Alternatively, a taxpayer who receives prior approval from the Comptroller may implement a system to report its future tax responsibilities based on a historical percentage calculated from a sample of transactions if: the system utilizes records provided by the person claiming the credit or reimbursement and the person who reported and remitted the tax to the Comptroller. (34 TAC Sec. 3.302(d))

- *Coupons, premiums, and trading stamps*

The value of coupons or certificates that are accepted by retailers as part of the selling price may be excluded from taxable sales, regardless of whether the retailer is reimbursed for the amount represented by the coupon or certificate.

Sales of taxable items to persons who give them as premiums with *bona fide* sales of other taxable items are not sales for resale, provided no additional charge is made for such premium. However, when the premiums are given with an additional charge, sales tax should be collected on the additional charge.

The redemption of trading stamps by exchanging merchandise for them is deemed to be a sale at retail of merchandise for a consideration, and trading stamp companies that sell tangible personal property or redeem trading stamps are treated as retailers. Retailers who redeem trading stamps must collect and remit sales tax. The tax is based on the redemptive value of the stamps surrendered, or the reasonable retail price of the taxable merchandise involved in the transaction, whichever is larger. The redemption of reward points in exchange for taxable items is also subject to sales tax.

Department of Revenue Comment: Daily Deals and Gift Certificates

Daily deals offered by sellers through third parties, such as social media networks and radio stations, are treated as gift certificates. Sales tax is not due on the sale of a deal by a third party. When the deal is redeemed for a taxable item, the deal is treated like cash given for the purchase of the item and sales tax is due on the full sales price, including any amount paid with the use of the deal. For example, a customer purchases a daily deal through an online site that offers $50 worth of food at a restaurant for $25. Tax is not due on the customer's purchase of the deal from the online site. When the customer redeems the deal at the restaurant, tax is due on the menu price of the meals and drinks. The value of the daily deal is then applied against that amount. (*Letter No. 201106112L,* Texas Comptroller of Public Accounts, June 2011; CCH Texas Tax Reports, ¶403-735)

CCH Comment: Voucher Seller Responsible for Tax Collection

A company that sold vouchers, redeemable for customized photo trading and postcards, through independent sellers was a direct sales organization responsible for the collection and remittance of Texas sales tax collected by the independent distributors. Receipts from the sale of the vouchers were essentially receipts for prepaid goods subject to sales tax. (*Decision of Comptroller of Public Accounts,* Hearing No. 37,308, February 24, 2000; CCH Texas Tax Reports, ¶402-121)

- *Trade-ins*

The value of tangible personal property taken as a trade-in is excluded from the sales price. However, a purchaser who issues a resale certificate for the purchase of a taxable item is liable for sales tax on the item's purchase price if the purchaser uses the item as a part of the excludable consideration on the purchase of another taxable item. A transaction that qualifies as a tax-free exchange exempt from federal income tax under IRC § 1031 does not automatically qualify as a valid trade-in transaction for

¶902

reducing the taxable value of the new item for Texas sales tax purposes. (*Letter*, Texas Comptroller of Public Accounts, No. 200903447L, March 30, 2009; CCH TEXAS TAX REPORTS, ¶403-574)

- *Delivery charges and packing costs*

Transportation or delivery charges incident to the sale, lease, or rental of taxable tangible personal property or the performance of taxable services are subject to sales tax, regardless of whether such charges are for transportation before or after the transaction, and regardless of whether such charges are stated separately from the sales price of the item.

Practitioner Comment: Part of the Package

Transportation is taxable when it is incident to the performance of a taxable service, pursuant to Tax Code § 151.007(a)(4). A remote airport parking service, Park 'N Fly, sought to exclude from sales tax its charges for transporting customers.

Because the shuttle service was a major part of its operating costs and was essential to its service, Park 'N Fly argued that its shuttle service was not a minor part of the service, should not be considered "incident to" parking services and should not be subject to sales tax.

The Third Court of Appeals in Austin opined that incidental and incident were not interchangeable, and that "incident to" in Tax Code § 151.007(a)(4) means "closely related to." The Court looked at the entire transaction and based on the facts (e.g., Park 'N Fly's shuttles ran from its parking lots to airport terminals and rates were based on the time parked in the lot regardless of whether customers used the shuttle service), the shuttle service was closely related to the parking service and subject to sales tax. (*Sharp v. Park 'N Fly of Texas, Inc.*, 969 S.W.2d 572 (Tex. App.—Austin 1998, pet. denied))

Adina Christian, Ryan

Separately stated postage charges are exempt when billed by a seller to a purchaser if the seller incurred the cost of the postage at the request of the purchaser to distribute taxable tangible personal property or taxable services to third-party recipients designated by the purchaser.

- *Installation charges*

Charges for installation of tangible personal property are part of the sales price, regardless of whether such charges are separately stated.

- *Installment, lay-away, and conditional sales*

Separately stated finance, carrying, and service charges or interest from credit sales are not part of the "sales price" subject to tax. Credit sales are sales in which payment of the purchase price is deferred, and includes installment sales, conditional sales contracts, and revolving credit accounts. Cash-basis sellers who make credit sales and charge interest on the credit extended, including sales tax, must pay tax on a portion of the interest collected on the deferred sales. A retailer that uses the accrual basis for sales tax purposes must pay tax on the entire amount of tax and must report the tax at the time the sale is made.

- *Returned goods and repossessions*

When a purchaser returns an item, the seller should refund the full amount of Texas sales tax to the purchaser even if the seller provides only a partial refund of the sales price. The seller may then apply for a credit or refund of the sales tax that was remitted to the Comptroller's Office. (*Letter*, Texas Comptroller of Public Accounts, No. 201005690L, May 19, 2010; CCH TEXAS TAX REPORTS, ¶403-617) Texas has a long-standing policy requiring direct sales organizations to collect and remit taxes on sales made by their independent distributors. When merchandise is returned by an independent seller or a customer of the independent seller, the direct selling company

Part III—Sales and Use Taxes

may apply for a sales tax refund or credit. (*Letter*, Texas Comptroller of Public Accounts, No. 201006689L, June 3, 2010; CCH Texas Tax Reports, ¶403-616)

When taxable items upon which tax has been paid are repossessed, the seller is entitled to a credit or reimbursement of the tax for that portion of the actual purchase price remaining unpaid. The deduction must not include any nontaxable charges that were a part of the original sales contract. Expenses incident to collecting, repossessing, or selling the repossessed item are not included in the deduction. If the repossessed item is subsequently sold, sales tax is due unless the sale is otherwise exempt. The purchaser must remit the tax directly to the Comptroller if the seller or other holder of the repossessed item fails to collect the tax.

¶903 Rate of Tax

> *Law:* Secs. 151.012, 151.023, 151.024, 151.025, 151.051, 151.0515, 152.001, 152.002, 152.021—152.023, 152.026, 158.051, 158.052, 158.057, 160.021—160.023, 161.002, Tax Code; 34 TAC Secs. 3.1281, 3.320, 3.481, 3.70, 3.741, 3.96 (CCH Texas Tax Reports, ¶60-110, 60-540, 60-570, 60-740).

The state tax rate is 6.25% of the sales price of the item sold. In lieu of the standard rate, special sales and use tax rates apply to motor vehicles, manufactured housing, and boats and boat motors.

- *Rate changes*

A tax rate change must take effect on the first day of a calendar quarter. In instances in which the performance of a taxable service begins before the effective date of a rate change but the performance of the service will not be complete until after the effective date, the rate change applies to the first billing period for the service performed on or after the effective date.

- *Motor vehicle sale, rental, and use taxes*

Persons who purchase a motor vehicle in Texas and resident domiciliaries, or persons doing business in Texas who purchase a motor vehicle outside Texas for use within Texas must pay tax equal to 6.25% of total consideration. "Total consideration" does not include:

— cash discounts;

— full cash or credit refunds for vehicles returned to the seller (also known as the "failure of sale");

— labor or services rendered in installing, applying, remodeling or repairing the vehicle sold;

— a finance, carrying or service charge or interest on credit extended under a conditional sale or other deferred payment contract;

— trade-ins;

— charges for transportation after the sale; or

— motor vehicle inventory tax.

CCH Practice Pointer: "Failure of Sale" Policy Clarified

A failure of sale occurs only if the entire amount received from the customer is fully refunded to the customer. In such instances, the motor vehicle sales and use tax paid will also be refunded. However, if the purchase price of dealer installed items is not refunded to the purchaser, the transaction will not qualify as a failure of sale and motor vehicle sales tax cannot be refunded. (*Letter No.* 200909449L, Texas Comptroller of Public Accounts, September 15, 2009)

Sellers, renters, and lessors of vehicles may also exclude the fair market value of a replaced or replacement vehicle under certain conditions.

In lieu of the 6.25% rate, a $90 use tax is imposed on a new resident who brings a vehicle into Texas that has been registered previously in the new resident's name in any other state or foreign country. A $5 tax is imposed on any transaction involving the even exchange of two motor vehicles, payable by each party to the transaction. A $25 use tax is imposed on any person to whom any metal dealer plate is issued. This tax is in lieu of any of the above taxes.

Gift of motor vehicle: A $10 tax is imposed on any gift of a motor vehicle payable by the person receiving the gift. The $10 Texas motor vehicle sales tax imposed on a gift of a motor vehicle is applicable only if (1) the person receives the vehicle from the person's spouse, parent or stepparent, grandparent or grandchild, child or stepchild, sibling, or guardian; (2) the person receives the vehicle from a decedent's estate; or (3) the recipient is an organization exempt from federal income taxation under IRC § 501(a) and § 501(c)(3). (Sec. 152.025, Tax Code)

To qualify for the gift tax rate, the donor and person receiving the vehicle must complete a joint, notarized Affidavit of Motor Vehicle Gift Transfer (Form 14-317) describing the transaction and the relationship between the parties. A joint statement that relates to the motor vehicle gift must be filed in person by the recipient of the gift or, as applicable, the person from whom the gift is received or a person authorized to act on behalf of the estate from which the gift is received. A motor vehicle title service may not be used to file the statement. The person who files the statement must present to the tax assessor-collector an unexpired valid identification document that bears the person's photograph.

Used vehicles: Special valuation rules apply when determining the tax due on the purchase of a used motor vehicle (¶ 902).

Off-road vehicles distinguished from street-legal vehicles: Off-road vehicles are subject to *sales tax* under Chapter 151 at a 6.25% state rate plus any local sales taxes up to 2%, all of which are remitted directly to the state by the dealers. Street-legal vehicles are subject to the *motor vehicle sales tax* under Chapter 152 at a 6.25% state rate only. (There is no local motor vehicle sales tax.) The tax is not remitted to the state but collected by local County Tax Assessor Collectors.

Local vehicle inventory taxes (VIT) are included in the total consideration paid for off-road vehicles and motorcycles, but not for street-legal vehicles and motorcycles. Similarly, documentary fees are part of the taxable transaction for purchases of off-road vehicles and off-road motorcycles, but not for purchases of street-legal vehicles or motorcycles. (*Letter*, Texas Comptroller of Public Accounts, No. 200605561L, May 9, 2006, CCH Texas Tax Reports, ¶ 403-065; *Letter*, Texas Comptroller of Public Accounts, No. 200610772L, October 2006, CCH Texas Tax Reports, ¶ 403-185)

Tax on rentals: Gross rental receipts from the rental of a motor vehicle are taxed at the rate of 10% for rentals of 30 days or less and 6.25% for the rental of a vehicle for longer than 30 days, but not more than 180 days. "Gross rental receipts" do not include separately stated charges for insurance, charges for damages occurring during the rental period, separately stated charges for motor fuel or discounts. (Sec. 152.026, Tax Code)

- Texas emissions reduction surcharge

Off-road, heavy duty, diesel equipment: Until August 31, 2013, a surcharge equal to 2% of the sales price or rental amount is imposed on the retail sale, lease, rental, or storage, use, or consumption of new or used off-road, heavy-duty diesel equipment, including mining equipment and excluding implements of husbandry used solely for agricultural purposes, and heavy duty diesel equipment used in oil and gas exploration and production (*Letter No.* 200611853L, Texas Comptroller of Public Accounts, November 3, 2006, CCH Texas Tax Reports, ¶ 403-226).

¶ 903

Part III—Sales and Use Taxes

On-road diesel motor vehicles: Until August 31, 2013, a surcharge equal to 2.5% of the total consideration is imposed on every retail sale, lease, or use of every on-road diesel motor vehicle that is over 14,000 pounds and is of a model year 1996 or earlier and that is sold or leased in Texas. The tax also applies to post-1996 model vehicles sold, leased, or used in Texas, but at a reduced rate of 1%.

The surcharge on off-road, heavy-duty diesel equipment is collected at the same time and in the same manner as the sales tax, and the tax on on-road diesel motor vehicles is collected at the same time and in the same manner as motor vehicle sales, rental, and use taxes.

- *Manufactured housing*

Manufacturers must collect a sales tax of 5% of 65% (or 0.0325%) of the sales price on the initial sale of a new manufactured home in Texas. A manufactured housing use tax is imposed on manufactured homes purchased new outside Texas and brought into Texas for use within one year from the date of purchase.

- *Boats and boat motors*

The boat and boat motor sales and use tax is imposed at a rate of 6.25% of the sales price paid, less any allowance for trade-ins. The boat and boat motor sales and use tax applies to retail sales of boats with a length of 65 feet or less (measured from end to end over the deck, excluding the sheer) including sales of sailboats, inboards, outboards, jet skis, and other personal watercraft.

The tax is also levied on the retail sale of outboard motors (gasoline or diesel) but not to electric motors (such as trolling motors) unless attached to a boat subject to boat tax and sold with that boat for a single price. The regular sales and use tax applies to sales of:

— boats greater than 65 feet in length;

— canoes;

— kayaks;

— inflatable boats and rafts;

— punts;

— boats designed to be propelled only by a paddle or pole;

— the rental or lease of a boat or boat motor;

— electric motors and accessories (such as life jackets or ladders), if sold separately; and

— the repair and remodeling of boats subject to the boat and boat motor sales and use tax. (*Notice*, Texas Comptroller of Public Accounts, May 2004, CCH TEXAS TAX REPORTS, ¶402-712)

A use tax at the same rate is imposed on a taxable boat or outboard motor that is purchased at retail outside Texas and used within Texas or brought into Texas for use by a Texas resident or other person who is domiciled or doing business in Texas. In lieu of the above taxes, a use tax is imposed on a new resident who brings a taxable boat or motor into Texas that had originally been purchased and owned by the new resident in any other state or foreign country. The tax is imposed at the rate of $15 for each taxable boat or motor.

- *Fireworks tax*

A sale of fireworks subject to sales and use taxes is also subject to an additional 2% fireworks tax.

The following are exempt from the fireworks tax, but not sales tax:

¶903

— a toy pistol, toy cane, toy gun, or other device that uses a paper or plastic cap;

— a model rocket or model rocket motor that is designed, sold, and used for the purpose of propelling a recoverable aero model;

— specified propelling or expelling charges;

— a novelty or trick noisemaker;

— a pyrotechnic emergency signaling device or distress signal;

— a fusee or railway torpedo for use by a railroad;

— a blank cartridge that is sold for use in a radio, television, film, or theater production, for signal or ceremonial purposes in athletic events, or for industrial purposes; or

— a pyrotechnic device that is sold for use by a military organization.

CCH Comment: Fireworks

Fireworks, not specifically exempt above, are subject to both the sales tax and the fireworks tax. (34 TAC Sec. 3.1281)

¶904 Local Taxes and Rates

Law: Secs. 321.002, 321.103, 321.104, 321.203, 321.205, 323.103—323.105, 323.203, 324.022, Tax Code (CCH Texas Tax Reports, ¶ 61-710, 61-730, 61-735).

Municipalities and counties are authorized to impose additional sales and use taxes. (Art. XI, Sec. 4 and Sec. 5, Tex. Const.) Local sales and use taxes are authorized for certain districts or for specified purposes (*e.g.*, short-term vehicle rentals, admissions tax, parking tax, etc.). Generally, the tax base is the same as the state's limited sales, excise, and use and the combined local rate may not generally exceed 2%, resulting in a maximum state and local tax rate of 8.25%.

CCH Practice Pointer: Collection of Local Taxes Clarified

A Comptroller letter sets forth the following four general rules for collecting local Texas sales and use taxes:

— First, sales tax takes precedence over use tax.

— Second, a seller can collect no more than 2% in total local taxes for all applicable jurisdictions.

— Third, if a seller collects a sales tax for a city, county, special purpose district (SPD), or transit authority, the seller may not collect a use tax for another local taxing jurisdiction of the same type. A seller may, however, collect more than one transit or SPD sales tax or multiple transit or SPD use taxes in relation to the same transaction.

— And fourth, the seller must collect the full amount of a local tax without exceeding the 2% cap; fractional collection is not permitted. In other words, a seller must collect all or none of a jurisdiction's tax. (*Letter No. 200710981L*, Texas Comptroller of Public Accounts, October 19, 2007, CCH Texas Tax Reports, ¶ 403-336)

- *Municipal sales and use taxes*

A municipality that has adopted the sales and use tax authorized by the Municipal Sales and Use Tax Act must impose the tax at the rate of 1%. A qualified municipality may vote to adopt an additional tax of up to 0.5%.

Certain municipalities may also impose a tax for crime prevention and control purposes at a rate not to exceed 0.5%.

Part III—Sales and Use Taxes

A 0.25% street maintenance sales and use tax may also be imposed, subject to voter approval. Municipalities may also create a municipal development corporation and may, subject to voter approval, impose a sales and use tax for the benefit of that corporation at the rate of tax of 0.125%, 0.25%, 0.375%, or 0.5%. However, any increase in the tax may not exceed 0.5%. (Sec. 379A.081, Local Government Code)

- *County sales and use taxes*

A county that has adopted the sales and use tax authorized by the County Sales and Use Tax Act must impose the tax at the rate of 0.5%, unless the county includes no territory within the limits of a municipality, in which case it must impose the tax at the rate of 1%. Certain counties may also impose a tax for crime prevention and control purposes at a rate not to exceed 0.5%. A county tax levied for the purpose of funding health services may be imposed at the rate of 0.5%, 0.625%, 0.75%, 0.875%, or 1%.

- *Development Corporation Act taxes*

A city adopting a local sales and use tax for the benefit of an industrial development corporation must adopt a rate of 0.125%, 0.25%, 0.375%, or 0.5%. (Art. 5190.6, Sec. 4A(d), R.C.S.) A city adopting a local sales and use tax for the benefit of a corporation building entertainment and sports facilities must also adopt a rate of 0.125%, 0.25%, 0.375%, or 0.5%. (Art. 5190.6, Sec. 4B(e), R.C.S.)

- *Transit authority sales and use taxes*

Metropolitan rapid transit authorities, regional transportation authorities, and county transportation authorities are allowed to levy local sales and use taxes at any of the following rates: 0.25%, 0.5%, 0.75%, and 1%. (Secs. 451.404, 452.401, 460.551, Transportation Code) City Transit Developments are allowed to levy local sales and use taxes at either of the following rates: 0.25% and 0.5%. (Sec. 453.401, Transportation Code)

- *Hospital district sales and use taxes*

Hospital districts that are authorized to impose property taxes may adopt a sales and use tax at any rate, in multiples of 0.125 of 1%, up to a maximum of 2%. (Secs. 285.061, 285.161, Health and Safety Code)

- *Health services sales and use taxes*

Subject to voter approval, counties having a population of 50,000 or less may impose a county health services sales and use tax, provided that the total local tax rate does not exceed 2%. (Sec. 324.021, Tax Code)

- *Special district taxes on residential gas and electricity*

Fire control, prevention, and emergency medical services district or a crime control and prevention district located in all or part of a municipality may adopt a local sales and use tax on the residential use of gas and electricity. The tax may be imposed on the sale, production, distribution, lease, rental, use, storage, or other consumption within the district of gas and electricity for residential use. The tax rate must be equal to the district's tax rate on all other sales of taxable items. (Sec. 321.1055, Tax Code)

- *Venue projects sales and use taxes*

Cities, counties, and venue districts formed by combinations of cities, counties, or both may impose a sales and use tax to finance venue projects at the following rates: of 0.125%, 0.25%, 0.375%, or 0.5%. (Sec. 334.083, Local Government Code)

¶904

Practitioner Comment: No Partial Tax Rates

Texas cities may adopt up to a 2% sales tax while counties, metropolitan transit authorities and city transit departments ("MTA/CTD"), and special purpose districts ("SPD") may also adopt sales and use taxes up to 1% each. All local sales taxes are collected based upon the location of the seller. Metropolitan transit authorities and city transit departments ("MTA/CTD") may adopt an additional 1% sales tax. MTA/CTD sales taxes are collected based upon the location of the purchaser. Although the combined tax rate at a particular location could be as high as 9.25%, by law, the total tax rate is limited to 8.25%. In cases where the combined rates exceed 8.25%, partial rates may not be collected.

For example, if a taxpayer located in a 1% city and 1% MTA/CTD jurisdiction purchases an item from a vendor located in a 1.5% city jurisdiction, the maximum amount of local tax that can be collected is 1.5%, not 2%. This results because the 1.5% city tax is due based upon the location of the vendor and the imposition of the 1% destination-based MTA/CTD tax would cause the total tax collected to exceed the maximum 8.25% rate. As a result, the MTA/CTD tax is not due and the taxpayer enjoys a .5% tax savings compared to the tax due on similar purchases from vendors located in the taxpayer's home city.

G. Brint Ryan, Ryan

- *Sourcing of sales*

For purposes of determining which city, county, or other taxing jurisdiction is entitled to the proceeds of the tax on a sale or on a particular use, specific tests are set forth to be applied in determining in which municipality, county, or taxing jurisdiction the sale was consummated or the use occurred. Detailed explanations and examples of local sourcing rules may be found in *Pub. 94-105, Guidelines for Collecting Sales and Use Tax*, Texas Comptroller of Public Accounts, February 2009.

Except as noted below, the sale of a taxable item, both tangible personal property and taxable services, occurs within the local taxing jurisdiction in which the seller's business is located. If a retailer has only one place of business in Texas, all of the retailer's retail sales are subject to sales tax in the jurisdiction in which the place of business is located. For retailers with more than one place of business in Texas, the sale is sourced to the location from where the retailer first accepts the order, provided that the order is placed in person by the purchaser or lessee of the taxable item. Prior to June 19, 2009, sales were sourced to the place of business from which the item was shipped. However, retailers should continue to collect local sales tax based on the "ship from" location on all delivery sales of taxable items that are shipped from a place of business in Texas when the order is not placed in person by the purchaser or lessee.

If a retailer has more than one place of business in Texas and the new sourcing provision does not apply, the sale is consummated at the place of business of the retailer:

— from which the retailer ships or delivers the item, if the retailer ships or delivers the item to a point designated by the purchaser or lessee such as when a purchaser places orders over the Internet, by telephone, or through the mail; or

— where the purchaser or lessee takes possession of and removes the item, if the purchaser or lessee takes possession of and removes the item from a place of business of the retailer.

Finally, if a retailer has more than one place of business in Texas and neither sourcing provision above applies, the sale is consummated at (1) the place of business of the retailer where the order is received or (2) if the order is not received at a

¶904

Part III—Sales and Use Taxes

retailer's place of business, the place of business from which the retailer's agent or employee who took the order operates.

The new sourcing provision does not apply if the taxable item is shipped or delivered from a warehouse that is a place of business of the retailer and the retailer has an economic development agreement with a municipality or county that provides certain prescribed information to the comptroller regarding each warehouse and place of business of the retailer. This exclusion expires September 1, 2014. (Sec. 321.203(c) and (d)).

A "place of business of the retailer" is defined as an established outlet, office, or location including a warehouse, storage yard, or manufacturing plant operated by the retailer or the retailer's agent or employee for the purpose of receiving orders for taxable items and includes any location (*e.g.*, a warehouse, storage yard, or manufacturing plant) at which three or more orders are received by the retailer during a calendar year.

Excluded from the definition of "place of business of the retailer" is an outlet, office, facility, or location that contracts with a retail or commercial business to process for that business invoices or bills of lading onto which sales tax is added if the Texas Comptroller of Public Accounts determines that the billing office functions to avoid sales and use taxes or to rebate a portion of the taxes to the contracting business.

If there is no place of business of the retailer because the Comptroller has made such a determination, the sale is consummated at the place of business of the retailer from whom the outlet, office, facility, or location purchased the taxable item for resale to the contracting business.

Purchasing office: Beginning September 1, 2011, the Comptroller will not recognize a purchasing office as a place of business of a retailer for purposes of sourcing local sales tax if (1) the office receives a rebate of local sales and use taxes or (2) a related entity (parent, subsidiary, or affiliate) is able to avoid or reduce its local tax liabilities by establishing or operating the purchasing office, through creating a new entity or moving an existing entity, in a location with a lower sales tax rate than the location where the purchasing functions were formerly performed. Special sourcing rules apply if a purchasing office location is disregarded for determining what local taxes are due.

CCH Comment: Treatment of Kiosks

For local sales and use tax purposes, a kiosk is not a considered a retailer's place of business. The term "kiosk" means a small stand-alone area or structure:

— that is used solely to display merchandise or to submit orders for taxable items from a data entry device;

— that is located entirely within a location that is a place of business of another retailer, such as a department store or shopping mall; and

— at which taxable items are not available for immediate delivery to a customer.

(Sec. 321.002(3), Tax Code)

A booth set up at a mall or street fair to sell taxable items is not a kiosk if customers can receive the items at the time of the sale. In these scenarios, the seller is operating a place of business and local sales tax is due based on the location of the booth at the time of the sale.

Drop shipments: When an order is received in Texas at a seller's place of business and then shipped directly to the customer's location from a third-party supplier, the seller should collect the local sales tax based on the place of business where the order is received. However, if the item is shipped from the seller's place of business or

¶904

warehouse, distribution center or other location located outside Texas, the seller must collect use tax based on where the product is delivered. (*Pub. 94-105, Guidelines for Collecting Sales and Use Tax*, Texas Comptroller of Public Accounts, February 2009; Letter, Texas Comptroller of Public Accounts, No. 200604633L, April 4, 2006, CCH Texas Tax Reports, ¶ 403-113)

> ***CCH Comment: Streamlined Sales and Use Tax Conformity***
>
> Texas is not participating in the Streamlined Sales and Use Tax Agreement (see ¶ 801). Sellers registering under the Agreement are not required to collect tax in Texas and Texas is not required to provide sellers with amnesty for uncollected taxes.

- *Specific sourcing rules*

    The following taxable items are sourced according to specific rules as follows:

    — *Amusement service:* the place where the performance or other deliver of the service takes place.

    — *Cable services:* the point of delivery to the consumer.

    — *Contractors:* A rule outlines the different sourcing rules applied depending upon whether the contract is a separated contract or a lump-sum contract, see 34 TAC Sec. 3.291.

    — *Florists:* the place where the order is received, regardless of whether the flowers are delivered inside or outside Texas.

    — *Garbage or other waste collection/removal services:* the location at which the garbage or waste is collected.

    — *Natural gas and electricity:* the point of delivery to the customer.

    — *Nonresidential real property repair and remodeling:* local taxes for both materials and labor sourced to job site's location.

    — *Telecommunication services (landline):* sourced to the location where the call originates, or if this information can not be obtained, to the location at which the service is billed.

    — *Telecommunication services (mobile):* sourced to the place of primary use (see ¶ 804).

Sales of telecommunications services sold based on a price that is measured by individual calls is sourced to the location where the call originates and terminates, or the location where the call either originates or terminates and at which the service address is also located. Except as provided, the sale of telecommunications services sold on a basis other than on a call-by-call basis is sourced to the location of the customer's primary place of use. A sale of post-paid calling services sold based on a price that is measured by individual calls is sourced to the location of the origination point of the telecommunications signal as first identified by the seller's telecommunications system or by information received by the seller from the seller's service provider if the system used to transport the signal is not that of the seller.

If a purchaser who has given a resale certificate makes any taxable use of the item purchased, the use or other consumption of the taxable item that subjected the taxable item to the tax is consummated at the place where the taxable item is stored or kept at the time of or just before the use or consumption.

¶ 905 Local Tax Rate Chart

The following chart shows the rates imposed by localities that levy a local sales and use tax, as of October 1, 2011. A Sales Tax Rate Locator can also be found on State Comptroller's Web site at http://ecpa.cpa.state.tx.us/atj/addresslookup.jsp.

Part III—Sales and Use Taxes

NAME	LOCAL CODE	LOCAL RATE	TOTAL RATE
Abbott	2109064	.015000	.082500
Hill Co	4109000	.005000	
Abernathy	2095024	.015000	.082500
Hale Co	4095006	.005000	
Abernathy	2095024	.015000	.082500
Lubbock Co	4152006	.005000	
Abilene (Jones Co)	2221012	.020000	.082500
Abilene (Taylor Co)	2221012	.020000	.082500
Ace			.067500
Polk Co	4187005	.005000	
Ackerly	2156020	.010000	.077500
Dawson Co	4058001	.005000	
Ackerly (Martin Co)	2156020	.010000	.072500
Acme			.067500
Hardeman Co	4099002	.005000	
Acton			.072500
Hood Co	4111006	.005000	
Hood County Development Dist No One	5111505	.005000	
Acuff			.067500
Lubbock Co	4152006	.005000	
Adamsville			.067500
Lampasas Co	4141000	.005000	
Addison (Dallas Co)	2057217	.010000	.082500
Dallas MTA	3057994	.010000	
Adkins (Bexar Co)			.067500
San Antonio MTA	3015995	.005000	
Adrian	2180020	.010000	.077500
Oldham Co	4180002	.005000	
Afton			.067500
Dickens Co	4063004	.005000	
Agnes			.067500
Parker Co	4184008	.005000	
Agua Dulce (Nueces Co)	2178051	.010000	.077500
Corpus Christi MTA	3178998	.005000	
Agua Nueva (Jim Hogg Co)			.082500
Jim Hogg Co	4124001	.010000	
Jim Hogg County Assistance District	5124519	.005000	
Jim Hogg County Health Services	5124500	.005000	
Aguilares			.067500
Webb Co	4240000	.005000	
Alamo (Hidalgo Co)	2108092	.020000	.082500
Alamo Beach			.067500
Calhoun Co	4029007	.005000	
Alamo Heights (Bexar Co)	2015021	.012500	.080000
San Antonio MTA	3015995	.005000	
Alba	2250043	.015000	.082500
Rains Co	4190000	.005000	
Alba	2250043	.015000	.082500
Wood Co	4250007	.005000	
Albany (Shackelford Co)	2209027	.020000	.082500
Albert			.067500
Gillespie Co	4086007	.005000	
Albion			.067500
Red River Co	4194006	.005000	
Aldine (Harris Co)			.072500
Houston MTA	3101990	.010000	
Aldine Community Improvement District	5101534	.010000	
Aledo	2184053	.015000	.082500
Parker Co	4184008	.005000	
Alexander			.067500
Erath Co	4072003	.005000	
Alfred			.067500
Jim Wells Co	4125000	.005000	
Algerita			.067500
San Saba Co	4206002	.005000	
Alice	2125028	.015000	.082500
Jim Wells Co	4125000	.005000	
Alief (Harris Co)			.072500
Houston MTA	3101990	.010000	
Allen (Collin Co)	2043072	.020000	.082500
Allenfarm			.067500
Brazos Co	4021005	.005000	
Allentown			.067500
Angelina Co	4003007	.005000	
Alleyton			.067500
Colorado Co	4045007	.005000	

¶905

Alma (Ellis Co)	2070112	.010000	.072500
Alpine	2022013	.015000	.082500
Brewster Co	4022004	.005000	
Altair			.072500
Colorado Co	4045007	.005000	
Rice Hospital District	5045506	.005000	
Alto	2037016	.015000	.082500
Cherokee Co	4037007	.005000	
Alto Springs			.067500
Falls Co	4073002	.005000	
Alton (Hidalgo Co)	2108172	.020000	.082500
Alum Creek			.067500
Bastrop Co	4011007	.005000	
Alvarado (Johnson Co)	2126054	.020000	.082500
Alvin	2020015	.015000	.082500
Brazoria Co	4020006	.005000	
Alvord	2249083	.015000	.082500
Wise Co	4249001	.005000	
Amarillo (Potter Co)	2188013	.020000	.082500
Amarillo (Randall Co)	2188013	.020000	.082500
Ames	2146096	.010000	.077500
Liberty Co	4146005	.005000	
Amherst (Lamb Co)	2140010	.012500	.075000
Ammansville			.067500
Fayette Co	4075000	.005000	
Amsterdam			.067500
Brazoria Co	4020006	.005000	
Anahuac (Chambers Co)	2036017	.010000	.077500
Chambers Co Health Ser	5036507	.005000	
Anchor			.067500
Brazoria Co	4020006	.005000	
Anderson	2093035	.012500	.080000
Grimes Co	4093008	.005000	
Andrews (Andrews Co)	2002017	.017500	.080000
Angleton	2020042	.015000	.082500
Brazoria Co	4020006	.005000	
Angus	2175107	.015000	.082500
Navarro Co	4175009	.005000	
Anna (Collin Co)	2043134	.020000	.082500
Annarose			.067500
Live Oak Co	4149002	.005000	
Annetta	2184099	.010000	.077500
Parker Co	4184008	.005000	
Annetta North	2184124	.0125000	.0800000
Parker Co	4184008	.005000	
Annetta South	2184115	.010000	.077500
Parker Co	4184008	.005000	
Annona	2194042	.010000	.077500
Red River Co	4194006	.005000	
Anson (Jones Co)	2127026	.020000	.082500
Anthony	2071022	.010000	.082500
El Paso Co	4071004	.005000	
El Paso Co Es Dis No2	5071503	.005000	
Anton (Hockley Co)	2110025	.010000	.072500
Appleby (Nacogdoches Co)			.072500
Nacogdoches County Hospital District	5174509	.010000	
Aquilla	2109108	.010000	.077500
Hill Co	4109000	.005000	
Aransas Pass	2205012	.010000	.082500
Aransas Co	4004006	.005000	
Aransas County Health Services	5004505	.005000	
Aransas Pass (Nueces Co)	2205012	.010000	.077500
Aransas Pass Municipal Develop Dist	5205502	.005000	
Aransas Pass (San Patricio Co)	2205012	.010000	.077500
Aransas Pass Municipal Develop Dist	5205502	.005000	
Archer City	2005023	.015000	.082500
Archer Co	4005005	.005000	
Arcola (Fort Bend Co)	2079131	.020000	.082500
Argenta			.067500
Live Oak Co	4149002	.005000	
Argyle (Denton Co)	2061104	.017500	.082500
Arlington (Tarrant Co)	2220095	.017500	.0800000
Arnett			.067500
Coryell Co	4050009	.005000	
Argyle Crime Control Dist	5061550	.002500	
Arney			.067500
Castro Co	4035009	.005000	
Arp	2212068	.010000	.077500
Smith Co	4212004	.005000	

¶905

Part III—Sales and Use Taxes

Art (Mason Co)			.072500
Mason County Health Services	5157500	.010000	
Arthur City			.067500
Lamar Co	4139004	.005000	
Asa			.067500
McClennan Co	4161005	.005000	
Asherton	2064030	.010000	.077500
Dimmit Co	4064003	.005000	
Ashland			.067500
Upshur Co	4230002	.005000	
Asia			.067500
Polk Co	4187005	.005000	
Aspermont (Stonewall Co)	2217018	.020000	.082500
Atascocita (Harris Co)			.072500
Houston MTA	3101990	.010000	
Atascosa (Bexar Co)			.067500
San Antonio MTA	3015995	.005000	
Ater			.067500
Coryell Co	4050009	.005000	
Athens (Henderson Co)	2107011	.020000	.082500
Atlanta (Cass Co)	2034028	.020000	.082500
Aubrey (Denton Co)	2061051	.020000	.082500
Augusta			.067500
Houston Co	4113004	.005000	
Aurora	2249136	.010000	.077500
Wise Co	4249001	.005000	
Austin (Travis Co)	2227016	.010000	.082500
Austin MTA	3227999	.010000	
Austin (Williamson Co)	2227016	.010000	.082500
Austin MTA	3227999	.010000	
Austin/Westbank Library Dist (Travis C	6227604	.010000	.082500
Austin MTA	3227999	.010000	
Austonio			.067500
Houston Co	4113004	.005000	
Austwell (Refugio Co)	2196040	.010000	.072500
Avery	2194024	.010000	.077500
Red River Co	4194006	.005000	
Avinger (Cass Co)	2034046	.015000	.077500
Avinger	2034046	.015000	.082500
Marion Co	4155003	.005000	
Axtell			.067500
McClennan Co	4161005	.005000	
Azle	2184035	.012500	.082500
Parker Co	4184008	.005000	
Azle Crm Control Dist	5184516	.002500	
Azle (Tarrant Co)	2184035	.012500	.077500
Azle Crm Control Dist	5184516	.002500	
Bagwell			.067500
Red River Co	4194006	.005000	
Bailey	2074109	.010000	.077500
Fannin Co	4074001	.005000	
Baileys Prairie	2020220	.010000	.077500
Brazoria Co	4020006	.005000	
Baileyville			.067500
Milam Co	4166000	.005000	
Baird (Callahan Co)	2030022	.015000	.077500
Balch Springs (Dallas Co)	2057119	.020000	.082500
Balcones Heights (Bexar Co)	2015030	.010000	.082500
San Antonio MTA	3015995	.005000	
Balcones Heights Crime Control Dist	5015502	.005000	
Ballinger	2200017	.015000	.082500
Runnels Co	4200008	.005000	
Balmorhea (Reeves Co)	2195032	.015000	.082500
Reeves County Hospital District	5195504	.005000	
Balsora			.067500
Wise Co	4249001	.005000	
Bammel (Harris Co)			.072500
Houston MTA	3101990	.010000	
Bandera	2010017	.015000	.082500
Bandera Co	4010008	.005000	
Bangs (Brown Co)	2025029	.017500	.080000
Bangs Municipal Development Dist	50255000	.002500	
Banquete (Nueces Co)			.067500
Corpus Christi MTA	3178998	.005000	
Barbarosa			.067500
Guadalupe Co	4094007	.005000	
Barclay			.067500
Falls Co	4073002	.005000	
Bardwell (Ellis Co)	2070149	.010000	.072500

¶905

Barkman			.067500
Bowie Co	4019009	.005000	
Barnes			.067500
Polk Co	4187005	.005000	
Barnum			.067500
Polk Co	4187005	.005000	
Barry			.067500
Navarro Co	4175009	.005000	
Bartlett	2246077	.010000	.077500
Bell Co	4014004	.005000	
Bartlett (Williamson Co)	2246077	.010000	.072500
Bartley Woods			.067500
Fannin Co	4074001	.005000	
Bartonville (Denton Co)	2061211	.017500	.080000
Bassett			.067500
Bowie Co	4019009	.005000	
Bastrop	2011025	.015000	.082500
Bastrop Co	4011007	.005000	
Bateman			.067500
Bastrop Co	4011007	.005000	
Battle			.067500
McClennan Co	4161005	.005000	
Bay City (Matagorda Co)	2158028	.020000	.082500
Bayou Vista (Galveston Co)	2084205	.017500	.080000
Bayside (Refugio Co)	2196031	.010000	.072500
Baytown (Chambers Co)	2101151	.012500	.080000
Chambers Co Health Ser	5036507	.005000	
Baytown (Harris Co)	2101151	.012500	.080000
Baytown Crime Control and Prevention Dist	5101632	.0012500	
Baytown Fire Control, Prevention, and Emerg. Med. Services Dist	5101623	.0012500	
Baytown Mun Dev Dist	5036516	.005000	
Bayview (Cameron Co)	2031183	.010000	.072500
Bazette			.067500
Navarro Co	4175009	.005000	
Beach City (Chambers Co)			.067500
Chambers Co Health Ser	5036507	.005000	
Beasley (Fort Bend Co)	2079060	.020000	.082500
Beaumont	2123011	.015000	.082500
Jefferson Co	4123002	.005000	
Beauxart Gardens			.067500
Jefferson Co	4123002	.005000	
Bebe			.067500
Gonzales Co	4089004	.005000	
Beckville (Panola Co)	2183027	.010000	.072500
Bedford (Tarrant Co)	2220102	.020000	.082500
Bedias	2093044	.012500	.080000
Grimes Co	4093008	.005000	
Bee Cave (Travis Co)	2227150	.020000	.082500
Bee House			.067500
Coryell Co	4050009	.005000	
Beeville	2013014	.015000	.082500
Bee Co	4013005	.005000	
Belfalls			.067500
Bell Co	4014004	.005000	
Bellaire (Harris Co)	2101026	.010000	.082500
Houston MTA	3101990	.010000	
Bellevue (Clay Co)	2039050	.010000	.072500
Bellmead	2161050	.015000	.082500
McClennan Co	4161005	.005000	
Bells (Grayson Co)	2091064	.020000	.082500
Bellville	2008020	.015000	.082500
Austin Co	4008002	.005000	
Belmont			.067500
Gonzales Co	4089004	.005000	
Belott			.067500
Houston Co	4113004	.005000	
Belton	2014040	.015000	.082500
Bell Co	4014004	.005000	
Belton/Salado Library District	6014601	.015000	.082500
Bell Co	4014004	.005000	
Ben Arnold			.067500
Milam Co	4166000	.005000	
Ben Bolt			.067500
Jim Wells Co	4125000	.005000	
Ben Franklin			.072500
Delta Co	4060007	.005000	
Delta Co Emergency Services District	5060506	.005000	

¶905

Part III—Sales and Use Taxes

Benavides (Duval Co)	2066038	.010000	.072500
Benbrook (Tarrant Co)	2220059	.015000	.082500
Benbrook Library District	5220610	.005000	
Bend			.067500
San Saba Co	4206002	.005000	
Benjamin (Knox Co)	2138032	.015000	.077500
Bennett			.067500
Parker Co	4184008	.005000	
Berea			.067500
Marion Co	4155003	.005000	
Bergheim			.067500
Kendall Co	4130003	.005000	
Bernardo			.067500
Colorado Co	4045007	.005000	
Berryville (Henderson Co)	2107128	.010000	.072500
Bertram (Burnet Co)	2027045	.017500	.080000
Best			.067500
Reagan Co	4192008	.005000	
Bethel			.067500
Anderson Co	4001009	.005000	
Bethel			.067500
Runnels Co	4200008	.005000	
Bettie			.067500
Upshur Co	4230002	.005000	
Beverly Hills	2161032	.015000	.082500
McClennan Co	4161005	.005000	
Bevil Oaks	2123084	.010000	.077500
Jefferson Co	4123002	.005000	
Biardstown			.067500
Lamar Co	4139004	.005000	
Big Bend Natl Park			.077500
Brewster Co	4022004	.005000	
Brewster Co Emergency Services District No. 1	5022503	.010000	
Big Lake	2192017	.015000	.082500
Reagan Co	4192008	.005000	
Big Sandy	2230039	.015000	.082500
Upshur Co	4230002	.005000	
Big Spring (Howard Co)	2114012	.020000	.082500
Big Wells	2064021	.010000	.077500
Dimmit Co	4064003	.005000	
Bigfoot			.067500
Frio Co	4082001	.005000	
Birch			.067500
Burleson Co	4026000	.005000	
Birome			.067500
Hill Co	4109000	.005000	
Birthright			.067500
Hopkins Co	4112005	.005000	
Biry			.067500
Medina Co	4163003	.005000	
Bishop (Nueces Co)	2178042	.015000	.082500
Corpus Christi MTA	3178998	.005000	
Blackfoot			.067500
Anderson Co	4001009	.005000	
Blackhill			.067500
Atascosa Co	4007003	.005000	
Blackwell (Coke Co)	2177034	.010000	.072500
Blackwell (Nolan Co)	2177034	.010000	.072500
Blanchard			.067500
Polk Co	4187005	.005000	
Blanco	2016020	.015000	.082500
Blanco Co	4016002	.005000	
Blandlake			.067500
San Augustine Co	4203005	.005000	
Blanket (Brown Co)	2025047	.012500	.075000
Blanton			.067500
Runnels Co	4200008	.005000	
Bleiblerville			.067500
Austin Co	4008002	.005000	
Blevins			.067500
Falls Co	4073002	.005000	
Bloomburg (Cass Co)	2034073	.010000	.072500
Blooming Grove	2175036	.010000	.077500
Navarro Co	4175009	.005000	
Bloomington			.067500
Victoria Co	4235007	.005000	
Blossom	2139068	.012500	.080000
Lamar Co	4139004	.005000	

¶905

Blue			.067500
Lee Co	4144007	.005000	
Blue Mound (Tarrant Co)	2220291	.010000	.082500
Fort Worth MTA	3220996	.005000	
Blue Mound Crime Control	5220665	.005000	
Blue Ridge (Collin Co)	2043063	.020000	.082500
Bluff Dale			.067500
Erath Co	4072003	.005000	
Blum	2109082	.010000	.077500
Hill Co	4109000	.005000	
Blumenthal			.067500
Gillespie Co	4086007	.005000	
Bluntzer (Nueces Co)			.067500
Corpus Christi MTA	3178998	.005000	
Boerne	2130012	.015000	.082500
Kendall Co	4130003	.005000	
Bogata	2194033	.010000	.082500
Red River Co	4194006	.005000	
Bogata Crime Control	5194505	.005000	
Boling			.067500
Wharton Co	4241009	.005000	
Bonham	2074038	.015000	.082500
Fannin Co	4074001	.005000	
Bonney			.067500
Brazoria Co	4020006	.005000	
Bonus			.067500
Wharton Co	4241009	.005000	
Booker (Lipscomb Co)	2148021	.015000	.077500
Booker (Ochiltree Co)	2148021	.015000	.077500
Boonsville			.067500
Wise Co	4249001	.005000	
Boquillas			.067500
Brewster Co	4022004	.005000	
Borden			.067500
Colorado Co	4045007	.005000	
Borderland			.072500
El Paso Co	4071004	.005000	
El Paso Co Es Dis No2	5071503	.005000	
Borger (Hutchinson Co)	2117019	.020000	.082500
Bosqueville			.067500
McClennan Co	4161005	.005000	
Boston			.067500
Bowie Co	4019009	.005000	
Bovina (Parmer Co)	2185025	.020000	.082500
Bowie (Montague Co)	2169034	.020000	.082500
Bowser			.067500
San Saba Co	4206002	.005000	
Boxelder			.067500
Red River Co	4194006	.005000	
Boyd			.067500
Fannin Co	4074001	.005000	
Boyd	2249029	.015000	.082500
Wise Co	4249001	.005000	
Boys Ranch			.067500
Oldham Co	4180002	.005000	
Bracken			.067500
Comal Co	4046006	.005000	
Brackettville	2136016	.010000	.082500
Kinney Co	4136007	.005000	
Kinney County Health Services	5136506	.005000	
Brad			.067500
Palo Pinto Co	4182000	.005000	
Bradford			.067500
Anderson Co	4001009	.005000	
Brady	2160015	.012500	.082500
McCulloch Co	4160006	.005000	
McCulloch County Hospital District	5160505	.002500	
Branchville			.067500
Milam Co	4166000	.005000	
Brandon			.067500
Hill Co	4109000	.005000	
Brashear			.067500
Hopkins Co	4112005	.005000	
Brazoria	2020131	.015000	.082500
Brazoria Co	4020006	.005000	
Brazos			.067500
Palo Pinto Co	4182000	.005000	
Brazos Country	2008075	.010000	.077500
Austin Co	4008002	.005000	

¶905

Part III—Sales and Use Taxes 137

Brazos Point			.067500
Bosque Co	4018000	.005000	
Breckenridge (Stephens Co)	2215010	.017500	.080000
Bremond (Robertson Co)	2198048	.020000	.082500
Brenham	2239012	.015000	.082500
Washington Co	4239003	.005000	
Briar			.067500
Parker Co	4184008	.005000	
Briar			.067500
Wise Co	4249001	.005000	
Briarcliff (Travis Co)	2227169	.010000	.072500
Briaroaks (Johnson Co)	2126107	.010000	.072500
Briary			.067500
Milam Co	4166000	.005000	
Bridge City	2181047	.015000	.082500
Orange Co	4181001	.005000	
Bridgeport	2249056	.015000	.082500
Wise Co	4249001	.005000	
Broaddus	2203023	.010000	.077500
San Augustine Co	4203005	.005000	
Brock			.067500
Parker Co	4184008	.005000	
Bronson			.067500
Sabine Co	4202006	.005000	
Bronte (Coke Co)	2041029	.020000	.082500
Brookeland			.067500
Sabine Co	4202006	.005000	
Brookshire (Waller Co)	2237014	.020000	.082500
Brookside Village	2020088	.010000	.077500
Brazoria Co	4020006	.005000	
Brookston			.067500
Lamar Co	4139004	.005000	
Browndell (Jasper Co)	2121031	.010000	.072500
Brownfield	2223010	.015000	.082500
Terry Co	4223001	.005000	
Brownsboro			.067500
Caldwell Co	4028008	.005000	
Brownsboro (Henderson Co)	2107093	.020000	.082500
Brownsville (Cameron Co)	2031076	.020000	.082500
Brownwood (Brown Co)	2025010	.020000	.082500
Bruceville Eddy	2161176	.010000	.077500
Falls Co	4073002	.005000	
Bruceville Eddy	2161176	.010000	.077500
McClennan Co	4161005	.005000	
Brumley			.067500
Upshur Co	4230002	.005000	
Brundage			.067500
Dimmit Co	4064003	.005000	
Bruni			.067500
Webb Co	4240000	.005000	
Brushy Prairie			.067500
Navarro Co	4175009	.005000	
Bryan	2021023	.015000	.082500
Brazos Co	4021005	.005000	
Bryson (Jack Co)	2119026	.010000	.072500
Buckholts	2166046	.010000	.077500
Milam Co	4166000	.005000	
Buckhorn			.067500
Austin Co	4008002	.005000	
Buda	2105031	.015000	.082500
Hays Co	4105004	.005000	
Buena Vista (Bexar Co)			.067500
San Antonio MTA	3015995	.005000	
Buffalo	2145015	.015000	.082500
Leon Co	4145006	.005000	
Buffalo Gap (Taylor Co)	2221067	.020000	.082500
Buffalo Springs	2152097	.010000	.077500
Lubbock Co	4152006	.005000	
Bug Tussle			.067500
Fannin Co	4074001	.005000	
Bula			.067500
Bailey Co	4009001	.005000	
Bullard	2212059	.015000	.082500
Cherokee Co	4037007	.005000	
Bullard	2212059	.015000	.082500
Smith Co	4212004	.005000	
Bulverde	2046042	.010000	.082500
Comal Co	4046006	.005000	
Bulverde Area Lib Dist	5046514	.005000	

¶905

Bunker Hill Village (Harris Co)	2101286	.010000	.082500
Houston MTA	3101990	.010000	
Burkburnett (Wichita Co)	2243025	.020000	.082500
Burke	2003070	.010000	.077500
Angelina Co	4003007	.005000	
Burleigh			.067500
Austin Co	4008002	.005000	
Burleson (Johnson Co)	2126045	.020000	.082500
Burleson (Tarrant Co)	2126045	.020000	.082500
Burlington			.067500
Milam Co	4166000	.005000	
Burnet (Burnet Co)	2027027	.020000	.082500
Burns			.067500
Bowie Co	4019009	.005000	
Burr			.067500
Wharton Co	4241009	.005000	
Burton	2239021	.010000	.077500
Washington Co	4239003	.005000	
Butler			.067500
Bastrop Co	4011007	.005000	
Byers (Clay Co)	2039023	.010000	.072500
Bynum	2109073	.010000	.077500
Hill Co	4109000	.005000	
Cactus (Moore Co)	2171030	.010000	.072500
Caddo Mills	2116056	.015000	.082500
Hunt Co	4116001	.005000	
Caldwell	2026019	.015000	.082500
Burleson Co	4026000	.005000	
Callisburg			.067500
Cooke Co	4049003	.005000	
Calvert (Robertson Co)	2198020	.020000	.082500
Camden			.067500
Polk Co	4187005	.005000	
Cameron	2166028	.015000	.082500
Milam Co	4166000	.005000	
Camilla			.067500
San Jacinto Co	4204004	.005000	
Camp Air (Mason Co)			.072500
Mason County Health Services	5157500	.010000	
Camp Verde			.067500
Kerr Co	4133000	.005000	
Camp Wood	2193016	.010000	.077500
Real Co	4193007	.005000	
Campbell	2116092	.012500	.080000
Hunt Co	4116001	.005000	
Campbellton			.067500
Atascosa Co	4007003	.005000	
Canadian (Hemphill Co)	2106012	.020000	.082500
Caney			.067500
Hopkins Co	4112005	.005000	
Caney City (Henderson Co)	2107066	.015000	.077500
Canton (Van Zandt Co)	2234044	.020000	.082500
Canutillo			.072500
El Paso Co	4071004	.005000	
El Paso Co Es Dis No2	5071503	.005000	
Canyon (Randall Co)	2191018	.020000	.082500
Canyon City			.082500
Comal Co	4046006	.005000	
Canyon Lake Community Lib Dist	5046505	.005000	
Comal Co Emergency Services District No. 3	5046523	.010000	
Canyon Lake			.082500
Comal Co	4046006	.005000	
Canyon Lake Community Lib Dist	5046505	.005000	
Comal Co Emergency Services District No. 3	5046523	.010000	
Carbon (Eastland Co)	2067064	.010000	.072500
Carbondale			.067500
Bowie Co	4019009	.005000	
Carey			.067500
Childress Co	4038006	.005000	
Carl			.067500
Navarro Co	4175009	.005000	
Carlos			.067500
Grimes Co	4093008	.005000	
Carls Corner	2109135	.015000	.082500
Hill Co	4109000	.005000	
Carlsbad			.067500
Tom Green Co	4226008	.005000	

¶905

Part III—Sales and Use Taxes   139

Carlton			.067500
Hamilton Co	4097004	.005000	
Carmine	2075055	.015000	.082500
Fayette Co	4075000	.005000	
Carmona			.067500
Polk Co	4187005	.005000	
Carrizo Springs	2064012	.015000	.082500
Dimmit Co	4064003	.005000	
Carrollton (Collin Co)	2057128	.010000	.082500
Dallas MTA	3057994	.010000	
Carrollton (Dallas Co)	2057128	.010000	.082500
Dallas MTA	3057994	.010000	
Carrollton (Denton Co)	2057128	.010000	.082500
Dallas MTA	3057994	.010000	
Carthage (Panola Co)	2183018	.020000	.082500
Cash			.067500
Hunt Co	4116001	.005000	
Cason			.067500
Morris Co	4172002	.005000	
Castle Hills (Bexar Co)	2015049	.012500	.082500
San Antonio MTA	3015995	.005000	
Castroville	2163030	.015000	.082500
Medina Co	4163003	.005000	
Cat Spring			.067500
Austin Co	4008002	.005000	
Catarina			.067500
Dimmit Co	4064003	.005000	
Cavitt			.067500
Coryell Co	4050009	.005000	
Cayote			.067500
Bosque Co	4018000	.005000	
Cayuga			.067500
Anderson Co	4001009	.005000	
Cedar Creek			.067500
Bastrop Co	4011007	.005000	
Cedar Hill (Dallas Co)	2057137	.020000	.082500
Cedar Hill (Ellis Co)	2057137	.020000	.082500
Cedar Park (Travis Co)	2246095	.020000	.082500
Cedar Park (Williamson Co)	2246095	.020000	.082500
Cedar Point (Chambers Co)			.067500
Chambers Co Health Ser	5036507	.005000	
Cedar Springs			.067500
Falls Co	4073002	.005000	
Cedar Springs			.067500
Upshur Co	4230002	.005000	
Cego			.067500
Falls Co	4073002	.005000	
Celeste	2116047	.012500	.080000
Hunt Co	4116001	.005000	
Celina (Collin Co)	2043090	.020000	.082500
Celina (Denton Co)	2043090	.020000	.082500
Center (Shelby Co)	2210024	.020000	.082500
Center Plains			.067500
Swisher Co	4219007	.005000	
Center Point			.067500
Camp Co	4032002	.005000	
Center Point			.067500
Kerr Co	4133000	.005000	
Center Point			.067500
Upshur Co	4230002	.005000	
Centerview			.067500
Leon Co	4145006	.005000	
Centerville	2145033	.015000	.082500
Leon Co	4145006	.005000	
Central			.067500
Angelina Co	4003007	.005000	
Central Gardens			.067500
Jefferson Co	4123002	.005000	
Central Heights (Nacogdoches Co)			.072500
Nacogdoches County Hospital District	5174509	.010000	
Cestohowa			.067500
Karnes Co	4128007	.005000	
Chalk Bluff			.067500
McClennan Co	4161005	.005000	
Chalk Mountain			.067500
Erath Co	4072003	.005000	
Chandler (Henderson Co)	2107100	.020000	.082500
Channing (Hartley Co)	2103015	.010000	.072500
Chapman Ranch (Nueces Co)			.067500

¶905

Corpus Christi MTA	3178998	.005000	
Chappell Hill			.067500
Washington Co	4239003	.005000	
Charleston			.072500
Delta Co	4060007	.005000	
Delta Co Emergency Services District	5060506	.005000	
Charlotte	2007058	.010000	.077500
Atascosa Co	4007003	.005000	
Chat			.067500
Hill Co	4109000	.005000	
Chatfield			.067500
Navarro Co	4175009	.005000	
Cheapside			.067500
Gonzales Co	4089004	.005000	
Cheek			.067500
Jefferson Co	4123002	.005000	
Cherokee			.067500
San Saba Co	4206002	.005000	
Cherry Spring			.067500
Gillespie Co	4086007	.005000	
Chester	2229032	.010000	.077500
Tyler Co	4229005	.005000	
Chesterville			.067500
Colorado Co	4045007	.005000	
Chesterville			.067500
Wharton Co	4241009	.005000	
Chico	2249065	.015000	.082500
Wise Co	4249001	.005000	
Chicota			.067500
Lamar Co	4139004	.005000	
Childress	2038015	.015000	.082500
Childress Co	4038006	.005000	
Chillicothe	2099020	.012500	.080000
Hardeman Co	4099002	.005000	
Chilton			.067500
Falls Co	4073002	.005000	
China	2123119	.015000	.082500
Jefferson Co	4123002	.005000	
China Grove (Bexar Co)	2015183	.010000	.077500
San Antonio MTA	3015995	.005000	
China Spring			.067500
McClennan Co	4161005	.005000	
Chireno (Nacogdoches Co)	2174046	.010000	.082500
Nacogdoches County Hospital District	5174509	.010000	
Chocolate Bayou			.067500
Brazoria Co	4020006	.005000	
Chriesman			.067500
Burleson Co	4026000	.005000	
Christine			.067500
Atascosa Co	4007003	.005000	
Christoval			.067500
Tom Green Co	4226008	.005000	
Churchill			.067500
Brazoria Co	4020006	.005000	
Cibolo	2094034	.015000	.082500
Guadalupe Co	4094007	.005000	
Cibolo Canyons Special Improvement Dist	5015557	.015000	
Cisco (Eastland Co)	2067019	.020000	.082500
Cistern			.067500
Fayette Co	4075000	.005000	
City By The Sea			.072500
Aransas Co	4004006	.005000	
Aransas County Health Services	5004505	.005000	
Clairette			.067500
Erath Co	4072003	.005000	
Clardy			.067500
Lamar Co	4139004	.005000	
Clarendon (Donley Co)	2065011	.020000	.082500
Clark			.067500
Liberty Co	4146005	.005000	
Clarks			.067500
Calhoun Co	4029007	.005000	
Clarksville	2194015	.015000	.082500
Red River Co	4194006	.005000	
Clarksville City	2092045	.010000	.077500
Gregg Co	4092009	.005000	
Clarksville City	2092045	.010000	.077500
Upshur Co	4230002	.005000	
Claude (Armstrong Co)	2006013	.010000	.072500

¶905

Part III—Sales and Use Taxes

Clawson			.067500
Angelina Co	4003007	.005000	
Clay			.067500
Burleson Co	4026000	.005000	
Claytonville			.067500
Swisher Co	4219007	.005000	
Clear Lake Shores (Galveston Co)	2084081	.017500	.080000
Clear Spring			.067500
Guadalupe Co	4094007	.005000	
Cleburne (Johnson Co)	2126027	.015000	.077500
Cleo (Kimble Co)			.067500
Kimble Co Emergency Services Dist	5134508	.005000	
Cleveland	2146014	.015000	.082500
Liberty Co	4146005	.005000	
Clifton	2018019	.015000	.082500
Bosque Co	4018000	.005000	
Clint	2071031	.010000	.082500
El Paso Co	4071004	.005000	
El Paso Co Es Dis No2	5071503	.005000	
Clinton			.067500
Hunt Co	4116001	.005000	
Clute	2020104	.015000	.082500
Brazoria Co	4020006	.005000	
Clyde (Callahan Co)	2030013	.020000	.082500
Coahoma (Howard Co)	2114021	.015000	.077500
Cochran			.067500
Austin Co	4008002	.005000	
Cockrell Hill (Dallas Co)	2057057	.010000	.082500
Dallas MTA	3057994	.010000	
Coffee City (Henderson Co)	2107146	.010000	.072500
Coke			.067500
Wood Co	4250007	.005000	
Coldspring	2204022	.015000	.082500
San Jacinto Co	4204004	.005000	
Coleman (Coleman Co)	2042028	.020000	.082500
College Hill			.067500
Bowie Co	4019009	.005000	
College Station	2021014	.015000	.082500
Brazos Co	4021005	.005000	
Colleyville (Tarrant Co)	2220237	.015000	.082500
Colleyville Crime Control District	5220629	.005000	
Collinsville (Grayson Co)	2091091	.020000	.082500
Colmesneil	2229023	.010000	.077500
Tyler Co	4229005	.005000	
Colony			.067500
Fayette Co	4075000	.005000	
Colorado City	2168017	.015000	.082500
Mitchell Co	4168008	.005000	
Columbus	2045016	.015000	.082500
Colorado Co	4045007	.005000	
Comal			.067500
Comal Co	4046006	.005000	
Comanche	2047023	.015000	.082500
Comanche Co	4047005	.005000	
Combes (Cameron Co)	2031094	.012500	.075000
Combine (Dallas Co)	2129079	.015000	.077500
Combine (Kaufman Co)	2129079	.015000	.077500
Comfort			.067500
Kendall Co	4130003	.005000	
Commerce	2116010	.015000	.082500
Hunt Co	4116001	.005000	
Como	2112032	.010000	.077500
Hopkins Co	4112005	.005000	
Comstock			.067500
Val Verde Co	4233009	.005000	
Comyn			.067500
Comanche Co	4047005	.005000	
Concan			.072500
Uvalde Co	4232000	.005000	
Uvalde County Health Services	5232509	.005000	
Concord			.067500
Cherokee Co	4037007	.005000	
Concord			.067500
Leon Co	4145006	.005000	
Cone			.067500
Crosby Co	4054005	.005000	
Connor			.067500
Madison Co	4154004	.005000	
Conroe (Montgomery Co)	2170022	.020000	.082500

¶905

Content			.067500
Runnels Co	4200008	.005000	
Converse (Bexar Co)	2015147	.015000	.082500
San Antonio MTA	3015995	.005000	
Cooks Point			.067500
Burleson Co	4026000	.005000	
Cookville			.067500
Titus Co	4225009	.005000	
Cool	2184106	.010000	.077500
Parker Co	4184008	.005000	
Coolidge (Limestone Co)	2147040	.010000	.072500
Cooper	2060016	.010000	.082500
Delta Co	4060007	.005000	
Delta Co Emergency Services District	5060506	.005000	
Copano Village			.072500
Aransas Co	4004006	.005000	
Aransas County Health Services	5004505	.005000	
Coppell (Dallas Co)	2057262	.017500	.082500
Coppell Crime Control Dist	5057501	.002500	
Coppell (Denton Co)	2057262	.017500	.082500
Coppell Crime Control Dist	5057501	.002500	
Copper Canyon (Denton Co)	2061275	.010000	.072500
Copperas Cove	2050018	.015000	.082500
Coryell Co	4050009	.005000	
Copperas Cove	2050018	.015000	.082500
Lampasas Co	4141000	.005000	
Corbet			.067500
Navarro Co	4175009	.005000	
Cordele			.067500
Jackson Co	4120005	.005000	
Corinth (Denton Co)	2061122	.017500	.082500
Corley			.067500
Bowie Co	4019009	.005000	
Corpus Christi (Nueces Co)	2178015	.013750	.082500
Corpus Christi MTA	3178998	.005000	
Corpus Christi Crime Control Dist	5178505	.001250	
Corpus Christi (San Patricio Co)	2178015	.013750	.082500
Corpus Christi MTA	3178998	.005000	
Corpus Christi Crime Control Dist	5178505	.001250	
Corral City (Denton Co)	2061293	.017500	.080000
Corrigan	2187023	.015000	.082500
Polk Co	4187005	.005000	
Corsicana	2175018	.015000	.082500
Navarro Co	4175009	.005000	
Coryell City			.067500
Coryell Co	4050009	.005000	
Cost			.067500
Gonzales Co	4089004	.005000	
Cotton Center			.067500
Hale Co	4095006	.005000	
Cottondale			.067500
Wise Co	4249001	.005000	
Cottonwood			.067500
Falls Co	4073002	.005000	
Cottonwood			.067500
Madison Co	4154004	.005000	
Cottonwood Shores (Burnet Co)	2027054	.015000	.082500
Cottonwood Shores Crime Control and Prevention District	5027508	.005000	
Cotulla (La Salle Co)	2142018	.020000	.082500
Coughran			.067500
Atascosa Co	4007003	.005000	
County Line			.067500
Camp Co	4032002	.005000	
County Line			.067500
Hale Co	4095006	.005000	
County Line			.067500
Lubbock Co	4152006	.005000	
Courtney			.067500
Grimes Co	4093008	.005000	
Cove (Chambers Co)	2036062	.010000	.077500
Chambers Co Health Ser	5036507	.005000	
Cove Spring			.067500
Cherokee Co	4037007	.005000	
Covington	2109126	.010000	.077500
Hill Co	4109000	.005000	
Cox			.067500
Upshur Co	4230002	.005000	
Coy City			.067500

¶905

Part III—Sales and Use Taxes

Karnes Co	4128007	.005000	
Crabbs Prairie			.067500
Walker Co	4236006	.005000	
Craft			.067500
Cherokee Co	4037007	.005000	
Crafton			.067500
Wise Co	4249001	.005000	
Crandall (Kaufman Co)	2129060	.020000	.082500
Crane (Crane Co)	2052016	.015000	.077500
Cranfills Gap	2018073	.010000	.077500
Bosque Co	4018000	.005000	
Crawford	2161121	.015000	.082500
McClennan Co	4161005	.005000	
Creedmoor (Travis Co)	2227089	.010000	.072500
Crescent			.067500
Wharton Co	4241009	.005000	
Crescent Valley			
Victoria Co	4235007	.005000	
Cresson	2111042	.010000	.077500
Hood Co	4111006	.005000	
Cresson (Johnson Co)	2111042	.010000	.072500
Cresson	2111042	.010000	.077500
Parker Co	4184008	.005000	
Crews			.067500
Runnels Co	4200008	.005000	
Crockett	2113013	.015000	.082500
Houston Co	4113004	.005000	
Crosbyton	2054014	.015000	.082500
Crosby Co	4054005	.005000	
Cross			.067500
Grimes Co	4093008	.005000	
Cross Plains (Callahan Co)	2030031	.020000	.082500
Cross Roads (Denton Co)	2061284	.017500	.080000
Cross Roads			.067500
Milam Co	4166000	.005000	
Crowell (Foard Co)	2078016	.017500	.080000
Crowley (Johnson Co)	2220228	.015000	.082500
Crowley Crime Control and Prevention Dist	5220718	.005000	
Crowley (Tarrant Co)	2220228	.015000	.082500
Crowley Crime Control and Prevention Dist	5220718	.005000	
Crystal City (Zavala Co)	2254012	.017500	.080000
Cuero (DeWitt Co)	2062032	.020000	.082500
Cumby	2112023	.015000	.082500
Hopkins Co	4112005	.005000	
Cuney	2037061	.015000	.082500
Cherokee Co	4037007	.005000	
Cunningham			.067500
Lamar Co	4139004	.005000	
Currie			.067500
Navarro Co	4175009	.005000	
Cushing (Nacogdoches Co)	2174037	.010000	.082500
Nacogdoches County Hospital District	5174509	.010000	
Cut			.067500
Houston Co	4113004	.005000	
Cut And Shoot (Montgomery Co)	2170086	.015000	.077500
Cuthand			.067500
Red River Co	4194006	.005000	
Cyclone			.067500
Bell Co	4014004	.005000	
Cypress			.067500
Franklin Co	4080003	.005000	
Cypress (Harris Co)			.072500
Houston MTA	3101990	.010000	
Cypress Mill			.067500
Blanco Co	4016002	.005000	
D Hanis			
Medina Co	4163003	.005000	
Dacosta			.067500
Victoria Co	4235007	.005000	
Daingerfield	2172011	.015000	.082500
Morris Co	4172002	.005000	
Daisetta	2146069	.010000	.077500
Liberty Co	4146005	.005000	
Dalby Springs			.067500
Bowie Co	4019009	.005000	
Dale			.067500
Caldwell Co	4028008	.005000	

Dalhart (Dallam Co)	2056012	.020000	.082500
Dalhart (Hartley Co)	2056012	.020000	.082500
Dallardsville			.067500
Polk Co	4187005	.005000	
Dallas (Collin Co)	2057011	.010000	.082500
Dallas MTA	3057994	.010000	
Dallas (Dallas Co)	2057011	.010000	.082500
Dallas MTA	3057994	.010000	
Dallas (Denton Co)	2057011	.010000	.082500
Dallas MTA	3057994	.010000	
Dallas (Kaufman Co)	2057011	.010000	.082500
Dallas MTA	3057994	.010000	
Dallas (Rockwall Co)	2057011	.010000	.082500
Dallas MTA	3057994	.010000	
Dalworthington Gardens (Tarrant Co)	2220264	.015000	.082500
Dalworthington Gdns Crime Cont Dist	5220601	.005000	
Damon			.067500
Brazoria Co	4020006	.005000	
Danbury	2020079	.010000	.077500
Brazoria Co	4020006	.005000	
Danciger			.067500
Brazoria Co	4020006	.005000	
Danevang			.067500
Wharton Co	4241009	.005000	
Darrouzett (Lipscomb Co)	2148030	.010000	.072500
Davilla			.067500
Milam Co	4166000	.005000	
Davisville			.067500
Leon Co	4145006	.005000	
Dawn			.067500
Deaf Smith Co	4059000	.005000	
Dawson	2175054	.012500	.080000
Navarro Co	4175009	.005000	
Dayton	2146023	.015000	.082500
Liberty Co	4146005	.005000	
Dayton Lakes			.067500
Liberty Co	4146005	.005000	
De Kalb	2019027	.015000	.082500
Bowie Co	4019009	.005000	
De Leon	2047014	.015000	.082500
Comanche Co	4047005	.005000	
De Soto (Dallas Co)	2057182	.020000	.082500
Dean (Clay Co)	2039069	.010000	.072500
Deanville			.067500
Burleson Co	4026000	.005000	
Decatur	2249010	.015000	.082500
Wise Co	4249001	.005000	
Deer Park (Harris Co)	2101268	.010000	.072500
Defense City			.067500
Bowie Co	4019009	.005000	
Del Rio	2233018	.015000	.082500
Val Verde Co	4233009	.005000	
Delhi			.067500
Caldwell Co	4028008	.005000	
Dell City (Hudspeth Co)	2115011	.010000	.072500
Delrose			.067500
Upshur Co	4230002	.005000	
Denison (Grayson Co)	2091019	.020000	.082500
Denning			.067500
San Augustine Co	4203005	.005000	
Dennis			.067500
Parker Co	4184008	.005000	
Denny			.067500
Falls Co	4073002	.005000	
Denson Spring			.067500
Anderson Co	4001009	.005000	
Denton (Denton Co)	2061024	.015000	.082500
Denton County Trans Authority	3061774	.005000	
Denver City (Yoakum Co)	2251024	.015000	.077500
Deport	2139022	.010000	.077500
Lamar Co	4139004	.005000	
Deport	2139022	.010000	.077500
Red River Co	4194006	.005000	
Derby			.067500
Frio Co	4082001	.005000	
Dermott			.067500
Scurry Co	4208000	.005000	
Detmold			.067500
Milam Co	4166000	.005000	

¶905

Part III—Sales and Use Taxes

Detroit	2194051	.010000	.077500
Red River Co	4194006	.005000	
Devers	2146112	.010000	.077500
Liberty Co	4146005	.005000	
Devine	2163012	.015000	.082500
Medina Co	4163003	.005000	
Dialville			.067500
Cherokee Co	4037007	.005000	
Diana			.067500
Upshur Co	4230002	.005000	
Diboll	2003025	.015000	.082500
Angelina Co	4003007	.005000	
Dickens	2063022	.015000	.082500
Dickens Co	4063004	.005000	
Dickinson (Galveston Co)	2084125	.015000	.077500
Dies			.067500
Tyler Co	4229005	.005000	
Dike			.067500
Hopkins Co	4112005	.005000	
Dilley	2082010	.015000	.082500
Frio Co	4082001	.005000	
Dilworth			.067500
Gonzales Co	4089004	.005000	
Dime Box			.067500
Lee Co	4144007	.005000	
Dimmitt	2035018	.015000	.082500
Castro Co	4035009	.005000	
Dinero			.067500
Live Oak Co	4149002	.005000	
Ding Dong			.067500
Bell Co	4014004	.005000	
Dinsmore			.067500
Wharton Co	4241009	.005000	
Direct			.067500
Lamar Co	4139004	.005000	
Divot			.067500
Frio Co	4082001	.005000	
Dodd City	2074092	.010000	.077500
Fannin Co	4074001	.005000	
Dodge			.067500
Walker Co	4236006	.005000	
Dogwood City			.067500
Smith Co	4212004	.005000	
Dolen			.067500
Liberty Co	4146005	.005000	
Domino (Cass Co)	2034055	.020000	.082500
Donna (Hidalgo Co)	2108047	.020000	.082500
Doole			.070000
McCulloch Co	4160006	.005000	
McCulloch County Hospital District	5160505	.002500	
Dorchester (Grayson Co)	2091171	.010000	.072500
Doss			.067500
Gillespie Co	4086007	.005000	
Dot			.067500
Falls Co	4073002	.005000	
Double Bayou (Chambers Co)			.067500
Chambers Co Health Ser	5036507	.005000	
Double Oak (Denton Co)	2061248	.010000	.072500
Doucette			.067500
Tyler Co	4229005	.005000	
Douglass (Nacogdoches Co)			.072500
Nacogdoches County Hospital District	5174509	.010000	
Douglassville (Cass Co)	2034082	.002500	.065000
Downing			.067500
Comanche Co	4047005	.005000	
Downsville			.067500
McClennan Co	4161005	.005000	
Drasco			.067500
Runnels Co	4200008	.005000	
Dreyer			.067500
Gonzales Co	4089004	.005000	
Driftwood			.070000
Hays Co	4105004	.005000	
Dripping Spgs Lib Dist	5105512	.002500	
Dripping Springs	2105040	.012500	.082500
Hays Co	4105004	.005000	
Dripping Spgs Lib Dist	5105512	.002500	
Driscoll (Nueces Co)	2178060	.015000	.082500
Corpus Christi MTA	3178998	.005000	

¶905

Dryden			.077500
Terrell Co	4222002	.015000	
Dubina			.067500
Fayette Co	4075000	.005000	
Dublin	2072012	.015000	.082500
Erath Co	4072003	.005000	
Duffau			.067500
Erath Co	4072003	.005000	
Dumas (Moore Co)	2171012	.020000	.082500
Duncanville (Dallas Co)	2057084	.020000	.082500
Dundee			.067500
Archer Co	4005005	.005000	
Dunlay			.067500
Medina Co	4163003	.005000	
Dunn			.067500
Scurry Co	4208000	.005000	
Duplex			.067500
Fannin Co	4074001	.005000	
Durango			.067500
Falls Co	4073002	.005000	
Eagle Lake	2045034	.010000	.082500
Colorado Co	4045007	.005000	
Rice Hospital District	5045506	.005000	
Eagle Pass	2159018	.010000	.082500
Maverick Co	4159009	.005000	
Maverick Co LFW and CDC District	5159508	.005000	
Early (Brown Co)	2025038	.020000	.082500
Earth (Lamb Co)	2140038	.015000	.077500
East Bernard			.080000
Wharton Co	4241009	.005000	
East Columbia			.067500
Brazoria Co	4020006	.005000	
East Mountain	2230048	.010000	.077500
Gregg Co	4092009	.005000	
East Mountain	2230048	.010000	.077500
Upshur Co	4230002	.005000	
East Tawakoni	2190019	.015000	.082500
Rains Co	4190000	.005000	
Easter			.067500
Castro Co	4035009	.005000	
Eastgate			.067500
Liberty Co	4146005	.005000	
Eastland (Eastland Co)	2067046	.015000	.082500
Eastland Memorial Hospital District	5067509	.005000	
Easton	2092090	.010000	.077500
Gregg Co	4092009	.005000	
Easton (Rusk Co)	2092090	.010000	.072500
Ebenezer			.067500
Camp Co	4032002	.005000	
Eckert			.067500
Gillespie Co	4086007	.005000	
Ector	2074074	.010000	.077500
Fannin Co	4074001	.005000	
Edcouch (Hidalgo Co)	2108136	.020000	.082500
Eden	2048013	.015000	.082500
Concho Co	4048004	.005000	
Edge			.067500
Brazos Co	4021005	.005000	
Edgecliff Village (Tarrant Co)	2220308	.010000	.072500
Edgewood (Van Zandt Co)	2234035	.020000	.082500
Edgeworth			.067500
Bell Co	4014004	.005000	
Edhube			.067500
Fannin Co	4074001	.005000	
Edinburg (Hidalgo Co)	2108010	.020000	.082500
Edmonson	2095051	.010000	.077500
Hale Co	4095006	.005000	
Edna	2120014	.015000	.082500
Jackson Co	4120005	.005000	
Edna Hill			.067500
Erath Co	4072003	.005000	
Edom (Van Zandt Co)	2234062	.010000	.072500
Egypt			.067500
Wharton Co	4241009	.005000	
El Campo	2241027	.015000	.082500
Wharton Co	4241009	.005000	
El Cenizo	2240037	.010000	.077500
Webb Co	4240000	.005000	
El Indio			.072500

¶905

Part III—Sales and Use Taxes

Maverick Co	4159009	.005000	
Maverick Co LFW and CDC District	5159508	.005000	
El Lago (Harris Co)	2101213	.010000	.082500
Houston MTA	3101990	.010000	
El Paso	2071013	.010000	.082500
El Paso CTD	3071889	.005000	
El Paso Co	4071004	.005000	
Eldorado	2207010	.010000	.082500
Schleicher Co	4207001	.005000	
Schleicher County Health Services	5207500	.005000	
Electra (Wichita Co)	2243043	.020000	.082500
Elevation			.067500
Milam Co	4166000	.005000	
Elgin	2011016	.015000	.082500
Bastrop Co	4011007	.005000	
Eliasville			.067500
Young Co	4252005	.005000	
Elk			.067500
McClennan Co	4161005	.005000	
Elkhart	2001036	.012500	.080000
Anderson Co	4001009	.005000	
Ellinger			.067500
Fayette Co	4075000	.005000	
Elliot			.067500
Wilbarger Co	4244006	.005000	
Elm Grove			.067500
Fayette Co	4075000	.005000	
Elm Grove			.067500
San Saba Co	4206002	.005000	
Elm Grove			.067500
Wharton Co	4241009	.005000	
Elm Mott			.067500
McClennan Co	4161005	.005000	
Elmendorf (Bexar Co)	2015192	.010000	.077500
San Antonio MTA	3015995	.005000	
Elmwood			.067500
Anderson Co	4001009	.005000	
Eloise			.067500
Falls Co	4073002	.005000	
Elsa (Hidalgo Co)	2108074	.020000	.082500
Elwood			.067500
Fannin Co	4074001	.005000	
Elwood			.067500
Madison Co	4154004	.005000	
Emberson			.067500
Lamar Co	4139004	.005000	
Emhouse	2175161	.010000	.077500
Navarro Co	4175009	.005000	
Emilee			.067500
Tyler Co	4229005	.005000	
Emmett			.067500
Navarro Co	4175009	.005000	
Emory	2190037	.015000	.082500
Rains Co	4190000	.005000	
Encinal (La Salle Co)	2142027	.020000	.082500
Encino (Brooks Co)			.067500
Brooks Co Health Services	5024501	.005000	
Energy			.067500
Comanche Co	4047005	.005000	
Engle			.067500
Fayette Co	4075000	.005000	
English			.067500
Red River Co	4194006	.005000	
Enloe			.072500
Delta Co	4060007	.005000	
Delta Co Emergency Services District	5060506	.005000	
Ennis (Ellis Co)	2070032	.015000	.077500
Enoch			.067500
Upshur Co	4230002	.005000	
Enochs			.067500
Bailey Co	4009001	.005000	
Enterprise			.067500
Cherokee Co	4037007	.005000	
Eola			.067500
Concho Co	4048004	.005000	
Era			.067500
Cooke Co	4049003	.005000	
Escobares (Starr Co)	2214075	.020000	.082500
Estelline (Hall Co)	2096023	.012500	.075000

¶905

Estes			.072500
Aransas Co	4004006	.005000	
Aransas County Health Services	5004505	.005000	
Etoile (Nacogdoches Co)			.072500
Nacogdoches County Hospital District	5174509	.010000	
Euless (Tarrant Co)	2220166	.017500	.082500
Euless Crime Control District	5220521	.002500	
Eulogy			.067500
Bosque Co	4018000	.005000	
Eureka	2175134	.010000	.077500
Navarro Co	4175009	.005000	
Eustace (Henderson Co)	2107075	.010000	.072500
Evant	2097031	.012500	.080000
Coryell Co	4050009	.005000	
Evant	2097031	.012500	.080000
Hamilton Co	4097004	.005000	
Evergreen			.067500
San Jacinto Co	4204004	.005000	
Everman (Tarrant Co)	2220246	.017500	.082500
Everman Crime Control and Prevention Dist	5220692	.002500	
Ewell			.067500
Upshur Co	4230002	.005000	
Eylau			.067500
Bowie Co	4019009	.005000	
Fabens			.072500
El Paso Co	4071004	.005000	
El Paso Co Es Dis No2	5071503	.005000	
Fair Oaks Ranch (Bexar Co)	2015254	.015000	.077500
Fair Oaks Ranch/ Bulverde Area Rural Library Dist.	6046603	.015000	.082500
Comal Co	4046006	.005000	
Fair Oaks Ranch	2015254	.015000	.082500
Kendall Co	4130003	.005000	
Fairdale			.067500
Sabine Co	4202006	.005000	
Fairfield (Freestone Co)	2081011	.020000	.082500
Fairlie			.067500
Hunt Co	4116001	.005000	
Fairview			.067500
Bosque Co	4018000	.005000	
Fairview (Collin Co)	2043027	.020000	.082500
Fairy			.067500
Hamilton Co	4097004	.005000	
Faker			.067500
Camp Co	4032002	.005000	
Falfurrias (Brooks Co)	2024011	.015000	.082500
Brooks Co Health Services	5024501	.005000	
Falls City	2128043	.010000	.077500
Karnes Co	4128007	.005000	
Fannett			.067500
Jefferson Co	4123002	.005000	
Farmers Branch (Dallas Co)	2057100	.010000	.082500
Dallas MTA	3057994	.010000	
Farmersville (Collin Co)	2043054	.020000	.082500
Farwell (Parmer Co)	2185034	.015000	.077500
Fashing			.067500
Atascosa Co	4007003	.005000	
Fate (Rockwall Co)	2199047	.015000	.082500
Rockwall Co Public Safety and Fire Assistance Dist	5199500	.005000	
Faught			.067500
Lamar Co	4139004	.005000	
Fayetteville	2075037	.012500	.080000
Fayette Co	4075000	.005000	
Fedor			.067500
Lee Co	4144007	.005000	
Fentress			.067500
Caldwell Co	4028008	.005000	
Ferris (Dallas Co)	2070023	.020000	.082500
Ferris (Ellis Co)	2070023	.020000	.082500
Fife			.070000
McCulloch Co	4160006	.005000	
McCulloch County Hospital District	5160505	.002500	
Figridge (Chambers Co)			.067500
Chambers Co Health Ser	5036507	.005000	
Fischer			.082500
Comal Co	4046006	.005000	
Canyon Lake Community Lib Dist	5046505	.005000	

¶905

Part III—Sales and Use Taxes 149

Comal Co Emergency Services District No. 3	5046523	.010000	
Fitze (Nacogdoches Co)			.072500
Nacogdoches County Hospital District	5174509	.010000	
Flagg			.067500
Castro Co	4035009	.005000	
Flat			.067500
Coryell Co	4050009	.005000	
Flatonia	2075046	.015000	.082500
Fayette Co	4075000	.005000	
Flats			.067500
Rains Co	4190000	.005000	
Flatwood (Eastland Co)			.067500
Eastland Memorial Hospital District	5067509	.005000	
Flint			.067500
Smith Co	4212004	.005000	
Flo			.067500
Leon Co	4145006	.005000	
Flora			.067500
Hopkins Co	4112005	.005000	
Florence (Williamson Co)	2246086	.017500	.080000
Floresville (Wilson Co)	2247030	.020000	.082500
Flowella (Brooks Co)			.067500
Brooks Co Health Services	5024501	.005000	
Flower Mound (Denton Co)	2061177	.015000	.082500
Flower Mound Crime Control Dist	5061578	.002500	
Flower Mound Fire Control Dist	5061587	.002500	
Floy			.067500
Fayette Co	4075000	.005000	
Floyd			.067500
Hunt Co	4116001	.005000	
Floydada (Floyd Co)	2077026	.017500	.080000
Fluvanna			.067500
Scurry Co	4208000	.005000	
Flynn			.067500
Leon Co	4145006	.005000	
Follett (Lipscomb Co)	2148049	.010000	.072500
Fords Corner			.067500
San Augustine Co	4203005	.005000	
Fordtran			.067500
Victoria Co	4235007	.005000	
Forest			.067500
Cherokee Co	4037007	.005000	
Forest Hill			.067500
Lamar Co	4139004	.005000	
Forest Hill (Tarrant Co)	2220200	.017500	.082500
Forest Hill Library Dist	5220638	.002500	
Forest Hill Crime Con	5220656	.000000	
Forney (Kaufman Co)	2129051	.020000	.082500
Forsan (Howard Co)	2114030	.010000	.072500
Fort Davis			.082500
Jeff Davis Co	4122003	.005000	
Jeff Davis County Health Services	5122502	.005000	
Jeff Davis Co Emergency Services District No. 1	5122511	.010000	
Fort Gates			.067500
Coryell Co	4050009	.005000	
Fort Stockton (Pecos Co)	2186015	.020000	.082500
Fort Worth (Denton Co)	2220031	.010000	.082500
Fort Worth MTA	3220996	.005000	
Fort Worth Crime Control District	5220503	.005000	
Fort Worth (Tarrant Co)	2220031	.010000	.082500
Fort Worth MTA	3220996	.005000	
Fort Worth Crime Control District	5220503	.005000	
Francitas			.067500
Jackson Co	4120005	.005000	
Franklin (Robertson Co)	2198039	.020000	.082500
Frankston	2001027	.015000	.082500
Anderson Co	4001009	.005000	
Frankston Lake			.067500
Anderson Co	4001009	.005000	
Fred			.067500
Tyler Co	4229005	.005000	
Fredericksburg	2086016	.015000	.082500
Gillespie Co	4086007	.005000	
Fredonia (Mason Co)			.072500
Mason County Health Services	5157500	.010000	
Freeport	2020051	.015000	.082500
Brazoria Co	4020006	.005000	

¶905

Freer (Duval Co)	2066010	.017500	.080000
Frelsburg			.067500
Colorado Co	4045007	.005000	
Freyburg			.067500
Fayette Co	4075000	.005000	
Friendship Village			.067500
Bowie Co	4019009	.005000	
Friendswood (Galveston Co)	2084054	.015000	.077500
Friendswood (Harris Co)	2084054	.015000	.077500
Frio Town			.067500
Frio Co	4082001	.005000	
Friona (Parmer Co)	2185016	.020000	.082500
Frisco (Collin Co)	2043036	.020000	.082500
Frisco (Denton Co)	2043036	.020000	.082500
Fritch (Hutchinson Co)	2117028	.017500	.082500
Fritch Crime Control Dist	5117509	.002500	
Fritch (Moore Co)	2117028	.017500	.082500
Fritch Crime Control Dist	5117509	.002500	
Frost	2175045	.010000	.077500
Navarro Co	4175009	.005000	
Frydek			.067500
Austin Co	4008002	.005000	
Fulbright			.067500
Red River Co	4194006	.005000	
Fulshear (Fort Bend Co)	2079104	.020000	.082500
Fulton	2004024	.010000	.082500
Aransas Co	4004006	.005000	
Aransas County Health Services	5004505	.005000	
Gainesville	2049012	.015000	.082500
Cooke Co	4049003	.005000	
Galena Park (Harris Co)	2101115	.010000	.072500
Gallatin			.067500
Cherokee Co	4037007	.005000	
Galveston (Galveston Co)	2084018	.020000	.082500
Ganado	2120023	.015000	.082500
Jackson Co	4120005	.005000	
Garden Ridge	2046024	.010000	.082500
Comal Co	4046006	.005000	
Comal Co Emergency Services District No. 6	5046532	.005000	
Gardendale (Ector Co)			.070000
Ector County Hospital District	5068508	.007500	
Garland			.067500
Bowie Co	4019009	.005000	
Garland (Collin Co)	2057173	.010000	.082500
Dallas MTA	3057994	.010000	
Garland (Dallas Co)	2057173	.010000	.082500
Dallas MTA	3057994	.010000	
Garland (Rockwall Co)	2057173	.010000	.082500
Dallas MTA	3057994	.010000	
Garner			.067500
Parker Co	4184008	.005000	
Garrett (Ellis Co)	2070130	.010000	.072500
Garrison (Nacogdoches Co)	2174028	.010000	.082500
Nacogdoches County Hospital District	5174509	.010000	
Garwood			.072500
Colorado Co	4045007	.005000	
Rice Hospital District	5045506	.005000	
Gatesville	2050027	.015000	.082500
Coryell Co	4050009	.005000	
Gause			.067500
Milam Co	4166000	.005000	
Gay Hill			.067500
Washington Co	4239003	.005000	
Geneva			.067500
Sabine Co	4202006	.005000	
George			.067500
Madison Co	4154004	.005000	
George West	2149011	.015000	.082500
Live Oak Co	4149002	.005000	
Georgetown (Williamson Co)	2246031	.020000	.082500
Gerald			.067500
McClennan Co	4161005	.005000	
Geronimo			.067500
Guadalupe Co	4094007	.005000	
Gholson	2161210	.015000	.082500
McClennan Co	4161005	.005000	
Giddings	2144016	.015000	.082500
Lee Co	4144007	.005000	

¶905

Part III—Sales and Use Taxes 151

Gillett			.067500
Karnes Co	4128007	.005000	
Gilmer	2230011	.015000	.082500
Upshur Co	4230002	.005000	
Gladewater	2092036	.015000	.082500
Gregg Co	4092009	.005000	
Gladewater	2092036	.015000	.082500
Upshur Co	4230002	.005000	
Glaze City			.067500
Gonzales Co	4089004	.005000	
Glen Flora			.067500
Wharton Co	4241009	.005000	
Glen Rose (Somervell Co)	2213012	.020000	.082500
Glenn Heights (Dallas Co)	2057253	.010000	.082500
Dallas MTA	3057994	.010000	
Glenn Heights (Ellis Co)	2057253	.010000	.082500
Dallas MTA	3057994	.010000	
Glenrio			.067500
Deaf Smith Co	4059000	.005000	
Glenwood			.067500
Upshur Co	4230002	.005000	
Glidden			.067500
Colorado Co	4045007	.005000	
Gober			.067500
Fannin Co	4074001	.005000	
Godley (Johnson Co)	2126090	.016250	.078750
Gold			.067500
Gillespie Co	4086007	.005000	
Golden			.067500
Wood Co	4250007	.005000	
Goldsmith (Ector Co)	2068027	.010000	.080000
Ector County Hospital District	5068508	.007500	
Goldthwaite (Mills Co)	2167018	.020000	.082500
Goliad (Goliad Co)	2088014	.015000	.082500
Goliad Municipal Development Dist	5088504	.005000	
Golinda	2073048	.015000	.082500
Falls Co	4073002	.005000	
Golinda	2073048	.015000	.082500
McClennan Co	4161005	.005000	
Gonzales	2089022	.015000	.082500
Gonzales Co	4089004	.005000	
Goodland			.067500
Bailey Co	4009001	.005000	
Goodlett			.067500
Hardeman Co	4099002	.005000	
Goodlow	2175116	.010000	.077500
Navarro Co	4175009	.005000	
Goodrich	2187050	.010000	.077500
Polk Co	4187005	.005000	
Goodville			.067500
Falls Co	4073002	.005000	
Gordon	2182037	.015000	.082500
Palo Pinto Co	4182000	.005000	
Goree (Knox Co)	2138041	.020000	.082500
Gorman (Eastland Co)	2067037	.020000	.082500
Graceton			.067500
Upshur Co	4230002	.005000	
Graford	2182055	.015000	.082500
Palo Pinto Co	4182000	.005000	
Graham	2252014	.015000	.082500
Young Co	4252005	.005000	
Granbury	2111015	.015000	.082500
Hood Co	4111006	.005000	
Grand Prairie (Dallas Co)	2220013	.017500	.082500
Grand Prairie Crime Control District	5220745	.002500	
Grand Prairie (Ellis Co)	2220013	.017500	.082500
Grand Prairie Crime Control District	5220745	.002500	
Grand Prairie (Tarrant Co)	2220013	.017500	.082500
Grand Prairie Crime Control District	5220745	.002500	
Grand Saline (Van Zandt Co)	2234026	.020000	.082500
Grandfalls (Ward Co)	2238022	.020000	.082500
Grandview			.067500
Dawson Co	4058001	.005000	
Grandview (Johnson Co)	2126018	.020000	.082500
Granger (Williamson Co)	2246040	.010000	.072500
Granite Shoals (Burnet Co)	2027036	.010000	.072500
Granjeno (Hidalgo Co)	2108207	.010000	.072500
Grapeland	2113022	.015000	.082500
Houston Co	4113004	.005000	

¶905

Grapetown			.067500
Gillespie Co	4086007	.005000	
Grapevine (Dallas Co)	2220022	.015000	.082500
Grapevine Crime Control District	5220736	.005000	
Grapevine (Denton Co)	2220022	.015000	.082500
Grapevine Crime Control District	5220736	.005000	
Grapevine (Tarrant Co)	2220022	.015000	.082500
Grapevine Crime Control District	5220736	.005000	
Gray			.067500
Marion Co	4155003	.005000	
Grays Prairie (Kaufman Co)	2129097	.010000	.072500
Green Lake			.067500
Calhoun Co	4029007	.005000	
Greenville	2116029	.015000	.082500
Hunt Co	4116001	.005000	
Greenwood			.067500
Gonzales Co	4089004	.005000	
Greenwood			.067500
Midland Co	4165001	.005000	
Greenwood			.067500
Wise Co	4249001	.005000	
Gregory (San Patricio Co)	2205085	.010000	.077500
Corpus Christi MTA	3178998	.005000	
Gresham			.067500
Smith Co	4212004	.005000	
Grey Forest (Bexar Co)	2015110	.012500	.075000
San Antonio MTA	3015995	.005000	
Grice			.067500
Upshur Co	4230002	.005000	
Griffin			.067500
Cherokee Co	4037007	.005000	
Griffing Park			.067500
Jefferson Co	4123002	.005000	
Groesbeck (Limestone Co)	2147022	.020000	.082500
Groom (Carson Co)	2033038	.020000	.082500
Groves	2123039	.015000	.082500
Jefferson Co	4123002	.005000	
Groveton (Trinity Co)	2228015	.020000	.082500
Grulla (Starr Co)	2214066	.010000	.072500
Gruver (Hansford Co)	2098021	.020000	.082500
Guadalupe			.067500
Victoria Co	4235007	.005000	
Guerra (Jim Hogg Co)			.082500
Jim Hogg Co	4124001	.010000	
Jim Hogg County Assistance District	5124519	.005000	
Jim Hogg County Health Services	5124500	.005000	
Gun Barrel City (Henderson Co)	2107057	.020000	.082500
Gunter (Grayson Co)	2091073	.020000	.082500
Gustine	2047032	.015000	.082500
Comanche Co	4047005	.005000	
Guys Store			.067500
Leon Co	4145006	.005000	
Hackberry (Denton Co)	2061257	.010000	.072500
Hagansport			.067500
Franklin Co	4080003	.005000	
Haid			.067500
Wharton Co	4241009	.005000	
Hainesville			.067500
Wood Co	4250007	.005000	
Hale Center	2095033	.015000	.082500
Hale Co	4095006	.005000	
Halfway			.067500
Hale Co	4095006	.005000	
Hall			.067500
San Saba Co	4206002	.005000	
Hallettsville (Lavaca Co)	2143017	.020000	.082500
Hallsburg	2161185	.010000	.077500
McClennan Co	4161005	.005000	
Hallsville (Harrison Co)	2102034	.010000	.072500
Halsted			.067500
Fayette Co	4075000	.005000	
Haltom City (Tarrant Co)	2220255	.017500	.082500
Haltom City Crime Control District	5220530	.002500	
Hamilton	2097013	.015000	.082500
Hamilton Co	4097004	.005000	
Hamlin (Fisher Co)	2127017	.020000	.082500
Hamlin (Jones Co)	2127017	.020000	.082500
Hamon			.067500
Gonzales Co	4089004	.005000	

¶905

Part III—Sales and Use Taxes

Hamshire			.067500
Jefferson Co	4123002	.005000	
Hankamer (Chambers Co)			.067500
Chambers Co Health Ser	5036507	.005000	
Happy (Randall Co)	2219025	.010000	.072500
Happy	2219025	.010000	.077500
Swisher Co	4219007	.005000	
Hardin	2146121	.010000	.077500
Liberty Co	4146005	.005000	
Harker Heights	2014068	.015000	.082500
Bell Co	4014004	.005000	
Harkeyville			.067500
San Saba Co	4206002	.005000	
Harlingen (Cameron Co)	2031012	.020000	.082500
Harmony			.067500
Anderson Co	4001009	.005000	
Harper			.067500
Gillespie Co	4086007	.005000	
Harriett			.067500
Tom Green Co	4226008	.005000	
Harris County Emergency Services District No. 21	5101614	.010000	
Harrison			.067500
McClennan Co	4161005	.005000	
Harrold			.067500
Wilbarger Co	4244006	.005000	
Hart	2035027	.015000	.082500
Castro Co	4035009	.005000	
Harvard			.067500
Camp Co	4032002	.005000	
Harwood			.067500
Gonzales Co	4089004	.005000	
Haskell (Haskell Co)	2104014	.020000	.082500
Haslet (Tarrant Co)	2220344	.020000	.082500
Hasse			.067500
Comanche Co	4047005	.005000	
Hastings			.067500
Brazoria Co	4020006	.005000	
Hatchel			.067500
Runnels Co	4200008	.005000	
Hawk Cove	2116118	.010000	.077500
Hunt Co	4116001	.005000	
Hawkins	2250052	.015000	.082500
Wood Co	4250007	.005000	
Hawley (Jones Co)	2127044	.017500	.080000
Hays	2105086	.010000	.077500
Hays Co	4105004	.005000	
Hearne (Robertson Co)	2198011	.020000	.082500
Heath (Rockwall Co)	2199038	.020000	.082500
Hebbronville (Jim Hogg Co)			.082500
Jim Hogg Co	4124001	.010000	
Jim Hogg County Assistance District	5124519	.005000	
Jim Hogg County Health Services	5124500	.005000	
Hebron (Denton Co)	2061337	.005000	.067500
Heckville			.067500
Lubbock Co	4152006	.005000	
Hedley (Donley Co)	2065020	.010000	.072500
Hedwig Village (Harris Co)	2101142	.010000	.082500
Houston MTA	3101990	.010000	
Heidenheimer			.067500
Bell Co	4014004	.005000	
Helena			.067500
Karnes Co	4128007	.005000	
Helotes (Bexar Co)	2015227	.015000	.077500
Hemphill	2202015	.015000	.082500
Sabine Co	4202006	.005000	
Hempstead (Waller Co)	2237023	.020000	.082500
Henderson (Rusk Co)	2201016	.020000	.082500
Henly			.067500
Hays Co	4105004	.005000	
Henning (Nacogdoches Co)			.072500
Nacogdoches County Hospital District	5174509	.010000	
Henrietta (Clay Co)	2039014	.020000	.082500
Henrys Chapel			.067500
Cherokee Co	4037007	.005000	
Hereford	2059019	.015000	.082500
Deaf Smith Co	4059000	.005000	
Hermleigh			.067500
Scurry Co	4208000	.005000	

¶905

Hewitt	2161041	.015000	.082500
McClennan Co	4161005	.005000	
Hickory Creek (Denton Co)	2061186	.020000	.082500
Hickory Creek			.067500
Hunt Co	4116001	.005000	
Hico	2097022	.015000	.082500
Hamilton Co	4097004	.005000	
Hidalgo (Hidalgo Co)	2108083	.020000	.082500
Higgins (Lipscomb Co)	2148012	.020000	.082500
High Hill			.067500
Fayette Co	4075000	.005000	
Highland			.067500
Erath Co	4072003	.005000	
Highland Park (Dallas Co)	2057146	.010000	.082500
Dallas MTA	3057994	.010000	
Highland Village (Denton Co)	2061220	.012500	.0825000
Denton County Trans Authority	3061774	.005000	
Hill Country Village (Bexar Co)	2015085	.020000	.082500
Hillcrest			.067500
Brazoria Co	4020006	.005000	
Hillcrest			.067500
Colorado Co	4045007	.005000	
Hillebrandt			.067500
Jefferson Co	4123002	.005000	
Hillister			.067500
Tyler Co	4229005	.005000	
Hillje			.067500
Wharton Co	4241009	.005000	
Hills			.067500
Lee Co	4144007	.005000	
Hillsboro	2109019	.015000	.082500
Hill Co	4109000	.005000	
Hilltop Lakes			.067500
Leon Co	4145006	.005000	
Hilshire Village (Harris Co)	2101080	.010000	.082500
Houston MTA	3101990	.010000	
Hitchcock (Galveston Co)	2084036	.020000	.082500
Hoard			.067500
Wood Co	4250007	.005000	
Hobson			.067500
Karnes Co	4128007	.005000	
Hockley (Harris Co)			.072500
Houston MTA	3101990	.010000	
Hockley Mine (Harris Co)			.072500
Houston MTA	3101990	.010000	
Hodgson			.067500
Bowie Co	4019009	.005000	
Holiday Lakes	2020202	.010000	.077500
Brazoria Co	4020006	.005000	
Holland	2014031	.012500	.080000
Bell Co	4014004	.005000	
Holliday	2005014	.010000	.077500
Archer Co	4005005	.005000	
Hollywood Park (Bexar Co)	2015138	.020000	.082500
Holman			.067500
Fayette Co	4075000	.005000	
Homer			.067500
Angelina Co	4003007	.005000	
Hondo	2163021	.015000	.082500
Medina Co	4163003	.005000	
Honey Grove	2074029	.015000	.082500
Fannin Co	4074001	.005000	
Hooks	2019054	.015000	.082500
Bowie Co	4019009	.005000	
Hopewell			.067500
Franklin Co	4080003	.005000	
Hopewell			.067500
Houston Co	4113004	.005000	
Horizon City	2071068	.015000	.082500
El Paso Co	4071004	.005000	
Horseshoe Bay (Burnet Co)	2027072	.017500	.080000
Horseshoe Bay (Llano Co)	2027072	.017500	.080000
Houston (Fort Bend Co)	2101017	.010000	.082500
Houston MTA	3101990	.010000	
Houston (Harris Co)	2101017	.010000	.082500
Houston MTA	3101990	.010000	
Houston (Montgomery Co)	2101017	.010000	.082500
Houston MTA	3101990	.010000	
Howardwick (Donley Co)	2065039	.010000	.072500

¶905

Part III—Sales and Use Taxes

Howe (Grayson Co)	2091055	.020000	.082500
Howellville (Harris Co)			.072500
Houston MTA	3101990	.010000	
Howland			.067500
Lamar Co	4139004	.005000	
Hoyte			.067500
Milam Co	4166000	.005000	
Hubbard	2109055	.015000	.082500
Hill Co	4109000	.005000	
Hudson	2003052	.015000	.082500
Angelina Co	4003007	.005000	
Hudson Oaks	2184071	.015000	.082500
Parker Co	4184008	.005000	
Hufsmith (Harris Co)			.072500
Houston MTA	3101990	.010000	
Hughes Springs (Cass Co)	2034019	.015000	.077500
Hughes Springs	2034019	.015000	.082500
Morris Co	4172002	.005000	
Hull			.067500
Liberty Co	4146005	.005000	
Humble (Harris Co)	2101222	.010000	
Houston MTA	3101990	.010000	
Hungerford			.067500
Wharton Co	4241009	.005000	
Hunt			.067500
Kerr Co	4133000	.005000	
Hunter			.067500
Comal Co	4046006	.005000	
Hunters Creek Village (Harris Co)	2101179	.010000	.082500
Houston MTA	3101990	.010000	
Huntington	2003034	.015000	.082500
Angelina Co	4003007	.005000	
Huntsville	2236015	.015000	.082500
Walker Co	4236006	.005000	
Hurlwood			.067500
Lubbock Co	4152006	.005000	
Hurst (Tarrant Co)	2220086	.015000	.082500
Hurst Crime Control District	5220512	.005000	
Hurst Springs			.067500
Coryell Co	4050009	.005000	
Hutchins (Dallas Co)	2057093	.020000	.082500
Hutto (Williamson Co)	2246059	.020000	.082500
Huxley (Shelby Co)	2210060	.010000	.072500
Hye			.067500
Blanco Co	4016002	.005000	
Iago			.067500
Wharton Co	4241009	.005000	
Idalou	2152033	.015000	.082500
Lubbock Co	4152006	.005000	
Impact (Taylor Co)	2221058	.010000	.072500
Inadale			.067500
Scurry Co	4208000	.005000	
Independence			.067500
Washington Co	4239003	.005000	
Indian Gap			.067500
Hamilton Co	4097004	.005000	
Indian Rock			.067500
Upshur Co	4230002	.005000	
Indianola			.067500
Calhoun Co	4029007	.005000	
Industry	2008066	.015000	.082500
Austin Co	4008002	.005000	
Inez			.067500
Victoria Co	4235007	.005000	
Ingleside (San Patricio Co)	2205021	.020000	.082500
Ingleside On The Bay (San Patricio Co)	2205110	.010000	.072500
Ingram	2133028	.015000	.082500
Kerr Co	4133000	.005000	
Iola	2093053	.012500	.080000
Grimes Co	4093008	.005000	
Iowa Colony	2020211	.010000	.077500
Brazoria Co	4020006	.005000	
Iowa Park (Wichita Co)	2243034	.020000	.082500
Ira			.067500
Scurry Co	4208000	.005000	
Iraan (Pecos Co)	2186024	.020000	.082500
Iredell	2018055	.010000	.077500
Bosque Co	4018000	.005000	
Ireland			.067500

¶905

Coryell Co	4050009	.005000	
Irene			.067500
Hill Co	4109000	.005000	
Ironton			.067500
Cherokee Co	4037007	.005000	
Irving (Dallas Co)	2057066	.010000	.082500
Dallas MTA	3057994	.010000	
Italy (Ellis Co)	2070096	.020000	.082500
Itasca	2109046	.015000	.082500
Hill Co	4109000	.005000	
Ivanhoe			.067500
Fannin Co	4074001	.005000	
Iverson			.067500
Hill Co	4109000	.005000	
Izoro			.067500
Lampasas Co	4141000	.005000	
Jacinto City (Harris Co)	2101160	.010000	.072500
Jacksboro (Jack Co)	2119017	.020000	.082500
Jacksonville	2037025	.015000	.082500
Cherokee Co	4037007	.005000	
Jamaica Beach (Galveston Co)	2084107	.010000	.072500
Jarrell (Williamson Co)	2246139	.020000	.082500
Jarvis College			.067500
Wood Co	4250007	.005000	
Jasper (Jasper Co)	2121022	.020000	.082500
Jasper County Development District No. 1	5121503	.005000	
Jayton (Kent Co)	2132010	.010000	.072500
Jean			.067500
Young Co	4252005	.005000	
Jeddo			.067500
Bastrop Co	4011007	.005000	
Jefferson	2155012	.015000	.082500
Marion Co	4155003	.005000	
Jenkins			.067500
Morris Co	4172002	.005000	
Jersey Village (Harris Co)	2101133	.015000	.082500
Jersey Village Crime Control Dist	5101525	.005000	
Jester			.067500
Navarro Co	4175009	.005000	
Jewett	2145042	.015000	.082500
Leon Co	4145006	.005000	
Jim Hogg Co	4124001	.010000	
Joaquin (Shelby Co)	2210033	.020000	.082500
Johnson City	2016011	.015000	.082500
Blanco Co	4016002	.005000	
Johntown			.067500
Red River Co	4194006	.005000	
Joliet			.067500
Caldwell Co	4028008	.005000	
Jolly (Clay Co)	2039041	.010000	.072500
Jollyville (Williamson Co)			.072500
Austin MTA	3227999	.010000	
Jones Creek	2020177	.010000	.077500
Brazoria Co	4020006	.005000	
Jones Creek			.067500
Wharton Co	4241009	.005000	
Jones Prairie			.067500
Milam Co	4166000	.005000	
Jonesboro			.067500
Coryell Co	4050009	.005000	
Jonesboro			.067500
Hamilton Co	4097004	.005000	
Jonestown (Travis Co)	2227105	.010000	.082500
Austin MTA	3227999	.010000	
Josephine (Collin Co)	2043107	.010000	.072500
Joshua (Johnson Co)	2126072	.020000	.082500
Jourdanton	2007030	.015000	.082500
Atascosa Co	4007003	.005000	
Judd			.067500
Palo Pinto Co	4182000	.005000	
Judson			.067500
Gregg Co	4092009	.005000	
Junction (Kimble Co)	2134018	.015000	.082500
Kimble Co Emergency Services Dist	5134508	.005000	
Juno			.067500
Val Verde Co	4233009	.005000	
Justin (Denton Co)	2061060	.020000	.082500
Kamey			.067500

¶905

Part III—Sales and Use Taxes

Calhoun Co	4029007	.005000	
Karnes City	2128016	.015000	.082500
Karnes Co	4128007	.005000	
Katemcy (Mason Co)			.072500
Mason County Health Services	5157500	.010000	
Katy (Fort Bend Co)	2101053	.010000	.082500
Houston MTA	3101990	.010000	
Katy (Harris Co)	2101053	.010000	.082500
Houston MTA	3101990	.010000	
Katy (Waller Co)	2101053	.010000	.082500
Houston MTA	3101990	.010000	
Kaufman (Kaufman Co)	2129024	.020000	.082500
Keechi			.067500
Leon Co	4145006	.005000	
Keene (Johnson Co)	2126081	.020000	.082500
Keeter			.067500
Wise Co	4249001	.005000	
Keller (Tarrant Co)	2220111	.017500	.082500
Keller Crime Control and Prevention District	5220683	.002500	
Kelsay (Jim Hogg Co)			.082500
Jim Hogg Co	4124001	.010000	
Jim Hogg County Assistance District	5124519	.005000	
Jim Hogg County Health Services	5124500	.005000	
Kelsey			.067500
Upshur Co	4230002	.005000	
Kemah (Galveston Co)	2084027	.020000	.082500
Kemp (Kaufman Co)	2129033	.017500	.080000
Kempner	2141037	.0125000	.080000
Lampasas Co	4141000	.005000	
Kendalia			.067500
Kendall Co	4130003	.005000	
Kendleton (Fort Bend Co)	2079088	.010000	.072500
Kenedy	2128025	.015000	.082500
Karnes Co	4128007	.005000	
Kenefick	2146103	.015000	.082500
Liberty Co	4146005	.005000	
Kennard	2113031	.010000	.077500
Houston Co	4113004	.005000	
Kennedale (Tarrant Co)	2220219	.020000	.082500
Kenney			.067500
Austin Co	4008002	.005000	
Kenwood Place (Harris Co)			.072500
Houston MTA	3101990	.010000	
Kerens	2175027	.015000	.082500
Navarro Co	4175009	.005000	
Kermit	2248011	.010000	.082500
Winkler Co	4248002	.005000	
Winkler County Health Services	5248501	.005000	
Kerrville	2133019	.015000	.082500
Kerr Co	4133000	.005000	
Kickapoo			.067500
Anderson Co	4001009	.005000	
Kilgore	2092027	.015000	.082500
Gregg Co	4092009	.005000	
Kilgore (Rusk Co)	2092027	.015000	.077500
Killeen	2014022	.015000	.082500
Bell Co	4014004	.005000	
Kimball			.067500
Bosque Co	4018000	.005000	
Kingsbury			.067500
Guadalupe Co	4094007	.005000	
Kingston			.067500
Hunt Co	4116001	.005000	
Kingsville	2137015	.015000	.082500
Kleberg Co	4137006	.005000	
Kingtown (Nacogdoches Co)			.072500
Nacogdoches County Hospital District	5174509	.010000	
Kiomatia			.067500
Red River Co	4194006	.005000	
Kirby (Bexar Co)	2015101	.012500	.080000
San Antonio MTA	3015995	.005000	
Kirbyville (Jasper Co)	2121013	.012500	.075000
Kirkland			.067500
Childress Co	4038006	.005000	
Kirtley			.067500
Fayette Co	4075000	.005000	
Kitalou			.067500
Lubbock Co	4152006	.005000	

¶905

Kittrell			.067500
Anderson Co	4001009	.005000	
Klein (Harris Co)			.072500
Houston MTA	3101990	.010000	
Klondike			.072500
Delta Co	4060007	.005000	
Delta Co Emergency Services District	5060506	.005000	
Knickerbocker			.067500
Tom Green Co	4226008	.005000	
Knippa			.072500
Uvalde Co	4232000	.005000	
Uvalde County Health Services	5232509	.005000	
Knollwood (Grayson Co)	2091162	.020000	.082500
Knox City (Knox Co)	2138014	.020000	.082500
Kohrville (Harris Co)			.072500
Houston MTA	3101990	.010000	
Kopperl			.067500
Bosque Co	4018000	.005000	
Kosse (Limestone Co)	2147059	.010000	.072500
Kountze (Hardin Co)	2100027	.020000	.082500
Kovar			.067500
Bastrop Co	4011007	.005000	
Kress	2219034	.010000	.077500
Swisher Co	4219007	.005000	
Krugerville (Denton Co)	2061159	.020000	.082500
Krum (Denton Co)	2061140	.017500	.0800000
Kurten	2021041	.010000	.077500
Brazos Co	4021005	.005000	
Kyle	2105013	.015000	.082500
Hays Co	4105004	.005000	
Kyote			.067500
Atascosa Co	4007003	.005000	
La Belle			.067500
Jefferson Co	4123002	.005000	
La Coste	2163058	.015000	.082500
Medina Co	4163003	.005000	
La Fayette			.067500
Upshur Co	4230002	.005000	
La Feria (Cameron Co)	2031049	.020000	.082500
La Grange	2075019	.015000	.082500
Fayette Co	4075000	.005000	
La Joya (Hidalgo Co)	2108145	.020000	.082500
La Junta			.067500
Parker Co	4184008	.005000	
La Marque (Galveston Co)	2084045	.020000	.082500
La Porte (Harris Co)	2101099	.017500	.080000
La Salle			.067500
Jackson Co	4120005	.005000	
La Vernia (Wilson Co)	2247012	.015000	.082500
La Vernia Municipal Development Dist	5247502	.005000	
La Villa (Hidalgo Co)	2108118	.010000	.072500
La Ward	2120032	.010000	.077500
Jackson Co	4120005	.005000	
Lacy Lakeview	2161096	.015000	.082500
McClennan Co	4161005	.005000	
Ladonia	2074056	.010000	.077500
Fannin Co	4074001	.005000	
Lagarto			.067500
Live Oak Co	4149002	.005000	
Lago Vista (Travis Co)	2227123	.010000	.082500
Austin MTA	3227999	.010000	
Laguna Park			.067500
Bosque Co	4018000	.005000	
Laguna Vista (Cameron Co)	2031110	.015000	.077500
Lajitas			.067500
Brewster Co	4022004	.005000	
Lake Bridgeport	2249092	.015000	.082500
Wise Co	4249001	.005000	
Lake Creek			.072500
Delta Co	4060007	.005000	
Delta Co Emergency Services District	5060506	.005000	
Lake Dallas (Denton Co)	2061015	.020000	.082500
Lake Jackson	2020097	.015000	.082500
Brazoria Co	4020006	.005000	
Lake Kiowa			.067500
Cooke Co	4049003	.005000	
Lake Worth (Tarrant Co)	2220040	.0175000	.0825500
Lake Worth Crime Control Dist	5220707	.002500	
Lakehills			.067500

¶905

Part III—Sales and Use Taxes 159

Bandera Co	4010008	.005000	
Lakeport	2092072	.010000	.077500
Gregg Co	4092009	.005000	
Lakeside (Tarrant Co)	2220175	.010000	.072500
Lakeside City	2005069	.010000	.077500
Archer Co	4005005	.005000	
Lakeside Village			.067500
Bosque Co	4018000	.005000	
Lakeview (Hall Co)	2096032	.010000	.072500
Lakeway (Travis Co)	2227061	.017500	.082500
Lake Travis Community Library Dist.	5227560	.002500	
Lakewood Harbor			.067500
Bosque Co	4018000	.005000	
Lakewood Village (Denton Co)	2061346	.015000	.082500
Lakewood Village Municipal Dev. Dist.	5061596	.005000	
Lamar			.072500
Aransas Co	4004006	.005000	
Aransas County Health Services	5004505	.005000	
Lamasco			.067500
Fannin Co	4074001	.005000	
Lamesa	2058010	.015000	.082500
Dawson Co	4058001	.005000	
Lamkin			.067500
Comanche Co	4047005	.005000	
Lampasas	2141019	.015000	.082500
Lampasas Co	4141000	.005000	
Lancaster (Dallas Co)	2057020	.020000	.082500
Lane City			.067500
Wharton Co	4241009	.005000	
Langtry			.067500
Val Verde Co	4233009	.005000	
Lanham			.067500
Hamilton Co	4097004	.005000	
Lannius			.067500
Fannin Co	4074001	.005000	
Laredo	2240019	.012500	.082500
Laredo CTD	3240885	.002500	
Webb Co	4240000	.005000	
Lassater			.067500
Marion Co	4155003	.005000	
Latch			.067500
Upshur Co	4230002	.005000	
Latexo	2113059	.010000	.077500
Houston Co	4113004	.005000	
Lavon (Collin Co)	2043269	.015000	.077500
Law			.067500
Brazos Co	4021005	.005000	
Lawn (Taylor Co)	2221085	.010000	.072500
League City (Galveston Co)	2084063	.017500	.080000
Leakey	2193025	.015000	.082500
Real Co	4193007	.005000	
Leander (Williamson Co)	2246102	.010000	.082500
Austin MTA	3227999	.010000	
Leary	2019090	.010000	.077500
Bowie Co	4019009	.005000	
Ledbetter			.067500
Fayette Co	4075000	.005000	
Leedale			.067500
Bell Co	4014004	.005000	
Leesburg			.067500
Camp Co	4032002	.005000	
Leesville			.067500
Gonzales Co	4089004	.005000	
Lefors (Gray Co)	2090038	.010000	.072500
Leggett			.067500
Polk Co	4187005	.005000	
Leming			.067500
Atascosa Co	4007003	.005000	
Leo			.067500
Lee Co	4144007	.005000	
Leon Junction			.067500
Coryell Co	4050009	.005000	
Leon Springs (Bexar Co)			.067500
San Antonio MTA	3015995	.005000	
Leon Valley (Bexar Co)	2015058	.013750	.081250
San Antonio MTA	3015995	.005000	
Leona	2145079	.010000	.077500
Leon Co	4145006	.005000	
Leonard	2074047	.015000	.082500

¶905

Fannin Co	4074001	.005000	
Leroy		2161201	.010000	.077500
McClennan Co	4161005	.005000	
Levelland (Hockley Co)	2110016	.020000	.082500
Levi			.067500
McClennan Co	4161005	.005000	
Levita			.067500
Coryell Co	4050009	.005000	
Lewisville (Dallas Co)	2061033	.012500	.080000
Denton County Trans Authority	3061774	.005000	
Lexington	2144025	.015000	.082500
Lee Co	4144007	.005000	
Liberty	2146032	.012500	.075000
Liberty Co	4146005	.005000	
Liberty City			.067500
Gregg Co	4092009	.005000	
Liberty Hill			.067500
Hill Co	4109000	.005000	
Liberty Hill			.067500
Milam Co	4166000	.005000	
Liberty Hill (Williamson Co)	2246111	.017500	.082500
Liberty Hill Public Library District	5246512	.002500	
Lilac			.067500
Milam Co	4166000	.005000	
Lily Island			.067500
Polk Co	4187005	.005000	
Lincoln			.067500
Lee Co	4144007	.005000	
Lincoln Park (Denton Co)	2061097	.020000	.082500
Lindale	2212022	.015000	.082500
Smith Co	4212004	.005000	
Linden (Cass Co)	2034037	.020000	.082500
Lindsay	2049030	.015000	.082500
Cooke Co	4049003	.005000	
Lingleville			.067500
Erath Co	4072003	.005000	
Linwood			.067500
Cherokee Co	4037007	.005000	
Lipan	2111024	.010000	.077500
Hood Co	4111006	.005000	
Lissie			.067500
Wharton Co	4241009	.005000	
Little Cypress			.067500
Orange Co	4181001	.005000	
Little Elm (Denton Co)	2061088	.020000	.082500
Little Hope			.067500
Wood Co	4250007	.005000	
Little River			.067500
Bell Co	4014004	.005000	
Little River Academy	2014102	.010000	.077500
Bell Co	4014004	.005000	
Littlefield (Lamb Co)	2140029	.017500	.080000
Live Oak (Bexar Co)	2015156	.020000	.082500
Liveoak			.067500
Palo Pinto Co	4182000	.005000	
Liverpool	2020033	.010000	.077500
Brazoria Co	4020006	.005000	
Livingston	2187014	.015000	.082500
Polk Co	4187005	.005000	
Llano (Llano Co)	2150017	.020000	.082500
Lochridge			.067500
Brazoria Co	4020006	.005000	
Locker			.067500
San Saba Co	4206002	.005000	
Lockett			.067500
Wilbarger Co	4244006	.005000	
Lockhart	2028017	.015000	.082500
Caldwell Co	4028008	.005000	
Lockney (Floyd Co)	2077017	.015000	.077500
Lodi			.067500
Marion Co	4155003	.005000	
Loebau			.067500
Lee Co	4144007	.005000	
Log Cabin (Henderson Co)	2107164	.010000	.072500
Lohn			.070000
McCulloch Co	4160006	.005000	
McCulloch County Hospital District	5160505	.002500	
Lolita			.067500
Jackson Co	4120005	.005000	

¶905

Part III—Sales and Use Taxes

Lometa	2141028	.015000	.082500
Lampasas Co	4141000	.005000	
London (Kimble Co)			.067500
Kimble Co Emergency Services Dist	5134508	.005000	
Lone Mountain			.067500
Upshur Co	4230002	.005000	
Lone Oak (Bexar Co)			.067500
San Antonio MTA	3015995	.005000	
Lone Oak	2116083	.010000	.077500
Hunt Co	4116001	.005000	
Lone Star	2172039	.010000	.077500
Morris Co	4172002	.005000	
Long Mott			.067500
Calhoun Co	4029007	.005000	
Long Point			.067500
Washington Co	4239003	.005000	
Longview	2092018	.015000	.082500
Gregg Co	4092009	.005000	
Longview (Harrison Co)	2092018	.015000	.077500
Loraine	2168026	.015000	.082500
Mitchell Co	4168008	.005000	
Lorena	2161103	.015000	.082500
McClennan Co	4161005	.005000	
Lorenzo	2054023	.010000	.077500
Crosby Co	4054005	.005000	
Los Fresnos (Cameron Co)	2031085	.020000	.082500
Los Indios (Cameron Co)	2031174	.010000	.072500
Los Ybanez	2058029	.010000	.077500
Dawson Co	4058001	.005000	
Losoya (Bexar Co)			.067500
San Antonio MTA	3015995	.005000	
Lott	2073020	.015000	.082500
Falls Co	4073002	.005000	
Louise			.067500
Wharton Co	4241009	.005000	
Lovelace			.067500
Hill Co	4109000	.005000	
Lovelady	2113040	.012500	.080000
Houston Co	4113004	.005000	
Loving			.067500
Young Co	4252005	.005000	
Lowake			.067500
Concho Co	4048004	.005000	
Lowry Crossing (Collin Co)	2043214	.010000	.072500
Loyola Beach			.067500
Kleberg Co	4137006	.005000	
Lubbock	2152015	.015000	.082500
Lubbock Co	4152006	.005000	
Lucas (Collin Co)	2043143	.010000	.072500
Luckenbach			.067500
Gillespie Co	4086007	.005000	
Lueders (Jones Co)	2127053	.010000	.072500
Lufkin	2003016	.015000	.082500
Angelina Co	4003007	.005000	
Luling	2028026	.015000	.082500
Caldwell Co	4028008	.005000	
Lumberton (Hardin Co)	2100045	.020000	.082500
Lyford (Willacy Co)	2245023	.010000	.072500
Lyons			.067500
Burleson Co	4026000	.005000	
Lytle	2007012	.015000	.082500
Atascosa Co	4007003	.005000	
Lytle (Bexar Co)	2007012	.015000	.077500
Lytle	2007012	.015000	.082500
Medina Co	4163003	.005000	
Lytton Springs			.067500
Caldwell Co	4028008	.005000	
Mabank (Henderson Co)	2129015	.020000	.082500
Mabank (Kaufman Co)	2129015	.020000	.082500
Macdona (Bexar Co)			.067500
San Antonio MTA	3015995	.005000	
Mackay			.067500
Wharton Co	4241009	.005000	
Macune			.067500
San Augustine Co	4203005	.005000	
Madisonville	2154013	.015000	.082500
Madison Co	4154004	.005000	
Magnet			.067500
Wharton Co	4241009	.005000	

¶905

Magnolia (Montgomery Co)	2170068	.020000	.082500
Magnolia			.067500
San Jacinto Co	4204004	.005000	
Magnolia Beach			.067500
Calhoun Co	4029007	.005000	
Mahl (Nacogdoches Co)			.072500
Nacogdoches County Hospital District	5174509	.010000	
Malakoff (Henderson Co)	2107020	.016250	.082500
Malakoff Crime Control and Prevention Dist	5107501	.003750	
Malone	2109037	.015000	.082500
Hill Co	4109000	.005000	
Malta			.067500
Bowie Co	4019009	.005000	
Manchester			.067500
Red River Co	4194006	.005000	
Manheim			.067500
Lee Co	4144007	.005000	
Mankins			.067500
Archer Co	4005005	.005000	
Manor (Travis Co)	2227034	.010000	.082500
Austin MTA	3227999	.010000	
Mansfield (Ellis Co)	2220120	.020000	.082500
Mansfield (Johnson Co)	2220120	.020000	.082500
Mansfield (Tarrant Co)	2220120	.020000	.082500
Manvel	2020186	.015000	.082500
Brazoria Co	4020006	.005000	
Maple			.067500
Bailey Co	4009001	.005000	
Mapleton			.067500
Houston Co	4113004	.005000	
Marathon			.067500
Brewster Co	4022004	.005000	
Marble Falls (Burnet Co)	2027018	.020000	.082500
Marfa (Presidio Co)	2189012	.017500	.080000
Marion	2094043	.015000	.082500
Guadalupe Co	4094007	.005000	
Markley			.067500
Young Co	4252005	.005000	
Marlin	2073011	.015000	.082500
Falls Co	4073002	.005000	
Marquez	2145060	.015000	.082500
Leon Co	4145006	.005000	
Marshall (Harrison Co)	2102016	.020000	.082500
Mart	2161078	.012500	.080000
McClennan Co	4161005	.005000	
Martin Springs			.067500
Hopkins Co	4112005	.005000	
Martindale	2028035	.010000	.077500
Caldwell Co	4028008	.005000	
Martinsville (Nacogdoches Co)			.072500
Nacogdoches County Hospital District	5174509	.010000	
Mason (Mason Co)	2157010	.010000	.082500
Mason County Health Services	5157500	.010000	
Massey Lake			.067500
Anderson Co	4001009	.005000	
Matador (Motley Co)	2173010	.020000	.082500
Mathis (San Patricio Co)	2205067	.020000	.082500
Matinburg			.067500
Camp Co	4032002	.005000	
Matthews			.072500
Colorado Co	4045007	.005000	
Rice Hospital District	5045506	.005000	
Maud	2019036	.015000	.082500
Bowie Co	4019009	.005000	
Mauriceville			.067500
Orange Co	4181001	.005000	
Maurin			.067500
Gonzales Co	4089004	.005000	
Maxdale			.067500
Bell Co	4014004	.005000	
Maxey			.067500
Lamar Co	4139004	.005000	
Maxwell			.067500
Caldwell Co	4028008	.005000	
Maydelle			.067500
Cherokee Co	4037007	.005000	
Mayfield			.067500
Hill Co	4109000	.005000	

¶905

Part III—Sales and Use Taxes

Maypearl (Ellis Co)	2070087	.017500	.080000
Maysfield			.067500
Milam Co	4166000	.005000	
McCoy			.067500
Atascosa Co	4007003	.005000	
Mc Dade			.067500
Bastrop Co	4011007	.005000	
Mc Gregor	2161112	.015000	.082500
McClennan Co	4161005	.005000	
McAdoo			.067500
Dickens Co	4063004	.005000	
McAllen (Hidalgo Co)	2108056	.020000	.082500
McBeth			.067500
Brazoria Co	4020006	.005000	
McCamey (Upton Co)	2231029	.015000	.077500
McClanahan			.067500
Falls Co	4073002	.005000	
McFaddin			.067500
Victoria Co	4235007	.005000	
McKinney (Collin Co)	2043045	.020000	.082500
McLean (Gray Co)	2090029	.015000	.077500
McLendon Chisholm (Rockwall Co)	2199065	.010000	.077500
Rockwall Co Public Safety and Fire Assistance Dist	5199500	.005000	
McMahan			.067500
Caldwell Co	4028008	.005000	
McNeil			.067500
Caldwell Co	4028008	.005000	
McNeil (Travis Co)			.072500
Austin MTA	3227999	.010000	
McQueeney			.067500
Guadalupe Co	4094007	.005000	
Meador Grove			.067500
Bell Co	4014004	.005000	
Meadow	2223029	.010000	.077500
Terry Co	4223001	.005000	
Meadows Place (Fort Bend Co)	2079168	.020000	.082500
Medicine Mound			.067500
Hardeman Co	4099002	.005000	
Medina			.067500
Bandera Co	4010008	.005000	
Meeker			.067500
Jefferson Co	4123002	.005000	
Meeks			.067500
Bell Co	4014004	.005000	
Megargel	2005041	.010000	.077500
Archer Co	4005005	.005000	
Melissa (Collin Co)	2043170	.020000	.082500
Melrose (Nacogdoches Co)			.072500
Nacogdoches County Hospital District	5174509	.010000	
Melvin	2160024	.010000	.080000
McCulloch Co	4160006	.005000	
McCulloch County Hospital District	5160505	.002500	
Memphis (Hall Co)	2096014	.020000	.082500
Menard	2164011	.015000	.082500
Menard Co	4164002	.005000	
Mendoza			.067500
Caldwell Co	4028008	.005000	
Menlow			.067500
Hill Co	4109000	.005000	
Mentz			.067500
Colorado Co	4045007	.005000	
Mercedes (Hidalgo Co)	2108038	.020000	.082500
Mercury			.070000
McCulloch Co	4160006	.005000	
McCulloch County Hospital District	5160505	.002500	
Mereta			.067500
Tom Green Co	4226008	.005000	
Meridian	2018028	.015000	.082500
Bosque Co	4018000	.005000	
Merit			.067500
Hunt Co	4116001	.005000	
Merkel (Taylor Co)	2221021	.020000	.082500
Mertens	2109117	.010000	.077500
Hill Co	4109000	.005000	
Mertzon (Irion Co)	2118018	.010000	.072500
Mesquite (Dallas Co)	2057039	.020000	.082500
Mesquite (Kaufman Co)	2057039	.020000	.082500
Mexia (Limestone Co)	2147013	.020000	.082500

¶905

Miami (Roberts Co)	2197012	.020000	.082500
Mico			.067500
Medina Co	4163003	.005000	
Middleton			.067500
Leon Co	4145006	.005000	
Midland	2165010	.015000	.082500
Midland Co	4165001	.005000	
Midlothian (Ellis Co)	2070050	.020000	.082500
Midway	2154022	.015000	.082500
Madison Co	4154004	.005000	
Milam			.067500
Sabine Co	4202006	.005000	
Milano	2166055	.015000	.082500
Milam Co	4166000	.005000	
Mildred	2175143	.010000	.077500
Navarro Co	4175009	.005000	
Miles	2200026	.015000	.082500
Runnels Co	4200008	.005000	
Miles	2200026	.015000	.082500
Tom Green Co	4226008	.005000	
Milford (Ellis Co)	2070121	.010000	.072500
Milheim			.067500
Austin Co	4008002	.005000	
Miller Grove			.067500
Hopkins Co	4112005	.005000	
Millers Cove	2225054	.010000	.077500
Titus Co	4225009	.005000	
Millersview			.067500
Concho Co	4048004	.005000	
Millican			.067500
Brazos Co	4021005	.005000	
Millsap	2184080	.010000	.077500
Parker Co	4184008	.005000	
Mims			.067500
Brazoria Co	4020006	.005000	
Mineola	2250016	.015000	.082500
Wood Co	4250007	.005000	
Mineral			.067500
Bee Co	4013005	.005000	
Mineral Wells	2182019	.015000	.082500
Palo Pinto Co	4182000	.005000	
Mineral Wells	2182019	.015000	.082500
Parker Co	4184008	.005000	
Minerva			.067500
Milam Co	4166000	.005000	
Mings Chapel			.067500
Upshur Co	4230002	.005000	
Mingus	2182046	.010000	.077500
Palo Pinto Co	4182000	.005000	
Minter			.067500
Lamar Co	4139004	.005000	
Mirando City			.067500
Webb Co	4240000	.005000	
Mission (Hidalgo Co)	2108065	.020000	.082500
Mission Valley			.067500
Victoria Co	4235007	.005000	
Missouri City (Fort Bend Co)	2079079	.010000	.082500
Houston MTA	3101990	.010000	
Missouri City (Harris Co)	2079079	.010000	.082500
Houston MTA	3101990	.010000	
Mixon			.067500
Cherokee Co	4037007	.005000	
Mobeetie (Wheeler Co)	2242035	.010000	.072500
Mobile City (Rockwall Co)	2199056	.010000	.077500
Rockwall Co Public Safety and Fire Assistance Dist	5199500	.005000	
Moffat			.067500
Bell Co	4014004	.005000	
Monahans (Ward Co)	2238013	.020000	.082500
Monkstown			.067500
Fannin Co	4074001	.005000	
Monroe City (Chambers Co)			.067500
Chambers Co Health Ser	5036507	.005000	
Mont Belvieu (Chambers Co)	2036053	.015000	.082500
Chambers Co Health Ser	5036507	.005000	
Mont Belvieu	2036053	.015000	.082500
Liberty Co	4146005	.005000	
Montalba			.067500
Anderson Co	4001009	.005000	

¶905

Part III—Sales and Use Taxes

Montell			.072500
Uvalde Co	4232000	.005000	
Uvalde County Health Services	5232509	.005000	
Montgomery (Montgomery Co)	2170040	.020000	.082500
Montgomery County Emergency Services District No. 1	5170610	.020000	
Montgomery County Emergency Services District No. 3	5170594	.020000	
Montgomery County Emergency Services District No. 9	5170585	.020000	
Monthalia			.067500
Gonzales Co	4089004	.005000	
Moody	2161087	.010000	.077500
McClennan Co	4161005	.005000	
Moore			.067500
Frio Co	4082001	.005000	
Mooresville			.067500
Falls Co	4073002	.005000	
Morales			.067500
Jackson Co	4120005	.005000	
Moran (Shackelford Co)	2209018	.010000	.072500
Morgan	2018064	.010000	.077500
Bosque Co	4018000	.005000	
Morgan Mill			.067500
Erath Co	4072003	.005000	
Morgans Point (Harris Co)	2101231	.015000	.077500
Morgans Point Resort	2014086	.012500	.080000
Bell Co	4014004	.005000	
Morris Ranch			.067500
Gillespie Co	4086007	.005000	
Morton (Cochran Co)	2040020	.015000	.077500
Moscow			.067500
Polk Co	4187005	.005000	
Mosheim			.067500
Bosque Co	4018000	.005000	
Moss Bluff			.067500
Liberty Co	4146005	.005000	
Moss Hill			.067500
Liberty Co	4146005	.005000	
Moulton (Lavaca Co)	2143026	.017500	.080000
Mound			.067500
Coryell Co	4050009	.005000	
Mound City			.067500
Anderson Co	4001009	.005000	
Mount Calm	2109144	.010000	.077500
Hill Co	4109000	.005000	
Mount Enterprise (Rusk Co)	2201043	.015000	.077500
Mount Enterprise			.067500
Wood Co	4250007	.005000	
Mount Lucas			.067500
Live Oak Co	4149002	.005000	
Mount Pleasant	2225018	.015000	.082500
Titus Co	4225009	.005000	
Mount Selman			.067500
Cherokee Co	4037007	.005000	
Mount Vernon	2080012	.015000	.082500
Franklin Co	4080003	.005000	
Mountain City	2105102	.010000	.077500
Hays Co	4105004	.005000	
Mountain Home			.067500
Kerr Co	4133000	.005000	
Mountain Springs			.067500
Cooke Co	4049003	.005000	
Muenster	2049021	.015000	.082500
Cooke Co	4049003	.005000	
Muldoon			.067500
Fayette Co	4075000	.005000	
Muleshoe	2009010	.015000	.082500
Bailey Co	4009001	.005000	
Mullin (Mills Co)	2167027	.010000	.072500
Mullins Prairie			.067500
Fayette Co	4075000	.005000	
Munday (Knox Co)	2138023	.020000	.082500
Murchison (Henderson Co)	2107119	.015000	.077500
Murphy (Collin Co)	2043161	.020000	.082500
Murray			.067500
Young Co	4252005	.005000	
Mustang	2175090	.015000	.082500
Navarro Co	4175009	.005000	

¶905

Mustang Ridge	2227178	.010000	.077500
Caldwell Co	4028008	.005000	
Mustang Ridge (Travis Co)	2227178	.010000	.072500
Myra			.067500
Cooke Co	4049003	.005000	
Nacogdoches (Nacogdoches Co)	2174019	.010000	.082500
Nacogdoches County Hospital District	5174509	.010000	
Nada			.072500
Colorado Co	4045007	.005000	
Rice Hospital District	5045506	.005000	
Nancy			.067500
Angelina Co	4003007	.005000	
Naples	2172020	.012500	.080000
Morris Co	4172002	.005000	
Nash	2019063	.015000	.082500
Bowie Co	4019009	.005000	
Nassau Bay (Harris Co)	2101204	.017500	.080000
Nassau Bay (Harris Co)			.082500
NASA Area Management Dist	5101641	.002500	
Natalia	2163049	.010000	.077500
Medina Co	4163003	.005000	
Navarro	2175170	.010000	.077500
Navarro Co	4175009	.005000	
Navarro Mills			.067500
Navarro Co	4175009	.005000	
Navasota	2093017	.015000	.082500
Grimes Co	4093008	.005000	
Nazareth	2035036	.015000	.082500
Castro Co	4035009	.005000	
Nechanitz			.067500
Fayette Co	4075000	.005000	
Neches			.067500
Anderson Co	4001009	.005000	
Nederland	2123048	.015000	.082500
Jefferson Co	4123002	.005000	
Needmore			.067500
Bailey Co	4009001	.005000	
Needville (Fort Bend Co)	2079024	.020000	.082500
Nell			.067500
Live Oak Co	4149002	.005000	
Nelsonville			.067500
Austin Co	4008002	.005000	
Nelta			.067500
Hopkins Co	4112005	.005000	
Nevada (Collin Co)	2043250	.0175000	.0800000
New Berlin	2094052	.010000	.077500
Guadalupe Co	4094007	.005000	
New Boston	2019045	.015000	.082500
Bowie Co	4019009	.005000	
New Braunfels	2046015	.015000	.082500
Cornal Co	4046006	.005000	
New Braunfels	2046015	.015000	.082500
Guadalupe Co	4094007	.005000	
New Caney (Montgomery Co)			.072500
East Montgomery Co Improvement Dist	5170512	.010000	
New Chapel Hill	2212086	.010000	.077500
Smith Co	4212004	.005000	
New Clarkson			.067500
Milam Co	4166000	.005000	
New Deal	2152042	.015000	.082500
Lubbock Co	4152006	.005000	
New Fairview	2249127	.015000	.082500
Wise Co	4249001	.005000	
New Hope (Collin Co)	2043241	.010000	.072500
New Hope			.067500
San Jacinto Co	4204004	.005000	
New Mine			.067500
Camp Co	4032002	.005000	
New Mountain			.067500
Upshur Co	4230002	.005000	
New Salem			.067500
Palo Pinto Co	4182000	.005000	
New Summerfield	2037052	.010000	.077500
Cherokee Co	4037007	.005000	
New Taiton			.067500
Wharton Co	4241009	.005000	
New Ulm			.067500
Austin Co	4008002	.005000	
New Waverly	2236024	.015000	.082500

¶905

Part III—Sales and Use Taxes

Location	Code	Rate	Total
Walker Co	4236006	.005000	
New Wehdem			.067500
Austin Co	4008002	.005000	
New Willard			.067500
Polk Co	4187005	.005000	
Newark (Tarrant Co)	2249047	.015000	.077500
Newark	2249047	.015000	.082500
Wise Co	4249001	.005000	
Newby			.067500
Leon Co	4145006	.005000	
Newcastle	2252032	.010000	.077500
Young Co	4252005	.005000	
Newgulf			.067500
Wharton Co	4241009	.005000	
Newsome			.067500
Camp Co	4032002	.005000	
Newton (Newton Co)	2176017	.020000	.082500
Neylandville	2116109	.010000	.077500
Hunt Co	4116001	.005000	
Nickel			.067500
Gonzales Co	4089004	.005000	
Niederwald	2105077	.010000	.077500
Caldwell Co	4028008	.005000	
Niederwald	2105077	.010000	.077500
Hays Co	4105004	.005000	
Nile			.067500
Milam Co	4166000	.005000	
Nix			.067500
Lampasas Co	4141000	.005000	
Nixon	2089013	.015000	.082500
Gonzales Co	4089004	.005000	
Nixon (Wilson Co)	2089013	.015000	.077500
Nocona (Montague Co)	2169016	.020000	.082500
Nolanville	2014095	.015000	.082500
Bell Co	4014004	.005000	
Nome	2123100	.010000	.077500
Jefferson Co	4123002	.005000	
Noonday	2212095	.010000	.077500
Smith Co	4212004	.005000	
Nordheim (DeWitt Co)	2062023	.010000	.072500
Normangee	2145024	.012500	.080000
Leon Co	4145006	.005000	
Normangee	2145024	.012500	.080000
Madison Co	4154004	.005000	
Normanna			.067500
Bee Co	4013005	.005000	
Norse			.067500
Bosque Co	4018000	.005000	
North Cleveland	2146050	.010000	.077500
Liberty Co	4146005	.005000	
North Prairie			.067500
Falls Co	4073002	.005000	
North Richland Hills (Tarrant Co)	2220184	.015000	.082500
No Richland Hills Crime Control Dist	5220549	.005000	
North Zulch			.067500
Madison Co	4154004	.005000	
Northlake (Denton Co)	2061319	.020000	.082500
Northrup			.067500
Lee Co	4144007	.005000	
Norton			.067500
Runnels Co	4200008	.005000	
Norwood			.067500
San Augustine Co	4203005	.005000	
Notrees (Ector Co)			.070000
Ector County Hospital District	5068508	.007500	
Novice			.067500
Lamar Co	4139004	.005000	
Noxville (Kimble Co)			.067500
Kimble Co Emergency Services Dist	5134508	.005000	
Nursery			.067500
Victoria Co	4235007	.005000	
O Brien (Haskell Co)	2104050	.010000	.072500
Oak Forest			.067500
Gonzales Co	4089004	.005000	
Oak Grove			.067500
Wood Co	4250007	.005000	
Oak Island (Chambers Co)			.067500
Chambers Co Health Ser	5036507	.005000	
Oak Leaf (Ellis Co)	2070158	.017500	.080000

¶905

Oak Point (Denton Co)	2061328	.017500	.080000
Oak Ridge	2049067	.015000	.082500
Cooke Co	4049003	.005000	
Oak Ridge North (Montgomery Co)	2170102	.020000	.082500
Oak Valley	2175125	.010000	.077500
Navarro Co	4175009	.005000	
Oakhurst			.067500
San Jacinto Co	4204004	.005000	
Oakland			.067500
Cherokee Co	4037007	.005000	
Oakland			.067500
Colorado Co	4045007	.005000	
Oakville			.067500
Live Oak Co	4149002	.005000	
Oakwood	2145051	.010000	.077500
Leon Co	4145006	.005000	
Occc			.067500
McClennan Co	4161005	.005000	
Odell			.067500
Wilbarger Co	4244006	.005000	
Odem (San Patricio Co)	2205058	.015000	.077500
Odessa (Ector Co)	2068018	.012500	.082500
Ector County Hospital District	5068508	.007500	
Odessa	2068018	.012500	.080000
Midland Co	4165001	.005000	
ODonnell	2153023	.010000	.077500
Dawson Co	4058001	.005000	
ODonnell	2153023	.010000	.077500
Lynn Co	4153005	.005000	
Oenaville			.067500
Bell Co	4014004	.005000	
Ogden			.067500
Comal Co	4046006	.005000	
Oglesby	2050036	.010000	.077500
Coryell Co	4050009	.005000	
Oilton			.067500
Webb Co	4240000	.005000	
Oklaunion			.067500
Wilbarger Co	4244006	.005000	
Old Boston			.067500
Bowie Co	4019009	.005000	
Old Brazoria			.067500
Brazoria Co	4020006	.005000	
Old Dime Box			.067500
Lee Co	4144007	.005000	
Old Larissa			.067500
Cherokee Co	4037007	.005000	
Old Ocean			.067500
Brazoria Co	4020006	.005000	
Old River Winfree (Chambers Co)	2036044	.015000	.082500
Chambers Co Health Ser	5036507	.005000	
Old River Winfree	2036044	.015000	.082500
Liberty Co	4146005	.005000	
Old Town Spring Improvement District	5101543	.010000	
Oldenburg			.067500
Fayette Co	4075000	.005000	
Olivia			.067500
Calhoun Co	4029007	.005000	
Olmos			.067500
Bee Co	4013005	.005000	
Olmos Park (Bexar Co)	2015067	.015000	.082500
San Antonio MTA	3015995	.005000	
Olney	2252023	.015000	.082500
Young Co	4252005	.005000	
Olton (Lamb Co)	2140047	.015000	.077500
Omaha	2172048	.010000	.077500
Morris Co	4172002	.005000	
Onalaska	2187032	.015000	.082500
Polk Co	4187005	.005000	
Opdyke West (Hockley Co)	2110052	.010000	.072500
OQuinn			.067500
Fayette Co	4075000	.005000	
Oran			.067500
Palo Pinto Co	4182000	.005000	
Orange	2181029	.015000	.082500
Orange Co	4181001	.005000	
Orange Grove	2125019	.015000	.082500
Jim Wells Co	4125000	.005000	
Orangefield			.067500

¶905

Part III—Sales and Use Taxes

Location	Code	Rate	Total
Orange Co	4181001	.005000	
Orchard (Fort Bend Co)	2079097	.020000	.082500
Ore City	2230020	.015000	.082500
Upshur Co	4230002	.005000	
Orient			.067500
Tom Green Co	4226008	.005000	
Orla (Reeves Co)			.067500
Reeves County Hospital District	5195504	.005000	
Osage			.067500
Coryell Co	4050009	.005000	
Oscar			.067500
Bell Co	4014004	.005000	
Osceola			.067500
Hill Co	4109000	.005000	
Otey			.067500
Brazoria Co	4020006	.005000	
Ottine			.067500
Gonzales Co	4089004	.005000	
Otto			.067500
Falls Co	4073002	.005000	
Overton (Rusk Co)	2201025	.015000	.077500
Overton	2201025	.015000	.082500
Smith Co	4212004	.005000	
Ovilla (Dallas Co)	2070103	.017500	.080000
Ovilla (Ellis Co)	2070103	.017500	.080000
Owentown			.067500
Smith Co	4212004	.005000	
Oyster Creek	2020159	.015000	.082500
Brazoria Co	4020006	.005000	
Paducah (Cottle Co)	2051017	.020000	.082500
Paige			.067500
Bastrop Co	4011007	.005000	
Paint Rock	2048022	.010000	.077500
Concho Co	4048004	.005000	
Palacios (Matagorda Co)	2158019	.020000	.082500
Palestine	2001018	.015000	.082500
Anderson Co	4001009	.005000	
Palestine			.067500
Polk Co	4187005	.005000	
Palito Blanco			.067500
Jim Wells Co	4125000	.005000	
Palm Valley (Cameron Co)	2031147	.010000	.072500
Palmer (Ellis Co)	2070069	.020000	.082500
Palmhurst (Hidalgo Co)	2108225	.015000	.077500
Palmview (Hidalgo Co)	2108163	.015000	.082500
Palmview Crime Control and Prevention District	5108528	.005000	
Palo Alto (Nueces Co)			.067500
Corpus Christi MTA	3178998	.005000	
Palo Pinto			.067500
Palo Pinto Co	4182000	.005000	
Paluxy			.067500
Hood Co	4111006	.005000	
Pampa (Gray Co)	2090010	.020000	.082500
Pancake			.067500
Coryell Co	4050009	.005000	
Pandale			.067500
Val Verde Co	4233009	.005000	
Panhandle (Carson Co)	2033010	.015000	.077500
Panna Maria			.067500
Karnes Co	4128007	.005000	
Panorama Village (Montgomery Co)	2170139	.012500	.075000
Pantego (Tarrant Co)	2220148	.020000	.082500
Papalote			.067500
Bee Co	4013005	.005000	
Paradise	2249118	.015000	.082500
Wise Co	4249001	.005000	
Paris	2139013	.015000	.082500
Lamar Co	4139004	.005000	
Park Springs			.067500
Wise Co	4249001	.005000	
Parker (Collin Co)	2043223	.010000	.072500
Pasadena (Harris Co)	2101035	.015000	.082500
Pasadena Crime Control District	5101516	.005000	
Patilo			.067500
Erath Co	4072003	.005000	
Patricia			.067500
Dawson Co	4058001	.005000	
Pattison (Waller Co)	2237050	.010000	.072500

¶905

Patton Village (Montgomery Co)	2170077	.010000	.082500
East Montgomery Co Improvement Dist	5170512	.010000	
Pattonville			
Lamar Co	4139004	.005000	.067500
Pawelekville			
Karnes Co	4128007	.005000	.067500
Pawnee			
Bee Co	4013005	.005000	.067500
Payne Springs (Henderson Co)	2107155	.017500	.080000
Pear Valley			.070000
McCulloch Co	4160006	.005000	
McCulloch County Hospital District	5160505	.002500	
Pearl			
Coryell Co	4050009	.005000	.067500
Pearland	2020024	.015000	
Brazoria Co	4020006	.005000	.082500
Pearland (Fort Bend Co)	2020024	.015000	.077500
Pearland (Harris Co)	2020024	.015000	.077500
Pearland (Harris Co)			.082500
Pearland Municipal Management Dist No. 1	5101650	.005000	
Pearland (Harris Co)			.082500
Spectrum Management Dist	5101696	.005000	
Pearsall	2082029	.015000	.082500
Frio Co	4082001	.005000	
Pearson			
Medina Co	4163003	.005000	.067500
Peaster			
Parker Co	4184008	.005000	.067500
Pecan Gap	2060025	.010000	.082500
Delta Co	4060007	.005000	
Delta Co Emergency Services District	5060506	.005000	
Pecan Gap	2060025	.010000	.077500
Fannin Co	4074001	.005000	
Pecan Hill (Ellis Co)	2070167	.010000	.072500
Pecangrove			.067500
Coryell Co	4050009	.005000	
Pecos (Reeves Co)	2195014	.015000	.082500
Reeves County Hospital District	5195504	.005000	
Peggy			
Atascosa Co	4007003	.005000	.067500
Pelham			
Navarro Co	4175009	.005000	.067500
Pelican Bay (Tarrant Co)	2220353	.010000	.072500
Pendleton			.067500
Bell Co	4014004	.005000	
Penelope	2109091	.010000	.077500
Hill Co	4109000	.005000	
Penitas (Hidalgo Co)	2108190	.015000	.082500
Penita Crime Control and Prevention District	5108537	.005000	
Penwell (Ector Co)			.070000
Ector County Hospital District	5068508	.007500	
Peoria			.067500
Hill Co	4109000	.005000	
Percilla			.067500
Houston Co	4113004	.005000	
Pernitas Point			.067500
Live Oak Co	4149002	.005000	
Perry			.067500
Falls Co	4073002	.005000	
Perryton (Ochiltree Co)	2179014	.020000	.082500
Perryville			.067500
Wood Co	4250007	.005000	
Peters			.067500
Austin Co	4008002	.005000	
Petersburg	2095042	.010000	.077500
Hale Co	4095006	.005000	
Petrolia (Clay Co)	2039032	.010000	.072500
Petronila (Nueces Co)	2178079	.010000	.072500
Pettibone			.067500
Milam Co	4166000	.005000	
Pettit			.067500
Comanche Co	4047005	.005000	
Pettus			.067500
Bee Co	4013005	.005000	
Petty			.067500
Lamar Co	4139004	.005000	
Pflugerville (Travis Co)	2227043	.015000	.082500

¶905

Part III—Sales and Use Taxes

Travis County Emergency Services District No.2	5227524	.005000	
Pflugerville (Williamson Co)	2227043	.015000	.077500
Pharr (Hidalgo Co)	2108127	.020000	.082500
Phelps			.067500
Walker Co	4236006	.005000	
Pickton			.067500
Hopkins Co	4112005	.005000	
Pidcoke			.067500
Coryell Co	4050009	.005000	
Pierce			.067500
Wharton Co	4241009	.005000	
Pierces Chapel			.067500
Cherokee Co	4037007	.005000	
Pilot Point (Denton Co)	2061042	.020000	.082500
Pine			.067500
Camp Co	4032002	.005000	
Pine Forest			.067500
Hopkins Co	4112005	.005000	
Pine Forest	2181074	.015000	.082500
Orange Co	4181001	.005000	
Pine Hill			.067500
Cherokee Co	4037007	.005000	
Pine Mills			.067500
Wood Co	4250007	.005000	
Pine Prairie			.067500
Walker Co	4236006	.005000	
Pine Valley			.067500
Angelina Co	4003007	.005000	
Pinehurst	2181065	.015000	.082500
Orange Co	4181001	.005000	
Pineland	2202024	.010000	.077500
Sabine Co	4202006	.005000	
Piney Point Village (Harris Co)	2101295	.010000	.082500
Houston MTA	3101990	.010000	
Pipe Creek			.067500
Bandera Co	4010008	.005000	
Pisek			.067500
Colorado Co	4045007	.005000	
Pittsburg	2032011	.015000	.082500
Camp Co	4032002	.005000	
Placedo			.067500
Victoria Co	4235007	.005000	
Placid			.070000
McCulloch Co	4160006	.005000	
McCulloch County Hospital District	5160505	.002500	
Plains (Yoakum Co)	2251015	.015000	.077500
Plainview	2095015	.015000	.082500
Hale Co	4095006	.005000	
Plainview			.067500
Sabine Co	4202006	.005000	
Plano (Collin Co)	2043018	.010000	.082500
Dallas MTA	3057994	.010000	
Plano (Denton Co)	2043018	.010000	.082500
Dallas MTA	3057994	.010000	
Plantersville			.067500
Grimes Co	4093008	.005000	
Pleak (Fort Bend Co)	2079140	.017500	.080000
Pleasant Grove			.067500
Falls Co	4073002	.005000	
Pleasant Hill			.067500
Polk Co	4187005	.005000	
Pleasant Valley (Wichita Co)	2243052	.010000	.072500
Pleasanton	2007049	.015000	.082500
Atascosa Co	4007003	.005000	
Pluck			.067500
Polk Co	4187005	.005000	
Plum			.067500
Fayette Co	4075000	.005000	
Plum Grove	2146041	.010000	.077500
Liberty Co	4146005	.005000	
Poesville			.067500
Bosque Co	4018000	.005000	
Point	2190028	.015000	.082500
Rains Co	4190000	.005000	
Point Blank	2204031	.010000	.077500
San Jacinto Co	4204004	.005000	
Point Comfort	2029034	.010000	.077500
Calhoun Co	4029007	.005000	

¶905

Guidebook to Texas Taxes

Point Venture (Travis Co)	2227196	.010000	.082500
Austin MTA	3227999	.010000	
Pollok			.067500
Angelina Co	4003007	.005000	
Ponder (Denton Co)	2061239	.017500	.080000
Ponta			.067500
Cherokee Co	4037007	.005000	
Pontotoc (Mason Co)			.072500
Mason County Health Services	5157500	.010000	
Pony			.067500
Runnels Co	4200008	.005000	
Poolville			.067500
Parker Co	4184008	.005000	
Port Alto			.067500
Calhoun Co	4029007	.005000	
Port Aransas (Nueces Co)	2178024	.015000	.082500
Corpus Christi MTA	3178998	.005000	
Port Arthur	2123020	.015000	.082500
Jefferson Co	4123002	.005000	
Port Arthur	2123020	.015000	.082500
Orange Co	4181001	.005000	
Port Isabel (Cameron Co)	2031058	.020000	.082500
Port Lavaca	2029025	.015000	.082500
Calhoun Co	4029007	.005000	
Port Neches	2123075	.015000	.082500
Jefferson Co	4123002	.005000	
Port O Connor			.067500
Calhoun Co	4029007	.005000	
Porter (Montgomery Co)			.072500
East Montgomery Co Improvement Dist	5170512	.010000	
Porter Springs			.067500
Houston Co	4113004	.005000	
Portland (Nueces Co)	2205076	.020000	.082500
Portland (San Patricio Co)	2205076	.020000	.082500
Posey			.067500
Lubbock Co	4152006	.005000	
Possum Kingdom Lake			.067500
Palo Pinto Co	4182000	.005000	
Post (Garza Co)	2085017	.020000	.082500
Post Oak			.067500
Houston Co	4113004	.005000	
Post Oak Bend (Kaufman Co)	2129104	.015000	.077500
Poteet	2007021	.015000	.082500
Atascosa Co	4007003	.005000	
Poth (Wilson Co)	2247049	.017500	.080000
Pottsboro (Grayson Co)	2091117	.020000	.082500
Pottsville			.067500
Hamilton Co	4097004	.005000	
Powderly			.067500
Lamar Co	4139004	.005000	
Powell			.067500
Navarro Co	4175009	.005000	
Poynor (Henderson Co)	2107137	.010000	.072500
Praesel			.067500
Milam Co	4166000	.005000	
Praha			.067500
Fayette Co	4075000	.005000	
Prairie Dell			.067500
Bell Co	4014004	.005000	
Prairie Hill			.067500
Washington Co	4239003	.005000	
Prairie Lea			.067500
Caldwell Co	4028008	.005000	
Prairie Point			.067500
Cooke Co	4049003	.005000	
Prairie View (Waller Co)	2237041	.017500	.082500
Prairie View Crime Control District	5237504	.002500	
Premont	2125037	.015000	.082500
Jim Wells Co	4125000	.005000	
Presidio (Presidio Co)	2189021	.020000	.082500
Primera (Cameron Co)	2031129	.020000	.082500
Primrose			.067500
Atascosa Co	4007003	.005000	
Princeton (Collin Co)	2043081	.020000	.082500
Pritchett			.067500
Upshur Co	4230002	.005000	
Proctor			.067500
Comanche Co	4047005	.005000	
Progreso (Hidalgo Co)	2108181	.020000	.082500

¶905

Part III—Sales and Use Taxes

Progreso Lakes (Hidalgo Co)	2108154	.015000	.077500
			.067500
Progress			
Bailey Co	4009001	.005000	
Prosper (Collin Co)	2043125	.020000	.082500
Providence			.067500
Polk Co	4187005	.005000	
Provident City			.067500
Colorado Co	4045007	.005000	
Pumphrey			.067500
Runnels Co	4200008	.005000	
Punkin Center			.067500
Dawson Co	4058001	.005000	
Purdon			.067500
Navarro Co	4175009	.005000	
Purmela			.067500
Coryell Co	4050009	.005000	
Pursley			.067500
Navarro Co	4175009	.005000	
Putnam (Callahan Co)	2030040	.010000	.072500
Pyote (Ward Co)	2238059	.010000	.072500
Pyron			.067500
Scurry Co	4208000	.005000	
Quanah	2099011	.015000	.082500
Hardeman Co	4099002	.005000	
Queen City (Cass Co)	2034064	.017500	.080000
Quemado			.072500
Maverick Co	4159009	.005000	
Maverick Co LFW and CDC District	5159508	.005000	
Quihi			.067500
Medina Co	4163003	.005000	
Quinlan	2116065	.015000	.082500
Hunt Co	4116001	.005000	
Quintana	2020195	.010000	.077500
Brazoria Co	4020006	.005000	
Quitaque (Briscoe Co)	2023012	.020000	.082500
Quitman	2250034	.015000	.082500
Wood Co	4250007	.005000	
Rabb (Nueces Co)			.067500
Corpus Christi MTA	3178998	.005000	
Rabbs Prairie			.067500
Fayette Co	4075000	.005000	
Raccoon Bend			.067500
Austin Co	4008002	.005000	
Rachel (Brooks Co)			.067500
Brooks Co Health Services	5024501	.005000	
Raisin			.067500
Victoria Co	4235007	.005000	
Raleigh			.067500
Navarro Co	4175009	.005000	
Ralls	2054032	.015000	.082500
Crosby Co	4054005	.005000	
Rancho Viejo (Cameron Co)	2031138	.010000	.072500
Randado (Jim Hogg Co)			.082500
Jim Hogg Co	4124001	.010000	
Jim Hogg County Assistance District	5124519	.005000	
Jim Hogg County Health Services	5124500	.005000	
Randolph			.067500
Fannin Co	4074001	.005000	
Ranger (Eastland Co)	2067028	.020000	.082500
Rankin (Upton Co)	2231010	.015000	.077500
Ransom Canyon	2152088	.005000	.072500
Lubbock Co	4152006	.005000	
Ratcliff			.067500
Houston Co	4113004	.005000	
Ratibor			.067500
Bell Co	4014004	.005000	
Ravenna	2074118	.010000	.077500
Fannin Co	4074001	.005000	
Ray Point			.067500
Live Oak Co	4149002	.005000	
Rayburn			.067500
Liberty Co	4146005	.005000	
Raymondville (Willacy Co)	2245014	.020000	.082500
Raywood			.067500
Liberty Co	4146005	.005000	
Reagan			.067500
Falls Co	4073002	.005000	
Red Oak (Ellis Co)	2070078	.020000	.082500
Red Ranger			.067500

¶905

Bell Co	4014004	.005000	
Red Rock			.067500
Bastrop Co	4011007	.005000	
Red Springs (Baylor Co)			.072500
Baylor County Hospital District	5012505	.010000	
Redbank			.067500
Bowie Co	4019009	.005000	
Redland			.067500
Angelina Co	4003007	.005000	
Redlawn			.067500
Cherokee Co	4037007	.005000	
Redlick			.067500
Bowie Co	4019009	.005000	
Redwater			.082500
Bowie Co	2019081 4019009	.015000 .005000	
Redwood			.067500
Guadalupe Co	4094007	.005000	
Reedville			.067500
Caldwell Co	4028008	.005000	
Reese			.067500
Cherokee Co	4037007	.005000	
Reese Village			.067500
Lubbock Co	4152006	.005000	
Refuge			.067500
Houston Co	4113004	.005000	
Refugio (Refugio Co)	2196013	.020000	.082500
Rek Hill			.067500
Fayette Co	4075000	.005000	
Reklaw	2201052 4037007	.010000 .005000	.077500
Cherokee Co			
Reklaw (Rusk Co)	2201052	.010000	.072500
Reliance			.067500
Brazos Co	4021005	.005000	
Reno	2139059	.010000	.082500
Lamar Co	4139004	.005000	
Reno Crime Control and Prevention District	5139503	.005000	
Reno	2184062	.012500	.080000
Parker Co	4184008	.005000	
Reno (Tarrant Co)	2184062	.012500	.075000
Retreat			.067500
Navarro Co	4175009	.005000	
Reynard			.067500
Houston Co	4113004	.005000	
Rhome	2249038	.015000	.082500
Wise Co	4249001	.005000	
Rhonesboro			.067500
Upshur Co	4230002	.005000	
Ricardo			.067500
Kleberg Co	4137006	.005000	
Rice (Ellis Co)	2175063	.012500	.075000
Rice	2175063	.012500	.080000
Navarro Co	4175009	.005000	
Richards			.067500
Grimes Co	4093008	.005000	
Richardson (Collin Co)	2057048 3057994	.010000 .010000	.082500
Dallas MTA			
Richardson (Dallas Co)	2057048 3057994	.010000 .010000	.082500
Dallas MTA			
Richland	2175072	.010000	.077500
Navarro Co	4175009	.005000	
Richland Hills (Tarrant Co)	2220157	.011250	.082500
Fort Worth MTA	3220996	.005000	
Richland Hills Crime Control and Prevention District	5220727	.003750	
Richland Springs			.067500
San Saba Co	4206002	.005000	
Richmond (Fort Bend Co)	2079042	.020000	.082500
Richwood	2020140	.012500	.080000
Brazoria Co	4020006	.005000	
Ridgeway			.067500
Hopkins Co	4112005	.005000	
Riesel	2161158	.012500	.080000
McClennan Co	4161005	.005000	
Rio Bravo	2240028	.010000	.077500
Webb Co	4240000	.005000	
Rio Frio			.067500
Real Co	4193007	.005000	
Rio Grande City (Starr Co)	2214020	.020000	.082500

¶905

Part III—Sales and Use Taxes

Location	Code	Rate	Total
Rio Hondo (Cameron Co)	2031067	.020000	.082500
Rio Vista (Johnson Co)	2126036	.015000	.077500
Riomedina			.067500
Medina Co	4163003	.005000	
Rising Star (Eastland Co)	2067055	.015000	.077500
River Oaks (Tarrant Co)	2220077	.015000	.082500
River Oaks Crime Control District	5220576	.005000	
Riverside	2236033	.015000	.082500
Walker Co	4236006	.005000	
Riviera			.067500
Kleberg Co	4137006	.005000	
Riviera Beach			.067500
Kleberg Co	4137006	.005000	
Roane			.067500
Navarro Co	4175009	.005000	
Roanoke (Denton Co)	2061131	.020000	.082500
Roans Prairie			.067500
Grimes Co	4093008	.005000	
Roaring Springs (Motley Co)	2173029	.020000	.082500
Robbins			.067500
Leon Co	4145006	.005000	
Robert Lee (Coke Co)	2041010	.020000	.082500
Robertson			.067500
Crosby Co	4054005	.005000	
Robinson	2161149	.015000	.082500
McClennan Co	4161005	.005000	
Robstown (Nueces Co)	2178033	.015000	.082500
Corpus Christi MTA	3178998	.005000	
Roby (Fisher Co)	2076027	.010000	.072500
Rochelle			.070000
McCulloch Co	4160006	.005000	
McCulloch County Hospital District	5160505	.002500	
Rochester (Haskell Co)	2104032	.010000	.072500
Rock Creek			.067500
McClennan Co	4161005	.005000	
Rock Hill			.067500
Wood Co	4250007	.005000	
Rock Island			.067500
Colorado Co	4045007	.005000	
Rockdale	2166037	.010000	.082500
Milam Co	4166000	.005000	
Rockdale Hospital District	5166509	.005000	
Rockland			.067500
Tyler Co	4229005	.005000	
Rockne			.067500
Bastrop Co	4011007	.005000	
Rockport	2004015	.010000	.082500
Aransas Co	4004006	.005000	
Aransas County Health Services	5004505	.005000	
Rocksprings (Edwards Co)	2069017	.017500	.080000
Rockwall (Rockwall Co)	2199029	.020000	.082500
Rocky Branch			.067500
Morris Co	4172002	.005000	
Rocky Hill			.067500
Falls Co	4073002	.005000	
Rocky Mound	2032020	.010000	.077500
Camp Co	4032002	.005000	
Rogers	2014059	.010000	.077500
Bell Co	4014004	.005000	
Rogers Hill			.067500
McClennan Co	4161005	.005000	
Rolling Meadows			.067500
Gregg Co	4092009	.005000	
Rollingwood (Travis Co)	2227052	.015000	.082500
Westbank Community Library District	5227506	.005000	
Roma (Starr Co)	2214011	.020000	.082500
Roman Forest (Montgomery Co)			.072500
East Montgomery Co Improvement Dist	5170512	.010000	
Romayor			.067500
Liberty Co	4146005	.005000	
Roosevelt (Kimble Co)			.067500
Kimble Co Emergency Services Dist	5134508	.005000	
Ropesville (Hockley Co)	2110034	.017500	.080000
Rosanky			.067500
Bastrop Co	4011007	.005000	
Roscoe (Nolan Co)	2177025	.020000	.082500
Rose City	2181056	.015000	.082500
Orange Co	4181001	.005000	
Rose Hill (Harris Co)			.072500

¶905

Houston MTA	3101990	.010000	
Rosebud	2073039	.015000	.082500
Falls Co	4073002	.005000	
Rosenberg (Fort Bend Co)	2079015	.020000	.082500
Rosenthal			.067500
McClennan Co	4161005	.005000	
Rosevine			.067500
Sabine Co	4202006	.005000	
Rosewood			.067500
Upshur Co	4230002	.005000	
Rosharon			.067500
Brazoria Co	4020006	.005000	
Ross	2161194	.010000	.077500
McClennan Co	4161005	.005000	
Rosser (Kaufman Co)	2129088	.010000	.072500
Rosston			.067500
Cooke Co	4049003	.005000	
Rossville			.067500
Atascosa Co	4007003	.005000	
Roswell			.067500
Bosque Co	4018000	.005000	
Rotan (Fisher Co)	2076018	.020000	.082500
Round Mountain	2016039	.010000	.082500
Blanco Co	4016002	.005000	
Blanco County North Library District	5016510	.005000	
Round Prairie			.067500
Navarro Co	4175009	.005000	
Round Rock (Travis Co)	2246022	.020000	.082500
Round Rock (Williamson Co)	2246022	.020000	.082500
Round Top	2075064	.015000	.082500
Fayette Co	4075000	.005000	
Rowena			.067500
Runnels Co	4200008	.005000	
Rowlett (Dallas Co)	2057235	.010000	.082500
Dallas MTA	3057994	.010000	
Rowlett (Rockwall Co)	2057235	.010000	.082500
Dallas MTA	3057994	.010000	
Roxton	2139040	.010000	.077500
Lamar Co	4139004	.005000	
Royse City (Collin Co)	2199010	.020000	.082500
Royse City (Rockwall Co)	2199010	.020000	.082500
Rucker			.072500
Comanche Co	4047005	.005000	
De Leon Hospital District	5047504	.005000	
Rule (Haskell Co)	2104041	.010000	.072500
Rumley			.067500
Lampasas Co	4141000	.005000	
Runaway Bay	2249109	.015000	.082500
Wise Co	4249001	.005000	
Runge	2128034	.015000	.082500
Karnes Co	4128007	.005000	
Rush Prairie			.067500
Navarro Co	4175009	.005000	
Rusk	2037034	.015000	.082500
Cherokee Co	4037007	.005000	
Rutersville			.067500
Fayette Co	4075000	.005000	
Rye			.067500
Brazos Co	4021005	.005000	
Rye			.067500
Liberty Co	4146005	.005000	
Sabinal	2232028	.010000	.082500
Uvalde Co	4232000	.005000	
Uvalde County Health Services	5232509	.005000	
Sachse (Collin Co)	2057191	.015000	.077500
Sachse (Dallas Co)	2057191	.015000	.077500
Sacul (Nacogdoches Co)			.072500
Nacogdoches County Hospital District	5174509	.010000	
Sadler (Grayson Co)	2091153	.010000	.072500
Saginaw (Tarrant Co)	2220139	.016250	.082500
Saginaw Crime Control District	5220585	.003750	
Saint Hedwig (Bexar Co)	2015218	.010000	.077500
San Antonio MTA	3015995	.005000	
Saint Jo (Montague Co)	2169025	.020000	.082500
Saint Paul (Collin Co)	2043232	.010000	.072500
Salado	2014120	.010000	.082500
Bell Co	4014004	.005000	
Salado Public Library District	5014503	.005000	
Salesville			.067500

¶905

Part III—Sales and Use Taxes

Palo Pinto Co	4182000	.005000	
Salmon			.067500
Anderson Co	4001009	.005000	
Saltillo			.067500
Hopkins Co	4112005	.005000	
Salty			.067500
Milam Co	4166000	.005000	
San Angelo	2226017	.015000	.082500
Tom Green Co	4226008	.005000	
San Antonio (Bexar Co)	2015012	.011250	.081250
San Antonio ATD	3015664	.002500	
San Antonio MTA	3015995	.005000	
San Augustine	2203014	.015000	.082500
San Augustine Co	4203005	.005000	
San Benito (Cameron Co)	2031021	.020000	.082500
San Diego (Duval Co)	2066029	.015000	.077500
San Diego Municipal Development Dist	5066500	.005000	
San Diego	2066029	.015000	.082500
Jim Wells Co	4125000	.005000	
San Elizario			.072500
El Paso Co	4071004	.005000	
El Paso Co Es Dis No2	5071503	.005000	
San Felipe	2008039	.015000	.082500
Austin Co	4008002	.005000	
San Gabriel			.067500
Milam Co	4166000	.005000	
San Juan (Hidalgo Co)	2108109	.020000	.082500
San Leanna (Travis Co)			.072500
Austin MTA	3227999	.010000	
San Marcos	2105022	.015000	.082500
Hays Co	4105004	.005000	
San Patricio (San Patricio Co)			.067500
Corpus Christi MTA	3178998	.005000	
San Pedro (Nueces Co)			.067500
Corpus Christi MTA	3178998	.005000	
San Saba	2206011	.015000	.082500
San Saba Co	4206002	.005000	
Sanctuary	2184133	.012500	.080000
Parker Co	4184008	.005000	
Sand Hill			.067500
Upshur Co	4230002	.005000	
Sanderson			.077500
Terrell Co	4222002	.015000	
Sandia			.067500
Jim Wells Co	4125000	.005000	
Sandy			.067500
Blanco Co	4016002	.005000	
Sandy Corner			.067500
Wharton Co	4241009	.005000	
Sandy Creek			.067500
Milam Co	4166000	.005000	
Sandy Fork			.067500
Gonzales Co	4089004	.005000	
Sandy Point			.067500
Brazoria Co	4020006	.005000	
Sanford (Hutchinson Co)	2117037	.010000	.072500
Sanger (Denton Co)	2061079	.020000	.082500
Sansom Park (Tarrant Co)	2220068	.015000	.082500
Sansom Park Crime Control District	5220674	.005000	
Santa Anna (Coleman Co)	2042019	.020000	.082500
Santa Clara	2094098	.010000	.077500
Guadalupe Co	4094007	.005000	
Santa Fe (Galveston Co)	2084116	.020000	.082500
Santa Rosa (Cameron Co)	2031030	.010000	.072500
Santo			.067500
Palo Pinto Co	4182000	.005000	
Saragosa (Reeves Co)			.067500
Reeves County Hospital District	5195504	.005000	
Sash			.067500
Fannin Co	4074001	.005000	
Satin			.067500
Falls Co	4073002	.005000	
Satsuma (Harris Co)			.072500
Houston MTA	3101990	.010000	
Sattler			.082500
Comal Co	4046006	.005000	
Canyon Lake Community Lib Dist	5046505	.005000	
Comal Co Emergency Services District No. 3	5046523	.010000	

¶905

Saturn			.067500
Gonzales Co	4089004	.005000	
Savoy	2074083	.015000	.082500
Fannin Co	4074001	.005000	
Sayers			.067500
Bastrop Co	4011007	.005000	
Schertz (Bexar Co)	2094025	.015000	.077500
Schertz	2094025	.015000	.082500
Comal Co	4046006	.005000	
Schertz	2094025	.015000	.082500
Guadalupe Co	4094007	.005000	
Schulenburg	2075028	.015000	.082500
Fayette Co	4075000	.005000	
Schumannsville			.067500
Guadalupe Co	4094007	.005000	
Schwab City			.067500
Polk Co	4187005	.005000	
Scotland	2005032	.015000	.082500
Archer Co	4005005	.005000	
Scottsville (Harrison Co)	2102043	.010000	.072500
Scroggins			.067500
Franklin Co	4080003	.005000	
Scurry (Kaufman Co)	2129122	.010000	.072500
Seabrook (Harris Co)	2101197	.015000	.082500
Seabrook Crime Control and Prevention Dist	5101570	.005000	
Seadrift	2029016	.015000	.082500
Calhoun Co	4029007	.005000	
Seagoville (Dallas Co)	2057208	.020000	.082500
Seagoville (Kaufman Co)	2057208	.020000	.082500
Seagraves (Gaines Co)	2083028	.020000	.082500
Sealy	2008011	.015000	.082500
Austin Co	4008002	.005000	
Seaton			.067500
Bell Co	4014004	.005000	
Seco Mines			.072500
Maverick Co	4159009	.005000	
Maverick Co LFW and CDC District	5159508	.005000	
Segno			.067500
Polk Co	4187005	.005000	
Segovia (Kimble Co)			.067500
Kimble Co Emergency Services Dist	5134508	.005000	
Seguin	2094016	.015000	.082500
Guadalupe Co	4094007	.005000	
Selden			.067500
Erath Co	4072003	.005000	
Selma (Bexar Co)	2015174	.015000	.082500
Selma Municipal Development District	5015520	.005000	
Selma	2015174	.015000	.082500
Comal Co	4046006	.005000	
Selma	2015174	.015000	.082500
Guadalupe Co	4094007	.005000	
Seminole (Gaines Co)	2083019	.015000	.077500
Serbin			.067500
Lee Co	4144007	.005000	
Seth Ward			.067500
Hale Co	4095006	.005000	
Seven Oaks	2187041	.010000	.077500
Polk Co	4187005	.005000	
Seven Pines			.067500
Upshur Co	4230002	.005000	
Seven Points (Henderson Co)	2107048	.020000	.082500
Seven Points (Kaufman Co)	2107048	.020000	.082500
Sexton			.067500
Sabine Co	4202006	.005000	
Seymore			.067500
Hopkins Co	4112005	.005000	
Seymour (Baylor Co)	2012015	.010000	.082500
Baylor County Hospital District	5012505	.010000	
Shady Grove			.067500
Angelina Co	4003007	.005000	
Shady Shores (Denton Co)	2061168	.010000	.072500
Shallowater	2152079	.010000	.077500
Lubbock Co	4152006	.005000	
Shamrock (Wheeler Co)	2242026	.017500	.080000
Sharp			.067500
Milam Co	4166000	.005000	
Shavano Park (Bexar Co)	2015209	.010000	.082500
San Antonio MTA	3015995	.005000	

¶905

Part III—Sales and Use Taxes

Shavano Park Crime Control District	5015511	.005000	
Shelby			.067500
Austin Co	4008002	.005000	
Shenandoah (Montgomery Co)	2170095	.015000	.082500
Shenandoah Municipal Dev. Dist.	5170665	.005000	
Shepherd	2204013	.015000	.082500
San Jacinto Co	4204004	.005000	
Sheridan			.072500
Colorado Co	4045007	.005000	
Rice Hospital District	5045506	.005000	
Sherman (Grayson Co)	2091028	.020000	.082500
Shiner (Lavaca Co)	2143044	.010000	.072500
Shirley			.067500
Hopkins Co	4112005	.005000	
Shiro			.067500
Grimes Co	4093008	.005000	
Shive			.067500
Hamilton Co	4097004	.005000	
Shoreacres (Chambers Co)	2101259	.012500	.080000
Chambers Co Health Ser	5036507	.005000	
Shoreacres (Harris Co)	2101259	.012500	.075000
Sidney			.067500
Comanche Co	4047005	.005000	
Siloam			.067500
Bowie Co	4019009	.005000	
Silsbee (Hardin Co)	2100018	.020000	.082500
Silver City			.067500
Navarro Co	4175009	.005000	
Silver City			.067500
Red River Co	4194006	.005000	
Silverton (Briscoe Co)	2023021	.017500	.080000
Simms			.067500
Bowie Co	4019009	.005000	
Simonton (Fort Bend Co)	2079122	.020000	.082500
Singleton			.067500
Grimes Co	4093008	.005000	
Sinton (San Patricio Co)	2205049	.020000	.082500
Sipe Springs			.067500
Comanche Co	4047005	.005000	
Sisterdale			.067500
Kendall Co	4130003	.005000	
Skellytown (Carson Co)	2033047	.012500	.075000
Skidmore			.067500
Bee Co	4013005	.005000	
Slaton	2152024	.015000	.082500
Lubbock Co	4152006	.005000	
Slide			.067500
Lubbock Co	4152006	.005000	
Slidell			.067500
Wise Co	4249001	.005000	
Slocum			.067500
Anderson Co	4001009	.005000	
Smetana			.067500
Brazos Co	4021005	.005000	
Smiley	2089031	.010000	.077500
Gonzales Co	4089004	.005000	
Smith Hill			.067500
Bowie Co	4019009	.005000	
Smith Point (Chambers Co)			.067500
Chambers Co Health Ser	5036507	.005000	
Smithland			.067500
Marion Co	4155003	.005000	
Smiths Bend			.067500
Bosque Co	4018000	.005000	
Smithson Valley			.067500
Comal Co	4046006	.005000	
Smithville	2011034	.015000	.082500
Bastrop Co	4011007	.005000	
Snook	2026037	.015000	.082500
Burleson Co	4026000	.005000	
Snow Hill			.067500
Polk Co	4187005	.005000	
Snyder	2208019	.015000	.082500
Scurry Co	4208000	.005000	
Socorro	2071059	.010000	.082500
El Paso Co	4071004	.005000	
El Paso Co Es Dis No2	5071503	.005000	
Soda			.067500
Polk Co	4187005	.005000	

Solms			.067500
Comal Co	4046006	.005000	
Somerset (Bexar Co)	2015165	.020000	.082500
Somerville	2026028	.015000	.082500
Burleson Co	4026000	.005000	
Sonora (Sutton Co)	2218017	.017500	.080000
Soules Chapel			.067500
Upshur Co	4230002	.005000	
Sour Lake (Hardin Co)	2100036	.020000	.082500
South Bend			.067500
Young Co	4252005	.005000	
South Elm			.067500
Milam Co	4166000	.005000	
South Houston (Harris Co)	2101188	.017500	.082500
South Houston Crime Control and Prevention District	5101552	.002500	
South Mountain			.067500
Coryell Co	4050009	.005000	
South Padre Island (Cameron Co)	2031101	.020000	.082500
South Purmela			.067500
Coryell Co	4050009	.005000	
South San Pedro (Nueces Co)			.067500
Corpus Christi MTA	3178998	.005000	
South Sulphur			.067500
Hunt Co	4116001	.005000	
South Texarkana			.067500
Bowie Co	4019009	.005000	
Southlake (Denton Co)	2220273	.015000	.082500
Southlake Crime Control District	5220594	.005000	
Southlake (Tarrant Co)	2220273	.015000	.082500
Southlake Crime Control District	5220594	.005000	
Southmayd (Grayson Co)	2091144	.020000	.082500
Southside Place (Harris Co)	2101062	.010000	.082500
Houston MTA	3101990	.010000	
Spanish Camp			.067500
Wharton Co	4241009	.005000	
Sparenberg			.067500
Dawson Co	4058001	.005000	
Sparks			.067500
Bell Co	4014004	.005000	
Spearman (Hansford Co)	2098012	.020000	.082500
Speegleville			.067500
McClennan Co	4161005	.005000	
Splendora (Montgomery Co)	2170059	.010000	.082500
East Montgomery Co Improvement Dist	5170512	.010000	
Spofford			.072500
Kinney Co	4136007	.005000	
Kinney County Health Services	5136506	.005000	
Spring (Harris Co)			.072500
Houston MTA	3101990	.010000	
Spring Branch			.072500
Comal Co	4046006	.005000	
Bulverde Area Lib Dist	5046514	.005000	
Spring Creek			.067500
Gillespie Co	4086007	.005000	
Spring Valley (Harris Co)	2101071	.010000	.082500
Houston MTA	3101990	.010000	
Spring Valley			.067500
McClennan Co	4161005	.005000	
Springfield			.067500
Anderson Co	4001009	.005000	
Springfield			.067500
Jim Wells Co	4125000	.005000	
Springhill			.067500
Navarro Co	4175009	.005000	
Springtown	2184017	.015000	.082500
Parker Co	4184008	.005000	
Spur	2063013	.015000	.082500
Dickens Co	4063004	.005000	
Spurger			.067500
Tyler Co	4229005	.005000	
Stafford (Fort Bend Co)	2079033	.020000	.082500
Stafford (Harris Co)	2079033	.020000	.082500
Stagecoach (Montgomery Co)	2170148	.010000	.072500
Stairtown			.067500
Caldwell Co	4028008	.005000	
Stamford (Haskell Co)	2127035	.020000	.082500
Stamford (Jones Co)	2127035	.020000	.082500
Stampede			.067500

¶905

Part III—Sales and Use Taxes

Bell Co	4014004	.005000	
Stamps			.067500
Upshur Co	4230002	.005000	
Stanton (Martin Co)	2156011	.017500	.080000
Staples			.067500
Guadalupe Co	4094007	.005000	
Startzville			.082500
Comal Co	4046006	.005000	
Canyon Lake Community Lib Dist	5046505	.005000	
Comal Co Emergency Services District No. 3	5046523	.010000	
Steep Hollow			.067500
Brazos Co	4021005	.005000	
Stellar			.067500
Fayette Co	4075000	.005000	
Stephen Creek			.067500
San Jacinto Co	4204004	.005000	
Stephenville	2072021	.015000	.082500
Erath Co	4072003	.005000	
Sterling City (Sterling Co)	2216019	.015000	.077500
Stinnett (Hutchinson Co)	2117046	.020000	.082500
Stockdale (Wilson Co)	2247021	.015000	.077500
Stoneham			.067500
Grimes Co	4093008	.005000	
Stonewall			.067500
Gillespie Co	4086007	.005000	
Stormville			.067500
Wood Co	4250007	.005000	
Stowell (Chambers Co)			.067500
Chambers Co Health Ser	5036507	.005000	
Stratford (Sherman Co)	2211014	.015000	.077500
Strawn	2182028	.015000	.082500
Palo Pinto Co	4182000	.005000	
Streeter (Mason Co)			.072500
Mason County Health Services	5157500	.010000	
Streetman (Freestone Co)	2081048	.012500	.075000
Streetman	2081048	.012500	.080000
Navarro Co	4175009	.005000	
Strickland			.067500
Sabine Co	4202006	.005000	
String Prairie			.067500
Bastrop Co	4011007	.005000	
Study Butte			.067500
Brewster Co	4022004	.005000	
Sudan (Lamb Co)	2140056	.015000	.077500
Suffolk			.067500
Upshur Co	4230002	.005000	
Sugar Land (Fort Bend Co)	2079051	.020000	.082500
Sullivan City (Hidalgo Co)	2108216	.015000	.082500
Sullivan City Crime Control and Prevention Dist	5108519	.005000	
Sulphur Bluff			.067500
Hopkins Co	4112005	.005000	
Sulphur Springs			.067500
Angelina Co	4003007	.005000	
Sulphur Springs	2112014	.015000	.082500
Hopkins Co	4112005	.005000	
Summerfield			.067500
Castro Co	4035009	.005000	
Summerville			.067500
Gonzales Co	4089004	.005000	
Sumner			.067500
Lamar Co	4139004	.005000	
Sun Valley	2139077	.010000	.077500
Lamar Co	4139004	.005000	
Sundown (Hockley Co)	2110043	.020000	.082500
Sunnyside			.067500
Castro Co	4035009	.005000	
Sunnyvale (Dallas Co)	2057244	.020000	.082500
Sunray (Moore Co)	2171021	.010000	.072500
Sunrise			.067500
Falls Co	4073002	.005000	
Sunrise Beach (Llano Co)	2150026	.010000	.072500
Sunset (Montague Co)	2169043	.000000	.062500
Sunset Valley (Travis Co)	2227070	.018750	.081250
Surfside Beach	2020168	.010000	.077500
Brazoria Co	4020006	.005000	
Swan			.067500
Smith Co	4212004	.005000	

¶905

Sweeny			.082500
Brazoria Co	2020122	.015000	
Sweeny Switch	4020006	.005000	
Live Oak Co	4149002	.005000	.067500
Sweetwater			.067500
Comanche Co	4047005	.005000	
Sweetwater (Nolan Co)	2177016	.020000	.082500
Swiss Alp			.067500
Fayette Co	4075000	.005000	
Sylvan			.067500
Lamar Co	4139004	.005000	
Tabor			.067500
Brazos Co	4021005	.005000	
Taft (San Patricio Co)	2205030	.017500	.080000
Tahoka	2153014	.015000	.082500
Lynn Co	4153005	.005000	
Talton			.067500
Wharton Co	4241009	.005000	
Talco	2225027	.010000	.077500
Titus Co	4225009	.005000	
Talty (Kaufman Co)	2129113	.017500	.080000
Tanglewood			.067500
Lee Co	4144007	.005000	
Tankersly			.067500
Tom Green Co	4226008	.005000	
Tarkington Prairie			.067500
Liberty Co	4146005	.005000	
Tarpley			.067500
Bandera Co	4010008	.005000	
Tatum (Panola Co)	2201034	.017500	.080000
Tatum (Rusk Co)	2201034	.017500	.080000
Taylor (Williamson Co)	2246013	.020000	.082500
Taylor Lake Village (Harris Co)	2101277	.010000	.082500
Houston MTA	3101990	.010000	
Taylor Town			.067500
Lamar Co	4139004	.005000	
Taylorsville			.067500
Caldwell Co	4028008	.005000	
Teague (Freestone Co)	2081020	.020000	.082500
Teaselville			.067500
Smith Co	4212004	.005000	
Tecula			.067500
Cherokee Co	4037007	.005000	
Telegraph (Kimble Co)			.067500
Kimble Co Emergency Services Dist	5134508	.005000	
Telephone			.067500
Fannin Co	4074001	.005000	
Telferner			.067500
Victoria Co	4235007	.005000	
Tell			.067500
Childress Co	4038006	.005000	
Temple	2014013	.015000	.082500
Bell Co	4014004	.005000	
Tenaha (Shelby Co)	2210042	.010000	.072500
Tennessee Colony			.067500
Anderson Co	4001009	.005000	
Terlingua			.067500
Brewster Co	4022004	.005000	
Terrell (Kaufman Co)	2129042	.020000	.082500
Terrell Hills (Bexar Co)	2015076	.010000	.077500
San Antonio MTA	3015995	.005000	
Terrys Chapel			.067500
Falls Co	4073002	.005000	
Texarkana	2019018	.015000	.082500
Bowie Co	4019009	.005000	
Texas City (Galveston Co)	2084090	.020000	.082500
Texline (Dallam Co)	2056021	.010000	.072500
The Colony (Denton Co)	2061195	.020000	.082500
The Colony/Denton Co Dev Dis 5 (Denton	6061603	.020000	.082500
The Grove			.067500
Coryell Co	4050009	.005000	
Thomas			.067500
Upshur Co	4230002	.005000	
Thompson (Harris Co)			.072500
Houston MTA	3101990	.010000	
Thompsons (Fort Bend Co)	2079113	.010000	.072500
Thompsonville			.067500
Gonzales Co	4089004	.005000	
Thorndale	2166019	.015000	.082500

¶905

Part III—Sales and Use Taxes

Milam Co	4166000	.005000	
Thorndale (Williamson Co)	2166019	.015000	.077500
Thornton (Limestone Co)	2147031	.010000	.072500
Thorntonville (Ward Co)	2238068	.010000	.072500
Thorp Spring			.067500
Hood Co	4111006	.005000	
Thrall (Williamson Co)	2246068	.012500	.075000
Three Rivers	2149020	.010000	.077500
Live Oak Co	4149002	.005000	
Throckmorton (Throckmorton Co)	2224019	.020000	.082500
Thurber			.067500
Erath Co	4072003	.005000	
Thurber			.067500
Palo Pinto Co	4182000	.005000	
Tiki Island (Galveston Co)	2084189	.010000	.072500
Tilmon			.067500
Caldwell Co	4028008	.005000	
Timpson (Shelby Co)	2210015	.010000	.077500
Timpson Public Library District	5210505	.005000	
Tioga (Grayson Co)	2091126	.020000	.082500
Tira			.067500
Hopkins Co	4112005	.005000	
Tivydale			.067500
Gillespie Co	4086007	.005000	
Toco	2139031	.010000	.077500
Lamar Co	4139004	.005000	
Todd Mission	2093026	.015000	.082500
Grimes Co	4093008	.005000	
Tokio			.067500
Terry Co	4223001	.005000	
Tolar	2111033	.015000	.082500
Hood Co	4111006	.005000	
Tom Bean (Grayson Co)	2091108	.020000	.082500
Tomball (Harris Co)	2101106	.020000	.082500
Tomball (Montgomery Co)	2101106	.020000	.082500
Tool (Henderson Co)	2107084	.010000	.072500
Topsey			.067500
Coryell Co	4050009	.005000	
Tornillo			.072500
El Paso Co	4071004	.005000	
El Paso Co Es Dis No2	5071503	.005000	
Tours			.067500
McClennan Co	4161005	.005000	
Town Center Econ Dev Zone No. 2	5170530	.010000	
Town Center Econ Dev Zone No. 3	5170549	.010000	
Towns Bluff			.067500
Tyler Co	4229005	.005000	
Toyah (Reeves Co)	2195023	.015000	.082500
Reeves County Hospital District	5195504	.005000	
Toyahvale (Reeves Co)			.067500
Reeves County Hospital District	5195504	.005000	
Travis			.067500
Falls Co	4073002	.005000	
Travis Peak (Travis Co)			.072500
Austin MTA	3227999	.010000	
Trawick (Nacogdoches Co)			.072500
Nacogdoches County Hospital District	5174509	.010000	
Trent (Taylor Co)	2221030	.010000	.072500
Trenton	2074010	.015000	.082500
Fannin Co	4074001	.005000	
Trinidad (Henderson Co)	2107039	.017500	.080000
Trinity (Trinity Co)	2228024	.020000	.082500
Trophy Club (Denton Co)	2061266	.020000	.082500
Troup	2212031	.015000	.082500
Cherokee Co	4037007	.005000	
Troup	2212031	.015000	.082500
Smith Co	4212004	.005000	
Troy	2014077	.015000	.082500
Bell Co	4014004	.005000	
Tucker			.067500
Anderson Co	4001009	.005000	
Tuleta			.067500
Bee Co	4013005	.005000	
Tulia	2219016	.015000	.082500
Swisher Co	4219007	.005000	
Tulsita			.067500
Bee Co	4013005	.005000	
Tunis			.067500
Burleson Co	4026000	.005000	

¶905

Tupelo			.067500
Navarro Co	4175009	.005000	
Turkey (Hall Co)	2096041	.020000	.082500
Turnersville			.067500
Coryell Co	4050009	.005000	
Turney			.067500
Cherokee Co	4037007	.005000	
Tuscola (Taylor Co)	2221076	.012500	.075000
Tye (Taylor Co)	2221049	.020000	.082500
Tyler	2212013	.015000	.082500
Smith Co	4212004	.005000	
Tynan			.067500
Bee Co	4013005	.005000	
Uhland	2105068	.015000	.082500
Caldwell Co	4028008	.005000	
Uhland	2105068	.015000	.082500
Hays Co	4105004	.005000	
Uncertain (Harrison Co)	2102052	.010000	.072500
Union			.067500
Scurry Co	4208000	.005000	
Union Grove	2230066	.010000	.077500
Upshur Co	4230002	.005000	
Union Hill			.067500
Upshur Co	4230002	.005000	
Union Valley	2116127	.010000	.077500
Hunt Co	4116001	.005000	
Universal City (Bexar Co)	2015129	.020000	.082500
University Park (Dallas Co)	2057075	.010000	.082500
Dallas MTA	3057994	.010000	
Upton			.067500
Bastrop Co	4011007	.005000	
Urbana			.067500
San Jacinto Co	4204004	.005000	
Utopia			.072500
Uvalde Co	4232000	.005000	
Uvalde County Health Services	5232509	.005000	
Uvalde	2232019	.010000	.082500
Uvalde Co	4232000	.005000	
Uvalde County Health Services	5232509	.005000	
Val Verde			.067500
Milam Co	4166000	.005000	
Valentine	2122012	.010000	.082500
Jeff Davis Co	4122003	.005000	
Jeff Davis County Health Services	5122502	.005000	
Valley Mills	2018037	.010000	.077500
Bosque Co	4018000	.005000	
Valley Mills	2018037	.010000	.077500
McClennan Co	4161005	.005000	
Valley View	2049049	.015000	.082500
Cooke Co	4049003	.005000	
Valley View			.067500
Upshur Co	4230002	.005000	
Van (Van Zandt Co)	2234053	.020000	.082500
Van Alstyne (Grayson Co)	2091037	.020000	.082500
Van Horn (Culberson Co)	2055013	.017500	.080000
Van Raub (Bexar Co)			.067500
San Antonio MTA	3015995	.005000	
Vance			.067500
Real Co	4193007	.005000	
Vancourt			.067500
Tom Green Co	4226008	.005000	
Vanderbilt			.067500
Jackson Co	4120005	.005000	
Vanderpool			.067500
Bandera Co	4010008	.005000	
Vanetia			.067500
Leon Co	4145006	.005000	
Vattman			.067500
Kleberg Co	4137006	.005000	
Vaughan			.067500
Hill Co	4109000	.005000	
Vega	2180011	.010000	.077500
Oldham Co	4180002	.005000	
Venus (Ellis Co)	2126063	.017500	.080000
Venus (Johnson Co)	2126063	.017500	.080000
Verdi			.067500
Atascosa Co	4007003	.005000	
Verhalen (Reeves Co)			.067500
Reeves County Hospital District	5195504	.005000	

¶905

Part III—Sales and Use Taxes

Veribest			.067500
Tom Green Co	4226008	.005000	
Vernon	2244015	.015000	.082500
Wilbarger Co	4244006	.005000	
Vick			.067500
Concho Co	4048004	.005000	
Victoria	2235016	.015000	.082500
Victoria Co	4235007	.005000	
Victory City			.067500
Bowie Co	4019009	.005000	
Vidor	2181010	.015000	.082500
Orange Co	4181001	.005000	
Vigo Park			.067500
Swisher Co	4219007	.005000	
Vilas			.067500
Bell Co	4014004	.005000	
Village of the Hills (Travis Co)	2227187	.007500	.082500
Travis Co. Emergency Service District 6	5227604	.010000	
Lake Travis Library Dist	5527560	.002500	
Vinton	2071077	.010000	.082500
El Paso Co	4071004	.005000	
El Paso Co Es Dis No2	5071503	.005000	
Violet (Nueces Co)			.067500
Corpus Christi MTA	3178998	.005000	
Voca			.070000
McCulloch Co	4160006	.005000	
McCulloch County Hospital District	5160505	.002500	
Volente (Travis Co)	2227212	.010000	.082500
Austin MTA	3227999	.010000	
Von Ormy (Bexar Co)	2015245	.020000	.082500
San Antonio MTA	3015995	.005000	
Voth			.067500
Jefferson Co	4123002	.005000	
Waco	2161023	.015000	.082500
McClennan Co	4161005	.005000	
Waelder	2089040	.010000	.077500
Gonzales Co	4089004	.005000	
Wake Village	2019072	.015000	.082500
Bowie Co	4019009	.005000	
Wakefield			.067500
Polk Co	4187005	.005000	
Waldeck			.067500
Fayette Co	4075000	.005000	
Waldrip			.070000
McCulloch Co	4160006	.005000	
McCulloch County Hospital District	5160505	.002500	
Walhalla			.067500
Fayette Co	4075000	.005000	
Wall			.067500
Tom Green Co	4226008	.005000	
Waller (Harris Co)	2237032	.020000	.082500
Waller (Waller Co)	2237032	.020000	.082500
Wallis	2008048	.015000	.082500
Austin Co	4008002	.005000	
Wallisville (Chambers Co)			.067500
Chambers Co Health Ser	5036507	.005000	
Walnut Springs	2018046	.010000	.077500
Bosque Co	4018000	.005000	
Warda			.067500
Fayette Co	4075000	.005000	
Wards Creek			.067500
Bowie Co	4019009	.005000	
Waring			.067500
Kendall Co	4130003	.005000	
Warlock			.067500
Marion Co	4155003	.005000	
Warren			.067500
Tyler Co	4229005	.005000	
Warren City	2092081	.010000	.077500
Gregg Co	4092009	.005000	
Warrenton			.067500
Fayette Co	4075000	.005000	
Washington			.067500
Washington Co	4239003	.005000	
Waskom (Harrison Co)	2102025	.010000	.072500
Watauga (Tarrant Co)	2220282	.015000	.082500
Watauga Crime Control District	5220567	.005000	
Water Valley			.067500
Tom Green Co	4226008	.005000	

¶905

Waxahachie (Ellis Co)	2070014	.020000	.082500
Weatherford	2184026	.015000	.082500
Parker Co	4184008	.005000	
Weaver			.067500
Hopkins Co	4112005	.005000	
Webberville (Travis Co)	2227203	.017500	.080000
Webster (Harris Co)	2101124	.020000	.082500
Weches			.067500
Houston Co	4113004	.005000	
Weimar	2045025	.015000	.082500
Colorado Co	4045007	.005000	
Weinert (Haskell Co)	2104023	.010000	.072500
Weir (Williamson Co)	2246148	.010000	.072500
Welch			.067500
Dawson Co	4058001	.005000	
Welcome			.067500
Austin Co	4008002	.005000	
Weldon			.067500
Houston Co	4113004	.005000	
Welfare			.067500
Kendall Co	4130003	.005000	
Wellborn			.067500
Brazos Co	4021005	.005000	
Wellington (Collingsworth Co)	2044017	.020000	.082500
Wellman			.067500
Terry Co	4223001	.005000	
Wells	2037043	.010000	.077500
Cherokee Co	4037007	.005000	
Weslaco (Hidalgo Co)	2108029	.020000	.082500
West	2161014	.015000	.082500
McClennan Co	4161005	.005000	
West Columbia	2020060	.015000	.082500
Brazoria Co	4020006	.005000	
West Lake Hills (Travis Co)	2227025	.015000	.082500
Westbank Community Library District	5227506	.005000	
West Mineola			.067500
Wood Co	4250007	.005000	
West Mountain			.067500
Upshur Co	4230002	.005000	
West Orange	2181038	.012500	.080000
Orange Co	4181001	.005000	
West Point			.067500
Fayette Co	4075000	.005000	
West Tawakoni	2116074	.015000	.082500
Hunt Co	4116001	.005000	
West University Place (Harris Co)	2101044	.010000	.082500
Houston MTA	3101990	.010000	
Westbrook	2168035	.010000	.077500
Mitchell Co	4168008	.005000	
Westfield (Harris Co)			.072500
Houston MTA	3101990	.010000	
Westlake (Denton Co)	2220371	.020000	.082500
Westlake (Tarrant Co)	2220371	.020000	.082500
Weston (Collin Co)	2043189	.010000	.072500
Westphalia			.067500
Falls Co	4073002	.005000	
Westway			.067500
Deaf Smith Co	4059000	.005000	
Westway			.072500
El Paso Co	4071004	.005000	
El Paso Co Es Dis No2	5071503	.005000	
Westworth Village (Tarrant Co)	2220326	.015000	.082500
Westworth Vil Crm Con	5220647	.005000	
Wetmore (Bexar Co)			.067500
San Antonio MTA	3015995	.005000	
Whaley			.067500
Bowie Co	4019009	.005000	
Wharton	2241018	.015000	.082500
Wharton Co	4241009	.005000	
Wheeler (Wheeler Co)	2242017	.015000	.077500
White City			.067500
Wilbarger Co	4244006	.005000	
White Deer (Carson Co)	2033029	.020000	.082500
White Hall			.067500
Bell Co	4014004	.005000	
White Hall			.067500
Grimes Co.	4093008	.005000	
White Oak	2092054	.015000	.082500
Gregg Co	4092009	.005000	

¶905

Part III—Sales and Use Taxes

White Rock			.067500
Hunt Co	4116001	.005000	
White Rock			.067500
San Augustine Co	4203005	.005000	
White Settlement (Tarrant Co)	2220193	.015000	.082500
White Settlement Crime Control Dist	5220558	.005000	
Whiteface (Cochran Co)	2040011	.015000	.077500
Whitehouse	2212040	.015000	.082500
Smith Co	4212004	.005000	
Whitesboro (Grayson Co)	2091082	.020000	.082500
Whitewright (Grayson Co)	2091046	.020000	.082500
Whitney	2109028	.015000	.082500
Hill Co	4109000	.005000	
Whitsett			.067500
Live Oak Co	4149002	.005000	
Whitson			.067500
Coryell Co	4050009	.005000	
Whitt			.067500
Parker Co	4184008	.005000	
Wichita Falls (Wichita Co)	2243016	.020000	.082500
Wickett (Ward Co)	2238031	.010000	.072500
Wilderville			.067500
Falls Co	4073002	.005000	
Wildorado			.067500
Oldham Co	4180002	.005000	
Williams			
Jefferson Co	4123002	.005000	
Willis (Montgomery Co)	2170031	.020000	.082500
Willow City			.067500
Gillespie Co	4086007	.005000	
Willow Grove			.067500
Bell Co	4014004	.005000	
Willow Oak			.067500
Upshur Co	4230002	.005000	
Willow Park	2184044	.015000	.082500
Parker Co	4184008	.005000	
Willow Springs			.067500
Fayette Co	4075000	.005000	
Willow Springs			.067500
San Jacinto Co	4204004	.005000	
Wills Point (Van Zandt Co)	2234017	.020000	.082500
Wilmer (Dallas Co)	2057164	.020000	.082500
Wilmeth			.067500
Runnels Co	4200008	.005000	
Wilson	2153032	.010000	.077500
Lynn Co	4153005	.005000	
Wimberley	2105095	.010000	.082500
Hays Co	4105004	.005000	
Wimberley Vil Lib Dist	5105503	.005000	
Winchester			.067500
Fayette Co	4075000	.005000	
Windcrest (Bexar Co)	2015094	.017500	.080000
Windom	2074065	.010000	.077500
Fannin Co	4074001	.005000	
Windthorst	2005050	.015000	.082500
Archer Co	4005005	.005000	
Windthorst (Clay Co)	2005050	.015000	.077500
Winedale			.067500
Fayette Co	4075000	.005000	
Winfield	2225036	.012500	.080000
Titus Co	4225009	.005000	
Wingate			.067500
Runnels Co	4200008	.005000	
Wink	2248020	.010000	.082500
Winkler Co	4248002	.005000	
Winkler County Health Services	5248501	.005000	
Winkler			.067500
Navarro Co	4175009	.005000	
Winnie (Chambers Co)			.067500
Chambers Co Health Ser	5036507	.005000	
Winnsboro	2250025	.015000	.082500
Franklin Co	4080003	.005000	
Winnsboro	2250025	.015000	.082500
Wood Co	4250007	.005000	
Winona	2212077	.015000	.082500
Smith Co	4212004	.005000	
Winters	2200035	.015000	.082500
Runnels Co	4200008	.005000	
Wixon Valley	2021032	.010000	.077500

¶905

Brazos Co	4021005	.005000	
Woden (Nacogdoches Co)			.072500
Nacogdoches County Hospital District	5174509	.010000	
Wolfe City	2116038	.015000	.082500
Hunt Co	4116001	.005000	
Wolfforth	2152051	.015000	.082500
Lubbock Co	4152006	.005000	
Womack			.067500
Bosque Co	4018000	.005000	
Woodbine			.067500
Cooke Co	4049003	.005000	
Woodbranch (Montgomery Co)			.072500
East Montgomery Co Improvement Dist	5170512	.010000	
Woodbury			.067500
Hill Co	4109000	.005000	
Woodcreek	2105059	.010000	.082500
Hays Co	4105004	.005000	
Wimberley Vil Lib Dist	5105503	.005000	
Woodlawn			.067500
Angelina Co	4003007	.005000	
Woodrow			.067500
Lubbock Co	4152006	.005000	
Woodsboro (Refugio Co)	2196022	.010000	.072500
Woodson (Throckmorton Co)	2224028	.010000	.072500
Woodville	2229014	.015000	.082500
Tyler Co	4229005	.005000	
Woodway	2161069	.015000	.082500
McClennan Co	4161005	.005000	
Wortham (Freestone Co)	2081039	.020000	.082500
Wright City			.067500
Smith Co	4212004	.005000	
Wrightsboro			.067500
Gonzales Co	4089004	.005000	
Wylie (Collin Co)	2043116	.020000	.082500
Wylie (Dallas Co)	2043116	.020000	.082500
Wylie (Rockwall Co)	2043116	.020000	.082500
Yancey			.067500
Medina Co	4163003	.005000	
Yantis	2250061	.015000	.082500
Wood Co	4250007	.005000	
Yard			.067500
Anderson Co	4001009	.005000	
Yarrelton			.067500
Milam Co	4166000	.005000	
Yoakum (DeWitt Co)	2143035	.020000	.082500
Yoakum (Lavaca Co)	2143035	.020000	.082500
Yorktown (DeWitt Co)	2062014	.015000	.077500
Youngsport			.067500
Bell Co	4014004	.005000	
Zabcikville			.067500
Bell Co	4014004	.005000	
Zavalla	2003043	.015000	.082500
Angelina Co	4003007	.005000	
Zipperlenville			.067500
Falls Co	4073002	.005000	
Zorn			.067500
Guadalupe Co	4094007	.005000	
Zuehl			.067500
Guadalupe Co	4094007	.005000	

¶906 Bracket Schedule

Law: Sec. 151.053, Tax Code (CCH Texas Tax Reports, ¶ 60-130).

The Comptroller is authorized to issue a bracket or rate schedule for sales that involve a fraction of a dollar. A fraction of one cent that is less than one-half of a cent is not collected, and a fraction of one cent that is equal to or more than one-half of a cent is collected as one cent of tax. The following bracket system has been issued for purposes of collecting the tax:

6.25% Tax Rate

Sale		Tax
$0.01 to $0.07		No tax
.08 to .23		1¢
.24 to .39		2¢
.40 to .55		3¢

¶906

Part III—Sales and Use Taxes

6.25% Tax Rate

Sale		Tax
.56 to	.71	4¢
.72 to	.87	5¢
.88 to	1.03	6¢

and so forth.

6.75% Tax Rate

Sale		Tax
$0.01 to	$0.07	No tax
.08 to	.22	1¢
.23 to	.37	2¢
.38 to	.51	3¢
.52 to	.66	4¢
.67 to	.81	5¢
.82 to	.96	6¢
.97 to	1.11	7¢

and so forth.

7% Tax Rate

Sale		Tax
$0.01 to	$0.07	No tax
.08 to	.21	1¢
.22 to	.35	2¢
.36 to	.49	3¢
.50 to	.64	4¢
.65 to	.78	5¢
.79 to	.92	6¢
.93 to	1.07	7¢

and so forth.

7.25% Tax Rate

Sale		Tax
$0.01 to	$0.06	No tax
.07 to	.20	1¢
.21 to	.34	2¢
.35 to	.48	3¢
.49 to	.62	4¢
.63 to	.75	5¢
.76 to	.89	6¢
.90 to	1.03	7¢

and so forth.

7.75% Tax Rate

Sale		Tax
$0.01 to	$0.06	No tax
.07 to	.19	1¢
.20 to	.32	2¢
.33 to	.45	3¢
.46 to	.58	4¢
.59 to	.70	5¢
.71 to	.83	6¢
.84 to	.96	7¢
.97 to	1.09	8¢

and so forth.

8% Tax Rate

Sale		Tax
$0.01 to	$0.06	No tax
.07 to	.18	1¢
.19 to	.31	2¢
.32 to	.43	3¢
.44 to	.56	4¢
.57 to	.68	5¢
.69 to	.81	6¢
.82 to	.93	7¢
.94 to	1.06	8¢

and so forth.

8.25% Tax Rate

Sale		Tax
$0.01 to	$0.06	No tax
.07 to	.18	1¢
.19 to	.30	2¢
.31 to	.42	3¢
.43 to	.54	4¢
.55 to	.66	5¢
.67 to	.78	6¢
.79 to	.90	7¢
.91 to	1.03	8¢

and so forth.

¶906

SALES AND USE TAXES

CHAPTER 10

EXEMPTIONS

¶ 1001	In General
¶ 1002	Exempt Property and Services
¶ 1003	Exempt Transactions
¶ 1004	Exempt Organizations and Persons
¶ 1005	Enterprise Zones and Similar Tax Incentives
¶ 1006	Exemption Certificates

¶ 1001 In General

The following paragraphs deal with exemptions from sales and use taxes, other than those exceptions and exclusions from tax noted in connection with the application of tax (¶ 802, 805) and the tax base (¶ 902).

Exemptions from use tax are generally the same as those provided for the sales tax. For specific use tax exemptions or exclusions, see ¶ 805.

Exempt property and services are discussed at ¶ 1002.

Generally, property or services that are subject to other taxes are exempt from sales and use taxes. Such property or services include the following:

— alcoholic beverages (¶ 1702);

— certain motor vehicles, trailers, semitrailers, and house trailers that are subject to, or exempt from, Texas motor vehicle sale, rental, and use tax (see ¶ 1002);

— motor fuels (¶ 1705);

— cement subject to cement production tax;

— insurance premiums subject to gross premiums tax (¶ 1704);

— mixed beverages, ice, or nonalcoholic beverages subject to the mixed beverage tax (¶ 1702);

— oil well services that are subject to the occupation tax under Subchapter E of Chapter 191 of the Tax Code; and

— sulfur subject to sulfur producer's tax (¶ 1709).

Exempt transactions are discussed at ¶ 1003. Exempt organizations and persons are discussed at ¶ 1004. Exemptions relating to Enterprise Zones are discussed at ¶ 1005. Exemption certificates are discussed at ¶ 1006.

¶ 1002 Exempt Property and Services

Law: Secs. 151.0035, 151.0048, 151.056, 151.057, 151.0101, 151.305, 151.308, 151.3101, 151.311, 151.3111, 151.312, 151.313, 151.314—151.320, 151.322—151.329, 151.329, 151.331, 151.333, 151.335, 151.336, 151.338, 151.340, 151.342, 151.347, 151.350, 151.3501, 151.351, 151.353, 151.355, 152.001, 152.081—152.089, 152.091—152.093, 160.0245, 321.105, 321.1055, Tax Code; 34 TAC Secs. 3.84, 3.284, 3.289, 3.293, 3.295, 3.296, 3.297, 3.298, 3.299, 3.300, 3.306, 3.308, 3.309, 3.310, 3.314, 3.330, 3.336, 3.350, 3.356, 3.357, 3.364, 3.365, 3.366, 3.369, 3.1281 (CCH Texas Tax Reports, ¶ 60-230, 60-250, 60-285, 60-290, 60-300, 60-310, 60-330, 60-350, 60-390, 60-445, 60-510, 60-520, 60-530, 60-540, 60-550, 60-570, 60-600, 60-620, 60-640, 60-645, 60-665, 60-720, 60-740, 60-750, 60-760, 61-710).

Sales and use tax exemptions apply to the following sales of items and/or services discussed below.

CCH Advisory: Exemptions for Natural Disaster Victims

The Comptroller has issued information concerning the exemptions available for repairs to both damaged residential and nonresidential property, purchases made by natural disaster victims with FEMA and nonprofit agency vouchers, fundraising exemptions, etc. (*Disaster Relief—Frequently Asked Questions,* Texas Comptroller of Public Accounts, http://www.window.state.tx.us/taxinfo/disaster_relief_faq.html).

- *Agricultural equipment, machinery, supplies*

Generally, animal life, feed, seed, insecticides, plants, fertilizer, farm machinery and equipment, and ice are exempt from sales and use taxes if the end product of the original sale will result in food for humans or if the end product will ordinarily be sold in the regular course of business.

Bins and cages: Bins used exclusively as containers in transporting fruit or vegetables from the field or place of harvest to a location where the items are processed, packaged, or marketed are also exempt. Poultry cages used exclusively for transporting poultry from a poultry farm to a location where the poultry is processed, packaged, or marketed are exempt as well.

Animals: Receipts from the sale, storage, use, or consumption of horses, mules, work animals, and animal life, the products of which ordinarily constitute food for human consumption, are generally exempt from tax.

Dairy farm structures: An exemption is allowed for tangible personal property incorporated into or attached to a structure that is located on a commercial dairy farm, is used or employed exclusively for the production of milk, and is either a free-stall dairy barn or a dairy structure used solely for maternity purposes.

Feed and seed: Feed, such as hay, corn, and oats, for farm, ranch and work animals, wildlife, and animals held for sale in the regular course of business is exempt from tax. Seeds and annual plants, the products of which ordinarily constitute food for human consumption, that are sold in the regular course of business, or used to produce feed for exempt animals, are also exempt.

Agricultural chemicals: Fertilizers, insecticides, herbicides, defoliants, desiccants, and fungicides exclusively used on a farm or ranch in the production of food for human consumption, animal feed, or other agricultural products sold in the regular course of business are exempt from tax.

Medicines for animals: A farmer or rancher may claim a sales tax exemption on the purchase of medications, tonics, restoratives or other therapeutic preparations for farm and ranch animals provided the medications are used exclusively on a farm or ranch. The medications and other therapeutic preparations may be purchased over the counter, and the farmer or rancher is not required to have a prescription in order to claim the exemption. (34 TAC Sec. 3.296(e))

Machinery and equipment: Machinery and equipment that are used exclusively on a farm or ranch in the building or maintaining of roads or water facilities, or in the production of food for human consumption, grass, animal feed, or other agricultural products sold in the regular course of business are exempt from tax. Machinery and equipment used exclusively in the processing, packing, or marketing of agricultural products by an original producer and pollution control equipment required as a result of these processes are also exempt.

Irrigation systems: Tangible personal property installed as a component of an underground irrigation system is exempt if used exclusively on a farm to produce food for human consumption; grass; feed for animals that ordinarily constitute food

¶1002

Part III—Sales and Use Taxes   **193**

for human consumption or for horses, mules, or work animals; or other agricultural products for sale.

Aircraft: Aircraft is exempt if sold to a person for use exclusively (at least 95% of the time) in connection with an agricultural use. Repair, remodeling, and maintenance services for such aircraft are also exempt as is machinery and equipment exclusively used in an agricultural aircraft operation. (Sec. 151.316(a)(10) and 151.328(a)(5), (b), and (h), Tax Code) The use of aircraft for predator control is not an exempt agricultural use under long-standing Comptroller policy. (*Decision*, Hearing No. 48,076, Texas Comptroller of Public Accounts, November 21, 2008, CCH TEXAS TAX REPORTS, ¶403-546)

Timber operations: The sale or use of machines, trailers, or semitrailers for use primarily for timber operations is exempt from Texas sales tax.

Purchases of seedlings, chemicals, machinery, and irrigation equipment used in commercial timber operations are exempt from sales tax.

CCH Pointer: Expansive application of timber operations exemption

The Comptroller has applied an expansive interpretation of the timber operations exemption. The exemption is not limited to the original producers but also extends to others, such as timber harvesters (lumberjacks). Although only original producers are eligible for the exemption for machinery and equipment used in processing, packing, or marketing timber products, no such limitation applies with respect to machinery, equipment, defoliants, desiccants, fertilizer, fungicides, herbicides, or insecticides exclusively used in the production of timber for sale.

Timber production includes activities to prepare the production site or to plant, cultivate, or harvest commercial timber that will be sold. It also includes construction, repair, and maintenance of private roads and lanes exclusively used for access to commercial timber sites. (*Letter No. 200804080L*, Texas Comptroller of Public Accounts, April 18, 2008, CCH TEXAS TAX REPORTS, ¶403-412)

Compliance Alert: Registration number required to claim agricultural and timber-related exemptions

Beginning January 1, 2012, a person claiming a Texas sales tax exemption on certain agricultural and timber-related items must include a registration number issued by the Comptroller of Public Accounts on the exemption certificate that the person provides to the seller. An online application form for a registration number can be found at: http://window.state.tx.us/taxinfo/taxforms/ap-228.pdf.

Exempt items that require a registration number and persons who are eligible for a registration number are listed in a comptroller website at: http://www.window.state.tx.us/taxinfo/taxpubs/ag_timber_exemption.html.

Exemption certificates and information for the agricultural and timber industries can be found at: http://window.state.tx.us/taxinfo/agriculture/index.html.

- *Amusement services*

The sale of an amusement service is exempt from sales tax if the service is exclusively provided:

 — by the state of Texas, or any political subdivision of Texas or the United States;

 — in a place that is included in the National Register of Historic Places, or is designated as a Recorded Texas Historic Landmark by the Texas Historical Commission;

 — by a nonprofit corporation or association, other than an entity described by IRC Sec. 501(c)(7) (clubs organized for pleasure, recreation, and other non-

¶1002

profitable purposes), if the proceeds do not go to the benefit of an individual except as part of the services of a purely public charity;

— by a nonprofit Texas corporation to encourage agriculture by maintaining public fairs and livestock exhibitions, if no individual receives a private benefit; or

— by an educational, religious, law enforcement, or charitable association or organization.

Example: Ticket Sales by NFL

Sales by the National Football League (NFL) of tickets to the 2011 Super Bowl game, which may be played in Arlington, Texas, would qualify for exemption from Texas state and local sales and use tax as the provision of an amusement service by a nonprofit association. A football game is an amusement service, and the NFL is a nonprofit organization under IRC § 501(c)(6). However, state and local tax would be due on sales of souvenirs, concession sales, programs, parking, and other taxable items. (*Letter No. 200702950L*, Texas Comptroller of Public Accounts, February 27, 2007, CCH TEXAS TAX REPORTS, ¶ 403-297)

Amusement or recreation services, including health club membership fees, are exempt if purchased under a written prescription of a licensed practitioner of the healing arts for the primary purpose of health maintenance or improvement. (Sec. 151.0028, Tax Code; 34 TAC Sec. 3.298(e)(1)) The written prescription must specify the type of treatment needed and a new prescription must be obtained each time a health club membership is renewed. A nurse is not considered a licensed practitioner of the healing arts. (*Decision of Comptroller of Public Accounts*, Hearing No. 46,983, May 29, 2007, CCH TEXAS TAX REPORTS, ¶ 403-317)

Although the use of a coin-operated machine to sell tickets or collect admission fees for taxable amusement services constitutes a taxable purchase or sale of the service, if the service itself (rather than admission to the amusement service) is provided by a coin-operated machine operated by the consumer, the amusement service is exempt from tax. Examples of nontaxable amusement services include pinball machines, video games, pool tables, and juke boxes.

Prepaid cards for music, games, and ring tones: The sale of a prepaid card other than a telephone prepaid calling card, which allows the purchaser to access and download music, ring tones, or video games, is not subject to sales or use tax because the card represents an intangible, that is, the right to a future purchase. Instead, tax is imposed when the card or access code is redeemed. (*Letter*, Texas Comptroller of Public Accounts, No. 200605591L, May 17, 2006, CCH TEXAS TAX REPORTS, ¶ 403-082)

CCH Advisory: Competitive Entry Fees

Entry fees charged for a competitive go-kart race are not taxable if: (1) the fee substantially exceeds what would normally be paid for using the facility, (2) a person is paying to compete in a race, and (3) part of the fee goes toward the cost of conducting the race and for prizes. Also, entry fees are not taxed if an individual would not normally use the facility or pay a fee except for the purpose of participating in the competitive event. (*Letter*, Texas Comptroller of Public Accounts, Letter No. 200408748L, August 17, 2004, CCH TEXAS TAX REPORTS, ¶ 402-744)

- *Bullion and coins*

Sales of gold, silver, or numismatic coins or of platinum, gold, or silver bullion are exempt from sales tax if the total sales price of all of the items sold is at least $1,000. The sales tax exemption for sales of $1,000 or more does not apply to jewelry or other items of adornment.

¶1002

Part III—Sales and Use Taxes

Also exempt are sales of official state of Texas coins that were produced under the State Purchasing and General Services Act and sold by a person under contract with the State Purchasing and General Services Commission.

- *Carriers*

The exemption for carriers is discussed below, under "Motor vehicles," and "Transportation equipment".

- *Clothing, backpacks, and school supplies*

Sales tax holiday: An annual, three-day sales tax holiday is allowed for backpacks and school supplies priced at $100 or less and purchased for use by elementary and secondary school students and for clothing and shoes with sales prices, including shipping and handling charges, of less than $100. In 2012, the sales tax holiday will begin at 12:01 a.m. on Friday, July 27, 2012, and end at 12 a.m. (midnight) Sunday, July 29, 2012. The sales tax holiday dates are established by first determining the earliest possible date a school district may begin instruction (the first Monday in August), then counting back eight days and finding the Friday before that date. Prior to 2012, the sales tax holiday began on the third Friday in August and ended at midnight on the following Sunday. The sales tax holiday exemption does not apply to accessories; special clothing or footwear, such as clothing and footwear used for sports or protective wear; nor to the rental of clothing or footwear. (Secs. 151.326 and 151.327, Tax Code)

CCH Practice Tip: Discounts, coupons, and two-for-ones

Discounts and coupons that bring the sales price below $100, enable the purchaser to buy the item tax-exempt. However, a two-for-one offer can not be used to average the items to enable both items to be purchased tax-exempt. For example, if a retailer advertises a buy-one get-one-free sale for a $120 pair of jeans, the tax would be due on $120. The transaction can not be split as two purchases of $60. Similarly, a buy one item, get the second item for 50% off, can not be averaged. (34 TAC Sec. 3.365)

An exemption certificate stating that school backpacks are purchased for use by students in a public or private elementary or secondary school is not required unless a purchaser buys 10 or more backpacks at a time. (Sec. 151.327, Tax Code; 34 TAC Sec. 3.365)

- *Computer/data processing services*

Data processing services are subject to sales and use tax, regardless of the ownership of the computer. However, 20% of the value of these services is exempt from tax.

Practitioner Comment: Services Performed With a Computer

Not all services performed using a computer are data processing services. In *Comptroller's Hearing* No. 30,695 (1995); CCH TEXAS TAX REPORTS, ¶401-859 and *Comptroller's Hearing* No. 32,269 (1995); CCH TEXAS TAX REPORTS, ¶402-588, a taxpayer used small electronic multi-memory calculators to perform inventory-counting services. The Administrative Law Judge noted that the taxpayer had previously provided the services without using a computer and the service was more than the entry, retrieval, storage, and manipulation of data into and from a computer. Accordingly, the use of the handheld computer by the taxpayer did not make its inventory-counting service a taxable data processing service. The computer merely facilitated the inventory-counting service, which is not a taxable service.

G. Brint Ryan, Ryan

Taxable "data processing services" are defined as word processing, data entry, data retrieval, payroll and business accounting data production, data search, information compilation, and other computerized data and information storage or manipula-

¶1002

tion. The term also includes the use of a computer or computer time for data processing, whether the processing is performed by the provider of the computer or computer time or by the purchaser or other beneficiary of the services.

Examples of taxable data processing services include:

— entry of inventory control data;

— maintenance of records of employee work time;

— filing payroll tax returns;

— preparing W-2 forms; and

— computing and preparing payroll checks.

Taxable data processing services also include emptying temporary folders and performing disk defragmentation. (*Letter*, Comptroller of Public Accounts, No. 200305893L, May 14, 2003, CCH TEXAS TAX REPORTS, ¶ 402-519)

Department of Revenue Comment: Data Processing vs. Information Services

A company was held to be providing information services rather than data processing services when it obtained, screened, transmitted, and sold personal information regarding candidates for dating services. This activity can be characterized as providing specialized or current information. This information service was not transformed into data processing simply because the taxpayer utilized electronic or computerized applications in gathering and transmitting the information. Although both information services and data processing services are taxable at 80% of their value, only a provider of information services may claim a tax exclusion for the sale of information that is (1) gathered on behalf of a particular client, (2) is of a proprietary nature to that client, and (3) may not be sold to others. The information sold by the taxpayer to dating services met all of the requirements for nontaxable proprietary information. When clients paid a fee to the taxpayer for each marketing lead, they obtained exclusive rights to those leads and the taxpayer guaranteed that it would not resell those leads to other dating services. (*Decision, Hearing No. 104,366*, Texas Comptroller of Public Accounts, July 21, 2011; CCH TEXAS TAX REPORTS, ¶ 403-760)

Bookkeeping services: When a bookkeeper merely enters data or records that were compiled or created by a client and does not analyze, review, or modify the results or apply his or her knowledge of accounting principles and tax laws, the services are taxable data processing services when performed using a computer. On the other hand, when a bookkeeper applies accounting or tax principles to produce financial reports, prepare tax returns, or create data or general ledger coding, he or she is providing nontaxable bookkeeping and accounting services. The use of a computer to perform nontaxable services would not make such services taxable. (*Letter*, Comptroller of Public Accounts, No. 200607779L, July 31, 2006, CCH TEXAS TAX REPORTS, ¶ 403-187).

Application development: The Comptroller has taken the position that charges for the development of custom applications for customers are taxable if the service provider retains ownership rights to the application's code, even if the application is developed from scratch and the customer receives exclusive rights to the application. If the software resides on the service provider's server and the customer uses the application on that server, the service provider must collect tax on 80% of the price of the application because the transaction is a data processing service. (*Letter*, Comptroller of Public Accounts, No. 200305893L, May 14, 2003, CCH TEXAS TAX REPORTS, ¶ 402-519).

Lap top rentals: The full rental charges for laptops rented to data processing customers were subject to sales tax. Because the rentals were not integral to the data processing service, the 20% exemption extended to data processing services did not apply to the rental of the laptops. (*Letter No. 200801068L*, Texas Comptroller of Public Accounts, January 17, 2008, CCH TEXAS TAX REPORTS, ¶ 403-396)

¶1002

Part III—Sales and Use Taxes

Training and support: Charges for teaching computer or software training classes at a customer's work site using the customer's existing computers and software are not taxable. However, charges for telephone or Internet technical support with respect to tangible personal property located in Texas are subject to sales and use taxes. (*Letter,* Comptroller of Public Accounts, No. 200305893L, May 14, 2003, CCH TEXAS TAX REPORTS, ¶402-519)

In contrast, consulting services (report design, software changes, etc.) provided in connection with data processing services are taxable because the services are provided in connection with the sale of taxable data processing. (*Letter No. 200801068L,* Texas Comptroller of Public Accounts, January 17, 2008, CCH TEXAS TAX REPORTS, ¶403-396)

Custom software: Custom software is tangible personal property and is generally taxable. However, charges to create a computer program from scratch for a customer who is given all and exclusive rights to the program are not taxable. In such a case, the programmer is an employee of the customer rather than a seller of software. (*Verizon North Inc. v. Combs, Texas Court of Appeals,* Third District, No. 03-08-00151-CV, May 22, 2009, CCH TEXAS TAX REPORTS, ¶403-555; *Decision of the Comptroller of Public Accounts,* Hearing No. 32,495, October 17, 1996, CCH TEXAS TAX REPORTS, ¶401-935; *Letter,* Texas Comptroller of Public Accounts, Letter No. 200109497L, September 25, 2001)

Software used in manufacturing: Software that is purchased, leased, or rented by a manufacturer for storage, use, or consumption may qualify for a manufacturing exemption from sales and use tax (see "Manufacturing" below). The exemption applies to software that becomes part of electronic control room equipment or computerized control units that are used to power, supply, support, or control equipment that is essential to manufacturing operations. This equipment must directly cause a chemical or physical change to the product that is being manufactured for sale or must be used in a pollution control process or in the generation of electricity.

Software services: Separately stated charges for instruction on the use of software are not subject to tax. In addition, nontaxable computer program services include the repair, maintenance, creation, and restoration of a computer program, including its development and modification, provided that the program was not sold by the person who performs the repair, maintenance, creation, or restoration service. However, the Comptroller has taken the position that charges for the initial setup of a computer and installation of system software are taxable charges for assembly, even if the service provider did not sell the hardware or software. (*Letter,* Comptroller of Public Accounts, No. 200305893L, May 14, 2003, CCH TEXAS TAX REPORTS, ¶402-519) In contrast charges for installation of computer equipment that was not connected with the sale of the equipment were not subject to Texas sales and use tax because installation services are not taxable services. (*Decision of the Comptroller of Public Accounts,* Hearing No. 42,587, April 1, 2005, CCH TEXAS TAX REPORTS, ¶402-922)

- *Construction*

New construction or improvements to residential real property are nontaxable services; however, the contractor is taxable as the consumer of the supplies and equipment used, including, in the case of lump-sum contracts, materials incorporated into the property. A contractor is not eligible for the manufacturing exemption on items used in the performance of a contract to improve real property. Real property services, such as landscaping and surveying, are taxable unless the service is purchased by a contractor as part of the improvement of real property with a new structure to be used as a residence or other improvement immediately adjacent to the new structure and used in the residential occupancy of the structure.

¶1002

CCH Comment: Ready Mix Concrete Services

Ready mix concrete contractors who both manufacture concrete for construction purposes and incorporate it into realty must separately state the price of the concrete and individually invoice the customer for each yard sold. The ready mix concrete contractor must also collect and remit tax on the concrete used or consumed. The tax rate is applied to the greater of the actual invoice price or the fair market value of the concrete on jobs other than public works projects. (Sec. 151.056(g), Tax Code)

Nontaxable new construction: New construction includes all new improvements to real property including initial finish out work to the interior or exterior of the improvement. An example would be a multiple story building that has only had its first floor finished and occupied. The initial finishing out of each additional floor prior to initial occupancy is considered new construction.

Practitioner Comment: Cubic Footage Counts

New construction includes the addition of new footage to an existing structure. New footage includes cubic footage, not just new square footage. In *Comptroller's Hearing* No. 36,375 (2000); CCH TEXAS TAX REPORTS, ¶20010626116, the replacement of a roof in a poultry processing plant was non-taxable new construction because the new roof, which was ten to twelve feet higher than the old roof, created new, usable cubic footage. The project was considered non-taxable new construction, despite the fact that no new floor space was created.

G. Brint Ryan, Ryan

CCH Advisory: Taxable vs. Nontaxable Construction

Repairs to apartment parking lots and condominium roof repairs were not subject to Texas sales and use taxes because they involved construction associated with residential buildings. Construction of fences, entrance monuments, entrance bridges, signs, and surrounding rock walls were not taxable landscaping services but new construction. The manufacture and installation of an aluminum sign, which *might* have been a replacement for an existing sign, was not new construction and was subject to tax. A project that involved both new construction and remodeling was taxed on the entire amount because the allocation of funds to each type of work could not be determined. (*Decision of Comptroller of Public Accounts*, Hearing No. 35,857, June 9, 1998; CCH TEXAS TAX REPORTS, ¶402-014).

Payments for the removal of an asphalt roadway located on a company's plant site and replacement with a concrete roadway were nontaxable new construction rather than taxable real property repair and remodeling services. Although the contract made reference to roadway repairs and described the agreement as a blanket repair contract, the contract called for the complete removal of the asphalt roadway and replacement by construction of a steel-reinforced concrete roadway and, therefore, provided for nontaxable new construction. (*Decision of Comptroller of Public Accounts*, Hearing No. 37,276, January 31, 2000; CCH TEXAS TAX REPORTS, ¶402-107)

A pipeline company's remedial installations of cathodic protection devices constituted taxable real property repair or remodeling services rather than nontaxable new construction. Installations of additional cathodic protection devices did not expand the capacity of existing pipelines, but rather prevented the pipelines from corroding. Excavation and backfilling services purchased in connection with the repair and recoating of underground pipelines did not qualify for exemption as unrelated services because the taxpayer did not contract for the excavation and backfilling services on a stand-alone basis. Rather, the excavation and backfilling services were a necessary and integral part of the taxable repair and recoating services. (*Chevron Pipeline Co. v. Strayhorn*, Texas Court of Appeals, Third District, No. 03-05-00449-CV, October 26, 2006; CCH TEXAS TAX REPORTS, ¶403-179)

¶1002

Part III—Sales and Use Taxes 199

Construction for exempt entities: Purchases by a contractor of tangible personal property are exempt if the items are used in performing a contract to improve the realty of one of the following organizations:

— a nonprofit religious, educational, or charitable organization;

— the U.S. government and its instrumentalities;

— a school district or a nonprofit hospital;

— the state of Texas or one of its political subdivisions; or

— the governments and political subdivisions of bordering states that provide similar exemptions benefiting Texas and its political subdivisions.

The exemption does not apply to materials purchased by a contractor for performance of lump-sum new construction projects on an Indian reservation if the incidence of the tax falls on a non-Indian in connection with transactions consummated outside the reservation. (*Decision of Comptroller of Public Accounts,* Hearing No. 43,233, June 5, 2006, CCH TEXAS TAX REPORTS, ¶ 403-144)

A specific exemption also applies to property, other than machinery or equipment and its accessories and repair and replacement parts, that is necessary and essential for the performance of the contract and that is completely consumed at the work site. Tangible personal property that is rented or leased for use in the performance of a contract does not qualify for the exemption because it cannot be completely consumed. To be considered "consumable" and exempt from sales tax, materials must be used up after one use.

The purchase of a taxable service for use in the performance of a contract for an improvement to realty that is performed for an exempt organization is exempt if the service is performed at the job site and (1) the contract expressly requires the specific service to be provided or purchased by the person performing the contract, or (2) the service is integral to the performance of the contract. (Sec. 151.311(c), Tax Code)

Practitioner Comment: Certain Indirect Costs Exempt for Federal and State Government Contractors

Government contractors may claim a resale exemption on purchases that are resold to federal and state governmental entities as direct costs in performing contracts. This exemption now applies to purchases of items used indirectly in performing government contracts. Qualifying contracts must contain language that explicitly and unambiguously conveys title of the indirect items to the exempt governmental entity. The exemption does not apply to capitalized equipment, rentals, computer software, and taxable services. (See *Strayhorn v. Raytheon E-Systems, Inc.*, 101 S.W.3d 558 (Tex. App. - Austin 2003, pet. denied), CCH TEXAS TAX REPORTS, ¶ 402-463)

Effective October 1, 2011, the definition of sale for resale was amended to limit the exemption. If the contractor provides non-taxable services, the contractor may not claim a resale exemption unless the goods or services will be resold to the Department of Defense, Department of Homeland Security, Department of Energy, NASA, CIA, NSA, National Oceanic and Atmospheric Administration, or National Reconnaissance Office. (See ¶ 1003)

G. Brint Ryan, Ryan

Restoration of historic sites: Restoration, repair, and remodeling services on an improvement to real property listed in the National Register of Historic Places is exempt from tax as long as the labor services are separately stated. Tangible personal property transferred by the service provider to the purchaser as part of the service remains subject to tax.

• *Containers*

The following types of containers are exempt from sales and use taxes:

¶ 1002

— containers sold with their contents if no sales tax is imposed on the price of the contents;

— empty nonreturnable containers sold to persons who fill the containers and sell the containers and contents together; and

— returnable containers sold with their contents or resold for refilling.

Exempt "containers" are glass, plastic, or metal bottles, cans, barrels, and cylinders. Wrapping, packing, and packaging supplies, as described in Tax Code Sec. 151.302(d) are not deemed to be containers. "Returnable container" means a container of a kind customarily returned for reuse by the buyer of the contents; "nonreturnable container" means any container other than a returnable container.

- *Court reporting services*

Court reporting services that relate to a notary public's or licensed court reporter's preparation of a document or other record in a civil or criminal suit are exempt from sales and use taxes if the document is (1) prepared for the use of a person participating in a suit or the court in which a suit or administrative proceeding is brought; and (2) sold to a person participating in the suit.

The exemption applies to a document or record on audio or video tape or a computer readable format and courtroom presentation of those items. The exemption includes qualified services by a video photographer who is not a court reporter and who videotapes or films a deposition, testimony, discovery document, or statement of fact pertaining to a civil or criminal suit.

- *Destination management services*

A qualified destination management company is the consumer of taxable items sold or otherwise provided under a qualified destination management services contract, and the destination management services provided under the contract are not considered taxable services. See ¶207 for definitions of "qualified destination management company" and "qualified destination management services contract." (Sec. 151.0565, Tax Code)

Also, see "Staff leasing services," below.

- *Employee services*

A service that is performed by an employee for his or her employer in the regular course of business is not subject to tax if the service is within the scope of the employee's duties and one for which the employee is paid his or her regular wages or salary. Services performed by temporary employment service employees are included in the exemption, provided:

— the services are to supplement the employer's existing work force;

— the services are ordinarily supplied by the employer's own employees;

— the employer provides all necessary supplies and equipment; and

— the temporary help is under the employer's direct or general supervision.

Also, see "Staff leasing services," below.

- *Energy conservation and environmental protection equipment*

Repair, remodeling, maintenance, or restoration services performed on tangible personal property are exempt if the service is required by law or by an order, rule, or regulation of a governmental or judicial entity in order to protect the environment or conserve energy.

Planning Note: Sales Tax Holiday for Energy-Efficient Product Purchases

Sales of certain energy efficient products are exempt from sales and use tax during the three-day Memorial Day weekend period each year. The sales must take place during

Part III—Sales and Use Taxes 201

the period beginning at 12:01 a.m. on the Saturday preceding the last Monday in May (Memorial Day) and ending at 11:59 p.m. on Memorial Day.

The exemption is available only for the following products that have received an Energy Star qualified product designation by the U.S. Environmental Protection Agency and Department of Energy:

- an air conditioner with a sales price of $6,000 or less;
- a clothes washer;
- a ceiling fan;
- a dehumidifier;
- a dishwasher;
- an incandescent or fluorescent light bulb;
- a programmable thermostat; and
- a refrigerator with a sales price of $2,000 or less. (Sec. 151.333, Tax Code)

- *Food*

In general, food products for human consumption are exempt from sales and use taxes. The exemption does not apply to:

— medicines, tonics, vitamins, or medicinal preparations in any form;

— foods or drinks ready for immediate consumption in or by restaurants, lunch counters, cafeterias, concession stands, caterers, vending machines, hotels, or similar places of business; or

— foods sold ready for immediate consumption from pushcarts, motor vehicles, or any other form of vehicle.

Also excluded from the food exemption are alcoholic beverages, carbonated and noncarbonated packaged soft drinks, diluted juices, ice, candy, drugs, and dietary supplements. These items are subject to tax. However, the sale of mixed beverages, including ice or nonalcoholic beverages that are mixed with, or are intended to be mixed with, alcoholic beverages, and gratuities collected on those sales, are not subject to sales tax if the receipts are subject to the mixed beverages tax (see ¶1702).

Gift cards and complimentary drinks: A restaurant's sale of a prepaid gift card is not subject to sales or use tax or Texas mixed beverage gross receipts tax because the card represents an intangible, i.e., the right to a future purchase. Instead, when the card is redeemed, sales tax is calculated on the amount attributable to the purchase of food and mixed beverage tax is calculated on the portion attributable to the purchase of mixed beverages. Complimentary mixed beverages provided by the restaurant, including mixed beverages purchased with complimentary gift cards, are subject to Texas use tax and not the mixed beverage gross receipts tax. (*Letter*, Comptroller of Public Accounts, No. 200603549L, March 23, 2006, CCH TEXAS TAX REPORTS, ¶403-062)

CCH Advisory: Packaging/Timing Is Everything

How an item is sold is key to whether the item is taxable or not. Consequently, in a letter to a bakery owner, the Comptroller took the position that doughnuts and other baked goods such as sales of pigs-in-a-blanket and biscuits, croissants and bagels with ingredients inside were not subject to tax unless the bakery provided plates, forks, or knives with the items. Even the fact that the bakery reheated the products for customers did not make those sales taxable, unless the bakery served the items on plates. In contrast, the Comptroller advised that sales of tacos and sandwiches, such as a biscuit-sausage sandwich, a bagel sandwich, or a croissant sandwich sold by the bakery would be subject to tax. (*Letter from Comptroller of Public Accounts*, No. 200402375L, February 4, 2004; CCH TEXAS TAX REPORTS, ¶402-650)

The term "food ready for immediate consumption" refers to food, beverages, or meals normally prepared, served, or sold by restaurants, lunch counters, cafeterias,

¶1002

etc., that, when sold, require no further preparation prior to consumption, even if not eaten immediately on the premises. Also subject to tax is:

— food sold in a heated state;

— two or more food ingredients mixed or combined by the seller for sale as a single item unless the food is only cut, repackaged, or pasteurized by the seller; and

— prepared foods and food products sold through vending machines (see ¶902 for the tax rate applicable to vending machine sales).

CCH Advisory: Pre- and Post-SST Agreement Conforming Amendments

Taxpayers should review whether various prepared items may now be subject to tax as a result of the SST Agreement amendments. For example, prior to the SST conforming amendments, sushi sold without eating utensils from a refrigerated case in the grocery section was not subject to tax. However, once the amendments were implemented on October 1, 2003, sushi rolled by a retailer on the grocery store premises is subject to tax, whereas sushi rolled off premises is not taxable unless it is sold with utensils. (*Letter from Comptroller of Public Accounts,* No. 200402371L, February 3, 2004; CCH TEXAS TAX REPORTS, ¶402-649)

Exempt food sales: The sale of food is exempt from tax under the following circumstances:

— food not ready for immediate consumption;

— sales of food, gum, or candy for 50¢ or less from a bulk vending machine;

— food sales (including soft drinks and candy but not alcoholic beverages) by schools, school associated groups, and state institutions, if (a) sold by religious organizations or sold at religious functions, (b) sold or served by public or private schools, school districts, student organizations, or parent-teacher associations in an elementary or secondary school during the regular school day, (c) sold or served by a parent-teacher association during a fund-raising sale, the proceeds of which do not benefit an individual, (d) sold by a member or volunteer of a nonprofit organization devoted to the exclusive purpose of education, or physical or religious training, and groups associated with public or private elementary or secondary schools as a part of a fund-raising drive sponsored by the organization for its exclusive use, (e) served to students, residents, or patients of hospitals, day-care centers, summer camps, and other state-licensed institutions, (f) served to permanent residents of a retirement facility at the retirement facility, or (g) provided at no cost to inmates by correctional facilities as part of the inmates' incarceration; and

— items purchased with food coupons under the food stamp program.

Taxable food sales: Tax is due on the sale of food, meals, and drinks under the following circumstances:

— prepared, sold, or served under the American plan by a hotel, boarding house, or other place of business, if separately stated (otherwise, hotel occupancy tax must be collected on the entire lump sum, or, if the lump-sum charge is not subject to hotel occupancy tax, sales tax must be collected on the portion of the lump-sum charge attributable to the meals; see ¶1707 for a discussion of the hotel occupancy tax);

— sold by universities, colleges, junior colleges, or other schools of higher learning;

— purchased ready for immediate consumption by a common carrier for the purpose of serving passengers traveling en route aboard the carrier; or

Part III—Sales and Use Taxes

— sold to a person confined in a correctional facility operated under the authority or jurisdiction of or under contract with the state of Texas or a political subdivision of the state.

See ¶ 902 for a discussion of the tax base for vending machine sales of food.

Employee meals and subsidies: Meals furnished by food service operators to employees immediately before, after or during a shift that are provided for the convenience of the employer are not taxable if the employee is involved in preparing or serving of food. An employer is not liable for tax on any subsidy paid to a food service operator unless the subsidy is specifically contingent on or included in the price of the meals served to employees or guests, or is the total consideration paid for the meals.

Free meals and beverages provided as promotional items to customers are taxable to a restaurant owner only to the extent tax would have been due on the original purchase price of the food or drinks from suppliers. If two meals are sold for the price of one, tax should be collected only on the amount charged.

Gratuities and tips: Voluntary tips/gratuities are exempt. Separately-stated mandatory gratuities of 20% or less are also exempt if disbursed to qualified employees. (Sec. 151.007(c)(7), Tax Code; 34 TAC Sec. 3.337)

Utilities used to prepare or store prepared food: The exemption for gas and electricity used in manufacturing does not include gas and electricity used to prepare or store prepared food.

- *Intercorporate services*

    See ¶ 1003.

- *Internet access*

The first $25 per month charged for Internet access is exempt from sales tax. The exemption applies whether the Internet access service is billed separately or is bundled with other services.

Sales of prepaid Internet access cards are exempt. However tax is imposed when the card is redeemed. (*Letter*, Texas Comptroller of Public Accounts, No. 200605591L, May 17, 2006, CCH Texas Tax Reports, ¶ 403-082)

CCH Advisory: Multiple Users

The exemption applies to the amount attributable to Internet access billed to a purchaser regardless of how many users the purchaser may have. Thus, if a company has 25 employees, only the first $25 billed to the company is exempt, not the first $25 attributable to each user.

Sales for resale: Resale certificates may be issued for a service if the buyer intends to transfer the service as an integral part of a taxable service provided by the buyer. For example, a provider of Internet access services may use a resale certificate when purchasing telecommunications services that are used to provide Internet access services. However, the service for which the resale certificate is issued must be an integral part of the taxable service.

Where taxable: If Internet access service is provided to and accessed by multistate customers with users in and outside Texas, the service is presumed to be used at the location from which the Internet is accessed and is not taxed in Texas to the extent that it is accessed outside Texas, as long as the method for allocation is reasonable and supported by business records. For local tax purposes, the location of the Internet access service provider determines whether local sales tax must be collected by the provider.

¶ 1002

Federal Internet Tax Freedom Act: The federal Internet Tax Freedom Act (ITFA) and its amendments (P.L. 105-277, 112 Stat. 2681, 47 U.S.C. 151 note, amended by P.L. 107-75, P.L. 108-435, P.L. 110-108) bars state and local governments from imposing multiple or discriminatory taxes on electronic commerce and taxes on Internet access for the period beginning on October 1, 1998, and ending on November 1, 2014. However, the moratorium imposed by the Act does not apply to Internet access taxes generally imposed and actually enforced prior to October 1, 1998, as long as the state has not, more than 24 months prior to the enactment of P.L. 110-108, repealed its tax on Internet access or issued a rule that it no longer applies such a tax.

"Internet access" means a service that enables users to connect to the Internet to access content, information, or other services, including the purchase, use, or sale of telecommunications by an Internet service provider to provide the service or otherwise enable users to access content, information, or other services offered over the Internet. It also includes incidental services such as home pages, electronic mail, instant messaging, video clips, and personal electronic storage capacity, whether or not packaged with service to access the Internet. However, "Internet access" does not include voice, audio or video programming, or other products and services using Internet protocol for which there is a charge, regardless of whether the charge is bundled with charges for "Internet access."

- *Laundry and cleaning services*

Generally, laundry, cleaning, and garment services are taxable personal services. However, sales tax is not due on personal services provided through coin-operated machines that are operated by the customer or performed by an employee for the employer, or on repairs to carpet in residential real property.

Hangers, safety pins, pins, inventory tags, staples, boxes, paper wrappers, and plastic bags sold to a launderer or dry cleaner to wrap or package a laundered or dry cleaned item are exempt from tax.

- *Lawn and yard services*

Individuals who are either under the age of 18 or age 65 or older or who are self-employed may provide nontaxable lawn and yard maintenance services if their total receipts from providing such services are $5,000 or less for the four most recent calendar quarters.

- *Manufacturing*

In general, tangible personal property that is purchased by a manufacturer for use as an ingredient or component part of a product manufactured, processed, or fabricated for ultimate sale at retail is exempt from sales and use taxes. Tangible personal property that is directly used or consumed in the actual manufacturing, processing, or fabrication of tangible personal property for ultimate sale is also exempt if:

(1) it is necessary or essential to such operation;

(2) its use or consumption directly makes or causes a chemical or physical change to the product being manufactured, processed, or fabricated for ultimate sale or to an intermediate or preliminary product that will become an ingredient or component part of the product being manufactured, processed, or fabricated for ultimate sale; or

(3) it is machinery, equipment, and replacement parts or accessories used or consumed in the actual manufacturing, processing, or fabrication of tangible personal property for ultimate sale if their use or consumption is necessary and essential to a pollution control process (*e.g.,* a vent hood covering food processing equipment such as a grill or fryer).

The phrase "tangible personal property for ultimate sale" limits the exemption to the manufacturing of products whose ultimate sale to customers is taxed as tangible personal property. The Texas Court of Appeals has held that switches and other equipment used by a local exchange carrier in providing telecommunications to customers did not qualify for a manufacturing exemption because the taxpayer's telecommunications product for sale constituted a service rather than tangible personal property. (*GTE Southwest, Inc., v. Combs*, Texas Court of Appeals, Third District, No. 03-08-00561-CV, June 3, 2010, CCH Texas Tax Reports, ¶ 403-610)

> ### CCH Comment: Where Manufacturing Occurs Immaterial?
> The Texas Comptroller of Public Accounts has held that manufacturing equipment shipped from outside the state and stored in Texas qualified for the manufacturing exemption. The Comptroller reasoned that no authority was provided for the Tax Division's assertion that a manufacturing exemption could only be claimed for machinery and equipment that was used in manufacturing in Texas. (*Decision, Hearing No. 44,798*, Texas Comptroller of Public Accounts, December 15, 2006, CCH Texas Tax Reports, ¶ 403-244)

Also exempt are (1) services performed directly on the product being manufactured prior to its distribution for sale for the purpose of making the product more marketable; and (2) tangible personal property used or consumed in a quality control process that tests tangible personal property that is being manufactured, processed, or fabricated for ultimate sale. A quality control process is a processing activity if it occurs before the manufactured product is packaged for sale.

In addition, an exemption applies to actuators, steam production equipment and its fuel, in-process flow-through tanks, cooling towers, generators, heat exchangers, electronic control room equipment, computerized control units, compressors, and hydraulic units that are used to power, supply, support, or control equipment that qualifies for exemption under category (2) above or that are used to generate electricity, chilled water, or steam for ultimate sale.

> ### CCH Comment: Equipment Must Be Used in Manufacturing By the Purchaser
> Two soft drink distributors were not entitled to a manufacturing exemption on their purchases of fountain equipment that they provided to retailers for use in preparing and selling the distributors' soda products to customers because the fountain equipment was used in manufacturing by the retailers, not the distributors. The retailers (bars and restaurants) agreed to purchase soda syrup, carbon dioxide, and cups from the distributors and to stock the fountain equipment with only the distributors' products. Even though the distributors remained the exclusive owners of the fountain equipment, they could not claim a manufacturing exemption for equipment used by other businesses. (*Laredo Coca-Cola Bottling Co. v. Combs*, Texas Court of Appeals, Third District, No. 03-09-00157-CV, April 15, 2010; CCH Texas Tax Reports, ¶ 403-599)

When manufacturing begins.—"Manufacturing" includes every operation beginning with the first stage in the production of tangible personal property and ending with the completion of tangible personal property that has the physical properties (including any packaging) that it retains when transferred by the manufacturer to someone else. The first stage of production does not include those acts in preparation for production. Thus, dragline equipment used to clear overburden above lignite that was eventually excavated did not qualify as manufacturing equipment, even though the removal of the overburden exposed the lignite to air, which began a chemical reaction that "enriched" the lignite and caused the lignite to crack making its extraction easier. The Comptroller held that this was not part of the production process, because the real purpose of removing the overburden was to enable the taxpayer to begin the extraction process and the other consequences of the removal were merely ancillary.

Similarly, a cement plant operator was denied the manufacturing exemption on its purchase of a coal mill that mixed and crushed coal and coke into a powder that fueled a kiln. The kiln was used to bake aggregate materials into semi-molten granules called clinker, which was cooled, mixed with gypsum, and sold as cement. The exemption was denied because the mill did not directly cause a chemical or physical change to an intermediate product that became an ingredient of the cement. Although silica ash, a residue from burning the coal/coke mix, was added to and became an ingredient of the clinker, this silica ash was produced in the kiln, not the coal mill. (*Decision of the Texas Comptroller of Public Accounts*, Hearing No. 46,434, April 25, 2008, CCH TEXAS TAX REPORTS, ¶ 403-480)

In contrast, blasting rock to create smaller rocks and allow the excavation of gravel was part of the actual production process, and equipment and dynamite used in such activities qualified for the manufacturing exemption. (*Decision of the Texas Comptroller of Public Accounts*, Hearing No. 42,128, January 20, 2004, CCH TEXAS TAX REPORTS, ¶ 402-690) This position was upheld by a Texas court of appeal in *Sabine Mining Company v. Strayhorn*, Texas Court of Appeals, 13th District, No. 13-06-330-CV, August 23, 2007, CCH TEXAS TAX REPORTS, ¶ 403-306.

Software: For purposes of the exemption, the manufacturing of computer software begins with the design and writing of the code or program for the software and includes the testing or demonstration of the software.

> **CCH Comment: Taxation of electronic design automation software**
>
> The Comptroller has held that an integrated chip manufacturer's use of electronic design automation (EDA) software to develop software is an exempt use for purposes of the software manufacturing exemption, while its use of the EDA software to develop hardware is a taxable divergent use. (*Letter No. 200808142L*, Texas Comptroller of Public Accounts, August 15, 2008, CCH TEXAS TAX REPORTS, ¶ 403-474)

Processing and fabrication.—Processing and fabrication are two activities that are performed during manufacturing. "Processing" refers to the physical application of materials and labor necessary to modify or change the characteristics of tangible personal property.

Processing does not include the repair of tangible personal property belonging to another by restoring it to its original condition, nor does it include remodeling or the mere packing, unpacking, or shelving of a product to be sold. Processing does not include remodeling, which is defined as making tangible personal property belonging to another over again, in a similar but different way, or to change the style, shape, or form, without causing a loss of its identity, or without causing the property to work in a new or different manner.

"Fabrication" means to make, build, create, produce, or assemble components of tangible personal property, or to make tangible personal property work in a new or different manner.

Film making/audio production.—"Manufacturing" specifically includes the production of a motion picture or a video or audio recording, a copy of which is sold or offered for ultimate sale, licensed, distributed, broadcast, or otherwise exhibited. "Manufacturing" also specifically includes the production of a publication for the dissemination of news of a general character and of a general interest that is printed on newsprint and distributed to the general public free of charge at a daily, weekly, or other short interval.

Leased equipment.—Items rented or leased for less than one year are not exempt.

> **Practitioner Comment: Leases of Manufacturing Equipment**
>
> The exemption for manufacturing equipment applies to leases and rentals of qualifying equipment, provided the lease term is one year or more. Bare rentals and short-term leases of qualifying equipment are taxable. Further, leases consummated prior to

¶ 1002

October 1, 1995, will not qualify for the manufacturing exemption at any time during their term, unless restructured. See Texas Tax Code § 151.318(e), Property Used in Manufacturing.

G. Brint Ryan, Ryan

The Comptroller's Office has viewed the actual term of the lease rather than the time that the equipment is at the customer's location to determine whether the exemption applies. A daily or monthly rental contract does not qualify for exemption even if the equipment remains at the customer's site for periods in excess of a year. Conversely, equipment that is contractually leased for a term of one year or more does not become taxable if the equipment breaks down or is removed from the lease prior to completion of the contract. In addition, equipment that is rented under contracts of a year or more are not taxable when moved to other sites by the customer as long as the use at the new sites also qualifies for the manufacturing exemption. (*Letter from Comptroller of Public Accounts,* No. 200402379L, February 7, 2004; CCH TEXAS TAX REPORTS, ¶ 402-663).

Leased equipment that is retained on a month-to-month basis after a contract of one year or more ends is subject to tax after the expiration of the one-year (or longer) contract. (*Letter from Comptroller of Public Accounts,* No. 200402379L, February 7, 2004; CCH TEXAS TAX REPORTS, ¶ 402-663).

An equipment rental contract that does not provide for an absolute termination date but, rather, continues indefinitely upon month-to-month payments until cancelled at will by either party upon 30 days' notice, does not qualify for exemption even if the contract stipulates that neither party may terminate the contract within the first 12 months. To be exempt, the rental contract must provide for a definite term with a specified beginning and ending date of one year or more. (*Letter from Comptroller of Public Accounts,* No. 201006692L, June 23, 2010; CCH TEXAS TAX REPORTS, ¶ 403-614).

Verbal contracts to lease equipment do not qualify for exemption, because they do not provide the documentation necessary to obtain the exemption. Verbal contracts are treated as month-to-month rentals if the charges are monthly or day rentals if the charges are daily. (*Letter from Comptroller of Public Accounts,* No. 200402379L, February 7, 2004; CCH TEXAS TAX REPORTS, ¶ 402-663).

Specifically exempt items.—The manufacturing exemption specifically includes the following items:

— ingredients or components;

— chemicals, catalysts, and other materials if used to produce or induce a chemical or physical change, to remove impurities, or to make the product more marketable;

— semiconductor fabrication cleanrooms and equipment;

— gas and electricity used directly in manufacturing (a person claiming an exemption for electricity used through a single meter must have a utility study performed to establish that the predominant use was an exempt use (34 TAC Sec. 3.295(e)));

— materials necessary or essential to the operation of machinery or equipment that is used in the actual manufacturing process (such as lubricants, explosives, and ice);

— safety apparel or work clothing;

— machinery and equipment rented or leased for the production of motion pictures or video or audio recordings; and

— pharmaceutical biotechnology cleanrooms and equipment that are installed as part of the construction of a new facility and on which construction began after July 1, 2003.

Practice Pointer: Treatment of Items Used in Food Preparation

Taxpayers involved in food preparation services should consult the Comptroller's listing of exempt and non-exempt items used by a food service provider for manufacturing food or drink for sale. (*Letter No. 200612897L*, Texas Comptroller of Public Accounts, December 12, 2006, CCH TEXAS TAX REPORTS, ¶ 403-240; *Letter No. 200805154L*, Texas Comptroller of Public Accounts, May 7, 2008, CCH TEXAS TAX REPORTS, ¶ 403-485)

Food processors may claim a manufacturing exemption for purchases of aprons, gloves, overalls/coveralls, shoe covers, sleeves, and smocks to be worn by their employees if the employer obtains prior written confirmation or approval from the Comptroller's office that the items are necessary to protect against contamination, are required by federal, state, or local sanitation laws or rules, and the items otherwise meet applicable safety standards. Food processors may submit work clothing exemption approval requests in writing to the Comptroller's Sales Tax Policy Division, P.O. Box 13528, Austin, Texas 78711-3528. (*Letter No. 200805081L*, Texas Comptroller of Public Accounts, May 2, 2008, ¶ 403-415)

Nonexempt items.—The manufacturing exemption does not apply to the following specific items:

— intraplant transportation equipment, including intraplant transportation equipment used to move a product or raw material in connection with the manufacturing process (see *Decision, Hearing No. 43,112*, Texas Comptroller of Public Accounts, April 14, 2008, CCH TEXAS TAX REPORTS, ¶ 403-406, for the treatment of certain gas well equipment), and specifically including all piping and conveyor systems; however, piping that is a component part of a single item of manufacturing equipment or pollution control equipment otherwise eligible for the exemption remains eligible, as does an automated storage and retrieval system (ASRS) that stored vehicle bodies on racks during vehicle manufacturing so that the sequence of bodies could be varied for different phases of assembly or manufacturing (*Decision, Hearing No. 44,798*, Texas Comptroller of Public Accounts, December 15, 2006, CCH TEXAS TAX REPORTS, ¶ 403-244);

— property used in the transmission or distribution of electricity;

— office equipment or supplies;

— equipment or supplies used in sales or distribution activities, research or development of new products, or transportation activities;

— other tangible personal property not used in an actual manufacturing, processing, or fabrication operation;

— machinery and equipment or supplies used to maintain or store tangible personal property; and

— items used in the performance of a contract to improve real property.

Practitioner Comment: The Lump-Sum Contract Trap

In instances where qualifying manufacturing equipment will be installed as an improvement to real property, the use of a lump-sum contract will result in the loss of the manufacturing exemption. Under Comptroller's Rules §§ 3.291(b)(12), Contractors, and 3.300(i), Manufacturing, neither the contractor nor the manufacturer may claim a manufacturing equipment exemption on manufacturing machinery or equipment installed under a lump-sum contract for new construction of real property. The use of a separated contract will allow the manufacturer to claim the exemption on qualifying property.

G. Brint Ryan, Ryan

Part III—Sales and Use Taxes   209

Divergent use.—The use of property exempted under the manufacturing exemption for uses other than qualifying purposes does not result in the imposition of sales and use taxes if the divergent use occurs after the fourth anniversary of the date the property is purchased. If the divergent use occurs during any month before the fourth anniversary of the date the property is purchased, tax is imposed equal to $1/48$ of the property's purchase price multiplied by the sales and use tax rate applicable at the time of the purchase. However, if the percentage of the divergent use is five percent or less of the total use of the property for that month, no tax is imposed.

The use of pharmaceutical biotechnology cleanrooms and equipment to manufacture, process, or fabricate a pharmaceutical biotechnology product that is not sold is not a divergent use if the use occurs during the certification process by the U.S. Food and Drug Administration.

CCH Caution: Use of manufacturing equipment to make warranty repair

A manufacturer is considered to be making a divergent use of exempt manufacturing equipment if, after its product has been packaged and sent to a customer, the manufacturer uses the equipment to make repairs on the product pursuant to the manufacturer's warranty. Any use of typically exempt manufacturing equipment to repair a product after the manufacturing process has ceased constitutes a divergent use that may trigger tax liability. (*Letter No. 201003824L*, Texas Comptroller of Public Accounts, March 15, 2010; CCH TEXAS TAX REPORTS, ¶ 403-625)

Wrapping, packing, and packaging supplies.—No sales or use tax is due on containers or packaging supplies purchased by manufacturers for use as a part of the completion of the manufacturing process. The manufacturing process is considered complete when the tangible personal property being produced has been packaged by the manufacturer as it will be sold. In addition, no sales tax is due on internal or external wrapping, packing, and packaging supplies sold to a person for the person's use in wrapping, packing, or packaging newspapers, including those distributed free of charge to the general public.

CCH Comment: Bags Used at Supermarket Checkout Counters

Paper and plastic bags purchased by a supermarket operator and used at checkout counters to hold items selected for purchase by customers are taxable as packaging supplies used by retailers in expediting or furthering a sale of tangible personal property. Bags used at the checkout point do not qualify for exemption as containers or packaging supplies purchased by manufacturers for use as a part of the completion of a manufacturing process, because any manufacturing or processing of grocery items has already been completed prior to that point. However, the Comptroller recognizes that processing activities may occur in certain areas of a grocery store, such as a bakery, delicatessen, or meat department, and packaging supplies used in these areas may be exempt if used in the completion of a manufacturing process. (*Decision, Hearing No. 49,001*, Texas Comptroller of Public Accounts, March 26, 2010; CCH TEXAS TAX REPORTS, ¶ 403-619)

- *Medical items*

Drugs and medicines prescribed or dispensed to humans or for animals by a doctor or other licensed member of the healing arts are exempt from sales and use tax. Items that merely treat an aesthetic issue and do not meet the definition of a drug or medicine are not exempt even if prescribed or dispensed by a physician. (*Letter No. 200807135L*, Texas Comptroller of Public Accounts, July 23, 2008, CCH TEXAS TAX REPORTS, ¶ 403-456) Over-the-counter drugs or medicines that are labeled with a Food and Drug Administration national drug code are also exempt, regardless of whether they are dispensed by licensed medical practitioners. Sales of medical devices are subject to tax. (*Letter No. 200803134L*, Texas Comptroller of Public Accounts, March 7, 2008, CCH TEXAS TAX REPORTS, ¶ 403-459)

¶1002

"Drugs and medicines" are products that:

— are intended for use in the diagnosis, cure, mitigation, treatment, or prevention of disease, illness, injury, or pain;

— are applied to the human body, or that humans ingest or inhale; and

— are not an appliance, device, or food.

The term does not include hardware of any kind, equipment, appliances, devices, or chemicals used to test bodily fluids and tissues.

The exemption includes over-the-counter drugs, vitamins, minerals, dietary/nutritional supplements, herbal medications (*Letter from Comptroller of Public Accounts,* Letter No. 200105211L, May 3, 2001; CCH TEXAS TAX REPORTS, ¶ 402-190), and essential oils used as a skin conditioner and massage lotions used to relieve muscle and joint pains. (*Letter from Comptroller of Public Accounts,* No. 200402360L, February 3, 2004; CCH TEXAS TAX REPORTS, ¶ 402-646)

Contact lens care products are exempt when purchased with a prescription from a licensed physician but are taxable when not sold under a doctor's prescription. Contact lens solution products (e.g., saline solutions, cleaners, chemical disinfecting products, and lubricating and rewetting drops) do not qualify as exempt over-the-counter (OTC) drugs or medicines because such products are classified as devices and not as drugs or medicines. (*Letter from Comptroller of Public Accounts,* Letter No. 201004828L, April 6, 2010; CCH TEXAS TAX REPORTS, ¶ 403-626)

Specified medical equipment and supplies are also exempt, including:

— braces;

— corrective lenses;

— hearing aids and audio loops;

— orthopedic appliances;

— prosthetic devices;

— dental devices;

— catheters that are inserted into a vein (hence epidural catheters are not exempt, see *Letter No. 200805079L,* Texas Comptroller of Public Accounts, May 2, 2008, CCH TEXAS TAX REPORTS, ¶ 403-411);

— surgically implanted ileostomy, colostomy, and ileal bladder appliances;

— hypodermic syringes and needles;

— wound dressings;

— therapeutic appliances, devices, and related supplies, including hot tubs and spas, when sold, leased, or rented to individuals under a prescription of a licensed practitioner of the healing arts;

— certain items used by blind or deaf persons;

— hospital beds;

— adjustable eating utensils for people who do not have full use or control of their hands or arms; and

— intravenous systems, supplies, and replacement parts used in the treatment of humans.

Veterinarians: Professional medical services performed by a veterinarian are not taxable. A drug or medicine is exempt when prescribed, orally or in writing, or dispensed by a veterinarian. Food prescribed by a veterinarian is exempt. Wound care dressings and supplies, as well as hypodermic needles and syringes are exempt. Dental devices are exempt; however, therapeutic appliances and devices prescribed by a veterinarian are not exempt. Microchip devices implanted in animals are taxable. Nonmedical pet grooming and maintenance services, including baths and nail trimmings, are taxable. (*Letter No. 201107187L,* Texas Comptroller of Public Accounts, July

Part III—Sales and Use Taxes **211**

15, 2011, CCH TEXAS TAX REPORTS, ¶ 403-754; *Letter No. 201107164L,* Texas Comptroller of Public Accounts, July 15, 2011, CCH TEXAS TAX REPORTS, ¶ 403-743)

- *Mining and drilling*

Drill pipe, casing, tubing, and other tangible personal property used exclusively for the exploration or production of oil, gas, sulfur, or other minerals offshore and outside Texas are exempt from tax. Drilling equipment that is built for exclusive use outside Texas is also exempt. In general, labor that is performed inside an oil well bore for the purpose of starting initial production or increasing production by working on the formation outside a well is not taxable.

The Comptroller has also ruled that materials used to assemble underwater seismic surveying equipment for use in deep sea oil and gas exploration outside the territorial limits of Texas were exempt from sales and use tax even though the materials were delivered to the purchaser for assembly within Texas. In addition, the return of the equipment for temporary storage in a Texas facility due to economic conditions or a need for repairs and/or routine maintenance did not constitute a taxable divergent use. (*Letter No. 200807119L,* Texas Comptroller of Public Accounts, July 17, 2008, CCH TEXAS TAX REPORTS, ¶ 403-454)

Equipment specifically used to process, reuse, or recycle wastewater that will be used in fracturing work performed at an oil or gas well is also exempt. (Sec. 151.355(7), Tax Code)

Oilfield portable units: Oilfield portable units are subject to the general sales tax but are exempt from motor vehicle sales and use tax and hotel occupancy tax. An oilfield portable unit is a bunkhouse, manufactured home, trailer, or semitrailer that is designed to be used for temporary lodging or as temporary office space and is used exclusively at an oil, gas, water disposal, or injection well site to provide sleeping accommodations or temporary work space for employees, contractors, or other workers. An oilfield portable unit does not require attachment to a foundation or to real property to be functional.

- *Motor vehicles*

Motor vehicles, trailers, semitrailers, and house trailers that are subject to Texas motor vehicle sales, rental, and use tax or that are exempt from that tax are exempt from the general sales and use taxes. Consequently, they are also exempt from local sales and use taxes.

The following are exempt from motor vehicle sales and use tax, including the tax on motor vehicle rentals:

— hydrogen power-capable vehicles with a fuel economy rating of at least 45 miles per gallon or fully hydrogen-powered vehicles;

— motor vehicles sold to, used by, or rented or leased to, a public agency;

— farm machinery, trailers or semitrailers for use primarily in farming and ranching, and for use in feed lots;

— machines, trailers, or semitrailers used primarily for timber operations, other than self-propelled vehicles used for transporting timber or timber products;

— vehicles modified within two years from the date of purchase for operation by handicapped persons. The Comptroller has taken the position that the exemption does not apply to leases of motor vehicles for under 180 days. (*Letter from Comptroller of Public Accounts,* Letter No. 200211584L, November 18, 2002; CCH TEXAS TAX REPORTS, ¶ 402-453) Acceptable proof that a person is orthopedically handicapped is outlined in 34 TAC Sec. 3.84 and applicable to sales occurring after 2009, the purchaser must present an exemption certificate demonstrating eligibility for the exemption at the time of purchase (Sec. 152.086, Tax Code);

¶1002

— driver training vehicles;

— fire trucks or ambulances purchased by volunteer fire departments, exempt nonprofit emergency medical service providers, or emergency medical service providers that are exempt from the motor vehicle registration fee for emergency medical service vehicles;

— motor vehicles used for religious purposes;

— interstate motor vehicles, trailers and semitrailers (see further discussion below);

— motor vehicles transported out of state prior to use;

— motor vehicles purchased, used, or rented by a qualified residential child-care facility and used primarily to transport the children;

— the rental of motor vehicles for re-rental; and

— salvage vehicles that have not been repaired. (*Notice*, Comptroller of Public Accounts, January 10, 2005, CCH TEXAS TAX REPORTS, ¶402-836)

Department of Revenue Comment: Vehicle Transported Outside State Prior to Use

A newly purchased vehicle that was driven from the dealership to the purchaser's residence and parked there for 22 days prior to being shipped to another country did not qualify for the motor vehicle sales tax exemption for vehicles that are purchased for use exclusively outside Texas. The purchaser clearly operated the vehicle in Texas for a purpose other than driving the vehicle out of the state. Parking was a use of the vehicle in Texas. Also, the purchaser's registration of the vehicle in Texas raised the presumption that the vehicle was purchased for use within Texas. (*Decision, Hearing No. 104,315*, Texas Comptroller of Public Accounts, January 11, 2011; CCH TEXAS TAX REPORTS, ¶403-676)

Interstate motor vehicles: Interstate motor vehicles, trailers, and semitrailers are not subject to Texas sale, rental, and use tax. For purposes of this exemption, an "interstate motor vehicle" is a motor vehicle operated in Texas and in another state or country for which registration fees could be apportioned if the motor vehicle were registered in a state or province of a country that is a member of the International Registration Plan.

Dealers and manufacturers: An exemption applies to a sale of a new motor vehicle to a franchised dealer who is authorized by law and by a franchise agreement to offer the vehicle for sale as a new vehicle and who acquires the vehicle either exclusively for sale or for purposes allowed under Ch. 503 of the Transportation Code.

CCH Advisory: Vehicle Registration vs. Titling

A licensed car dealer may purchase a motor vehicle for resale without incurring a tax liability. The vehicle must be held exclusively for resale and no other use made. When a dealer titles and registers a vehicle, the registration creates a presumption of use.

However, dealers may title a vehicle tax-free for "resale purposes only" as long as the vehicle is not registered. If a dealer registers the vehicle it indicates an intent to use the vehicle, and the dealer owes motor vehicle sales tax.

These procedures do not apply to vehicles that still have a Manufacturer's Certificate of Origin. Only dealers authorized to sell new motor vehicles may acquire a new motor vehicle for resale tax free, and only the make of vehicle they are franchised to sell. Motor vehicle tax is due on the purchase of a new vehicle when purchased by an independent motor vehicle dealer or a dealer franchised to sell a different make of vehicle, even if the vehicle is being held strictly for resale. Motor vehicle sales tax is due if a used car dealer titles a vehicle with a Manufacturer's Certificate of Origin for any reason. (*Letter from*

Part III—Sales and Use Taxes 213

Texas Comptroller of Public Accounts, No. 200403450L, March 19, 2004; CCH TEXAS TAX REPORTS, ¶402-669).

Also exempt is:

— the sale of a used motor vehicle in which the purchaser is a dealer who holds a dealer's general distinguishing number and who acquires the vehicle either for the exclusive purpose of resale or for other allowable purposes; and

— the sale to a franchised dealer of a new motor vehicle that is removed from the dealer's inventory for the purpose of entering into a contract to lease the vehicle to another person if, immediately after executing the lease, the franchised dealer transfers title of the vehicle and assigns the lease contract to the lessor.

Automotive repair: The repair, maintenance, or restoration of a motor vehicle is exempt. However, parts used during the repair, maintenance, or restoration of the vehicle are subject to tax.

CCH Tip: Treatment of AirCheckTexas Program Payments

The amount of a grant received by a purchaser under the AirCheckTexas program is excluded from the total consideration paid for a motor vehicle and therefore is not subject to Texas motor vehicle sales tax. The AirCheckTexas program, administered by participating counties, provides vehicle replacement grants and vehicle repair assistance to low-income individuals with polluting vehicles. The maximum grant amount is $3,500. Parts used to repair qualifying motor vehicles under the AirCheckTexas program are subject to state sales tax. However, no sales tax is due on repair parts that are paid for with funds paid directly to the service provider by a county participating in the program. Payments received from the county should be applied to taxable parts first. Tax is due on taxable repair parts above the amount of the county payment. Exemption certificates are not required. (*Tax Policy News, Vol. XVIII, Issue 12*, Texas Comptroller of Public Accounts, December 2008)

Motor vehicle tinting services are an exempt maintenance service, not a taxable remodeling service or a taxable purchase of vehicle accessories. (*Decision of the Texas Comptroller of Public Accounts*, Hearing No. 43,661, March 12, 2004, CCH TEXAS TAX REPORTS, ¶402-694).

If a repairperson repairs a component part of a vehicle, such as a starter or alternator, that the customer will place on the vehicle from which the part was removed, the labor is considered to be motor vehicle repair, which is not taxable. The customer should provide an exemption certificate that clearly states that the repaired part is being placed on the vehicle from which it was removed. On the other hand, if the repairperson repairs or rebuilds a component part that the customer will place in inventory or install on a vehicle other than the vehicle from which the part was removed, the labor is considered to be the repair of tangible personal property, which is taxable. (*Letter*, Comptroller of Public Accounts, No. 200610752L, October 12, 2006; CCH TEXAS TAX REPORTS, ¶403-173).

No tax is due on parts or labor furnished by the manufacturer to repair a motor vehicle, private aircraft, or tangible personal property in general under a manufacturer's warranty or recall campaign. The Texas Comptroller has determined that a warranty will exist for sales tax purposes only if (1) the repairs to motor vehicles were performed pursuant to a written warranty; or (2) the repairs were performed pursuant to an implied warranty within seven calendar days of the vehicle purchase. However, materials used in a repair to an "as is," "checked and certified" used vehicle under "goodwill" warranty do not qualify for the exemption. (*Decision of the Texas Comptroller of Public Accounts*, Hearing No. 39,916, March 22, 2004, CCH TEXAS TAX REPORTS, ¶402-696).

¶1002

- *Publishing, broadcasting, and motion pictures*

Newspapers: Sales of newspapers are exempt from tax. A "newspaper" means a publication that is printed on newsprint, the average sales price of which for each copy over a 30-day period does not exceed $1.50, and that is printed and distributed at daily, weekly, or other short intervals of four weeks or less for the dissemination of news of a general character and of a general interest. The Comptroller has determined that monthly publications do not qualify as exempt newspapers. (*Letter from Texas Comptroller of Public Accounts*, No. 200401317L, January 8, 2004; CCH Texas Tax Reports, ¶ 402-630)

"Newspaper" does not include magazines, handbills, circulars, flyers, sales catalogs, or other items that are printed to the special order of the customer, unless the item is distributed as part of a newspaper and delivered by the printer directly to the person responsible for the distribution of the newspaper. Tangible personal property that will become an ingredient or component part of such item is also exempt.

A transaction involving a sale of a newspaper that has been produced, fabricated, or printed to the special order of a customer is exempt if the customer (1) is responsible for gathering substantially all of the information contained in the newspaper and for formulating the design, layout, and format of the newspaper; and (2) would be entitled to the exemption for property used in newspaper production if it owned its own printing facility.

Practitioner Comment: Printed Materials Processed Out of State

Effective October 1, 2003, Section 151.011(a) was amended to overturn the court of appeals holding in Morton Buildings, which created an exclusion from use tax for items purchased and fabricated out-of-state into self-constructed assets later transported into Texas. However, the legislation contained a narrow exclusion for printed materials, providing that "use" does not include "printed materials that have been processed, fabricated, or manufactured into other property or attached to or incorporated into other property." The Comptroller implemented the exclusion by allowing an exemption from use tax for raw materials, such as paper and ink purchased and fabricated out of state into printed materials and later brought into Texas.

In *Southwestern Bell Yellow Pages v. Combs*, Texas Court of Appeals, Third District, No. 03-07-00638-CV (Tex. App. – Austin, January 30, 2009, pet. denied), the court rejected the taxpayer's contention that printing "services" constituted "printed material" excluded from use tax pursuant to Tex. Tax Code § 151.011(a). The Comptroller argued that the printed-material exclusion applied to raw materials, but not to printing. In ruling against the taxpayer, the court went further than the Comptroller, stating that Tex. Tax Code § 151.011(a) applies only to "printed material that serves as a component of some other finished product . . . "

34 TAC § 3.346 provides that raw materials incorporated into printed materials outside Texas will be subject to use tax unless the materials become components of some other finished product.

G. Brint Ryan, Ryan

Magazines: Subscriptions to magazines that are sold for a semiannual or longer period are also exempt if the magazines are entered as second class mail. "Magazine" is defined as a publication that is usually paperbacked and sometimes illustrated, that appears at a regular interval, and that contains stories, articles, and essays by various writers as well as advertisements.

Periodicals and writings published or distributed by nonprofit religious, philanthropic, charitable, historical, scientific, and similar organizations, excluding educational organizations, are exempt from tax. The exemption also extends to material written in Braille and audio recordings of writings and periodicals that are recorded and distributed by such organizations.

¶ 1002

Part III—Sales and Use Taxes 215

> ### CCH Comment: Controlled Circulation Magazines
> A "controlled circulation magazine," which is a magazine paid for by the advertisers rather than by the recipients of the magazine, is required to collect sales tax from advertisers on the basis of the sales price of the magazine. However, according to a Texas Court of Appeals, sales tax would apply only to any "premium" amount charged to advertisers to have the magazines delivered to a specified group of readers. (*Sharp, Comptroller of Public Accounts et al. v. Cox Texas Publications, Inc.* (TexCtApp, 1997), 943 SW2d 206; CCH TEXAS TAX REPORTS, ¶401-944)

Electrical transcriptions: Charges for producing an electrical transcription are exempt from sales tax. Any charges for making copies of an electrical transcription are subject to sales tax. The term "electrical transcription" refers to any master tape, disc, or other item, other than motion picture film or video tape, capable of reproducing sound when used in conjunction with electrical equipment and manufactured to produce copies or other recordings.

Motion pictures, videos, or audio recordings or broadcasts: Property, including gas and electricity, used in the production of a motion picture, video, audio recording or broadcast that becomes an ingredient or component part of the end result or that is consumed during production is exempt from tax. In addition, the sale of motion picture, video, or audio master set by the producer is also exempt.

Media production facility: A sale, lease, or rental of a taxable item to a qualified person is exempt from sales and use tax for a maximum of two years if the item is used for the following:

— for the construction, maintenance, expansion, improvement, or renovation of a media production facility at a qualified media production location;

— to equip a media production facility at a qualified media production location; or

— for the renovation of a building or facility at a qualified media production location that is to be used exclusively as a media production facility.

(Sec. 151.3415, Tax Code)

"Media production facility," "qualified person," "qualified media production location", and other key terms are defined under the Media Production Development Zone Act within the Government Code at Sec. 485A.001, Gov't Code *et seq.*

Television stations: A television station is not liable for tax on amounts paid either for the copyright license to broadcast film or the tax assessed on the original cost of the film. Tangible personal property sold to digital television broadcast stations is also exempt if the property is necessary for the entity to comply with TV transmission standards.

- *Repair services*

Sales tax is not due on labor to repair tangible personal property damaged within a disaster area if the amount of the charge for the labor is separately itemized and if the property was damaged by the condition that caused the area to be declared a disaster area.

> ### CCH Comment: 2011 Wildfire Victims
> Taxpayers whose homes or businesses were damaged or destroyed by wildfires in the state are not required to pay sales tax on certain fire recovery-related expenses. In addition, businesses may be granted tax extensions of up to 90 days while they clean up fire damage. Fire recovery-related expenses exempt from state and local sales tax include:
>
> — the cost of labor to repair fire damage to nonresidential property, including offices, stores, and other commercial buildings;

¶1002

— the cost of labor for residential repairs;

— services used to restore fire-damaged property (e.g., dry cleaning of clothing and draperies, carpet cleaning, furniture cleaning, and appliance repairs);

— charges for cutting damaged or dead trees (but charges to haul away trees and limbs are taxable); and

— purchases made with vouchers or debit cards provided by relief organizations such as the Red Cross and Salvation Army (but purchases made with cash or personal funds are taxable).

Additional information about wildfire-related tax issues and other resources to assist taxpayers are provided in a comptroller webpage at: http://www.window.state.tx.us/disaster/. (*News Release*, Texas Comptroller of Public Accounts, September 8, 2011)

The repair, remodeling, maintenance, or restoration of computer programs that are not sold by the person performing the service is exempt from tax.

Automotive repairs are exempt (see "Motor vehicles," above). Also certain repairs to aircraft and vessels are exempt (see "Transportation equipment," below).

- *Staff leasing services*

Services performed by assigned employees of a staff leasing company (also known as a "professional employer organization") for a client company under a written contract that provides for shared employment responsibilities between the staff leasing company and the client company for the assigned employees are exempt from sales and use taxes if the following tests are met:

— at least 75% of the assigned employees performing services under a staff leasing contract were previously employees of the client company for a period of at least three months immediately prior to commencement of the contract;

— none of the assigned employees were employed previously by the staff leasing company (unless the previous employment was through a shared employment relationship) or by an entity that previously provided or currently provides taxable services to the client company; and

— a shared employment relationship exists between the client company and the staff leasing company as to the assigned employees.

CCH Advisory: Start-Up Companies

When the client company has been in operation for less than one year and that circumstance is not due to a change in legal entity, merger, or corporate reorganization, a staff leasing contract need not comply with the first requirement that at least 75% of the assigned employees performing services under the contract were previously employees.

- *Telecommunications services and fees*

The following telecommunications services, other than mobile telecommunication services (see ¶804), are not subject to sales and use taxes:

— long distance services that are not both originated from and billed to a telephone number or billing or service address within Texas;

— broadcasts to the general public by FCC-licensed commercial radio or television stations;

— telecommunications services purchased for resale;

— telegraph services that are not both originated from and billed to a person within Texas; and

— access to a local exchange telephone company's network by a regulated provider of telecommunications services.

¶1002

Part III—Sales and Use Taxes

In addition, sales tax does not apply to 911 emergency service fees and equalization surcharges. (*Letter from Texas Comptroller of Public Accounts*, No. 200204977L, April 16, 2002; CCH Texas Tax Reports, ¶402-301) Direct-to-home satellite cable television service programming transmitted or broadcast directly to a customer's premises, including a residence, hotel, or motel, without use of ground receiving or distribution equipment, except at the subscriber's premises or in the uplink process to the satellite, is not subject to local tax under §602 of the Telecommunications Act of 1996. (34 TAC Sec. 3.313)

Nontaxable charges combined with, and not separately stated from, taxable telecommunications service charges on a customer's bill or invoice are subject to tax unless the provider can identify the portion of the charges that are nontaxable through the provider's books and records kept in the regular course of business.

- *Transportation equipment*

Certain aircraft and ships and vessels are exempt from sales and use taxes. Also, some repair services related to such property are exempt.

Aircraft: The following sales or uses of aircraft are exempt from tax:

— a sale to persons using the aircraft as a certificated or licensed carrier;

— a sale to a foreign government or a nonresident;

— a sale to a person who has a sales tax permit and uses the aircraft for the purpose of providing FAA-approved flight instruction that is designed to lead to a qualified FAA pilot certificate;

— aircraft rented by a student enrolled in an FAA-approved flight training course, if the aircraft is used for flight training, including solo flights, supervised by an instructor; or

— a sale in Texas to a person for use and registration in another state or nation, but only if the aircraft is not used in Texas before the sale for any purpose other than flight training or transporting the aircraft out of state. After the sale, the new owner can take lessons on how to fly the plane and fly the plane out of state without incurring a sales tax liability.

Department of Revenue Comment: Aircraft Purchaser Must Hold Common Carrier Certificate

A corporation's purchase of an aircraft through a series of transactions involving multiple entities did not qualify for exemption as a sale of aircraft to a person that uses the aircraft as a certificated or licensed carrier of persons or property, because the purchaser was not certificated or licensed by the FAA as a carrier of persons or property. The purchaser had structured the transaction so that the aircraft was operated by other entities that were certified and licensed as common carriers. However, the exemption is available only when the purchaser itself holds a common carrier certificate. (*Decision, Hearing No. 102,986,* Texas Comptroller of Public Accounts, January 21, 2011, CCH Texas Tax Reports, ¶403-689)

Department of Revenue Comment: Aircraft Must Be Listed in Operations Specifications Report

An air carrier's purchase of a helicopter did not qualify for tax exemption as aircraft used by a certificated or licensed carrier in transporting persons or property because the helicopter was not listed in the purchaser's Operations Specifications Report (OSR). The fact that the purchaser held a carrier certificate was not by itself sufficient. Federal Aviation Regulations prohibit a certificate holder from using aircraft that are not listed in its OSR. (*Decision, Hearing No. 102,678,* Texas Comptroller of Public Accounts, October 25, 2010, CCH Texas Tax Reports, ¶403-677)

Practitioner Comment: Aircraft Purchased for Use and Registration Outside of Texas

To claim the exemption found in Tax Code § 151.328(f) for aircraft purchased for use and registration outside Texas, a purchaser must complete a Texas Aircraft Exemption Certificate—Out-of-state Registration and Use. Comptroller's Rule 3.297(c)(9)(A) provides that the seller must give the completed certificate to the Comptroller within 30 days of the sale.

In Comptroller's Hearing No. 35,911 (1997), the Administrative Law Judge upheld tax assessed on the sale of an aircraft to a California purchaser because the purchaser did not sign the certificate when purchasing the airplane and the seller did not provide the certificate to the Comptroller within 30 days of the sale. Because Tax Code § 151.328(f) specifically provides that the purchaser must sign the certificate when purchasing the aircraft and Comptroller's Rule 3.297 specifically provides that the certificate must be sent to the Comptroller within 30 days, certificates provided after that date are not valid for purposes of the exemption.

G. Brint Ryan, Ryan

Practitioner Comment: Test Flights

Although it's true that before a sale a buyer can "test drive" a plane without incurring a Texas sales tax liability, more importantly, after the sale, the new owner can take lessons on how to fly the plane and fly the plane out of state without incurring a Texas sales tax liability.

Adina Christian, Ryan

Maintenance and repair: The repair, remodeling, maintenance, and restoration of aircraft is exempt. Machinery, tools, supplies, and equipment that are used or consumed exclusively in such repair, remodeling, or maintenance of aircraft, aircraft engines, and component parts by or for a licensed or certificated carrier or a person providing FAA-recognized flight instruction are also exempt. Also exempt is tangible personal property permanently affixed to such aircraft and property pumped, poured, or placed in the aircraft for normal aircraft operations, such as gases and lubricants.

Exemption for persons overhauling, retrofitting, or repairing jet turbine aircraft engines and their component parts: Persons who overhaul, retrofit, or repair jet turbine aircraft engines and their component parts are entitled to an exemption on the purchase of machinery, equipment, replacement parts, or accessories that have a useful life of more than six months. The exemption also applies to supplies, including aluminum oxide, nitric acid, and sodium cyanide, used in electrochemical plating or a similar process that are used or consumed in the overhauling, retrofitting, or repairing.

Ships and vessels: The sale by a builder of a ship or vessel that is in excess of eight tons displacement and used exclusively in a commercial enterprise is exempt from sales and use taxes. Materials, equipment, or component parts of exempt ships or vessels are also exempt, as are materials and labor used in repairing the vessels. (*Decision of the Texas Comptroller of Public Accounts*, Hearing No. 39,662, August 30, 2001, CCH Texas Tax Reports, ¶ 402-231)

Materials and supplies, including ship stores and sea stores, that are purchased by the owner or operator of a vessel operating in foreign or interstate commerce are exempt if the property is loaded on the vessel and used to maintain or operate the vessel or if it becomes a component part of the vessel.

Boats or boat motors sold to or used by a volunteer fire department or other volunteer emergency fire or medical service department, company, or association are exempt from boat and boat motor sales and use tax.

¶ 1002

Part III—Sales and Use Taxes

Also see "Motor vehicles," above.

Rolling stock: Rolling stock, locomotives, and fuel and supplies essential to the operation of locomotives and trains are exempt from sales and use taxes. Electricity, natural gas, and other fuels used or consumed predominantly in the repair, maintenance, or restoration of rolling stock are also exempt from sales and use taxes. (Sec. 151.331, Tax Code) In upholding the denial of the exemption for repair and replacement parts for two ship unloaders that operated on rails, a Texas Court of appeal held that the rolling stock exemption does not apply to any equipment mounted on rails. (*Reynolds Metals Company v. Combs*, Texas Court of Appeals, Third District, No. 03-07-00709-CV, April 8, 2009, CCH TEXAS TAX REPORTS, ¶403-553)

- *Utilities*

Gas and electricity are exempt from state and most local sales and use taxes when sold for residential use. Certain municipalities that adopted local sales tax before October 1, 1979, and certain special purpose districts (SPDs) associated with those municipalities, may opt to impose local tax on the residential use of natural gas and electricity. Campground owners may submit exemption certificates claiming predominant residential use to utility companies without performing utility studies. (*Sales of Utilities for Use in Campgrounds*, Texas Comptroller of Public Accounts, September 15, 2008, CCH TEXAS TAX REPORTS, ¶403-490) Gas and electricity used in manufacturing (see above), other than the preparation or storage of prepared food, are also exempt. If natural gas or electricity is used during a regular monthly billing period for both exempt and nonexempt purposes under a single meter, the predominant use of the gas or electricity determines whether it will be totally exempt or totally nonexempt. Generally, a person claiming that the predominant use of gas or electricity through a single meter is an exempt use must have a utility study performed to establish that the predominant use is an exempt use.

> **Practitioner Comment: The Account Name Matters**
>
> Under the Comptroller's interpretation, the exemption for natural gas and electricity requires that the purchaser, rather than the end user, be engaged in the actual exempt activity such as manufacturing or agriculture. Thus, if a building owner is engaged predominantly in manufacturing, the use of electricity in the building is exempt. However, if the building owner rents the building to another manufacturer and passes through the charges for electricity to the tenant, the building owner cannot claim a manufacturing or resale exemption, but must pay sales tax on the electricity. See *Comptroller's Hearing* No. 36,187 (1999), CCH TEXAS TAX REPORTS, ¶402-587 and *Direlco, Inc. v. Bullock*, 711 S.W.2d 360 (Ct. App., Austin 1986, writ ref'd n.r.e.); CCH TEXAS TAX REPORTS, ¶400-257. In order to overcome this limitation, the user of qualifying electricity or natural gas can purchase the natural gas or electricity in its own name directly from the utility and claim the exemption.
>
> G. Brint Ryan, Ryan

Electricity, natural gas, and other fuels used or consumed predominately in the repair, maintenance, or restoration of rolling stock are exempt. Gas and electricity are also exempt when used in mining, agriculture (see above), the repair of jet turbine engines (see above under "Transportation equipment"), under a national defense or national security-related electronics contract, or timber operations. See *Letter No. 200901277L*, Texas Comptroller of Public Accounts, January 5, 2009, CCH TEXAS TAX REPORTS, ¶403-542 for a discussion of the treatment of electricity by nurseries.

In general, sales of water are exempt from sales and use taxes. Equipment and services used exclusively for water conservation purposes are likewise exempt.

- *Vending-machine sales*

The following items that are sold through bulk vending machines for a total of 50¢ or less are exempt from sales and use taxes:

¶1002

— food or candy, other than beverages;

— chewing gum; or

— childrens' toys.

A "bulk vending machine" is a vending machine that randomly dispenses unsorted items, either one at a time or in approximately equal quantities.

Only half the proceeds of food vending-machine sales are taxable (¶902) except receipts from candy and soft drink sales, which are fully taxable.

- *Waste removal*

The removal or collection of the following types of waste is not taxable:

— hazardous waste (as identified or listed by the administrator of the federal Environmental Protection Agency or by any other appropriate federal or state agency);

— industrial solid waste (as defined in Health and Safety Code, Chapter 361) other than garbage or municipal solid waste (see *Southern Plastics, Inc., v. Combs, Texas Court of Appeals,* Third District, No. 03-08-00149-CV, July 1, 2009, CCH TEXAS TAX REPORTS, ¶403-562);

— waste material resulting from oil, gas, or geothermal exploration or production;

— domestic sewage or an irrigation return flow, to the extent the sewage or return flow does not constitute garbage or rubbish;

— industrial discharges subject to regulation by permit issued pursuant to Chapter 26 of the Texas Water Code; and

— radioactive waste that requires specific licensing under Article 4590f of the Texas Civil Statutes.

Department of Revenue Comment: Computer Monitor Disposal Fees

Computer monitor disposal fees are subject to Texas sales tax as taxable waste disposal fees because, according to a 2006 EPA publication, computer monitors are no longer regulated as hazardous waste. Formerly, computer monitor disposal fees were exempt because the monitors used to contain cathode ray tubes-CRTs, which quallified as hazardous waste. (*Letter 201105050L,* Comptroller of Public Accounts, May 18, 2011, CCH TEXAS TAX REPORTS, ¶403-714)

¶1003 Exempt Transactions

Law: Secs. 151.006, 151.052, 151.151, 151.156, 151.157, 151.1575, 151.158, 151.302, 151.304, 151.306, 151.307, 151.3071, 151.346, Tax Code; 34 TAC Secs. 3.285, 3.316, 3.323, 3.331, 3.358 (CCH TEXAS TAX REPORTS, ¶¶60-450, 60-590, 60-650).

Comparable Federal: Sec. 1504.

Certain transactions, such as resales and occasional sales, are exempt from taxation in Texas, as discussed below.

A service performed on an item of tangible personal property is generally exempt if the sale, lease or rental of the property would be exempt from tax because of the nature of the property, its use, or a combination of its nature and use.

- *Resales*

The sale for resale of a taxable item is exempt from sales and use taxes. Tangible personal property that is used to perform a taxable service is not considered resold unless the care, custody, and control of the property is transferred to the purchaser of the service.

¶1003

Part III—Sales and Use Taxes

Transfer of possession: In determining whether a transaction qualifies for a resale exemption, a taxpayer must demonstrate that care, custody, and control was transferred. Consequently a provider of public pay phones could not claim a resale exemption for purchases of telephone equipment, because the care, transfer, and control of the equipment was transferred only on a temporary basis. (*Decision of Comptroller of Public Accounts*, Hearing No. 38,980, February 26, 2001; CCH TEXAS TAX REPORTS, ¶402-178) Similarly, a resale exemption was denied for purchases of specified cable equipment purchased by a cable service provider, because the terms of the contract between the cable service provider and its customers did not specify that the customer obtained control over the equipment. (*Decision of Comptroller of Public Accounts*, Hearing Nos. 38,038—042, January 5, 2001; CCH TEXAS TAX REPORTS, ¶402-171)

The opposite conclusion was reached by a Texas court of appeal in *Sharp v. Clearview Cable TV, Inc.*, 960 S.W.2d 424 (Tex CtApp 1998); CCH TEXAS TAX REPORTS, ¶401-978. See (*Decision of Comptroller of Public Accounts*, Hearing No. 41,730, January 15, 2004; CCH TEXAS TAX REPORTS, ¶402-660) for a similar ruling concerning a country club's purchase of lockers to be rented to its members.

> **Compliance Note: Transfer of Software to Customers**
>
> A Web hosting service provider's purchases of software licenses from Microsoft did not qualify for a resale exemption because the taxpayer did not subsequently transfer primary care over the software to customers. The taxpayer owned data centers and computer servers used by its customers. After the taxpayer installed the Microsoft operating system (OPS) software on a server, it gave the customer the administrator password which enabled the customer to remotely access the server, customize the software, install new applications, or even lock out the taxpayer. To be entitled to a resale exemption, the taxpayer had to show that it had transferred the care, custody, and control of the software to its customers. Although customers acquired primary custody and control over the software, the taxpayer did not transfer primary care over the software. The taxpayer actively participated in the maintenance of the OPS even after access was handed over to the customer. The taxpayer patched the software with updates released by Microsoft and monitored the server and OPS for malfunctions. (*Decision*, Hearing No. 100,478, Texas Comptroller of Public Accounts, December 21, 2010; CCH TEXAS TAX REPORTS, ¶403-695)

"Sale for retail" defined: The term "sale for resale" is defined as a sale of tangible personal property or a taxable service to a purchaser who acquires the property for the purpose of reselling, leasing, renting, or transferring it to another person in the United States, its possessions or territories, or in Mexico. The resale item must be sold in the normal course of business and in the form or condition in which it was acquired or as an attachment to, or integral part of, other tangible personal property or taxable services. Tangible personal property purchased for the purpose of leasing or renting it is not a sale for resale if the leasing or renting of such property is incidental to the leasing or renting of real estate.

> **Compliance Note: Transfer of Toy Prizes As Part of Amusement Service**
>
> An owner of coin-operated amusement crane machines that contained plush toy prizes that patrons attempted to retrieve by operating a mechanical arm and claw inside the machine was entitled to a resale exemption on its purchase of toys used to stock the machines because the toys were transferred to its customers as an integral part of a taxable amusement service. Under the Tax Code, amusement services are considered taxable even though an exemption is allowed for amusement services provided through coin-operated machines. The care, custody, and control of every plush toy was eventually transferred to the taxpayer's customers in satisfaction of the resale exemption requirement, even though not every customer obtained a toy each time he or she played the game. (*Roark Amusement & Vending, L.P. v. Combs*, Texas Court of Appeals, Third

¶1003

District, Austin, No. 03-10-00105-CV, January 26, 2011; CCH Texas Tax Reports, ¶403-664).

A resale sale also includes a sale of a taxable service performed on tangible personal property for sale by the purchaser of the service and a sale of tangible personal property to a purchaser who acquires it for the purpose of transferring it as an integral part of a taxable service. A transfer of a wireless voice communication device (cell phone) as an integral part of a taxable service is a sale for resale if payment for the service is a condition for receiving the device. (Sec. 151.006(a) and (b), Tax Code; 34 TAC Sec. 3.285)

CCH Comment: Purchase of Services to Satisfy Lease Obligations

An airline company did not qualify for a sale for resale exemption when it purchased taxable janitorial and maintenance services from third-party providers to fulfill the airline's lease obligation to keep its airport leased premises in a clean condition. The airports merely leased terminal space to the airline with the requirement that the airline maintain the space. The airline's decision to purchase janitorial and maintenance services from third-party providers rather than perform the services itself did not transform its obligation under the lease into a sale of janitorial and maintenance services to the airports. The airports did not purchase janitorial or maintenance services from the airline, and the airline's fulfillment of its lease obligation did not constitute a sale to the airports. (*Delta Air Lines, Inc. v. Combs*, Texas Court of Appeals, Third District, No. 03-09-00312-CV, August 3, 2010; CCH Texas Tax Reports, ¶403-623)

Resale certificates: A purchaser may issue a resale certificate to a seller in lieu of paying sales or use tax on purchases for resale. The resale certificate must show the name and address of the purchaser, the number of the purchaser's sales tax permit, a description of the item, the purchaser's signature, and the date. If an application for a sales tax permit is pending, the purchaser should so indicate and include the application date. The certificate of an out-of-state purchaser must show the purchaser's out-of-state registration number instead of the sales tax number. A resale certificate may not be signed by a purchaser who does not know at the time of purchase whether the item will be resold, leased, rented, or used for some other purpose.

Purchases to perform nontaxable service: Effective October 11, 2011, a resale exemption may not be claimed on a sale of property or service to a purchaser who acquires the property or service for the purpose of performing a service that is not taxed, regardless of whether title transfers to the service provider's customer, unless the property or service is purchased for the purpose of reselling it to the United States in a contract or subcontract with any branch of the Department of Defense, Department of Homeland Security, Department of Energy, National Aeronautics and Space Administration, Central Intelligence Agency, National Security Agency, National Oceanic and Atmospheric Administration, or National Reconnaissance Office to the extent allocated and billed to the contract with the federal government.

Compliance Note: Resale Exemption on Federal Contracts

Effective October 1, 2011, a resale exemption may be claimed by a purchaser who acquires property for the purpose of transferring it as an integral part of performing a contract, or a subcontract of a contract, with the federal government only if the purchaser (1) allocates and bills to the contract the cost of the property as a direct or indirect cost and (2) transfers title to the property to the federal government under the contract and applicable federal acquisition regulations.

Part III—Sales and Use Taxes

- *Occasional sales*

Occasional sales of taxable items are exempt from both sales and use taxes. The exemption for occasional sales does not apply to the rental or lease of taxable items.

> **Practitioner Comment: Documenting Occasional Sale**
>
> The Comptroller has created Form 01-917, Statement of Occasional Sale, for use in documenting certain occasional sale transactions. Although the form is not required, the Comptroller recommends that the seller complete the form for the purchaser, and that the purchaser retain the complete form for at least four years from the date of the transaction. (*Comptroller's Letter No. 200711090L* (2007))
>
> *Adina Christian, Ryan*

One or two sales of taxable items at retail, or 10 or fewer sales of admissions to amusement services, during a 12-month period by a person who does not habitually engage, or hold himself or herself out as engaging, in the business of selling taxable items at retail or providing amusement services are occasional sales.

> **CCH Comment: Application of 12-Month Period**
>
> The 12-month period allowed for occasional sales is not based on a calendar year but, rather, on the 12-month period encompassing a sale date. However, the Comptroller has taken the position that all sales made within a 12-month period would be taxable if a seller planned any of them in advance, because a seller who plans a series of transactions is engaged in the business of selling taxable items. (*Letter*, Comptroller of Public Accounts, 200310180L, October 16, 2003, CCH TEXAS TAX REPORTS, ¶ 402-595)

Generally, maquiladoras are disqualified from making any tax-free occasional sales (see below).

Personal or family use items: An occasional sale includes the sale by an individual of tangible personal property that was originally purchased by the individual or a member of the individual's family for the personal use of the individual or the individual's family. To qualify for the exemption, the following conditions must be met:

— the individual does not hold and is not required to hold a seller or retailer permit;

— the individual does not employ an auctioneer, broker, or factor, other than an online auction, to sell the property; and

— the total receipts from such sales in a calendar year do not exceed $3,000. (Sec. 151.304(b)(5), Tax Code)

> **Department of Revenue Comment: Seller May Not Be Engaged in Selling Taxable Items**
>
> An occasional sale exemption cannot be claimed if the seller is engaged in the business of selling, leasing, or renting taxable items. In this instance, a fabric manufacturer's sale of an aircraft did not qualify for an occasional sale exemption, because it sold the fabrics it manufactured throughout the world. The occasional sale exemption did not apply even though the aircraft was not the type of item that the seller normally sold. (*Decision, Hearing No. 103,801*, Texas Comptroller of Public Accounts, December 20, 2010; CCH TEXAS TAX REPORTS, ¶ 403-671)

Mergers, consolidations, and acquisitions: The sale in a single transaction of the entire operating assets of a business or of a separate division, branch, or identifiable segment of a business is an occasional sale provided that the income and expenses attributable to the separate division, branch, or segment could be separately ascertained from the books of account or records.

¶ 1003

Practitioner Comment: Entire Doesn't Always Mean Entire

The sale of the entire operating assets of a business or of a separate division, branch, or identifiable segment of a business is an occasional sale and is exempt from sales and use tax under Texas Tax Code § 151.304, Occasional Sales; Comptroller's Rule § 3.316, Occasional Sales. However, in *Comptroller's Hearing* No. 32,398 (1994); CCH TEXAS TAX REPORTS, ¶ 402-589, "entire" didn't mean "entire." A taxpayer who purchased all but 16 assets in an asset purchase involving approximately 25,000 assets qualified for the occasional sale exemption. The ALJ determined that the 16 assets were merely *de minimis* and that the occasional sale exemption applied.

G. Brint Ryan, Ryan

Three or more sales of a business or identifiable segment of a business within a 12-month period will not result in the loss of the occasional sale exemption.

"Operating assets" means tangible personal property used exclusively by the enterprise in providing the product or service, but does not mean tangible personal property maintained and used both for general business purposes and by the specific enterprise. The term does not include inventory and intangible property.

CCH Caution: Auction Sale

The Comptroller has taken the position that purchases of all the operating assets of a liquidating corporation made during an auction were not exempt occasional sales if purchased piece by piece. In order for the exemption to apply, the items must be purchased in one transaction and not in a series of transactions. (*Decision of Comptroller of Public Accounts,* Hearing No. 17,644, March 15, 1988; CCH TEXAS TAX REPORTS, ¶ 400-724)

Transfer with substantially similar ownership: The transfer, other than a lease or rental, of all or substantially all the property used in the course of an activity is an occasional sale if there is no change in the real or ultimate ownership of the property. Ownership is "substantially similar" if the person transferring the property owns 80% or more of the stock of the corporation to which the transfer is being made, or if 80% of the stock of the transferring corporation is owned by the transferee. "Substantially all" the property means at least 80% of the total property.

Practitioner Comment: Comptroller May Disregard Transitory Entity

In Comptroller's Letter No. 200611755L (2006), the Comptroller reversed its long-standing policy of allowing certain tax-planning strategies to avoid sales or use tax on airplanes. Effective December 1, 2006, the Comptroller will analyze all transactions in which an entity was formed to purchase an airplane and transfer it to a related entity in a non-taxable manner. If the Comptroller determines that the method of transfer does not have a business purpose other than tax avoidance, the agency will assess use tax.

Adina Christian, Ryan

Intercorporate services: An otherwise taxable service exchange between affiliated entities (at least one of which is a corporation) that file a single consolidated federal income tax return for the tax year in which the transaction occurs is exempt from sales and use taxes. The term, "affiliated entities," includes those that would be classified as affiliated under IRC Sec. 1504 but for the exclusions contained in that section.

The exemption is not applicable to services that would have been taxable under the law as it existed on September 1, 1987. These services are:

— amusement services;

— cable television services;

¶1003

Part III—Sales and Use Taxes   **225**

   — personal services;

   — motor vehicle parking and storage;

   — the repair, remodeling, maintenance, or restoration of tangible personal property except maintenance of computer software and those services excluded from tax by Tax Code, 151.0101(a)(5); and

   — telecommunications services.

Moreover, services that are exempt under this provision and tangible personal property that is transferred as an integral part of such exempt services may not be purchased for resale by the providing company.

A limited partnership that elects to be treated as a corporation under the check-the-box provisions of the Internal Revenue Code may qualify for the intercorporate services exemption if the limited partnership reports its income on a single consolidated federal income tax return with other affiliated entities. Similarly, a limited liability company (LLC) that checks the box to report as a disregarded entity for federal income tax purposes may qualify for the intercorporate services exemption if the disregarded entity's income is reported by the parent company on a single consolidated federal income tax return with other affiliated entities. However, the exemption does not apply to a partnership that reports its income to the IRS on Form 1065. (*Letter,* Texas Comptroller of Public Accounts, No. 200212621L, December 9, 2002, CCH TEXAS TAX REPORTS, ¶ 402-444)

Joint ownership transfers: A sale of an interest in tangible personal property is exempt if the transferee, either before or after the sale, owns a joint or undivided interest in the property with the transferor. The sale must be made under the terms of a good faith bona fide contractual relationship, and the seller must have paid sales or use tax on the tangible personal property at the time of the purchase. The exemption does not apply to sales between related corporations or other entities if the only joint ownership is through ownership of the corporation stock.

Also, see the discussion of research and development ventures at ¶ 1005.

- *Out-of-state shipments*

Tangible personal property shipped by the seller to a point outside Texas is exempt from sales tax if the shipment is made by the seller by means of:

   — the seller's facilities;

   — delivery by the seller to a carrier for shipment to a consignee at a point outside Texas; or

   — delivery by the seller to a forwarding agent for shipment to a location in another state of the United States or its territories or possessions.

Property that is sold to a common carrier and shipped by the carrier to its out-of-state facilities in its business as an out-of-state carrier is also exempt. If delivery is made to a carrier for shipment to a location outside the United States, the seller must maintain the same documents that are required to show proof of export (see below).

Services performed for use outside Texas are wholly exempt from sales tax. This exemption does not apply to services performed outside Texas for use within the state. Services performed for use both inside and outside Texas are exempt to the extent that they are for use outside Texas.

It is presumed that printed materials that are distributed by the U.S. Postal Service singly or in sets addressed to individuals other than the purchaser will be used in Texas, requiring Texas printers and/or sellers to collect Texas sales and use tax on these materials. If the materials are for distribution to both in-state and out-of-state recipients, the presumption may be overcome if the purchaser of the printed materials issues an exemption certificate and agrees to pay tax on the materials distributed in Texas.

¶1003

- *Imports and exports*

Tangible personal property that is exported from Texas is exempt from state taxation by virtue of the Import and Export clause of the U.S. Constitution. Property acquired outside Texas is exempt from use tax if the sale, use, or storage of the property would be exempt had it been sold, leased, or rented in Texas.

Persons who purchase taxable items in Texas for export may seek a refund of taxes paid on those items so long as they provide the necessary proof of export documentation and the applicable waiting period has passed.

Electronic audio equipment that is exempt from sales and use taxes because it was purchased for use outside of the United States remains exempt, even if it is installed in Texas.

Proof of export: When an exemption is claimed for property exported beyond the U.S. territorial limits, the retailer is responsible for obtaining proof of exportation. Except in the case of purchases by a maquiladora enterprise (discussed below), exemption certificates, affidavits, or statements from the purchaser that the goods will be exported are not sufficient. Proof of export may be shown only by one of the following:

— A copy of a bill of lading issued by a licensed and certified carrier that shows the seller as consignor, the buyer as consignee, and a delivery point outside the U.S. territorial limits;

— Documentation provided by a licensed U.S. customs broker that certifies that delivery was made to a point outside the United States;

— Import documents from the country of destination showing that the property was imported into a country other than the United States;

— A copy of an original airway, ocean, or railroad bill of lading and a copy of the freight forwarder's receipt if an air, ocean, or rail freight forwarder takes possession of the property in Texas; or

— A maquiladora exemption certificate issued by a maquiladora enterprise and a copy of its maquiladora export permit.

Custom brokers: Only a licensed customs broker or an employee of a licensed customs broker may issue and sign a valid export certification form for purposes of establishing proof of export (item (2) above). A "licensed customs broker" is a U.S. customs broker who is registered with the Comptroller. A customs broker is required to obtain a license from the Comptroller and pay an annual $300 license fee (prorated on a $75 per quarter basis) for each place of business before issuing documentation supporting a sales and use tax exemption for tangible personal property exported to another country. In addition, to ensure payment of any sales and use tax owed each applicant must post a bond or other security in the amount of $5,000, plus an additional $1,000 for each place of business from which the customs broker intends to issue export certification forms.

The Comptroller must maintain a password-protected website that licensed customs brokers must use to prepare documentation to show the Texas sales and use tax exemption of tangible personal property exported outside the United States. A customs broker must submit quarterly reports to the Comptroller stating: (1) the total value of the property and the total amount of the corresponding tax for which the customs broker issued certificates of export; and (2) the total amount of tax refunded in accordance with certificates of export. The quarterly report is due on the 20th day of the month following the end of each calendar quarter reporting period. A penalty of $500 will be imposed for each report filed after the due date.

A licensed customs broker may issue documentation certifying that delivery of property was made to a point outside the territorial limits of the United States only if the customs broker:

¶1003

Part III—Sales and Use Taxes

— watches the property cross the U.S. border;

— watches the property being placed on a common carrier for delivery outside the United States; or

— verifies, by various means listed in Sec. 151.1575, that the purchaser is transporting the property to a destination outside United States.

The documentation must include:

— the customs broker's name and address;

— the customs broker's license number;

— the purchaser's name and address;

— the name and address of the place at which the property was purchased;

— the date and time of the sale;

— a description and the quantity of the property;

— the sales price of the property;

— the foreign country destination of the property, which may not be the place of export;

— the date and time at which the customs broker watched the property cross the U.S. border, at which the customs broker watched the property being placed on a common carrier for delivery outside of the United States, or at which the property is expected to arrive in the foreign country destination, as stated by the purchaser;

— a signed declaration stating that the customs broker is a licensed Texas customs broker and that the customs broker, or an authorized employee, inspected the property and the original receipt for the property; and

— an export certification stamp issued by the Comptroller.

A customs broker who fails to comply with export documentation requirements may be required to pay the Comptroller the amount of any sales tax refunded plus a penalty of $500 to $5,000.

Export certification stamps are issued by the Comptroller for a charge of $2.10 per stamp.

Purchaser identification number: Customs brokers must request a purchaser identification number from purchasers who are transporting property to a destination outside the United States. A purchaser identification number is defined as a number issued by the purchaser's country of residence for purposes of identification. (34 TAC Sec. 3.360)

Maquiladora enterprises: A maquiladora enterprise or its agent may make tax-free purchases in Texas of tangible personal property for immediate export to Mexico. Items may be stored in Texas prior to export to Mexico without incurring tax liability.

The term "maquiladora enterprise" is a Mexican-chartered business entity authorized by the Mexican government to make duty-free imports of raw materials, component parts, and other property into Mexico to be used in the manufacture, processing, and assembly of items for export from Mexico.

To qualify for tax-free purchases, a maquiladora enterprise must:

— obtain from the Comptroller's office a numbered maquiladora export permit;

— provide the Comptroller with a copy of the maquiladora authorization issued by the Mexican government; and

— post any bond or security required by the Comptroller sufficient to ensure the payment of state and local sales and use taxes.

¶1003

A maquiladora export permit holder may make tax-free purchases of goods for export to Mexico by providing the supplier with a blanket exemption certificate and a copy of the maquiladora export permit issued by the Comptroller.

Maquiladoras are disqualified from making any tax-free occasional sales, except a sale of all or an identifiable part of a business or a transfer of property without substantial change in ownership.

Each maquiladora export permit holder must file quarterly reports of tax-free and taxable purchases and must pay tax for any goods that are used or consumed in Texas (¶1103).

¶1004 Exempt Organizations and Persons

Law: Secs. 151.309, 151.310, 151.311, 151.321, 151.332, 151.337, 151.341, Tax Code; 34 TAC Secs. 3.315, 3.316, 3.322 (CCH Texas Tax Reports, ¶60-420, 60-430, 60-580).

Comparable Federal: Sec. 501.

In general, taxable items that are sold, leased, rented to, used, stored, or consumed by religious, educational, or charitable organizations and certain other non-profit and public service organizations are exempt from sales and use taxes.

The exemption for periodicals and writings published and distributed by non-profit religious, philanthropic, charitable, historical, scientific, and other similar organizations is discussed at ¶1002.

Construction on exempt property or for exempt entities is exempt unless the construction is for the use or benefit of a non-exempt entity (¶1002).

CCH Practice Tip: Contractor Lump-Sum Contracts with Exempt Entities

Purchases by a contractor of tangible personal property are exempt if the items are used in performing a contract to improve the realty of one of the following organizations:

— a nonprofit religious, educational, or charitable organization;

— the U.S. government and its instrumentalities;

— a school district or a nonprofit hospital;

— the state of Texas or one of its political subdivisions; or

— the governments and political subdivisions of bordering states that provide similar exemptions benefiting Texas and its political subdivisions.

A specific exemption also applies to property that is necessary and essential for the performance of the contract and that is completely consumed at the work site. Consumable materials must be material that is completely consumed after being used once for its intended purpose (e.g., tape). (34 TAC Sec. 3.291) Tangible personal property that is rented or leased for use in the performance of a contract does not qualify for the exemption, because it cannot be completely consumed.

Also exempt are services necessary to the performance of the contract that are performed at the job site. (Sec. 151.311(c), Tax Code)

Organizations must have a letter of exemption from the Comptroller and must provide an exemption certificate to the contractor. (34 TAC Sec. 3.291)

Qualification for exemption: To qualify for exempt status, an organization must satisfy all of the following requirements:

— the organization must be organized or formed solely to conduct one or more exempt activities;

— the organization must devote its operations exclusively to one or more exempt activities;

— the organization must dedicate its assets in perpetuity to one or more exempt activities;

— no profit or gain may pass directly or indirectly to any private shareholder or individual; and

— all compensation of officers and employees must be commensurate with the services actually rendered to the organization.

Religious, charitable, and educational organizations: An organization that qualifies for exemption from federal income tax under IRC Sec. 501(c)(3), (c)(4), (c)(8), (c)(10), or (c)(19) may qualify for exemption from sales and use taxes. An exemption also applies to qualified bingo equipment purchased by these entities.

An organized group of persons regularly associating for the sole purpose of holding, conducting, and sponsoring religious services may qualify for exemption. An organization that is based on nontheistic belief systems may qualify for the exemption. (*Ethical Society of Austin v. Strayhorn*, 110 S.W.3d 458 (Tex. CtApp 2003), denial of petition for review, Texas Supreme Court, No. 03-0479, April 23, 2004, CCH TEXAS TAX REPORTS, ¶402-484) However, an organization that merely supports or encourages religion as an incidental purpose or that has only a general purpose of furthering religious work may not qualify for exempt status unless the organization qualifies under another provision.

A charitable or eleemosynary organization that devotes substantially all of its activities to the alleviation of poverty, disease, pain, and suffering by providing food, clothing, medicine, medical treatment, shelter, or psychological counseling directly to indigent or similarly deserving members of society may qualify for exemption. The organization's funds must be derived primarily from sources other than fees or charges for its services.

An educational organization whose activities are devoted solely to systematic instruction may qualify for exemption. The organization must have (1) a regularly scheduled curriculum and faculty, and an enrolled student body or students in attendance where the activities are regularly conducted; or (2) activities consisting solely of presenting discussion groups, forums, panels, lectures, or similar programs.

Tax-free sales: A religious, charitable, or eleemosynary exempt organization, including organizations that qualify for exemption under IRC Sec. 501(c)(3), (4), (8), (10), or (19), and each bona fide chapter of such an organization may hold two tax-free sales or auctions during a calendar year, each of which may last for one day only. If two exempt organizations hold a joint sale or auction event for two days, both organizations are deemed to have used up their two days of tax-free sales or auctions. (*Letter No. 200606661L*, June 23, 2006, CCH TEXAS TAX REPORTS, ¶403-129) The exemption applies only to items sold by such organizations for a sales price of $5,000 or less. The storage, use, or consumption of a taxable item acquired tax-free at the sale or auction is exempt from the use tax until the item is resold or transferred.

An exempt organization must provide the vendor with an exemption certificate when purchasing, leasing, or renting an item that is necessary to an exempt function of the organization.

Nonprofit youth athletic organizations: A nonprofit athletic organization engaged exclusively in providing athletic competition among persons under 19 years of age may qualify for exemption if no financial benefit goes to an individual or shareholder. Such organizations may sell, or contract for the sale of, concessions at an event conducted by the organization without loss of exempt status.

Chambers of commerce, tourist promotion agencies: A chamber of commerce or a convention and nonprofit tourist promotional agency that represents at least one Texas city or county may qualify for exemption if no part of the earnings inures to the benefit of a private shareholder or other individual.

Development and health facilities corporations: Nonprofit corporations formed under the Development Corporation Act of 1979, the Health Facilities Development Act of 1981, the Texas Hospital Equipment Financing Act of 1983, or the Agricultural

¶1004

Development Act of 1983 are exempt from sales and use taxes when purchasing items for their exclusive use and benefit. These organizations do not have to prove exempt status. The exemption does not apply to items that are purchased by such corporations to be lent, sold, leased, or rented.

Electric and telephone cooperatives: An electric cooperative formed under the Electric Cooperative Corporation Act or a telephone cooperative formed under the Telephone Cooperative Act and nonprofit electric and telephone cooperatives located outside Texas may qualify for exemption.

Parent/teacher associations: If the PTA is the actual seller of an item, the sale may qualify for exemption during the two one-day tax-free sales available in a calendar year to certain exempt organizations, including PTAs. A PTA is the seller when it purchases inventory from a vendor and resells the items at its own profit or loss. (See *Combs v. Entertainment Publications, Inc.*, Texas Court of Appeals, Third District, No. 03-08-00474-CV, June 12, 2009, CCH TEXAS TAX REPORTS, ¶403-559) However, if the PTA merely acts as an agent for the seller, the tax-free sale provisions do not apply and sales tax must be collected based on the sales price to the customer unless another exemption applies. The PTA is an agent and not a seller when it takes orders for the vendor and receives a commission from the vendor, such as a share or split of the proceeds. This is often the case for items such as school pictures, books, and gift wrap. (*Letter No. 200704926L*, Texas Comptroller of Public Accounts, April 25, 2007, CCH TEXAS TAX REPORTS, ¶403-269) Additional information is available in the Texas Comptroller's Publication 94-183, *School Fundraisers and Texas Sales Tax*.

Senior citizens organizations: Sales of tangible personal property produced exclusively by persons who are at least 65 years old and that are sold at a qualified sale as part of a fundraising drive are exempt from sales and use taxes. All net proceeds must go either to the nonprofit organization or to the person who produced the taxable item sold. An organization that is created for the purpose of providing assistance to the elderly may conduct not more than four tax-exempt fundraising drives during the calendar year, for an aggregate total of no more than 20 days. Any sale occurring after the fourth drive or the 20th day is not exempt.

University and college student organizations: Sales of taxable items by a qualified student organization are exempt from sales tax if the student organization (1) sells the items at a one-day-only sale, the primary purpose of which is to raise funds for the organization; and (2) holds not more than one sale each month for which an exemption is claimed. The exemption applies only to items sold by such organizations for a sales price of $5,000 or less. The exemption limitations do not apply if the item is manufactured by or donated to the organization.

In addition, the first $5,000 of a qualified student organization's total receipts from sales of taxable items in a calendar year is exempt regardless of how or when they are sold. The storage, use, or consumption of a taxable item acquired tax-free under this exemption is exempt from use tax until the item is resold or subsequently transferred.

A student organization qualifies for the sales tax exemption if it:

— is affiliated with an institution of higher education or a private or independent college or university that is located in Texas and accredited by a recognized accrediting agency;

— has a primary purpose other than engaging in business or performing an activity designed to make a profit; and

— files a certification with the Comptroller of Public Accounts as required.

- *Governmental entities*

Generally, sales to the United States and to state and local governmental units are exempt from sales and use taxes.

¶1004

> ### CCH Advisory: Travel Expenses May Be Taxable
> A person traveling on official business for an exempt governmental entity must pay sales tax on taxable purchases. Sales tax must be paid whether the person is reimbursed on a *per diem* basis or reimbursed for actual expenses incurred. Agencies of the state of Texas may request a refund of hotel occupancy tax (¶1707) paid by the agency or reimbursed to an employee on a state travel voucher.

U.S. government: Sales to the U.S. government, its instrumentalities, and agencies are totally exempt. Purchases by a contractor of tangible personal property and taxable services are exempt if the items are used in performing a contract to improve the realty of the U.S. government or its instrumentalities. Similar exemption criteria apply as that applied for the exemption for purchases by contractors performing work for exempt entities. See the discussion above.

> ### CCH Caution: Purchases by Contractor
> A contractor may claim an exemption for items purchased to be used directly in performing a contract with the U.S. government as well as a sale for resale exemption for purchases of tangible overhead items allocated as indirect costs to multiple contracts with the federal government. (*Strayhorn v. Raytheon E-Systems, Inc.*, Texas Court of Appeals, Third District, No. 03-02-00346-CV, January 30, 2003, CCH Texas Tax Reports, ¶402-463)

The American National Red Cross and its local chapters are instrumentalities of the federal government and therefore may not be required by Texas to collect Texas sales or use tax on their sales of tangible personal property. However, this prohibition against requiring instrumentalities of the federal government from collecting a state's sales or use tax does not create an exemption for the taxable items sold. Thus, a purchaser owes use tax on the items if the items are stored, used, or consumed in Texas, unless another exemption applies. (*Letter No. 201106066L*, Texas Comptroller of Public Accounts, June 10, 2011, CCH Texas Tax Reports, ¶403-716)

State and local governments: Items sold, leased, or rented to, or stored or used by the state of Texas, or by its unincorporated agencies and instrumentalities, counties, cities, special districts, or other political subdivisions, are exempt from sales and use taxes. In addition, items sold, leased, stored, or used by a state or a governmental unit of a state that borders Texas are exempt if the bordering state or governmental unit exempts or does not impose a tax on similar sales to Texas or its political subdivisions.

There is no sales tax on any fee charged for furnishing copies of a public document under the Open Records Act or for furnishing copies of a document not open to public inspection, such as a college furnishing an academic transcript.

Fire departments: A volunteer fire company, department, or association is exempt from tax.

Public schools: Any college or university created or authorized by the state of Texas is an exempt organization. Items sold, leased, stored, or used by such organizations are exempt from sales and use taxes. Colleges, universities, and public schools are not required to collect sales tax on parking permits and fees charged to their students, faculty, or staff for parking. However, charges to the general public for parking are taxable.

Foreign diplomatic personnel: Foreign diplomatic personnel who are stationed in the United States are exempt from the payment of Texas sales or use tax if they hold a photo-identification card issued by the U.S. State Department. The exemption does not apply to gas or utility purchases and diplomatic exemption cards are not transferable.

¶1004

In the summer of 2011, the U.S. Department of State issued a newly designed Diplomatic Tax Exemption Card to authorize exemptions from Texas sales, occupancy, restaurant/meal, and other similar taxes. The exemptions apply to eligible purchases, official and personal, of foreign diplomatic and consular missions and their members in the United States.

The previous exemption cards used a blue or yellow stripe to visually convey to vendors the level of tax exemption privileges that a cardholder was authorized to receive. On the new cards, the blue/yellow stripes have been replaced with an image of an owl, an eagle, a buffalo, or a deer.

— An owl image signifies that the card is for official purchases, and the cardholder/mission is eligible for tax exemptions without restriction.

— A buffalo image signifies that the card is for official purchases, and the cardholder/mission's eligibility for tax exemptions is restricted.

— An eagle image signifies that the card is for personal purchases, and the cardholder is eligible for tax exemptions without restriction.

— A deer image signifies that the card is for personal purchases, and the cardholder's eligibility for tax exemptions is restricted.

The new card also describes the cardholder's level of entitlement to tax exemption privileges on the front and back sides of the card. (*Letter No. 201106068L*, Texas Comptroller of Public Accounts, June 6, 2011, CCH TEXAS TAX REPORTS, ¶ 403-719)

- *Native Americans*

In general, a taxable item that is sold, leased, or rented to, or stored, used, or consumed by a tribal council or a business owned by a tribal council of the Alabama-Coushatta Indian Tribe, the Kickapoo Indian Tribe, or the Tigua Indian Tribe is exempt from sales and use taxes. An exemption certificate or purchase order from the tribal council is sufficient proof of the exempt sale. The exempt status of a tribe or tribal council does not pass through to individual tribal members. Tribal councils of federally recognized tribes and their employees traveling on official business may also claim an exemption from hotel occupancy tax. (*Letter No. 201005670L*, Texas Comptroller of Public Accounts, May 14, 2010; CCH TEXAS TAX REPORTS, ¶ 403-611)

Sales, leases, or rentals that are made within the boundaries of the reservation by a tribal council or a business owned by a tribal council of these tribes are exempt from sales tax if the taxable item being sold was made by a member of the tribe, and if the taxable item is a cultural artifact of the tribe.

All sales that are made off the reservation and the sales of items that are not cultural artifacts that are made on the reservation are taxable.

See ¶ 1005 for a discussion of enterprise zones and research and development ventures. See ¶ 1003 for maquiladora enterprises. See ¶ 1002 for exempt amusement services.

¶ 1005 Enterprise Zones and Similar Tax Incentives

Law: Secs. 151.334, 151.348, 151.429, 151.4291, 151.431, Tax Code; 34 TAC Secs. 3.326, 3.329, 3.331 (CCH TEXAS TAX REPORTS, ¶ 60-360, 60-510, 60-530, 61-610).

Texas offers sales and use tax incentives for certain businesses operating in enterprise zones. Other tax incentives are provided for qualified hotel projects, cooperative research and development ventures, businesses qualifying as defense readjustment projects in readjustment zones, property taxes paid to certain school districts located in reinvestment zones (¶ 411), and wages paid to certain employees receiving financial assistance (¶ 2002).

Part III—Sales and Use Taxes   **233**

- *Refunds for enterprise zone projects*

An enterprise project designated by the Texas Governor's Office of Economic Development and Tourism qualifies for a refund of state sales and use taxes for each "new permanent job" or "retained job" that the enterprise project provides for a "qualified employee" during the period of its designation as an enterprise project. The refund amounts for an enterprise project ranges from $2,500 for capital investments of between $40,000 to $399,999 up to $7,500 for capital investments of $250 million or more.

"New permanent job" means a new employment position created by a qualified business at the qualified business site not earlier than the 90th day before the date the business's project or activity is designated as an enterprise project. The job must provide at least 1,820 employment hours per year to qualified employee and must also have existed or will exist at the qualified business site for the longer of the duration of the project's designation period or at least three years after the date on which a state enterprise zone benefit is received. A "qualified employee" is a person who works for a qualified business and performs at least 50% of his or her services for the business in the enterprise zone.

Qualifying purchases: The refund applies to sales taxes paid on all taxable items purchased for use at the qualified business site related to the project or activity. The purchases must be made by the enterprise project during the period in which a business is designated as an enterprise project or up to 90 days before the designation. (Sec. 151.429(a), Tax Code; 34 TAC Sec. 3.329(c))

Practitioner Comment: Separated Contract Required

Purchases of qualifying materials made under a lump-sum contract are ineligible for the sales and use tax incentive available to qualifying Enterprise Zone or Defense Readjustment Zone projects. In order for an enterprise project or a defense readjustment project to avail itself of certain sales tax refunds, the project must enter into a separated contract, and the charges for items that qualify for enterprise project or defense readjustment project refunds must be separately stated. See Comptroller's Rule §3.329, Enterprise Projects, Enterprise Zones, and Defense Readjustment Zones.

G. Brint Ryan, Ryan

CCH Caution: Purchases by Contractor

A contractor working for an enterprise project may not claim the exemption for purchases of materials used on a job for an enterprise contract under the auspices of an agency relationship. A contract between an owner and a general contractor does not create an agency for purposes of allowing purchases by the general contractor to qualify as exempt purchases by an enterprise project. (*Decision of the Texas Comptroller of Public Accounts,* Hearing No. 40,091, October 10, 2001, CCH TEXAS TAX REPORTS, ¶402-240)

Credit limitations: The maximum tax refund that an enterprise project may apply for in a state fiscal year is $250,000, increased to $500,000 if the project is located in a double jumbo enterprise zone, and to $750,000 if the project is located in a triple jumbo enterprise zone. A double jumbo enterprise zone project is a project that invests between $150 million and under $250 million in the project and is designated as such by the Texas Economic Development Bank. A taxpayer must invest $250 million or more in the project to qualify for a designation as a triple jumbo enterprise project by the Economic Development Bank. (Sec. 2303.407, Govt. Code; Sec. 151.429, Tax Code) An enterprise project that has been allocated the maximum number of jobs for purposes of the sales tax refund may not receive an additional and concurrent enterprise project designation, with an additional maximum job allocation and related tax benefits, in the same enterprise zone. (*Opinion of the Texas Attorney General,* Opinion No. JC-0567, October 29, 2002, CCH TEXAS TAX REPORTS, ¶402-419)

¶1005

Carryovers: Any excess refund claim may be carried forward to a subsequent year, but the carryover must be applied for prior to the end of the state fiscal year immediately following the state fiscal year in which the designation as an enterprise project expires or is removed.

Claim procedure: Refund claims must be in writing and must indicate the period for which the refund is claimed. Claims may be filed annually (covering the period of September through August of each fiscal year) or semiannually (covering the periods of September—February and March—August).

Maintenance of effort: The refund is conditioned on the enterprise project maintaining at least the same level of employment of qualified employees that existed at the time it qualified for a refund and for three years from that date.

One-time refund for job retention: A qualified business operating in an enterprise zone for at least three consecutive years is entitled to a one-time refund of sales and use taxes paid on purchases of equipment and machinery for use in the enterprise zone. In general, a "qualified business" means an entity that is engaged in or has provided substantial commitment to initiate the active conduct of a trade or business in an enterprise zone and:

— has at least 25% of its new employees in the zone who are residents of a zone within the jurisdiction of the zone's governing body or are economically disadvantaged;

— is a qualified hotel project that is owned by a municipality with a population of 1.5 million or more or by a nonprofit municipally sponsored local government corporation that is created under the Texas Transportation Corporation Act; or

— is a builder that has demonstrated (a) proficiency in residential construction in the state by providing five satisfactory home references for properties constructed by it in the preceding three years, (b) financial stability, and (c) participation in a 10-year insured warranty program.

To be eligible for the refund, the business must retain at least 10 jobs held by qualified employees during the year, as certified by a local governing body to the Comptroller's office. The refund is limited to $500 for each qualified employee retained, up to a limit of $5,000 for each qualified business.

- *Qualified hotel projects*

During the first 10 years after a "qualified hotel project" is open for occupancy, the owner of a qualified hotel project is entitled to receive a rebate, refund, or payment of 100% of sales and use taxes paid or collected by the qualified hotel project or businesses located in the project.

A "qualified hotel project" is a hotel that is proposed to be constructed by a municipality or a nonprofit municipally sponsored local government corporation created under the Texas Transportation Corporation Act and that is within 1,000 feet of a convention center owned by a municipality having a population of 1.5 million or more. The term includes shops, parking facilities, and any other facilities ancillary to the hotel.

CCH Comment: Hotel Project May Be Private Entity

A "qualified hotel project" includes a private entity *selected* by a municipality. Thus, a "qualified hotel project" is not restricted to a hotel owned by a municipality or a municipally sponsored corporation, and includes a hotel owned by a private entity. (*Attorney General Letter Opinion* No. 95-085, December 15, 1995; CCH TEXAS TAX REPORTS, ¶ 401-887)

¶ 1005

Part III—Sales and Use Taxes

- *Cooperative research and development ventures*

Items that are sold by a joint research and development venture to an entity that participated in the venture are exempt from sales and use taxes if the items were created, developed, or substantially modified by or for the venture, including items that were developed as a result of research and/or development agreements entered into by the venture with third parties. In addition, any items that are *purchased* by the venture for its stated purpose are exempt if the venture's public disclosure notification of its purpose, filed as required by federal law, was published in the *Federal Register* on either January 17, 1987, or May 19, 1988, and if the items have a useful life exceeding six months when placed in service by the venture.

- *Carbon dioxide capture and sequestration project*

A sales and use tax exemption is enacted for qualified components used in connection with an advanced clean energy project under the Health and Safety Code or a clean energy project under the Natural Resources Code. The components must be installed to capture carbon dioxide from an anthropogenic emission source, transport or inject carbon dioxide from such a source, or prepare carbon dioxide from such a source for transportation or injection. In addition, the carbon dioxide must be sequestered in Texas either (1) as part of an enhanced oil recovery project that qualifies for a severance tax rate reduction; or (2) in a manner that creates a reasonable expectation that at least 99% of the carbon dioxide will remain sequestered from the atmosphere for at least 1,000 years.

- *Defense readjustment projects*

A business designated as a defense readjustment project by the Texas Department of Economic Development is eligible for a refund of state sales and use taxes paid on purchases of the following:

— equipment or machinery sold to the defense readjustment project for use in a readjustment zone;

— building materials sold to the defense readjustment project for use in remodeling, rehabilitating, or constructing a structure in a readjustment zone;

— labor for remodeling, rehabilitating, or constructing a structure by the defense readjustment project in a readjustment zone; and

— electricity and natural gas purchased and consumed in the normal course of business in the readjustment zone.

The amount of refund that may be claimed is equal to $2,500 for each new permanent job or job that has been retained by the defense readjustment project for a qualified employee, up to $250,000 in a state fiscal year. If the defense readjustment project qualifies in a state fiscal year for a refund in excess of $250,000, the project may apply for a refund of the excess amount in a subsequent year, subject to the $250,000 limitation each year, but may not apply for refund after the end of the state fiscal year immediately following the state fiscal year in which the project's designation as a defense readjustment project expires or is removed. Also, the total amount that may be refunded to a project may not exceed an amount calculated by multiplying $250,000 by the number of state fiscal years during which the project created one or more jobs for qualified employees.

Items purchased by a defense readjustment project after it is designated as a project or within 90 days before its designation are eligible for the refund.

¶1005

¶1006 Exemption Certificates

Law: Secs. 141.001, 151.054, 151.155, Tax Code; 34 TAC Secs. 3.286, 3.287 (CCH Texas Tax Reports, ¶61-020).

A purchaser may issue an exemption certificate to a seller in lieu of paying sales or use tax if the transaction qualifies for exemption.

A resale certificate must be issued for items purchased for resale (¶1003). Direct payment permits are discussed at ¶1106.

Beginning January 1, 2012, a person claiming an exemption on certain agricultural and timber-related items must include a registration number issued by the Comptroller of Public Accounts on the exemption certificate that the person provides to the seller. (¶1002)

- *Taxable use of items obtained under an exemption certificate*

A purchaser that uses an item for a purpose other than that stated in the exemption certificate is liable for sales tax on the value of the taxable item for any period of divergent use.

The penalty for improper use of exemption certificates is discussed at ¶1306.

- *Seller's good faith*

A sale is exempt if the seller receives in good faith from a purchaser either an exemption certificate or a resale certificate from a purchaser in the business of selling, leasing, or renting taxable items. The resale certificate must state that the item purchased is to be sold or transferred as an integral part of a taxable service, in the regular course of the purchaser's business.

A retailer must be familiar with the exemptions that are available for the items the retailer sells. A retailer may accept a blanket exemption certificate from a purchaser who purchases only items that are exempt.

CCH Advisory: Common Audit Issues

A properly executed exemption certificate should be in the seller's possession at the time of the sale. Simply having permit numbers on file without properly completed certificates does not relieve the seller of the responsibility for collecting tax. Deductions claimed based on the certificates are disallowed if the seller fails to obtain exemption certificates within 60 days from written demand by the Comptroller.

Practitioner Comment: 61 Days Is Too Late

During an audit, the Comptroller requires that all certificates be submitted within 60 days of a seller receiving written notice from the Comptroller ("60-day letter"). Certificates submitted after the 60-day period are disallowed. The law does not provide for an extension or waiver of the 60-day period and taxpayers should make sure their certificates are complete and accounted for prior to the commencement of an audit. See Section 151.054(e) and Rules 3.282(1)(2), 3.285(b)(4) and 3.287(d)(4).

G. Brint Ryan, Ryan

- *Form of certificate*

The certificate must be in substantially the form that the Comptroller of Public Accounts adopts by reference. Copies may be obtained from the Comptroller's website at http://www.window.state.tx.us/taxinfo/taxforms/01-forms.html or by writing the Comptroller of Public Accounts, Tax Policy Division, 111 West 6th Street, Austin, TX 78701-2913, or requested by calling 1-800-252-5555 (in Austin, call 512-463-4600, and for Telecommunication Device for the Deaf (TDD), call 1-800-248-4099).

Part III—Sales and Use Taxes

The Multistate Tax Commission has adopted a uniform sales and use tax exemption certificate that is accepted by Texas.

Practitioner Comment: Incomplete Exemption Certificates Invalid

Comptroller's Rule 3.287 provides that a properly completed exemption certificate must be obtained on a timely basis and must include certain specific information as proof to the seller that the purchase was exempt from tax. Certificates that do not contain all of the information required by Comptroller's Rule 3.287(f) are considered incomplete and will be disallowed regardless of when they are obtained or submitted.

G. Brint Ryan, Ryan

¶1006

SALES AND USE TAXES

CHAPTER 11

RETURNS, PAYMENTS, RECORDS, ADMINISTRATION

¶1101	In General
¶1102	Returns and Payments
¶1103	Due Dates, Extensions, Discounts
¶1104	Prepayment of Taxes
¶1105	Vendor Registration
¶1106	Direct Payment Permits
¶1107	Recordkeeping Requirements
¶1108	Audits
¶1109	Absorption of Tax Prohibited
¶1110	Administration

¶1101 In General

Law: 34 TAC Sec. 3.286 (CCH Texas Tax Reports, ¶61-210).

The amount of sales tax must be separately stated on the bill, contract, or invoice to the customer, or the seller must provide a written statement to the customer that the stated price includes sales or use tax. Out-of-state sellers must identify the tax as Texas sales tax or Texas use tax.

In general, a seller computes the sales tax by multiplying the total receipts from all sales of taxable property and services by the percentage rate of the sales tax. However, certain vendors may use an optional method (¶1102).

Generally sales and use tax returns and payments are due monthly, quarterly, or annually (¶1103). Retailers are allowed discounts for timely filing of returns. An additional discount is allowed for prepayment of taxes (¶1104).

Every retailer, wholesaler, distributor, manufacturer, or other person who sells, leases, rents, or transfers ownership of taxable items for a consideration in Texas is required to obtain a sales tax permit (¶1105). Out-of-state sellers engaged in business in Texas must obtain a permit for purposes of collecting the use tax. Direct payment permits are discussed at ¶1106.

Taxpayers are required to keep records for specified periods of time (¶1107).

A retailer's absorption of the tax is prohibited (¶1109).

For electronic payment requirements see ¶1805.

¶1102 Returns and Payments

Law: Secs. 151.027, 151.403, 151.406—151.408, 151.410—151.414, 151.423, 151.424, 151.430, 151.462, Tax Code; 34 TAC Secs. 3.286, 3.302, 3.328 (CCH Texas Tax Reports, ¶61-220).

The following persons are required to file sales and use tax returns:

— a person subject to sales tax;

— a retailer engaged in business in Texas who is required to collect use tax; and

— a person who acquires a taxable item, the storage, use, or consumption of which is subject to use tax, if the person did not pay the use tax to a retailer or other authorized person.

Two or more businesses operating under a single taxpayer number must file a consolidated return.

A tax report or return must be signed by the person required to file it or by the person's authorized agent.

- *Accounting basis for reports*

Taxpayers may use the cash basis, accrual basis, or any generally recognized accounting basis that correctly reflects the operation of the business. The use of any other accounting method requires the prior written approval of the Comptroller. A taxpayer that uses a generally recognized accounting basis that accurately reflects the operation of the business may file the tax reports on the same basis as that used for the taxpayer's regular books.

- *Optional reporting methods for certain vendors*

In general, a seller computes the sales tax by multiplying the total receipts from all sales of taxable property and services by the percentage rate of the sales tax. However, any retailer who can establish that 50% or more of total receipts arise from individual transactions in an amount upon which no tax is produced and who has obtained written approval from the Comptroller may exclude those receipts from such sales when reporting and paying the tax.

Retail grocers and certain other vendors are eligible for alternate methods of reporting and paying sales tax. For purposes of these provisions, the term "retail grocer" is defined as a person who sells food at retail to be consumed off-premises, and who sells household supplies and nondurable household goods, but whose receipts from any other tangible personal property do not exceed 5% of total receipts.

Percentage of sale method: The following taxpayers may use a reporting method based on a percentage of sales:

— any retail grocer;

— any vendor who operates a separate grocery department that has separately auditable records; and

— any other vendor whose taxable receipts from the sale of taxable items are less than 10% of total receipts.

Retail grocers whose gross receipts do not exceed $100,000 per calendar year may pay tax based on 15% of total receipts.

- *WebFile*

Texas businesses may file their Texas sales and use tax returns online using the Comptroller's WebFile system. Taxpayers required to submit their sales and use taxes using electronic funds transfer (see ¶1805), must file their returns electronically. To use the system, a taxpayer must complete an online sales tax return. Once the form has been submitted, the system scans it for any errors and calculates the amount of sales tax due. The taxpayer may submit payment by a Discover, American Express, or MasterCard credit card or may have the payment electronically deducted from the taxpayer's bank account. If the taxpayer remits payment by electronic funds transfer, the taxpayer may select a date, on or before the due date, for the sales tax to be automatically paid.

The WebFile system is accessible through the Comptroller's website at www.window.state.tx.us/webfile .

¶1102

Part III—Sales and Use Taxes

- *Direct payment permit holders*

Direct payment permit holders (¶1106) may be eligible to report their sales and use taxes liability utilizing a percentage-based reporting method by which the taxpayer categorizes specified purchase transactions, reviews an agreed upon sample of invoices in that category to determine the percentage of taxable transactions, and uses that percentage to calculate the amount of tax to be reported. Taxpayers approved by the Comptroller to use this method must continue to use this method for a three-year period. However, approval may be revoked if the percentage used is no longer representative because of a change in law or in the taxpayer's business operations.

- *Information returns*

Persons who have information relating to the sale of a taxable item, the storage, use, or consumption of which is subject to use tax, may be required by the Comptroller to file a special use tax report. The report must contain the name and address of the purchaser of the property, the sales price, the date of the sale, and other information required by the Comptroller.

- *Alcoholic beverage sales report*

By the 25th day of each month, each brewer, manufacturer, wholesaler, distributor, or package store local distributor of alcoholic beverages must electronically file a report with the Comptroller which contains certain information for the preceding calendar month's sales, including the monthly net sales made to a retailer for each outlet or location covered by a separate retail permit or license number.

- *Refunds*

The amount of refund due a sales tax permit or use tax collection permit holder who overpaid tax to either the Comptroller or another retailer may be computed by using a projection based on a sampling of transactions. The sampling method used must comply with generally accepted sampling methods approved by the Comptroller. Reimbursement for overpaid amounts may be taken as a credit on the retailer's sales tax returns or by filing a claim for refund (¶2002).

- *Confidentiality of returns*

Records, reports, and other instruments required to be furnished for sales or use tax purposes are confidential and not open to public inspection. However, disclosure of confidential information is allowed under certain circumstances. In addition to the disclosure allowed under the general administrative provisions (¶1804), with respect to sales and use taxes only, confidential information may be used:

— by another state officer or law enforcement officer, a tax official of another state, an official of the United States if a reciprocal agreement exists, or a tax official of the United Mexican States;

— by a taxpayer or a taxpayer's representative if the document is the copy of a report or other paper filed by the taxpayer;

— for the publication of statistics classified to prevent the identification of a particular report or items in a particular report;

— by the Attorney General or the Comptroller in an action against the taxpayer who furnished the information;

— for the delivery to a successor, receiver, executor, administrator, assignee, or guarantor of a taxpayer of information about items included in the measure and amounts of any unpaid tax or amounts of tax, penalties, and interest required to be collected; or

— by a municipality with a population of less than 50,000 that has adopted a sales and use tax, to verify the amount of sales and use taxes paid to it during the preceding or current calendar year by each person doing business in the

¶1102

municipality who annually remits to the Comptroller state and local sales tax payments of more than $100,000.

Also, confidential information may be used if it is information set forth in a lien or a permit.

¶1103 Due Dates, Extensions, Discounts

Law: Secs. 151.401, 151.405, 151.423, Tax Code; 34 TAC Sec. 3.68, 3.286, 3.1281 (CCH Texas Tax Reports, ¶¶ 61-220).

Generally sales and use tax returns and payments are due monthly, quarterly, or annually. Every taxpayer required to file a city, county, or metropolitan transit authority/city transit department sales and use tax return must file it at the same time that the state sales and use tax return is filed.

Monthly: Generally, sales and use taxes must be paid and reported to the Comptroller by the 20th day of the month following the end of the calendar month being reported, unless a taxpayer reports and pays or prepays taxes quarterly (see ¶1104 for prepayment of taxes). The Comptroller may require a seller, retailer, or purchaser to file returns or pay taxes on other than a monthly basis if necessary to ensure the payment or facilitate the collection of taxes due.

Quarterly: If a taxpayer owes less than $500 for a calendar month or $1,500 for a calendar quarter, the taxes are due and payable on the 20th day of the month following the end of the quarter.

Annually: If the taxpayer owes less than $1,000 during a calendar year, the taxpayer may apply to the Comptroller to file on a yearly basis. If authority is granted, the return and payment are due on or before January 20 of the following calendar year.

• *Motor vehicle sales and use tax*

Motor vehicle sales tax must be paid to the tax collector-assessor in the county where the vehicle is registered by the 20th working day after the day that the motor vehicle is delivered to the purchaser. Motor vehicle use tax is due on the 20th working day after the day that the motor vehicle is brought into Texas. However, for commercial vehicles the motor vehicle sales or use tax is not due until the 20th working day after the date the motor vehicle is equipped with a body or other equipment that enables the motor vehicle to be eligible to be registered under the Transportation Code. A member of the U.S. military, a reserve unit of the U.S. military, the Texas National Guard, or the National Guard of another state who is on active military duty under an order of the president of the United States must pay motor vehicle sales or use tax no later than 60 county working days after the date of receipt of the vehicle.

The tax on the sale price of a seller-financed vehicle must be paid to the Comptroller by the seller as the proceeds of the sale are received from the purchaser. However, if a seller factors, assigns, or otherwise transfers the right to receive payments from a purchaser under an installment contract, all unpaid tax is due on the total consideration not reported at the time the agreement is transferred. The seller must report and submit the tax in the report period in which the right to receive the payment is transferred. The seller may not take a deduction in the amount of tax due if a transfer at a discount is made. (Sec. 152.047(g), Tax Code)

This due-on-sale provision does not apply in situations in which the seller/dealer:

— pledges the loans as collateral for the sale of bonds if the nonpayment risk remains with the seller;

— sells a purchaser's account to a related (using an 80% ownership test) finance company; or

¶1103

Part III—Sales and Use Taxes   **243**

— grants a security interest in a purchaser's account but retains custody and control of the account and the right to receive payments under the security agreement. (Secs. 152.047, 152.0472, Tax Code)

The seller still remains liable for collecting and remitting the tax when the purchaser's account is transferred to a related finance company. (*Letter No. 200708956L*, Texas Comptroller of Public Accounts, August 14, 2007, CCH Texas Tax Reports, ¶403-309) The Comptroller will establish a registration system for related finance companies and may charge an annual registration fee that does not exceed $1,500. (Sec. 152.0475, Tax Code)

- *Fireworks tax*

A seller must report and remit fireworks tax by August 20 on sales that occur during the following periods: (1) May 1 through May 5 if the sales location is not more than 100 miles from the Texas-Mexico border and in a county that has approved such sales; or (2) June 24 through July 4. A seller must report and remit fireworks tax by February 20 on sales that occur from December 20 through January 1.

The prepayment and timely filing discounts do not apply to the fireworks tax. (34 TAC Sec. 3.1281)

- *Extensions of time*

Extensions of time for filing returns and making tax payments are discussed in Chapter 18, "Administration, Reports, and Payment" at ¶1803.

- *Discounts*

Retailers may deduct a discount of $1/2\%$ of the tax due from their returns if the return and tax payment are timely. The discount is a reimbursement for the expenses incurred in collecting sales and use taxes. For retailers who prepay the tax, an additional 1.25% discount is available. See ¶1104 for a discussion of prepayment of taxes.

Yearly and monthly filing requirements, prepayment procedures, and discounts for timely filing do not apply to holders of direct payment permits (¶1106).

¶1104 Prepayment of Taxes

Law: Secs. 151.424, 151.425, Tax Code; 34 TAC Sec. 3.286 (CCH Texas Tax Reports, ¶61-230).

A discount of 1.25% of the amount due may be retained by monthly or quarterly filers who prepay their sales tax. The prepayment must be a reasonable estimate of state and local tax liability or at least 90% of the total tax due or the actual net tax that was paid for the same reporting period of the immediately preceding year.

- *Due dates of prepayments*

Quarterly filers must make their prepayments by the 15th day of the second month of the quarter for which the tax is due. Monthly filers must prepay by the 15th of the month.

By the 20th day of the month following the end of the period for which a prepayment was made, the taxpayer must file a return that shows the actual tax liability and must remit any balance due in excess of the prepayment. The taxpayer will receive an overpayment notice or a refund warrant if the prepayment exceeds the actual liability.

- *Penalties and interest*

All discounts are forfeited and a mandatory 5% penalty is imposed if a taxpayer fails to file the quarterly or monthly return and payment by the due date. An additional mandatory 5% penalty is imposed after 30 days' delinquency. After 60 days' delinquency, interest begins to accrue at the rate set out at ¶1909.

¶1104

• *Prepayment of tax in August 2013*

In August 2013, a taxpayer who reports sales and use taxes on a monthly basis and who pays taxes by electronic funds transfer must remit a tax prepayment by August 20th (for the July 2013 reporting period) that is equal to 25% of the amount the taxpayer owes for the July reporting period. This one-time tax prepayment is in addition to the amount the taxpayer is otherwise required to remit during August. The taxpayer may then take a credit in the amount of the tax prepayment on the tax report due in September 2013. Taxpayers who normally prepay taxes based on a reasonable estimate of tax liability under Sec. 151.424 are not subject to this special tax prepayment.

¶1105 Vendor Registration

Law: Secs. 151.106, 151.201—151.205, 151.251, 151.252, 151.254, 151.256, 151.262, Tax Code; Sec. 54.07, Alc. Bev. Code; 34 TAC Secs. 3.286, 3.327 (CCH Texas Tax Reports, ¶60-260, 61-240).

Every retailer, wholesaler, distributor, manufacturer, or other person who sells, leases, rents, or transfers ownership of taxable items for a consideration in Texas is required to obtain a sales tax permit. Out-of-state sellers engaged in business in Texas must obtain a permit for purposes of collecting use tax.

• *Sales tax permit*

Any person who desires to be a seller in Texas must apply to the Comptroller for a separate permit for each place of business in the state.

The term "place of business" is defined as an outlet, office, or location operated by the seller for the purpose of receiving orders for taxable items. Warehouses, storage yards, and manufacturing plants are not considered places of business unless the seller receives three or more orders in a calendar year at the location. A person who has traveling salespersons operating from a central location need obtain only one permit. A person who operates two or more types of business under the same roof needs only one permit.

The permit is valid only for the person and the place of business to which it applies and is nonassignable.

When issued, a sales tax permit is valid indefinitely; however, the permit may be canceled if no business activity is reported for 12 consecutive months. The term "no business activity" is defined as zero total sales, zero taxable sales, and zero taxable purchases.

A person who engages in business without a permit is subject to penalties (¶1306). The Attorney General may sue to enjoin a person who does not have a valid permit from selling taxable items.

Out-of-state wineries must obtain a Texas sales tax permit and a direct shipper's permit in order to sell and deliver wine to Texas consumers. Permit holders must maintain complete sales and delivery records for at least five years.

Application for permit: The application for a permit must be on a form prescribed by the Comptroller (AP-201), include the name and address of the business and other information required by the Comptroller, and be signed by the owner. The application may also be completed on-line at: http://www.window.state.tx.us/taxpermit. The applicant must also file adequate security for the payment of the taxes (see discussion below). The permit is issued without charge.

Suspension, revocation, reissuance: The Comptroller may revoke or suspend the sales tax permit of a person who fails to comply with the law. Such person is entitled to 20 days' written notice of the time and place of the hearing on the matter. At the hearing, the person must show why the permit should not be revoked or suspended. Written notice of the revocation or suspension must be given to the permit holder either personally or by mail. A taxpayer may appeal a revocation or suspension in the same manner that appeals are made from a final deficiency determination (¶ 2005).

A new permit may be issued if the Comptroller is satisfied that the person will comply with the tax laws and rules and such person provides sufficient security (see discussion below).

Temporary permits: The Comptroller may issue a temporary permit for up to 14 days. It expires without notice on the stated expiration date.

- *Use tax collection permits*

A retailer engaged in business in Texas who sells a taxable item for storage, use, or consumption in Texas must register for a use tax collection permit and provide security for payment of taxes. The term "retailer engaged in business in Texas" is explained at ¶ 803.

- *Security requirements*

Applicants for sales tax or use tax collection permits and permit holders who have been delinquent in paying taxes or filing reports must file adequate security with the Comptroller for the payment of state, city, and MTA sales and use taxes otherwise the permit or registration will be suspended or revoked.

Exemptions: A permit holder or use tax registrant is entitled to a return of the security if the person has complied with the required conditions for two consecutive years. Persons who received sales tax permits or were registered as retailers before 1974, and who are not delinquent are also exempt from filing security.

Amount of security: The bond or security is generally equal to the greater of $100,000 or four times the average monthly tax liability. An itinerant vendor may be required to post a bond at a minimum amount of $500.

The Comptroller may require the posting of a new or additional bond if the Comptroller determines at any time that the amount of the bond on file is inadequate.

¶ 1106 Direct Payment Permits

Law: Secs. 151.417, 151.4171, 151.419—151.422, Tax Code; 34 TAC Sec. 3.288 (CCH Texas Tax Reports, ¶ 61-250).

Holders of direct payment permits may issue blanket exemption certificates in lieu of paying taxes when purchasing, leasing, or renting taxable items. Items purchased under a direct payment permit must be for the purchaser's own use and not for resale. The blanket exemption certificate covers all future sales of taxable items to the permit holder and relieves the seller of the obligation of collecting sales or use tax.

All direct payment permit holders must file direct payment returns, regardless of whether they have taxes to report.

In instances when items are stored prior to use, a direct pay permit holder may elect to accrue and report both Texas state use tax and local use tax based on either first storage or first use, as long as the use taxes are reported in a consistent manner. That is, if a taxpayer elects to accrue state use tax based on the location of first use, then the local use tax must also be accrued and allocated based on the location where first use occurs. When applying for a direct pay permit, an applicant must indicate the type of accounting method that will be used for the accrual of Texas use taxes. This accounting method will be used in the event of an audit to determine the proper allocation and remittance of local use taxes. (*Letter No. 200805278L*, Texas Comptroller of Public Accounts, May 29, 2008, released February 2009, CCH Texas Tax Reports, ¶ 403-543)

- *Application for permit*

A direct payment permit application (AP-101) may be obtained from the Comptroller's Web site at: http://www.window.state.tx.us/taxinfo/taxforms. An applicant must agree to do the following:

— accrue and pay use tax on the storage and use of all taxable nonexempt items purchased, leased, or rented by the permit holder;

— pay the taxes monthly on or before the 20th day of the month following the end of each calendar month; and

— waive the discount for the collection of taxes under the direct payment permit.

The application must also describe the accounting method to be used for distinguishing taxable from exempt transactions and the records establishing that the applicant purchases annually at least $800,000 worth of taxable items not for resale.

- *Cancellation of permit*

The permit may be canceled at the initiative of the Comptroller upon written notice by registered mail. The cancellation is not appealable. A permit holder may also voluntarily relinquish the permit. In either case, the permit holder must immediately notify each seller to whom a blanket exemption certificate had been given that the direct payment or exemption certificate is no longer valid. The failure to so notify is deemed a failure and refusal to pay the taxes.

CCH Advisory: Refund of Use Tax

A direct payment taxpayer is entitled to a refund of use tax paid on tangible personal property that is acquired for storage or use if the taxpayer resells, leases, or rents the item to another before making any use of the property. However, a taxpayer is not entitled to a refund of the tax amounts paid or remitted on unused tangible personal property that is discarded or destroyed, because the refund applies only to property that is resold, leased, or rented. The issue is not whether the property will be used, but whether it has been resold, leased, or rented without having been used. (*Decision of Comptroller of Public Accounts,* Hearing No. 23,618, July 9, 1990; CCH TEXAS TAX REPORTS, ¶ 401-234)

Taxpayers holding a direct payment permit must also file a separate refund claim for overpaid use taxes even if they have already filed a similar claim for overpaid sales taxes. The Comptroller's Office has ruled that the pendency of an administrative hearing involving a taxpayer's Texas sales tax liability did not toll the limitations period for the taxpayer's filing of a direct payment refund claim involving use tax for the same period because each matter involved a different type of tax. (*Decision of Comptroller of Public Accounts,* Hearing No. 44,383, May 4, 2006, CCH TEXAS TAX REPORTS, ¶ 403-145)

¶ 1107 Recordkeeping Requirements

Law: Sec. 151.025, Tax Code; 34 TAC Sec. 3.281 (CCH TEXAS TAX REPORTS, ¶ 61-260).

All sellers of taxable items and services and all persons storing, using, or consuming taxable items in Texas must keep the following records, in the form required by the Comptroller:

— records of all gross receipts, including documentation in the form of receipts, shipping manifests, invoices, and other pertinent papers, from each sale, rental, lease, taxable service, and taxable labor transaction occurring during each reporting period;

— records in the form of receipts, shipping manifests, invoices, and other pertinent papers of all purchases of taxable items from every source made during each reporting period;

Part III—Sales and Use Taxes

— records in the form of receipts, shipping manifests, invoices, and other pertinent papers that substantiate each authorized claimed deduction or exclusion; and

— records in the form of sales receipts, invoices, or other equivalent records showing all sales and use tax, and any money represented to be sales and use tax, received or collected on each sale, rental, lease, or service transaction during each reporting period.

The Comptroller has authorized the use of microfiche and pdf files for purposes of storing exemption certificates. (*Letter*, Texas Comptroller of Public Accounts, No. 200605573L, May 17, 2006, CCH TEXAS TAX REPORTS, ¶ 403-073)

Records must be kept for at least four years unless the Comptroller authorizes destruction at an earlier date. Exemption and resale certificates must be kept for four years following completion of the last sale covered by the certificate.

The Comptroller will estimate the tax liability on the basis of the information available, including the records of suppliers, if a person fails to keep accurate records. The Comptroller's policy concerning missing records is to assume that all transactions are taxable, unless extraordinary circumstances can be established. A taxpayer's move is not considered to be an extraordinary circumstance, however, the Comptroller has granted relief when records were misfiled during a merger. (*Decision of Comptroller of Public Accounts,* Hearing No. 41,876, January 14, 2004; CCH TEXAS TAX REPORTS, ¶ 402-664)

¶ 1108 Audits

Law: Secs. 111.0042, 111.0075, 151.023, 151.0231, Tax Code; 34 TAC Secs. 3.282, 3.368 (CCH TEXAS TAX REPORTS, ¶ 61-420).

The Comptroller or his or her representative may examine, copy, and photograph the books, records, papers, and equipment of any person who sells taxable items or who is liable for use tax and may investigate the character of the taxpayer's business to verify the accuracy of a report or to determine the amount of tax required to be paid. In addition, the Comptroller may, upon 10 days' notice, require a taxpayer to produce for inspection the books, records, papers, and returns relating to the taxable activity stated in the notice.

Both sellers and purchasers may be audited and assessed relative to any transaction on which tax was due but has not been paid and both remain liable until the tax, penalty, and interest have been paid. An audit may be conducted at any time during regular business hours at the discretion of the Comptroller or his authorized representative.

Sampling: The Comptroller is authorized to use sample auditing methods to determine tax liability. Sampling methods are appropriate if:

— the records are so voluminous that a detailed audit is impractical;

— the taxpayer's records are incomplete; or

— the cost of a detailed audit would be unreasonable in relation to the benefits derived.

The sample must reflect as nearly as possible the normal conditions under which the business was operated during the audit period. Before a sample technique may be used to establish a tax liability, the taxpayer must be given written notification of the sampling procedure to be used.

- *Resale and exemption certificates*

Resale and exemption certificates are the only acceptable proof that taxable items are purchased for resale or qualify for exemption. Resale and exemption certificates should be available at the time of the audit. Certificates acquired after the audit begins are subject to independent confirmation before the deductions will be allowed.

¶ 1108

Any deductions claimed that require resale or exemption certificates will be disallowed if a seller is not in possession of resale or exemption certificates within 60 days after the date on which the Comptroller gives written notice that certificates for particular periods or transactions are required.

Department of Revenue Comment: Claiming Credit for Taxes Paid by Subcontractors

At an audit for unpaid taxes on commercial remodeling jobs, a general contractor was denied a credit for sales taxes that it claimed were previously paid by its subcontractors on materials and were included in subcontract prices that the general contractor passed on to the owner of the property. The taxpayer had not issue resale certificates to the subcontractors. To qualify as a tax-included contract, there must be a written statement that the stated price includes sales or use taxes. Contracts, bills, or invoices that only state "all taxes" included are not specific enough to relieve either party of its sales and use tax responsibilities. In this case, the taxpayer submitted invoices that contained, in separate line items for taxes, the designation "INC." This documentation fell short of the required proof. Sales or use taxes were not specifically identified. Moreover, the comptroller submitted evidence that the taxpayer's subcontractors did not hold sales tax permits and did not remit any sales taxes. (*Decision, Hearing No. 101,939*, Texas Comptroller of Public Accounts, June 29, 2011, CCH TEXAS TAX REPORTS, ¶ 403-758)

- *Multistate audits*

Because Texas is a member of the Multistate Tax Compact, a taxpayer may be subject to multistate audits of sales and use tax liability.

- *Managed audits*

A taxpayer may enter into an agreement with the Comptroller that allows the taxpayer to conduct a managed audit of the taxpayer's business to determine the taxpayer's sales and use tax liability for specified transactions occurring during a set period of time. Penalties will be abated and interest may be waived on any amount identified to be due by the Comptroller's office when verifying the audit results. However, penalties and interest will still be imposed if there is fraud or willful evasion of tax involved or if the taxpayer does not remit to the Comptroller's office any amount of tax actually collected.

Practitioner Comment: Managed Audit Requests on a Short Fuse

The Texas Managed Audit program is one of the most advantageous managed audit programs available to taxpayers in any state. Among other benefits, the program provides complete or partial waiver of penalty and interest for audits successfully conducted under the terms of the managed audit program. Under prior policy, taxpayers could request participation in the managed audit program at any time prior to the commencement of field work.

Effective April 12, 2007, Managed Audit requests must be made within thirty (30) days of the issuance of an Audit Notification Letter. Requests made after thirty (30) days will not be considered by the Comptroller. This policy change puts a very valuable program on a very short fuse for taxpayers.

The Managed Audit Program is authorized under Texas Tax Code § 151.0231, Managed Audits.

G. Brint Ryan, Ryan

In determining whether to authorize a taxpayer to conduct managed audits, the Comptroller may consider:

— the taxpayer's history of tax compliance;

— the amount of time and resources the taxpayer has available to dedicate to the audit;

Part III—Sales and Use Taxes 249

— the extent and availability of the taxpayer's records; and
— the taxpayer's ability to pay any expected liability.

Practitioner Comment: Overlooked Refunds May Be Lost

A taxpayer's failure to identify and claim a refund of an overpayment of tax for any period covered by a managed audit before the managed audit becomes final is a waiver of any demand against the Comptroller for an alleged overpayment of tax. The only exception to this policy is in cases where a court invalidates a statutory provision, rule, or agency policy or in cases where the Comptroller invalidates or modifies a rule or agency policy. Therefore, regardless of the applicable limitations period, all refunds not claimed during the managed audit are lost. Taxpayers should consider this provision of the managed audit agreement carefully before requesting a managed audit. The Managed Audit Program is authorized under Texas Tax Code § 151.0231, Managed Audits.

G. Brint Ryan, Ryan

- *Use of audit information*

A person who obtains public information relating to taxpayer audits must wait until the sixth day after the date the Comptroller made the information available to the person before using the information to solicit business or employment for pecuniary gain. Penalties are provided for violation of this provision. According to a legislative report, the purpose of the provision is to prevent a situation in which a taxpayer is contacted by tax consultants before the taxpayer is aware that a tax audit has been ordered.

¶1109 Absorption of Tax Prohibited

Law: Sec. 151.704, Tax Code; 34 TAC Sec. 3.286 (CCH Texas Tax Reports, ¶61-210).

A retailer may not advertise or state to a customer or to the public that the retailer will assume, absorb, or refund any part of the tax or will not add the tax to the sales price. Retailers who do so are subject to a penalty (¶1306).

¶1110 Administration

Texas has uniform procedures for the administration of all taxes administered by the Comptroller of Public Accounts (¶1802), including sales and use taxes. They establish a single set of rules and procedures for refunds, credits, deficiency assessments, protests and appeals, report filing dates, interest on deficiencies and refunds, extensions of time, lien priorities, and periods of limitations. These provisions are discussed in detail in Part VII, "Administration and Procedure," beginning at ¶1801.

SALES AND USE TAXES

CHAPTER 12

CREDITS

	¶1201	In General
	¶1202	Credit for Tax Paid to Another State
	¶1203	Credit for Tax Paid on Property Subsequently Resold
	¶1204	Credits for Contractors and Repairpersons
	¶1205	Temporary Credit for Real Property Contributed to Institution of Higher Education

¶1201 In General

Texas allows several credits against sales and use taxes. Discussed in the following paragraphs are the credit for taxes paid to another state (¶1202), the credit for tax paid on property subsequently resold (¶1203), credits allowed to contractors and repairpersons (¶1204), and the temporary credit for real property contributed to institutions of higher education (¶1205).

In addition to these credits, discounts are provided for timely payment of taxes (¶1103) and for prepayment of taxes (¶1104). Also, tax incentives are available for enterprise zone projects, qualified hotel projects, cooperative research and development ventures, and defense readjustment projects (¶1005).

A refund of sales and use taxes (and other taxes) is authorized for wages paid by a taxpayer to employees who receive state financial assistance and for whom the taxpayer provides or pays for a portion of the cost of qualifying health benefit coverage (¶2002).

¶1202 Credit for Tax Paid to Another State

Law: Sec. 151.303, Tax Code; 34 TAC Secs. 3.61, 3.338, 3.346 (CCH Texas Tax Reports, ¶61-270).

As a member of the Multistate Tax Compact, Texas allows as a credit against Texas use tax any combined amounts of legally imposed sales and use taxes paid on the same property to another state or a political subdivision of another state, if such other state provides a similar credit for Texas taxpayers. The credit is allowed even if the other state is not a member of the Multistate Compact.

The credit is first applied against the amount of use tax due the Metropolitan Transit Authority or city transit department (see ¶904 for a discussion of local and transit district taxes), then against county use tax due, if any, then against the amount of any city use tax due, and finally, against state use tax.

Sales tax imposed by Texas will not be refunded because of a subsequent payment of use tax to another state. However, Texas will refund or credit, to the extent of the payment, use tax that is subsequently paid to another state if the other state's use tax was imposed because the item was used in that state prior to its use in Texas.

Credit against Texas use tax will not be allowed for sales tax paid to another state if the tax was not legally due and payable to that state.

A credit against Texas use tax will not be allowed for any gross receipts tax imposed on retailers in another state that is not customarily separated from the sales price and is not passed on directly to customers as tax.

A Texas motor vehicle sales and use tax credit is allowed for sales or use tax paid to another state or a political subdivision of another state on a motor vehicle. Credit is not allowed for payment of a foreign country's tax, custom or duty tax, or import tax. Also, credit is not allowed against the state's new resident tax or the Texas Emissions Reduction Plan (TERP) surcharge.

¶1203 Credit for Tax Paid on Property Subsequently Resold

Law: Sec. 151.427, Tax Code; 34 TAC Sec. 3.338 (CCH Texas Tax Reports, ¶61-270).

A seller who acquires tangible personal property for storage or use, pays the tax, and subsequently sells, leases, or rents the item in the regular course of business before making a taxable use of the property may take a credit for the amount of tax paid to the supplier. The seller must not have made any use of the item other than retaining, displaying, or demonstrating it while holding it for sale.

The purchaser must have a receipt from a Texas retailer or other seller authorized to collect Texas sales and use taxes, reflecting the tax paid and the selling price of the item purchased. A purchaser may claim a credit on a return for a later period or by filing an amended return.

A credit for local sales and use tax may also be claimed, provided the tax paid to the supplier was for the same local taxing jurisdiction to which the purchaser is required to remit tax. Local tax paid to a supplier in a local taxing jurisdiction other than the one in which the taxable items are subsequently resold must be recovered from the supplier.

¶1204 Credits for Contractors and Repairpersons

Law: 34 TAC Sec. 3.338 (CCH Texas Tax Reports, ¶61-270).

A contractor improving real property under a separate contract may claim a tax credit for Texas sales and use taxes paid to a supplier on items incorporated into the property being improved. However, a credit is not allowed if sales or use tax liability is not incurred in the subsequent incorporation of the taxable item into real property. For example, no sales or use tax liability is incurred when the contract is with an exempt organization; therefore, tax paid to a supplier for taxable items may not be claimed as a credit on the contractor's return.

A contractor's credit for tax paid to a supplier will be limited to the amount of tax otherwise due to be reported by the contractor on the subsequent incorporation of the same tangible personal property into real property on which an improvement is performed.

A person repairing motor vehicles or private aircraft may claim a credit on the purchaser's return for tax paid to suppliers if the repairs are performed pursuant to a separated (not a lump-sum) contract.

¶1205 Temporary Credit for Real Property Contributed to Institution of Higher Education

Law: Sec. 111.110, Tax Code (CCH Texas Tax Reports, ¶61-270).

A special credit is allowed against sales and use taxes for 50% of the fair market value of a parcel of real estate transferred by the taxpayer to an institution of higher education by August 31, 1996, if the Comptroller issued a credit to the taxpayer and specified conditions were met. Five percent or less of the total credit may be claimed in any calendar year for 20 years after the credit was issued.

¶1203

SALES AND USE TAXES

CHAPTER 13

COLLECTION OF TAX

¶ 1301	In General
¶ 1302	Assessments
¶ 1303	Collection Suits
¶ 1304	Judgments
¶ 1305	Statute of Limitations
¶ 1306	Penalties and Interest

¶ 1301 In General

The following paragraphs discuss only those collection provisions that are specifically applicable to sales and use taxes. General provisions that apply to all taxes administered by the Comptroller (¶ 1802), including sales and use taxes, are discussed in Part VII, "Administration and Procedure," beginning at ¶ 1801.

A deficiency determination may be made by the Comptroller if no return is filed (¶ 1302). Generally, the assessment must be made within four years (¶ 1305).

The Comptroller may bring suit to collect unpaid sales and use taxes, penalties, and interest (¶ 1303). Generally, a suit must be brought within three years (¶ 1305). Once the state obtains a judgment, it may file a lien on all real property owned or subsequently acquired by the defendant in any county in the state (¶ 1304).

Penalties and interest are discussed at ¶ 1306. For a discussion of the Comptroller's authority to settle or waive the penalty or interest on unpaid tax if the taxpayer exercised reasonable diligence in attempting to comply with the tax laws, see ¶ 1903.

> *CCH Pointer: Detrimental reliance*
>
> The Comptroller will waive the following Texas sales and use tax, penalties, and interest when a purchaser has proven detrimental reliance on advice or information provided by the Comptroller's office in relation to taxable purchases:
>
> — all penalties and interest;
>
> — tax on materials directly utilized and consumed in the performance of a service or sale of a product for an unrelated third party;
>
> — tax on indirect materials or services if the taxpayer can prove that these items were used in computing prices or bids; and
>
> — tax on assets or tools directly used in the performance of services or sales may be partially exempted based upon their purchase dates and the remaining life of the assets.
>
> In addition, a full waiver and possible ongoing waiver will be considered if a taxpayer can prove that the Comptroller's advice was used in a decision to locate facilities in Texas. (*Letter No. 200712099L*, Texas Comptroller of Public Accounts, December 13, 2007, received June 2008, CCH Texas Tax Reports, ¶ 403-427)

CCH Advisory: Personal Liability of Corporate Officers

A corporate officer was personally liable for Texas sales tax, municipal sales tax, and transit authority sales tax collected by the corporation but not remitted to the state because the officer had control over the corporation's financial affairs and caused the corporation to breach its fiduciary duty to remit the tax to the state. The corporation held the taxes in trust for the benefit of the state and the officer, acting as the corporation's agent, was also a trustee of the state's tax money who could be held liable for any unremitted amounts. (*Mink*, Texas Court of Appeals, Third District, No. 03-98-00032-CV, February 11, 1999; CCH TEXAS TAX REPORTS, ¶ 402-043)

¶1302 Assessments

Law: Secs. 151.503—151.505, 151.508, 151.511, Tax Code (CCH TEXAS TAX REPORTS, ¶ 61-410).

The Comptroller may compute the tax due using any information available if no return is filed. Deficiency determinations may be issued for one or more periods, and more than one determination may be issued for a single period. A deficiency determination other than a jeopardy determination becomes final 30 days after the date the determination was served unless a petition for redetermination (¶ 2003) is filed in the meantime.

The Comptroller may make a determination before the due date of a tax payment or return if a business is discontinued.

- *Offsets*

In making a determination, the Comptroller may offset an overpayment against an underpayment or penalty and interest for the same or other periods. Any interest accrued on the overpayments is included in the offset.

- *Redetermination*

The Comptroller may decrease the amount of a tax determination at any time before the determination becomes final and may increase such amount if the increase is asserted at or before a hearing on redetermination. A taxpayer is entitled to a 30-day continuance if such an additional claim is asserted.

¶1303 Collection Suits

Law: Secs. 151.515, 151.601—151.603, 151.605, Tax Code (CCH TEXAS TAX REPORTS, ¶ 61-510).

The Comptroller, through the Attorney General, may bring an action to collect unpaid sales and use taxes, penalties, and interest in a Texas court or in another state or federal court. An action brought in Texas may be brought in the county where the person owing the tax resides or has a place of business, or in Travis County.

No bond or affidavit is required before the issuance of a writ of attachment. A Comptroller's certificate showing the delinquency is *prima facie* evidence of the determination and amount of the tax, penalties, and interest, the delinquency of the amounts, and the Comptroller's compliance in computing and determining the amounts.

¶1304 Judgments

Law: Sec. 151.608, Tax Code (CCH TEXAS TAX REPORTS, ¶ 61-500).

Once the state obtains a judgment, it may file a lien on all real property owned or subsequently acquired by the defendant in any county in the state. The lien will be in effect for 10 years after the date of judgment unless the lien is released or discharged before then.

Part III—Sales and Use Taxes

A prior judgment is not a bar to a subsequent suit for additional taxes, penalties, and interest accruing after the prior judgment, if the suit is brought before the expiration of the limitation period (¶ 1305). Execution on a tax judgment may issue in the same manner as an execution under other judgments.

¶ 1305 Statute of Limitations

Law: Sec. 151.607, Tax Code; 34 TAC Secs. 3.325, 3.339 (CCH Texas Tax Reports, ¶ 61-510, 61-520, 61-610).

In general, the limitations period for assessing taxes is four years from the date the tax becomes due and payable. The deficiency notice must be served or mailed within four years of the last day of the calendar month following the close of the taxpayer's regular reporting period, or after the report is filed whichever is later. However, prior to the expiration of the limitations period, the Comptroller and the taxpayer may agree in writing to an extension. A refund claim filed within six months after the date on which a deficiency determination becomes final is within the limitations period for all items included in the deficiency determination.

Practitioner Comment: Refund Contentions Not Pled Are Lost

House Bill 2425, Laws 2003, sharply limited the statute of limitations for filing refund claims. The amended language provides the period to file a refund claim is only held open for "issues that were contested." Taxpayers can no longer rely on the tolling provisions that applied during the pendency of a redetermination or administrative hearing under prior law. Accordingly, unless all refund contentions are pled prior to the expiration of the four-year statute of limitations or any applicable limitations extension agreement, such refunds will be lost.

G. Brint Ryan, Ryan

- *Seizure of property*

The Comptroller may seize and sell the property of a delinquent taxpayer, in order to satisfy taxes, penalties, and interest due, within three years after the deficiency determination becomes due and payable, the jeopardy determination becomes final, or the redetermination decision becomes final.

- *Suit for collection*

A suit for collection may be brought at any time within three years after (1) a deficiency determination becomes final; (2) the last recording of a lien; or (3) a jeopardy determination becomes final. The Comptroller may collect taxes, penalties and interest at any time in case of fraud and misrepresentation.

¶ 1306 Penalties and Interest

Law: Secs. 151.512, 151.703—151.705, 151.707—151.709, 151.711, 152.106, Tax Code; 34 TAC Sec. 3.286 (CCH Texas Tax Reports, ¶ 61-410, 61-530).

The following penalties and interest apply.

- *Civil penalties*

Failure to report or pay tax: A person who fails to file a report or pay a tax by the due date must pay a penalty of 5% of the amount due. If the delinquency continues for more than 30 days, an additional 5% penalty is imposed.

Late-filed tax report: An additional $50 penalty will be assessed for the late filing of certain tax reports due on or after October 1, 2011. The penalty is in addition to any other applicable penalty and will be assessed regardless of whether the taxpayer subsequently files the report or whether any taxes or fees were due for the reporting period. The taxes and fees affected by this additional penalty include sales and use tax, hotel occupancy tax, mixed beverage gross receipts tax, motor vehicle gross rental receipts tax, motor vehicle seller finance sales tax, the off-road, heavy-duty diesel equipment surcharge tax, and the 911 prepaid wireless emergency service fee.

Fraud: A 50% penalty will be added if all or part of a deficiency is due to fraud or intent to evade taxes. (Sec. 111.061, Tax Code)

- Criminal penalties

An indictment or information must be brought within four years after the commission of the offense.

Retailer advertising assumption of tax: A retailer who directly or indirectly advertises, holds out, or states to a customer that the retailer will assume, absorb, or refund part of the tax or will not add the tax to the sales price commits a misdemeanor punishable by a fine of not more than $500 (¶ 1109). A car dealer who performs such acts is guilty of a class C misdemeanor.

Failure to collect use tax or issue receipt: A retailer who engages in business in Texas and who makes a sale of a taxable item for storage, use, or consumption in Texas commits a misdemeanor punishable by a fine of not more than $500 if the retailer does not collect use tax and give the purchaser a receipt.

Failure to remit taxes collected: A person who intentionally or knowingly fails to pay to the Comptroller sales and use taxes collected by that person commits:

— a Class C misdemeanor if the unpaid tax is less than $50;

— a Class B misdemeanor if the unpaid tax is from $50 to $499;

— a Class A misdemeanor if the unpaid tax is from $500 to $1,499;

— a state jail felony if the unpaid tax is $1,500 or more but less than $20,000; and

— a felony of the first degree if the unpaid tax is $200,000 or more.

Improper use of exemption or resale certificate: A person who intentionally or knowingly makes a false entry in, or fraudulent alteration of, an exemption or resale certificate, who presents a false certificate, or who intentionally fails to provide the comptroller with certain records that document a taxpayer's taxable sale of items that had been obtained using a resale certificate commits:

— a Class C misdemeanor if the amount of tax avoided is less than $20;

— a Class B misdemeanor if the tax avoided is $20 or more, but less than $200;

— a Class A misdemeanor if the tax avoided is $200 or more, but less than $750;

— a felony in the third degree if the tax avoided is $750 or more, but less than $20,000; and

— a felony in the second degree if the tax avoided is $20,000 or more.

It is also an offense to intentionally conceal, remove, or impair the veracity or legibility of an exemption or resale certificate or to unreasonably impede the availability of a certificate.

Selling without a permit: A person or officer of a corporation commits a misdemeanor if the person or corporation engages in business in Texas without a permit or after the permit has expired. The misdemeanor ranges from a Class C misdemeanor for a first offense to a Class A misdemeanor punishable by up to one year in jail and/or a fine of $4,000 for more than three offenses. Each day a person or an officer of a corporation operates a business without a permit or with a suspended permit is considered a separate offense.

Failure to furnish report: A person who refuses to furnish a required report commits a misdemeanor. The misdemeanors range from a Class C misdemeanor for a

Part III—Sales and Use Taxes

first offense to a Class A misdemeanor subject to a fine of up to $4,000 for a three or more offenses.

Falsifying records: A person who intentionally or knowingly conceals, destroys, makes a false entry in, or fails to make an entry in records that are required to be made or kept is guilty of a third-degree felony.

Failure to produce records for inspection: A person who fails to produce records for the Comptroller's inspection is guilty of a Class C misdemeanor. Each day that the person fails to produce the records after requested is a separate offense.

- *Interest*

Unpaid taxes draw interest beginning 60 days after the date on which the tax became due and payable to the state. The yearly interest rate on all delinquent taxes is listed at ¶1909. The Comptroller of Public Accounts has the authority to waive interest on delinquent taxes, including delinquent sales and use taxes (¶1903).

¶1306

PART IV

INHERITANCE TAXES

CHAPTER 14
ESTATE AND GENERATION-SKIPPING TAXES

¶ 1401	The Law
¶ 1402	Rates and Exemptions
¶ 1403	Charitable Exemptions
¶ 1404	Computation
¶ 1405	Additional Estate Tax
¶ 1406	Taxable Transfers
¶ 1407	Settlement of Domiciliary Disputes
¶ 1408	Property Subject to Tax
¶ 1409	Deductions
¶ 1410	Return and Assessment
¶ 1411	Payment and Refund
¶ 1412	Notice and Waivers
¶ 1413	Generation Skipping Transfer Tax

¶1401 The Law

The inheritance tax, summarized below, is imposed by Title 2, Chapter 211, Tax Code. The inheritance tax and generation-skipping transfer (GST) tax do not apply where the date of death is on or after January 1, 2005. However, the state inheritance and GST tax laws have not been repealed.

Complete details are contained in CCH Inheritance, Estate and Gift Tax Reports.

¶1402 Rates and Exemptions

General: An estate tax is assessed in an amount equal to the federal estate tax credit for state death taxes. The credit is as follows:

MAXIMUM FEDERAL CREDIT

Adjusted Taxable Estate (After $60,000 Exemption) From	To	Credit =	+	%	Of Excess Over
$0	$40,000	$0		0	$0
40,000	90,000	0		0.8	40,000
90,000	140,000	400		1.6	90,000
140,000	240,000	1,200		2.4	140,000
240,000	440,000	3,600		3.2	240,000
440,000	640,000	10,000		4.0	440,000
640,000	840,000	18,000		4.8	640,000
840,000	1,040,000	27,600		5.6	840,000
1,040,000	1,540,000	38,800		6.4	1,040,000
1,540,000	2,040,000	70,800		7.2	1,540,000
2,040,000	2,540,000	106,800		8.0	2,040,000
2,540,000	3,040,000	146,800		8.8	2,540,000
3,040,000	3,540,000	190,800		9.6	3,040,000
3,540,000	4,040,000	238,800		10.4	3,540,000
4,040,000	5,040,000	290,800		11.2	4,040,000
5,040,000	6,040,000	402,800		12.0	5,040,000
6,040,000	7,040,000	522,800		12.8	6,040,000
7,040,000	8,040,000	650,800		13.6	7,040,000
8,040,000	9,040,000	786,800		14.4	8,040,000
9,040,000	10,040,000	930,800		15.2	9,040,000
10,040,000	....	1,082,800		16.0	10,040,000

¶1403 Charitable Exemptions

Charitable, religious, etc., exemptions provided in the federal law are allowable under the Texas law.

¶1404 Computation

Residents.— A tax equal to the amount of the federal credit is imposed on the transfer at death of the property of every resident. If the estate of a resident is subject to a death tax imposed by another state or states for which a federal credit is allowable, the amount of the tax due is reduced by the lesser of (1) the amount of the death tax paid the other state or states and that is allowable as the federal credit; or (2) an amount determined by multiplying the federal credit by a fraction, the numerator of which is the value of the resident's gross estate less the value of the property of a resident that is included in the gross estate and the denominator of which is the value of the resident's gross estate.

Nonresidents.— A tax is imposed equal to an amount determined by multiplying the federal credit by a fraction, the numerator of which is the value of property located in Texas that is included in the gross estate and the denominator of which is the value of the nonresident's gross estate.

Aliens.— A tax is imposed which is an amount determined by multiplying the federal credit by a fraction, the numerator of which is the value of the property located in Texas that is included in the gross estate and the denominator of which is the value of the alien's gross estate.

¶1405 Additional Estate Tax

Since Texas' estate tax is designed to absorb the federal estate tax credit for state death taxes paid, it does not have a separate additional estate for federal credit.

¶1403

Part IV—Inheritance Taxes

¶1406 Taxable Transfers

Residents.— Transfers are taxable when made by:

—will;

—intestate law;

—grant or gift to take effect in possession or enjoyment at or after death.

Special types of property interests are treated as follows:

—dower and curtesy do not exist in Texas;

—community property is taxable only to the extent of $1/2$ the value thereof upon the death of either spouse;

—bequest to an executor, in lieu of commission, is taxable to the extent that it exceeds reasonable compensation;

—jointly held property with right of survivorship is subject to tax on the death of a joint tenant to the extent of the value of the tenancy contributed by the decedent less any consideration from the other joint tenants; gifts to a joint tenancy are presumed attributable to all tenants equally;

—tenancies by the entirety do not exist in Texas;

—property in which the decedent had a general power of appointment at the time of death is subject to tax;

—life insurance proceeds receivable by the executor are taxable;

—life insurance proceeds receivable by beneficiaries other than the estate are taxable if the decedent had any of the incidents of ownership are taxable;

—retirement benefits are taxable as under federal law.

Nonresidents.— The same transfers are taxable in the case of nonresident decedents as in the case of resident decedents.

¶1407 Settlement of Domiciliary Disputes

There is a provision for compromise of state death taxes in cases where there is a dispute over the question of decedent's domicile.

¶1408 Property Subject to Tax

Residents.— Real property and tangible personal property within the state and intangible personal property wherever situated are taxable if made the subject of a taxable transfer.

Nonresidents.— All property within the jurisdiction of the state, real or personal, corporeal or incorporeal, and any interest therein, is subject to tax. Provision is made, however, for the reciprocal exemption of intangibles of nonresident decedents. In addition, bank accounts and savings and loan association accounts or shares are not subject to tax which are owned by nonresidents who are citizens of foreign countries and not doing business in Texas or which are owned by nonresident citizens of the United States who reside in a foreign country and are not doing business in Texas.

¶1409 Deductions

Residents.— The following items are deductible in the estate of a resident decedent:

—debts of the estate;

—funeral expenses and charges incident to the last illness;

—expenses of administration;

—executor's fees;

—attorney's fees;

—court costs accruing in connection with the assessment and collection of the tax;

—Federal, state, county and municipal taxes due at the time of death.

The federal estate tax deductions are built into the Texas law. These include:

—the unified credit;

—the marital deduction;

—losses from casualty or theft during administration; and charitable transfers.

A full statement in duplicate of the facts authorizing deductions must be set out under oath by the executor or administrator. One copy must be filed with the County Clerk and the other with the Comptroller.

Nonresidents.— Debts due on the Texas estate and cost of Texas administration are deductible in the estates of nonresident decedents.

¶1410 Return and Assessment

Jurisdiction.— The Comptroller of the state determines the tax. A redetermination hearing may be maintained before the Comptroller and the taxpayer has the right to appeal questions of valuation to the district court of the county.

Return.— A final tax return must be filed within 9 months of the date of the decedent's death. If complete information is not available at that time, a supplementary report may be filed later. Within 30 days after receiving information or notice of the final assessment and determination of the value of the estate assessed and determined by the federal government for the purpose of fixing the federal estate tax, the personal representative must make a report of the value to the Comptroller. If the Comptroller is not satisfied with the returns or the amount of the tax required to be paid, he may recompute the tax. He may have the value of any property appraised or reappraised. A hearing may be obtained before the Comptroller for a redetermination of the tax. A valuation question may be appealed to the district court of the county. In nonresident estates the same procedure is followed as in the case of resident decedents. The Comptroller's office is at Austin, Texas.

Final determination.— The Comptroller recomputes the tax if he is not satisfied with the returns, amount of tax or valuation.

¶1411 Payment and Refund

Time for payment.— Payment is due within nine months of decedent's death. If the date of the filing of the federal estate return and payment of the federal estate tax is extended, then the date for payment and return for the state of Texas is also extended. The personal representative of the estate shall notify the comptroller within 30 days after the extension is granted by the Internal Revenue Service. The taxes are payable to the Treasurer of the state through the Comptroller.

Receipt for payment.— The Comptroller shall issue proper receipt for payment of the tax and deliver it to the party making the payment or to his attorney of record.

Interest and discount.— Interest at a rate to be determined annually, based on the prime rate plus 1% (8.25% (0.02260% per day) for 2006 is added to estate taxes that are not paid within 9 months from the date of the decedent's death. From September 1, 1991, through December 31, 1999, the rate was set at 12% per year, and, prior to September 1, 1991, the rate was set at 10% per year. No final account is allowable until the taxes are paid. There is a penalty of 5% of the taxes due if the taxes

Part IV—Inheritance Taxes

are not paid when due. If the amount that is delinquent is not paid within 30 days after the due date, a penalty of an additional 5% of the delinquent amount is due.

Liability for payment.— No domestic corporation or association, executor, administrator, or trustee shall deliver any property to any legatee or heir until the estate tax is paid or a release of the tax is secured from the Comptroller. Failure to comply with this requirement renders the corporation, executor, etc., and its bondsmen liable for the tax, penalty, interest and cost of collection. All persons acquiring any portion of an estate subject to estate tax for federal credit are personally liable for the taxes.

Refunds.— If a tax, penalty or interest has been unlawfully or erroneously collected, the Comptroller will credit such collection against any other taxes due and refund the remainder. A written tax refund claim may be filed with the Comptroller, stating the grounds upon which the claim is based, within 4 years of its due date or 6 months after a deficiency determination becomes final, whichever is later. The date for filing a refund claim may be extended by up to 24 months under written agreement. The taxpayer must receive 20 days' notice of a hearing, if so requested. The Comptroller's decision is final 20 days (15 days prior to September 1, 1991) after issuance, unless a rehearing is requested in writing, specifying each ground of error and setting out the amount of the refund sought. If the rehearing motion is denied, the taxpayer may file suit for refund in the district court within 30 days after such denial. The amount of the refund sought must be set out in the petition, with copies of the rehearing motion attached to such petition and to the copy of the petition served upon the Comptroller. The only issues that may be raised in the suit are the grounds of error contained in the rehearing motion. Penalties and interest paid solely as a result of payments timely mailed, but postmarked after the due date, may be refunded by the Comptroller. If the court finds that all or part of the money paid under protest was unlawfully demanded, the overpayment will be refunded with the pro rata interest earned on that amount by issuance of a tax refund warrant to the taxpayer. Effective September 1, 2005, refunds will include interest at the lesser of (1) the prime rate on the first business day of January of each year plus 1% or (2) the annual rate of interest earned on state treasury deposits during December of the previous year (4.06825% (0.0115% per day). The interest will be paid from 60 days after the due date. The Comptroller may recover erroneously made refunds within 4 years of the refund date.

¶1412 Notice and Waivers

Residents.— The personal representative of a decedent's estate may not transfer or deliver any of the decedent's property toany person unless a tax determined on the property is paid. The personal representative, other person responsible for the payment of the tax, or bondsman of a representative or other person who violates this provision is liable for the tax, a related penalty, interest, and the costs of the collection of the tax, penalty, and interest. A corporation, bank, stock transfer agent, safe deposit institution or other depository or institution, or person in actual or constructive possession of any property of the decedent as agent of the decedent or custodian of the property or any similar relationship such as debtor, bailor, or lessor (other than a personal representative, spouse, transferee, trustee, person in possession of property by reason of the exercise or release of a power of appointment, legatee, devisee, heir, or beneficiary who has received the property) is not liable for any tax penalty or interest.

Nonresidents.— Waivers are not required.

¶1413 Generation Skipping Transfer Tax

Texas imposes a generation skipping transfer tax for federal credit.

¶1413

PART V

PROPERTY TAXES

CHAPTER 15
PROPERTY TAXES

¶1501	Scope of Chapter
¶1502	Imposition of Tax
¶1503	Property Subject to Tax
¶1504	Exemptions
¶1505	Valuation, Appraisal, and Assessment
¶1506	Payment of Taxes
¶1507	Collection of Tax
¶1508	Penalties and Interest
¶1509	Taxpayer Remedies
¶1510	Abatements, Limitations, and Deferrals
¶1511	Credits

¶1501 Scope of Chapter

The Texas property tax is imposed on all privately held real property, on business tangible personal property, and on intangible property of certain savings and loan associations and insurance companies. Generally, tangible personal property that is not held or used for the production of income is exempt from property taxation, although there is a limited local option to tax such property. Texas has no state property tax.

This chapter is intended to be a general survey of the property taxes and is not intended to provide detailed coverage. It outlines primarily the property subject to taxation, the assessment procedure, the basis of the tax, and the requirements for filing returns and making payments.

¶1502 Imposition of Tax

Law: Secs. 1.04(12), 6.01, 6.03, 111.301, Tax Code; 34 TAC Sec. 9.4037 (CCH Texas Tax Reports, ¶20-010, 20-070, 20-405, 20-700).

The tax is imposed by appraisal districts at the county level and by cities, towns, school districts, hospital districts, and the like.

Property taxes are administered by the Comptroller of Public Accounts.

CCH Comment: *Constitutionality of School Financing System*

In 2003, the Texas Supreme Court upheld the right of school districts to challenge the constitutionality of Texas' school financing system on the basis that the state's control of the property system is so pervasive that for all intents and purposes it is the state, rather than the local districts, that impose the property tax. Under Texas' constitution, the state is prohibited from imposing a property tax. (*West Orange-Cove Consolidated I.S.D. v. Alanis*, Texas Supreme Court, No. 02-0427, 46 Tex. Sup. J. 724, May 29, 2003, CCH Texas Tax Reports, ¶402-519) In 2004, a Texas trial court held that the Texas public school finance system was unconstitutional, violating provisions of the Texas State Constitution relating to local property taxation and education. The court issued an injunction to take effect sometime in 2005 providing that state funding of public schools cease unless the legislature conformed the school finance system to meet the constitutional stan-

¶1502

dards. The Texas Supreme Court upheld the lower court's finding but extended the effective date of the lower court's injunction until June 1, 2006. (*Neeley v. West Orange-Cove Consolidated Independent School District*, 176 S.W.3d 746 (Tex.SCt 2005), CCH TEXAS TAX REPORTS, ¶402-974)

In 2006, the Texas Legislature enacted major tax reform that revamped the current franchise tax (see ¶101 et seq.), raised the cigarette tax rate (see ¶1703) and made major reductions in the property tax rate. H.B. 1, Laws 2006, provides for property tax relief through state aid to school districts. The legislation effectively reduces the maximum local school property tax rate from $1.50 per $100 assessed valuation to $1.33 per $100 valuation in the fall of 2006, and to $1 per $100 in the fall of 2007. In addition, school districts are authorized to raise their tax rates by 4 cents in 2006 for local programs.

Abatements of property tax are available for property located in reinvestment zones (¶1510).

A refund is allowed for state sales and use taxes and state franchise taxes paid in a calendar year for which the taxpayer has also paid property taxes to a school district on certain property that is located in a reinvestment zone (¶411, 1005).

- *Tax rate*

A taxing unit must adopt a tax rate for the current year and notify the assessor of the rate before the later of September 30 or the 60th day after the date the certified appraisal roll is received by the taxing unit. For a taxing unit that does not adopt a rate by the required date, the tax rate for that tax year is the lower of the effective tax rate calculated for that tax year or the tax rate adopted by the taxing unit for the preceding tax year.

CCH Comment: Tax Increase Notice and Voting Requirements

A municipality or a county must comply with specified public notice and voting requirements prior to adopting a budget that will require raising more revenue from property taxes than in the previous year. A separate vote of the governing body is required to ratify the property tax increase reflected in the budget. This vote is in addition to and separate from the vote to adopt the budget or a vote to set the tax rate. If the county or municipality maintains an Internet Web site, the proposed budget must be posted on the Web site. (Secs. 102.005, 102.007, Local Gov't Code)

The rate is set by formula based on the prior year's rate. The taxing unit may not adopt a tax rate that exceeds the lower of the rollback tax rate or 103% of the effective tax rate without a public hearing and a vote by its governing body. The tax rate is an aggregate rate of tax imposed by counties, cities, and special taxing districts.

Notice to property owners regarding a taxing unit's calculated tax rates must include a statement that the adoption of a tax rate equal to the effective tax rate would result in an increase or decrease, as applicable, in the amount of taxes imposed by the taxing unit as compared to last year's levy, and the amount of the increase or decrease. The notice must also include the percentage difference in the appraised value of the property for the current year as compared to the fifth year before the current tax year. (34 TAC Sec. 9.4037)

CCH Practice Pointer: Online Service Providing Tax and Other Economic Data Available

An online research service called Economic Data for Growth and Expansion (EDGE) that provides data and analysis useful in revenue planning, financial analysis, economic forecasting, and site location decisions is available on the Comptroller's website at http://www.window.state.tx.us/taxes/. The EDGE service can supply property tax and sales tax rates for areas in Texas, as well as tax rate and tax collection trends over time. The service also provides information about tax programs available in a community, including property tax information, such as tax increment reinvestment zones;

¶1502

Part V—Property Taxes

property tax value limitations (commonly known as H.B. 1200 agreements); and sales taxes, including 4A and 4B economic development sales taxes.

¶1503 Property Subject to Tax

Law: Secs. 11.01, 11.02, 11.14, 21.01, 21.02, 21.021, 21.06 Tax Code (CCH Texas Tax Reports, ¶20-105—20-105, 20-110, 20-125, 20-305, 20-275).

In general, all real property located in the state is taxable. Texas also taxes:

— tangible personal property if located in the state for longer than a temporary period;

— tangible personal property temporarily located outside Texas belonging to a Texas resident; and

— tangible personal property used continually, whether regularly or irregularly, in Texas.

> ### CCH Pointer: Period of examination
>
> In determining whether Texas has the jurisdiction to subject property to taxation, the decision as to whether property was continually used in Texas must be made by looking back to the year before the tax year at issue. (*Alaska Flight Services, LLC v. Dallas Central Appraisal District*, 261 S.W.3d 884 (Tex. Ct App. 2008), CCH Texas Tax Reports, ¶403-482)

However, because Texas exempts most tangible personal property that is not used in the production of income, only business personal property and manufactured/mobile-type homes are subject to tax. Intangible personal property is not taxable except for property of certain savings and loan associations and insurance companies.

Real and personal property is generally taxable by a taxing unit if it is located in the unit on January 1.

Texas does not designate classes of taxable property.

- *Taxable situs of property*

Different situs rules apply, dependent on the type of property involved.

Real property: Real property is generally taxable by a taxing unit if it is located in the unit on January 1.

Tangible personal property: Subject to certain exceptions, tangible personal property is generally taxable by a taxing unit if any of the following conditions are satisfied:

(1) the property is located in the unit on January 1 for longer than a temporary period;

(2) the property is temporarily outside the taxing unit on January 1 but is normally located in the unit;

(3) the property is not located in any one place for more than a temporary period and is normally returned to the unit between uses elsewhere; or

(4) if the property does not have a situs based on factors (1) through (3) and the owner of nonbusiness property resides in the taxing unit or the owner of business property maintains his or her principal place of business in a taxing unit.

¶1503

CCH Advisory: Exemptions for Business Property

A business's tangible personal property that may potentially have taxable situs within a taxing unit by virtue of being located in the taxing unit on January 1 for longer than a temporary period may instead qualify for a tax exemption:

— as freeport goods detained in Texas for up to 175 days for assembling, storing, manufacturing, processing, or fabricating purposes (see ¶1504);

— as goods moving in interstate commerce; or

— goods held in a foreign trade zone, either as either imported goods held in the zone for certain purposes or as goods produced in the United States and held in the zone for exportation.

Vessels and aircraft: Different rules apply for determining the taxable situs of special-purpose vessels or other watercraft that are not used as instrumentalities of commerce, for railroad rolling stock, and for commercial aircraft. A special-purpose vessel or other watercraft that is not used as an instrumentality of commerce is deemed located on January 1 for more than a temporary period in the taxing unit in which it was physically located for the longest period during the year preceding the tax year or for 30 days, whichever is longer. If the watercraft is not deemed to be in any taxing unit for more than a temporary period, then it is deemed to be located in the taxing unit where the watercraft is normally located or returned, where the owner resides for nonbusiness property, or at the principal place of business for business property.

Railroad rolling stock: Rolling stock of a railroad that operates in another state is allocated to Texas on the basis of the proportion of the rolling stock's total market value that fairly reflects its use in the state during the preceding tax year. Use is determined either on the basis of the property stored/used in the state or the percentage of track line miles in the state.

Commercial aircraft: The value of commercial aircraft used both inside and outside Texas is subject to allocation by formula. The allocable portion of the aircraft's total fair market value that is taxable in Texas is presumed to be the fair market value of the aircraft multiplied by a fraction, the numerator of which is the product of multiplying 1.5 times the number of revenue departures by the aircraft from Texas during the preceding year, and the denominator of which is the greater of either (1) 8,760; or (2) the numerator. To be entitled to allocation, the taxpayer must provide information showing entitlement to allocation at the time of its report to the appraisal district (see ¶1505). (*SLW Aviation, Inc. v. Harris County Appraisal District*, 105 S.W.3d 99 (Tex. CtApp 2003), CCH TEXAS TAX REPORTS, ¶402-499)

Oil rigs: A portable drilling rig designed for land-based oil or gas drilling or exploration operations is taxable by the taxing unit in which the rig is located on January 1 if the rig was located in the appraisal district that appraises property for the unit for the preceding 365 consecutive days. If the drilling rig was not located in the appraisal district where it is located on January 1 for the preceding 365 days, it is taxable by the taxing unit in which the owner's principal place of business in the state is located on January 1. (Sec. 21.02, Tax Code) Previously, a Texas court of appeals had ruled that oil rigs were taxable in the county in which the taxpayer's principal place of business was located and not in the county in which the rigs were located temporarily. The rigs were constantly moved from one temporary location to another. Accordingly, the rigs were not taxable in the county that was not the taxpayer's place of business because they were at their January 1 location only temporarily. (*Patterson-UTI Drilling Co. LP, LLLP v. Webb County Appraisal District*, 182 S.W.3d 14 (Tex. CtApp 2005), CCH TEXAS TAX REPORTS, ¶402-957)

¶1503

Part V—Property Taxes

Intangible property: Intangible property is generally taxable by a taxing unit if the owner of the property resides in the unit on January 1. However, when the property is normally used for business purposes outside the taxing unit, it is taxable by each taxing unit in which it is used.

¶1504 Exemptions

Law: Secs. 11.12, 11.13, 11.14, 11.145, 11.146, 11.15, 11.16, 11.161, 11.17, 11.18, 11.181, 11.182, 11.184, 11.19, 11.20, 11.21, 11.22, 11.23, 11.24, 11.25, 11.251, 11.254, 11.26, 11.27, 11.271, 11.28, 11.29, 11.30, 11.31, 11.32, 11.41, 11.42, 11.43, 11.439, 21.031, 23.135, 23.76, Tax Code; 34 TAC Sec. 9.415 (CCH TEXAS TAX REPORTS, ¶20-115, 20-165, 20-190, 20-195, 20-205, 20-235, 20-285, 20-270, 20-275, 20-285, 20-295, 20-300, 20-320, 20-505).

With certain exceptions, a person who does not qualify for an exemption on January 1 will not receive the exemption that year.

Certain exemptions, such as the exemptions for veterans and for community service clubs, must be claimed annually; other exemptions, such as the exemption for residence homesteads and charitable organizations, need not be claimed in years subsequent to initial qualification. No exemption claim need be made for public property, property exempt by federal law, household goods and personal effects, family supplies, farm products, implements of husbandry, and automobiles.

The following are the main exemptions from the property tax (see ¶1503 for the exemption relating to tangible personal property):

Public property: Property owned by the United States and property owned by the State of Texas or by a political subdivision thereof is exempt if the property is used for public purposes. The portion of property of a Texas institution of higher education that is used for public purposes is exempt even if the property is used for both public and private purposes. The public property exemption also applies to property owned by the Texas state or local governments, including a leasehold or other possessory interest in the property that is held or occupied by a religious organization if the property is used primarily as a place of regular religious worship and is reasonably necessary for engaging in religious worship.

CCH Comment: "Public Purpose" Clarified

Even though revenues generated by the private commercial use of a public building were used to benefit county residents, this was not enough to satisfy the public use requirement necessary to qualify the building for the public property exemption. (*Opinion of the Texas Attorney General,* No. JC-0311, November 30, 2000, received March 2001, CCH TEXAS TAX REPORTS, ¶402-161)

Property that is exempt from ad valorem taxation by federal law also qualifies for exemption. This includes property granted a free trade zone exemption. (Sec. 11.12, Tax Code)

Property owned by charitable organizations: An exemption applies to property owned and used by charitable organizations that exist exclusively for religious, charitable, scientific, literary, or educational purposes and are engaged exclusively in performing one or more of the following functions without considering the beneficiary's ability to pay:

— providing medical care;

— providing support or relief to orphans, delinquent, dependent, or handicapped children needing residential care, abused or battered spouses or children needing temporary shelter, the poor, or victims of natural disasters;

— providing support to elderly persons or to the handicapped;

— preserving a historical landmark or site;

— promoting or operating a museum, zoo, library, theater of the dramatic or performing arts, or symphony orchestra or choir;

— promoting or providing humane treatment of animals;

— acquiring, storing, transporting, selling, or distributing water for public use;

— providing a volunteer fire department;

— promoting the athletic development of boys or girls under 18 years old;

— preserving or conserving wildlife;

— promoting educational development through loans or scholarships;

— providing halfway house services;

— providing permanent housing and related social, health care, and educational facilities for persons age 62 or older;

— promoting or operating an art gallery, museum, or collection that is open to the public;

— providing for the organized solicitation and collection for distribution through gifts, grants, and agreements to nonprofit charitable, educational, religious, and youth organizations that provide direct human, health, and welfare services;

— performing biomedical or scientific research or biomedical or scientific education for the benefit of the public;

— operating a public television station or a qualified public interest radio station;

— providing housing for low-income and moderate-income families, for unmarried individuals 61 years of age or older, for handicapped individuals, and for families displaced by urban renewal;

— providing housing and related services to persons who are 62 years of age or older in a retirement community, if the retirement community provides independent living services, assisted living services, and nursing services to its residents on a single campus (a license to occupy a dwelling unit in a tax-exempt retirement community is not a taxable leasehold or other possessory interest in real property);

— providing assistance to ambulatory health care centers; or

— acquiring, holding, and transferring unimproved real property under an urban land bank program.

The qualifications for charitable organizations engaged primarily in the above activities are eased in those jurisdictions that have adopted an authorizing ordinance. This exemption may only be claimed upon approval by the Comptroller and lasts only for five years, but may be renewed upon application by the organization.

In addition, beginning with taxes due in 2010, the exemption applies to certain corporations that are not qualified charitable organizations but are exempt from federal income taxes under IRC Sec. 501(a) by being listed as an exempt entity under IRC Sec. 501(c)(2); hold title to the property; and turn over income generated by the property to a qualified charitable organization. (Sec. 11.184(l), Tax Code)

Real property owned by a charitable organization and leased to an institution of higher education is exempt from taxation to the same extent as the property would be exempt if the property were owned by the institution. (Sec. 11.184(p), Tax Code)

The exemptions include real property owned by a charitable organization consisting of an incomplete improvement that is under active construction or other physical preparation designed and intended to be used exclusively by the qualified

¶1504

Part V—Property Taxes

charitable organization, and the land on which the incomplete improvement located that will be reasonably necessary for the use of the improvement. Incomplete improvements may not be exempted for more than five years (three years applicable to ad valorem taxes imposed for a tax year that begins prior to January 1, 2010). Physical preparation includes architectural or engineering work, soil testing, land clearing activities, site improvement work necessary for the construction of the improvement, or an environmental or land use study relating to the construction.

A similar exemption is available to qualifying nonprofit economic development corporations. (Sec. 11.231, Tax Code)

Local entities are prohibited from imposing property taxes on land that is owned by a religious organization and that is leased for use as a school or that will be used to expand or construct a place of religious worship, so long as the land produces no revenue for the religious organization.

Cooperative student housing: A Texas real and personal property tax exemption applies to the property owned and used exclusively by an organization providing housing on a cooperative basis to college students if:

— the organization is a tax-exempt entity listed under IRC Sec. 501(c)(3);

— membership in the organization is open to all students enrolled in the institution and is not limited to those chosen by current members of the organization;

— the organization is governed by its members; and

— the members of the organization share the responsibility for managing the housing.

Family supplies: Family supplies for home or farm use are exempt.

Farm products and implements: Farm products, including livestock and poultry, produced and owned by, and in the hands of, a producer are exempt. Nursery products are farm products if they are in a growing state. Machinery and equipment that are used in the production of farm or ranch products are also exempt.

Timber falls under the farm products exemption from property tax. "Timber," for this exemption, means standing timber or timber that has been harvested and, on January 1 of the tax year, is located on the real property on which it was produced and is under the ownership of the person who owned it when it was standing. Implements of husbandry used in the production of timber are also exempt from property tax. The imposition of additional property taxes (rollback taxes) is waived for a change of use of qualified timber land if the land is (1) changed for use as the owner's residence; (2) owned by a religious organization and converted to a religious use within five years; or (3) under specified conditions, used by a nonprofit cemetery organization.

Freeport goods: Freeport goods are exempt from tax. (Sec. 11.251, Tax Code) "Freeport" goods are property that is:

— acquired in or imported into Texas to be forwarded outside the state, whether or not the intention to forward the property outside Texas is formed or the destination to which the property is forwarded is specified when the property is acquired in or imported into Texas;

— detained in Texas for assembling, storing, manufacturing, processing, or fabricating purposes by the person who acquired or imported the property; and

— transported outside Texas within 175 days after the date the person acquired or imported the property into Texas.

Goods-in-transit: An exemption applies to personal property that is:

¶1504

— ired in or imported into Texas to be forwarded to another location in outside the state;

— ined at a location in Texas in which the owner of the property does direct or indirect ownership interest for assembling, storing, manufac- ocessing, or fabricating purposes by the person who acquired or imported the property; and

— is transported to another location in Texas or outside the state not later than 175 days after the person acquired the property in or imported the property into the state.

The exemption does not include oil, natural gas, petroleum products, aircraft, dealer's motor vehicle inventory, dealer's vessel and outboard motor inventory, dealer's heavy equipment inventory, or retail manufactured housing inventory. In addition, the governing body of a taxing unit may provide for the taxation of goods-in-transit. (Sec. 11.254, Tax Code) However, a taxing jurisdiction may not tax goods in interstate commerce in violation of the U.S. Commerce Clause. This was the basis of the Texas Court of Appeals ruling in *Peoples Gas, Light, and Coke Co. v. Harrison Central Appraisal District* 270 S.W.3d 208 (Tex. CtApp2008), CCH TEXAS TAX REPORTS, ¶403-492, in which the court held that a local taxing district was prohibited from assessing local property taxes on natural gas stored at an underground Texas storage facility that was part of the interstate pipeline system because the gas was in interstate commerce.

Homesteads: Texas provides the following seven different kinds of property tax exemptions for residence homesteads:

(1) A family or a single individual is entitled to an exemption from county taxes of $3,000 of the assessed value of a residence homestead;

(2) An individual is entitled to an exemption from school district taxes of $15,000 of the appraised value of his or her residence homestead (however, in some school districts $10,000 of the $15,000 may not apply);

(3) In addition to the exemption in (2) above, an individual who is disabled or is age 65 or older is entitled to an exemption from school district taxes of $10,000 of the appraised value of his or her residence homestead;

(4) In addition to the exemptions listed in (2) and (3) above, an individual who is disabled or is age 65 or older or, the individual's surviving spouse, if the surviving spouse was at least age 55 when the deceased spouse died, is entitled to an exemption from taxes imposed by a taxing unit for not less than $3,000 of the appraised value of the individual's residence homestead, if the exemption is adopted either by the governing body of a taxing unit or by a majority of the voters at an election called by the governing body on the petition of at least 20% of qualified voters who voted in the preceding election of the taxing unit;

(5) In addition to all the above exemptions, an individual is entitled to an exemption from taxation by a taxing unit of a percentage of the appraised value of his or her residence homestead. The governing body of a taxing unit must adopt such an exemption by July 1. The percentage adopted by any taxing unit must not exceed 20%, but may not amount to less than $5,000 of the homestead's appraised value;

(6) School district taxes are "frozen," for disabled taxpayers and taxpayers age 65 or older, at the level imposed on the residence the first year the taxpayer qualified the residence for exemption. The school tax freeze limitation for a residence homestead may be transferred to a different residence homestead by either the taxpayer or the taxpayer's surviving spouse who was at least 65 years old when the deceased spouse died; and

¶1504

Part V—Property Taxes

(7) Counties, cities, towns, and junior college districts are authorized to establish a property tax freeze on residence homesteads of taxpayers who are disabled and taxpayers who are 65 years old or older. The governing body of a taxing unit may not repeal or rescind such a tax limitation once established. However, taxing units may increase taxes on a residence homestead owned by an elderly or disabled individual based on increased value because of improvements to the homestead, other than repairs.

Eligibility for, and the amount of, a residence homestead exemption for any tax year is generally determined by the claimant's qualifications on January 1. A person claiming an exemption must file an application form by May 1 with the chief appraiser of the district in which the subject property is located. However, the chief appraiser may approve a late application if it is filed not later than one year after the date the taxes on the homestead became delinquent. An exemption under category (3) or (4) above is effective immediately on qualification for the exemption, and a person who qualifies for an exemption under category (3) or (4) above may apply to the chief appraiser for the exemption up until the first anniversary of the date the person qualified for the exemption.

Once a homestead exemption is allowed, it need not be claimed in subsequent years, and the exemption applies to the property until:

— the property changes ownership;

— the person no longer qualifies for the exemption; or

— the chief appraiser delivers a written notice that a new application form is required to confirm the person's qualification.

Joint or community owners may not each receive an exemption for the same residence homestead in the same year. An eligible disabled person who is age 65 or older may not receive both a disabled and an elderly residence homestead exemption, but may choose either. A person may not receive a residence homestead exemption for more than one residence homestead in the same year. Special rules apply to the taxation of a residence that qualified for the residence homestead exemption for elderly taxpayers if the owner qualifies a different property for the exemption during the same tax year.

A residence homestead, in addition to structures and mobile homes, may also consist of an interest in real property created through the ownership of stock in a corporation incorporated under Texas's Cooperative Association Act to provide dwelling places to its stockholders.

A taxpayer may still claim a resident homestead exemption even though the taxpayer temporarily stops occupying the structure as a principal residence so long as the taxpayer does not establish a different principal residence and:

— the absence is for a period of less than two years and the taxpayer intends to return and occupy the structure as the taxpayer's principal residence; or

— the absence is caused by the taxpayer's military service outside the United States as a member of the armed forces or by the taxpayer's residency in a facility that provides services related to health, infirmity, or aging.

Similarly, a homestead exemption is not lost if a taxpayer does not live in the home due to wind or water damage if the taxpayer begins active construction or other physical preparation no later than one year after the damage occurred. The exemption during this period of non-occupancy is only available for two years. Additional tax may be owed if the taxpayer sells the property before completing construction or repairs. (Sec. 11.135, Tax Code)

Medical center developments: All real and personal property owned by a nonprofit corporation, as defined in the Texas Non-Profit Corporation Act, and held for use in

¶1504

the development of a medical center is exempt from all Texas property taxes until completion of the medical center, so long as the property is not leased or otherwise used with a view to profit. In a Texas county with a population of 3.3 million or more, all real and personal property owned by a nonprofit corporation and held for use in either the operation or the development of a medical center is exempt.

Personal property: All tangible personal property that is not held or used for the production of income, other than manufactured homes, is exempt. The exemption does not apply to a structure that is substantially affixed to real estate and that is used or occupied as a residential dwelling.

Travel trailers that are not held or used for the production of income qualify for the exemption. An exemption applies to one motor vehicle owned by an individual that is used in the course of the individual's occupation or profession and is also used for personal activities of the owner that do not involve the production of income. (Sec. 11.253, Tax Code) Leased motor vehicles are also exempt if the lessee does not hold the vehicle for the production of income and the vehicle is used primarily for activities that do not involve the production of income. However, municipalities still have the option to tax leased vehicles.

CCH Advisory: Household Goods May Still Be Exempt

In a taxing unit that has opted to tax nonincome-producing property, the exemption for family supplies for home or farm use (see above) may be especially important.

Income producing property with a taxable value of less than $500 is also exempt. All property in each taxing unit is aggregated to determine taxable value.

Mineral interests: A mineral interest that has a taxable value of less than $500 is exempt. All property in each taxing unit is aggregated to determine taxable value.

Offshore drilling equipment: Mobile marine drilling equipment designed for the offshore drilling of oil and gas wells that is being stored in a county or body of water bordering the Gulf of Mexico is exempt. To qualify for the exemption, the equipment must:

— be stored in a county bordering on the Gulf of Mexico or on a bay or other body of water immediately adjacent to the Gulf of Mexico;

— not be stored for the sole purpose of repair or maintenance; and

— not be used to drill a well at the location at which it is being stored.

Pollution control equipment: Facilities or devices used for air, water, or land pollution control are exempt from property tax if approved by the Texas Natural Resource Conservation Commission. The exemption applies to land acquired after January 1, 1994, and to any structure, building, installation, excavation, machinery, equipment, or device that is used, constructed, acquired, or installed to comply with federal, state, or local environmental protection agency regulations. The exemption extends to any attachment, addition, reconstruction, replacement, or improvement of such property. However, the exemption is not available to persons solely on the basis that they manufacture or produce a product or provide a service that prevents, monitors, controls, or reduces pollution. Motor vehicles and property subject to a tax abatement agreement executed before 1994, and property used for residential, recreational, park, or scenic uses are also ineligible for the exemption.

Practitioner Comment: Pollution Control Property Exemption

While the Texas property tax exemption for pollution control property has been in effect since the 1995 tax year, many property owners continue to pay annual property taxes on pollution control property that would otherwise qualify for the exemption. The exemption, which is outlined in Section 11.31 of the Texas Property Tax Code, is for real or

Part V—Property Taxes   **275**

personal property that is constructed or installed for the control of air, water, or land pollution. The exemption covers a wide range of pollution control property from simple dust control systems to more environmentally friendly manufacturing equipment.

In order to qualify for the exemption, a property owner must first file an "Application for Use Determination for Pollution Control Property" with the Texas Commission on Environmental Quality. The application requires a description of the pollution control property and a citation of the relevant rule, regulation or statutory provision being met by the pollution control property. Upon approval of this application, the commission will issue a "Use Determination" approving the pollution control property for exemption from local property taxation. The property owner is then required to file the determination along with an "Application for Pollution Control Property Tax Exemption" with the central appraisal district in which the property is located. [CCH Note: The application requirements are eased and expedited for property that is listed on a Commission of Environmental Quality preapproved list of pollution control property.]

While no further applications on approved pollution control property are required to be filed with the state or with central appraisal districts for subsequent tax years, applications are required to be filed on new pollution control property installed in subsequent years.

John R. Ferrell, Ryan

Solar and wind-powered energy devices: The amount of the appraised value of property arising from the installation or construction of a solar or wind-powered energy device is exempt if the device is primarily for the production and distribution of energy for on-site use. Applications for exemption must be filed before May 1.

Vessels and watercraft: A vessel or other watercraft used as an instrumentality of commerce or a special-purpose vessel or other watercraft not used as an instrumentality of commerce that is used outside Texas and is in this state solely to be converted, repaired, stored, or inspected does not have a taxable situs in Texas. Similarly, a vessel or other watercraft to be used as an instrumentality of commerce or a special-purpose vessel or other watercraft not to be used as an instrumentality of commerce that is under construction in this state and/or tangible personal property that will be incorporated into or attached to a such a watercraft also does not create a taxable situs in Texas. Nonincome-producing vessels and watercraft are exempt personal property.

Veterans: A full property tax exemption is available for a veteran's residential homestead if the taxpayer received a 100% disability compensation due to a service-related disability and a rating of 100% disability or of individual unemployability from the U.S. Department of Veterans Affairs. The full exemption is available if the property is owned as community property with the veteran's spouse, but only that portion of the residence owned by the veteran is eligible for exemption if the property is owned jointly with another person not as community property. (Sec. 11.131, Tax Code) Currently, the surviving spouse of an eligible veteran does not qualify to receive the 100% residence homestead exemption, but may qualify for a partial exemption as outlined below.

Veterans who are partially disabled qualify for exemptions for any property they own based on the percent of their disability rating. The exemption amounts for any property owned by qualifying disabled veterans are as follows:

— a disabled veteran with a disability rating of at least 10% may claim an exemption ranging from $5,000 to $12,000, depending on the veteran's disability rating;

— a disabled veteran is entitled to an exemption equal to $12,000 of assessed property value of a property the veteran owns if he or she is age 65 or older and has a disability rating of at least 10%, is totally blind in one or both eyes, or has lost the use of one or more limbs;

¶1504

— the surviving spouse of a deceased disabled veteran who has not remarried may claim the amount the veteran was entitled to at time of death; and

— the surviving spouse and unmarried children under age 18 of an individual who dies while on active duty are entitled to an exemption of up to $5,000.

(Sec. 11.22, Tax. Code)

CCH Advisory: Interplay Between Full and Partial Exemption

A 100% disabled veteran who qualifies for the $12,000 exemption under Property Tax Code Section 11.22 may apply the $12,000 exemption to another property he or she owns, other than his or her residence homestead. (*Release*, Texas Comptroller of Public Accounts, August 2009)

A taxpayer may claim either the first and second exemption, but not both. An exemption may be claimed by an individual for only one property, and the same property must be used for every taxing unit in which the individual claims the exemption.

Exemption application.—The application for the partial exemption must be filed before May 1 on forms prepared by appraisal and tax offices. However, a late application will be accepted if it is filed not later than the first anniversary of the earlier of the date (a) the property taxes were paid; or (b) the taxes became delinquent. Once the exemption is allowed, it need not be claimed in subsequent years and applies until the property changes ownership or the claimant's qualification for the exemption changes. However, the chief appraiser may require a person allowed one of the exemptions in a prior year to file a new application for purposes of confirming the person's current qualification for the exemption. (Sec. 11.43(c), Tax Code)

Regulation 34 TAC Sec. 9.415 provides a listing of all the model application forms to be used to file for an exemption.

The application for the full exemption homestead exemption for tax year 2009 should be filed with the veteran's appraisal district using the "temporary" Comptroller Form 50-764, Application for Residence Homestead Exemption for Disabled Veteran with 100 Percent Disability. A veteran may also use a form provided by his or her appraisal district. ("Release," Texas Comptroller of Public Accounts, August 2009)

¶1505 Valuation, Appraisal, and Assessment

Law: Secs. 22.01, 22.23-22.26, 23.23, 23.41, 23.52, 23.521, 23.55, 23.73, 23.81, 23.83, 25.25, 41.11, 41.12 Tax Code; 34 TAC Sec. 9.3031 (CCH Texas Tax Reports, ¶20-605—20-715).

Taxable property is assessed at its market value as of January 1 of the tax year. Real property must be appraised at least once every three years.

The Texas Constitution requires that taxation and assessment be equal and uniform and all property must be taxed in proportion to its value. The chief appraiser must consider the cost, income, and market data comparison methods of appraisal in determining the market value of taxable property and must use the method he or she considers most appropriate. However, each property must be appraised based upon the individual characteristics that affect the property's market value, and all available evidence that is specific to the value of the property must be considered in determining the property's market value. (Sec. 23.01, Tax Code) In determining the market value of real property, other than rental income property, the appraiser must exclude from that value the value of any tangible personal property, including trade fixtures, intangible personal property, or other property that is not subject to appraisal as real property.

¶1505

Part V—Property Taxes 277

"Market value" is the price at which a property would transfer for cash or its equivalent under prevailing market conditions. This is true for leasehold interests as well. Although the rent paid may be an indication of the value of the leasehold interest, an independent determination of what the leasehold interest would command on the open market must also be made. (*Panola County Fresh Water Supply District No. 1 v. Panola County Appraisal District et al.*, 69 S.W.3d 278 (Tex. CtApp 2002), CCH TEXAS TAX REPORTS, ¶402-254) Comparable sales used to determine market value should be those sales occurring within the last 24 months, unless there were not enough sales to comprise a representative sample. Comparable property that was sold at a foreclosure sale or that has declined in value because of a declining economy may not be excluded from comparable sales. (Sec. 23.013, Tax Code)

When a property's appraised value is reduced at a protest hearing, the new reduced amount becomes the appraised value for the following year, unless the chief appraiser is able to establish by substantial evidence that the property's value has increased. (Sec. 23.01, Tax Code)

Practitioner Comment: Texas Manufacturing Inutility and Property Tax Valuation

Value loss occurs when the operating level of a property is less than full production capacity. While a similar condition is commonly called "vacancy" when referring to commercial real estate, this reduced production is known as "inutility" when referring to manufacturing and other operating industrial properties. Income is directly related to production, so lower capacity utilization results in lower property income and, therefore, lower property value. The external obsolescence causing the decline in value (economic conditions, foreign competition, environmental regulations) may be temporary or permanent.

Most commonly, value loss due to temporary inutility is measured by capitalizing the income loss due to the external obsolescence into an estimate of the loss in total property value. In order to estimate income loss, the absorption rate of the unused capacity and the capitalization/discount rate must be determined. If the condition causing inutility is permanent, the replacement cost new estimate may be based on the current production level rather than actual plant capacity. This has the effect of "right sizing" the plant value estimate to reflect current economic conditions.

Most physical depreciation formulas and guidelines used by assessors and appraisers assume a uniform or constant utility over the useful life of the asset. An economic obsolescence adjustment is necessary to compensate for the fact that utilization and economic return may not be uniform.

Lester C. Rhodes, Ryan

- *Omitted property*

If the chief appraiser discovers real property that was omitted from the appraisal roll in any one of the five preceding years or personal property that was omitted from the appraisal roll in any one of the two preceding years, he or she must appraise the property as of January 1 of each year that it escaped taxation.

- *Rendition statements and property reports*

All tangible personal property used for the production of income that a person owns or manages and controls as a fiduciary on January 1 must be rendered for taxation. The rendition statement and property report must be filed with the central appraisal office in which the property is taxable after January 1 and on or before April 15. It must be signed by the person who is required to file the statement or report, or, for a corporation, by a designated corporate officer, agent, or employee.

A listing of the various rendition statement forms available for different industries and different types of property is found in regulation 34 TAC Sec. 9.3031.

¶1505

For exempt property or for property for which an application for exemption is filed, the rendition statement must be filed within 30 days from the date the exemption is terminated or the exemption application is denied.

Practitioner Comment: Personal Property Rendition Statement Requirements

The requirements for the filing of annual personal property rendition statements are summarized as follows:

—A property owner must file a rendition statement with the appropriate central appraisal district prior to April 15th of each tax year. However, a chief appraiser of a central appraisal district is required to extend the filing deadline, upon written request by the property owner prior to April 15th, to May 15th of each tax year. Also, if a property owner can show good cause in writing, a chief appraiser can further extend the filing deadline by an additional 15 days;

—The property owner's rendition statement is required to include the name and address of the owner, the property's physical location or taxable situs, a description of the type and category of property including inventory and quantity of each type of inventory, and also the owner's good faith estimate of the market value of the property for each tax year. In lieu of reporting a good faith estimate of market value, the owner has the option of reporting the historical cost of the property by acquisition year;

—A property owner that is regulated by the Public Utility Commission of Texas, the Railroad Commission of Texas, the Federal Surface Transportation Board, or the Federal Energy Regulatory Commission is considered to be in compliance with this section if the owner provides, upon written request by a central appraisal district's chief appraiser, a copy of its annual regulatory report to the chief appraiser;

— If personal property located in a central appraisal district has a total value, in the property owner's opinion, of $20,000 or less, the owner is not required to report a good faith estimate of value or acquisition costs in the rendition statement;

—If a property owner has 50 employees or less, its good faith estimate of market value may be based on net book values used for federal income tax purposes;

—A property owner that provides property information to an outside appraisal firm representing a central appraisal district is not required to file a rendition statement;

—A property owner's failure to file a rendition statement before the required due date of a current tax year will result in a penalty of ten percent (10%) of the total taxes assessed on the owner's property for that tax year;

—Upon written request by a chief appraiser, a property owner must provide, within 21 days of the request, additional information or documentation to support how the owner's good faith estimate of market value was determined. Failure to comply with a chief appraiser's request will result in the same ten percent (10%) penalty for failure to file a rendition statement;

—Should a court of law determine that a property owner filed a fraudulent rendition statement or provided fraudulent information to a central appraisal district, a property owner will be fined a penalty of 50% of the total taxes assessed on the owner's property for the subject tax year.

John R. Ferrell, Ryan

CCH Comment: Streamlined Rendition Process Available

A taxpayer whose information contained in the most recently filed rendition statement is accurate for the current tax year may comply with the rendition requirements by filing a rendition statement on a form prescribed by the Comptroller of Public Accounts on which the person has checked a box to affirm that the information continues to be complete and accurate. (Sec. 22.01(l), Tax Code)

Part V—Property Taxes

- *Specially assessed property*

Texas provides for assessment of five types of property at its present-use value, rather than at market value. These are agricultural use land; timberland; open-space land; recreational, park, and scenic land; and public access airport property. Special appraisal rules also apply to real property interests in oil or gas in place.

Agricultural use land: All land owned by natural persons that is designated for agricultural use must be assessed considering only factors relative to the agricultural use. The classification of agricultural land will also be determined by its "productive capacity". The constitution defines "agricultural use" to mean the raising of livestock or growing of crops, fruit, flowers, and other products of the soil under natural conditions as a business venture for profit, when the business is the primary occupation and source of income of the owner. The Tax Code states that "agriculture" means the use of land to produce plant or animal products (including fish or poultry) under natural conditions.

The term does not include the processing of plant or animal products after harvesting or the production of timber or forest products. Land used for residential purposes or a purpose inconsistent with agricultural use and land that secures a home equity loan cannot be designated for agricultural use.

Special rules apply to appraising a parcel of land used for single-family residential purposes and contiguous to agricultural or open-space land if owned by the same person or related persons.

Land that is located in a county with a population of 35,000 or less and that includes a greenhouse for growing florist items solely for wholesale purposes may be designated as land for agricultural use if the land otherwise qualifies for agricultural use designation and the owner of the land does not use the land in conjunction with or contiguous to land used to conduct retail sales of florist items.

CCH Practice Pointer: Impact of Drought

Effective January 1, 2010, a land's designation as agricultural use is not impacted when the land ceases to be devoted principally to agricultural use as a result of a governor-declared drought provided that the taxpayer intends to return the land to agricultural use when the declared drought ceases. (Sec. 23.522, Tax. Code)

Open-space land: Open-space land devoted to farm, ranch, or wildlife management purposes is valued on the basis of its productive capacity. "Open-space land" is land that (1) is currently devoted principally to agricultural use "to the degree of intensity generally accepted in the area," and (2) for property other than property used for wildlife management purposes, has been devoted principally to agricultural use or to the production of timber or forest products for five of the preceding seven years. The term also includes land that is used principally as an ecological laboratory by a public or private college or university. Property must satisfy rules developed by the Texas Parks and Wildlife Department to qualify for open-space land devoted to wildlife management.

Property taxes on qualified agricultural and open-space land subject to a temporary quarantine of at least 90 days established by the Texas Animal Health Commission due to the tick infestation is subject to proration, and upon written request by the landowner, the land will be reappraised for each year the land was or is under quarantine.

An additional tax will be imposed if the use of land that has been appraised as open-space land changes. Notice must be provided to the owner. The amount of the tax is the difference between the taxes imposed for the five years preceding the year in which the change of use occurs and the tax that would have been imposed had the

¶1505

land been taxed on the basis of market value in those years, plus interest at an annual rate of 7%.

Timberland: Open-space land devoted to timber production is valued on the basis of its productive capacity. Land qualifies for appraisal as timberland if it (1) is "currently and actively devoted principally to production of timber or forest products to the degree of intensity generally accepted in the area with intent to produce income," and (2) has been devoted principally for five of the preceding seven years to the production of timber or forest products or to agricultural use that would qualify it for appraisal as open-space or agricultural use land.

Timberland on which harvesting is restricted for aesthetic, conservation, water protection, or plant or animal protection may qualify for appraisal as restricted-use timber land. The land must be in an aesthetic management zone, critical wildlife habitat zone, or streamside management zone. The appraised value is one-half of what it would have been appraised at under normal circumstances. An application must be filed with the chief appraiser by May 1.

Timber falls under the farms products exemption from Texas property tax (see ¶1504, under "Farm products and implements").

Recreational, park, and scenic land: In appraising recreational, park, and scenic land, the chief appraiser may not consider any factors other than those relating to the value of the land as restricted for such use. "Recreational, park, or scenic use" means use for individual or group sporting activities; park or camping activities; development of historical, archaeological, or scientific sites; or the conservation and preservation of scenic areas. To qualify, the land must be at least five acres in size and the term of the deed restriction must be at least 10 years.

Public access airport property: The chief appraiser may not consider any factors other than those relating to the value of the property as restricted public access airport property. "Public access airport property" is privately owned airport property that is regularly used by the public, or which regularly provides services to the public in connection with airport purposes.

Oil and gas property: A real property interest in oil or gas in place may be appraised by a method that takes into account the future income from the sale of the oil or gas. In such an instance, the method must use the average price of the oil or gas from the interest for the preceding calendar year multiplied by a market condition factor. (Sec. 23.175, Tax Code) (A rule provides guidance in calculating the present value of oil and gas properties using discounted future income. (34 TAC Sec. 9.4031)) The Comptroller must calculate the market condition factor by a certain method and publish the results. If no oil or gas was produced from the interest during any month of the preceding calendar year, the average price for comparable oil or gas for that month may be used instead.

- *Residence homesteads*

The appraised value of a residence homestead for a particular tax year may not exceed the lesser of (1) the market value of the property for the most recent tax year that the market value was determined by the appraisal office, or (2) the sum of:

— 10% of the appraised value of the property for the preceding tax;

— the appraised value of the property for the preceding year; and

— the market value of all new improvements to the property.

This limitation takes effect as to a residence homestead on January 1 of the tax year following the first tax year the owner qualifies the property for a residence homestead exemption.

A replacement structure for a structure that was rendered uninhabitable or unusable by a casualty or by mold or water damage will not be counted as a new

¶1505

Part V—Property Taxes

improvement, unless it is a significant improvement over the replaced structure as that structure existed before the casualty or damage occurred.

> ### CCH Practice Pointer: Tax Notice Deadlines
> The chief appraiser is required to deliver notice of appraised value to owners of single-family residences by April 1 and notice of appraised value to owners of other property by May 1. (Sec. 25.19, Tax Code)

- *Appraisal review board*

    The duties of an appraisal review board are to:

    — determine protests initiated by property owners;

    — determine challenges initiated by taxing units;

    — correct clerical errors in the appraisal records and the appraisal rolls;

    — act on motions to correct appraisal rolls;

    — determine whether an exemption, partial exemption, or special appraisal was improperly granted; and

    — take other actions specifically authorized or required by statute.

    If the appraisal review board finds that appraisals are not substantially uniform or that records do not conform to the law in some other respect, the board must direct the chief appraiser to make the reappraisals or corrections in the appraisal records or appraisal roll necessary to conform the records to the board's determination or decision.

    The appraisal review board must, by July 20 (August 30 in counties with a population of at least 1 million people):

    — hear and determine all or substantially all timely filed protests;

    — determine all timely filed challenges;

    — submit a list of approved changes in the appraisal records to the chief appraiser; and

    — approve such records.

    Written notice must be given to a property owner of any proposed change in the records ordered by the board that increases the tax liability of the owner not later than the date the board approves the appraisal records. Failure to deliver the notice nullifies the change in the records to the extent applicable to that property owner.

- *Appraisal roll corrections*

    The appraisal roll may be changed only in the following instances:

    (1) by the chief appraiser at any time to correct a name or address, a determination of ownership, a description of property, multiple appraisals of a property, or a clerical error or other inaccuracy as prescribed by board rule that does not increase the amount of tax liability;

    (2) by the appraisal review board for any of the proceeding five years, on motion of the chief appraiser or a property owner, to correct (a) a clerical error that affects a property owner's liability for tax, (b) multiple appraisals of a property in a single tax year, (c) the inclusion of property that does not exist in the form or at the location indicated in the roll (this type of motion may be filed regardless of whether the property owner protested before the appraisal review board under Tax Code Ch. 41 (see ¶1509), or (d) (effective September 1, 2011) an error in which property is shown as owned by a person who did not own the property on January 1 of that tax year;

    (3) to reflect a determination on a taxpayer protest or court order; or

¶1505

(4) by the appraisal review board, on motion filed by the chief appraiser or a property owner, to correct an error that resulted in an incorrect appraised value that exceeds by more than one-third the correct appraised value. However, such a change may not be made if the property is the subject of a protest by the property owner before the appraisal review board or if the appraised value of the property was established under a written agreement between the property owner or the owner's agent and the appraisal district.

If the chief appraiser and the property owner do not agree to the correction before the 15th day after a motion is filed with the appraisal review board, a party bringing a motion described in instances (2) or (4) above may request a hearing before the appraisal review board. However, the property owner must comply with the payment requirements for district court appeals discussed at ¶1509.

CCH Advisory: Challenge to Interstate Allocations

A taxpayer may not seek an appraisal roll correction to address an interstate allocation of its airplane because an appraisal roll correction can only be made if the property did not exist at the location at all, not if the amount of time allocated to the location is improper. (*Corsicana Company, Inc. v. Dallas Central Appraisal District et al.*, Texas Court of Appeals, No. 05-01-00759, February 21, 2002, CCH TEXAS TAX REPORTS, ¶402-268; *CIT Leasing Corp. v. Tarrant Appraisal Review Board*, Texas Court of Appeals, No. 2-02-294-CV, July 17, 2003, CCH TEXAS TAX REPORTS, ¶402-548)

- *Chief appraiser appeals*

The chief appraiser may appeal appraisal review board orders determining taxpayer protests orders if: (1) the protest involved a determination of the property's appraised or market value of less than $1 million according to the order; or (2) for any other taxpayer protest, the property to which the protest applies has an appraised value of less than $1 million according to the appraisal roll for the current year, unless the chief appraiser alleges that the taxpayer or a person acting on behalf of the taxpayer committed fraud, made a material misrepresentation, or presented fraudulent evidence in the hearing before the board.

¶1506 Payment of Taxes

Law: Secs. 23.125, 31.02, 31.03, 31.031, 31.032, 31.04, 31.05, 31.072, Tax Code (CCH TEXAS TAX REPORTS, ¶20-335, 89-102, 89-108, 89-188).

In general, tax bills for the current year are mailed by the assessor by October 1 and the taxes become delinquent if not paid by the following February 1. County taxpayers who prefer to pay the tax in two equal installments may do so by paying the first installment by December 1 and the remainder by the following July 1, if the taxing unit has adopted the split-payment option. Taxpayers may obtain a discount for early payment if discount plans have been adopted by taxing units.

CCH Practice Tip: Deferred Payments for Military

Eligible military personnel serving on active duty in any branch of the U.S. Armed Forces during a war or national emergency may pay delinquent Texas property taxes without penalty or interest no later than the 60th day after the earliest of the following:

— the person is discharged from active military service;

— the person returns to Texas for more than 10 days;

— the person returns to nonactive duty status in the reserves; or

— the war or national emergency ends.

Eligible military personnel includes individuals on active military duty in Texas and members of the reserves placed on active military duty who were transferred out of the state as a result of a war or national emergency. A person is considered to be on active

Part V—Property Taxes 283

military duty if the person is covered by the Service members' Civil Relief Act or the Uniformed Services Employment and Reemployment Rights Act of 1994 (38 U.S.C. Secs. 4301 *et seq.*), as amended.

The deferred payment provisions apply only to property owned on the date the person was transferred out of Texas and to property the person inherited or acquired as a gift after that date.

- *Four-installment payment option for disabled or senior homeowners*

Home owners who are either disabled or at least 65 years old, and who qualify for a residence homestead exemption from school district taxes (¶1504), have the option of paying their property taxes in four equal installments, with the first one-quarter payment being due before the property tax delinquency date, February 1, and the remainder in equal installments before April 1, June 1, and August 1 of the year following the calendar year in which the taxes were imposed.

A notice of intent to make such installment payments must be submitted by the claimant before the delinquency date and accompany the first payment. The installment payment option applies only to taxes imposed on property that the taxpayer owns and occupies as a residence. No interest or penalties are due on the last three installment payments if all such requirements are met.

Disabled veterans or recipients of the Purple Heart, the Congressional Medal of Honor, the Bronze Star Medal, the Silver Star, the Legion of Merit, or a service cross awarded by a branch of the United States armed forces may make installment payments of their property taxes.

The penalty for failure by a disabled or elderly person to make a timely installment payment of property taxes on a residence homestead is 6%.

- *Four-installment payment option for property damaged by disaster*

Certain taxpayers whose residential real property or whose business real or personal property is located in a disaster area and is damaged as a direct result of the disaster may elect to pay one-fourth or more of a taxing unit's property taxes on the property before the February 1 delinquency date and pay the remaining taxes in three equal installments without penalty or interest. The last three installments will be due before March 31, May 31, and July 31. This installment payment option is available only to (1) a person who owns real property that consists of fewer than five living units and that is the owner's residence homestead or is used for residential purposes; and (2) small businesses with annual gross receipts of less than $5 million (adjusted for inflation beginning with the 2010 tax year). The installment payment option is also limited to property taxes that are imposed on the property by a taxing unit before the first anniversary of the disaster. (Sec. 31.032, Tax Code)

- *Installment payments of delinquent taxes*

The collector for a taxing unit may enter into a written installment agreement with a taxpayer for the payment of delinquent tax, penalty, and interest (see ¶1507 for details on delinquencies). Such an agreement, limited to a period of three years or less, constitutes an irrevocable admission of liability for the tax, penalty, and interest subject to the agreement. Interest at the rate of 1% per month, as well as the penalty imposed (¶1508) accrue on the unpaid balance during the period of the agreement.

Execution of an agreement prevents seizure of property or the filing of suits by the collecting authorities during the period of installment collection, provided the property owner meets the conditions of the agreement and pays any other property taxes owed to the taxing unit when due; see ¶1507 for a discussion of seizures and suits.

¶1506

- *Discounts for early payment*

Two types of early-payment discounts may be adopted by taxing units, alternatively or in tandem: fixed-date plans and open-date plans. Discounts are not available to taxpayers who elect the split-payment option (see above).

Fixed-date plan: The fixed-date plan, applicable regardless of the date tax bills are mailed, permits the taxpayer to reduce the tax by the following stated percentages if the tax is paid within certain months: 3% in October; 2% in November; and 1% in December.

Open-date plan: Under the open-date discount plan, applicable only when tax bills are mailed after September 30, the taxpayer may take a 3% discount if the tax is paid during the next full calendar month following the date the tax bills were mailed, a 2% discount in the second full calendar month, and 1% discount in the third full calendar month.

Taxing units may adopt both discounts, in which case the fixed-date plan applies unless the tax bills are mailed after September 30, in which case the open-date plan is effective.

- *Prepayments by dealers*

A motor vehicle dealer who owes current year vehicle inventory taxes or a dealer of vessels and outboard motors who owes current year vessel and outboard motor inventory taxes must make monthly property tax prepayments. Monthly tax prepayment requirements also apply to dealers' inventories of heavy equipment and to retailers' inventories of manufactured housing.

- *Services performed in lieu of payment*

The governing body of a taxing unit or school district may permit qualified individuals to perform services for the taxing unit or school district in lieu of paying Texas property or school taxes.

An individual age 65 or older may be allowed to perform services for the taxing unit in order to satisfy, in whole or in part, the property taxes due on his or her homestead. The services are performed under a contract with the taxing unit and the individual will not be considered an employee nor be entitled to any employee benefits including workers compensation. The taxpayer will receive credit equal to the federal hourly minimum wage for each hour of service performed and the services must be completed within one year of the delinquency date for the taxes due.

Qualified individuals may be allowed to perform teaching duties at junior high schools or high schools in lieu of school taxes owed on a residence homestead. Pursuant to a written contract, the individual is entitled to a maximum credit of $500 per semester or $1000 for a course in which a student receives a full year's credit for one semester of study. An individual may not receive credit for more than two courses in any school year. The individual must meet state standards in order to teach but is not considered an employee nor is he or she entitled to any employee benefits, including workers compensation. Businesses may also qualify for the school tax credit and assign an employee of the business to perform teaching services subject to the above credit maximums.

¶1507 Collection of Tax

Law: Secs. 31.01, 31.02, 31.04, 32.01, 33.05, 33.06, 33.21, 33.22, 33.23, 33.24, 33.25, 33.41, 33.91, 33.911, 34.21, 34.22, 34.23, Tax Code (CCH Texas Tax Reports, ¶89-162, 89-164, 89-172, 89-176, 89-180).

In general, taxes are delinquent if not paid before February 1 of the year following imposition. For tax bills mailed to a taxpayer after January 10, the delinquency date for the taxes shown on that bill will be postponed to the first day of the

¶1507

Part V—Property Taxes

next month that will provide a period of at least 21 days after the mailing of the tax bill within which to pay the taxes before they become delinquent. If the taxing unit has adopted "open-date" discounts (¶1506), the delinquency date is postponed to the first day of the next month following the fourth full calendar month following the date tax bills were mailed. For example, if a tax bill was mailed December 15, the delinquency date would be May 1.

The property tax delinquency date is postponed to February 1 of the first year that will provide a 180-day period after the date the tax bill was mailed in which to pay the taxes if the bill includes taxes for one or more preceding tax years because the property was erroneously omitted from the tax roll in those years.

All taxes, penalties, and interest on property are automatically a lien on the property as of January 1 of each year.

A taxpayer may be allowed to make installment payments of delinquent taxes (¶1506). Taxpayers who are at least age 65 or who are disabled may defer collection activities on delinquent property taxes on their resident homesteads (¶1510). See ¶1506 for a discussion of the deferral available to military personnel.

- *Seizure of personal property*

The personal property of a taxpayer may be seized for the payment of a delinquent tax, penalty, and interest owed on a property. Personal property subject to seizure includes tangible personal property, cash on hand, notes or accounts receivable (including rents and royalties), demand or time deposits, and certificates of deposit, but excludes current wages in possession of an employer.

After a tax becomes delinquent, the tax collector or peace officer may apply for a tax warrant authorizing seizure of property in any county in which the person liable for the tax has personal property. The court must issue the warrant if the collector shows by affidavit that the person whose property he or she seeks to seize (1) is delinquent in the amount stated; or (2) that the property on which tax has been or will be imposed is about to be removed from the county or sold in a liquidation sale in connection with the cessation of a business and there is no other known property from which the tax may be satisfied. (Sec. 33.21)

Seizure of property, or the sale of property that has been seized, may be prevented by the delivery to the collector of a cash or surety bond conditioned on payment of the tax before delinquency. The bond amount is determined by the collector, but may not exceed an amount greater than the tax imposed or a reasonable estimate of the tax to be imposed.

After property has been seized, the collector must serve a written notice as soon as possible, stating the time and place of the sale, to any person with an interest in the property, as well as to the person against whom a tax warrant has been issued. However, failure to send or receive the notice does not affect the validity of the sale or title to the seized property.

- *Seizure of real property*

A municipality or a county may seize and sell a person's real property for payment of delinquent property taxes, penalties, and interest associated with the property, after giving notice to the person, if:

— the property is in a municipality or county, is less than one acre, and has been abandoned for at least one year;

— the taxes on the property are delinquent either for each of the preceding five years or, for property within a municipality, each of the preceding three years if a lien on the property has been created in favor of the municipality for the cost of remedying a health or safety hazard on the property; and

¶1507

— the tax collector determines that seizure of the property would be in the best interest of the municipality.

CCH Advisory: Sales of Homestead

A homestead may be sold to collect unpaid taxes, penalties, and interest. However, a homestead may not be sold to collect delinquent public improvement district (PID) assessments. The Texas Attorney General has taken the position that the protection afforded homesteads from tax sales for delinquent PID assessments does not extend to assessments levied prior to a taxpayer claiming a homestead exemption. Thus, a homestead may be sold for assessments levied against a developer prior to a homeowner purchasing the home. (*Opinion of the Texas Attorney General*, No. GA-0237, August 25, 2004, CCH TEXAS TAX REPORTS, ¶ 402-748)

The seizure and sale may not be set aside or voided because of any error in determination. These seizure and sale provisions are in addition to the general provisions governing delinquent tax suits and tax sales.

Property is presumed to have been abandoned for at least one year if, during that period, the property has remained vacant and a lawful act of ownership has not been exercised, such as mowing grass, repairing a structure, removing debris, or other forms of upkeep or maintenance. The tax collector may rely on the affidavit of any competent person with personal knowledge of the facts in determining whether property has been abandoned or is vacant.

An assessor or collector who has not provided notice of potential seizure by mailing the owner a bill for delinquent taxes may provide notice by serving a copy of the application for a tax warrant to each person known to have an interest in the property. If the official cannot determine ownership of the property, notice may be published in a local newspaper. Under certain circumstances, the official may post notice at the county courthouse and two other public places. An affidavit by the assessor or collector testifying that notification has been made may serve as proof of notification. Failure to send or receive notice does not affect the validity of the sale of the seized property.

A person who owes delinquent taxes to the county or any school district or municipality in the county is ineligible to purchase property at a tax sale.

- *Suits to collect taxes*

At any time after a real or personal property tax becomes delinquent, a taxing unit may file a suit to foreclose the lien securing payment of the tax or any other lien on the property in favor of the taxing unit, or to enforce personal liability for the taxes owed. The suit must be filed in a court of competent jurisdiction in the county in which the tax was imposed. The court may grant injunctive relief if the taxing unit demonstrates that the property is about to be removed from the county or transferred to a third party.

Taxpayers who are at least age 65 or who are disabled may defer or abate a suit to collect delinquent property taxes on their resident homesteads.

- *Statutes of limitations*

Personal property may not be seized and a suit may not be filed to collect a tax on personal property that has been delinquent more than four years or to collect a tax on real property that has been delinquent more than 20 years.

- *Redemption of real property after tax sale*

Homestead or agricultural land: Real property sold at a tax sale that was used as the residence homestead of the owner or was land designated for agricultural use

¶1507

Part V—Property Taxes 287

may be redeemed by the owner within two years of the date on which the purchaser's deed is filed for record. The owner must pay the purchaser:

— the amount the purchaser bid for the property;

— the amount of the deed recording fee; and

— the amount paid by the purchaser as taxes, penalties, interest, and costs on the property; plus

— a redemption premium of 25% of the aggregate total if the property is redeemed during the first year of the redemption period or 50% if the property is redeemed during the second year of the redemption period.

The same principles apply if the purchaser at the tax sale was a taxing unit that has resold the property, except that if the amount paid by the owner is less than the amount of the judgment for taxes, the owner must pay the difference.

Property purchased by a taxing unit that has not been resold may be redeemed by the original property owner within two years by paying the taxing unit the lesser of:

— the amount of the judgment against the property; or

— the market value of the property as specified in that judgment, plus the amount of the fee for filing the taxing unit's deed and the amount spent by the taxing unit as costs on the property if the property was judicially foreclosed and bid off to the taxing unit.

For property seized and bid off to the taxing jurisdiction, the original property owner must pay the lesser of:

— the amount of the taxes, penalties, and interest, and costs for which the warrant was issued; or

— the market value of the property as specified in the warrant, plus the amount of the fee for filing the taxing unit's deed and the amount spent by the taxing unit as costs on the property.

Property that is not a homestead or agricultural land: The owner may redeem the property in the same manner and by paying the same amounts, except that the owner's right of redemption must be exercised within six months after the date on which the purchaser's or taxing unit's deed is filed for record, and the redemption premium payable by the owner to a purchaser other than a taxing unit may not exceed 25%.

Mineral interests: The period during which the former owner of a mineral interest that was sold for unpaid property taxes may buy back the mineral interest is two years.

¶1508 Penalties and Interest

Law: Secs. 11.251, 11.439, 22.28-22.30, 33.01, 33.011, 33.04, 33.07, 33.55, Tax Code (CCH TEXAS TAX REPORTS, ¶ 89-204, 89-206, 89-210).

A delinquent tax incurs a 6% penalty for the first calendar month it is delinquent, plus 1% for each additional month or portion of a month it remains unpaid prior to July 1. On July 1, the total penalty becomes 12% of the delinquent tax, including a delinquent second payment under the split-payment option, regardless of the number of months of delinquency.

In lieu of the penalty discussed above, a penalty of 50% of a taxpayer's delinquent tax is incurred, regardless of the number of months the tax is delinquent, if the tax is delinquent because certain homestead exemptions were claimed by the taxpayer to which the taxpayer was not entitled. The 50% penalty does not apply if the

¶1508

exemption was granted by the appraisal district or board and not at the request or application of the property owner.

Under certain circumstances, a taxing unit or appraisal district that contracts with an attorney to collect delinquent taxes may impose a special "additional penalty" in an amount equal to the collection costs (i.e., the compensation paid the attorney).

In addition to penalties, interest accrues at 1% for each month or portion of a month the tax remains unpaid.

Taxpayers who fail to file a rendition statement or property report (¶1505) by the applicable deadline are subject to a penalty equal to 10% of the total amount of taxes imposed. An additional penalty, equal to 50% of the total amount of taxes, is imposed if a court determines that the taxpayer filed a false statement or report with the intent to commit fraud or tax evasion. The chief appraiser may waive the penalties if he or she determines that the person exercised reasonable diligence to comply with or has substantially complied with the requirements. A written request for waiver must be sent to the chief appraiser not later than June 1 or 30 days after the date the person received notification of the penalty.

A 10% penalty is imposed against taxpayers that fail to file the required inventory or property tax records necessary to support its freeport exemption application within 30 days of an appraiser's request and against those taxpayers who file a late freeport exemption application. The penalty must be paid to each affected taxing district and is imposed on the difference between the amount of tax imposed by the taxing unit on the inventory or property and the amount that would have been imposed otherwise.

A delinquent tax continues to accrue penalties and interest as long as the tax remains unpaid, regardless of whether a judgment has been rendered for the delinquent tax.

- *Waiver of penalties and interest*

A taxing unit must waive penalties and may waive interest on a delinquent tax if an act or omission of an officer, employee, or agent of the taxing unit, or of the appraisal district in which the taxing unit participates, caused the taxpayer's failure to pay the tax before delinquency. The taxpayer, however, must have paid the tax within 21 days from the date the taxpayer knew or should have known of the delinquency. A request for a waiver of penalties and interest must be made before the 181st day after the delinquency date.

In addition, interest and penalties will be waived by a taxing unit on a tax bill that is returned undelivered to the taxing unit by the U.S. Postal Service if:

— the taxing unit does not send another bill at least 21 days before the delinquency date and the taxpayer establishes that it furnished the appraisal district with a current mailing address before September 1 of the year in which the tax is assessed; or

— the tax bill was returned because of an act or omission of an officer, employee or agent of the taxing unit or of the appraisal district and the taxing unit or appraisal district did not send another tax bill at least 21 days before the delinquency date to the proper address. The taxpayer must request such a waiver before the 181st day after the delinquency date. The waiver is unavailable if the tax bill was sent to an incorrect mailing address furnished by the taxpayer. The taxpayer must pay the outstanding taxes within 21 days of receipt of a bill at the taxpayer's correct address.

Electronic funds transfer: Penalties and interest on delinquent tax will be waived if:

¶1508

Part V—Property Taxes

— the tax was payable by electronic funds transfer;

— the taxpayer's failure to pay the tax before the delinquency date was caused by an error in the transmission of the funds; and

— the tax was paid not later than the 21st day after the date the taxpayer knew or should have known of the delinquency.

¶1509 Taxpayer Remedies

Law: Secs. 31.11, 31.111, 31.12, 41.41, 41A.01, 41A.03, 41A.10, 42.01, 42.06, 42.21, 42.22, 42.225, 42.26, 42.43, 43.03, Tax Code (CCH TEXAS TAX REPORTS, ¶¶ 89-204, 89-224, 89-228, 89-234, 89-236).

A property owner may protest before the appraisal review board any action of the appraisal office that adversely affects the owner, including the determination of the market value of the property, unequal appraisal, denial of an exemption, or a determination that the owner's land may not be designated agricultural use land, open-space land, or timberland. Only agents for whom a taxpayer has submitted a written-authorization may represent a taxpayer before the appraisal review board. (Sec. 1.111, Tax Code)

A written notice of protest must be filed with the appraisal review board before May 1 (June 1 for non-single family resident property owners) or not later than 30 days after the valuation notice was delivered to the property owner, whichever is later. However, owners of single-family residences who file a notice of protest after the deadline but before the appraisal review board approves the appraisal records are entitled to a hearing and determination of the protest if they file the notice before June 1. (Sec. 41.44, Tax Code) An informal hearing is held to determine the protests.

Any agreement between a property owner or the property owner's agent and the chief appraiser of an appraisal district is final. An appraisal review board may not review or reject such an agreement. (Sec. 41.01(b), Tax Code) Nor may such an agreement be appealed to the courts. (*Verm v. Harris Country Appraisal District*, Texas Court of Appeals, Fourteenth District, No. 14-06-01046-CV, July 1, 2008, CCH TEXAS TAX REPORTS, ¶ 403-438)

Practitioner Comment: Changes in Property Appraisal Requirements

In 2009, the Texas Legislature passed Senate Bill 771 which implemented changes to Section 23.01 (Appraisals Generally) of the State of Texas Property Tax Code. As part of these changes, Section 23.01 (b) was amended to require chief appraisers to consider all available evidence that is specific to the property being appraised in their market value determination process.

Also, more importantly, the addition of Subsection (c) to Section 23.01 prohibits a chief appraiser from increasing the appraised value of a property in a tax year immediately following the tax year in which the appraised value of the property was reduced and finalized under the appeal remedies set out in Subtitle F of the property tax code. However, a chief appraiser may increase the appraised value of the property in the following tax year if the increase is "reasonably" warranted by reliable and substantial evidence. Further, the burden of proof to support an increase in an appraised value of the property in the following tax year is the responsibility of the chief appraiser.

John R. Ferrell, Ryan

CCH Advisory: Access to Information

A property owner has a right of access to information about the property prepared by a private appraisal firm and obtained by the appraisal district from the firm. The owner also has a right of access to information in the possession of the firm that is not in the

¶1509

possession of the appraisal district. (*Opinion of the Texas Attorney General*, Opinion No. JC-0424, October 19, 2001, CCH TEXAS TAX REPORTS, ¶402-244)

- *Court appeals*

A property owner may appeal an appraisal review board order or a Comptroller's order determining a protest in district court. The owner must file a written notice of the appeal with the body issuing the order within 15 days of receiving notice of the order and must petition for review with the district court within 60 days of receiving notice of the order or at any time after the hearing but before the 60-day deadline. (Sec. 42.21(a), Tax Code)

> **CCH Pointer: Pilot Administrative Appeals Program Available**
>
> Effective January 1, 2010, a three-year pilot program allows taxpayers to appeal their property tax appraisals from the appraisal review board in certain counties to the State Office of Administrative Hearings rather than appealing to the district court. The pilot program only applies to property with an appraised value of $1 million or more that is located in Bexar, Cameron, Dallas, El Paso, Harris, Tarrant, and Travis counties. To make an appeal under the program, taxpayers are required to file with the chief appraiser of the appraisal district within 30 days of receiving notice of an appraisal review board decision. (Sec. 2003.901, et seq., Tax Code)

The district court must grant relief on the ground that property is appraised unequally in comparison to the level of other property in the appraisal district if the appraised value varies at least 10% from the median level of appraisal of either (1) a reasonable and representative sample of other properties in the appraisal district, or (2) a sample of appraisal district properties consisting of a reasonable number of other properties similarly situated, or of the same general kind or character as, the property subject to the protest. Relief must also be granted on the ground that a property is appraised unequally if the appraised value of the property exceeds the median appraised value of a reasonable number of comparable properties appropriately adjusted.

> **CCH Comment: Unequal Value vs. Market Value**
>
> If a conflict exists between taxation at market value and equal and uniform taxation, a Texas court of appeal has held that equal and uniform taxation must prevail. (*United Investors Realty Trust*, 47 S.W.3d 648 (Tex. CtApp 2001), CCH TEXAS TAX REPORTS, ¶402-174)

The filing of an appeal does not affect the delinquency date for payment of the tax. A property owner must generally pay, before the delinquency date, the lesser of (1) the amount of taxes due on the portion of the taxable value of the property that is not in dispute, or (2) the amount of taxes due on the property under the order from which the appeal is taken. (Sec. 42.08, Tax Code)

> **CCH Pointer: Failure to timely pay no bar to appeal of total assessment**
>
> A taxpayer that paid its taxes after the due date was not barred from pursuing its appeal in district court because the taxpayer was disputing whether it owed any taxes at all. Thus, the amount not in dispute was zero and the taxpayer's failure to timely pay did not bar his appeal. (*C.I.T. Leasing Corp. v. Dallas Central Appraisal District*, Texas Court of Appeals, Fifth District, No. 05-06-01546-CV, December 13, 2007, CCH TEXAS TAX REPORTS, ¶403-356)

Attorney's fees: A taxpayer who prevails in a judicial appeal on the ground of excessive or unequal appraisal may be awarded reasonable attorney's fees, not to exceed the greater of $15,000 or 20% of the amount by which the property owner's tax

¶1509

liability is reduced as a result of the appeal. The attorney's fees may not to exceed the lesser of $100,000 or the total amount by which the property owner's tax liability is reduced as a result of the appeal. (Sec. 42.29, Tax Code) The Texas appellate courts are split as to whether the awarding of such fees is mandatory or discretionary; see *Aaron Rents v. Travis Central Appraisal District*, 212 S.W.3d 665 (TX CtApp 2006), CCH TEXAS TAX REPORTS, ¶ 403-152.

- *Binding arbitration*

Practitioner Comment: Binding Arbitration, an Alternative to Property Tax Litigation

In the appeal of a determination made by an appraisal review board, Section 9.804 of the State of Texas Property Tax Code provides for a binding arbitration process as an alternative to filing a lawsuit in district court. Only real property, and not personal property, is subject to the binding arbitration process, and then, only when the property is valued at $1 million or less or if the property qualifies as the owner's residence homestead. The basis of any appeal under this section can only concern the issue of the appraised or fair market value of the property and cannot involve any other matters of dispute such as unequal appraisal, special valuation assessments, or exemptions.

In order to take advantage of the binding arbitration process, a property owner must file a Request for Binding Arbitration form along with a $500 deposit payable by certified check, cashiers check, or money order to the Texas Comptroller of Public Accounts, with the appropriate central appraisal district within 45 days after the date that the property owner receives the appraisal review board order determining protest. Alternatively, the property owner may request expedited arbitration which allows for only one hour of testimony at the hearing but reduces the deposit fee to $250. Failure to submit the required deposit fee with the request form will result in the dismissal of the application. The request form can be obtained from the Texas Comptroller of Public Accounts' website or from a central appraisal district. If the form is filed by a property owner's agent, written authorization signed by the owner must accompany the form when filed.

The comptroller will notify both the appropriate appraisal district and the property owner that it has received and approved the application for arbitration. The property owner and the appraisal district will have 20 days to agree on an arbitrator or to notify the comptroller that the parties are unable to agree on an arbitrator. If the parties are unable to agree on an arbitrator, the comptroller will select an arbitrator on their behalf. The arbitrator must make every effort to complete the arbitration within 120 days of being selected.

The arbitrator will deliver hearing procedures and will determine the level of formality used during the arbitration hearing. The hearing itself may be held in person, in writing, or via teleconference.

If the arbitrator finds that taxes on the property under arbitration are delinquent, the appraisal review board order was not related to real property with an appraised or market value of $1 million or less (unless the property qualifies as the owner's residence homestead), or the property owner filed a lawsuit in district court for the same property, then the request for binding arbitration will be dismissed. With the dismissal of a request for binding arbitration by an arbitrator, the comptroller is required to refund the deposit less 10% for the comptroller's administrative costs.

Within 20 days of the arbitration hearing, the arbitrator is required to make a final determination of the appraised or market value for the property under arbitration. If the arbitrator's determination is nearer to the property owner's opinion of the appraised or market value for the property, the comptroller is required to refund the property owner's deposit. The central appraisal district is then required to pay the arbitrator's fee. If the arbitrator's determination is closer to the central appraisal district's value, the arbitrator's fee will be paid from the property owner's deposit fee. In either case, 10% of the deposit is retained by the comptroller to cover its administrative costs.

John P. Skidmore, Ryan

¶1509

- *Refunds*

A tax collector must mail a notice of overpayment along with a refund application to taxpayers who submitted payments exceeding, by $5 or more, the amount of property tax owed for a tax year. In addition, in the case of duplicative tax payments, a refund must be issued to the person who erred in making a payment and no refund claim is required. However, if an appraiser makes a correction to the tax roll eliminating a multiple appraisal of the property, a refund may only be issued up to four years after the year of the correction.

Taxpayers may apply to the tax collector for a refund of an overpayment or erroneous payment of property taxes. Refund claims must be made within three years after the date of payment. Local governments may extend the refund filing deadline by up to two years on a showing of good cause by the taxpayer, unless the overpayment was caused by a change of exemption status or correction of a tax roll. Refunds of overpayments or erroneous payments may be made by the tax collector without approval by the taxing unit's governing body if the amount is less than (1) $5,000 to be paid by a county of 1.5 million or more; or (2) less than $500 in all other taxing units ($2,500 if the collector collects taxes for more than one taxing jurisdiction). Property owners may file a motion with the governing body of a taxing unit at any time for the correction of mathematical errors in the computation of their property tax and receive a refund of the amount erroneously paid. (Sec. 31.11, Tax Code)

CCH Advisory: Preliminary Steps to Formal Protests

Prior to instituting the formal protest process, a good first step in most cases is to review the assessor's valuation records, which are public records, for neighboring and/or comparable properties to confirm whether any glaring inconsistencies are evident. For example, if the other properties have been assigned relatively higher values, that may caution against proceeding with a protest to avoid the risk of having an appraised value increased or otherwise alerting the assessor to what may essentially be a favorable appraisal.

It also may be useful to directly contact the assessor to discuss what factors the assessor considered in valuing the property, as this may alert the parties to obvious valuation errors that the assessor may be willing to correct without requiring the property owner to pursue a formal protest.

- *Interest on refunds*

For refunds of $5 or more, no interest is due on the amount refunded if the refund is paid on or before the 60th day after the date the liability for the refund arises. If, however, the refund is not paid within the 60-day period, interest accrues on the refund from the date on which liability for the refund arises until it is paid, at the rate of 1% per month, or part of a month, that the refund is unpaid.

A taxing unit that does not make a refund, including interest, before the 60th day after the date the chief appraiser certifies a correction to the appraisal roll must pay interest on the amount refunded at an annual rate of 12%, calculated from the delinquency date of the taxes until the date the refund is made. Moreover, a taxpayer who prevails in a suit to compel a refund, including interest, that is filed on or after the 180th day after the date that the chief appraiser certifies the appraisal roll is entitled to court costs and reasonable attorney's fees.

¶1510 Abatements, Limitations, and Deferrals

Law: Secs. 33.06, 33.065, 312.001—402, 313.001—054, Tax Code (CCH Texas Tax Reports, ¶20-170, 20-215, 20-315).

In addition to the property tax exemptions listed at ¶1504, Texas law provides certain tax abatements and deferrals.

- *Deferral for senior citizens*

An individual who is age 65 or older and owns and occupies a residence homestead on which a tax is delinquent may defer collection activities, defer or abate a suit to collect the delinquent tax, or abate a sale to foreclose a tax lien. However, a tax lien remains, and interest at the rate of 8% continues to accrue during the period that collection of taxes is deferred or abated. In general, no penalty may be imposed during the deferral period. However, those that were imposed prior to the application for deferral/abatement are preserved. The additional penalty for collection costs may be imposed only if the taxes for which collection is deferred remain delinquent 181 days after the deferral period expires.

To obtain a deferral for the collection of delinquent taxes, the taxpayer must file the affidavit with the chief appraiser of the appraisal district in which the property is located. To obtain an abatement of a pending suit to collect delinquent taxes, the taxpayer must file the affidavit in the court in which the suit is pending. To obtain an abatement of a pending sale to foreclose a tax lien, the taxpayer must file the affidavit with the chief appraiser of the appraisal district in which the property is located and the collector for the taxing unit that requested the order of sale or the attorney representing the respective taxing unit for the collection of delinquent taxes and the officer charged with selling the property by the fifth day before the date of the sale.

The surviving spouse of a deceased individual who qualified for a deferral or abatement of activities may continue to claim the abatement or deferral until the 181st day after the date the surviving spouse no longer owns and occupies the property as a residence homestead if:

— the property was the residence homestead of the deceased spouse when the deceased spouse died;

— the surviving spouse was at least 55 years of age when the deceased spouse died; and

— the property was the residence homestead of the surviving spouse when the deceased spouse died.

- *Deferral for residence homestead appreciation*

An individual taxpayer may defer, or abate a suit to collect, delinquent property taxes imposed on the portion of the appraised value of a residence homestead that exceeds 105% of the appraised value of the property for the preceding year. Abatement or deferral is not allowed if taxes are delinquent on the non-appreciated portion of the home. For new improvements made to the property, the tax deferral or abatement is allowed for delinquent taxes imposed on the portion of the residence homestead that exceeds the sum of (1) 105% of the property's appraised value for the preceding year; and (2) the market value of the new improvements.

The total amount of taxes that may be deferred from collection must be reduced if (1) the collection of tax on a property was deferred in a prior tax year; and (2) the sum of 105% of the property's appraised value for the preceding year plus the market value of new improvements to the property exceeds the property's appraised value for the current tax year. The amount of taxes that may be deferred is reduced by an amount calculated by multiplying the taxing unit's tax rate for the current tax year by the amount by which the sum described in the preceding sentence (105% of the

¶1510

property's appraised value for the preceding year, plus the market value of new improvements to the property) exceeds the appraised value of the property.

Tax liens, interest and penalties, defenses: While collection of tax is deferred, a tax lien remains on the property and interest continues to accrue at a rate of 8%.

- *Abatement of taxes for property located in a reinvestment zone*

Until September 1, 2009, eligible municipalities and counties may enter into tax abatement agreements with owners of real or personal property, located in designated reinvestment zones. Municipalities may also enter into an agreement with a leasehold interest holder in tax-exempt real property. An agreement with a municipality may not exceed ten years and the owner must make specific improvements or repairs to the property. According to the Texas Attorney General's Office, although the abatement period may not last longer than 10 years, the municipality and the taxpayer may agree to have the abatement period commence at a later time. (*Opinion No. GA-0734*, Texas Attorney General, August 6, 2009, CCH TEXAS TAX REPORTS, ¶403-567)

A tax abatement agreement takes effect on January 1 of the tax year after the date the improvements or repairs required of the owner in the agreement are substantially completed. Any property subject to such an agreement may not be located in an improvement project financed by tax increment bonds.

A municipality may also agree to exempt tangible personal property located on the real property in each year of the agreement, other than (1) personal property already located on the real property before the period covered by the agreement; and (2) inventory and supplies.

- *Limitations on appraisals for school district taxes for qualified investments*

Through December 31, 2011, school districts may enter into agreements to limit school district property taxes imposed on taxable entities that make qualified investments in their communities. To qualify, the taxable entity must use the property in connection with manufacturing, research and development, a clean coal project, an advanced clean energy project, renewable energy electric generation, electric power generation using integrated gasification combined cycle technology, or nuclear electric power generation. The property must be IRC Sec. 1245 property that is used in connection with the manufacturing, processing, or fabrication in a cleanroom environment of a semiconductor property or a building or portion of a building that houses such property. The property must also be located in a reinvestment zone or an enterprise zone and the land that the property is situated upon must not be the subject of a tax abatement agreement with the school district.

CCH Pointer: Real property lessee eligible for property tax limitation

The Texas Attorney General has taken the position stated that a person meeting the other requirements of the Texas Economic Development Act who owns qualified property, including a building or other improvement or tangible personal property, is eligible to apply for a property tax appraisal limitation on the person's qualified property, irrespective of whether the person owns or leases the land on which the qualified property is located. (*Opinion No. GA-0665*, Texas Attorney General, September 16, 2008, CCH TEXAS TAX REPORTS, ¶403-491)

In addition, the taxpayer must make at least a minimum investment amount in the property and create at least 25 new jobs (10 jobs in certain rural school districts), 80% of which are permanent full-time positions that are covered by a group health benefit of which the business offers to pay at least 80% of the premiums and that pay at least 110% of the county average weekly wage for manufacturing jobs. The amount of the minimum qualified investment required ranges from $20 million in counties with a taxable value of property in the district of less than $100 million to $100

¶1510

million for counties with a taxable value of property in the district of $10 billion or more. Lower minimum investment amounts apply in certain rural school districts. Furthermore, the taxpayer must maintain a viable presence in the school district for at least three years after the date the limitation on appraised value of the owner's property expires.

Taxpayers must submit Form 50-296, Application for Appraised Value Limitation on Qualified Property, to the school district for review. The district has 120 days to review the application, although the period may be extended. (34 TAC Secs. 9.1051, 9.1053) If a taxpayer's application, to enter into a limitation agreement is approved by a school district, the taxpayer's property taxes are limited to the lesser of the market value of the property or the amount agreed to by the school district. The minimum amount agreed to by the school district is the same as the minimum investment amount discussed above. The limitation applies to each of the first eight tax years that begin after the applicable qualifying time period. The "applicable qualifying time period" is the first two tax years (seven tax years for a nuclear power generation facility; five years for qualified clean energy projects) that begin on or after the date a person's application for a limitation on appraised value is approved. A taxpayer who violates the terms of an agreement is required to pay back taxes on the property's full market value plus penalties and interest.

¶1511 Credits

Law: Secs. 313.101—105, Tax Code (CCH Texas Tax Reports, ¶20-170).

In addition to the limitation on appraised value of a persons' qualified property discussed at ¶1510, a person may also claim a tax credit from the school district that approved the limitation. If approved, the credit is equal to the amount of property taxes paid the school district that were imposed on the portion of the appraised value of the qualified property that exceeds the limitation amount agreed to in each year in the applicable qualifying time period. The "applicable qualifying time period" means the first two tax years that begin on or after the date a person's application for a limitation on appraised value is approved.

To receive the credit, a taxpayer must apply to the school district before September 1 of the year immediately following the applicable qualifying time period. The credit is applied in the second and subsequent six tax years that begin after the date the application is approved in an amount equal to $1/7$ of the total amount of tax credit that the person is entitled to, up to 50% of the total amount of property taxes due on the property by the school district. Any amount remaining is credited against the taxpayer's taxes in the first year after the date the person's eligibility for the limitation expires, up to the total amount of taxes due to the school district.

The credit is scheduled to expire on December 31, 2011.

PART VI

MISCELLANEOUS TAXES

CHAPTER 16
UNEMPLOYMENT COMPENSATION

¶ 1601	The Law
¶ 1602	Coverage
¶ 1603	Tax Rates
¶ 1604	Returns and Reports
¶ 1605	Benefits

¶ 1601 The Law

The Texas Unemployment Compensation Act is administered by the Texas Workforce Commission, 101 E. 15th St., Austin, Texas 78778. Telephone (512) 463-2222.

¶ 1602 Coverage

Employer.—One who pays wages of $1,500 or more during any calendar quarter in the current or preceding calendar year, or employs at least one individual on each of 20 days during the current or preceding calendar year, each day being in a different calendar week. Generally, an employer who is subject to the FUTA is automatically an employer under the Texas law.

Employment.—Service, including service in interstate commerce, performed for wages or under any contract of hire, written or oral, express or implied, with exceptions listed below.

Services performed for wages constitute "employment" unless and until it is shown that the individual is free from control or direction over the performance of the services both under his contract and in fact.

Services by certain agent-drivers or commission-drivers and traveling or city salesmen are covered, service on or in connection with an American vessel or aircraft is covered also if management and control of that vessel or aircraft is within Texas.

"Employment" can include services performed by U.S. citizens outside the U.S., even if the employer has no place of business in the U.S., if the employer is a resident of Texas, is a corporation organized under the laws of Texas, or is a partnership or trust mainly based in Texas, or, under some circumstances, simply if the benefit claim is filed in Texas.

Exemptions.—:

— Insurance agents wholly on commission basis.

— Interns in employ of hospital who have completed 4-year course in state-chartered or approved medical school.

— Newspaper and shopping news carriers under 18.

— Relatives, i.e., services performed by individual in employ of son, daughter, or spouse, or by child under 21 in employ of parent.

— Service covered by federal unemployment compensation system.

— Service for a school, college, or university by a student in regular attendance.

— Service by a student enrolled at a nonprofit or public educational institution in a full-time work-study program. Not applicable to a program established for an employer or group of employers.

— Service for a hospital by a patient of the hospital.

— Student nurses in employ of hospital or training school who are attending state-chartered or approved training school.

— Service on a fishing vessel with a crew of fewer than 10 if each crew member's reimbursement is a share of the catch and such services are excluded under FUTA.

— Service performed as a direct seller if the individual is engaged in the business of in-person sales of consumer products to a buyer on a buy-sell, deposit-commission, or similar basis for resale in the home or other than in a permanent retail establishment; substantially all the remuneration is directly related to sales or other output rather than to number of hours worked; and there is a written contract providing that the individual is not treated as an employee for federal tax purposes.

— Service performed by a full-time student in the employ of an organized camp is excluded if the camp did not operate for more than 7 months in either the current or preceding calendar years or had average gross receipts in any 6 months in the preceding calendar year that were not more than 33 1/3% of its receipts for the other 6 months and the student performed services for the camp for fewer than 13 weeks in the calendar year.

— Real estate broker or salesperson if the individual is engaged in performing acts or transactions comprehended in the definition of "real estate broker," the individual is licensed as a real estate broker or salesperson, substantially all the remuneration is directly related to sales or other output and not to number of hours worked, and the services are performed under a written contract that provides that the individual is not treated as an employee for federal tax purposes.

— Instructors of persons licensed or seeking licensure as real estate brokers or salespersons if the individual is instructing an educational program or course approved by the Texas Real Estate Commission and his services are performed under a written contract providing that he is not treated as an employee for federal tax purposes.

— Traveling or city salesperson (other than as provided above), or independent contractor for wholesaler or sales representative of consumer goods, performing services in connection with trade market facility, or agent-driver or commission driver engaged on a full-time basis in the solicitation on behalf of and the transmission to a principal or orders from wholesaler, retailer, etc.

— Product demonstrators, if certain conditions are met.

— Services performed at a trade market for a wholesaler or sales representative of a wholesaler or manufacturer of consumer goods under a written contract, or as a salesman for a wholesaler of consumer goods if the wholesaler maintains a regular or seasonal place of business at a trade market facility in a city with a population of more than 750,000.

— Private for-profit delivery or courier services, if certain conditions are met.

— Service performed for a private for-profit person or entity by a landman if the individual is engaged primarily in negotiating for the acquisition or divestiture of mineral rights or business agreements that provide for the explora-

¶1602

Part VI—Miscellaneous Taxes

tion or development of minerals, substantially all remuneration is directly related to the completion of the specific tasks contracted for rather than to the number of hours worked, and the services are performed under a written contract that provides that the landman is to be treated as an independent contractor.

(See also exclusions under "Government and nonprofit employers.")

Agricultural and domestic employers.—Farm and ranch labor is covered if performed by a seasonal worker employed on a truck farm, orchard, or vineyard, or if performed by any other farm and ranch laborer employed by an employing unit that paid cash wages of $6,250 in any quarter of the current or preceding calendar year or employed three or more individuals in such employment for some portion of a day on some 20 days during the current or preceding calendar year. Farm and ranch labor performed by migrant workers is covered. Farm and ranch labor, if performed by a seasonal worker, is covered employment under the same conditions as if the seasonal worker were a migrant worker, provided that the seasonal worker is working for a farmer, ranch operator, or labor agent who employs migrant workers and is doing the same work at the same time at the same place as migrant workers. If a labor agent furnishes farm and ranch laborers, the labor agent is liable for the payment of taxes as if the labor agent were the employer of the workers, without regard to the right of control or other factors used to determine an employer-employee relationship; however, if the labor agent does not pay taxes, the person with whom the labor agent contracts for the services of the farm and ranch laborers is jointly and severally liable with the labor agent for the payment of taxes.

Domestic service in a private home, local college club or local chapter of a college fraternity or sorority is covered if performed for an employing unit that paid wages of $1,000 or more for such services in any quarter of the current or preceding calendar year.

Government and nonprofit employers.—Coverage is mandatory for the following services: nonprofit organizations exempt from federal income tax which employ four or more individuals on each of 20 days during the current or preceding calendar year, each day being in a different week; and for the state, any branch or department thereof, or any instrumentality of the state. Political subdivisions of the state are also mandatorily covered. Other government services are not covered.

Service for a nonprofit organization, the state, or a political subdivision do not include the following:

(1) Church or organization operated primarily for religious purposes and which is controlled by a church.

(2) Religious duties of minister or member of a religious order.

(3) Patients and certain blind individuals performing services in a rehabilitation facility or sheltered workshop.

(4) Individual receiving unemployment work-relief or work-training under a program financed by a federal agency or an agency of a state or political subdivision.

(5) Inmate of a custodial or penal institution owned or operated by the State or a political subdivision.

(6) Elected officials.

(7) Members of a legislative body or the judiciary.

(8) Temporary employees serving in case of fire, storm, snow, earthquake, flood or similar emergency.

(9) Individuals serving in certain major nontenured policymaking or advisory positions.

¶1602

Nonprofit organizations may finance the payment of benefits by the regular contributions method or the reimbursement method. The state and political subdivisions may elect to pay contributions or use the reimbursement method. Under reimbursement financing, payments must equal the full amount of regular benefits and 50% (100% for governmental employers) of extended benefits paid to claimants. An employer that elects the reimbursement method may be required to execute and file a surety bond.

Wages.—Remuneration for personal services, including the cash value of all remuneration in any medium other than cash and gratuities received by an employee to the extent that they are considered wages under the FUTA.

Term "wages" does not include the following:

(1) Remuneration over $9,000 paid to an individual with respect to employment in a calendar year, counting remuneration paid by employer's predecessor (if joint application for transfer of experience has been approved) and for service in another state. ("Wages" for benefit purposes is a different amount.)

(2) Payments to an individual or his dependents under a plan or system established by the employer on account of retirement, sickness, accident, disability, etc. Also other retirement payments, including amounts paid by the employer for insurance or annuities or into a fund.

(3) Payment of employees' FICA tax without deduction from wages.

(4) Payments from, to, or under trust, annuity, or bond-purchase plan exempt from federal income tax.

(5) Noncash remuneration to an employee for service not in the course of the employer's trade or business.

(6) Payments for sickness or accident disability or medical or hospitalization expenses made over six months after separation.

(7) Stand-by pay (other than vacation or sick pay) made to an employee 65 years of age or older if no work was performed in the period for which the payment was made.

¶1603 Tax Rates

Standard rate.—2.7%. Maximum possible rate is 8.25% for 2011. No employee tax.

Experience rates.—Employer's contribution rate for any calendar year will be determined under experience-rating provisions if its account has been chargeable with benefits during each month of the preceding four calendar quarters. A new employer pays the greater of the rate established for that year for its industry group or 2.7%; however, note that new employers pay 2.6% for the period in which the employing training investment tax is in effect.

Employer contribution rates are determined through the Experience Tax Rate formula: The sum of General Tax Rate + Replenishment Tax Rate + Employment and Training Investment Assessment. Some years may also include a Deficit Tax Rate. The process and terms involved are as follows:

The General Tax Rate is based on unemployment insurance claims charged to an employer's account. It is the product of each employer's Benefit Ratio and the Replenishment Ratio (a Statewide multiplier), multiplied by 100% and rounded up to the next tenth.

To determine an employer's benefit ratio for a year, its total chargebacks for the 36-consecutive-month period ending on the current October 1 (the computation date) are computed and then divided by the total amount of its taxable wages for the same period. The quotient is the employer's benefit ratio for the next year. If employer has

¶1603

Part VI—Miscellaneous Taxes

less than 3 years but at least 4 calendar quarters of compensation experience throughout which his account has been chargeable with benefits, his benefit ratio is percentage equal to total of chargebacks divided by total taxable wages for all completed calendar months immediately preceding date on which his tax rate is determined. "Benefit wages" do not include wages paid to worker whose separation was required by federal or Texas law or by Texas ordinance or to worker whose separation was due to disqualifying circumstances, provided employer fulfills separation reporting requirements.

Since the benefit ratio is determined from the amount of an employer's chargebacks and taxable wages for the past three years, chargebacks must be defined before going on to the actual tax rate formula. When benefit payments are made to claimants the benefits which they receive are charged to the account of their base period employer (or employers). Benefits so charged are designated as "chargebacks," and total chargebacks to an employer's account are therefore the total amount of benefits charged to its account. If claimants do not collect all the benefits to which they are entitled, the employers' chargebacks will be a lower amount, since only benefits actually paid may be charged to their accounts.

After the benefit ratio is determined, another formula is used to determine the replenishment ratio. This ratio is the quotient of the total amount of benefits that are effectively charged to employers' accounts and paid from the Fund during the 12 months ending September 30 of the preceding year, plus one-half of the amount of benefits paid during that period that are not charged to an employer's account, that are charged to employers' accounts after they have reached maximum liability because of the maximum tax rate or that are charged but considered not collectible, divided by the total amount of benefits paid during the 12 months ending September 30 of the preceding year that are effectively charged to employers' accounts. The numerator of the replenishment ratio is reduced by (1) benefit warrants cancelled, (2) repayment of benefits that have been overpaid, and (3) benefits paid that are repayable from reimbursing employers, the federal government or any other governmental entity.

There is a table in the law that gives the rates automatically once both the benefit ratio and the replenishment ratio have been determined. The table of rates has been extended by the Commission to include rates as high as 6.0%.

The final elements of the formula include the Replenishment Tax Rate and the Employment and Training Investment Assessment. The former is based on statewide benefits and taxed wages and is applicable to all employers to cover unemployment claims not charged to a specific employer. This tax varies inversely from year to year, to statewide economic conditions.

Finally, the Employment and Training Investment Assessment is a rate of 0.10% and is set according to State Law. It is the same for each employer entitled to an experience rate.

A Deficit Assessment may be imposed in some years. This tax is calculated by multiplying the statewide Deficit Ratio by the sum of an employer's prior year's General, Deficit, and Replenishment Tax Rates. The Deficit Tax may not exceed 2.0%.

For 2011, the Replenishment Ratio is 1.28, the Replenishment Tax Rate is 0.56 %, the Employment Training Assessment Rate is 0.10%, and the interest tax rate is 0.0%.

An employer classified in the North American Industrial Classification System Manual as a crop preparation services or cotton ginning employer may elect to pay contributions at a total fixed rate of 5.4%, the general tax rate applicable to the employer plus the deficit assessment and replenishment tax rate, or any other tax rate applicable to the employer.

¶1603

SUTA dumping.—Effective September 1, 2005, a successor employing unit that acquires compensation experience and that is an experience-rated employer on the date of and during the period preceding the acquisition will pay contributions from the date of the acquisition until the end of the calendar year at the rate applicable to the successor on the date of acquisition. A successor employer unit that is not an experience-rated employer will pay contributions from the date of the acquisition until the next contribution rate computation date at the highest rate applicable at the time of the acquisition to any predecessor that is a party to the acquisition.

In the case of a partial acquisition, if the Commission determines that the part of the organization, trade, or business transferred is definitely identifiable and segregable and that compensation experience can be specifically attributed to that part of the organization, trade, or business, the contribution rate of the successor must be computed: (1) based on the successor's experience for the part of the organization, trade, or business that was not acquired by the transfer; and (2) for the part of the organization, trade, or business acquired through the transfer.

If in either instance of acquisition, the Commission determines that the transfer was accomplished solely or primarily for the purpose of obtaining a lower contribution rate, the successor's contribution rate must be determined under Section 204.006.

Any person who recklessly, knowingly, or intentionally defeats, evades, or circumvents these provisions or if the person recklessly, knowingly, or intentionally attempts, aids and abets and attempt, or advises another to defeat, evade, or circumvent these provisions commits a Class A misdemeanor offense. An employer who commits an offense may be assessed a civil penalty in an amount equal to two percent of wages for the year during which the violation occurred and for three years following that year. A person, other than an employer, who commits an offense may be assessed a civil penalty of not more than $5,000 for a first offense and not more than $5,000 for each subsequent offense.

Voluntary payments.—An employer for whom the Commission has computed an experience rate as of October 1 of a calendar year that is effective for the succeeding calendar year may elect to make a voluntary payment of contributions to the Commission. The amount of the voluntary contribution may be equal to all or part of the employer's chargebacks during the period ending September 30 that are used in computing the employer's experience rate for the succeeding calendar year. Upon receiving a voluntary contribution, the Commission must reduce the employer's chargebacks by an amount equal to the contribution and must then recompute the experience rate applicable to that employer for the succeeding calendar year.

An employer who elects to make a voluntary contribution for the recomputation of its experience rate must make the contribution not later than the 30th day after the date on which the Commission mails to the employer the annual notice of the employer's experience rate. The employer may not revoke the contribution after the date on which the Commission uses the contribution to recompute its experience rate. Note that the Commission may not compute a new experience rate for an employer or reduce an employer's experience rate based on a voluntary contribution made by the employer after the expiration of the 120th day of the calendar year for which the rate is effective.

¶1604 Returns and Reports

Tax and wage.—Employers Quarterly Report, Form C-3, is due quarterly on or before last day of following month. Detailed quarterly wage report is also required on Form C-3. Note that certain domestic employers may elect to report quarterly wages on an annual basis. Employers reporting wages for 10 or more employees are required to file electronically, using Internet wage reporting, QuickFile, or magnetic media.

¶1605 Benefits

Base period.—First 4 of last 5 calendar quarters preceding first day of benefit year; first 4 of last 5 calendar quarters preceding the quarter in which a medically verifiable illness began or injury occurred that precluded an individual from working during the major part of any base period quarter, if the individual files an initial claim for benefits not later than 24 months after the date on which the illness or injury began or occurred.

Benefit year.—52-consecutive-week period beginning with the effective date of first valid initial claim and thereafter, the period of 52 consecutive weeks beginning with the effective date of the next valid initial claim after the termination of the last preceding benefit year.

Weekly benefit amount.—$1/25$ of highest quarterly base-period wages, less wages in excess of $5 or 25% of benefit amount (whichever amount is higher), computed to next higher multiple of $1. The maximum weekly benefit amount is determined annually as 47.6% of the statewide average weekly wage and the minimum weekly benefit amount is determined annually as 7.6% of the statewide average weekly wage.

The maximum for the year beginning 10/1/2011 increases to $426 and the minimum increases to $61.

An employer may participate in a shared work program designed to reduce unemployment by allowing certain employees to collect benefits if they share the work remaining after a reduction in the total number of hours of work and a corresponding reduction in wages.

Maximum total benefits.—Lesser of 26 times weekly benefit amount or 27% of base-period wages. For claims effective on and after October 1, 2011, the maximum total benefit amount is $11,076. In addition, during periods of high unemployment, payment of extended benefits at claimant's regular weekly benefit rate.

Benefit eligibility.—Requirements: (1) Registered for work and filed claim for benefits; (2) base-period benefit wage credits of at least 37 × his weekly benefit amount and wage credits in at least 2 calendar quarters, and if he has had a prior benefit year, he must have earned wages equal to 6 × his weekly benefit amount subsequent to the beginning of the prior benefit year; (3) be able and available for work; (4) serve waiting period of 1 week after filing initial claim (waiting week is compensable if paid benefits of at least 3 × weekly benefit amount); and (5) participate in reemployment services if required.

No benefits may be paid to instructors, researchers, or principal administrators of an educational institution during school vacation periods or during paid sabbatical leaves based on service with such institutions.

Benefits are not payable to an individual performing services in a nonprofessional capacity for an educational institution during periods between academic years or terms if there is reasonable assurance that he will perform services in the second year or term. Retroactive payments of benefits may be claimed if no work is offered in the second year or term.

A disqualification similar to those in the foregoing two paragraphs applies to individuals performing services in an educational institution while in the employ of an educational service agency.

Benefits are not payable to a professional athlete for periods between sport seasons if there is a reasonable assurance that he will perform services in both seasons.

Benefits are not payable to an alien unless he has been lawfully admitted for permanent residence or is otherwise permanently residing in the United States under color of law.

Benefits may not be denied to an individual in approved training because of the availability for work requirement or the disqualification for refusal of suitable work without good cause.

Benefits may not be denied solely on the basis of pregnancy or termination of pregnancy.

Disqualifications—Period.—

Discharge for misconduct connected with last work, voluntary leaving without good cause or refusal of suitable work without good cause—until the individual has returned to work and has either worked for 6 weeks or earned wages equal to 6 × his weekly benefit amount.

An individual who leaves work to move with a spouse from the area in which he or she worked is disqualified for not less than 6 nor more than 25 benefit periods.

No disqualification if leaving is due to medically verified illness of individual or individual's minor child (but only if there is no reasonable alternative care available for the child and the employer refused to allow the individual a reasonable amount of time off during the illness), injury, disability or pregnancy, where individual is still available for work.

No disqualification for an individual who is partially unemployed and who resigns to accept other employment that the individual reasonably believes will increase his or her weekly wage.

Military personnel who do not reenlist may not be considered to have left work voluntarily without good cause.

No disqualification for claimant whose work-related reason for separation is urgent, compelling and of a necessitous nature, so as to make separation involuntary.

A temporary employee of a temporary help firm is deemed to have left the last work voluntarily without good cause connected with the work if the employee does not contact the firm for reassignment on completion of an assignment; the employee is not deemed to have left work voluntarily without good cause unless the employee has been advised of the obligation to contact the firm on completion of assignments and that benefits may be denied for failure to do so.

Labor dispute—duration.

Securing benefits through nondisclosure or misrepresentation—forfeiture of benefit rights for remainder of year.

Receipt of wages in lieu of notice, workers' compensation benefits, or old-age social security benefits—unemployment benefits reduced by the amount of such other payments.

Receipt of governmental or other pension or retirement pay from base period employer unless the amount is less than the amount of unemployment benefits to which claimant is entitled—unemployment benefits reduced by amount of pension or retirement pay. Automatic conformity with the FUTA is provided.

Corporate officer who is a majority or controlling shareholder and who is involved in the sale of the corporation, is a limited or general partner who is involved in the sale or is the selling proprietor—benefit period occurring from the date of the sale until the date that the officer is employed and eligible for benefits based on wage credits from the new employment.

¶1605

Part VI—Miscellaneous Taxes

Discharge from last work on basis of refusal to provide services included within the course and scope of the employment to an individual infected with a communicable disease—until the claimant has returned to work and either worked for 6 weeks or earned wages equal to 6 × his weekly benefit amount. No disqualification unless the employer made available to the claimant the facilities, equipment, training, and supplies necessary to preclude the infection of the claimant with the communicable disease.

MISCELLANEOUS TAXES

CHAPTER 17
OTHER STATE TAXES

¶1701	Scope of Chapter
¶1702	Alcoholic Beverages Taxes
¶1703	Cigarette and Tobacco Products Taxes
¶1704	Insurance Taxes
¶1705	Motor Fuel Taxes
¶1706	Motor Vehicle Registration Fees
¶1707	Hotel Occupancy Tax
¶1708	Utilities Taxes
¶1709	Severance Taxes
¶1710	Environmental Taxes and Fees
¶1711	Sexually Oriented Business Admission Fee

¶1701 Scope of Chapter

This chapter deals with the Texas taxes that have not been previously discussed. The discussion here will indicate in general terms the persons subject to tax, the basis and rate of tax, and payments and reports due. Uniform administrative procedure provisions apply to all taxes administered by the Comptroller of Public Accounts (¶1802). These procedures are discussed in Part VII, "Administration and Procedure," beginning at ¶1801.

¶1702 Alcoholic Beverages Taxes

Law: Secs. 1.04, 5.50, 11.09, 12.02, 14.02, 16.02, 18.02, 19.02, 20.02, 21.02, 22.02, 23.02, 24.02, 25.02, 25.03, 26.02, 27.02, 27.12, 28.02, 29.02, 30.02, 31.02, 32.02, 33.02, 33.22, 34.02, 35.02, 36.02, 37.02, 38.04, 39.04, 40.02, 41.02, 42.02, 43.02, 44.02, 45.02, 46.02, 48.02, 52.02, 62.02, 63.02, 64.02, 65.02, 66.02, 67.02, 68.02, 69.02, 70.02, 71.02, 72.02, 73.02, 74.02, 201.03, 201.06, 201.07, 201.42, 201.43, 201.48, 201.49, 201.71, 203.03, 203.08, 203.09, 203.10, Alc. Bev. Code; Secs. 183.021, 183.022, Tax Code (CCH TEXAS TAX REPORTS, ¶35-001, 35-050, 35-150).

Persons subject to tax: Taxes are imposed on all alcoholic beverages over 0.5% alcohol by weight, intoxicating and nonintoxicating. A tax is imposed on gross receipts of permittees from the sale, preparation, or service of mixed beverages or ice or nonalcoholic beverages intended to be mixed with alcoholic beverages. This includes bar set-up fees. (*Letter,* Texas Comptroller of Public Accounts, No. 200111608L, November 14, 2001, CCH TEXAS TAX REPORTS, ¶402-241) An agent of the permittee is not liable for the mixed beverage tax. (*Myers v. Texas,* 169 S.W.3d 731 (Tex. CtApp 2005), CCH TEXAS TAX REPORTS, ¶402-931)

> *CCH Practice Tip: Treatment of hotel corkage service*
>
> Hotel corkage fees charged for corkage service provided on the licensed premises of a mixed beverage permit holder is subject to the mixed beverage tax. However, if the corkage service is not provided on the licensed premises, then the corkage fee is not subject to mixed beverage tax but could be subject to sales tax if the hotel provides food. (*Letter No. 200804100L,* Texas Comptroller of Public Accounts, April 10, 2008, CCH TEXAS TAX REPORTS, ¶403-430)

An exemption equal to 25% of the tax imposed on beer is provided for manufacturers whose annual production of beer in Texas does not exceed 75,000 barrels per year. No exemption is available for charitable organizations that sell alcohol at a fundraising event. However, for an appreciation event with an open bar where no money is exchanged or tickets sold, the nonprofit organization does not owe mixed beverage gross receipts tax, but must pay Texas sales tax on the purchase of the alcoholic beverages. (*Letter,* Texas Comptroller of Public Accounts, No. 200108673L, August 28, 2001, CCH Texas Tax Reports, ¶ 402-253)

Rate: The tax on beer is $6 per barrel or .193548 per gallon. A tax of 22¢ is imposed upon every prescription for liquor that is filled by a pharmacist. The tax on mixed beverages, or ice or nonalcoholic beverages for use in mixed beverages, is 14% of gross receipts. The rates for liquor are as follows:

Beverage	Rate per Gallon	Beverage	Rate per Gallon
Distilled spirits	$2.40	Still wine (more than 14% alcohol by volume)	0.408
(Minimum tax, 12.2¢ per package containing 1/2 pint, 5¢ per package containing 2 oz. or less)		Sparkling wine	0.516
Still wine (not over 14% alcohol by volume)	0.204	Malt liquor (more than 4% alcohol by weight)	0.198

Alcoholic beverages served on passenger trains and aircraft in Texas are exempt from sales and use taxes and in lieu of those taxes are subject to a tax of 5¢ per individual serving. Texas residents importing liquor or beer into Texas for their own personal use are subject to a 50¢ administrative fee.

Payments and reports: The taxes on distilled spirits, vinous liquor, ale, and malt liquor are payable to the Comptroller, together with any required sworn statement of taxes due, on the 15th of the month following the first sale. A 2% discount is allowed to permittees for nondelinquent taxes.

The tax on beer is due and payable on the 15th day of the month following the month in which the first taxable sale occurs. A 2% discount is allowed permittees for nondelinquent taxes. Mixed beverage permittees must file a return and pay the tax to the Comptroller on or before the 20th day of every month.

Alcoholic beverage licensees are required to keep source records regarding the Texas mixed beverage gross receipts tax for four years. If the ink on thermal cash register tapes deteriorates in a period less than four years, an alternative method of maintaining the records must be devised. (*Letter,* Comptroller of Public Accounts, No. 200502980L, February 3, 2005, CCH Texas Tax Reports, ¶ 402-867)

¶1703 Cigarette and Tobacco Products Taxes

Law: Secs. 154.021, 154.022, 154.024, 154.041, 154.043, 154.050, 154.052, 154.111, 154.152, 154.204, 154.210, 154.305, 155.021, 155.0211, 155.022, 155.023, 155.024, 155.049, 155.103, 155.111, 155.184, Tax Code; Sec. 404.095(a), (b), and (c), Govt. Code; 34 TAC Secs. 3.1205, 16.2, 16.3 (CCH Texas Tax Reports, ¶ 55-001, 55-010, 55-020, 55-030, 55-040, 55-110, 55-120, 55-130, 55-140).

Texas imposes taxes on cigarettes and other tobacco products.

- *Cigarette tax*

Persons subject to tax: A tax is imposed on all cigarettes used or otherwise disposed of in Texas. The tax is paid by the person making the first sale in Texas. The following are exempt: (1) cigarettes imported in quantities of 200 or less for personal use; and (2) bonded stock to be disposed of in interstate commerce. Cigarettes sold on Indian reservations to tribal members are also exempt. (*Letter,* Texas Comptroller of Public Accounts, No. 200405554L, May 4, 2004, CCH Texas Tax Reports, ¶ 402-700)

Part VI—Miscellaneous Taxes

A Texas cigarette tax rule explains the registration and other requirements applicable to sellers making delivery sales of cigarettes to Texas consumers from within or without the state. A "delivery sale" is one in which the purchaser submits the order by telephone, mail, or Internet and the cigarettes are delivered by mail or another delivery service. Sellers are required to register with the Comptroller's office, collect and pay taxes, affix tax stamps to cigarette packages, verify that the purchaser is at least 18 years old, provide a disclosure notice to the purchaser, and comply with shipping and reporting requirements. Penalties are applicable to various violations.

CCH Advisory: Interstate Transactions

A person who transports cigarettes or causes cigarettes to be transported from Texas for sale in another state must affix the cigarette tax stamp required by the state in which the cigarettes are to be sold and must pay any other cigarette tax imposed by the other state before transporting the cigarettes. However, the transporter may not affix a tax stamp to cigarettes as required by another state or pay any other excise tax on the cigarettes imposed by the other state if the other state prohibits such actions or prohibits the sale of the cigarettes.

Additionally, a person who transports cigarettes from Texas for sale in another state must submit a report to the Texas Attorney General by the 15th day after the end of each calendar quarter that identifies (1) the quantity of cigarettes, by brand style, transported in the preceding calendar quarter; and (2) the name and address of each recipient of the cigarettes.

Rate: Cigarettes weighing not more than 3 lbs. per 1,000 are taxed at the rate of $70.50 per 1,000. This equals a rate of $1.41 per pack of 20 cigarettes and a rate of $1.76 per pack of 25 cigarettes. Cigarettes weighing more than 3 lbs. per 1,000 are taxed at the rate of $72.60 per 1,000. A discount of 3% of the face value of stamps is allowed.

Payments and reports: The tax is paid by means of stamps purchased by distributors from the Comptroller of Public Accounts. Payment must be made within 30 days from the date the stamps and an accompanying invoice are received by the distributor. At the close of each biennium, payment for stamps purchased or received on or before August 31 of that fiscal year must be received in the Comptroller's office in full on or before August 31 of that fiscal year.

Cigarette distributors and manufacturers who sell cigarettes to a permit holder in Texas must file a report with the Comptroller on or before the end of each month for the previous month.

- *Cigar and tobacco products tax*

Persons subject to tax: A tax is imposed when a permit holder receives cigars or tobacco products, which includes snuff, chewing tobacco, pipe tobacco, and loose tobacco for rolling cigarettes, for the purpose of making a first sale. Cigars and tobacco products brought into Texas in amounts selling at retail for 25¢ or less and intended for personal use are exempt. A tax is imposed on manufacturers at the time the tobacco products are first transferred in connection with a purchase, sale, or exchange for value in intrastate commerce.

Rate: The rate for cigars weighing not more than 3 lbs. per 1,000 is 1¢ per each 10 cigars. The rate for cigars weighing more than 3 lbs. per 1,000 and retailing for not more than 3.3¢ each is $7.50 per 1,000. For cigars with substantially no nontobacco ingredients weighing more than 3 lbs. per 1,000 and retailing for over 3.3¢ each, the rate is $11 per 1,000. The rate for cigars with a substantial amount of nontobacco ingredients weighing more than 3 lbs. per 1,000 and retailing for over 3.3¢ each is $15 per 1,000.

¶1703

The rate for tobacco products other than cigars is $1.10 per ounce in fiscal year 2010, $1.13 per ounce in fiscal year 2011, $1.16 per ounce in fiscal year 2012, $1.19 per ounce from September 1, 2012, to December 1, 2013, and $1.22 per ounce after December 1, 2013. Prior to the 2010 fiscal year, the rate for chewing tobacco, snuff, or smoking tobacco was 40% of factory list price.

Payment and reports: The tax is paid by the distributor when the report is filed. All tobacco product distributors and manufacturers must file a report with the Comptroller of Public Accounts on or before the last day of each month for the previous month.

¶1704 Insurance Taxes

Law: Arts. 1.10, 1.14-2, 1.14-3, 1.35B, 4.10, 4.11A(5), 4.11A(10), 4.11B, 4.11C, 4.17, 4.63, 4.65—4.68, 5.12, 5.24, 5.49, 5.91, 9.46, 9.48, 20A.33, 21.07-6, 21.28-C, 21.28-D, 21.49(19), 23.08A, 26.14A, Secs. 222.002, 223.003, 281.004, Insur. Code; Sec. 101.252, Civil Stats.; Sec. 4413(37), Civil Stats. Tit. 70 (CCH Texas Tax Reports, ¶¶88-001, 88-015, 88-030, 88-045, 88-060).

Persons subject to tax: An annual gross premium receipts tax must be paid by every insurance carrier, including Lloyd's and reciprocal exchanges or interinsurance exchanges, and any other organization or concern receiving gross premiums from the business of fire, marine, marine inland, accident, credit, title, livestock, fidelity, guaranty, surety, casualty, employers' liability, or any other kind of insurance. The tax does not apply to:

— premium receipts received from the business of life insurance, personal accident insurance, life and accident insurance, or health and accident insurance for profit, written by life insurance companies, life and accident insurance companies, health and accident insurance companies, or for mutual benefit or protection of the state;

— fraternal benefit associations or societies in the state, nonprofit group hospital service plans, stipulated premium companies, or mutual assessment associations, companies or corporations;

— purely cooperative or mutual fire insurance companies carried on by the members thereof solely for the protection of their own property and not for profit; and

— title insurance companies.

Every insurance carrier receiving premiums from the business of life, accident, or health insurance, including variable life insurance, credit life insurance, and credit accident and health insurance for profit or otherwise or for mutual benefit or protection, in Texas must pay an annual tax on its gross premiums. The tax does not apply to local mutual aid associations, fraternal benefit associations, and societies that limit their membership to one occupation.

Title insurance companies receiving premiums from the business of title insurance must pay a tax on those premiums in lieu of all other taxes except maintenance taxes assessed by the Department of Insurance and property taxes.

Applicable to health benefit plans that are delivered, issued for delivery, amended or renewed after 2003, health carriers that enter into contracts with health group cooperatives to provide health benefit plan coverage are exempt from Texas insurance premiums tax for two years with respect to the premiums received for coverage provided to each uninsured employee and dependent.

Part VI—Miscellaneous Taxes   **311**

CCH Comment: Insurance Companies Subject to Other Taxes

The Texas Court of Appeals has rejected an insurance company's contention that, under the applicable statute, no taxes may be imposed on insurance companies other than insurance gross premiums tax and ad valorem tax. The insurance company was seeking refunds of numerous taxes, including sales taxes and franchise taxes. Had the insurance company been successful, the state would have been potentially liable for up to $2 billion in refund claims to all affected insurance companies. (*United Services Automobile Association v. Rylander,* 124 S.W.3d 722 (Tex. CtApp 2003), petition for review denied, Texas Supreme Court, September 10, 2004, CCH Texas Tax Reports, ¶402-957)

Texas imposes a "retaliatory tax" on foreign insurance companies determined by a measurement of the amount a foreign insurer's state of incorporation would impose in taxes, fees, and assessments on a Texas insurer, in the aggregate, for insurance written in the other state, as compared to the amount Texas would impose on the foreign insurer. For example, if Texas provides an exemption from its gross premiums tax on insurance companies that another state does not, foreign insurers from that state would be required to include the amount of the difference in taxation schemes in their retaliatory tax calculation. (*Letter,* Comptroller of Public Accounts, No. 200502976L, February 1, 2005, CCH Texas Tax Reports, ¶402-851)

CCH Comment: Retaliatory Tax Upheld

The Texas Supreme Court has held that the calculation of the Texas retaliatory tax on foreign title insurance companies did not violate the Equal Protection Clauses of the U.S. Constitution or the Texas Constitution because the distinction between the retaliatory tax's treatment of foreign and domestic insurers was rationally related to a legitimate government purpose—compensation for higher out-of-state tax obligations imposed on Texas insurers. (*First American Title v. Strayhorn,* 258 S.W.3d 627, 51 Tex. Sup. Ct. J. 880, May 16, 2008, CCH Texas Tax Reports, ¶403-413, *petition for cert. denied,* U.S. Supreme Court, Dkt. 08-721, May 4, 2009)

Basis of tax: Gross premium receipts for insurance companies other than life, accident, and health are generally the total gross amount of premiums actually written during the tax year on each and every kind of insurance or risk written upon property or risks located in Texas, except premiums actually written by other licensed companies for reinsurance, less return premiums and dividends paid policyholders with no deduction for premiums paid for reinsurance.

Property and casualty insurance is taxed on a "written basis," recognizing the effective date of the coverage and including for each tax year all premiums to be charged for the policy. For example, the taxable premiums for calendar year 2008 on a 12-month policy with an effective date of October 1, 2008, with monthly premiums of $100 would be $1,200. (*Tax Policy News,* Vol. XVII, Issue 12, Texas Comptroller of Public Accounts, December 2007)

Generally, for purposes of the tax on life, accident, and health insurance companies, "gross premiums" is the total gross amount of all premiums, membership fees, assessments, dues, and any other considerations for such insurance received during the tax year on such insurance covering persons located in Texas. The following are deducted from this amount: returned premiums, any dividends applied to purchase paid-up additions to insurance or to shorten the endowment or premium payment period, and those premiums received from insurance carriers for reinsurance (there is no deduction for premiums paid for reinsurance).

¶1704

> **CCH Practice Tip: Allocation of premiums**
>
> Insurers licensed in Texas must allocate premiums according to the requirements of the applicable tax statutes in the Insurance Code without regard to National Association of Insurance Commissioners (NAIC) guidelines or Statutory Accounting Principles (SAP). (*Tax Policy News, Vol. XVIII, Issue 1*, Texas Comptroller of Public Accounts, January 2008)
>
> Premiums from indemnity insurance policies are sourced to an insured business's headquarters. (*Tax Policy News, Vol. XVIII, Issue 1*, Texas Comptroller of Public Accounts, January 2008)

Fees charged in lieu of commissions are also included in the gross premiums subject to tax. (*Letter*, Comptroller of Public Accounts, No. 200604550L, April 1, 2006, CCH Texas Tax Reports, ¶ 403-057)

Excluded from gross premiums subject to tax are premiums received from the state of Texas or U.S. Treasury for insurance contracted for the purpose of providing welfare benefits and premiums paid on group health, accident, and life policies in which the group covered by the policy consists of a single nonprofit trust established to provide coverage primarily for municipal or county employees of Texas.

Rate: The tax on insurance companies other than title, life, accident, and health is 1.6% of premium receipts.

Except for the tax on the first $450,000 of gross premiums of life insurers and the tax on gross revenues of health maintenance organizations, the tax on life, accident, and health insurance companies is 1.75% of gross premiums. Gross revenues of health maintenance organizations are taxed at 1.75% except that the tax rate is one-half of such rates on the first $450,000 of gross revenues. A tax is imposed on life insurers on the first $450,000 of gross premiums at a rate equal to one-half of the basic premiums tax rate as provided above for life insurers.

The tax on title insurance companies is 1.35% of annual premiums received for title insurance written on property located in Texas. For unauthorized insurers, independently procured insurance, and surplus lines insurers, the tax rate is 4.85%. The independently procured insurance tax does not apply to premiums for individual life or individual disability insurance.

> **CCH Advisory: Independently Procured Insurance Tax**
>
> A Texas court of appeals ruled that the independently procured insurance tax was unconstitutional under the federal McCarran-Ferguson Act and the U.S. Supreme Court's ruling in *State Board of Insurance v. Todd Shipyards Corp.*, 370 U.S. 451 (1962). The tax was imposed against an out-of state corporation's insurance on its Texas property procured through an out-of-state insurance company. (*Dow Chemical Co. v. Rylander*, 38 S.W.3d 741 (Tex.App.-Austin 2001, *pet. denied*), *cert. denied*, 151 L.Ed.2d 383, 122 S.Ct. 466 (2001); CCH Texas Tax Reports, ¶ 402-148)

> **Practitioner Comment: Survival of the Independently Procured Insurance Tax**
>
> If the *only* connection with the state is the location of the risk that is being insured, no independently procured insurance tax (IPIT) is due. The Comptroller's position, even assuming that the insurance policy was negotiated entirely outside the state, is discussed in Publication 98-376 (01/2007) and can be found on the Comptroller's Web site at www.cpa.state.tx.us/taxinfo/taxpubs/tx98_376.html. It provides that IPIT is due if any contact with Texas applies, including but not limited to:
>
> — policies paid for in Texas;
>
> — policies or other documents related to the policies that are issued or delivered in Texas;

¶1704

Part VI—Miscellaneous Taxes

— risk investigations or credit checks that are conducted in Texas prior to or subsequent to the issuance of the policies; and

— loss and claims adjustments, other investigations or payments that occur in Texas.

A taxpayer challenged the imposition of the tax upon a company headquartered in Texas. After the district court ruled in the taxpayer's favor, the court of appeals reversed the decision by determining that "as applied" the tax did not violate Due Process or the McCarran-Ferguson Act. The taxpayer filed a Petition for Review with the Texas Supreme Court in June 2007, which was denied in August 2008. (*Combs v. STP Nuclear Operating Co.*, 239 S.W. 3d 264 (Tex. App.—Austin 2007, pet. denied))

Sandi Farquharson, Ryan

In addition to the above taxes, an annual assessment is collected by the Comptroller from each insurer to defray the costs of creating, administering, and operating the office of Public Insurance Counsel.

Exemptions: Gross premiums taxes on insurance companies are levied in lieu of all other taxes based on gross receipts.

The share of Medicare premiums paid by the federal government are also exempt from gross premiums insurance tax, but amounts paid directly by individuals for their portion of the premiums are subject to tax. (*Letter*, Comptroller of Public Accounts, No. 200603502L, March 17, 2006, CCH Texas Tax Reports, ¶ 403-031)

An exemption also applies to premiums received on property or events covered by liability insurance that are insured by a Native American tribe if the property or event is located on an Indian reservation. (*Letter*, Comptroller of Public Accounts, No. 200512378L, December 2, 2005, CCH Texas Tax Reports, ¶ 402-993)

Credits: A credit against insurance gross premiums tax may be taken for most examination and evaluation fees paid to the State of Texas by an insurance company in the taxable year. The credit or an offset may not be paid by a domestic and a foreign insurance company for fees or examination expenses paid to another state or an examination expense paid in a different tax year.

An insurer that is a member of the Life, Accident, Health and Hospital Service Guaranty Association may assign or transfer a credit against premium tax to another member insurer if (1) an acquisition, merger, or total assumption of reinsurance has occurred between the insurers; or (2) the Commissioner of Insurance approves the assignment or transfer by order. A member insurer must report the assignment or transfer to the Comptroller on or before the later of November 1 or the 60th day after the date of the assignment or transfer.

Insurance companies that invest in certified capital companies that provide venture capital to small, early-stage businesses engaged in specified, non-retail, real estate, insurance, banking, or professional service activities, may claim a nonrefundable credit against insurance gross premiums tax. The credit is equal to the amount of qualified investment made, but only 25% of the credit may be claimed in any taxable year, beginning with the tax report due March 1, 2009, for the 2008 tax year.

To claim the credit, the insurance company must complete an allocation claim that must be filed with the Comptroller by the certified capital company on the date specified by the Comptroller. Credits are subject to recapture if the certified capital company is decertified.

Payments and reports: All companies pay the tax to the Comptroller and file their annual reports on or before March 1. A semiannual prepayment of tax must be made on March 1 and August 1 by insurers with net tax liability for the previous calendar year in excess of $1,000.

¶ 1704

Surplus lines insurers pay the tax with their semiannual reports due within 30 days after January 1 and July 1. The tax on independently procured insurance is due with the report.

Unauthorized insurance premium tax is due before March 1 next succeeding the calendar year in which the insurance was so effectuated, continued, or renewed.

¶1705 Motor Fuel Taxes

Law: Secs. 162.001, 162.002, 162.003, 162.004, 162.005, 162.006, 162.007, 162.008, 162.010, 162.011, 162.012, 162.013, 162.014, 162.015, 162.016, 162.101, 162.102, 162.103, 162.104, 162.105, 162.106, 162.108, 162.109, 162.110, 162.112, 162.113, 162.114, 162.115, 162.116, 162.117, 162.118, 162.119, 162.120, 162.121, 162.122, 162.123, 162.124, 162.125, 162.126, 162.127, 162.1275, 162.128, 162.201, 162.202, 162.2025, 162.203, 162.204, 162.205, 162.206, 162.207, 162.208, 162.209, 162.210, 162.211, 162.212, 162.213, 162.214, 162.215, 162.216, 162.217, 162.218, 162.219, 162.220, 162.221, 162.222, 162.223, 162.224, 162.225, 162.226, 162.227, 162.2275, 162.228, 162.229, 162.230, 162.231, 162.232, 162.233, 162.234, 162.235, 162.301, 162.302, 162.3021, 162.3022, 162.303, 162.304, 162.305, 162.306, 162.307, 162.308, 162.309, 162.310, 162.311, 162.401, 162.402, 162.403, 162.404, 162.405, 162.406, 162.407, 162.408, 162.409, 162.410, 162.501, 162.502, 162.5025, 162.503, 162.504, 162.5045, 162.505, Tax Code; Sec. 16.001, 16.002, 16.003, 16.004, 16.005, 16.006, Agriculture Code; Secs. 161.062, 162.062, Utilities Code (CCH Texas Tax Reports, ¶ 40-001, 40-003, 40-005, 40-007, 40-009, 40-011).

Texas imposes three major motor fuel taxes: the Gasoline Tax; the Diesel Fuel Tax; and the Liquefied Gas Tax. Effective July 1, 1995, Texas participates in the International Fuel Tax Agreement (IFTA).

Gasoline Tax: The Texas gasoline tax is imposed on any liquid or combination of liquids blended together, offered for sale, sold, used, or capable of use as fuel for a gasoline-powered engine, including gasohol, aviation gasoline, and blending agents. The gasoline tax, however, does not apply to racing gasoline, diesel fuel, aviation jet fuel, or liquefied gas. (Sec. 162.001, Tax Code)

The Texas gasoline tax is generally imposed on the supplier or permissive supplier of the gasoline (which may include terminal operators) Under specific circumstances, importers, blenders, and interstate truckers may also be liable for collection or payment of the tax. (Sec. 162.101, Tax Code) A backup tax may also be imposed on certain nonexempt uses (including uses by consumers) in which the gasoline tax was not paid. (Sec. 162.103, Tax Code)

In each subsequent sale of gasoline on which the tax has been paid, the amount of the tax is added to the selling price so that the tax is paid ultimately by the person using or consuming the gasoline. Gasoline is considered to be used when it is delivered into a motor vehicle's fuel supply tank. (Sec. 162.1025, Tax Code)

People engaged in many activities related to the use or distribution of motor fuels are required to obtain an appropriate state license (including suppliers, permissive suppliers, distributors, importers, terminal operators, exporters, blenders, motor fuel transporters, aviation fuel dealers, and interstate truckers). (Sec. 162.105, et seq, Tax Code)

The gasoline tax is imposed in the below instances.

The gasoline tax is imposed on the removal of gasoline from the bulk transfer/terminal system or removal from the terminal using the terminal rack (other than by bulk transfer). The supplier or permissive supplier is liable for and is required to collect the gasoline tax from those who order withdrawal at the terminal rack or the bulk transfer terminal system. (Sec. 162.101(a) and (c), Tax Code)

The gasoline tax is also imposed on the importation of gasoline into Texas for delivery to a destination in the state (other than by bulk transfer). The supplier or permissive supplier is liable for and is required to collect the gasoline tax from those

Part VI—Miscellaneous Taxes

who import the gasoline into Texas. If the seller of the gasoline is not a supplier of permissive supplier, then liability falls on the importer who must pay the gasoline tax. (Sec. 162.101(b), Tax Code)

The gasoline tax is also imposed on the importation of gasoline into Texas in the motor vehicle supply tanks of a person required to be licensed as an interstate trucker. The interstate trucker is liable for and is required to pay the gasoline tax. (Sec. 162.101(d), Tax Code)

The gasoline tax is also imposed on the blending of gasoline at the point gasoline blended fuel is made in Texas outside the bulk transfer/terminal system. The blender is liable for and is required to pay the gasoline tax. The number of gallons of gasoline blended fuel on which the tax is imposed is equal to the difference between the number of gallons of blended fuel made and the number of gallons of previously taxed gasoline used to make the blended fuel. (Sec. 162.101(e), Tax Code)

A backup tax is imposed at the same rate as the gasoline tax on certain nonexempt uses in which the gasoline tax was not paid. Specifically, the backup tax is imposed on:

(1) a person who obtains a refund of tax on gasoline by claiming the gasoline was used for an off-highway purpose, but actually uses the gasoline to operate a motor vehicle on a public highway;

(2) a person who operates a motor vehicle on a public highway using gasoline on which tax has not been paid;

(3) a person who sells to the ultimate consumer gasoline on which tax has not been paid and who knew or had reason to know that the gasoline would be used for a taxable purpose; and

(4) a nonexempt person who acquires gasoline on which tax has not been paid from any source in this state.

(Sec. 162.103, Tax Code)

The gasoline tax rate is 20 cents for each net gallon or fractional part on which the tax is imposed. (Sec. 162.102, Tax Code) The tax rate for the backup tax is the same as the gasoline tax rate. (Sec. 162.103, Tax Code) An additional tax or refund on inventories of 2,000 or more gallons may apply following an increase or reduction in gasoline tax rate. (Sec. 162.015, Tax Code)

The Texas gasoline tax is a consumption tax targeting gasoline sold in Texas used to propel vehicles on public roads in the state. Therefore, exemptions to the gasoline tax include uses or sales of gasoline where the fuel is not used to propel a vehicle on public roads in Texas or sales made to an exempt purchaser. Exemptions include:

— Fuel sold to the U.S. government (Sec. 162.104(a)(1), Tax Code);

— Fuel sold for public school transportation (Sec. 162.104(a)(2) and (3), Tax Code; 34 TAC 3.448);

— Exported gasoline (Sec. 162.104(a)(7), Tax Code; Sec. 162.104, Tax Code);

— Gasoline transfers between suppliers (Sec. 162.104(a)(5), Tax Code);

— Gasoline used for aviation fuel (Sec. 162.104(a)(6), Tax Code);

— Gasoline sold to a volunteer fire department (Sec. 162.104(a)(8), Tax Code); and

— Nonprofit electric and telephone cooperatives (Sec. 161.062, Utilities Code; Sec. 162.062, Utilities Code).

Taxpayers are required to file a return, accompanied by payment of tax reported due, with the Texas Comptroller of Public Accounts on or before the 25th day of the month following the end of the calendar quarter. (Sec. 162.114, Tax Code) Electronic

¶1705

reporting is available for both IFTA-licensed and non-IFTA taxpayers, at http://www.window.state.tx.us/taxinfo/etf/etf.html.

The state mandates that specific information be included on returns filed with the comptroller. (Sec. 162.116, Tax Code (suppliers and permissive suppliers); Sec. 162.118, Tax Code (distributors); Sec. 162.119, Tax Code (importers); Sec. 162.120, Tax Code (terminal operators); Sec. 162.121, Tax Code (fuel transporters); Sec. 162.122, Tax Code (exporters); Sec. 162.123, Tax Code (blenders); Sec. 162.124, Tax Code (interstate truckers))

Licensed distributors and importers are required to remit applicable gasoline taxes for fuel removed from the terminal rack to the supplier or permissive supplier. Licensed distributors or importers may elect to defer payment of the tax until two days before the supplier or permissive supplier is required to remit the tax to the comptroller. Timely payment of the applicable taxes to supplier or permissive suppliers entitles licensed distributors or importers to retain a percentage of the tax owed for administrative expenses (see "Credits, Refunds, and Reimbursements" below). (Sec. 162.113, Tax Code)

A claim for a refund generally must be filed before the first anniversary of the first day of the calendar month following the purchase, use, delivery, or export, whichever period expires latest. (Sec. 162.128, Tax Code) The right to receive a refund or take a credit is not assignable. (Sec. 162.125(h), Tax Code) Refund claims must filed with the comptroller and contain certain information. (Sec. 162.127, Tax Code) The following credits are available for the gasoline tax:

— Administrative expenses for licensed distributors and importers (Sec. 162.113(e), Tax Code);

— Collection allowance for suppliers and permissive suppliers (Sec. 162.116(b), Tax Code);

— Credit for taxes not remitted (Sec. 162.116(c), Tax Code);

— Gasoline for the exclusive use of the U.S. government (Sec. 162.125(a) and (c), Tax Code);

— Gasoline used exclusively for public school transportation (Sec. 162.125(a) and (c), Tax Code; 34 TAC 3.448; Sec. 162.1275, Tax Code);

— Exported gasoline (Sec. 162.125(a) and (c), Tax Code; Sec. 162.125(f), Tax Code; Sec. 162.128(a), Tax Code);

— Gasoline sold to aviation fuel dealers (Sec. 162.125(a) and (c), Tax Code);

— Gasoline transfers between suppliers (Sec. 162.125(b), Tax Code);

— Off-highway use (Sec. 162.125(c), Tax Code; 34 TAC 3.433);

— Gasoline used in interstate trucking (Sec. 162.125(d), Tax Code; Sec. 162.128(b), Tax Code);

— Gasoline used for auxiliary power units or power take-off equipment (Sec. 162.125(e), Tax Code; 34 TAC 3.435);

— Gasoline lost by fire, theft, or accident (Sec. 162.125(f), Tax Code; Sec. 162.128(a), Tax Code);

— Gasoline used by a transit company (Sec. 162.125(g), Tax Code; 34 TAC 3.431);

— Gasoline used by a volunteer fire department (Sec. 162.125(g-1), Tax Code);

— Credit related to retail sale to certain purchasers (Sec. 162.125(j), Tax Code); and

— Refund for bad debts and credits for nonpayment (Sec. 162.126, Tax Code; 34 TAC 3.442).

¶1705

Part VI—Miscellaneous Taxes

Diesel Fuel Tax: Texas imposes three major motor fuel taxes: the Gasoline Tax; the Diesel Fuel Tax; and the Liquefied Gas Tax. Effective July 1, 1995, Texas participates in the International Fuel Tax Agreement (IFTA). The Texas diesel fuel tax is imposed on any kerosene or another liquid, or a combination of liquids blended together, offered for sale, sold, used, or capable of use as fuel for the propulsion of a diesel-powered engine, including products commonly referred to as kerosene, light cycle oil, #1 diesel fuel, #2 diesel fuel, dyed or undyed diesel fuel, aviation jet fuel, renewable diesel, biodiesel, distillate fuel, cutter stock, or heating oil. The diesel fuel tax, however, does not apply to gasoline, aviation gasoline, or liquefied gas. (Sec. 162.001, Tax Code)

The Texas diesel fuel tax is generally imposed on the supplier or permissive supplier of the gasoline (which may include terminal operators) Under specific circumstances, importers, blenders, and interstate truckers may also be liable for collection or payment of the tax. (Sec. 162.201, Tax Code) A backup tax may also be imposed on certain nonexempt uses (including uses by consumers) in which the gasoline tax was not paid. (Sec. 162.203, Tax Code)

In each subsequent sale of gasoline on which the tax has been paid, the amount of the tax is added to the selling price so that the tax is paid ultimately by the person using or consuming the gasoline. Gasoline is considered to be used when it is delivered into a motor vehicle's fuel supply tank. (Sec. 162.2025, Tax Code)

People engaged in many activities related to the use or distribution of motor fuels are required to obtain an appropriate state license (including suppliers, permissive suppliers, distributors, importers, terminal operators, exporters, blenders, motor fuel transporters, aviation fuel dealers, interstate truckers, and dyed diesel fuel bonded users). (Sec. 162.205, et seq, Tax Code)

The diesel fuel tax is imposed in the below instances.

The diesel fuel tax is imposed on removal of fuel from the bulk transfer/terminal system or removal from the terminal using the terminal rack (other than by bulk transfer). The supplier or permissive supplier is liable for and is required to collect the tax from those who order withdrawal at the terminal rack or the bulk transfer terminal system. (Sec. 162.201(a) and (c), Tax Code)

The diesel fuel tax is also imposed on the importation of fuel into Texas for delivery to a destination in the state (other than by bulk transfer). The supplier or permissive supplier is liable for and is required to collect the gasoline tax from those who import the fuel into Texas. If the seller of the gasoline is not a supplier of permissive supplier, then liability falls on the importer who must pay the tax. (Sec. 162.201(b), Tax Code)

The diesel fuel tax is also imposed on the importation of diesel fuel into Texas in the motor vehicle supply tanks of a person required to be licensed as an interstate trucker. The interstate trucker is liable for and is required to pay the diesel fuel tax. (Sec. 162.201(d), Tax Code)

The diesel fuel tax is also imposed at the point diesel fuel is blended to make blended fuels in Texas outside the bulk transfer/terminal system. The blender is liable for and is required to pay the diesel fuel tax. The number of gallons of diesel blended fuel on which the tax is imposed is equal to the difference between the number of gallons of blended fuel made and the number of gallons of previously taxed diesel used to make the blended fuel. (Sec. 162.201(e), Tax Code)

A backup tax is imposed at the same rate as the diesel fuel tax on certain nonexempt uses in which the tax was not paid. Specifically, the backup tax is imposed on:

(1) a person who obtains a refund of tax on diesel fuel by claiming the fuel was used for an off-highway purpose, but actually uses the fuel to operate a motor vehicle on a public highway;

¶1705

(2) a person who operates a motor vehicle on a public highway using diesel fuel on which tax has not been paid;

(3) a person who sells to the ultimate consumer diesel fuel on which tax has not been paid and who knew or had reason to know that the fuel would be used for a taxable purpose; and

(4) a nonexempt person who acquires diesel fuel on which tax has not been paid from any source in this state.

(Sec. 162.203, Tax Code)

The diesel fuel tax rate is 20 cents for each net gallon or fractional part on which the tax is imposed. (Sec. 162.202, Tax Code) The tax rate for the backup tax is the same as the diesel fuel tax rate. (Sec. 162.203, Tax Code) An additional tax or refund on inventories of 2,000 or more gallons may apply following an increase or reduction in tax rate. (Sec. 162.015, Tax Code)

The Texas diesel fuel tax is a consumption tax targeting diesel sold in Texas used to propel vehicles on public roads in the state. Therefore, exemptions to the tax include uses or sales of fuel where the fuel is not used to propel a vehicle on public roads in Texas or sales made to an exempt purchaser. The following exemptions apply to the diesel fuel tax:

— Fuel sold to the U.S. government (Sec. 162.204(a)(1), Tax Code);

— Fuel sold for public school transportation (Sec. 162.204(a)(2) and (3), Tax Code; 34 TAC 3.448);

— Exported fuel (Sec. 162.204(a)(7), Tax Code; Sec. 162.204, Tax Code);

— Diesel fuel transfers between suppliers (Sec. 162.204(a)(5), Tax Code);

— Diesel fuel used for aviation (Sec. 162.204(a)(6), Tax Code);

— Diesel fuel sold to a volunteer fire department (Sec. 162.204(a)(14), Tax Code);

— Nonprofit electric and telephone cooperatives (Sec. 161.062, Utilities Code; Sec. 162.062, Utilities Code);

— Certain deliveries of dyed diesel fuel (Sec. 162.204(a)(8), Tax Code; Sec. 162.204(a)(10), Tax Code; Sec. 162.204(a)(11), Tax Code; Sec. 162.206, Tax Code);

— Off-highway use (Sec. 162.204(a)(8), Tax Code; Sec. 162.235, Tax Code; 34 TAC 3.433; 34 TAC 3.438; 34 TAC 3.440);

— Blended diesel fuels (Sec. 162.204(a)(9), Tax Code);

— Dyed kerosene (Sec. 162.204(a)(12), Tax Code); and

— Fuel for certain commercial passenger transporters (Sec. 162.204(a)(13), Tax Code).

Taxpayers are required to file a return, accompanied by payment of tax reported due, with the Texas Comptroller of Public Accounts on or before the 25th day of the month following the end of the calendar quarter. (Sec. 162.215, Tax Code) Electronic reporting is available for both IFTA-licensed and non-IFTA taxpayers, at http://www.window.state.tx.us/taxinfo/etf/etf.html.

The state mandates that specific information be included on returns filed with the comptroller. (Sec. 162.217, Tax Code (suppliers and permissive suppliers); Sec. 162.219, Tax Code (distributors); Sec. 162.220, Tax Code (importers); Sec. 162.221, Tax Code (terminal operators); Sec. 162.222, Tax Code (fuel transporters); Sec. 162.223, Tax Code (exporters); Sec. 162.224, Tax Code (blenders); Sec. 162.225, Tax Code (interstate truckers); Sec. 162.226, Tax Code (dyed diesel fuel bonded users))

Licensed distributors and importers are required to remit applicable diesel fuel taxes for fuel removed from the terminal rack to the supplier or permissive supplier.

¶1705

Part VI—Miscellaneous Taxes

Licensed distributors or importers may elect to defer payment of the tax until two days before the supplier or permissive supplier is required to remit the tax to the comptroller. Timely payment of the applicable taxes to supplier or permissive suppliers entitles licensed distributors or importers to retain a percentage of the tax owed for administrative expenses (see "Credits, Refunds, and Reimbursements" below). (Sec. 162.214, Tax Code)

A claim for a refund generally must be filed before the first anniversary of the first day of the calendar month following the purchase, use, delivery, or export, whichever period expires latest. (Sec. 162.230, Tax Code) The right to receive a refund or take a credit is not assignable. (Sec. 162.227(g), Tax Code) Refund claims must filed with the comptroller and contain certain information. (Sec. 162.229, Tax Code) The following credits and refunds are available for the diesel fuel tax:

— Administrative expenses for licensed distributors and importers (Sec. 162.214(e), Tax Code);

— Collection allowance for suppliers and permissive suppliers (Sec. 162.217(b), Tax Code);

— Credit for taxes not remitted (Sec. 162.217(c), Tax Code);

— Fuel for the exclusive use of the U.S. government (Sec. 162.227(a) and (c), Tax Code);

— Fuel used exclusively for public school transportation (Sec. 162.227(a) and (c), Tax Code; 34 TAC 3.448; Sec. 162.2275, Tax Code);

— Exported diesel fuel (Sec. 162.227(a), Tax Code; Sec. 162.227(e), Tax Code; Sec. 162.230(a), Tax Code);

— Diesel fuel sold to aviation fuel dealers (Sec. 162.227(a) and (c), Tax Code);

— Diesel fuel transfers between suppliers (Sec. 162.227(b), Tax Code);

— Use as feedstock (Sec. 162.227(c-1), Tax Code);

— Use in oil or gas industry (Sec. 162.227(c-1), Tax Code; Sec. 162.227(c-2), Tax Code);

— Off-highway use (Sec. 162.204(a)(8), Tax Code; Sec. 162.235, Tax Code; Sec. 162.235, Tax Code; 34 TAC 3.433; 34 TAC 3.438; 34 TAC 3.440);

— Diesel fuel used in interstate trucking (Sec. 162.227(d), Tax Code; Sec. 162.230(b), Tax Code);

— Diesel fuel lost by fire, theft, or accident (Sec. 162.227(e), Tax Code; Sec. 162.230(a), Tax Code);

— Diesel fuel used by a transit company (Sec. 162.227(f), Tax Code);

— Diesel fuel used by a volunteer fire department (Sec. 162.227(f-1), Tax Code);

— Credit related to retail sale to certain purchasers (Sec. 162.227(j), Tax Code); and

— Refund for bad debts and credits for nonpayment (Sec. 162.228, Tax Code; 34 TAC 3.442).

Aviation Fuel Tax: Texas does not have a separate motor fuel excise tax for aviation fuels. Aviation gasoline is covered by the statutory definition of "gasoline" and, therefore, is subject to the Texas Gasoline Tax. (Sec. 162.001, Tax Code) However, aviation gasoline delivered to a licensed dealer for use in the fuel supply tanks of aircraft or aircraft servicing equipment is exempt from the gasoline tax. (Sec. 162.104(a)(6), Tax Code) Aviation jet fuel is covered by the statutory definition of "diesel fuel" and, therefore, is subject to the Texas Diesel Fuel Tax. (Sec. 162.001, Tax Code) However, aviation jet fuel delivered to a licensed dealer for use in the fuel

¶1705

supply tanks of aircraft or aircraft servicing equipment is exempt from the diesel fuel tax. (Sec. 162.204(a)(6), Tax Code)

A55 / A-21: The taxability of A55 or A-21 motor fuel is not specifically addressed under Texas motor fuel laws. However, the diesel portion of blended fuels are subject to the regular Texas diesel fuel tax. The water portion of a blended diesel fuel is exempt from the diesel fuel tax. (Sec. 162.204(a)(6), Tax Code)

Biodiesel: Texas defines biodiesel as a motor fuel that is mono-alkyl esters of long chain fatty acids derived agricultural products, vegetable oils, recycled greases, biomass, or animal fats or the wastes of those products or fats, and is intended for use in engines that are designed to run on conventional, petroleum-derived diesel fuel. The definition also requires that biodiesel meet the federal registration requirements under the Clean Air Act (42 U.S.C. § 7545) and meet the requirements of American Society for Testing and Materials (ASTM) specification D-6751. (Sec. 16.001, Agricultural Code)

Biodiesel is covered by the statutory definition of "diesel fuel" and, therefore, is technically subject to the Texas diesel fuel tax. (Sec. 162.001, Tax Code) However, the Texas comptroller of Public Accounts interprets the partial exemption on blending agents as an exemption for pure biodiesel (B-100) fuel and as an exemption for the biodiesel portion of a blended biodiesel fuel (*e.g.,* B-5, B-20) with any petroleum-based diesel portion of the blended fuel being taxed at the standard diesel fuel rate. (Sec. 162.204(a)(6), Tax Code; 34 TAC 3.443; *Notice on IFTA Reporting of Biodiesel Fuel,* Texas Comptroller of Public Accounts, CCH Texas State Tax Reporter, ¶ 403-642)

Texas also regulates the production of biodiesel through the Fuel Ethanol, Renewable Methane, Biodiesel, and Renewable Diesel Production Incentive Program. Under the program, plants producing fuel ethanol, renewable methane, biodiesel, or renewable diesel receive grant money but in exchange must pay a fee in an amount equal to 3.2 cents per gallon of fuel ethanol or MMBtu of renewable methane and 1.6 cents for each gallon of biodiesel produced. (Sec. 16.001 et al, Agricultural Code)

Compressed natural gas (CNG): Compressed natural gas is covered by the statutory definition of "liquefied gas" and, therefore, is subject to the Texas liquefied gas tax (see, explanation under LNG) and is taxed at the same rate. (Sec. 162.001, Tax Code)

E-85: In Texas, E-85 as well as other blends of gasoline and motor fuel alcohol (excluding denaturants and water) are covered by the statutory definition of "gasoline" and, therefore, are subject to the Texas gasoline tax and are taxed at the same rate of 20 cents per gallon. (Sec. 162.001, Tax Code, see definitions for "alcohol", "fuel grade ethanol", "gasohol", and "gasoline")

Ethanol: In Texas, ethanol and other motor fuel alcohol (excluding denaturants and water) are covered by the statutory definition of "gasoline" and, therefore, is subject to the Texas gasoline tax and is taxed at the same rate of 20 cents per gallon. (Sec. 162.001, Tax Code, see definitions for "alcohol", "fuel grade ethanol", "gasohol", and "gasoline")

Gasohol: Gasohol is a blended motor fuel composed of gasoline and motor fuel alcohol. (Sec. 162.001, Tax Code) In Texas, gasohol is covered by the statutory definition of "gasoline" and, therefore, is subject to the Texas gasoline tax and is taxed at the same rate. (Sec. 162.001, Tax Code, see definitions for "alcohol", "fuel grade ethanol", "gasohol", and "gasoline")

Liquefied Natural Gas (LNG): Texas imposes a liquefied gas tax on the use of liquefied gas for the propulsion of motor vehicles on Texas public highways at a rate of 15 cents per gallon. (Sec. 162.301, Tax Code) The tax applies to all combustible gases that exist in the gaseous state at 60 degrees Fahrenheit and at a pressure of 14.7

¶1705

Part VI—Miscellaneous Taxes

pounds per square inch absolute, excluding gasoline or diesel fuel. (Sec. 162.001, Tax Code)

The liquefied gas tax is generally collected and remitted by licensed liquefied gas dealers and interstate truckers. (Sec. 162.304, Tax Code; Sec. 162.308, Tax Code) Specific licensing and decal display requirements may apply to the use of liquefied gas-propelled motor vehicles, including vehicles equipped to use liquefied gas interchangably with other fuels. (Sec. 162.302, Tax Code; Sec. 162.303, Tax Code; Sec. 162.305, Tax Code; Sec. 162.306, Tax Code; Sec. 162.307, Tax Code; 34 TAC 3.434; 34 TAC 3.436)

The liquefied gas tax does not apply to the sale or use of liquefied petroleum gas to a public school district or county in Texas. (Sec. 162.3021, Tax Code; 34 TAC 3.448) In addition, the tax does not apply to certain use of liquefied gas fuels by metropolitan rapid transit authorities. (Sec. 162.3022, Tax Code)

A person using a liquefied gas-propelled motor vehicle that is required to be licensed for use on Texas public highways must prepay the liquefied gas tax on an annual basis. (Sec. 162.302, Tax Code) Licensed dealers and interstate truckers must file a report and remit payment on or before the 25th day of the month following the end of each calendar quarter. (Sec. 162.310, Tax Code)

For the expense associated with collecting, accounting for, reporting, record keeping, and timely remitting the tax, licensed dealers of liquefied gas fuels may retain 1 percent of the tax collected and interstate truckers may retain AA percent. (Sec. 162.308, Tax Code)

Liquefied Petroleum Gas (LPG): Liquefied petroleum gas is covered by the statutory definition of "liquefied gas" and, therefore, is subject to the Texas liquefied gas tax (see, explanation under LNG) and is taxed at the same rate. (Sec. 162.001, Tax Code)

M-85: In Texas, M-85 as well as other blends of gasoline and motor fuel alcohol (excluding denaturants and water) are covered by the statutory definition of "gasoline" and, therefore, is subject to the Texas gasoline tax and are taxed at the same rate of 20 cents per gallon. (Sec. 162.001, Tax Code, see definitions for "alcohol", "fuel grade ethanol", "gasohol", and "gasoline")

Methanol: In Texas, methanol as well as other motor fuel alcohols (excluding denaturants and water) are covered by the statutory definition of "gasoline" and, therefore, is subject to the Texas gasoline tax and are taxed at the same rate of 20 cents per gallon. (Sec. 162.001, Tax Code, see definitions for "alcohol", "fuel grade ethanol", "gasohol", and "gasoline")

Propane: Propane gas is covered by the statutory definition of "liquefied gas" and, therefore, is subject to the Texas liquefied gas tax (see, explanation under LNG) and is taxed at the same rate. (Sec. 162.001, Tax Code)

International Fuel Tax Agreement (IFTA): Effective July 1, 1995, Texas participates in the International Fuel Tax Agreement (IFTA), discussed below. Citations (e.g., R212) in this discussion of IFTA are to the IFTA Articles of Agreement (e.g., R212), Audit Manual (e.g., A310), or Procedures Manual (e.g., P410), each of which can be reviewed on the International Fuel Tax Association Web site. IFTA does not apply in the states of Alaska or Hawaii; the District of Columbia; or the Canadian provinces of Yukon Territory, Northwest Territory, or Nunavut.

The IFTA is a tax collection agreement among the 48 contiguous states and member Canadian provinces. The agreement is intended to provide uniform administration of motor fuels use taxation laws with respect to qualified motor vehicles operated in more than one member jurisdiction. Concepts at the core of the agreement include:

¶1705

— base jurisdiction;

— retention of sovereign authority to exercise substantive tax authority over matters such as tax rates and exemptions; and

— uniform definition of vehicles to which the agreement applies.

(R130.100)

For purposes of IFTA, "base jurisdiction" means the member jurisdiction where qualified motor vehicles are based for vehicle registration purposes and where:

— operational control and operational records of a licensee's qualified motor vehicles are maintained or can be made available; and

— some travel is accrued by qualified motor vehicles within the licensee's fleet.

The commissioners of two or more affected jurisdictions may allow a person to consolidate several fleets that otherwise would be based in two or more jurisdictions. (R212)

A "qualified motor vehicle" is a motor vehicle used, designed, or maintained for transportation of persons or property, and either:

— having two axles with a gross vehicle or registered gross vehicle weight over 26,000 pounds or 11,797 kilograms;

— having three or more axles, regardless of weight; or

— used in combination and the gross vehicle or the registered vehicle weight of the combined vehicle weight exceeds 26,000 pounds or 11,797 kilograms.

"Qualified motor vehicle" does not include recreational vehicles. (R245)

"Motor fuel" means all fuels placed in the supply tank of qualified motor vehicles. (R239)

Generally, persons based in a member jurisdiction operating a qualified motor vehicle in two or more member jurisdictions are required to be licensed under this Agreement. (R305) In lieu of such motor fuel tax licensing, persons may elect to satisfy motor fuels use tax obligations on a trip-by-trip basis. (R310) Persons required to register must file an application for licensing with their base jurisdiction and annually must renew their licenses, which expire December 31. (R610)

Generally, licensees must preserve records related to quarterly tax returns for four years from the later of the tax return due date or filing date. (IFTA Procedure Manual, P510.100) The records must be made available to any member jurisdiction upon request. (IFTA Procedure Manual, P520.100)

Generally, licensees must file a quarterly report on or before the last day of the month immediately following the close of each calendar quarter, even if no operations were conducted or no taxable fuel was used during the reporting period. (R930.100, R960.100) However, a licensee whose operations total less than 5,000 miles or 8,000 kilometers in all member jurisdictions other than the base jurisdiction during 12 consecutive months may ask to report on an annual basis. The request must be approved by the base jurisdiction. (R930.200) If the request is approved, the licensee's annual return will be due on January 31 following the close of the annual tax reporting period. (R960.100)

Licensees must pay all taxes due to all member jurisdictions with the remittances payable to the base jurisdictions on the same dates that reports are due. (R910) Payments may be made by hand delivery, postal service delivery, or by electronic means approved by the base jurisdiction. (R960)

¶1705

Part VI—Miscellaneous Taxes

The timely filing of the tax return and the payment of taxes due to the base jurisdiction for all member jurisdiction discharges the responsibility of the licensee for filing of tax returns and payment of individual taxes to all member jurisdictions. (R920)

Licensees can claim a tax-paid credit on the IFTA tax return for fuel purchased at retail only when the fuel is placed into the fuel tank of a qualified motor vehicle and the purchase price includes fuel tax paid to a member jurisdiction. (R1010) For storage fuel purchased in bulk, a credit can be claimed on the IFTA return only when:

— the fuel is placed into the fuel tank of a qualified motor vehicle;

— the bulk storage tank is owned, leased, or controlled by the licensee; and either

— the purchase price of the fuel includes fuel tax paid to the member jurisdiction where the bulk fuel storage tan is located; or

— the licensee has paid fuel tax to the member jurisdiction where the bulk fuel storage tank is located.

(R1020.200)

Licensees can receive full credit or refund for tax-paid fuel used outside the jurisdiction where the fuel was purchased. The base jurisdiction must allow credits and issue refunds for all of its licensees on behalf of all member jurisdictions, as long as the licensee has satisfied all tax liability, including audit assessments, to all member jurisdictions. (R1100) If a credit is not refunded, it shall be carried over to offset the licensee's liabilities for the earlier of:

(1) the time at which the credit is fully offset; or

(2) eight calendar quarters.

(R1120.100) A licensee may apply an overpayment generated in one jurisdiction to taxes owed to another jurisdiction. (R1120.200)

If a refund is paid more than 90 days after an application was made, the refund is subject to interest at the rate of 1% per month or part of a month calculated from the date the refund was due. (R1150)

A base jurisdiction may, among other things, assess tax against any licensee that:

— fails, neglects, or refuses to file a tax return when due;

— fails to make records available upon written request; or

— fails to maintain records from which the licensee's true liability can be determined.

The assessment made by the base jurisdiction will be presumed correct. (R1200)

For failing to file a tax return, filing a late tax return, or underpaying taxes due, a licensee may be assessed a penalty equaling the greater of $50.00 or 10% of delinquent taxes. Nothing in the IFTA limits the authority of a base jurisdiction to impose any other penalties provided by the laws of the base jurisdiction. (R1220)

The base jurisdiction shall assess interest on qualifying delinquent taxes at the rate of 1% per month. (R1230.100) Interest will be calculated separately for each jurisdiction from the date tax was due for each month or fraction of a month. (1230.300) All interest collected shall be remitted to the appropriate jurisdiction. (R1230.400)

A base jurisdiction may waive penalties for reasonable cause. If the base jurisdiction's laws permit waiver of interest and a licensee demonstrates that a tax return was filed late due to misinformation given by the base jurisdiction, the base jurisdiction may waive interest, also. However, to waive interest for another jurisdiction, the base jurisdiction must receive written approval from that jurisdiction. (R1260)

¶1705

While each base jurisdiction must audit its licensees on behalf of all member jurisdictions, other jurisdictions are not precluded from also auditing those licensees. (R1310) Audits conducted by member jurisdictions must be in compliance with IFTA Articles of Agreement, Procedures Manual, and Audit Manual. (R1330)

While IFTA has appeal procedures for licensees, those procedures only apply if the base jurisdiction does not have provisions for appeals of actions or audit findings. (R1400)

In order to appeal an action or audit finding, a licensee must make a written request for a hearing within 30 days after service of notice of the original action or finding. (R1410) The hearing must be held "expeditiously," and the base jurisdiction must give at least 20 days' notice of the time and place of the hearing. (R1420)

The licensee may appear in person and/or be represented by counsel and may produce witnesses, documents, or other pertinent material. (R1430.100) If the licensee appeals an assessment for one or more jurisdictions, the base jurisdiction will be responsible for participating in the appeal on behalf of the other jurisdictions. (R1430.200) The base jurisdiction will notify the licensee of the findings of fact and the ruling on the appeal. (R1440)

An appeal of any jurisdiction's findings will proceed in accordance with that jurisdiction's laws. (R1450.100) In the case of an audit, the licensee may request any or every jurisdiction to audit the licensee's records. Each jurisdiction can accept or deny the request, and those electing to audit the record will audit only for its own portion of the licensee's operations. (R1450.200)

CCH Comment: Hurricane Ike disaster relief

Licensed diesel fuel suppliers, permissive suppliers, and distributors operating within areas of southeast Texas affected by Hurricane Ike could sell undyed diesel fuel free from motor fuel tax if the fuel was purchased between September 19, 2008, and October 14, 2008, for use in off-highway equipment. Purchasers were required to use of an affidavit supplied by the Comptroller or by the seller on its monthly tax return. (*Special Tax Mailing*, Texas Comptroller of Public Accounts, September 25, 2008)

¶1706 Motor Vehicle Registration Fees

Law: Secs. 502.002, 502.101, 502.158, 502.161, 502.162, 502.163, 502.165, 502.166, 502.167, 502.1675, 502.168, 502.170, 502.171, 502.172, 502.173, 502.174, 502.175, 502.177, 502.276, 502.278, 502.351, 502.352, 502.353, Trans. Code (CCH TEXAS TAX REPORTS, ¶¶50-110, 50-120).

Motor vehicles must be registered. Application for registration is made to the Department of Transportation through the county assessor-collector in which the applicant resides. Motor vehicles are registered annually on a staggered registration system.

The minimum registration fee is $5. An additional 30¢ is added to the cost of each license plate, set of plates, or other registration device to pay for the cost of reflectorized plates. A $1 service charge may be imposed by a county assessor-collector for registration. The registration fee for a motor vehicle (other than a passenger car, a truck with a manufacturer's rated carrying capacity of two tons or less, or a truck-tractor or commercial motor vehicle combination) is increased by 11% if the vehicle has a diesel motor.

The commissioners court of any county may impose an additional fee of not to exceed $10 for registering a vehicle in the county and an additional child safety fee not to exceed $1.50. A $1 transfer fee is charged to the purchaser on the transfer of any vehicle by a person other than a dealer.

¶1706

The fee for a passenger vehicle ranges from $40.50 to $58.50 depending on the vehicle's model year. Fees for other vehicles vary by weight.

Foreign commercial vehicles owned by residents of the United States, Canada, or Mexico may be issued a temporary permit for a fee of $25 for a 72-hour permit or $50 for a 144-hour permit.

Nonresident trucks transporting farm products pay 1/12th of the annual registration fee for a temporary registration permit that is valid for up to 30 days.

- *Texas emissions reduction plan surcharge*

In addition to the registration fees discussed above, a surcharge is imposed on the registration of a truck-tractor or commercial motor vehicle in an amount equal to 10% of the total registration fees. The fee expires on August 31, 2008. The surcharge does not apply to recreational vehicles (RVs) that are not held or used for the production of income.

¶1707 Hotel Occupancy Tax

Law: Secs. 111.006, 151.429(h), 156.001, 156.051, 156.052, 156.053, 156.101, 156.102, 156.103, 156.104, 156.151, 156.152, 156.153, 156.202, 156.203, 351.001, 351.002, 351.0025, 351.003, 351.004, 351.005, 351.006, 352.001, 352.002, 352.003, 352.004, 352.005, 352.007, 352.107, 383.001—383.040, Tax Code; Secs. 334.251—334.258, 334.253(c), 335.001—335.075, Local Govt. Code; Sec. 2303.003(8), Govt. Code; 34 TAC Secs. 3.161, 3.162, 3.163 (CCH TEXAS TAX REPORTS, ¶ 33-303, 33-305, 33-309, 33-312, 33-314, 33-317, 33-319, 33-327).

Persons subject to tax: A tax is levied on the cost of occupancy or "the use or possession, or the right to the use or possession of any room or rooms in a hotel for any purposes" when charges are $15 or more. Manufactured homes are included in the definition of a hotel (34 TAC Sec. 3.161(a)(3)). The tax is imposed on the occupant and collected by the hotel. Also, the hotel occupancy tax must be collected for the rental of meeting and banquet rooms located in a building having sleeping accommodations. The tax does not apply to hospitals, sanitariums, nursing homes, or dormitories or other housing facilities owned or leased and operated by an institution of higher education.

CCH Practice Tip: Questions Answered

The Comptroller's Office has responded to a series of questions from a hotel operator concerning what services and fees are subject to tax. In answering the questionnaire, the Comptroller indicated that as a general rule, the following are subject to tax:

- guaranteed no show charges;
- attrition fees;
- package fees in which room fees are not separately stated;
- rooms for resale;
- banquet/meeting services;
- pet charges and cleaning fees;
- rollaway bed charges; and
- refrigerator charges are subject to tax.

Conversely, complimentary rooms, early and late departure fees, cancellation fees, and separately stated child care services are not subject to tax. The questionnaire also addresses exemptions for permanent residents, government employees, and charitable, religious, and educational organizations and food and beverage taxes charged by hotels. (*Letter*, Texas Comptroller of Public Accounts, No. 200307797L, July 10, 2003, CCH TEXAS TAX REPORTS, ¶ 402-556)

In addition, charges assessed against hotel guests for damage from smoking in the room or taking items such as hair dryers, linens, pillows, and wastebaskets are subject to

Texas hotel occupancy tax rather than sales tax. (*Letter No. 200804069L*, Texas Comptroller of Public Accounts, April 22, 2008, CCH TEXAS TAX REPORTS, ¶ 403-399).

Exemptions: Permanent residents are exempt from both state and local hotel occupancy taxes. A "permanent resident" is any occupant who has or will have a right to the occupancy of any room or rooms in a hotel for at least 30 consecutive days, without any interruption of payment for the period. The use of hotel reward points to receive some complimentary room rentals for part of a 30-day period does not impact the 30-day residency period, the issue is occupancy not how the room is paid for. (*Letter*, Texas Comptroller of Public Accounts, No. 200404428L, April 7, 2004, CCH TEXAS TAX REPORTS, ¶ 402-683) A company that reserves and pays for hotel rooms for more than 30 consecutive days qualifies for the permanent resident exemption, even if different individuals use the rooms during the period. (*Letter*, Texas Comptroller of Public Accounts, No. 200412936L, December 21, 2004, CCH TEXAS TAX REPORTS, ¶ 402-832) An occupant who rents a hotel room for the entire month of February does not qualify for the exemption because February never has 30 days. (*Letter*, Texas Comptroller of Public Accounts, No. 200502994L, February 2, 2005, CCH TEXAS TAX REPORTS, ¶ 402-859).

CCH Advisory: Establishment of Permanent Residency

Guests who provide the hotel with written notification that they will occupy a room for 30 or more consecutive days are considered permanent residents beginning on the first day of occupancy, whereas guests who do not provide such notification are not permanent residents until the 31st day of occupancy and must pay tax on the first 30 days.

Rental of an additional room by a permanent resident is not automatically exempt. The permanent resident must provide the hotel with written notice of his or her intent to occupy the additional room for 30 or more consecutive days and then occupy the additional room for the next 30 days. Without the written notice, tax would be due on the first 30 days of the rental. (*Letter*, Comptroller of Public Accounts, No. 200605604L, May 31, 2006, CCH TEXAS TAX REPORTS, ¶ 403-093.)

There is no resale exemption for purposes of the hotel occupancy tax. Thus, a hotel that must rent rooms from another hotel to accommodate its overbooked guests must pay the applicable room charges plus tax to the other hotels. If the amount the taxpayer collected from the overbooked guests is greater than the amount the taxpayer pays to the other hotels, the taxpayer must also report the difference as taxable room receipts. (*Letter No. 200808141L*, Texas Comptroller of Public Accounts, August 1, 2008, CCH TEXAS TAX REPORTS, ¶ 403-473).

Exempt entities, agencies, and institutions: Also exempt from all Texas hotel occupancy taxes are certain governmental entities, agencies, and institutions. Qualified religious, charitable, and educational organizations are also exempt from the state hotel occupancy tax provided they receive a Comptroller's letter of hotel tax exemption. IRC Sec. 501(c)(3) organizations are not automatically exempt from the tax. Furthermore, the exemption applies only to the state hotel occupancy tax, not to municipal or county hotel occupancy taxes. The exemption for institutions of higher education applies only to Texas institutions.

The following governmental entities are exempt from all Texas state and local hotel occupancy taxes: the United States, the State of Texas, and agencies, institutions, boards, and commissions of the state, other than non-Texas institutions of higher education. However, certain exempt governmental entities may be required to pay hotel occupancy tax and then apply for a refund no later than two years after the end of the fiscal year in which the travel occurred. Officers or employees of the exempt federal and state governmental entities listed above are exempt from the state,

¶ 1707

Part VI—Miscellaneous Taxes

municipal, and county taxes when traveling or when otherwise engaged in the course of official duties.

Officers or employees of *federal* governmental entities are eligible for a hotel occupancy tax exemption only if the governmental entity makes a direct payment to the hotel for the price of the room. All *state* officers or employees who are entitled to reimbursement for the cost of lodging and for whom a special provision or exception to the general rate of reimbursement under the General Appropriations Act is not applicable must pay the tax. The governmental entity with whom the employee is associated must then claim a refund of the tax. A state employee for whom the special provision or exception to the general rate of reimbursement under the General Appropriations Act is applicable is not required to pay the tax provided the employee has a photo identification verifying his or her identity and exempt status. As a federal employee, an active duty member of the military is exempt from Texas hotel occupancy tax when traveling on official business. (*Letter*, Texas Comptroller of Public Accounts, No. 200412935L, December 15, 2004, CCH TEXAS TAX REPORTS, ¶402-864)

CCH Comment: Hotel guest's federal ID card may not be copied

The Texas Comptroller has offered advice on how a hotel operator can verify a federal employee's exemption from paying hotel occupancy tax. Because federal law prohibits a person from making a copy of a U.S. government identification card, verification of the exemption can be written on the exemption certificate presented by the guest or on the guest folio or other hotel record indicating who stayed in the room. For example, the hotel clerk can write *ID card verified* on the exemption certificate along with a date and the clerk's signature or initials. (*Letter No. 201004674L*, Texas Comptroller of Public Accounts, April 9, 2010, CCH TEXAS TAX REPORTS, ¶403-618)

State officials, judicial officers, heads of state agencies, the Executive Director of the Legislative Council, the Secretary of the Senate, state legislators, legislative employees, members of state boards and commissions, and designated employees of the State of Texas who present a Hotel Tax Exemption Photo Identification Card when traveling on official state business are exempt from the hotel occupancy tax. State agency, institution, board, or commission employees who have not been issued a Hotel Tax Exemption Photo Identification Card must pay the hotel occupancy tax.

A Hotel Tax Exemption Photo Identification Card includes (1) any photo identification card issued by a state agency that states "EXEMPT FROM HOTEL OCCUPANCY TAX, under Sec. 156.103(d), Tax Code," or similar wording; or (2) a Hotel Tax Exemption Card that states "when presented with a photo identification card issued by a Texas agency, the holder of this card is exempt from state, municipal, and county hotel occupancy tax, Sec. 156.103(d), Tax Code," or similar wording.

Diplomatic personnel of a *foreign* government who present an appropriate Tax Exemption Card issued by the U.S. Department of State are also exempt from the tax.

An exemption may only be taken if a valid exemption certificate is provided. The Comptroller produces a list on its Internet website of entities that have been provided a letter of exemption. This information can be found at http://www.window.state.tx.us/taxinfo/exempt/xmptsearch.html.

Hotel owners and operators may accept, in good faith, hotel occupancy tax exemption certificates when presented with appropriate support documentation. For federal government entities, that documentation is a valid government identification card. (*Letter*, Texas Comptroller of Public Accounts, No. 200407688L, July 19, 2004, CCH TEXAS TAX REPORTS, ¶402-731)

Basis and rate: The state hotel occupancy tax is imposed at the rate of 6% of the price paid for a room in a hotel. The price of the room does not include the cost of

¶1707

food served by the hotel or the cost of personal services performed by the hotel, except charges for cleaning or readying the room for occupancy. If charges for such benefits are included in the price of the lodging they must be separately stated on the customer's bill or the entire amount will be subject to tax. As reimbursement for the cost of collection, the hotel may deduct and keep 1% of the tax otherwise due. However, if the tax is not paid when due or the report is not filed when due, the one-percent reimbursement for collection costs may not be taken.

A hotel fee that allows a guest to modify a prepaid reservation by changing the occupancy dates without moving the reservation to another hotel is subject to hotel occupancy tax. If a prepaid guest moves to another hotel property within the corporation's same family of brands, hotel tax is due on the changed reservation fee if the guest changes the reservation within 30 days of the date of arrival and the guest pays the consideration necessary to have occupied the room. The hotel that held the original reservation should treat the changed reservation fee as a cancellation fee in its records. (*Letter No. 201007850L*, Texas Comptroller of Public Accounts, July 26, 2010; CCH TEXAS TAX REPORTS, ¶403-628)

Cities and some counties can each levy local hotel taxes, generally at rates varying up to 7%; sports and community venue projects can levy hotel taxes at rates varying up to 2%, except for Dallas County which can impose a hotel venue tax at a rate of up to 3%. For example, in Houston there is 6% state tax, 7% Houston tax, 2% Harris County tax and a 2% Harris County/Houston Sports Authority tax.

Additional taxes may be imposed by county development districts and by cities, counties, or venue districts for venue projects.

CCH Comment: Online Travel Companies' Hotel Tax Liability Based on Discounted Room Rate

Local hotel occupancy taxes were imposed on the discounted room rates that hotels charged online travel companies (OTCs) rather than on the marked-up room rates that consumers paid to the OTCs. Hotels charged the OTC a discounted room rate, to which the OTC added a "markup" to arrive at the online rate displayed on the OTC's website. The OTC charged the consumer's credit card for the marked-up rate. The hotel later invoiced the OTC for the room charge at the discounted rate plus local hotel occupancy taxes based on that amount. The local taxing authorities claimed that hotel tax should have been due on the amount that a consumer paid the OTC. The local taxes at issue were imposed on the "cost of occupancy," a term that was not defined. The court held that this phrase could be reasonably interpreted as the amount paid by an OTC to a hotel on the occupant's behalf for the right to use a room. The hotels offered rooms and occupancy in exchange for payment. An OTC, on the other hand, did not have rooms or occupancy but, rather, a website. (*City of Houston v. Hotels.Com, L.P.*, Texas Court of Appeals, Fourteenth District, Houston, No. 14-10-00349-CV, October 25, 2011, CCH TEXAS TAX REPORTS, ¶403-769)

Payments and reports: Monthly payment and returns are required unless the taxpayer owes less than $500 for the calendar month or $1,500 for a calendar quarter, in which case payment and reporting are required on a calendar quarter basis. Monthly returns and payments are due on or before the 20th day of the following month, and quarterly returns and payments are due on the 20th day after the end of the calendar quarter.

— A 5% penalty is imposed if the report is not filed or the payment not made when due.

— An additional 5% penalty is assessed if payment is not made within 30 days of the due date.

Audit and additional penalty: If a hotel operator fails to pay municipal hotel occupancy taxes, the municipality may conduct an audit and hold the hotel operator liable for (1) attorney fees, (2) audit costs if the tax has been delinquent for at least two municipal fiscal quarters, and (3) a 15% penalty if the tax has been delinquent for at least one municipal fiscal quarter. Municipalities are authorized to use previous years' tax filings to estimate the amount of tax due.

Qualified hotel projects: The owner of a qualified hotel project is entitled to receive a rebate, refund, or payment of 100% of the state hotel occupancy taxes paid by hotel customers during the first 10 years after the qualified hotel project is open for initial occupancy in the enterprise zone. See ¶1005 for a discussion of qualified hotel projects.

¶1708 Utilities Taxes

Law: Sec. 771.0712, Health & Safety; Secs. 182.021, 182.022, 182.024, 182.026, 182.081, 182.082, 182.083, Tax Code; Secs. 1.351, 1.352, 1.353, 3.604, 3.606, Art. 1466c-0, V.A.C.S.; Art. 6060, Tit. 102, Revised Civil Stats.; Sec. 5.235, Water Code (CCH TEXAS TAX REPORTS, ¶60-720, 80-001, 80-010, 80-020, 80-030, 80-040, 80-050, 80-055, 80-060).

Persons subject to tax: A tax is imposed on each utility company located in an incorporated city or town having a population of more than 1,000. A "utility company" is a person who operates a gas, electric light, electric power, waterworks, or water and light plant used for local sale and distribution that is located within an incorporated city or town in Texas. Retail electric providers that make local sales within an incorporated city or town must pay the tax. (Sec. 182.021, Tax Code) Utility companies owned and operated by any city, town, or county or water improvement or conservation district are exempt. A tax is also imposed on telecommunications utilities.

Exemptions: The sale of electricity generated by an advanced clean energy project is not subject to the utility gross receipts tax.

Basis and rate: The taxes are based on gross receipts of each company as shown by its report. Gas, electric light, power, or waterworks companies are taxed at the following rates:

— in towns with populations of 1,000 to 2,499, the rate is 0.581%;

— in cities with populations of 2,500 to 9,999, the rate is 1.07%;

— in cities with populations of 10,000 or more, the rate is 1.997%; and

— all utilities beginning business on or after the first day of a quarter, the rate is $50 for the first quarter.

Administrative expense assessment: In addition, each public utility within the jurisdiction of the Public Utility Commission of Texas, including interexchange telecommunications carriers, and retail electric providers are subject to an assessment equal to $1/6$ of 1% of gross receipts from rates charged the ultimate consumer in Texas.

Telecommunication Infrastructure Fund assessments: Until September 1, 2008, annual assessments are imposed on each telecommunications utility and each commercial mobile service provider doing business in Texas. The assessments are imposed at the rate of 1.25% of the taxable telecommunications receipts of each telecommunications utility and commercial mobile service provider that is subject to the assessment, unless the amount deposited in the Telecommunications Infrastructure Fund reaches $1.5 billion. If the Comptroller determines that $1.2 billion or more, excluding interest and loan repayments, has already been deposited to the Fund, the Comptroller must impose the assessment during the next fiscal year at a rate estimated as sufficient to result in total deposits to the fund of not more than $1.5 billion. The last assessment must be paid in October 2008.

Water or sewer utility regulatory assessments: Every public utility that provides potable water or sewer utility service must collect a regulatory assessment from each retail customer at the rate of 1% of the charge for retail water or sewer service. A water supply or sewer service corporation and a district providing potable water or sewer utility service must collect a regulatory assessment from each retail customer at the rate of 1/2% of the charge for retail water or sewer service.

Payments and reports: Reports are to be filed with the State Comptroller on the last days of January, April, July, and October. Tax payments must accompany quarterly reports. The administrative expense assessment is due August 15 or may be paid quarterly on August 15, November 15, February 15, and May 15 of each year.

9-1-1 emergency fees: Several 911-related charges are imposed monthly under the Health and Safety Code, including (1) the 9-1-1 Emergency Service Fee, (2) the 9-1-1 Wireless Emergency Service Fee, and (3) the 9-1-1 Equalization Surcharge. Effective June 1, 2010, a statute requires retail sellers of prepaid wireless telecommunications service to collect from customers a prepaid wireless 9-1-1 emergency service fee, equal to 2% of the purchase price of each prepaid wireless telecommunications service that permits a person to access to 9-1-1 emergency communications services. (Sec. 771.0712, Health & Safety Code; *Letter,* Texas Comptroller of Public Accounts, No. 201005823L, May 13, 2010; CCH TEXAS TAX REPORTS, ¶ 403-622)

The 911 emergency service fee applies to wireless telecommunications connections that are purchased on a prepaid basis as well as a postpaid basis. The original statute imposes the fee on all wireless connections and contains no language limiting its scope based on the manner in which the user purchases the connection. The fact that the Legislature subsequently enacted a prepaid wireless 911 service fee (Health and Safety Code § 771.0712) was not proof that the original fee (Health and Safety Code § 771.0711) did not cover prepaid wireless service. Postpaid customers typically pay a monthly bill for the connection and services used in the preceding month, usually measured in minutes. On the other hand, prepaid customers pay for their wireless connection and service in advance by purchasing a handset and a wireless card for a fixed dollar amount or a fixed number of minutes of service. (*Commission on State Emergency Communications v. TracFone Wireless, Inc. and Virgin Mobile USA, LP,* Texas Court of Appeals, Third District, Austin, No. 03-10-00111-CV, May 5, 2011; CCH TEXAS TAX REPORTS, ¶ 403-701)

¶1709 Severance Taxes

> *Law:* Secs. 201.001, 201.051—201.055, 201.057, 201.058, 201.059, 201.101—201.106, 201.201, 201.2015, 201.202, 201.203, 201.2035, 201.204, 201.205, 201.251, 202.001, 202.002, 202.003, 202.052, 202.053, 202.054, 202.056, 202.057, 202.058, 202.059, 202.060, 202.061, 202.151, 202.1515, 202.152—202.156, 202.201, 202.202, 202.251, 203.001—203.003, 204.002—204.008, Tax Code; Secs. 81.111, 81.116, 81.117, 89.047, Nat. Res. Code; 34 TAC Secs. 3.14, 3.16, 3.20, 3.21, 3.22, 3.31, 3.33—3.38, 3.41, 3.50 (CCH TEXAS TAX REPORTS, ¶ 37-301).

Texas imposes taxes on the production of oil, gas, and sulfur.

- *Oil production tax*

Persons subject to tax: The oil production tax, the additional tax on crude petroleum, and the regulatory fee on crude petroleum production are the primary liability of the producer and a liability of the first and subsequent purchasers. The tax is generally withheld by the first purchaser from payments to the producer and then remitted to the state. The tax is borne ratably by all interested parties, including royalty interests. Producers or purchasers must withhold from payments to the interested parties the proportionate amount of tax due from each party.

Exemptions: Royalty interests owned by specified governmental entities are not subject to the tax on oil production. Oil produced from Texas wells that have been inactive for at least two or three years is exempt from the oil production tax. The exemption applies to hydrocarbons produced from a well during a 10-year period if the Texas Railroad Commission designates the well as a "two-year inactive well" or a

Part VI—Miscellaneous Taxes

"three-year inactive well." Hydrocarbons that are produced in Texas from a well that is subject to an agreement under Natural Resources Code, concerning Texas Experimental Research and Recovery Activity (TERRA), and that are produced under a license issued under TERRA are also exempt from the oil production tax. A five-year, 50% exemption is available to operators of certain qualifying leases on the lease's qualified incremental production. Finally, an exemption applies to oil incidentally produced in association with the production of geothermal energy.

Basis and rate: The oil production tax is imposed at a rate of 4.6% of the market value of oil produced in Texas, or 4.6¢ for each barrel of 42 standard gallons of oil produced, whichever formula results in the greater amount of tax. The additional tax is imposed on crude petroleum in the amount of $3/16$ of 1¢ on each barrel of 42 standard gallons of petroleum produced. A special reduced oil production tax rate of 2.3% (called the "recovered oil tax rate") applies to oil produced from a new enhanced oil recovery project or from a coproduction project and to incremental production caused by the expansion of an existing enhanced recovery project. The reduced rate may only be claimed by a taxpayer who receives approval from the Texas Railroad Commission prior to commencing project operations.

An additional 50% reduction in the rate is available for up to 30 years if in the process of oil recovery the project uses carbon dioxide that is captured from an anthropogenic source in Texas, that would otherwise be released into the atmosphere as industrial emission, that is measurable at the source of capture and is sequestered in one or more geological formations in this state following the enhanced oil recovery process. The reduction may be reduced if a portion of the carbon dioxide used does not satisfy the above criteria because it is not anthropogenic. To qualify, a taxpayer must receive certification from the Texas Railroad Commission and/or the Texas Commission on Environmental Quality and must submit the certification along with an application for the reduced rate to the Comptroller of Public Accounts. Amounts paid prior to approval by the Comptroller may be credited. (Sec. 202.0545, Tax Code)

The oil-field cleanup regulatory fee on crude petroleum production is imposed at the rate of $5/16$ of 1¢ per 42-gallon barrel produced in Texas.

Credits: Taxpayers who use enhanced efficiency equipment in the production of oil may claim a credit of up to 10% of the cost of the equipment, not to exceed $1,000 per well. The equipment must be purchased and installed between September 1, 2005, and September 1, 2013. (Sec. 202.061, Tax Code)

Three levels of tax credits are provided for oil production from qualified low-producing oil leases for any given month. The level depends on average taxable oil prices, adjusted to 2005 dollars, based on applicable price indices of the previous three months. An operator of a qualifying low-producing oil lease is entitled to a 25% tax credit if the average taxable oil price is above $25 per barrel but not more than $30. The credit increases to 50% if the price is above $22 per barrel but not more than $25, and to 100% if the price is $22 or less. (Sec. 202.058, Tax Code)

Payments and reports: On or before the 25th day of each calendar month, each producer and first purchaser of oil must file reports containing information about oil produced or purchased during the preceding calendar month. Payment of tax is due with the report.

In addition, a producer also must file a Crude Oil Special Tax Report with the Comptroller to report where and how much oil has been used, lost, stolen, possessed, or otherwise unaccounted for by the producer after the oil has been produced and measured. The producer must also pay the oil production tax on such oil. The report must be filed by the 25th day of the month following the month in which the oil has been used, lost, stolen, possessed, or otherwise not taken into account.

¶1709

- *Gas production tax*

    Persons subject to tax: The tax on gas production is imposed on the producer, but is paid by the first purchaser who takes delivery of the gas at the production site. The severance tax on gas is borne ratably by all interested parties, including royalty interest holders.

    Exemptions: Royalty interests owned by specified governmental entities are not subject to the tax on gas production. The gas production tax is not imposed on gas (1) injected into Texas soil, unless sold for injection; (2) produced from oil wells simultaneously with oil and lawfully vented or flared; (3) used for lifting oil, unless sold for that purpose; and (4) oil incidentally produced in association with the production of geothermal energy.

    High-cost gas produced from a well that is spudded or completed after August 31, 1996, is entitled to a *reduction* of the tax for the first 120 consecutive calendar months (regardless of whether or not a well produces oil or gas during any or all such months) beginning on the first day of production, or until the cumulative value of the tax reduction equals 50% of the drilling and completion costs incurred for the well, which ever occurs first.

    An operator who increases production by marketing gas from an oil well or lease that previously was released into the air for 12 months or more pursuant to the rules of the Texas Railroad Commission is entitled to an exemption from the gas production tax on the production that results from the marketing of such gas for the life of the well or lease.

    In addition, the same exemptions allowed against the oil production tax for three-year inactive wells and two-year inactive wells, TERRA wells, and certain incremental production techniques are allowed against the gas production tax (see above).

    Credits: The credit against the oil production tax for low-producing oil wells (discussed above) may also be claimed against the gas production tax.

    Basis and rate: The gas production tax is imposed at a rate of 7.5% of the market value of gas produced and saved in Texas by the producer. Market value is the value of gas at the mouth of the well and is determined by ascertaining the producer's actual marketing costs and subtracting those costs from the producer's gross cash receipts from the sale of the gas. The oil-field cleanup regulatory fee on gas is $1/15$ of 1¢ per thousand cubic feet produced and saved in the state. For cash sales, the amount of tax charged is included in the tax base.

> *Practitioner Comment: Marketing Cost Deduction Reduces Taxable Value*
>
> The market value of gas is its value at the mouth of the well from which it was produced (Tex Tax Code §201.101 (Vernon 2002)). Market value is determined by subtracting those costs necessary to get the gas to market from the producer's gross cash receipts received from the sale of the gas. The marketing cost deduction reduces the gross taxable value prior to the application of either the full tax rate or the reduced tax rate applicable to qualifying high-cost gas production. The marketing cost deduction may not reduce net taxable value below zero. Companies are not required to claim a marketing cost deduction, but those that do so may significantly reduce their tax liability.
>
> Qualifying marketing costs include, but are not limited to, compression, sweetening, dehydration, gas gathering costs, third party gas processing costs, and other direct expenses found necessary to get the gas to market. Note that some functions, such as compression, may be considered both a marketing and a production function. In such cases, a supportable allocation may be required before the expense may be claimed. Both qualifying external (3rd party) expenses as well as qualifying internally allocated expenses may be claimed. The Texas Comptroller of Public Accounts ("The Comptroller") has established that direct labor costs for company and/or contract pumpers may

¶1709

be claimed at standard percentages (50% for gas wells and 25% for oil wells). Such standard percentages may be claimed even if supported with limited documentation. However, a producer may be successful in claiming a higher percentage if more comprehensive support documentation is available to substantiate the claim. Such support may include, but not be limited to, detailed information obtained from interviewing 3rd party as well as company personnel who have day-to-day knowledge of the particular lease operation, or other such suitable support data such as detailed lease inventories, lease schematics, or other visual evidence. Additionally, indirect labor costs may be claimed as allowable overhead provided that such costs are supportable through company records and can be directly associated with the handling of the gas at the marketing facility. Flat rate overhead computed based on production or industry accounting standards are not considered to be associated with the marketing facility and as such are not allowable.

The Comptroller has traditionally published that the outlet of the initial separator is the bright line test for establishing where production functions end and marketing functions begin. However, in some instances costs incurred prior to initial separation may be claimed (such as line heaters). Flowline expenditures are allowable based on an allocation as determined by the ratio of natural gas to crude oil production. While initial separation functions are not considered allowable marketing costs, second stage separation or gas scrubbing activities may qualify for the deduction.

Qualifying marketing costs also include depreciation expense (as determined on a straight line basis over ten (10) years and allowing for a ten percent (10%) salvage value and return on investment (allowable at a rate of 6%) calculated on qualifying marketing equipment that has been capitalized by the operator. Marketing equipment typically includes, but is not limited to, compressors (except for those used to enhance production), line heaters, glycol/dehydration units, gas gathering lines, gas processing facilities, amine plants, and gas sales meters. For marketing equipment obtained through acquisition, a market value must be assigned to the individual piece of equipment in order for allowable depreciation and return on investment deductions to apply. Allocations after the fact are not allowable.

Finally, lease use gas consumed to power the above-mentioned qualifying marketing equipment may also be claimed as a marketing cost deduction provided the severance tax had been paid on it when produced.

William M. Samuels, Ryan

Payments and reports: Payment of the gas production tax is due with the report at the Comptroller's office on the 20th day of the second month following the month of production. Any producer having an average monthly tax liability of less than $200 may pay the tax annually rather than monthly. Annual payment is due on or before February 20 for the preceding calendar year. However, if a producer who has been designated as an annual filer accumulates tax liability of $2,400 or more during a calendar year, the producer must remit the tax due on or before the 20th day of the second month following the month in which the producer's accumulated tax liability reached or exceeded $2,400 and must remit tax monthly thereafter.

- Sulfur production tax

Persons subject to tax: The sulfur production tax is imposed on the sulfer producer.

Basis and rate: The tax is imposed at a rate of $1.03 per long ton or fraction of a long ton of sulfur produced in Texas.

Payments and reports: A producer must file quarterly reports and pay the tax due on or before the last day of each January, April, July, and October.

¶1709

¶1710 Environmental Taxes and Fees

Law: Secs. 361.013, 361.0135, 361.134—361.137, 382.062, 382.0621, 401.011, 402.272, Health and Safety Code; Sec. 91.605, Nat. Res. Code; Secs. 26.011, 26.0291, Water Code; 25 TAC Secs. 205.44, 205.51, 289.126; 31 TAC Secs. 305.503, 335.323—335.325, 335.328 (CCH Texas Tax Reports, ¶33-505, 33-510, 33-515, 33-525, 33-530).

Texas imposes certain fees for environmental regulation and protection purposes, including solid waste disposal and transportation fees; hazardous waste facility, generator, and disposal fees; and fees for disposal of radioactive wastes, under programs administered by the Texas Commission on Environmental Quality. A coastal protection fee is also imposed on motor fuels (¶1705).

- *Solid waste disposal fees*

The solid waste disposal fee is $1.25 per ton received for disposal at a municipal solid waste landfill if the solid waste is measured by weight. If the solid waste is measured by volume, the fee for compacted solid waste is 40¢ per cubic yard or, for uncompacted solid waste, 25¢ per cubic yard received for disposal at a municipal solid waste landfill.

An operator of a public or private solid waste facility may obtain a refund of 15% of its solid waste disposal fee payments to purchase or lease equipment to compost yard waste for return to beneficial use. A 20% refund is allowed if the operator bans disposal of yard waste at the facility altogether.

Transporters of municipal solid waste who are required to register with the Commission will be charged an annual registration fee by the Commission. The Commission must adopt a fee schedule by rule. The fee must be reasonably related to the volume or type of waste transported, or both, and may not be less than $25 or more than $500.

- *Industrial and hazardous waste*

Permit fees: A fee on every applicant for an industrial solid waste or hazardous waste permit may be imposed in an amount not less than $2,000 or more than $50,000. Renewal fees may be less than $2,000. In addition, the Commission is authorized to impose fees in amounts from $25 through $75,000 for applications, operating permits, and inspections for facilities that emit air contaminants and that are not subject to the federal Clean Air Act.

Inspection fees: Annual waste treatment inspection fees are charged each permittee. The maximum fee that may be assessed is generally $11,000 ($15,000 upon delegation of national pollutant discharge elimination system permit authority to the Commission).

Generation fees: An annual generation fee is assessed against generators of Class I industrial solid waste or hazardous waste on the basis of the volume of waste generated during a calendar year. The amount of the fee is between $50 and $50,000 for hazardous waste, or $10,000 for nonhazardous waste. There is no fee if waste generated is under one ton. An annual fee is also imposed on oil and gas hazardous waster generators according to volume of hazardous waster generated.

Facility fees: An annual facility fee is assessed on each person who holds one or more Class I industrial solid waste or hazardous waste permits and each facility operating a Class I industrial solid waste or hazardous waste management unit subject to permit requirements. The minimum fee for a facility authorized to manage only nonhazardous waste is $500; the maximum fee is $5,000.

Hazardous waste management fee: Each owner or operator of a commercial or noncommercial hazardous waste facility is assessed a fee, which may not exceed $20 per ton, for hazardous materials that are stored, processed, or disposed of at the facility for a charge.

¶1710

Part VI—Miscellaneous Taxes

Payments and reports: Hazardous waste management fees must be reported and paid to the Texas Water Commission by the 25th day of the month following the end of the month for which payment is due. A quarterly report and payment may be made if the fee owed is less than $50 for a calendar month or less than $150 for a calendar quarter.

- *Radioactive materials*

Fees for licenses for radioactive material disposal are imposed by the Texas Commission on Environmental Quality. In addition, the Commission must collect a fee from persons who seek to dispose of low-level radioactive waste. The Commission is required to issue a fee schedule and set minimum and maximum annual fees on the basis of the projected annual volume, and relative hazards, of the low-level waste generated by users of radioactive materials.

- *Manufacturers and sellers of hazardous substances*

A registration statement must be filed with the Texas Department of Health by manufacturers of hazardous substances whose products are distributed in Texas. The fee for filing the statement is $150 for each initial statement and each annual refiling.

Retail sellers of abusable glues and aerosol paints must obtain a $25 glue and paint permit for each location at which such products may be sold. The fee for annual renewal of the permit is also $25.

- *Lead-acid batteries*

A fee is imposed on wholesale and retail sales of lead-acid batteries containing lead and sulfuric acid and not sold for resale. A tax is also imposed on the storage, use, or other consumption in Texas of a lead-acid battery, unless purchased for resale or unless the fee has been paid. The fee equals $2 for batteries of 6 to 12 volts and $3 for batteries of 12 volts or more. The sale of a lead-acid battery is exempt from the fee if it (1) has dimensions totaling less than 15 inches; (2) is sealed to prevent any access to its interior without destroying the battery; and (3) has a rating of less than 10 ampere-hours.

An automotive oil sales fee is also imposed (¶1705).

¶1711 Sexually Oriented Business Admission Fee

Law: Secs. 47.051-053, Bus. & Comm. Code. (CCH TEXAS TAX REPORTS, ¶33-101).

CCH Comment: Adult Entertainment Business Fee Upheld

A Texas fee on businesses that offered live nude entertainment in combination with alcohol consumption on the premises did not violate the right to free speech under the First Amendment. Reversing a decision by the state court of appeals, the Texas Supreme Court held that the fee was content-neutral and satisfied the U.S. Supreme Court's test for content-neutral restrictions on symbolic speech. The court rejected the claim that the fee was a content-based tax that had to satisfy a constitutional strict scrutiny test. The fee was not directed at any expressive content in nude dancing, but, rather, at the negative secondary effects of nude dancing when alcohol was being consumed (e.g., sexual assault and abuse, prostitution, and disorderly conduct). The $5 fee per customer admitted was a minimal restriction on a business, and the business could avoid the fee by offering nude entertainment without allowing alcohol to be consumed. The case was remanded to the trial court to consider issues raised by the respondents under the Texas Constitution. *Combs v. Texas Entertainment Association, Inc., and Karpod, Inc..* Texas Supreme Court, No. 09-0481, August 26, 2011, CCH TEXAS TAX REPORTS, ¶403-747)

Persons subject to tax: The Texas admissions fee is imposed on a sexually oriented business. The business has discretion to determine the manner in which it derives the money to pay the fee and is not required to impose a fee on customers. (Sec. 47.052, Bus & Comm. Code) See ¶902 regarding the relationship of the fee to the sales tax.

¶1711

"Sexually oriented business" means a nightclub, bar, restaurant, or similar commercial enterprise that (1) provides live nude entertainment or live nude performances for an audience of two or more individuals; and (2) authorizes on-premises consumption of alcoholic beverages. (Sec. 47.051, Bus. & Comm. Code)

Fee rate: The fee is equal to $5 for each entry by each customer admitted to the business. (Sec. 47.052, Bus & Comm Code)

Payment: The fee must be remitted and reported to the Comptroller on a quarterly basis. (Sec. 47.053, Bus. & Comm. Code)

¶1711

PART VII

ADMINISTRATION AND PROCEDURE

CHAPTER 18
ADMINISTRATION, REPORTS, AND PAYMENT

¶1801	Overview of Administration and Procedure
¶1802	Administrative Agencies
¶1803	Reports and Payment
¶1804	Records and Confidentiality
¶1805	Electronic and Credit Card Payments

¶1801 Overview of Administration and Procedure

The general administrative provisions applicable to taxes administered by the Comptroller of Public Accounts (¶1802) are codified as Chapters 111—113 of the Tax Code. They establish a single set of rules and procedures for:

— refunds (¶2002);

— credits (¶2002);

— deficiency assessments (¶1901);

— protests and appeals (¶2003, 2005);

— report filing dates (¶1803);

— interest on deficiencies and refunds (¶1909, 2004);

— extensions of time (¶1803);

— lien priorities (¶1904);

— records (¶1804);

— requirements for electronic fund transfer payments (¶1805); and

— periods of limitations (¶1901).

They also establish rules for:

— record keeping (¶1804);

— settlement of tax claims and penalties (¶1903);

— deficiency assessments (¶1901);

— tax liens and levy (¶1904);

— seizure and sale of property (¶1905);

— injunctions (¶1908, 2006); and

— penalties (¶1909).

The provisions of Chapters 111—113 are also applicable to local sales and use taxes.

Some of the taxes that are subject to the provisions of the general administrative provisions contain some administrative and collection provisions applicable only to those particular taxes. The special administrative and collection provisions that relate to only one tax are discussed in the chapters covering that tax.

¶1801

¶1802 Administrative Agencies

Law: Secs. 111.001, 111.0021, Tax Code (CCH TEXAS TAX REPORTS, ¶89-082).

The following is a description of tax administrative bodies in Texas. The Secretary of State is also included because the Secretary of State administers and collects certain corporate organization and qualification fees; see Part VIII, "Doing Business in Texas."

The administrative bodies maintain offices in the state capital, Austin. See also the directory of Texas resources in Chapter 21, which provides addresses, phone numbers, e-mail addresses, and websites for all Texas taxing agencies.

Comptroller of Public Accounts: The Comptroller of Public Accounts is the chief tax administrator in Texas.

The Comptroller's office administers and collects the following taxes: alcoholic beverages tax (with Alcoholic Beverage Commission); cement tax; cigarette and tobacco taxes; controlled substances tax; estate tax; franchise tax; gasoline tax; general property tax (with local officers); hospital assessments; hotel occupancy tax; insurance tax (with Department of Insurance); lead-acid battery tax; mixed beverage tax; natural gas production tax; oil production tax; oil well service tax; petroleum tax; property tax on transportation business intangibles; public utilities tax (with Public Service Commission); sales and use taxes; severance beneficiary tax; and sulfur tax.

Secretary of State: The Secretary of State administers and collects the corporate organization and qualification fees (¶2201, ¶2202).

Alcoholic Beverage Commission: The Alcoholic Beverage Commission, with the Comptroller of Public Accounts and local officers, administers and collects the alcoholic beverage and bingo taxes.

Public Utility Commission: The utility tax is administered by this Commission (with Comptroller).

Department of Insurance: The Commissioner of Insurance administers the insurance tax with the Comptroller.

Texas Commission on Environmental Quality: This Commission administers hazardous waste fees and solid waste fees.

Railroad Commission: The Commission administers hazardous oil and gas waste generation fee provisions.

Workforce Commission: The Workforce Commission administers and collects the unemployment insurance tax.

Department of Transportation: The Department administers motor vehicle registration (with county officials) and motor carrier provisions.

Local taxing officers: The local taxing officers administer and collect the following taxes: general property tax (with Comptroller of Public Accounts); motor vehicle registration (with Department of Transportation); motor vehicle sales or use tax (with the Comptroller).

¶1803 Reports and Payment

Law: Secs. 111.051, 111.053—111.058, Tax Code; 34 TAC Secs. 3.1, 3.9 (CCH TEXAS TAX REPORTS, ¶89-102, 89-110).

The law imposing each tax contains provisions setting a payment due date and report filing date for that particular tax (the due date for a particular tax is discussed in the chapter of this *Guidebook* that covers the tax). However, the Comptroller has the authority to set dates other than those prescribed by statute; these dates prevail over

Part VII—Administration and Procedure **339**

those set by law. The only due dates that cannot be changed are those for paying and reporting state sales and use taxes (¶1103).

Weekends and holidays: If the last day for filing a report or making a payment of state tax falls on a Saturday, Sunday, or legal holiday, the report or payment is considered timely if made on the next day that is not a weekend or legal holiday.

Timeliness: A properly addressed report is considered filed at the time it is mailed or placed in the hands of a common or contract carrier. The postmark, or the receipt from a contract or common carrier, is *prima facie* evidence of the date on which the report was filed or payment made, but a different date may be established by competent evidence.

A report or tax payment is considered to be timely if a person exercises reasonable diligence to comply and, through no fault of the person, the report is not filed or payment is not made on time (see ¶1903 for a discussion of reasonable diligence). If a correct report and full tax payment is made within ten days after the filing date, the Comptroller has 90 days to assess penalty and interest (¶1909). If the Comptroller fails to assess penalty and interest, they are waived.

Restricted or conditional payments: Unless otherwise authorized, a taxpayer may not place any limits or restrictions on checks or money orders remitted to pay any taxes, penalties, or interest. (Sec. 111.051, Tax Code)

- *Electronic filing*

A taxpayer who paid $50,000 or more during the previous fiscal year must file reports electronically during the current fiscal year if the taxpayer has received a notice from the Comptroller at least 60 days prior to the report due date informing the taxpayer that electronic filing will be required. Waivers may be granted upon written request. (Sec. 111.0626, Tax. Code; 34 TAC Sec. 3.9)

Taxpayers required to make electronic payments of sales and use taxes, oil production tax, gas production tax, or payments under the International Fuel Tax Agreement (IFTA) must also file their returns electronically. (Sec. 111.0626, Tax. Code)

For a complete listing of the electronic filing requirements, see the Comptroller's Web site at: http://www.window.state.tx.us/webfile/required.html.

- *Extensions*

The Comptroller may grant a reasonable extension of time, not to exceed 45 days, for filing a tax report. To qualify, the taxpayer must submit to the Comptroller a written request with an explanation, prior to the due date for filing the return, and pay at least 90% of the estimated tax due at the time of the request.

If the extension request is denied, no late filing penalty (¶1909) is imposed if the report and payment are made within 10 days of the date of the denial. No interest is charged on late payment for the first 60 days (¶1909). The extension provisions apply to all taxes administered by the Comptroller except inheritance taxes.

The Comptroller may grant to individuals who are victims of a natural disaster an extension of time of up to 90 days for filing a report or paying a tax. The request for the extension must be given to the Comptroller before the expiration of 90 days after the original due date of the tax report. Penalty and interest for late filing are waived during the extended period.

CCH Practice Tip: Relief for Taxpayers Affected by Disasters

Businesses affected by disasters may postpone paying taxes owed to the state. Businesses will, upon request, be granted an extension of 90 days to file tax returns. (*Disaster Relief—Frequently Asked Questions*, Texas Comptroller of Public Accounts, http://www.window.state.tx.us/taxinfo/disaster_relief_faq.html)

¶1803

¶1804 Records and Confidentiality

Law: Secs. 111.006, 111.0036, 111.0041, Tax Code (CCH Texas Tax Reports, ¶89-136).

All tax records required to be kept by a taxpayer must be open for inspection by the Comptroller, the attorney general, or their authorized representative for four years. This retention period supersedes all others except the period set forth for the maintenance of sales records by a pistol dealer.

• *Confidentiality and disclosure*

Generally, any information from a federal income tax return or information secured, derived, or obtained by the Comptroller or the Attorney General during the course of an examination of the taxpayer's books, records, papers, officers, or employees is confidential.

However, under certain circumstances, confidential information may be:

— subpoenaed or used in a judicial or administrative proceeding in which Texas, another state, or the federal government is a party;

— used by the Comptroller or the Attorney General to enforce state taxation provision;

— disclosed to a municipality or county only for use in the enforcement or administration of its local hotel occupancy tax; or

— examined by a state officer, a law enforcement officer of Texas, a tax official of another state, a tax official of Mexico, an official of the United States, or an authorized representative of any of those officers or officials and, for an official of another state, the United States, or Mexico, a reciprocal agreement to allow such examinations exists.

Additional circumstances allowing disclosure apply to sales and use taxes only (¶1102).

The Comptroller is authorized to contract with another person to perform tax audits in one or more states that are not covered by a field office of the Comptroller. The Comptroller may provide that person with any confidential information in the Comptroller's custody relating to a taxpayer if the information is necessary to the audit of the taxpayer and if the Comptroller is not prohibited from sharing the information under an agreement with another state or the federal government. A person who receives such confidential information, and each employee or agent of that person, is subject to each prohibition against disclosure of confidential information that applies to the Comptroller or the Comptroller's employees and is subject to the same penalties and sanctions for improper disclosure that would apply to the Comptroller or an employee of the Comptroller.

It is a misdemeanor for the Comptroller or the Comptroller's employees, present or past, to disclose information on a federal return. A maximum $1,000 penalty or a one-year sentence, or both, is imposed following a conviction.

¶1805 Electronic and Credit Card Payments

Law: Secs. 111.062, 111.063, 111.0625, 111.0626, Tax Code; 34 TAC Sec. 3.9 (CCH Texas Tax Reports, ¶89-106, 89-108).

Taxpayers that paid $10,000 or more during the preceding fiscal year for the following taxes must make payments by electronic funds transfer (EFT) if the Comptroller reasonably expects the taxpayer will pay at least that amount during the current fiscal year:

— local sales and use taxes;

— direct payment sales taxes;

Part VII—Administration and Procedure

- gas and oil severance taxes;
- franchise taxes;
- gasoline and diesel fuel taxes;
- hotel occupancy taxes;
- insurance premium taxes;
- mixed beverage gross receipts taxes;
- motor vehicle rental taxes;
- telecommunications infrastructure fund assessments.

The Comptroller may add or delete the taxes impacted by this requirement if the Comptroller finds that the action is necessary. Also a waiver is available to taxpayers unable to comply due to hardship, impracticality, or other reason. (Sec. 111.0625, Tax Code; 34 TAC Sec. 3.9) See the Comptroller's Web site for the latest information: http://www.window.state.tx.us/webfile/required.html.

CCH Practice Tip: Combined groups

A combined group is required to electronically transmit payments if any member of the group receives notice that it is required to make payment electronically. (*Tax Policy News*, Vol. XVIII, Issue 5, Texas Comptroller of Public Accounts, May 2008)

Taxpayers who pay $100,000 or more in franchise tax must make their electronic payments via TEXNET. Taxpayers who paid $10,000 or more, but less than $100,000, can make their electronic payments by credit card or WebEFT when using WebFile, or may pay electronically via the Internet or telephone if they enroll in TEXNET. (*Tax Policy News*, Vol. XVIII, Issue 5, Texas Comptroller of Public Accounts, May 2008)

- *Penalties*

The Comptroller may impose a penalty of 5% of the tax due on a person who fails to pay by EFT or file electronically. This penalty is in addition to any other penalty provided by law.

A separate provision further states that a person's failure to transfer payment amounts by electronic funds transfer or to comply with the Comptroller's rules concerning electronic funds transfer may result in the assessment of a penalty by the state agency of 5% of the payment amount.

- *Protested tax payments*

The Comptroller may not require a protested tax payment to be made by an electronic funds transfer. Taxpayers who wish to submit protested tax payments by means of electronic funds transfer must deliver to one of the Comptroller's offices in Austin, within 24 hours of payment, a written statement of protest identifying the date of electronic payment, the taxpayer number, and the amount paid.

- *Credit card payments*

The Comptroller is authorized to accept a credit card in payment of a delinquent tax and related penalties and interest. The Comptroller may also accept a credit card payment for any service fee charged by the Comptroller, including the fee charged for an account status certificate, a no-tax-due certificate, postage, copies of documents or microfilm, written evidence of the Comptroller's records, research, labor, and a minerals tax history or extract. The Comptroller may impose a processing fee on taxpayers that use a credit card to pay the above taxes or fees.

¶1805

ADMINISTRATION AND PROCEDURE

CHAPTER 19
COLLECTION OF TAX

¶ 1901	Deficiency Assessments and Jeopardy Assessments
¶ 1902	Demand of Security for Tax
¶ 1903	Settlement of Tax Claims and Penalties
¶ 1904	Tax Liens and Levy
¶ 1905	Seizure and Sale of Property
¶ 1906	Suit to Collect Delinquent Taxes
¶ 1907	Assignment of Tax Claims
¶ 1908	Injunction and Revocation
¶ 1909	Penalties and Interest

¶1901 Deficiency Assessments and Jeopardy Assessments

Law: Secs. 111.008—111.009, 111.016, 111.020, 111.022, 111.024, 111.201, 111.203, 111.204, 111.205, 111.2051, 111.206, 111.207, Tax Code (CCH Texas Tax Reports, ¶ 89-144, 89-164, 89-166, 89-168, 89-228).

A written notice of the deficiency determination must be mailed or delivered personally to the taxpayer. Service is complete when the notice is deposited in the U.S. mail. A deficiency determination becomes final 30 days after the date on which the service of the notice of determination is completed unless a petition for redetermination (¶ 2003) is filed by the taxpayer. A deficiency determination is due and payable 10 days after it becomes final, and if not paid, a 10% penalty is added to the amount of the determination.

The Comptroller must issue a jeopardy determination that is due and payable immediately if the Comptroller believes that the collection of a tax required to be paid to the state, or the amount due for a tax period, is jeopardized by delay. A jeopardy determination becomes final on the expiration of 20 days after the day on which notice of the jeopardy determination is served by personal service or mail unless a petition for redetermination is filed in that time. A penalty of 10% of the amount and interest due is assessed if a jeopardy determination becomes final without payment being made.

- *Statute of limitations*

Generally, the Comptroller has four years from the date a tax becomes due and payable to make an assessment of any state tax. The period starts on the day after the last day a payment is required by the chapter of the Tax Code imposing the tax. In determining the expiration date for the limitations period, the following periods are not considered:

— the period following a tax payment made under protest, but only if a lawsuit is timely filed in accordance with Chapter 112;

— the period during which a judicial proceeding is pending to determine the amount of tax due;

— the period during which a redetermination proceeding or refund hearing is pending before the Comptroller; and

— the period during which a Title 11 bankruptcy case is pending.

The regular four-year limitations period does not apply, and the Comptroller may assess a tax *at any time* if:

— the taxpayer files a false or fraudulent report with intent to evade the tax;

— no report for the tax has been filed; or

— information in the report contains a gross error and the amount of additional tax is 25% or more greater than the amount initially reported.

Extension of limitations period: Taxpayers can consent to an extension of the limitations period for a deficiency assessment, refund claim, or for suit following a deficiency assessment.

Practitioner Comment: Tolling and the Commencement of a Bankruptcy Case

Texas Tax Code Sec. 111.207(c) includes a provision suspending limitations after a federal bankruptcy case commences under the United States Code, Title 11, but unlike Sec. 111.207(a), it only addresses assessments or collections. It is unclear whether this constitutes an express exception to the general rule that refunds or credits can be requested at any time before the expiration of the period during which the Comptroller may assess a deficiency covered in Sec. 111.107(a).

Sandi Farquharson, Ryan

Practitioner Comment: An Agreement to Waive the Statute of Limitations Does Not Toll Limitations

In determining the limitations expiration date for assessments or credits/refunds, the period covered by an agreement to extend the limitations period (assuming it is signed prior to the expiration of the limitations period) is only effective through the date stated in the agreement. In the absence of other circumstances that would toll limitations or give rise to an applicable exception, the period during which the agreement is in place must also be counted in determining whether limitations has expired.

Sandi Farquharson, Ryan

A single agreement cannot extend the limitations period for more than 24 months, although additional extension agreements may be made. The limitations period may be extended if:

— there is a possibility of a revenue loss without an extension;

— the taxpayer or the Comptroller needs time to complete or prepare an audit;

— circumstances beyond the control of the taxpayer or the Comptroller make an audit impractical or burdensome for either party without an extension; or

— an administrative or judicial determination is pending on an issue of law involved in an audit.

If a taxpayer has filed a timely refund claim, then notwithstanding the expiration of any limitations period, the Comptroller may assess a tax until the later of (1) four years after the date on which the claim is filed with the Comptroller; or (2) the expiration of the regular limitations period that applies to the assessment of a tax. This period of time for assessment is limited to the period of time and type of tax for which the refund is sought. The limitations period for filing a timely refund claim is not extended or tolled by the additional time for making assessments. The Texas Comptroller has taken the position that the filing of an Amended Statement of Grounds for a refund triggers another four year limitations period. (*Decision*, Hearing No. 44,870, Texas Comptroller of Public Accounts, March 5, 2008, CCH Texas Tax Reports, ¶ 403-545)

¶1901

Part VII—Administration and Procedure

The four-year limitations period does not apply when the amount of tax liability is affected by a final determination in an administrative proceeding of a local, state, or federal regulatory agency (including the Internal Revenue Service), or by a final determination in a judicial proceeding arising from such an administrative proceeding. The taxpayer must file a detailed report of the determination with the Comptroller within 120 days of its finality; the Comptroller then has one year from receipt of the report to assess a deficiency or to sue for collection. If the report is not filed within the 120-day period, the one-year limitation period begins upon receipt of the report or upon discovery of the determination, whichever is sooner.

If the final determination or investigation results in an overpayment, the limitations period for refunds and credits is likewise extended.

Practitioner Comment: Informally Reviewed Refunds

A refund claim filed before June 20, 2003, that is informally reviewed and resolved tolls limitations prior to the repeal of Tax Code Sec. 111.207(d). See *Strayhorn v. Willow Creek Resources, Inc.*, 161 S.W.3d 716 (Tex. App.—2005, no pet.). After June 20, 2003, the combination of Tax Code Sec. 111.1042 and the amendment to Sec. 111.207(a)(3) that replaced the phrase "redetermination proceeding" with "redetermination or refund hearing" may prevent an informal review of a claim from tolling limitations.

Sandi Farquharson, Ryan

- *Business successor liability*

A buyer of a business or stock of goods must withhold from the purchase price an amount sufficient to pay tax owed by the seller. The amount must be withheld by the purchaser until the seller provides the purchaser with either a receipt from the Comptroller showing that the tax has been paid or a certificate stating that no tax is due.

The purchaser of a business or stock of goods who fails to withhold such amount from the purchase price of the business or goods is liable, up to the value of the purchase price of the business, for the taxes owed by the business seller. Additionally, a purchaser is not relieved from liability even if he or she withholds amounts if (1) the amount withheld from the purchase price is not sufficient to fully satisfy the liability of the seller of the business or stock of goods, and (2) the purchase price paid to the seller for the business or stock of goods is not reasonably equivalent to the value of the business or stock of goods. Finally, a contract of sale providing that the purchaser is not responsible for the debts of the seller does not alter a purchaser's statutory liability for state taxes owed by the seller.

A purchaser need not buy all of a predecessor's assets to have business successory liability imposed. (*Decision of Comptroller of Public Accounts*, Hearing No. 44,506, January 12, 2006, CCH TEXAS TAX REPORTS, ¶403-034)

The statute of limitations on enforcement of the purchaser's liability for failure to withhold tax due from the business seller begins to run when, whichever occurs last, (1) the former owner of the business sells the business or stock of goods, or (2) a determination is made against the former business owner.

Request for statement from Comptroller: The purchaser of a business may request that the Comptroller issue a certificate stating that no tax is due from the business seller, or, in the alternative, issue a statement of the amount that must be paid before such a certificate may be issued. The Comptroller must issue the certificate or statement within 60 days after receiving the request or within 60 days after the records of the business seller are made available for audit, whichever period expires later. In any event, the Comptroller must issue the certificate or statement within 90 days after the date of receiving the request from the purchaser. The purchaser is released from the obligation to withhold from the purchase price the amount of state

¶1901

taxes due from the business seller if the Comptroller fails to mail the certificate or statement within the applicable period.

Fraudulent or sham transfers: A person who acquires a business or the assets of a business from a taxpayer through a fraudulent transfer or a sham transaction is liable for any tax, penalty, and interest owed by the taxpayer.

CCH Caution: Personal Liability

Texas is following a trend among states to hold corporate officers and directors, partners, and even employees personally liable for unpaid taxes. Any person who is under a duty to perform an act with respect to the collection, accounting, or payment of a tax or money to the state is considered a "responsible person" subject to personal liability. Currently, Texas limits personal liability to those taxes collected for and held in trust for the state, such as sales and use taxes and motor fuel taxes. Under Texas law, these responsible persons are liable for the payment of these "trust" taxes if they wilfully fail to pay or cause to be paid the tax or money collected. (Sec. 111.016(b), Tax. Code) However, many states that initially limited personal liability to "trust" taxes have expanded personal liability to *any* taxes owed to the state. Taxpayers should be on alert that Texas may follow this trend in the near future.

- *Officer liability*

Individual officers, managers, and directors of business are subject to personal liability for fraudulent tax evasion, to the extent the Comptroller was unable to secure any tax, penalty, and interest due from the entity. (Sec. 111.0611, Tax. Code) However, individuals who had been corporate officers when a corporation's Texas franchise tax report was due, but who resigned before the corporate debt was incurred after the report was not filed, were not personally liable for the corporation's debts. (*Paccar Financial Corp. v. Potter*, Texas Court of Appeals, Fifth District, No. 05-05-00403-CV, October 31, 2007, CCH TEXAS TAX REPORTS, ¶403-338)

¶1902 Demand of Security for Tax

Law: Sec. 111.012, Tax Code (CCH TEXAS TAX REPORTS, ¶89-178).

A taxpayer may be required to provide security or establish a tax escrow account at a bank or other financial institution if the Comptroller believes that the tax payment due is insecure. If security is required, the amount and form of the security as calculated by the Comptroller may not exceed twice the amount of taxes estimated to be due from the taxpayer during the succeeding 12 months. Security may be in the form of cash deposits, surety bonds, or any other security acceptable to the Comptroller. The Comptroller may not require a taxpayer to establish a tax escrow account unless the Comptroller has determined that the taxpayer remitted or should have remitted a monthly average of $500 or more in tax collected from the taxpayer's customers during the preceding six months.

Some individual tax statutes also require the posting of security; see the discussions of specific taxes for details.

¶1903 Settlement of Tax Claims and Penalties

Law: Secs. 111.101—111.103, Tax Code (CCH TEXAS TAX REPORTS, ¶89-186).

The Comptroller is authorized to settle a claim for tax, penalty, or interest before the filing of a redetermination petition (¶2003) if the total costs of collection would exceed the total amount due. The Comptroller may also settle a claim for refund of tax, penalty, or interest if the total costs of defending a denial of the claim would exceed the total amount claimed.

The Comptroller may settle a claim for a tax, penalty, or interest only if the taxpayer exercised "reasonable diligence" in complying with the provisions of the

¶1902

Part VII—Administration and Procedure **347**

Tax Code. The issue of what constitutes "reasonable diligence" is heavily litigated. The Comptroller has indicated several factors for determining "reasonable diligence" including:

— the size and tax sophistication of the taxpayer;

— the clarity or ambiguity of the statutes and rules applicable to a particular case;

— whether the taxpayer has been audited before, and if so, whether the same or similar errors were uncovered; and

— the relative size of the deficiency with respect to tax remitted on returns and whether orderly and complete records were kept. (*Decision of Comptroller of Public Accounts,* Hearing No. 19,095, September 23, 1986; CCH TEXAS TAX REPORTS, ¶ 89-186.65)

In most of the litigated cases, the major factors have been the last two listed above. In the majority of cases in which the taxpayer was successful in obtaining a waiver, it was the taxpayer's first audit. (*Decision of Comptroller of Public Accounts,* Hearing No. 19,685, October 13, 1986; CCH TEXAS TAX REPORTS, ¶ 89-186.66, *Decision of Comptroller of Public Accounts,* Hearing No. 17,087, December 18, 1986; CCH TEXAS TAX REPORTS, ¶ 89-186.667) The taxpayer was also successful when the amount of the deficiency was much lower than the deficiency uncovered in a prior audit. (*Decision of Comptroller of Public Accounts,* Hearing No. 19,529, October 21, 1986; CCH TEXAS TAX REPORTS, ¶ 89-186.662)

¶ 1904 Tax Liens and Levy

Law: Secs. 111.021, 111.0102, 113.001, 113.0021, 113.006—113.008, 113.101, 113.105, Tax Code (CCH TEXAS TAX REPORTS, ¶ 89-172, 89-176).

All taxes, fines, interest, and penalties constitute a general lien on all property, real and personal, that is subject to execution and that, at the time the lien attaches, belongs to the taxpayer. The lien attaches on the day the tax becomes due and payable and continues until the tax secured by the lien has been paid. The state tax lien on personal property and real estate also attaches to personal property and real estate acquired by the taxpayer beginning on the first day of the period for which the lien is filed by the state.

The filing and recording of a state tax lien by the Comptroller with the county clerk serves as a public record of the existence of the lien. One tax lien notice is sufficient to cover all taxes of any nature administered by the Comptroller that may have accrued before or after the filing of the notice.

Bona fide purchasers, mortgagees, holders of a deed of trust, judgment creditors, and other lienholders whose rights in the delinquent taxpayer's property arise before a notice of tax lien is filed are not affected by a subsequently filed state tax lien.

The provisions concerning state tax liens apply not only to state taxes imposed under Title 2 of the Tax Code (¶ 1802), but also to taxes and fees that the Comptroller is required to collect under laws not included in Title 2.

- *Release of lien*

A tax lien is released upon payment of the taxes, penalties, and interest secured by the lien as well as all other taxes, penalties, interest, fees, or sums that the taxpayer owes the state and that are administered or collected by the Comptroller. A lien may also be released by the Comptroller, on approval of the Attorney General, for a specific piece of real or personal property, conditioned on payment of a reasonable cash market value on the specific property, as determined by the Comptroller.

- *Levy by notice to third person*

The Comptroller may, by notice, freeze the transfer of assets owned by a delinquent taxpayer and held, controlled, or owed to the taxpayer by a third person, and then, by notice, levy on such assets if a taxpayer is delinquent in the payment of a state tax, or has not paid an amount claimed in a determination made against him or her. The notice may be given at any time within three years after the tax payment becomes delinquent or within three years after the last recording of a state tax lien against the delinquent taxpayer. The notice must state the amount of taxes, penalties, and interest due and owing, and the additional amount of penalties and interest that will accrue by operation of law in a period not to exceed 30 days. The notice is, in the case of a credit, bank, or savings account or deposit, effective only up to the amount specified in the notice.

The person receiving the notice must within 20 days after receiving the notice advise the Comptroller of each asset belonging to the delinquent taxpayer that is possessed or controlled by the person receiving the notice, and of each debt owed by the person receiving the notice to the delinquent taxpayer. The person receiving the notice may not transfer or dispose of the asset or debt of the delinquent taxpayer possessed, controlled, or owed by the person receiving the notice for a period of 60 days after receipt of the notice without the consent of the Comptroller. The person may not avoid or attempt to avoid compliance with the notice by filing an interpleader action in court and depositing the delinquent's or person's funds or other assets into the registry of the court. A person who disposes of the asset before the expiration of the 60-day period is liable to the state for the amount of the delinquency stated in the notice plus an additional penalty equal to 50% of the amount sought to be frozen or levied. (Sec. 111.021, Tax Code)

Within the last 45 days of the 60-day period during which the transfer or disposal of property of a delinquent taxpayer in the possession or control of a third person is prohibited under a notice of freeze, the Comptroller may levy on the asset or debt so held or owed by the third person on whom the notice of freeze was served. The person receiving the notice of levy, on receipt of the notice, must transfer the asset belonging to the delinquent taxpayer to the Comptroller or pay to the Comptroller the amount owed by such person to the delinquent taxpayer. A person acting upon a notice of levy is discharged from any obligation or liability to the delinquent taxpayer.

- *Action to challenge collection efforts*

A suit brought to challenge or avoid a collection action or state tax lien must be brought in the district courts of Travis County. (Sec. 111.0102, Tax Code)

¶1905 Seizure and Sale of Property

Law: Secs. 111.017—111.019, 111.0102, Tax Code (CCH Texas Tax Reports, ¶¶89-162, 89-176).

Before the expiration of three years after a person becomes delinquent in the payment of any state tax, the Comptroller may seize and sell at public auction any real and personal property of the person that is not exempt from execution. The delinquent taxpayer must receive notice at least 20 days before the date of the sale. The notice must also be published for at least ten days before the date of the sale in a newspaper of general circulation published in the county in which the seized property is to be sold. However, publication of notice in a newspaper is not required if the estimated value of the property to be sold is less than $40,000. For property valued at less than $40,000, the Comptroller may notify potential buyers of the seized property by any means that is reasonable and cost-effective to the state under the circumstances.

The Comptroller may sell seized property at public auction, as provided in the notice, and may deliver to the purchaser a bill of sale for personal property sold and a deed for real property sold. The bill of sale or deed vests in the purchaser the interest or title in the property held by the delinquent taxpayer. The Comptroller may leave unsold property at the place of sale at the risk of the delinquent taxpayer.

- *Interference with seizure and sale procedures*

A person who obstructs or interfere with the Comptroller's seizure of the property of a delinquent taxpayer by trespass, removal, destruction, or other actions is subject to a Class A misdemeanor. (Sec. 111.017, Tax Code)

¶1906 Suit to Collect Delinquent Taxes

Law: Secs. 111.010, 111.013, 111.108, 111.202, Tax Code (CCH TEXAS TAX REPORTS, ¶89-180).

The Comptroller of Public Accounts, through the Attorney General, has three years from the date a deficiency or jeopardy determination becomes due and payable, or from the last recording of a lien, in which to file suit to collect delinquent taxes, penalties, and interest. A judgment in favor of the state bears interest at the rate of 10% per year from the day the judgment was signed to the date of satisfaction. Suit may be brought in the district courts of Travis County, in a federal court, or in the court of another state.

The taxpayer may deny a claim for taxes, penalties, or interest only by filing a sworn statement that specifically identifies the amounts at issue and asserts that they are not due.

- *Burden of proof*

Texas law expressly provides that a Comptroller's certificate of delinquency is prima facie evidence of the stated amount and the delinquency of the taxes, penalties and interest, after all just and lawful offsets, payments, and credits. The Comptroller's delinquency certificates create a presumption of the correctness of the taxing authority's claim, which the taxpayer has the burden to overcome. If unrebutted, the certificates are sufficient to establish as a matter of law, the amount the taxpayer owes. In order to overcome the presumption of correctness, the taxpayer must provide evidence "tending to support the contrary as would be conclusive, or evidence which would be so clear and positive it would be unreasonable not to give effect to it as conclusive." (*Wimmer v. State of Texas*, Texas Court of Appeals, Third District, No. 03-03-00135-CV, February 5, 2004, CCH TEXAS TAX REPORTS, ¶402-640)

- *Suit to recover erroneous refunds*

The Comptroller may bring suit to recover erroneously paid refunds, or an erroneously allowed credit in a jeopardy or deficiency determination, within four years after the date of the refund or credit. The four-year period for suing to recover erroneous refunds or credits does not extend or toll the limitations period allowed to a taxpayer for filing a refund claim.

¶1907 Assignment of Tax Claims

Law: Secs. 111.251, 111.252, 111.254, Tax Code (CCH TEXAS TAX REPORTS, ¶89-172).

The state's rights, liens, judgments, and remedies to enforce the payment of delinquent taxes may be assigned to one who voluntarily pays another's tax, fine, penalty, and interest or pays on a judgment for those taxes. Upon payment, the assignee becomes subrogated to and succeeds to the state's enforcement rights. The taxpayer must be given 30 days' prior notice of the assignment by certified mail. Assignments may be reassigned, and all the state's rights, liens, judgments, and remedies pass to each person receiving a reassignment, if notice of the assignment is given and reassignment is not limited in writing.

¶1908 Injunction and Revocation

Law: Secs. 111.0046, 111.047, 111.011, Tax Code (CCH Texas Tax Reports, ¶89-236).

The Texas Attorney General may sue for an injunction prohibiting a taxpayer from continuing business operations until delinquent withholding reports are filed or tax paid.

The Attorney General must also bring suit for an injunction prohibiting such practice against a person engaged in a business that involves the receipt, collection, or withholding of a tax who either (1) receives, collects, or withholds more tax than authorized by law; or (2) receives, collects, or withholds money under a false claim that it is a tax authorized by law. Prior to filing suit against such a taxpayer, the Attorney General must send written notice by certified mail requesting that the person cease any wrongful collections and must allow 15 days from the date of the notice for compliance.

Venue: Either suit is brought in Travis County.

- *Refusal or revocation of permits or licenses*

The Comptroller must refuse to issue or renew any permit or license of a person who is either not permitted or licensed as required by law for a different tax or activity administered by the Comptroller, or currently delinquent in the payment of any tax collected by the Comptroller. The Comptroller may also establish minimum age requirements to apply for permits or licenses.

Also, if a person fails to comply with the Tax Code or with a rule of the Comptroller, the Comptroller may revoke or suspend any permit or license issued by the Comptroller to such person after a hearing has been held. The Comptroller must give 20 days' written notice of the time and place of a hearing on the proposed revocation or suspension to the permittee or licensee. After the hearing, the Comptroller must give written notice of the revocation or suspension of a permit or license to the holder of the permit or license.

A taxpayer may appeal the revocation or suspension of a permit or license in the same manner that appeals are made from a final deficiency determination (¶2003). A new permit or license may not be issued to a former holder of a revoked permit or license unless the Comptroller is satisfied that the former holder will comply with provisions of the Tax Code and with rules of the Comptroller relating to the Tax Code.

¶1909 Penalties and Interest

Law: Secs. 111.002, 111.0021, 111.060, 111.061, Tax Code (CCH Texas Tax Reports, ¶89-192, 89-202, 89-208).

Civil and criminal penalties for failure to report or to pay taxes on time are imposed by the law for each specific tax; see the discussions of the specific taxes for details. However, a provision applicable to all state taxes imposed under Title 2 of the Tax Code (¶1802) states that noncompliance with a Comptroller's rule adopted for the enforcement of the provisions of Title 2 is subject to a forfeiture of between $25 to $500 for each day the violation continues. Any other provision of the Tax Code that imposes a different penalty for violation of a Comptroller's rule prevails. The general provisions concerning penalties apply not only to state taxes imposed under Title 2, but also to other taxes or fees that the Comptroller is required to collect.

A general penalty of 5% of the tax due is imposed for failure to timely report or to pay a state or local tax authorized under the Tax Code. An additional 5% penalty is imposed if the failure to file the report or pay the tax continues for more than 30 days. An additional penalty of 50% of the tax due is imposed if the failure to file or pay is the result of fraud or an intent to evade the tax. The additional 50% penalty is also

Part VII—Administration and Procedure

imposed if a taxpayer alters, destroys, or conceals any record, document, or thing, or presents to the Comptroller any altered or fraudulent record, document, or thing, or otherwise engages in fraudulent conduct, for the apparent purpose of affecting the course or outcome of an audit, investigation, redetermination, or other proceeding before the Comptroller.

Another provision applicable to all taxes imposes a 10% penalty on any deficiency assessment not paid within 10 days after it becomes final or within 20 days after a Comptroller's decision in a redetermination hearing becomes final (¶2003).

A person is guilty of a Class A misdemeanor if he or she obstructs, hinders, impedes, or interferes with the Comptroller's seizure of a delinquent taxpayer's property. (Sec. 111.017, Tax Code)

- *Interest*

Interest on delinquent state taxes is imposed at the prime rate plus 1% per year. Delinquent taxes begin to draw interest 60 days after the date due. The 60-day grace period does not apply to taxes imposed on the sale, rental, or use of motor vehicles, or under motor fuels tax cooperative agreements with other states. The rate for the 2009 and 2010 calendar years was 4.25%.

Practitioner Comment: Why You May Be Paying a Higher Rate

For delinquent taxes that were due before January 1, 2000, the interest rate does not vary annually and is set at 12%, even if the tax remains unpaid during the periods January 1, 2000, forward. For most taxes due on or after January 1, 2000, the rate will vary annually. See applicable rates at: http://window.state.tx.us/taxinfo/int_rate.html.

Sandi Farquharson, Ryan

ADMINISTRATION AND PROCEDURE

CHAPTER 20
TAXPAYER REMEDIES

¶2001	Taxpayer's Choice of Remedies
¶2002	Refunds, Credits, and Offsets
¶2003	Redetermination After Deficiency Assessment
¶2004	Suit for Refund
¶2005	Suit to Protest Tax
¶2006	Tax Injunction

¶2001 Taxpayer's Choice of Remedies

Following a deficiency assessment, a dissatisfied taxpayer may take the following actions:

— file a petition for redetermination and obtain an administrative hearing before the Comptroller (¶2003);

— pay the deficiency assessment under protest and sue to recover the taxes without a prior administrative hearing (¶2005); or

— post security for the deficiency and sue for an injunction (¶2006).

A taxpayer who discovers that a tax has been erroneously paid and no deficiency assessment has been made may file a claim for refund and obtain an administrative hearing before the Comptroller.

¶2002 Refunds, Credits, and Offsets

Law: Secs. 301.103, 301.104, 301.106, Labor Code; Secs. 111.064, 111.104, 111.1042, 111.105, 111.107, 111.109, 111.206, 111.207, 112.060, Tax Code; 34 TAC Secs. 3.2, 3.4 (CCH TEXAS TAX REPORTS, ¶5-106, 89-204, 89-224).

Taxes, penalties, or interest that have been unlawfully or erroneously collected are first applied against any amount due from the taxpayer; any excess is refunded. This offset procedure applies to all taxes and license fees collected or administered by the Comptroller, except those sales and use taxes paid for the purchase of machinery and equipment used in manufacturing or for machinery or equipment used in the repair of jet turbine aircraft engines (¶1002).

No tax, penalty, or interest may be refunded to a person who has collected the amount from another person until the amount collected is first refunded to the party from whom it was originally collected.

In addition, the Comptroller may subtract the amount of delinquent taxes owed by a taxpayer under a tax administered or collected by the Comptroller from any amount due the taxpayer from the state and may issue a warrant for the difference. Amounts deemed to be current wages owed to the taxpayer by the state are specifically excluded from this offset procedure. Written notice must be given to the taxpayer at least 20 days before the date of the offset.

- *Refund for wages paid to employees receiving financial assistance*

A refund of any tax paid to the state, administered by the Comptroller (¶1802), and deposited to the general revenue fund without dedication is authorized for wages paid by a taxpayer to employees who receive state financial assistance and for whom the taxpayer provides or pays for a portion of the cost of qualifying health benefit coverage. The refund may be claimed against the following taxes paid, or collected and remitted, in the calendar year for which the refund is sought: franchise tax, state sales and use tax (but not local sales and use taxes), boat and boat motor sales and use tax, manufactured housing sales and use tax, public utility gross receipts tax, and hotel occupancy tax.

The amount of the refund is 20% of total wages, up to $10,000 per employee, paid or incurred by the taxpayer for an employee's services rendered during the employee's first year of employment for the taxpayer. Refunds are allowed on a calendar year basis. A refund for a calendar year may not exceed the amount of net tax paid by the taxpayer to the state, after any other applicable tax credits, in that calendar year.

Procedure: Taxpayers must apply to the Texas Workforce Commission on or after January 1 but before April 1 for a tax refund voucher for wages paid during the prior calendar year to an employee receiving financial assistance. A taxpayer is eligible for a voucher if the taxpayer pays wages to an employee who is a Texas resident and if the Texas Workforce Commission certifies that the employee received state financial assistance and services on or before the first day of employment by the taxpayer.

Qualification: Wages paid by an employer to an employee will qualify for the tax refund if the employer provides and pays, for the employee's benefit, "a part of" the cost of coverage under:

— a health plan provided by a health maintenance organization established under the Texas Health Maintenance Organization Act;

— a health benefit plan approved by the Texas Commissioner of Insurance; or

— a self-funded or self-insured employee welfare benefit plan that provides health benefits and is established in accordance with the federal Employee Retirement Income Security Act of 1974. ("ERISA," 29 U.S.C. § § 1001 *et seq.*)

- *Refund claims*

In general, a request for a refund or credit for an overpayment of a state tax must be made within four years from the date the tax becomes due and payable. However, a person may not refile a refund claim for the same transaction or item, tax type, period, and ground or reason that was previously denied by the Comptroller. Other exceptions to the limitations period are listed at ¶1901. In the case of erroneous payment, the refund claim and its denial is a prerequisite to suit for refund (¶2004); but if payment is made under protest (¶2005), filing a refund claim with the Comptroller is optional and not a condition to a refund suit.

Limitations period: The claim may be filed only by the person who directly paid the tax or by the person's attorney, assignee, or other successor and must be filed before the expiration of the applicable limitation period, or within six months after a jeopardy or deficiency determination becomes final, whichever period is later. The limitation period, however, can be extended by agreement of the Comptroller and the taxpayer (¶1901).

Practitioner Comment: Refund Contentions Not Pled Are Lost

House Bill 2425, Laws 2003, sharply limits the statute of limitations for filing refund claims. The amended language provides the period to file a refund claim is only held open for "issues that were contested." Taxpayers can no longer rely on the tolling provisions that applied during the pendency of a redetermination or administrative

¶2002

Part VII—Administration and Procedure

hearing under prior law. Accordingly, unless all refund contentions are pled prior to the expiration of the four-year statute of limitations or any applicable limitations extension agreement, such refunds will be lost.

G. Brint Ryan, Ryan

See ¶1106 for a discussion of the tolling provisions for taxpayers that hold direct payment permits.

Appeal of denial: A person claiming a refund of taxes, interest, or penalties may request a hearing within 30 days from the date of denial. The person is entitled to 20 days' notice of the time and place of the hearing. During the hearing, the Comptroller may not consider any evidence submitted after the date set for submission of evidence.

The Comptroller may grant or deny a refund claim through an informal review, which is not a hearing or contested case and does not impair the right to a hearing on a refund claim.

- *Interest on refunds and credits*

Interest on refunds and on credits of erroneously paid taxes is allowed at the prime rate plus 1% for periods beginning 60 days after the payment date or the due date of the tax report, whichever is later, and ending on either the date of allowance of a credit or a date not more than 10 days before the date of the refund warrant. For tax refunds claimed after September 1, 2005, the interest rate is the lesser of (1) the prime rate on the first business day in January of each year plus 1%; or (2) the annual rate of interest earned on state treasury deposits during December of the previous year.

The interest rate for 2009 is 2.511% (4.764% for 2008, 5.066% for 2007, 4.06825% for 2006, and 6.25% for 2005).

The provisions regarding interest on refunds and credits do not apply to real or personal property tax or to the Comptroller's cooperative agreements with other states for the exchange of information and auditing of interstate motor fuel users.

Practitioner Comment: The Short Life of Equality in Interest Rates

Effective September 1, 2005 interest on tax refunds is no longer calculated solely at the prime rate of interest plus 1%. Interest on tax refunds is calculated at the lesser of the annual rate of interest earned on deposits in the state treasury (historically a rate lower than the prime rate) during December of the previous calendar year or the prime rate of interest plus 1%.

As with prior law, no interest is paid on refunds for report periods prior to January 1, 2000. For a refund claimed before September 1, 2005, and granted for a report period due on or after January 1, 2000, the rate of interest remains at the prime rate of interest plus 1%. With this change, the law again creates a differential between the rate of interest paid on tax refunds and tax deficiencies, an inequity Texas Comptroller Carole Strayhorn eliminated during her first term in office. (See Section 111.064, Tax Code S.B. 1570, Laws 2005)

G. Brint Ryan, Ryan

¶2003 Redetermination After Deficiency Assessment

Law: Secs. 111.0081, 111.009, 111.022, Tax Code; 34 TAC Secs. 1.5, 1.6, 1.8, 1.13, 1.21, 1.27, 1.28 (CCH TEXAS TAX REPORTS, ¶¶ 89-228, 89-234).

Practitioner Comment: DRO Conference Replaced by IAR

Comptroller Susan Combs, addressing the deficiencies of the former Dispute Resolution Officer (DRO) conference, has established a new dispute resolution program. The new Internal Audit Review (IAR) conference is designed to resolve tax disputes prior to administrative hearing. Unlike the former DRO conference, the IAR process allows taxpayers to meet with Comptroller personnel not assigned to the Audit Division and not involved in the audit process. The IAR conference is available for most non-agreed audits, except for cases where no records are provided or where a tax policy determination has been issued on the matter in dispute by the Comptroller's Tax Policy Division.

Procedures for the IAR are summarized in Comptroller's Audit Directive 53 adopted May 17, 2007.

G. Brint Ryan, Ryan

If a taxpayer is dissatisfied with the results of the IAR conference, the taxpayer may request mediation prior to filing an appeal with the State Office of Administrative Hearings. See the Comptroller's Web site for additional information: http://www.window.state.tx.us/taxinfo/taxprocess/.

Petitions for redetermination of a deficiency assessment or refund claim denial must be filed before the expiration of 30 days after service of the notice of a deficiency assessment or refund denial or within 20 days after the date a notice of a jeopardy assessment is served on the taxpayer. If no petition for redetermination is filed, the deficiency determination is final upon expiration of the filing period.

The petition must include a statement of grounds that sets out in detail the reason the taxpayer does not agree with the deficiency or jeopardy determination. The Comptroller allows a taxpayer that has timely requested redetermination pursuant to raise any issue to challenge the assessment and to raise any credit issues to offset the same. An extension of the due date for submitting a request for redetermination and a statement of grounds may be granted if filed prior to the deadline, but only in cases of emergency or extraordinary circumstances.

If the determination or billing is amended, or a refund or credit is issued, the action will become final 20 days after notification, unless the taxpayer files another petition for redetermination. An amended billing or determination is payable 20 days after it becomes final unless otherwise specified. (34 TAC Sec. 1.8) If the Assistant General Counsel does not accept the taxpayer's petition, the counsel will prepare a position letter outlining his or her position regarding each of the taxpayer's contentions. A taxpayer must accept or reject the position letter within 45 days of receipt, unless an extension is granted. A taxpayer that rejects the position letter must submit the selection form along with two copies of its reply setting forth all of its arguments in support of its position and all supportive documents, affidavits, and other evidence. The Position Letter may be modified. A new 45-day period for acceptance or rejection by the taxpayer begins on the day the modified Position Letter is dated. Additional details concerning the procedures and timelines for filing responses and modified position letters are contained in 34 TAC Secs. 1.7 through 1.10.

Practice Tip: Tax Appeals Transferred to State Office of Administrative Hearings

Applicable to hearings filed after June 15, 2007, the Tax Division of the State Office of Administrative Hearings (SOAH) is statutorily required to hear all contested tax cases in relation to the collection, receipt, administration, and enforcement of all taxes imposed under the Tax Code and any other tax, fee, or other amount that the Comptroller is required to collect, receive, administer, or enforce under other law provisions.

Part VII—Administration and Procedure

Procedures relating to cases filed before June 15, 2007, will continue as they existed prior to that date or as provided by an interagency cooperation contract entered into between the comptroller and SOAH and in effect on that date.

Hearings related to the following items are not considered contested tax cases that will be heard by the SOAH:

— property valuation study hearings;
— certain unclaimed property issues;
— forfeiture of a right to do business;
— a certificate of authority;
— articles of incorporation;
— the penalty for failing to file a report more than two times;
— the Comptroller's refusal to settle a contested tax issue; and
— a request for or revocation of a tax exemption.

An administrative law judge in the Tax Division will issue a proposal for decision for each hearing conducted that includes findings of fact and conclusions of law. The proposal for decision must also include the legal reasoning and other analysis considered by the judge in reaching the decision.

The Comptroller may change a finding of fact or conclusion of law made by the administrative law judge, or vacate or modify an order, if the Comptroller:

— finds that the ALJ did not properly apply or interpret applicable law, then existing comptroller rules or policies, or prior administrative decisions, or issued a finding of fact that is not supported by a preponderance of the evidence;
— determines that a Comptroller policy or a prior administrative decision on which the ALJ relied is incorrect.

A taxpayer can elect between either an oral hearing or a written submission hearing. If no election is made, the default is the case being docketed by SOAH as a written submission hearing. Requests for conversion may be considered. Only the Comptroller can refer a case to SOAH by filing a Request to Docket a Case Form. However, procedural or other preliminary disputes can be referred to SOAH by either party.

The administrative law judge must give the taxpayer at least 20 days' notice before a hearing is held or the record is closed. If a party has additional arguments and evidence to file, they should request leave to make such a filing. The motion should be filed no later than 7 days before the oral hearing or record close date. The length of each hearing is limited to two hours, but the administrative law judge may, on a showing of good cause, schedule a longer hearing.

Within 30 days after the record of the hearing is closed, the administrative law judge will prepare a proposal for decision and serve it on the parties. Under 1 TAC Sec. 155.59, any party may file exceptions and a brief within 15 days, and the other party will have 15 days to reply. An additional 3 days is provided if the proposal for decision is served by mail. The proposal for decision can either be amended, or the administrative law judge may issue a letter to the Comptroller with a recommendation regarding the disposition of each of the exceptions.

The proposal for decision of the administrative law judge is not effective until it is approved by the Comptroller. The Comptroller's decision will be sent to the taxpayer and is final 20 days from the date it is served on the taxpayer. If a motion for rehearing is filed, the Comptroller's decision becomes final on the date the motion is overruled.

The amount of a deficiency determination is due and payable 20 days after a Comptroller's decision in a redetermination hearing becomes final. If not so paid, a penalty of 10% is added to the amount of the determination.

¶2003

If a hearing is requested on the redetermination petition, a hearing will be granted and the taxpayer given at least 20 days' notice of the hearing date. The Comptroller's decision on the petition for redetermination becomes final 20 days after it is served on the taxpayer. The amount of a deficiency determination is due and payable 20 days after a Comptroller's decision in a redetermination hearing becomes final and if not so paid, a penalty of 10% is added to the amount of the determination.

Hearing procedure: For hearings filed after June 14, 2007, the rules and procedures established by the Texas Administrative Procedure Act govern the conduct of the redetermination hearings. Under these rules, notice of the hearing must be given at least 10 days in advance of the hearing and rules of evidence generally apply. Hearings are confidential and not open to the public and all taxpayer identification information must be kept confidential. (Sec. 2003.101, et seq.)

Practitioner Comment: Beware of the Waiver of Motion for Rehearing

In *El Paso Natural Gas v. Strayhorn, Comptroller*, 208 S.W.3d 676 (Tex. App. 2006), CCH TEXAS TAX REPORTS, ¶ 403-169, the taxpayer signed a Waiver of Motion for Rehearing shortly after a decision was issued in a redetermination case in order to expedite its refund. In order to pursue other unsolved issues, the taxpayer subsequently filed a refund request exactly six months after the date the Decision became final as stated in the Order of the Decision, which would constitute a timely refund claim. The Court of Appeals held that the filing of the Waiver of Motion for Rehearing constituted a new final date for the Decision and that the subsequent refund claim was not within the statute of limitations because the refund claim was filed more than six months after the final date of the decision using the new final date determined by the Waiver of Motion for Rehearing.

Eric L. Stein, Ryan

¶2004 Suit for Refund

Law: Secs. 112.001, 112.151, 112.1512, 112.155, 112.156, Tax Code (CCH TEXAS TAX REPORTS ¶ 89-224).

A person may sue the Comptroller following denial of a refund claim if the person has (1) filed a refund claim; (2) filed a motion for rehearing that has been denied; and (3) paid any additional tax found due in a jeopardy or deficiency assessment.

Suit must be brought against both the Comptroller and the Attorney General and filed in a district court in Travis County within 30 days after the Comptroller's denial of a rehearing motion. The state may counterclaim in a taxpayer's refund suit if the counterclaim relates to taxes or fees imposed under the same statute and during the same period as the taxes or fees that are the subject of the suit. The counterclaim must be filed no later than the 30th day before the date set for trial.

Practitioner Comment: Judgment Interest

Tax Code Sec. 112.155(c) entitles a taxpayer to interest on the amount included in a judgment in the taxpayer's favor. The interest accrues beginning on the date the tax was paid. The rate of interest paid varies and is based upon the amount of interest that would be due if the tax had been deposited in the suspense account of the Comptroller.

Sandi Farquharson, Ryan

The rule of *res judicata* applies only when the issues and the liability periods in controversy are the same as were finally decided in a previous judgment entered in a Texas court of record in a suit between the same parties.

Part VII—Administration and Procedure

¶2005 Suit to Protest Tax

Law: Secs. 112.051—112.054, 112.056, 112.060, 112.108, Tax Code; 34 TAC Sec. 3.9 (CCH Texas Tax Reports, ¶89-236).

A taxpayer who is required to pay any tax or fee administered by the Comptroller (¶1802) and who believes that such a tax is erroneous or unlawful may file a written protest along with the payment of the tax.

Practitioner Comment: Omission of Basis for the Claim Is Not a Curable Defect

The protest letter included with the payment may not have to state that a "refund" is requested (but should state so, if applicable), but does have to state the grounds for the claim. Merely stating that an amount is being paid under protest does not give the district court jurisdiction to determine the claim, but is sufficient for a declaratory judgment claim on purely constitutional grounds. (*Local Neon Co., Inc. v. Strayhorn*, 2005 Tex. App. LEXIS 4667 (Tex. App.—Austin 2005), CCH Texas Tax Reports, ¶402-925)

Sandi Farquharson, Ryan

In the case of the corporation franchise tax for a regular annual period, if an extension to file has been granted and the report is filed within the extension period, the protest may be filed with the report to cover the entire amount of tax paid for the period, and the suit for recovery of the entire amount of tax paid for the period may be filed before the 91st day after the date the report was filed.

Taxpayers who are required to pay taxes by means of electronic funds transfer (¶1805) may make protested payments by other means if a written statement of protest accompanies the nonelectronic payment.

A taxpayer who files an oath of inability to pay a tax, penalties, and interest due may be excused from the requirement of prepayment of a state tax as a prerequisite to appeal if the court, after notice and hearing, finds that such prepayment would constitute an unreasonable restraint on the party's right of access to the courts.

Protest payments must be made within the time period set out for the filing of refund claims (¶2002); generally, that is within four years from the date the tax was due and payable. The taxpayer must bring suit in a state district court in Travis County to recover the tax within 90 days of filing the protest. The suit must be brought against the public official charged with the duty of collecting the tax or fee, the Comptroller, and the attorney general.

Any taxes that become due prior to the trial court proceeding and during the appeal of the decision must be paid on time. Prior to trial, a taxpayer who objects to continued liability on the same grounds as stated in the original written protest may file a written protest with payment and may then amend the original petition to the trial court at any time until five days before the date of the court hearing or may elect to file a separate suit for the additional protested taxes. Pending the result of an appeal, the taxpayer must continue to make payments under protest, but is not required to file suit on the additional payments; however, the taxpayer is bound by the final court decision.

Interest is allowed on amounts ordered to be refunded.

¶2006 Tax Injunction

Law: Secs. 112.101—112.108, Tax Code (CCH Texas Tax Reports, ¶89-236).

Texas prohibits a legal action for the issuance of a restraining order or injunction to prevent the assessment or collection of any state tax or fee administered or collected by the Comptroller (¶1802) or a statutory penalty for failure to pay a tax or fee, unless the applicant for the injunction or restraining order meets specified filing requirements. The applicant must file with the Attorney General at least five days before filing suit a statement of the grounds on which the order or injunction will be sought and an assurance that either one of the two following conditions has been met:

— payment of all taxes, fees, and penalties due the state is made to the public official who collects them; or

— a bond is filed for double the amount of fees, taxes, or penalties that are due or may accrue during the injunction period. The amount of the bond must be accepted by the Attorney General and by the judge of the court granting the order or injunction.

However, after a taxpayer files an oath of inability to pay a tax, penalties, and interest due, the taxpayer may be excused from the requirement of prepayment of a state tax as a prerequisite to appeal if the court, after notice and hearing, finds that such prepayment would constitute an unreasonable restraint on the taxpayer's right of access to the courts.

A court may not issue a restraining order or consider the issuance of an injunction that prohibits the assessment or collection of a state or local tax or fee unless the applicant for the order or injunction shows irreparable injury and the lack of another adequate remedy and that he or she has a reasonable likelihood of prevailing on the merits of the claim.

Except for a restraining order or injunction issued under Secs. 112.101—112.108, Tax Code, a court is prohibited from issuing a restraining order, injunction, declaratory judgment, writ of mandamus, or prohibition order requiring the payment of taxes or fees into the registry or custody of the court, or other similar legal or equitable relief against the state or a state agency relating to the applicability, assessment, collection, constitutionality, or amount of a tax or fee.

The state may bring a counterclaim in a suit for a temporary or permanent injunction if the counterclaim relates to taxes or fees imposed under the same statute and if the counterclaim is filed no later than the 30th day before the date set for trial.

Records listing the taxes accruing during the effective period of the injunction or order must be maintained by the taxpayer after a restraining order or injunction has been issued by the court.

- *Report required*

On the first Monday of each month during the period the order or injunction is effective, the applicant must file a report with the state officer responsible for collecting the tax to which the order or injunction applies. The monthly report, made on prescribed forms, must contain the following information:

— the amount of tax accruing;

— a description of the total purchases, receipts, sales, and other dispositions of all commodities, products, materials, and articles on which the tax is levied or by which the tax is measured;

— the name and address of each person who purchased the product or service; and

— a complete record of stamps or tickets used, sold, or handled if the tax was paid by the use of stamps or tickets.

- *Additional security*

If a bond to ensure collection of taxes subject to injunction is not filed, the applicant is required to make ongoing payments into the suspense account for taxes, fees, and penalties as they accrue and before they become delinquent.

An additional bond must be filed upon a determination by the Attorney General that the amount of the bond previously filed is insufficient to cover double the amount of taxes, fees, and penalties accruing after the restraining order or injunction is granted.

¶2006

Part VII—Administration and Procedure

- *Dismissal of injunction*

An affidavit stating that the applicant has failed to comply with or has violated a provision relating to tax injunctions may be filed by the Attorney General or the state officer responsible for collecting the tax in the court that granted the injunction or restraining order. Notice of the filing must be given to the applicant by the clerk of the court; a hearing must be held within five days of service or as soon as the court can hear it. If the court finds that the applicant, prior to disposition of the suit by the court of last resort, has failed to file a report, keep records, file an additional bond on demand, or pay additional fees, taxes, or penalties, it *must* dismiss the application and dissolve the order or injunction.

If a restraining order or injunction is dismissed or dissolved, the Treasurer may demand immediate payment of the tax from the taxpayer or sureties if a bond was given to secure payment; or, if no bond was filed, the Treasurer may transfer the amounts due from the suspense account to the proper fund to which the taxes, fees, and penalties are allocated.

Taxes remaining unpaid after demand for payment may be recovered in an action by the Attorney General against the applicant and his or her sureties in a court of competent jurisdiction of Travis County, or in any other court having jurisdiction.

ADMINISTRATION AND PROCEDURE

CHAPTER 21
TEXAS RESOURCES

Comptroller of Public Accounts, Lyndon B. Johnson Bldg., 111 E. 17th St., Austin, TX 78774-0100
- General Information 800-252-5555
- Tax Practitioners 800-248-4093
- Forms 800-531-1441
  - *Mailing address:* PO Box 13528, Capitol Station, Austin, TX 78711-3528
  - *Internet:* www.cpa.state.tx.us

Alcoholic Beverage Commission, 5806 Mesa Dr., Austin, TX 78731
- Main number 512-206-3333
  - *Mailing address:* PO Box 13127, Austin, TX 78711
  - *Internet:* http://www.tabc.state.tx.us/default.htm

Department of Insurance, 333 Guadalupe, Austin, TX 78701
- Phone .... 512-463-6169 (local), 800 578-4677
  - *Mailing address:* PO Box 149104, Austin, TX 78714-9104
  - *Internet:* http://www.tdi.state.tx.us/

Department of Transportation, 125 E. 11th St., Austin, TX 78701-2483
- Motor Vehicle Division 512-416-4800
  - *Mailing address:* 125 E. 11th St., Austin, TX 78701-2483
  - *Internet:* http://www.dot.state.tx.us/

Public Utility Commission, 1701 N. Congress Ave., Austin, TX 78711-3326
- Phone 512-936-7000
  - *Mailing address:* PO Box 13326, Austin, TX 78711-3326
  - *Internet:* http://www.puc.state.tx.us/

Railroad Commission, 1701 N. Congress, Austin, TX 78711
- General Information 512-463-7288
  - *Mailing address:* PO Box 12967, Austin, TX 78711-2967
  - *Internet:* http://www.rrc.state.tx.us/

Secretary of State, State Capital, Rm. 1E.8, Austin, TX 78701
- Receptionist 512-463-5770
  - *Mailing address:* PO Box 12887, Austin, TX 78711-2887
  - *Internet:* http://www.sos.state.tx.us/

State Office of Administrative Hearings, 300 West 15th Street, Room 504
    Phone 512-475-4993
    Facsimile 512-475-4994
        Mailing address: P.O. Box 13025, Austin, TX 78711-3025
    Internet: http://www.soah.state.tx.us

Workforce Commission, 101 E. 15th St., Austin, TX 78778-0001
    Tax Department—Austin .... 800-832-9394 (option 2)
    Internet: http://www.twc.state.tx.us/

- *Regional offices*

    There are 36 regional offices as follows:

    Abilene
    209 South Danville Dr., Suite C202
    Abilene, Tx 79605-1464
    Phone: (915) 695-4323

    Amarillo
    Park West Office Center, Building A, Suite 220
    7120 IH-40 West
    Amarillo, Tx 79106-2519
    Phone: (806) 358-0148

    Austin Central
    111 West 6th St.
    P.O. Box 684843
    Austin, Tx 78768-4843
    Phone: (512) 463-3961

    Austin TPS
    208 East 16th St., Room G-22
    P.O. Box 13528
    Austin, Tx 78711-3528
    Phone: (512) 936-6105

    Beaumont
    6440 Concord
    Beaumont, Tx 77708-4315
    Phone: (409) 899-4650

    Belton
    2429 North Main
    Belton, Tx 76513-1517
    Phone: (254) 933-7577

    Brownsville (Temporarily Closed)
    955 West Price Rd.
    Brownsville, Tx 78520-8703
    Phone: (956) 542-8426

Bryan
1713 BRoadmoor, Suite 300
Bryan, Tx 77802-5220
Phone: (979) 776-5200

Corpus Christi
209 South Danville Dr., Suite C202
Abilene, Tx 79605-
Phone: (915) 695-4323

Dallas Northesat
9241 LBJ Freeway, Suite 205
Dallas, Tx 75243-3451
Phone: (972) 671-7166

Dallas Southeast
1331 East Highway 80, Suite 2
Mesquite, Tx 75150-5709
Phone: (972) 289-3400

Dallas Southwest
7222 South Westmoreland Rd., 100
Dallas, Tx 75237-2983
Phone: (972) 709-4357

Denton
400 South Carroll Blvd., Suite 1000
Denton, Tx 76201-5929
Phone: (940) 891-4790

El Paso
401 East Franklin Ave., Suite 160
El Paso, Tx 79901
Phone: (915) 834-5660

Euless
831 West Euless Blvd., Suite 5
Euless, Tx 76040-4436
Phone: (817) 858-6022

Fort Worth
4040 Fossil Creek Blvd., Suite 100
Fort Worth, Tx 76137-2747
Phone: (817) 847-6201

Houston North
16630 Imperial Valley, Suite 227
Houston, Tx 77060-3411
Phone: (281) 820-6055

Houston Northwest
1919 North Loop West, Suite 510
Houston, Tx 77008-1354
Phone: (713) 868-9112

Houston Southeast
650 FM 1959
Houston, Tx 77034-5420
Phone: (281) 484-6533

Houston Southwest
6220 Westpark, Suite 240
Houston, Tx 77057-7371
Phone: (713) 266-4063

Laredo
1202 Del Mar Blvd., Suite 1
Laredo, Tx 78041-2400
Phone: (956) 722-2859

Longview
Judson Plaza, Suite 150
1121 Judson Rd.
Longview, Tx 75601-5119
Phone: (903) 236-7797

Lubbock
Plaza West Office Building, Suite 404
4630 50th St.
Lubbock, Tx 79414-3599
Phone: (806) 792-1895

Lufkin
3213 South Medford, Suite 204
Lufkin, Tx 75901-5759
Phone: (936) 634-2621

McAllen
3231 North McColl Rd.
McAllen, Tx 78501-5538
Phone: (956) 687-9227

Odessa
4682 East University
Odessa, Tx 79762-8104
Phone: (915) 550-3027

San Angelo
3127 Executive Dr.

Part VII—Administration and Procedure

San Angelo, Tx 76904-6801
Phone: (915) 942-8364

San Antonio Northeast
14145 Nacogdoches Rd., Suite 1
San Antonio, Tx 78247-1920
Phone: (210) 646-0399

San Antonio Northwest
9515 Console, Suite 102
San Antonio, Tx 78229-2042
Phone: (210) 616-0067

San Antonio Southwest
123 Southwest Military Dr.
San Antonio, Tx 78221-1613
Phone: (210) 924-6434

Sherman
One Grand Centre Building, Suite 110
Sherman, Tx 75090-2672
Phone: (903) 893-0692

Tyler
3800 Paluxy Dr., Suite 300
Tyler, Tx 75703-1661
Phone: (903) 534-0333

Victoria
3003 North Cameron St.
Victoria, Tx 77901-3931
Phone: (361) 575-2874

Waco
801 Austin Ave., Suite 810
Waco, Tx 76701-1919
Phone: (254) 755-7709

Wichita Falls
710 Lamar, Suite 425
Wichita Falls, Tx 76301-6842
Phone: (940) 761-4141

• *Property taxes*

Appraisal districts in each county, as the body primarily responsible for assessing Texas property taxes, are the principal source of specific property tax information and appropriate forms. The following list provides contact information for each of the appraisal districts in the state:

Anderson County Appraisal District; Box 279, Palestine Texas 75802-0279; 903-723-2949.

Andrews County Appraisal District; 600 N. Main, Andrews, Texas 79714-5207; 915-523-9111.

Angelina County Appraisal District; Box 2357, Lufkin Texas 75902-2357; 409-634-8456.

Aransas County Appraisal District; 601 S. Church St., Rockport Texas 78382-2513; 512-729-9733.

Archer County Appraisal District; Box 1141, Archer City Texas 76351-1141; 940-574-2172.

Armstrong County Appraisal District; Drawer 835, Claude Texas 79019-0835; 806-226-4481.

Atascosa County Appraisal District; Box 139, Poteet Texas 78065-0139; 830-742-3591.

Austin County Appraisal District; 5 E. Amelia St., Bellville Texas 77418-1521; 409-865-9124.

Bailey County Appraisal District; 302 Main St., Muleshoe Texas 79347-3614; 806-272-5501.

Bandera County Appraisal District; Box 1119, Bandera Texas 78003-1119; 830-796-3039.

Bastrop County Appraisal District; Drawer 578, Bastrop Texas 78602-0578; 512-321-3925.

Baylor County Appraisal District; 101 S. Washington St., Seymour Texas 76380-2866; 940-888-5636.

Bee County Appraisal District; Box 1262, Beeville Texas 78104-1262; 512-358-0193.

Bell County Appraisal District; Box 390, Belton Texas 76513-0390; 254-939-5841.

Bexar County Appraisal District; Box 830248, San Antonio Texas 78283-0248; 210-224-8511.

Blanco County Appraisal District; Box 338, Johnson City Texas 78636-0338; 830-868-4013.

Borden County Appraisal District; Box 298, Gail Texas 79738-0298; 806-756-4484.

Bosque County Appraisal District; Box 393, Meridian Texas 76665-0393; 254-435-2304.

Bowie County Appraisal District; Box 6527, Texarkana Texas 75505-6527; 903-793-8936.

Brazoria County Appraisal District; 500 N. Chenango St., Angleton Texas 77515-4650; 409-849-7792.

Brazos County Appraisal District; 1673 Briarcrest Dr., #A-101, Bryan Texas 77802-2749; 409-774-4100.

Brewster County Appraisal District; Box 1231, Alpine Texas 79831-1231; 915-837-2558.

Briscoe County Appraisal District; Box 728, Silverton Texas 79257-0728; 806-823-2161.

Brooks County Appraisal District; Drawer A, Falfurrias Texas 78355-0901; 512-325-5681.

Part VII—Administration and Procedure **369**

Brown County Appraisal District; 403 Fisk Ave., Brownwood Texas 76801-2929; 915-643-5676.

Burleson County Appraisal District; Box 1000, Caldwell Texas 77836-1000; 409-567-4671.

Burnet County Appraisal District; Drawer E, Burnet Texas 78611-0140; 512-756-8291.

Caldwell County Appraisal District; Box 59, Lockhart Texas 78644-0059; 512-398-2391.

Calhoun County Appraisal District; Box 48, Port Lavaca Texas 77979-0048; 512-552-4560.

Callahan County Appraisal District; Box 806, Baird Texas 79504-0806; 915-854-1165.

Cameron County Appraisal District; Box 1010, San Benito Texas 78586-1010; 956-399-9322.

Camp County Appraisal District; Box 739, Pittsburg Texas 75686-0739; 903-856-6538.

Carson County Appraisal District; Box 970, Panhandle Texas 79068-0970; 806-537-3569.

Cass County Appraisal District; Box 1150, Linden Texas 75563-1150; 903-756-7545.

Castro County Appraisal District; 204 S.E. 3rd (Rear), Dimmitt Texas 79027-2612; 806-647-5131.

Chambers County Appraisal District; Box 1520, Anahuac Texas 77514-1520; 409-267-3795.

Cherokee County Appraisal District; Box 494, Rusk Texas 75785-0494; 903-683-2296.

Childress County Appraisal District; Box 13, Childress Texas 79201-0013; 940-937-6062.

Clay County Appraisal District; 101 E. Omega St., Henrietta Texas 76365-3437; 940-538-4311.

Cochran County Appraisal District; 109 S.E. 1st St., Morton Texas 79346-3101; 806-266-5584.

Coke County Appraisal District; Box 2, Robert Lee Texas 76945-0002; 915-453-4528.

Coleman County Appraisal District; Box 914, Coleman Texas 76834-0914; 915-625-4155.

Collin County Appraisal District; 2404 K Ave., Plano Texas 75074-5911; 972-578-5200.

Collingsworth County Appraisal District; 800 W. Ave., Rm. 104, Wellington Texas 79095-3037; 806-447-5172.

Colorado County Appraisal District; Box 10, Columbus Texas 78934-0010; 409-732-8222.

Comal County Appraisal District; Box 311222, New Braunfels Texas 78131-1222; 830-625-8597.

Comanche County Appraisal District; Box 6, Comanche Texas 76442-0006; 915-356-5253.

Concho County Appraisal District; Box 68, Paint Rock Texas 76866-0068; 915-732-4389.

Cooke County Appraisal District; 200 W. California St., Gainesville Texas 76240-3905; 940-665-7651.

Coryell County Appraisal District; Box 142, Gatesville Texas 76528-0142; 254-865-6593.

Cottle County Appraisal District; Box 459, Paducah Texas 79248-0459; 806-492-3345.

Crane County Appraisal District; 511 W. 8th St., Crane Texas 79731-3036; 915-558-1021.

Crockett County Appraisal District; Drawer H, Ozona Texas 76943-2507; 915-392-2674.

Crosby County Appraisal District; Box 479, Crosbyton Texas 79322-0479; 806-675-2356.

Culberson County Appraisal District; Box 550, Van Horn Texas 79855-0550; 915-283-2977.

Dallam County Appraisal District; Box 592, Dalhart Texas 79022-0592; 806-249-6767.

Dallas County Appraisal District; 2949 N. Stemmons Fwy., Dallas Texas 75247-6195; 214-631-0520.

Dawson County Appraisal District; Box 797, Lamesa Texas 79331-0797; 806-872-7060.

Deaf Smith County Appraisal District; Box 2298, Hereford Texas 79045-2298; 806-364-0625.

Delta County Appraisal District; Box 47, Cooper Texas 75432-0047; 903-395-4118.

Denton County Appraisal District; Box 2816, Denton Texas 76202-2816; 940-566-0904.

Dewitt County Appraisal District; Box 4, Cuero Texas 77954-0004; 512-275-5753.

Dickens County Appraisal District; Box 119, Dickens Texas 79229-0119; 806-623-5216.

Dimmit County Appraisal District; 402 N. 7th St., Carrizo Springs Texas 78834-3157; 830-876-3480.

Donley County Appraisal District; Box 1220, Clarendon Texas 79226-1220; 806-874-2744.

Duval County Appraisal District; Box 809, San Diego Texas 78384-0809; 512-279-3305.

Eastland County Appraisal District; Box 914, Eastland Texas 76448-0914; 254-629-8597.

Ector County Appraisal District; 1301 E. 8th St., Odessa Texas 79761-4703; 915-332-6834.

Edwards County Appraisal District; Box 858, Rocksprings Texas 78880-0378; 830-683-4189.

Ellis County Appraisal District; Box 878, Waxahachie Texas 75165-0878; 972-937-3552.

El Paso County Appraisal District; 5801 Trowbridge El Paso Texas 79925; 915-780-2000.

Part VII—Administration and Procedure **371**

Erath County Appraisal District; Box 94, Stephenville Texas 76401-0094; 254-965-7301.

Falls County Appraisal District; Drawer 430, Marlin Texas 76661-0430; 254-883-2543.

Fannin County Appraisal District; Route 4, Box 366, Bonham Texas 75418; 903-583-8701.

Fayette County Appraisal District; Box 836, La Grange Texas 78945-0836; 409-968-8383.

Fisher County Appraisal District; Box 516, Roby Texas 79543-0516; 915-776-2733.

Floyd County Appraisal District; Box 249, Floydada Texas 79235-0249; 806-983-5256.

Foard County Appraisal District; Box 419, Crowell Texas 79227-0419; 940-684-1225.

Fort Bend County Appraisal District; 2801-B F Terry Blvd., Rosenberg Texas 77471-5600; 281-344-8623.

Franklin County Appraisal District; Box 720 Mount Vernon Texas 75457-0720; 903-537-2286.

Freestone County Appraisal District; Box 675, Fairfield Texas 75840-0675; 903-389-5510.

Frio County Appraisal District; Box 1129, Pearsall Texas 78061-1129; 830-334-4163.

Gaines County Appraisal District; Box 490, Seminole Texas 79360-0490; 915-758-3263.

Galveston County Appraisal District; Box 3647, Texas City Texas 77592-3647; 409-935-1980.

Garza County Appraisal District; Drawer F, Post Texas 79356-0290; 806-495-3518.

Gillespie County Appraisal District; Box 429, Fredericksburg Texas 79624-0429; 830-997-9807.

Glasscock County Appraisal District; Box 89, Garden City Texas 79739-0089; 915-354-2580.

Goliad County Appraisal District; Box 34, Goliad Texas 77963-0034; 512-645-2492.

Gonzales County Appraisal District; Box 867, Gonzales Texas 78629-0867; 830-672-2879.

Gray County Appraisal District; Box 836, Pampa Texas 79066-0836; 806-665-0791.

Grayson County Appraisal District; 205 N. Travis, Sherman Texas 75090-5922; 903-893-9673.

Gregg County Appraisal District; 1333 E. Harrison Rd., Longview Texas 75604-5537; 903-238-8823.

Grimes County Appraisal District; Box 489, Anderson Texas 77830-0489; 409-873-2163.

Guadalupe County Appraisal District; 3000 N. Austin St., Seguin Texas 78155-7379; 830-372-2871.

Hale County Appraisal District; Box 29, Plainview Texas 79073-0029; 806-293-4226.

Hall County Appraisal District; 721 Robertson St., Memphis Texas 79245-3345; 806-259-2393.

Hamilton County Appraisal District; 119 E. Henry St., Hamilton Texas 76531-1909; 254-386-8945.

Hansford County Appraisal District; Box 519, Spearman Texas 79081-0519; 806-659-5575.

Hardeman County Appraisal District; Box 388, Quanah Texas 79252-0388; 940-663-2532.

Hardin County Appraisal District; Box 670, Kountze Texas 77625-0670; 409-246-2507.

Harris County Appraisal District; Box 920975, Houston Texas 77292-0975; 713-683-9200.

Harrison County Appraisal District; Box 818, Marshall Texas 75671-0818; 903-935-1991.

Hartley County Appraisal District; Box 405, Hartley Texas 79044-0405; 806-365-4515.

Haskell County Appraisal District; Box 467, Haskell Texas 79521-0467; 940-864-3805.

Hays County Appraisal District; 21001 N. IH-35, Kyle Texas 78640-9998; 512-268-2522.

Hemphill County Appraisal District; Box 65, Canadian Texas 79014-0065; 806-323-8022

Henderson County Appraisal District; Box 430, Athens Texas 75751-0430; 903-675-9296.

Hidalgo County Appraisal District; Box 632, Pharr Texas 78577-0632; 956-781-1545.

Hill County Appraisal District; Box 416, Hillsboro Texas 76645-0416; 254-582-2508.

Hockley County Appraisal District; Box 1090, Levelland Texas 79336-1090; 806-894-9654.

Hood County Appraisal District; Box 819, Granbury Texas 76048-0819; 817-573-2471.

Hopkins County Appraisal District; 109 College St., Sulphur Springs Texas 75482-2801; 903-885-2173.

Houston County Appraisal District; Box 112, Crockett Texas 75835-0112; 409-544-9655.

Howard County Appraisal District; Box 1151, Big Spring Texas 79721-1151; 915-263-8301.

Hudspeth County Appraisal District; Box 429, Sierra Blanca Texas 79851-0429; 915-369-4118

Hunt County Appraisal District; Box 1339, Greenville Texas 75403-1339; 903-454-3510.

Hutchinson County Appraisal District; Box 5065, Borger Texas 79008-5065; 806-274-2294.

Part VII—Administration and Procedure

Irion County Appraisal District; Box 980, Mertzon Texas 76941-0980; 915-835-3551.
Jack County Appraisal District; Box 958, Jacksboro Texas 76058-0958; 940-567-6301.
Jackson County Appraisal District; 411 N. Wells, Rm. 109, Edna Texas 77957-2734; Phone:512-782-7115
Jasper County Appraisal District; Box 1300, Jasper Texas 75951-1300; 409-384-2544.
Jeff Davis County Appraisal District; Box 373, Fort Davis Texas 79734-0373; 915-426-3210.
Jefferson County Appraisal District; Box 21337, Beaumont Texas 77720-1337; 409-840-9944.
Jim Hogg County Appraisal District; Box 459, Hebbronville Texas 78361-0459; 512-527-4033.
Jim Wells County Appraisal District; Box 607, Alice Texas 78333-0607; 512-668-9656.
Johnson County Appraisal District; 109 N. Main St., Cleburne Texas 76031-4941; 817-558-8100.
Jones County Appraisal District; Box 348, Anson Texas 79501-0348; 915-823-2422.
Karnes County Appraisal District; 915 S. Panna Maria, Karnes City Texas 78118-4106; 830-780-2433.
Kaufman County Appraisal District; Box 819 Kaufman Texas 75142-0819; 972-932-6081.
Kendall County Appraisal District; Box 788, Boerne Texas 78006-0788; 830-249-8012.
Kenedy County Appraisal District; Box 705, Bastrop Texas 78602-0705; 512-321-1695.
Kent County Appraisal District; Box 68, Jayton Texas 79528-0068; 806-237-3066.
Kerr County Appraisal District; Box 1885, Kerrville Texas 78029-1885; 830-895-5223.
Kimble County Appraisal District; Box 307, Junction Texas 76849-0307; 915-446-3717.
King County Appraisal District; Box 117, Guthrie Texas 79236-0117; 806-596-4588.
Kinney County Appraisal District; Box 1377, Bracketville Texas 78832-1377; 830-563-2323.
Kleberg County Appraisal District; Box 1027, Kingsville Texas 78364-1027; 512-595-5775.
Knox County Appraisal District; Box 47, Benjamin Texas 79505-0047; 940-454-3891.
Lamar County Appraisal District; Box 400, Paris Texas 75461-0400; 903-785-7822.
Lamb County Appraisal District; Box 950, Littlefield Texas 79339-0950; 806-385-6474.
Lampasas County Appraisal District; Box 175, Lampasas Texas 76550-0175; 512-556-8138.

LaSalle County Appraisal District; Drawer O, Cotulla Texas 78014-1530; 830-879-2547.

Lavaca County Appraisal District; Box 386, Hallettsville Texas 77964-0386; 512-798-4396.

Lee County Appraisal District; 218 E. Richmond, Giddings Texas 78942-4130; 409-542-9618.

Leon County Appraisal District; Box 536, Centerville Texas 75833-0536; 903-536-2252.

Liberty County Appraisal District; Box 10016, Liberty Texas 77575-0016; 409-336-5722.

Limestone County Appraisal District; Drawer 831, Groesbeck Texas 76642-0831; 254-729-3009.

Lipscomb County Appraisal District; Box 128, Darrouzett Texas 79024-0128; 806-624-2881.

Live Oak County Appraisal District; Box MM, George West Texas 78022-2370; 512-449-2641.

Llano County Appraisal District; 103 E. Sandstone, Llano Texas 78643-2039; 915-247-3065.

Loving County Appraisal District; Box 352, Mentone Texas 79754-0352; 915-377-2201.

Lubbock County Appraisal District; Box 10542, Lubbock Texas 79408-3542; 806-762-5000.

Lynn County Appraisal District; Box 789, Tahoka Texas 79373-0789; 806-998-5477.

Madison County Appraisal District; Box 1328, Madisonville Texas 77864-1328; 409-348-2783.

Marion County Appraisal District; Box 690, Jefferson Texas 75657-0690; 903-665-2519.

Martin County Appraisal District; Box 1349, Stanton Texas 79782-1349; 915-756-2823.

Mason County Appraisal District; Box 1119, Mason Texas 76856-1119; 915-347-5989.

Matagorda County Appraisal District; Box 179, Bay City Texas 77404-0179; 409-244-2031.

Maverick County Appraisal District; Box 2628, Eagle Pass Texas 78853-2628; 830-773-0255.

McCulloch County Appraisal District; 104 N. College St., Brady Texas 76825-4437; 915-597-1627.

McLennan County Appraisal District; Box 2297, Waco Texas 76703-2297; 254-752-9864.

McMullen County Appraisal District; Box 38, Tilden Texas 78072-0038; 512-274-3685.

Medina County Appraisal District; 1410 Ave. K, Hondo Texas 78861-1300; 830-741-3035.

Menard County Appraisal District; Box 1058, Menard Texas 76859-1058; 915-396-4784.

Part VII—Administration and Procedure

Midland County Appraisal District; Box 908002, Midland Texas 79708-8002; 915-699-4991.

Milam County Appraisal District; Box 769, Cameron Texas 76520-0769; 254-697-6638.

Mills County Appraisal District; Box 565, Goldthwaite Texas 76844-0565; 915-648-2253.

Mitchell County Appraisal District; Box 358, Colorado City Texas 79512-0358; 915-728-5028.

Montague County Appraisal District; Box 121, Montague Texas 76251-0121; 940-894-6011.

Montgomery County Appraisal District; Box 2233, Conroe Texas 77305-2233; 409-756-3354.

Moore County Appraisal District; Box 717, Dumas Texas 79029-0717; 806-935-4193.

Morris County Appraisal District; Box 563, Daingerfield Texas 75638-0563; 903-645-5601.

Motley County Appraisal District; Box 779, Matador Texas 79244-0779; 806-347-2273.

Nacogdoches County Appraisal District; 216 W. Hospital St., Nacogdoches Texas 75961-5144; 409-560-3447.

Navarro County Appraisal District; Box 3118, Corsicana Texas 75151-3118; 903-872-6161.

Newton County Appraisal District; Drawer X, Newton Texas 75966-1520; 409-379-3710.

Nolan County Appraisal District; Box 1256, Sweetwater Texas 79556-1256; 915-235-8421.

Nueces County Appraisal District; 201 N. Chaparral, Corpus Christi Texas 78401-2503; 512-881-8022.

Ochiltree County Appraisal District; 825 S. Main, Ste. 100, Perryton Texas 79070-3556; 806-435-9623.

Oldham County Appraisal District; Drawer 310, Vega Texas 79092-0310; 806-267-2442.

Orange County Appraisal District; Box 457, Orange Texas 77630-0457; 409-745-4777.

Palo Pinto County Appraisal District; Box 250, Palo Pinto Texas 76484-0250; 940-659-1281.

Panola County Appraisal District; 2 Ball Park Rd., Carthage Texas 75633-3225; 903-693-2891.

Parker County Appraisal District; 188 W. Columbia St., Weatherford Texas 76086-4312; 817-596-0077.

Parmer County Appraisal District; Box 56, Bovina Texas 79009-0056; 806-238-1405.

Pecos County Appraisal District; Box 237, Fort Stockton Texas 79735-0237; 915-336-7587.

Polk County Appraisal District; 312 N. Washington Ave., Livingston Texas 77351-3240; 409-327-2174.

Potter County Appraisal District; Box 7190, Amarillo Texas 79114-7190; 806-358-1601.

Presidio County Appraisal District; Box 879, Marfa Texas 79843-0879; 915-729-3431.

Rains County Appraisal District; Box 70, Emory Texas 75440-0070; 903-473-2391.

Randall County Appraisal District; Box 7190, Amarillo Texas 79114-7190;Phone 806-358-1601.

Reagan County Appraisal District; Box 8, Big Lake Texas 76932-0008; 915-884-3275.

Real County Appraisal District; Box 158, Leaky Texas 78873-0158; 830-232-6248.

Red River County Appraisal District; Box 461, Clarksville Texas 75426-0461; 903-427-4181.

Reeves County Appraisal District; Box 1229, Pecos Texas 79772-1229; 915-445-5122.

Refugio County Appraisal District; Box 156, Refugio Texas 78377-0156; 512-526-5994.

Roberts County Appraisal District; Box 458, Miami Texas 79059-0458; 806-868-5281.

Robertson County Appraisal District; Box 998, Franklin Texas 77856-0998; 409-828-5800.

Rockwall County Appraisal District; 106 N. San Jacinto, Rockwall Texas 75087-2508; 972-771-2034.

Runnels County Appraisal District; Box 524, Ballinger Texas 76821-0524; 915-365-3583.

Rusk County Appraisal District; Box 7, Henderson Texas 75653-0007; 903-657-3578.

Sabine County Appraisal District; Box 137, Hemphill Texas 75948-0137; 409-787-2777.

San Augustine County Appraisal District; 122 N. Harrison, San Augustine Texas 75972-1906; 409-275-3496.

San Jacinto County Appraisal District; Box 1170, Coldspring Texas 77331-1170; 409-653-4479.

San Patricio County Appraisal District; Box 938, Sinton Texas 78387-0938; 512-364-5402.

San Saba County Appraisal District; 423 E. Wallace St., San Saba Texas 76877-3527; 915-372-5031.

Schleicher County Appraisal District; Box 936, Eldorado Texas 76936-0936; 915-853-2617.

Scurry County Appraisal District; 2612 College Ave., Snyder Texas 79549-3334; 915-573-8549.

Shackelford County Appraisal District; Box 565, Albany Texas 76430-0565; 915-762-2207.

Shelby County Appraisal District; 724 Shelbyville St., Center Texas 75935-3736; 409-598-6171.

Sherman County Appraisal District; Box 239, Stratford Texas 79084-0239; 806-396-5566.

Part VII—Administration and Procedure 377

Smith County Appraisal District; 245 S. SE Loop 323, Tyler Texas 75702-6456; 903-510-8600.

Somervell County Appraisal District; 112 Allen Dr, Glen Rose Texas 76043-9998; 254-897-4094.

Starr County Appraisal District; Box 137, Rio Grande City Texas 78582-0137; 956-487-5613.

Stephens County Appraisal District; Box 351, Breckenridge Texas 76424-0351; 254-559-8233.

Sterling County Appraisal District; Box 28, Sterling City Texas 76951-0028; 915-378-7711.

Stonewall County Appraisal District; Box 308, Aspermont Texas 79502-0308; 940-989-3363.

Sutton County Appraisal District; 300 E. Oak St., Sonora Texas 76950-3106; 915-387-2809.

Swisher County Appraisal District; Box 8, Tulia Texas 79088-0008; 806-995-4118.

Tarrant County Appraisal District; 2315 Gravel Rd., Fort Worth Texas 76118-6951; 817-284-0024.

Taylor County Appraisal District; Box 1800, Abilene Texas 79604-1800; 915-676-9381.

Terrell County Appraisal District; Box 747, Sanderson Texas 79848-0747; 915-345-2251.

Terry County Appraisal District; Box 426, Brownfield Texas 79316-0426; 806-637-6966.

Throckmorton County Appraisal District; Box 788, Throckmorton Texas 76483-0788; 940-849-5691.

Titus County Appraisal District; Box 528, Mount Pleasant Texas 75456-0528; 903-572-7939.

Tom Green County Appraisal District; Box 3307, San Angelo Texas 76902-3307; 915-658-5575.

Travis County Appraisal District; Box 149012, Austin Texas 78714-9012; 512-834-9317.

Trinity County Appraisal District; Box 950, Groveton Texas 75845-0950; 409-642-1502.

Tyler County Appraisal District; Drawer 9, Woodville Texas 75979-0009; 409-283-3736.

Upshur County Appraisal District; Box 280, Gilmer Texas 75644-0280; 903-843-3041.

Upton County Appraisal District; Box 1110, Mc Camey Texas 79752-1110; 915-652-3221.

Uvalde County Appraisal District; 209 N. High St., Uvalde Texas 78801-5207; 830-278-1106.

Val Verde County Appraisal District; Box 1059, Del Rio Texas 78841-1059; 830-774-4602.

Van Zandt County Appraisal District; Box 926, Canton Texas 75103-0926; 903-567-6768.

Victoria County Appraisal District; 1611 E. North St., Victoria Texas 77901-7052; 512-576-3621.

Walker County Appraisal District; Box 1798, Huntsville Texas 77342-1798; 409-295-0402.

Waller County Appraisal District; Box 159, Katy Texas 77492-0159; 281-396-6100.

Ward County Appraisal District; Box 905, Monahans Texas 79756-0905; 915-943-3224.

Washington County Appraisal District; Box 681, Brenham Texas 77834-0681; 409-277-6528.

Webb County Appraisal District; Box 719, Laredo Texas 78042-0719; 956-718-4091.

Wharton County Appraisal District; Box 1068, Wharton Texas 77488-1068; 409-532-8931.

Wheeler County Appraisal District; Box 1200, Wheeler Texas 79096-1200; 806-826-5900.

Wichita County Appraisal District; Box 5172, Wichita Falls Texas 76307-5172; 940-322-2435.

Wilbarger County Appraisal District; Box 1519, Vernon Texas 76384-1519; 940-553-1857.

Willacy County Appraisal District; Rt 2 Box 256, Raymondville Texas 78580-9802; 956-689-5979.

Williamson County Appraisal District; Box 1120, Georgetown Texas 78627-1120; 512-930-3787.

Wilson County Appraisal District; Box 849, Floresville Texas 78114-0849; 210-393-3065.

Winkler County Appraisal District; Box 1219, Kermit Texas 79745-1219; 915-586-2832.

Wise County Appraisal District; 206 S. State St., Decatur Texas 76234-1837; 940-627-3081.

Wood County Appraisal District; Box 518, Quitman Texas 75783-0518; 903-763-4891.

Yoakum County Appraisal District; Box 748, Plains Texas 79355-0748; 806-456-7101.

Young County Appraisal District; Box 337, Graham Texas 76450-0337; 940-549-2392.

Zapata County Appraisal District; Box 2315, Zapata Texas 78076-2315; 956-765-9971.

Zavala County Appraisal District; 323 W. Zavala, Crystal City Texas 78839-3240; 830-374-3475.

PART VIII

DOING BUSINESS IN TEXAS

CHAPTER 22

FEES AND TAXES

| ¶ 2201 | Domestic Corporation Costs |
| ¶ 2202 | Foreign Corporation Costs |

¶ 2201 Domestic Corporation Costs

Law: Art. 10.01, Business Corporation Act (CCH Texas Tax Reports, ¶ 1-250, 1-610).

The following are the fees and costs required to be paid by domestic corporations. See ¶ 2202 for the requirements for foreign corporations.

- *Initial fees and taxes*

Fees for filing articles of incorporation, amendments and name reservations are as follows:

—Filing articles of incorporation of a domestic corporation $300

—Filing amendment of articles of incorporation of a domestic corporation $150

—Filing restated articles of incorporation of a domestic corporation $300

—Filing application for reservation of corporate name $40

—Filing notice of transfer of reserved corporate name $15

Fees charged by the Secretary of State for performing corporate services are as follows:

SERVICE PERFORMED	FEE
Filing articles of merger	$300
Filing application of foreign corporation for certificate of authority	$750
Filing application of foreign corporation for amended certificate of authority	$150
Filing application for registration or renewal of corporate name	$75
Filing statement of change of registered office or agent, or both, or of address of agent	$15
Filing statement relating to establishing or cancellation of shares	$15
Filing statement of reduction of stated capital	$15
Filing articles of dissolution	$40
Filing application for withdrawal	$15
Filing certificate from home state that foreign corporation is no longer in existence in said state	$15
Maintaining a record of service of process upon Secretary of State as agent	$40
Filing an instrument not otherwise provided for	$15

¶ 2202 Foreign Corporation Costs

Law: Art. 10.01, Business Corporation Act (CCH Texas Tax Reports, ¶ 2-300).

The following are the fees and costs to which foreign corporations are subject. See ¶ 2201 for those applicable to domestic corporations.

- *Initial fees and taxes*

Statutory filing fees required for documents relating to transactions of foreign corporations are as follows:

Articles of merger	$300
Certificate of authority	$750
Amended certificate of authority	$150
Reservation of corporate name	$40
Transfer of reservation	$15
Registration or renewal of corporate name	$75
Home state certificate of corporate non-existence	$15

Additional fees for services of the Secretary of State are listed at ¶2201.

PART IX

UNCLAIMED PROPERTY

CHAPTER 23
UNCLAIMED PROPERTY

¶2301 Unclaimed Property

"Escheat" is the vesting of title to property in the state. (Sec. 71.001, Prop. Code) The Texas statutes relating to escheat of unclaimed property are codified as Title 6, Chapters 71, 72, 73, 74, 75, and 76, Texas Property Code. Some of the provisions are drawn from the Uniform Unclaimed Property Acts of 1954 and 1981.

> *CCH Comment: Potential federal/state conflict*
>
> Escheat is an area of potential federal/state conflict. A federal statute may preempt state escheat provisions. For instance, it has been federal policy that the Employee Retirement Income Security Act of 1974 (ERISA) (particularly Sec. 514(a)) generally preempts state laws relating to employee benefit plans. Thus, funds of missing participants in a qualified employee benefit plan stay in the plan pursuant to the federal executive policy that state escheat laws are preempted by ERISA. (*Advisory Opinion, 94-41A*, Department of Labor, Pension and Welfare Benefit Administration, Dec. 7, 1994) However, some states have challenged the federal position on this and similar narrowly delineated situations. Thus, practitioners are advised that a specific situation where federal and state policy cross on the issue of escheat may, at this time, be an area of unsettled law.

In the case of federal tax refunds, IRC Sec. 6408 disallows refunds if the refund would escheat to a state.

- *"Unclaimed" property*

"Unclaimed" property subject to escheat includes the following:

(1) real and personal property of an individual who dies intestate and without heirs (Sec. 71.001, Prop. Code);

(2) personal property presumed to be abandoned (Sec. 72.101, Prop. Code); and

(3) mineral proceeds that have remained unclaimed by the owner for more than three years. (Sec. 75.101, Prop. Code)

- *Presumptions of abandonment*

Actual abandonment of property may be proved at any time, but since unclaimed property is usually held under circumstances in which ownership of the property is unknown or uncertain, Texas law provides the following presumptive periods for abandonment:

18-month property

Utility deposits (Sec. 72.1017, Prop. Code) .... 18 months

Three-year property

Personal property, generally (Sec. 72.101, Prop. Code) .... 3 years

Gift certificates, gift cards (Sec. 72.1016, Prop Code) .... 3 years

Uncashed checks (Sec. 73.102, Prop. Code) .... 3 years

Proceeds from sale of minerals (Sec. 75.101, Prop. Code) .... 3 years

Child support payments (1 TAC Sec. 55.142)...................... 3 years

Money orders (Sec. 72.102, Prop. Code) .... 3 years

Bank accounts (checking, savings, and matured certificates of deposit) (Sec. 73.101, Prop. Code) .... 3 years

Five-year property

Bank accounts (generally) (Sec. 73.101, Prop. Code) .... 5 years

Safe deposit boxes (Sec. 73.101, Prop. Code) .... 5 years

Seven-year property

Intestate succession (Sec. 71.002, Prop. Code) .... 7 years

Fifteen-year property

Traveler's checks (Sec. 72.102, Prop. Code) .... 15 years

Utility deposits. Effective September 1, 2011, a refundable money deposit paid to a utility service as a condition of initiating service is presumed abandoned 18 months after the refund check was payable to the owner, the owner's last communication with the utility, or the date the utility issued the check if no claim to the check has been asserted or exercised. However, there is no presumed abandonment for two years after an owner provides documentation to the utility of being called to active military service during the above 18-month period. (Sec. 72.1017, Prop Code)

Abandoned personal property—In general. Unless a different period is prescribed, personal property is presumed abandoned if the existence and location of its owner is unknown to the holder for more than three years and a claim to the property has not been asserted or an act of ownership has not been exercised within that period. Unclaimed investment accounts (stocks, mutual funds), insurance proceeds, and credit balances or refunds would fall within this category. (Sec. 72.101, Prop. Code) A holder of unclaimed property may establish knowledge of the owner's whereabouts by recording any owner-generated activity relating to that property. The mailing of correspondence by a holder to the last-known address of the property owner and the nonreturn of such mail to the holder is insufficient to establish that the holder has knowledge of the owner's whereabouts. (34 TAC Sec. 13.3)

Special periods apply to the following properties.

Stored value cards. A "stored value card" includes a gift card or gift certificate, and is defined as a record that evidences a promise made for monetary consideration by the seller or issuer that goods or services will be provided to the owner in the value shown on the record. The card is prefunded, and its value is reduced on redemption. (Sec. 35.42, Bus. and Com. Code)

If the existence and location of the owner of a stored value card is unknown to the holder of the property, the card is presumed abandoned to the extent of its unredeemed and uncharged value on the earlier of (1) the card's expiration date; (2) the third anniversary of the date the card was issued, if the card is not used after it is issued, or the date the card was last used or value was last added to the card; or (3) the first anniversary of the date the card was issued, if the card is not used after it is issued, or the date the card was last used or value was last added to the card, if the card's value represents wages. (Sec. 72.1016, Prop. Code)

Checks (excluding traveler's checks). A check (excluding a traveler's check) is presumed abandoned on the latest of (1) the third anniversary of the date on which the check was payable; (2) the third anniversary of the date the issuer or payor of the check last received documented communication from the payee of the check; or (3) the third anniversary of the date the check was issued if, according to the issuer's

¶2301

Part IX—Unclaimed Property

knowledge and records, a claim to the check has not been asserted or an act of ownership has not been exercised by the payee. (Sec. 73.102, Prop. Code)

Sale of minerals. All mineral proceeds held or owed by the holder of the mineral property and that have remained unclaimed by the owner for more than three years after they became payable or distributable are presumed abandoned. (Sec. 75.101, Prop. Code)

Child support payments. Effective October 11, 2010, child support payments being held for disbursement by the state or a local registry may be reported as unclaimed property if, after three years from the date the child support payments have been held, there has been no contact by the property owner and attempts to locate the owner have failed. If the person to whom the child support payments are owed is deceased, payments may be reported as unclaimed property after three years from the date of death, if there has been no claim to the payments by a caretaker, emancipated child, or executor of the owner's estate. The reporting of the unclaimed payments may be deferred to the next reporting period, if information on the location of the owner is present. Reporting may, however, only be deferred until the end of the second deferral year. (1 TAC Sec. 55.142)

Bank account. A bank account is generally presumed abandoned if it has been inactive for at least five years and the location of the depositor of the account is unknown. An account becomes inactive beginning on the date of the depositor's last transaction or correspondence concerning the account. However, if the account is a checking or savings account or is a matured certificate of deposit, the account is presumed abandoned if the account has been inactive for at least three years. (Sec. 73.101, Prop. Code)

Safe deposit box in a bank. A safe deposit box in a bank is presumed abandoned if it has been inactive (a safe deposit box becomes inactive on the date a rental is due but not paid) for at least five years and the owner is unknown. (Sec. 73.101, Prop. Code)

Money orders. A money order is presumed abandoned three years after its date of issue, the owner's last communication with the issuer, or the date of the last writing indicating the owner's interest in the money order, whichever is latest. Prior to September 1, 2011, the abandonment period was seven years. (Sec. 72.102, Prop. Code) If a holder imposes service, maintenance, or other charges on a money order prior to the time of presumed abandonment, such charges may not exceed $1 per month. (Sec. 72.103, Prop. Code)

Traveler's checks. A traveler's check is presumed abandoned 15 years after its date of issue, the owner's last communication with the issuer, or the date of the last writing indicating the owner's interest in the check, whichever is latest. (Sec. 72.102, Prop. Code)

Intestate property. For escheat purposes, the presumptive period relating to intestate property is seven years. Thus, an individual who is absent from his residence for seven years or more and is not known to exist is presumed dead. (Sec. 71.002, Prop. Code) A lack of heirs is presumed if within the seven-year period preceding the court's determination, a lawful claim to the decedent's property has not been asserted and a lawful act of ownership has not been exercised. (Sec. 71.004, Prop. Code) Payment of taxes on the property is an exercise of a lawful act of ownership. (Sec. 71.005, Prop. Code) Intestacy is presumed if no will has been recorded or probated in the county where the individual's property is located by the seventh anniversary of his or her death. (Sec. 71.003, Prop. Code)

Wages. Unclaimed wages are presumed abandoned if, for longer than one year, the holder of the wages is unaware of the existence and location of the person to whom the wages are owed, there are no claims to the wages, and no one has exercised any act of ownership of the wages. The term "wages" is defined as

¶2301

compensation owed by an employer for (1) labor or services rendered by an employee, whether computed on a time, task, piece, commission, or other basis, or (2) vacation pay, holiday pay, sick leave pay, parental leave pay, or severance pay owed to an employee under a written agreement with or written policy of the employer. (Sec. 72.101, Property Code)

Proceeds of demutualization of insurance company. Property distributable during a demutualization or related reorganization of an insurance company is presumed abandoned one year after the date the property became distributable if, at the time of the first distribution, (1) the last known address of the owner is known to be incorrect or the post office returns as undeliverable the distribution or statements related to the distribution and (2) the owner has not communicated with the holder of the property regarding the interest, as evidenced by a written document, memorandum, or other record on file with the holder or its agents. (Sec. 72.101, Property Code)

- *Obligations of holder of unclaimed property*

Report filing, delivery. Any person who, on June 30, holds property that is presumed abandoned must file a report of that property and deliver the property to the Comptroller by November 1, although the Comptroller may set an earlier date for the delivery of the contents of a safe deposit box. (Sec. 74.101, Prop. Code; Sec. 74.301, Prop. Code) After delivery, the state assumes custody of the property and responsibility for its safekeeping. (Sec. 74.304, Prop. Code)

Due diligence. A holder of abandoned property must preserve the property and may not deduct service, maintenance, or other charges from the value of the property. (Sec. 72.103, Prop. Code; Sec. 73.003, Prop. Code; Sec. 75.102, Prop. Code)

- *Recovery of escheated property*

Intestate property. Property that has escheated to the state by reason of intestacy may be recovered by suing for its recovery. The suit must be filed within two years (real property) or four years (personal property) of the date of the final judgment of the escheat proceeding. (Sec. 71.301, Prop. Code; Sec. 71.303, Prop. Code)

All other property. The owner of personal property that has been delivered to a depository or to the Comptroller as unclaimed property may file a claim for such property (or for the cash proceeds, if the property has been sold). (Sec. 74.501, Prop. Code; Sec. 74.502, Prop. Code) If the owner is aggrieved by the decision on his claim, he may appeal the decision to a district court. (Sec. 74.506, Prop. Code)

- *Administrator*

The Texas Unclaimed Property Program is administered by the Comptroller of Public Accounts. Inquiries should be directed to the Comptroller of Public Accounts; Unclaimed Property Division; Research and Correspondence Section; P.O. Box 12019; Austin, TX 78711-2019. Phone: 1-800-654-FIND (3463).

- *Waiver of interest and penalties*

The Comptroller may waive penalty and interest imposed on delinquent property if the holder delivering the property to the Comptroller was required to deliver the property on or before November 1, 1997. (Sec. 74.707(c), Prop. Code)

¶2301

LAW AND RULE LOCATOR

This finding list shows where sections of Texas statutory law and administrative rules referred to in the *Guidebook* are discussed.

TAX CODE

Law Sec.	Discussion at ¶
Property Tax	
1.04	1502
6.01	1502
6.03	1502
11.01	1503
11.02	1503
11.12—11.14	1504
11.14	1503, 1504
11.145	1504
11.146	1504
11.15	1504
11.16	1504
11.161	1504
11.17	1504
11.18	1504
11.181	1504
11.182	1504
11.184	1504
11.19—11.25	1504
11.251	1504, 1508
11.254	1504
11.26	1504
11.27	1504
11.271	1504
11.28—11.32	1504
11.41—11.43	1504
11.439	1504, 1508
21.031	1504
22.01	1505
22.23—22.26	1505
22.28—22.30	1505
23.125	1506
23.135	1504
23.23	1505
23.41	1505
23.52	1505
23.521	1505
23.522	1505
23.55	1505
23.73	1505
23.76	1504
23.81	1505
23.83	1505
25.21	1504
25.25	1505
31.01	1507
31.02	1506, 1507
31.03	1506
31.031	1506
31.032	1506
31.04	1506, 1507
31.05	1506
31.072	1506
31.11	1509

Law Sec.	Discussion at ¶
31.111	1509
31.12	1509
32.01	1507
33.01	1508
33.011	1508
33.04	1508
33.05	1507
33.06	1507, 1510
33.065	1510
33.07	1508
33.21—33.25	1507
33.41	1507
33.55	1508
33.91	1507
33.911	1507
34.21—34.23	1507
41.41	1509
41A.01	1509
41A.03	1509
41A.10	1509
42.01	1509
42.06	1509
42.21	1509
42.22	1509
42.225	1509
42.26	1509
42.43	1509
43.03	1509
Enforcement and Collection	
111.001	1802
111.002	1909
111.0021	1802, 1904, 1909
111.0036	1804
111.0041	1804
111.0042	1108
111.0046—111.0047	1908
111.006	1707, 1804
111.008—111.009	1901
111.0081	2003
111.009	2003
111.010	1906
111.011	1908
111.012	1902
111.013	1906
111.016	1901
111.017—111.019	1905
111.020	1901
111.022	1901, 2003
111.024	1901
111.046—111.047	1908
111.051	1803
111.0511	1803
111.053—111.058	1803
111.060	1909

385

Law Sec.	Discussion at ¶	Law Sec.	Discussion at ¶
111.061	1306, 1909	151.052	802, 1003
111.061	1901	151.053	905
111.062	1805	151.054	1006
111.063	1805	151.056	1002
111.101—111.103	602, 1903, 1904, 1905	151.0565	207, 1002
111.104	2002	151.057	1002
111.1042	2002	151.059	803
111.105	2002	151.061	804
111.107	2002	151.101	902
111.108	1906	151.101—151.105	804, 805
111.109	404, 2002	151.106	1105
111.110	1205	151.107—151.108	803
111.201	1901	151.151	1003
111.202	1906	151.154	902
111.203—111.206	1901	151.155	1006
111.2051	1901	151.156	1003
111.206	1901, 2002	151.157	1003
111.207	1901, 2002	151.1575	1003
111.251	1907	151.158	1003
111.252	1907	151.201—151.205	1105
111.254	1907	151.251	1105
111.301	407, 1502	151.252	1105
111.302	407	151.254	1105
112.001	2004	151.256	1105
112.051—112.054	2005	151.262	1105
112.056	2005	151.302	802, 1003
112.060	2002, 2005	151.303	1202
112.101—112.108	2006	151.304	1003
112.108	2005	151.305	1002
112.151	2004	151.306	1003
112.1512	2004	151.307	1003
112.155	2004	151.3071	1003
112.156	2004	151.308	1002
113.001	1904	151.309	1004
113.0021	1904	151.310	1004
113.006—113.008	1904	151.3101	1002
113.101	1904	151.311	1002, 1004
113.105	1904	151.3111	1002
Multistate Tax Compact		151.312	1002
141.001	302, 801, 1006	151.313	1002
142.001—142.011	801	151.314—151.320	1002
Sales, Excise and Use Taxes		151.321	1004
151.0028	804	151.322—151.327	1002
151.0033—151.0036	804	151.328	1002
151.0038	804	151.329	1002
151.0039	804	151.330	805
151.0045	804	151.331	1002
151.0047	804	151.332	1004
151.0048	804, 1002	151.335	1002
151.005	802	151.336	1002
151.006	802, 1003	151.337	1004
151.007	902	151.338	1002
151.008	802, 803	151.340	1002
151.009	802	151.341	1004
151.010	802, 902	151.3415	1002
151.0101	804, 1002	151.342	1002
151.011	805	151.346	1003
151.012	903	151.347	1002
151.021	801	151.348	1005
151.023	903, 1108	151.350	1002
151.0231	1108	151.351	1002
151.024	802, 903	151.353	1002
151.025	903, 1107	151.401	1103
151.027	1102	151.403	1102
151.051	802, 902, 903	151.405	1103
151.0515	903	151.406—151.408	1102
		151.410	1102

Law and Rule Locator

Law Sec.	Discussion at ¶
151.410—151.414	1102
151.411	902, 1102
151.417	1106
151.4171	1106
151.419—151.422	1106
151.423	1102, 1103
151.424	1102, 1104
151.425	1104
151.426	902
151.4261	902
151.427	1203
151.428	902
151.429	1005, 1707
151.4291	1005
151.430	1102
151.431	1005
151.462	1102
151.503—151.505	1302
151.508	1302
151.511	1302
151.512	1306
151.515	1303
151.601—151.603	1303
151.605	1303
151.607	1305
151.608	1304
151.703—151.705	1306
151.704	1109
151.707—151.709	1306
151.711	1306
152.001	903, 1002
152.002	903
152.021—152.023	903
152.025	903
152.026	903
152.0412	902
152.081—152.089	1002
152.091—152.093	1002
152.106	1306

Motor Fuel Taxes

Law Sec.	Discussion at ¶
162.101	1705
162.102	1705
162.104	1705
162.105	1705
162.106	1705
162.114	1705
162.116	1705
162.119	1705
162.125	1705
162.126	1705
162.201	1705
162.204	1705
162.205	1705
162.206	1705
162.215	1705
162.217	1705
162.227	1705
162.228	1705
162.301	1705
162.302	1705
162.3021	1705
162.308	1705

[Cigarette and Tobacco Products Taxes]

Law Sec.	Discussion at ¶
154.021	1703
154.022	1703
154.024	1703
154.041	1703
154.043	1703
154.050	1703
154.052	1703
154.111	1703
154.152	1703
154.204	1703
154.210	1703
154.305	1703
155.021	1703
155.0211	1703
155.022	1703
155.023	1703
155.024	1703
155.049	1703
155.103	1703
155.111	1703
155.184	1703

Hotel Occupancy Tax

Law Sec.	Discussion at ¶
156.001	1707
156.051—156.053	1707
156.101—156.104	1707
156.151—156.153	1707
156.202	1707
156.203	1707

Manufactured Housing Sales and Use Tax

Law Sec.	Discussion at ¶
158.051	903
158.052	903
158.057	903
160.021—160.023	903
160.0245	1002
161.002	903

Franchise Tax

Law Sec.	Discussion at ¶
171.0001	202, 205, 507
171.001	102, 103, 104, 501
171.0011	102
171.002	102, 103, 104, 202, 204
171.021	102
171.005	102
171.006	104
171.051—171.087	104
171.088	104
171.101	103, 202,
171.1011	202, 207
171.1012	205
171.1013	204
171.1014	507
171.1015	103
171.1016	102
171.102	207
171.103 (Former)	303
171.1055	303
171.106	303, 765
171.107	104, 206
171.109	103, 504
171.110	504
171.111	402
171.112	302, 303, 504
171.1121	202, 205, 303, 504
171.113	204
171.151—171.154	501
171.152	502
171.1531	503
171.158	503
171.201	504
171.202	504, 505
171.2022	504

Law Sec.	Discussion at ¶	Law Sec.	Discussion at ¶
171.203	504	202.251	1709
171.2035	504	**Sulfur Production Tax**	
171.204	504, 601	203.001—203.003	1709
171.205	601	**Tax Credit for New Field Discoveries**	
171.206—171.210	506	204.002—204.008	1709
171.211	601	**Inheritance Tax**	
171.212	504, 602	312.001—402	1510
171.251—171.258	504, 604	313.001—54	1510
171.259	608	313.101—105	1511
171.260	608	**Local Taxation**	
171.301	605	321.002	904
171.302	605	321.103	904
171.303—171.308	607	321.104	904
171.308	604	321.1055	904
171.309	606	321.203	904
171.310	605	321.205	904
171.311—171.315	606	323.103—323.105	904
171.316	608	323.203	904
171.317	608	324.022	904
171.351	603	**[Local Hotel Occupancy Tax]**	
171.352	603	351.001—351.006	1707
171.353	607	352.0025	1707
171.354	603	352.001—352.005	1707
171.355	603	352.007	1707
171.361	506	352.107	1707
171.362	505, 602	**County Development Districts**	
171.363	602	383.001—383.040	1707
171.721—171.731	405	**[MISCELLANEOUS TAXES]**	
171.751—171.761	406	**Alcoholic Beverages Code**	
171.815—171-825	403	1.04	1702
[Utilities Taxes]		5.50	1702
182.021	1708	11.09	1702
182.022	1708	12.02	1702
182.024	1708	14.02	1702
182.026	1708	16.02	1702
182.081—182.083	1708	18.02	1702
Mixed Beverage Tax		19.02	1702
183.021	1702	20.02	1702
183.022	1702	21.02	1702
Gas Production Tax		22.02	1702
201.001	1709	23.02	1702
201.051—201.055	1709	24.02	1702
201.058	1709	25.02	1702
201.059	1709	25.03	1702
201.101—201.106	1709	26.02	1702
201.201	1709	27.02	1702
201.2015	1709	27.12	1702
201.202	1709	28.02	1702
201.203	1709	29.02	1702
201.2035	1709	30.02	1702
201.204	1709	31.02	1702
201.205	1709	32.02	1702
201.251	1709	33.02	1702
Oil Production Tax		33.22	1702
202.001—202.003	1709	34.02	1702
202.052—202.055	1709	35.02	1702
202.056	1709	36.02	1702
202.057	1709	37.02	1702
202.058	1709	38.04	1702
202.059	1709	39.04	1702
202.060	1709	40.02	1702
202.061	1709	41.02	1702
202.151	1709	42.02	1702
202.1515	1709	43.02	1702
202.152—202.156	1709	44.02	1702
202.201	1709	45.02	1702
202.202	1709	46.02	1702

Law and Rule Locator

Law Sec.	Discussion at ¶
48.02	1702
52.02	1702
54.07	1105
62.02	1702
63.02	1702
64.02	1702
65.02	1702
66.02	1702
67.02	1702
68.02	1702
69.02	1702
70.02	1702
71.02	1702
72.02	1702
73.02	1702
74.02	1702
101.252	1704
201.03	1702
201.06	1702
201.07	1702
201.42	1702
201.43	1702
201.48	1702
201.49	1702
201.71	1702
203.03	1702
203.08	1702
203.09	1702
203.10	1702

Government Code

404.095	1703
490.352	409
2303.003	1707

Health and Safety Code

361.013	1710
361.0135	1710
361.134—361.137	1710
371.062	1705
382.062	1710
382.0621	1710
401.011	1710
402.272	1710

Insurance Code

Art. 1.10	1704
Art. 1.14-2	1704
Art. 1.14-3	1704
Art. 1.35B	1704
Art. 4.10	1704
Art. 4.11A	1704
Art. 4.11B	1704
Art. 4.11C	1704
Art. 4.17	1704
Art. 4.63	1704
Art. 4.65—4.68	1704
Art. 5.12	1704
Art. 5.24	1704
Art. 5.49	1704
Art. 5.91	1704
Art. 9.46	1704
Art. 9.48	1704
Art. 20A.33	1704
Art. 21.07-6	1704
Art. 21.28-C	1704
Art. 21.28-D	1704
Art. 21.49	1704
Art. 23.08-A	1704
Art. 26.14A	1704

Law Sec.	Discussion at ¶
222.002	1704
223.003	1704
281.004	1704

Labor Code

301.101—301.107	404
301.103	2002
301.104	2002
301.106	2002

Local Government Code

334.251—334.258	1707
335.001—335.075	1707

Natural Resources Code

40.154	1705
40.155	1705
81.111	1709
81.116	1709
81.117	1709
89.047	1709
91.605	1710

Transportation Code

502.002	1706
502.101	1706
502.158	1706
502.161—502.163	1706
502.165—502.168	1706
502.170—502.175	1706
502.177	1706
502.276	1706
502.278	1706
502.351—502.353	1706

Water Code

5.235	1708
26.011	1710
26.0291	1710
26.342	1705
26.3574	1705
26.361	1705

REVISED CIVIL STATUTES
Public Utilities

1.351—1.353, Art. 1466c-0	1708
3.604—3.606, Art. 1466c-0	1708
Art. 6060, Tit. 102	1708

RULES

25 TAC	Discussion at ¶
205.44	1710
205.51	1710
289.126	1710

31 TAC

305.503	1710
335.323—335.325	1710
335.328	1710

34 TAC

1.5	2003
1.6	2003
1.13	2003
1.21	2003
1.27	2003
1.28	2003
3.1	1803
3.2	1803
3.4	2002
3.5	602
3.9	1803, 1805, 2005
3.14—3.16	1709

25 TAC	Discussion at ¶	25 TAC	Discussion at ¶
3.20—3.22	1709	3.356	1002
3.31	1709	3.357	1002
3.33—3.38	1709	3.358	1003
3.41	1709	3.360	1003
3.50	1709	3.364	1002
3.70	903	3.365	1002
3.79	902	3.366	1002
3.84	1002	3.481	903
3.96	903	3.541	104
3.1205	1703, 1103	3.544	501, 502, 504, 602
3.1281	903, 1103	3.545	505
3.161	1707	3.546	103
3.162	1707	3.550	203
3.281	1107	3.551	204
3.282	1108	3.552	207
3.284	1002	3.553	204
3.285	1003	3.554	103
3.286	803, 902, 1006, 1101, 1102, 1103, 1104, 1105, 1109, 1306	3.555	205,
		3.558	205
3.287	1006	3.559	204
3.288	1106	3.560	103
3.289	1002	3.562	202, 204, 205
3.293	902, 1002	3.563	103, 204
3.294	1707	3.565	204, 503
3.295—3.300	1002	3.566	104
3.302	902, 1102	3.567	502
3.303	902, 1102	3.568	503
3.306	1002	3.570	604
3.308	1002	3.575	505
3.309	1002	3.581	103, 303
3.310	804, 1002	3.582	104
3.314	1002	3.583	104
3.316	1003, 1004	3.584	202, 501, 504
3.320	903	3.586	103
3.322	1004	3.587	202
3.323	1003	3.588	205
3.325	1305	3.589	501
3.327	1105	3.590	507
3.328	1102	3.592	102
3.329	1005	3.594	402
3.330	1002	3.741	903
3.331	1003, 1005	3.1281	1103
3.336	1002	9.415	1504
3.338	1202, 1203, 1204	9.3031	1505
3.339	1305	9.4037	1502
3.346	805, 902, 1202	16.2	1703
3.350	1002	16.3	1703
3.541	104		

TOPICAL INDEX

References are to paragraph (¶) numbers.

A

Abatements
- property tax ... 1510

Absorption of tax
- sales and use taxes
  - prohibition ... 1108

Accounting methods
- franchise tax ... 202,
  - allocation and apportionment ... 303
  - federal/state key feature comparison ... 45
- sales and use taxes
  - accounting basis for reports ... 1102

Accounting periods
- franchise tax 202, ... 205
- federal/state key feature comparison ... 45

Administration and procedure
- administrative agencies ... 1802
- assignment of tax claims ... 1907
- business successor liability ... 1901
- confidentiality ... 1804
- credit card payments ... 1805
- credits ... 2002
- deficiency assessments ... 1901
  - redetermination ... 2003
- due dates ... 1803
- electronic funds transfer ... 1805
- extensions ... 1803
- hearings ... 2003
- in general ... 1801
- injunctions ... 1908; 2006
- interest, deficiencies ... 1909
  - deficiencies ... 1909
  - interest ... 2002
- jeopardy assessments ... 1901
- levy ... 1904
- liens ... 1904
- offsets ... 2002
- payment ... 1803
  - credit card and electronic funds transfer ... 1805
- penalties ... 1909
  - payment ... 1805
- personal liability ... 1901
- records ... 1804
- refunds ... 2002
- returns ... 1803
- revocation of permits, licenses ... 1908
- sales and use taxes ... 1109
- security for tax ... 1902
- seizure and sale of property ... 1905
- settlements ... 1903
- statute of limitations, deficiencies ... 1901
- suit for refund ... 2004
- suit to collect ... 1303; 1305; 1906
- suit to protest tax ... 2005
- taxpayer remedies ... 2001
  - redetermination after deficiency assessment ... 2003
  - refunds, credits, and offsets ... 2002
  - suit for refund ... 2004
  - suit to protest tax ... 2005
  - tax injunction ... 2006
- unemployment compensation ... 1602

Administrative agencies
- administration and procedure ... 1802

Administrative expense assessment
- utilities taxes ... 1708

Agricultural use land
- property tax
  - assessment ... 1505

Agriculture
- property tax ... 1505
- sales and use taxes
  - exemptions ... 1002

Aircraft
- property ... 1204
- sales and use taxes
  - credits, certain repairs ... 1204
  - exemptions ... 1002

Alcoholic beverages taxes ... 1702

Allocation and apportionment
- accounting methods ... 303
- franchise tax
  - apportionment formula ... 303
  - in general ... 301
  - sourcing rules ... 303
  - UDITPA ... 302

Alternative minimum tax
- franchise tax
  - federal/state key feature comparison ... 45

Amended returns ... 504

Amnesty ... 1909

Amortization
- franchise tax ... 205
- federal/state key feature comparison ... 45

Amusement services
- sales and use taxes ... 804
- exemptions ... 1002

Animals
- sales and use taxes
  - exemptions ... 1002

Appeals
- franchise tax
  - judgment of forfeiture ... 607
- property tax ... 1509

Apportionment formula
- franchise tax ... 303

Appraisals
- property tax ... 1505
  - review board ... 1505, 1509

Arbitration
- property tax ... 1509

Attorneys
- franchise (margin) tax ... 767

Attorneys fees
- property tax
  - excessive appraisals ... 1509

Assessments
- administration and procedure
  - deficiency assessments and jeopardy assessments ... 1901
- estate tax ... 1409
- property tax ... 1505
- sales and use taxes ... 1302
- utilities taxes ... 1708

Asset expense election
- franchise tax ... 205
- federal/state key feature comparison ... 45

Assignment of tax claims ... 1907

Auctions
- administration and procedure
  - sale of seized property ... 1905
- sales and use taxes ... 1003

Audits ... 1108
- internal audit review ... 2003

Automotive oil
- motor fuel taxes
  - sales fee ... 1705

Automotive repair
- sales and use taxes
  - exemption ... 1002

AUT

B

Bad debt deduction
- franchise tax ... 205
- - federal/state key feature comparison ... 45
- sales and use tax ... 902

Banking corporations
- franchise tax ... 103
- - charter revocation ... 608

Banking institutions
- franchise tax
- - federal/state key feature comparison ... 45

Basis of tax
- estate tax ... 1401
- franchise tax ... 201 et seq.
- - deductions in computation ... 204-207
- gas production tax ... 1709
- gross premiums tax
- - insurance companies ... 1704
- hotel occupancy tax ... 1707
- motor fuel taxes ... 1705
- oil production tax ... 1709
- property tax ... 1501
- sales and use taxes
- - bad debts ... 902
- - bracket schedule ... 906
- - coupons, premiums, and trading stamps ... 902
- - in general ... 901
- - local tax rate chart ... 905
- - local tax rates ... 904
- - rate of tax ... 903
- - tax base ... 902
- - trade-ins ... 902
- sulfur production tax ... 1709
- utilities taxes ... 1708

Batteries, lead-acid
- environmental taxes and fees ... 1710

Benefits
- unemployment compensation
- - employee's benefits ... 1606

Binding arbitration
- property tax
- - taxpayer remedies ... 1509

Bins and cages
- sales and use taxes
- - exemptions ... 1002

Boats and boat motors
- sales and use taxes ... 903

Bonds
- amortization
- - franchise federal/state key feature comparison ... 45
- premiums, amortization
- - franchise federal/state key feature comparison ... 45

Bracket schedules
- sales and use taxes ... 906

Broadcasting
- sales and use taxes
- - exemptions ... 1002

Business incentives
- franchise tax ... 55
- insurance premiums tax ... 65
- sales and use taxes ... 60

Business successors
- successor liability ... 1901

C

Cable television services
- sales and use taxes ... 804

Capital assets and investments
- franchise tax
- - credit ... 403, 406

Capital gains and capital losses
- franchise tax
- - federal/state key feature comparison ... 45

Capital investments
- franchise tax
- - credit ... 403; 406

Certificate of authority
- franchise tax
- - forfeiture ... 605; 606; 607

Chambers of commerce
- sales and use taxes
- - exemptions ... 1004

Charitable contributions
- franchise tax
- - federal/state key feature comparison ... 45

Charitable organizations
- franchise tax exemption ... 104
- sales and use tax exemption ... 1004
- property tax exemption ... 1504

Charter
- franchise tax
- - forfeiture ... 605; 606; 607
- - revocation, banking corporation or savings and loan associations ... 608

Chemicals, agricultural
- sales and use taxes
- - exemptions ... 1002

Cigarette and tobacco products taxes ... 1703

Claim procedure
- administration and procedure
- - settlement, tax claims and penalties ... 1903
- sales and use taxes
- - refunds ... 1005

Clean energy project
- franchise tax ... 409

Clean-fuel vehicles
- franchise tax
- - federal/state key feature comparison ... 45

Clothing and backpacks
- sales and use taxes
- - exemption ... 1002

Coastal protection fee ... 1705

Coins and bullion
- sales and use taxes
- - exemptions ... 1002

Collection of tax
- administration and procedure
- - assignment of tax claims ... 1907
- - deficiency assessments ... 1901
- - injunctions ... 1908
- - interest, delinquent tax ... 1909
- - jeopardy assessments ... 1901
- - levy ... 1904
- - liens ... 1904
- - offsets ... 2002
- - penalties ... 1909
- - refunds ... 2002
- - revocation of permits, licenses ... 1908
- - security for tax ... 1902
- - seizure and sale of property ... 1905
- - settlements ... 1903
- - statute of limitations, deficiencies ... 1901
- - suit to collect ... 1906
- franchise tax ... 601
- - banks, revocation of charter ... 608
- - forfeiture, charter or certificate of authority ... 605; 606; 607
- - forfeiture, corporate privileges ... 604
- - interest ... 602
- - penalties ... 602
- - suit to enforce ... 603
- property tax ... 1507
- sales and use taxes ... 1301
- - assessments ... 1302
- - collection suits ... 1303; 1305
- - interest ... 1306
- - judgments ... 1304
- - penalties ... 1306
- - statute of limitations ... 1305

Collection suits
- administration and procedure ... 1906

BAD

Topical Index

References are to paragraph (¶) numbers.

Collection suits—continued
. franchise tax 603
. property tax 1507
. sales and use taxes 1303; 1305

Combined reports
. franchise (margin) tax 507

Compensation
. franchise (margin) tax deduction 204

Computation of tax
. estate taxes 1403
. franchise tax . . . . 202 et seq.

Computers, services, and software
. franchise tax 303
. sales and use taxes
. . exemptions 1002

Confidentiality
. administration and procedure 1804
. franchise tax 506
. sales and use taxes 1102

Consolidated returns
. franchise tax 501
. . federal/state key feature comparison 45

Construction
. sales and use taxes
. . exemptions 1002
. . lump sum contracts 1002
. . sourcing rules for local taxes 904

Containers
. sales and use taxes
. . exemptions 1002

Contractors and repairpersons
. sales and use taxes
. . credit 1204

Cooperative credit associations
. franchise tax
. . exemption 104

Corporate distributions and adjustments
. franchise tax
. . federal/state key feature comparison 45

Corporate officer, director liability
. franchise tax 604
. in general 1902

Corporate privileges
. franchise tax
. . forfeiture 604

Corporations—see Franchise tax, Franchise (margin) tax; see also specific types

County sales and use taxes—see Local taxes

Coupons, premiums, and trading stamps
. sales and use taxes 902

Cost of goods sold
. franchise (margin) tax deduction 766

Court action
. administration and procedure
. . taxpayer remedies 2003; 2004; 2005; 2006
. property tax
. . taxpayer remedies 1509

Court-reporting services
. sales and use taxes
. . exemptions 1002

CPA audit program
. sales and use tax liability 1108

Credit card payments 1805

Credit reporting services
. sales and use taxes 804

Credit unions
. franchise tax
. . exemptions 104

Credits
. administration and procedure 2002
. estate tax
. . maximum federal credit 1402

Credits—continued
. franchise tax 401
. . business loss carryovers 402
. . capital investment 403; 406
. . clean energy project 409
. . economic development 403, 406
. . employees receiving financial assistance 55; 404
. . federal/state key feature comparison 45
. . job creation 45; 406
. . research and development 45
. federal/state key feature comparison
. . franchise tax 45
. insurance premiums tax 1704
. property tax 1511
. sales and use taxes 1201
. . contractors and repairpersons 1204
. . property subsequently resold 1203
. . real property contributed to institution of higher
learning 1205
. . tax paid to another state 1202

Crude Oil Special Tax Report 1709

D

Data processing services
. sales and use taxes 804
. . exemptions 1002

Dealers
. property tax
. . prepayment 1506

Debt collection services
. sales and use taxes 804

Deductions
. franchise tax . . . . 204 et seq.

Defense readjustment project
. franchise tax
. . federal/state key feature comparison 45
. sales and use taxes
. . refunds 1005

Deferrals
. property tax
. . military personnel 1506
. . residence homestead appreciation 1510
. . senior citizens 1510

Deferred compensation plans
. franchise tax 205
. . federal/state key feature comparison 45

Deficiency assessments
. administration and procedure 1901
. . redetermination 2003

Definitions
. administration and procedure
. . reasonable diligence 1903
. franchise tax
. . corporation 103
. . gross receipts 303
. . passive entity 104
. . qualified business 408
. . strategic investment area 406
. hotel occupancy tax
. . hotel 1707
. . permanent resident 1707
. property tax
. . agricultural use 1505
. . agriculture 1505
. . freeport goods 1504
. . market value 1505
. . public access airport property 1505
. . public purpose 1504
. . recreational, park, or scenic use 1505
. sales and use taxes
. . bad debts 902
. . credit sales 902
. . electrical transcriptions 1002
. . enterprise project 1005
. . manufacturing 1002
. . maquiladora enterprise 1003
. . no business activity 1105
. . place of business 1105

DEF

Topical Index

References are to paragraph (¶) numbers.

Definitions—continued
. sales and use taxes—continued
.. purchase ... 802
.. qualified business ... 1005
.. qualified employee ... 1005
.. qualified hotel project ... 1005
. receipts ... 902
. retail grocer ... 1102
. retailer ... 802
. sale ... 802
. sales for resale ... 1003
. sales price ... 902
. seller ... 802
.. tangible personal property ... 802
. total consideration ... 903
. unemployment compensation ... 1603
. utilities taxes
.. utility company ... 1708

Delinquent taxes
. administration and procedure
.. credit card payments ... 1805
.. seizure and sale of property ... 1905
. property tax ... 1508
.. installment payments ... 1506

Delivery charges and packing costs
. sales and use taxes ... 902

Depletion
. franchise tax ... 205
.. federal/state key feature comparison ... 45

Depreciation
. franchise tax ... 205
.. federal/state key feature comparison ... 45
.. franchise (margin) tax ... 764

Destination management companies
. franchise tax ... 1301
.. defined ... 207
.. total revenue exclusion ... 203, 207
. sales and use tax exemption ... 1002

Detrimental reliance
. sales and use taxes ... 1301

Development Corporation Act ... 104; 904; 1102

Development corporations
. sales and use taxes
.. exemptions ... 1004
.. reports ... 1102

Diesel fuel
. motor fuel taxes ... 1705

Direct payment permits
. sales and use taxes ... 1106

Disabled access expenditures
. franchise tax
.. federal/state key feature comparison ... 45

Disabled homeowners
. property tax
.. installment payment option ... 1506
.. school district taxes exemption ... 1504

Disaster damage to property
. property tax
.. installment payments ... 1506

Discounts
. cigarette and tobacco products taxes ... 1703
. property tax
.. early payment discounts ... 1506
. sales and use taxes ... 1103

Dividends
. franchise tax ... 203
.. federal/state key feature comparison ... 45
. franchise (margin) tax deduction ... 761

Doing business
. domestic corporations
.. fees and taxes ... 2201
. foreign corporations
.. fees and taxes ... 2202

Domestic corporations
. doing business in Texas
.. fees and taxes ... 2201

Domiciliary disputes
. estate tax ... 1406

Due dates
. administration and procedure ... 1803
. alcoholic beverages taxes ... 1702
. cigarette and tobacco products taxes ... 1703
. estate ... 1410
. fireworks tax ... 1103
. franchise tax
.. extensions ... 505
.. payments ... 502
.. withdrawal, merger, consolidation, conversion ... 503
. gas production tax ... 1709
. gross premiums tax
.. insurance companies ... 1704
. hotel occupancy tax ... 1707
. motor fuel taxes ... 1705
. oil production tax ... 1709
. property tax ... 1506
. sales and use taxes ... 1103
.. extensions ... 1803
.. prepayments ... 1104
. sulfur production tax ... 1709
. utilities taxes ... 1708

E

Early payment discounts
. property tax ... 1506

Economic development
. franchise tax
.. credits ... 403; 406

Electric and telephone cooperatives
. sales and use taxes
.. exemptions ... 1004
. franchise tax
.. exemption ... 104

Electrical transcriptions
. sales and use taxes
.. exemptions ... 1002

Electronic filing
. sales and use taxes ... 1803

Electronic funds transfer (EFT) ... 1805

Employee compensation
. franchise tax ... 204; 205

Employee retirement plan services
. franchise tax
.. apportionment ... 303

Employee services
. sales and use taxes
.. exemptions ... 1002

Employees
. unemployment compensation
.. benefits ... 1606

Employers
. administration and procedure
.. refund, wages paid to employees receiving financial assistance ... 2002
. unemployment compensation
.. employers subject to tax ... 1603
.. exempt employers and employment ... 1604
.. returns ... 1607

Empowerment zones
. franchise tax
.. federal/state key feature comparison ... 45

Energy conservation
. sales and use taxes
.. exemptions ... 1002

Enterprise zones
. franchise tax
.. credits ... 403
.. refund, job creation ... 408
. hotel occupancy tax
.. qualified hotel projects ... 1707
. sales and use taxes ... 1005

Environmental protection
. environmental taxes and fees ... 1705; 1710

DEL

Topical Index
References are to paragraph (¶) numbers.

Environmental protection—continued
. sales and use taxes
. . exemptions 1002
Environmental remediation costs
. franchise tax 205
. . federal/state key feature comparison 45
Environmental taxes and fees 1705; 1710
Equipment
. property tax
. . prepayment, dealers' inventories of heavy equipment 1506
Estate tax
. additional 1404
. assessment 1409
. basis of tax 1401
. computation of tax 1403
. deductions 1408
. domiciliary disputes, settlement 1406
. due dates 1407
. exemptions 1402
. . charitable 1402
. imposition of tax 1401
. in general 1401
. interest 1410
. liability for taxes 1410
. notice 1411
. payment 1410
. property subject to tax 1407
. rates 1402
. refunds 1407
. returns 1409
. transfers, taxable 1405
. waivers 1411
Exclusions
. sales and use taxes
. . exclusions from sales price 902
Exempt corporations
. franchise tax 104
Exempt organizations
. franchise tax 104
. . federal/state key feature comparison 45
Exemption certificates 1005
Exemptions
. alcoholic beverages taxes 1702
. cigarette and tobacco products taxes 1703
. environmental taxes and fees 1705; 1710
. estate tax 1402
. franchise tax 104
. gas production tax 1709
. hotel occupancy tax 1707
. motor fuel taxes 1705
. oil production tax 1709
. property tax 1504; 2307
. sales and use taxes 1006; 1106
. . agricultural 1002
. . aircraft 1002
. . amusement services 1002
. . animals 1002
. . automotive repair 1002
. . bins and cages 1002
. . broadcasting 1002
. . bullion 1002
. . chambers of commerce 1004
. . charitable organizations 1004
. . chemicals, agricultural 1002
. . clothing 1002
. . coins 1002
. . computer hardware, software, and services 1002
. . construction 1002
. . containers 1002
. . court-reporting services 1002
. . development corporations 1004
. . dry cleaning 1002
. . educational organizations 1004
. . electric and telephone cooperatives 1004
. . employee services 1002
. . energy conservation equipment 1002
. . environmental protection equipment . . . 1002
. . exemption certificates 1006; 1106
. . feed and seed 1002

Exemptions—continued
. sales and use taxes—continued
. . fire departments 1004
. . fireworks 903
. . food 1002
. . foreign diplomatic personnel 1004
. . governmental entities 1004
. . health facilities corporations 1004
. . imports and exports 1003
. . in general 1001
. . intercorporate services 1003
. . internet access 1002
. . interstate motor vehicles 1002
. . irrigation systems 1002
. . joint ownership transfers 1003
. . laundry and cleaning services 1002
. . lawn services, certain persons 1002
. . machinery and equipment 1002
. . magazines 1002
. . manufacturing 1002
. . maquiladora enterprise 1003
. . medical items 1002
. . mining and drilling 1002
. . motion pictures 1002
. . motor vehicle dealers and manufacturers . . 1002
. . motor vehicles 1002
. . Native Americans 1004
. . new construction 1002
. . newspapers 1002
. . nonprofit organizations 1004
. . occasional sales 1003
. . out-of-state shipments 1003
. . packaging supplies 1002
. . penalties, improper use 1306
. . public schools 1004
. . publishing and broadcasting 1002
. . recording studios 1002
. . recordkeeping requirements 1107
. . religious organizations 1004
. . repairs, computer 1002
. . repairs, disaster 1002
. . resale certificates 1003; 1108
. . resales 1003
. . research and development ventures 60; 1005
. . restoration of historic sites 1002
. . sales prohibited by federal law 1003
. . senior citizens' organizations 1004
. . ships and vessels 1002
. . staff-leasing services 1002
. . telecommunications services 1002
. . television stations 1002
. . Texas National Research Laboratory Commission . . 1004
. . timber operations 1002
. . tourist promotion agencies 1004
. . transportation equipment 1002
. . university and college student organizations . . 1004
. . utilities 1002
. . vending-machine sales 1002
. . waste removal 1002
. . water and water conservation equipment . . 1002
. . wrapping, packing, and packaging supplies . . 1002
. . unemployment compensation 1603
. . utilities taxes 1708

Exports—see Imports and exports
Extensions
. administration and procedure 1803
. extension of limitations period 1901
. franchise tax 505
. sales and use taxes 1103
Extraterritorial income exclusion
. franchise tax
. . federal/state key feature comparison 45

F

Family supplies
. property tax
. . exemption 1504
Farmers and farming
. franchise tax
. . exemption 104

FAR

Topical Index
References are to paragraph (¶) numbers.

Farmers and farming—continued
. property tax
. . exemption 1504

Federal/state key feature comparisons
. franchisee tax 45

Feed
. sales and use taxes
. . exemption 1002

Fees and taxes
. doing business in Texas
. . domestic corporations 2201
. . foreign corporations 2202

Fire departments
. sales and use taxes
. . exemption 1004

Financial asset securitization investment trusts (FASITs)
. franchise tax
. . federal/state key feature comparison 45

Fireworks
. fireworks tax 903
. . due date 1103
. . exemptions 903

Food
. sales and use taxes
. . exemptions 1002
. . tax base, vending machine food 902

Foreign commercial vehicles
. motor vehicle registration fee 1706

Foreign corporations
. doing business in Texas
. . fees and taxes 2202

Foreign diplomatic personnel
. sales and use taxes
. . exemption 1004

Foreign source income
. franchise tax
. . federal/state key feature comparison 45

Foreign tax credit
. franchise tax
. . federal/state key feature comparison 45

Forfeiture of charter
. franchise tax 605
. . corporate privileges 604
. . judicial 607
. . nonjudicial 606

Forfeiture of corporate privileges
. franchise tax 604

Franchise tax
. accounting periods and methods 202
. . federal/state key feature comparison 45
. allocation and apportionment
. . apportionment formula 303
. . in general 301
. . margin tax 303
. . UDITPA 302
. alternative minimum tax
. . federal/state key feature comparison 45
. asset expense deduction 205
. . federal/state key feature comparison 45
. bad debt deduction 203
. . federal/state key feature comparison 45
. banking corporations 103;608
. banking institutions
. . federal/state key feature comparison 45
. basis of tax
. . computation, margin . . . . 201 et seq.
. . deductions in computation 204-206
. . in general 201
. capital gains and looses
. . federal/state key feature comparison 45
. charitable contributions
. . federal/state key feature comparison 45
. charter, certificate of authority, forfeiture 605; 606; 607
. clean-fuel vehicles
. . federal/state key feature comparison 45
. collection of tax 601
. . banks, revocation of charter 608

Franchise tax—continued
. collection of tax—continued
. . forfeiture, charter or certificate of authority . . 605; 606; 607
. . forfeiture, corporate privileges 604
. . interest 602
. . penalties 602
. . suit to enforce 603
. corporate distributions and adjustments
. . federal/state key feature comparison 45
. corporate privileges, forfeiture 604
. corporations subject to tax 103
. credits 401; 770
. . capital investment 403; 406
. . clean energy project 409
. . deferred compensation plans 204; 205
. . federal/state key feature comparison 45
. . franchise (margin) tax . . . . 401 et seq.
. depletion 205
. . federal/state key feature comparison 45
. depreciation 205
. . federal/state key feature comparison 45
. disabled access expenditures
. . federal/state key feature comparison 45
. dividends 203
. . federal/state key feature comparison 45
. . economic development 45; 403; 406
. . employees receiving financial assistance . . . 45
. . job creation 45; 406
. . research and development 45
. . Texas Youth Commission, wages 2305
. deductions . . . . 204—207
. due dates 502
. environmental remediation costs 205
. . federal/state key feature comparison 45
. exempt organizations
. . federal/state key feature comparison 45
. . exemptions 104
. extraterritorial income
. . federal/state key feature comparison 45
. federal credits
. . federal/state key feature comparison 45
. foreign source income
. . federal/state key feature comparison 45
. gains
. . federal/state key feature comparison 45
. insurance companies
. . federal/state key feature comparison 45
. intangibles, amortization
. . federal/state key feature comparison 45
. interest on deficiencies 602
. interest on indebtedness
. . federal/state key feature comparison 45
. interest on state obligations
. . federal/state key feature comparison 45
. limited liability companies 103; 106
. losses
. . business loss carryover credit 402
. . federal/state key feature comparison 45
. net operating loss
. . federal/state key feature comparison 45
. overview 101
. payment of tax
. . due dates 502
. . reports 504
. penalties
. . forfeiture of charter . . . . 605—607
. . forfeiture of corporate privileges 604
. . in general 601; 602
. . revocation of charter of banking corporation . 608
. . suit to enforce tax 603
. pollution control facilities, amortization 205
. . federal/state key feature comparison 45
. privilege periods 501
. rate of tax 102
. refund, wages paid employees receiving financial assistance 404
. refunds
. . in general 2002
. . job creation in enterprise zone 408
. . reinvestment zone property taxes 407
. reports 504
. . combined 507
. . confidentiality 506

FED

Topical Index

References are to paragraph (¶) numbers.

Franchise tax—continued
. research expenses 205
. . federal/state key feature comparison 45
. returns and payment
. . confidentiality 506
. . due dates 502
. . extensions 505
. . privilege periods 501
. . reports 504
. . withdrawal, merger, consolidation, conversion 503
. S corporations 103;105
. . federal/state key feature comparison 45
. savings and loan associations 103
. start-up expenditures, amortization
. . federal/state key feature comparison 45
. suit to enforce 603
. tax base 201
. . alternative computation method 102
. . computation deductions . . . . 204—207
. tax evasion
. . federal/state key feature comparison 45
. tax liens 604
. tax paid deduction 205
. . federal/state key feature comparison 45
. taxpayer remedies
. . in general 701
. . refund, job creation in enterprise zone 408
. . refund, reinvestment zone property taxes 407
Fraud
. sales and use taxes 1306
Freeport goods
. sales and use tax exemption 1504

G

Gains
. franchise tax
. . federal/state key feature comparison 45
Gas production tax 1709
Gasoline
. motor fuel taxes 1705
Generally accepted accounting principles
. franchise tax
. . accounting methods 202
. . computation, gross receipts 303
Generation-skipping transfer tax 1401; 1412
Goods-in-transit
. property tax exemption 1504
Governmental entities
. sales and use tax exemption 1004
Gratuities 902
Gross premiums tax 1704

H

Hazardous waste fees 1710
Hazardous waste removal
. sales and use taxes
. . exemption 1002
Health care institutions
. franchise (margin) tax exclusions 207
Health care providers
. franchise (margin) tax exclusions 207
Health facilities corporations
. sales and use taxes
. . exemption 1004
Homeowners
. property tax
. . installment payments for disabled or senior
      homeowners 1506
Homesteads
. property tax
. . appraised value, residential homestead 1505
. . exemption 1504
. . payment deferral on appreciation 1510

Hospital district sales and use taxes—see Local taxes
Hospital laundry cooperative associations
. franchise tax
. . exemption 104
Hotel occupancy tax 1707
Hotel projects, qualified
. sales and use taxes
. . refunds 1005
Household goods
. property tax
. . exemption 1504
Housing finance corporations
. franchise tax
. . exemption 104

I

Imports and exports
. sales and use taxes
. . exemptions 1003
Imposition of tax
. alcoholic beverages taxes 1702
. cigarette and tobacco products taxes 1703
. estate tax 1401
. franchise tax 101; 103
. motor fuel taxes 1705
. property tax 1502
. sales tax 802
. use tax 805
Incentives—see Business incentives
Incidence of tax
. sales tax 802
. use tax 805
Industrial waste fees 1710
Industrial waste removal
. sales and use taxes
. . exemption 1002
Information returns
. sales and use taxes 1102
Information services
. sales and use taxes 804
Inheritance tax—see Estate tax
Injunctions
. administration and procedure 1908; 2006
Insolvent taxpayer
. administration and procedure
. . settlement of tax claims and penalties 1903
Installation charges
. sales and use taxes 902
Installment, lay-away, and conditional sales
. sales and use taxes 902
Installment payments
. property taxes 1506
Insurance companies
. franchise tax
. . exemptions 104
. . federal/state key feature comparison 45
. gross premiums tax 1704
. credits 104
. . retaliatory tax 1704
Insurance services
. sales and use taxes 804
Intangibles
. franchise tax
. . apportionment 303
. sales and use taxes tax
. . sourcing of sales 904
Intangibles, amortization
. franchise tax
. . federal/state key feature comparison 45
Intercorporate services
. franchise (margin) tax 303; 507

INT

398 Topical Index

References are to paragraph (¶) numbers.

Intercorporate services—continued
. sales and use taxes
. . exemptions 1003

Interest
. administration and procedure
. . delinquent taxes 1909
. . refunds 2002
. estate tax 1410
. franchise tax
. . delinquent taxes 602
. . indebtedness 45; 205
. . state and local obligations
. . in general 1909
. property tax
. . delinquencies 1508
. . refunds 1509
. sales and use taxes
. . unpaid taxes 1306

Internal audit review 2003

International Fuel Tax Agreement (IFTA) 1705

Internet access services
. sales and use taxes
. . exemption 1002
. . nexus 803
. . taxation of 804

Interstate Income Law—see Public Law 86-272

Interstate motor vehicles
. sales and use taxes
. . exemption 1002

Investment companies
. franchise tax
. . exemption, open-end investment companies 104

Irrigation systems
. sales and use taxes
. . exemption 1002

J

Jeopardy assessments
. administration and procedure 1901

Joint ownership transfers
. sales and use taxes
. . exemption 1003

Joint ventures
. franchise tax 103

Judgments
. sales and use taxes
. . collection 1304

L

Laundry and cleaning
. sales and use taxes
. . exemptions 1002

Lawn and yard care
. sales and use taxes
. . exemptions 1002

Leases
. sales and use taxes
. . application of tax 802
. . manufacturing exemption 1002
. . tax base 902

Legal service providers
. franchise (margin) tax 207

Lending institutions
. franchise (margin) tax 207

Liability for tax
. administration and procedure
. . personal liability, unpaid corporate taxes 1901
. estate tax 1410
. franchise tax
. . during forfeiture 604

Liens, tax
. administration and procedure 1904

Liens, tax—continued
. franchise tax 604
. property tax 1507

Limited liability companies (LLCs)
. franchise tax 103; 106
. . apportionment by corporate member 303
. . basis of tax 106
. . determining surplus 106
. . tax rate 102

Liquefied gas
. motor fuel taxes 1705

Liquidations
. administration and procedure
. . settlement of tax claims and penalties 1903
. sales and use taxes 1003

Local tax rate chart 905

Local taxes
. sales and use taxes 904
. tax rate chart 905

Lodges
. franchise tax
. . exemption 104

Losses
. franchise tax
. . credit for business losses 402
. . federal/state key feature comparison 45

Lump sum contracts
. sales and use taxes
. . construction 1004

M

Machinery and equipment
. sales and use taxes
. . exemptions 1002

Magazines
. sales and use taxes
. . exemption 1002

Managed audits
. sales and use taxes 1108

Manufactured housing
. property tax
. . prepayment, retailers' inventories 1506
. sales and use taxes 903

Manufacturing
. environmental taxes and fees
. . hazardous substances 1710
. sales and use taxes
. . exemptions 1002

Margin, Franchise Tax—see Franchihse Tax
. apportionment 303
. basis of tax 202
. combined reports 507
. compensation deduction 204
. computation of tax 201
. . starting point for computation 202
. cost of goods sold deduction 205
. credits . . . . 401 et seq.
. entities subject to tax 103
. deductions and exclusions 203; 206
. exempt entities 104
. health care institutions and service providers 207
. lending institutions 207
. legal service providers 207
. overview 101
. rate of tax 102
. returns and payments 501

Maquiladora enterprises
. sales and use taxes 1003

Marketing associations
. franchise tax
. . exemption 104

Media production facility
. sales and use tax
. . exemption 1002

INT

Topical Index

References are to paragraph (¶) numbers.

Medical equipment
. sales and use taxes
. . exemptions 1002

Mergers, consolidations, and acquisitions
. franchise tax 503
. sales and use taxes 1003

Military personnel
. property tax
. . deferral 1506

Minerals
. property tax
. . exemption 1504

Mining and drilling
. gas production tax
. . credits, new fields 1709
. oil production tax
. . credits, new fields 1709
. sales and use taxes
. . exemptions 1002

Mobile telecommunications 804

Motor fuel taxes 1705

Motion pictures
. sales and use taxes
. . exemption 1002

Motor vehicle dealers and manufacturers
. property tax
. . prepayment 1506
. sales and use taxes
. . exemptions 1002

Motor vehicle parking services
. sales and use taxes 804

Motor vehicles
. emissions reduction plan surcharge 903;1706
. property tax exemption 1504
. registration fees 1706
. sales and use taxes
. . basis of tax 902
. . credit, certain repairs 1204
. . exemption 1002
. . gift 903
. . off-road vehicles 903
. . rate 903

Multistate Tax Compact
. franchise tax 302
. sales and use taxes 801; 803; 1202

Municipal sales and use taxes—see Local taxes

N

Native Americans
. sales and use taxes 1004

Net operating loss
. franchise tax
. . business loss carryover credit 402
. . federal/state key feature comparison 45

Net taxable capital
. franchise tax
. . nexus requirement 103

Net taxable earned surplus
. franchise tax
. . nexus requirement 103

Newspapers
. sales and use taxes
. . exemption 1002

Nexus
. franchise tax 103; 302
. loss, additional tax 102
. sales and use taxes 803; 1003

Nonproductive personal property
. property tax
. . exemption 1504

Nonprofit organizations
. franchise tax
. . exemptions 104

Nonprofit organizations—continued
. hotel occupancy tax
. . exemptions 1707
. property tax
. . exemptions 1504
. sales and use taxes
. . exemptions 1004
. unemployment compensation
. . exemptions 1603

Nonprofit youth athletic organizations
. sales and use taxes
. . exemptions 1004

Nonresidents
. estate tax 1402
. . computation of tax 1403
. . deductions 1408
. . domiciliary disputes, settlement 1403
. . property subject to tax 1407
. . taxable transfers 1405
. motor vehicle registration fee 1706

Notice
. estate tax 1411

O

Occasional sales
. sales and use taxes
. . exemptions 1003

Offsets 1302; 2002

Oil-drilling equipment
. property tax
. . exemption 1504
. sales and use taxes
. . exemptions 1002

Oil-field cleanup regulatory fee 1709

Oil production tax 1709

Open-end investment companies
. franchise tax
. . exemption 104

Open-space land
. property tax
. . assessment 1505

Out-of-state shipments
. sales and use taxes
. . exemptions 1003

Ownership information report
. franchise tax 504

P

Packaging supplies
. sales and use tax exemption 1002

Parking and storage services
. sales and use taxes 804

Partnerships
. franchise tax 103

Passenger vehicles
. motor vehicle registration fee 1706

Payment of tax
. administration and procedure 1803
. . credit card and electronic funds transfer payments . . . 1805
. alcoholic beverages taxes 1702
. cigarette and tobacco products taxes . . . 1703
. environmental taxes and fees 1710
. estate tax 1410
. franchise tax
. . confidentiality 506
. . due dates 502
. . extensions 505
. . privilege periods 501
. . reports 504
. . withdrawal, merger, consolidation, conversion . . . 503
. gas production tax 1709
. gross premiums tax
. . insurance companies 1704
. hotel occupancy tax 1707

PAY

Topical Index

References are to paragraph (¶) numbers.

Payment of tax—continued
- motor fuel taxes 1705
- oil production tax 1709
- property tax 1506
- sales and use taxes
  - absorption of tax, prohibition 1108
  - administration 1109
  - direct payment permits 1106
  - discounts 1103
  - due dates 1103
  - extensions 1803
  - generally 1101; 1102
  - prepayment of taxes 1104
  - recordkeeping requirements 1107
  - vendor registration 1105
- sulfur production tax 1709
- unemployment compensation 1605
- utilities taxes 1708

Penalties
- administration and procedure 1909
- electronic funds transfer payment 1805
- settlements, tax claims and penalties 1903
- franchise tax
  - forfeiture of charter .... 605—607
  - forfeiture of corporate privileges 604
  - in general 601; 602
  - revocation of charter of banking corporation 608
  - suit to enforce tax 603
- hotel occupancy tax 1707
- property tax 1508
- sales and use taxes 1306

Personal property
- property tax exemption 1504

Personal services
- sales and use taxes 804

Persons subject to tax
- alcoholic beverages taxes 1702
- cigarette and tobacco products taxes 1703
- franchise tax
  - corporations 103
  - taxable entities 103
- gas production tax 1709
- gross premiums tax
  - insurance companies 1704
- hotel occupancy tax 1707
- oil production tax 1709
- sulfur production tax 1709
- unemployment compensation 1603
- utilities taxes 1708

Petroleum products
- motor fuel taxes
  - delivery fee 1705

Pollution control equipment
- property tax exemption 1504

Pollution control facilities, amortization
- franchise tax
  - federal/state key feature comparison 45

Prepayment of taxes
- property tax
  - dealers 1506
- sales and use taxes 1104

Private security services
- sales and use taxes 804

Privilege periods
- franchise tax
  - payments 501

Procedure—see Administration and procedure

Property
- administration and procedure
  - seizure of property 1905
- estate tax 1407
- sales and use taxes
  - credit, contractors and repairpersons ... 1204
  - credit, property subsequently resold 1203
  - seizure of property 1305

Property subject to tax 1503
- estate tax 1407

Property tax
- abatements 1510
- appeals 1509
- appraisal 1505
- appraisal review board 1505; 1509
- arbitration 1509
- assessment 1505
- collection of tax 1507
- credits 1511
- damaged property 1506
- deferrals 1510
- delinquencies 1507
- discounts for early payments 1508
- due dates 1506
- exemptions 1504
- homesteads 1504
- imposition of tax 1501; 1502
- in general 1501
- installment payments 1506
- notice requirements 1505
- interest 1508
- payment 1506
- penalties 1508
- personal property 1504
- prepayment of taxes 1506
- property subject to tax 1503
- rate of tax 1502
- redemption of real property 1507
- refunds 1509
- rendition statements 1505
- reports 1505
- seizure and sale 1507
- statute of limitations, collection 1507
- suit to collect tax 1507
- tax liens 1507
- taxpayer remedies 1509
- valuation 1505

Public access airport property
- property tax
  - assessment 1505

Public Law 86-272
- franchise tax 103

Public property
- property tax
  - exemption 1504

Public schools
- sales and use taxes
  - exemption 1004

Public Utility Commission of Texas 1708

Publishing
- sales and use taxes
  - exemptions 1002

Q

Qualified hotel project
- hotel occupancy tax
  - refund 1707
- sales and use taxes 1005

Qualified subchapter S subsidiaries (QSSS) 205

R

Radioactive waste disposal 1002; 1710

Railway companies
- franchise tax
  - exemption 104

Rate of tax
- alcoholic beverages taxes 1702
- cigarette and tobacco products taxes 1703
- estate tax 1402
- franchise tax 102
- gas production tax 1709
- gross premiums tax
  - insurance companies 1704
- hotel occupancy tax 1707
- motor fuel taxes 1705
- motor vehicle registration fees 1706
- oil production tax 1709

PEN

Topical Index

401

References are to paragraph (¶) numbers.

Rate of tax—continued
. property tax 1502; 1505
. sales and use taxes 903
. . bracket schedules 906
. . local 904; 905
. sulfur production tax 1709
. unemployment compensation 1604
. utilities taxes 1708

Real estate investment trusts (REITS)
. franchise tax 104
. . federal/state key feature comparison 45

Real estate mortgage investment companies (REMICs)
. franchise tax 104
. . federal/state key feature comparison 45

Real property
. property tax
. . exemptions 1504
. . seizure of property 1507
. . subject to tax 1503
. sales and use taxes
. . services 804

Real property repair and remodeling services
. sales and use taxes 804

Real property services
. sales and use taxes 804

Recording studios
. sales and use taxes
. . exemption 1002

Recordkeeping requirements
. administration and procedure 1804
. franchise tax
. . audit and examination 601
. sales and use taxes 1107

Recreational, park, and scenic land
. property tax
. . assessment 1505

Redemption of property
. property tax 1507

Redetermination
. administration and procedure
. . deficiency assessment 2003
. . settlement of tax claims and penalties 1903
. sales and use taxes 1302

Refunds
. administration and procedure
. . suit for refund 2004
. . suit to collect erroneous refunds 1906
. . wages, employees needing financial assistance 2002
. environmental taxes and fees 1710
. franchise tax
. . in general 701
. . job creation in enterprise zone 408
. . reinvestment zone property taxes 407
. . wages, employees needing financial assistance 404
. hotel occupancy tax
. . qualified hotel projects 1707
. estate tax 1410
. property tax 1509
. . reinvestment zones 407, ; 1502
. sales and use taxes 1102
. . defense readjustment projects 1005
. . job creation in enterprise zone 1005
. . qualified hotel projects 1005
. . reinvestment zone property taxes 1005; 1502
. . use tax 1106; 1201

Regulated investment companies (RICs)
. franchise tax 303
. . federal/state key feature comparison 45

Reinvestment zones
. franchise tax
. . refund 407
. property tax
. . abatements 1502
. . refund 1509

Religious organizations
. franchise tax exemption 104
. property tax exemption 1504
. sales and use tax exemption 1004

Reorganization, corporate
. franchise tax 503

Repair services
. sales and use taxes 804
. . credit, contractors and repairpersons 1204
. . exemptions 1002

Reporting periods
. franchise tax 501

Reports—see Returns

Repossessions—see Returned goods and repossessions

Resale certificates
. sales and use taxes
. . exemptions 1003
. . penalties, improper use 1306
. . recordkeeping requirements 1107

Resales
. sales and use taxes
. . exemptions 1003

Research and development
. sales and use taxes
. . cooperative venture exemption 1005

Research expenses
. franchise tax 205
. . federal/state key feature comparison 45

Residents
. alcoholic beverages taxes 1702
. estate tax
. . computation of tax 1403
. . deductions 1408
. . property subject to tax 1407
. . taxable transfers 1405
. hotel occupancy tax
. . permanent resident 1707

Retirement plan services
. franchise tax 103

Returned goods and repossessions
. sales and use taxes 902

Returns
. administration and procedure 1803
. alcoholic beverages taxes 1702
. cigarette and tobacco products taxes 1703
. environmental taxes and fees 1710
. franchise tax
. . confidentiality 506
. . due dates 502
. . extensions 505
. . final report 504
. . privilege periods 501
. . reports 504
. . withdrawal, merger, consolidation, or conversion . . . 503
. gas production tax 1709
. gross premiums tax
. . insurance companies 1704
. hotel occupancy tax 1707
. motor fuel taxes 1705
. oil production tax 1709
. sales and use taxes
. . absorption of tax, prohibition 1108
. . administration 1109
. . confidentiality 1102
. . direct payment permits 1106
. . discounts 1103
. . due dates 1103
. . extensions 1803
. . generally 1101; 1102
. . information returns 1102
. . prepayment 1104
. . recordkeeping requirements 1107
. . vendor registration 1105
. sulphur production tax 1709
. unemployment compensation 1605
. utilities taxes 1708
. WebFile 1102

Revival of charter or certificate of authority
. franchise tax 605; 606; 607

Revival of corporate privileges
. franchise tax 604

REV

402 Topical Index

References are to paragraph (¶) numbers.

Revocation of permits or licenses
. administration and procedure 1908

S

S corporations
. franchise tax 103; 105
. . basis of tax 202, ... 204; 205
. . federal/state key feature comparison 45
. . reportable federal taxable income

Safe harbor leases
. franchise tax
. . federal/state key feature comparison 45

Sales and use taxes
. absorption of tax, prohibition 1108
. administration 1109
. alcoholic beverage sales reports 1102
. amusement services 804
. application, sales tax 802
. assessments 1302
. audits 1108
. bad debts 902
. boats and boat motors 903
. bracket schedule 906
. collection of tax 1301
. collection suits 1303; 1305
. confidentiality of returns 1102
. county transportation authorities 904
. coupons, premiums, trading stamps 902
. credits 1201
. . contractors and repairpersons 1204
. . property subsequently resold 1203
. . real property contributed to institution of higher
    learning 1205
. . return sales 1201
. . tax paid to another state 1202
. delivery charges 902
. direct payment permits 1102; 1106
. discounts 1103
. due dates, returns and payments 1103
. electronic form of delivery 802
. enterprise zones 1005
. exclusions 902
. exemption certificates 1006; 1106
. exemptions
. . organizations and persons 1004
. . property and services 1002
. . transactions 1003
. extensions of time 1803
. fireworks 903
. imports and exports 1003
. incidence of sales tax 802
. information returns 1102
. installation charges 902
. installment sales 902
. interest 1306
. judgments 1304
. local tax rate chart 905
. local tax rates 904
. manufactured housing 903
. mobile telecommunication services 804
. motor vehicles 903
. . standard presumptive value 902
. municipalities 904
. nexus 803
. occasional sales 1003
. offsets 1302
. out-of-state vendors 803
. overview 801
. payment of tax 1102
. . due dates 1103
. . prepayment 1104
. penalties 1306
. prepayment of taxes 1104
. purchase 802
. rate of tax 903
. receipts 902
. recordkeeping requirements 1107
. records 1107
. repair services 1002
. repossessions 902
. resale certificates 1003
. resales 1003

Sales and use taxes—continued
. retail grocer 1102
. retailer 802
. returned goods 902
. returns 1102
. . due dates 1103
. . in general 1101
. . prepayment 1104
. . WebFile 1102
. sale 802
. sales price 902
. sales tax permit 1105
. security requirements 1105
. seller 802
. services, taxable 804
. settlement of tax claims 801
. sourcing of local sales 904
. statute of limitations, collection 1305
. storage 805
. Streamlined sales and use tax agreement 801
. tax base 902
. tax holiday 1002
. trade-ins 902
. Uniform Sales and Use Tax Administration Act . . . 801
. use tax 805
. use tax collection permit 1105
. vendor registration 1105
. web hosting 803
. WebFile 1102

Sales tax permit 1105

Savings and loan associations
. franchise tax 103

School district taxes
. property tax
. . exemption 1504

Security
. administration and procedure
. . demand of security for tax 1902
. sales and use taxes
. . requirements, sales or use tax collection permits 1105

Security services
. sales and use taxes 804

Seed
. sales and use taxes
. . exemption 1002

Seizure of property
. administration and procedure 1905
. property tax 1507
. sales and use taxes 1305

Seller
. environmental taxes and fees
. . hazardous substances 1710
. sales and use taxes 802

Senior citizens
. sales and use taxes
. . exemptions 1004

Senior homeowners
. property tax
. . deferrals 1510
. . installment payment option 1506
. . school district taxes exemption 1504

Service of process 603

Services
. sales and use taxes 804; 1002
. . intercorporate 1003
. utilities taxes 1708

Settlement
. administration and procedure
. . tax claims and penalties 1903

Severance taxes—see Gas production tax; see also Oil production tax; see also Sulfur production tax

Sewer services
. utilities taxes 1708

Sexually-oriented business fee 1711

Shipment from out of state
. use tax 805

REV

Topical Index

References are to paragraph (¶) numbers.

Ships and vessels
. sales and use taxes
. . exemption 1002

Solar energy devices
. franchise tax
. . deductions 206
. . exemption, installers 104
. property tax
. . exemption 1504

Solid waste
. environmental taxes and fees
. . disposal fees 1710
. franchise tax
. . exemption, sludge recycling corporations 104
. sales and use taxes
. . exemption, removal 1002

Staff-leasing services
. franchise (margin) tax 202; 207
. sales and use taxes
. . exemptions 1002

Start-up expenditures, amortization
. franchise tax
. . federal/state key feature comparison 45

Statute of limitations
. administration and procedure
. . deficiencies 1901
. . suit to collect 1906
. . suit to recover erroneous refunds 1906
. property tax 1507
. sales and use taxes 1305

Storage tax
. sales and use taxes 805

Streamlined sales and use tax agreement
. sales and use taxes 801

Student loan corporations
. franchise tax
. . exemption 104

Subsidiaries
. franchise tax
. . investments 103

Suits
. administration and procedure
. . collection 1906
. . recovery, erroneous refunds 1906
. . refunds 2004
. . tax protest 2005
. franchise tax 603
. property tax
. . collection 1507
. sales and use taxes
. . collection 1303; 1305

Sulfur production tax 1709

T

Tangible personal property
. property tax
. . exemptions 1504
. . seizure of property 1507
. . subject to tax 1503
. sales and use taxes 802
. . value as trade-in 902

Tax evasion
. franchise tax
. . federal/state key feature comparison 45

Tax levy
. administration and procedure 1904

Tax liens
. administration and procedure 1904
. franchise tax 604
. property tax 1507

Taxes paid deduction
. franchise tax
. . federal/state key feature comparison 45

Taxpayer protest
. administration and procedure 1805
. . suit to protest 2005
. property tax 1509

Taxpayer remedies
. administration and procedure 2001
. . credits 2002
. . hearings 2003
. . injunction 2006
. . offsets 2002
. . redetermination 2003
. . refunds 2002
. . suit for refund 2004
. . suit to protest tax 2005
. estate tax
. . refunds 1410
. franchise tax
. . in general 701
. property tax 1509
. sales and use taxes
. . credits .... 1201—1204
. . refunds, enterprise zone projects 1005
. . use tax refund 1106

Taxpayers subject to tax
. franchise tax 103

Telecommunications Infrastructure Fund
. utilities taxes 1708

Telecommunications services
. sales and use taxes 804
. . mobile telecommunication services 804
. . exemptions 1002
. utilities taxes
. . telecommunications utilities 1708

Telephone answering services
. sales and use taxes 804

Telephone cooperative corporations
. franchise tax
. . exemption 104

Television stations
. sales and use taxes
. . exemption 1002

Texas Experimental Research and Recovery Activity (TERRA) 1709

Texas National Research Laboratory Commission
. franchise tax
. . exemptions 104
. sales and use taxes
. . exemption 1004

Texas Natural Resources Commission 1710

Timber operations
. sales and use taxes
. . exemption 1002

Timberland
. property tax
. . assessment 1505

Tips
. sales and use taxes 90

Tourist promotion agencies
. sales and use taxes
. . exemptions 1004

Trade-ins
. sales and use taxes 902

Transfers
. estate tax 1405

Transit authority sales and use taxes—see Local taxes

Transportation equipment
. sales and use taxes
. . exemptions 1002

True object test
. sales and use taxes 804

U

UDITPA
. franchise tax 302

UDI

Topical Index
References are to paragraph (¶) numbers.

Unclaimed property 2301

Unemployment compensation
. administration 1602
. benefits 1606
. coverage 1603
. definitions 1603
. disqualification period 1606
. employers subject to tax 1603
. exemptions 1603
. experience rates 1604
. imposition of tax 1602
. in general 1601
. labor disputes 1606
. payment of tax 1605
. rates 1604
. reports 1605
. returns 1605
. wages 1603

University and college student organizations
. sales and use taxes
. . exemption 1004

Use tax—see also Sales and use taxes
. overview 805
. penalties 1306
. rate of tax 903
. refund 1106

Use tax collection permit 1105

Utilities
. sales and use taxes
. . exemptions 1002
. . utilities taxes 1708

V

Valuation
. property tax 1505

Vending-machines sales
. sales and use taxes
. . exemptions 1002
. . tax base, vending machine food 902

Vendors
. sales and use taxes
. . optional reporting methods 1102
. . vendor registration 1105

Venue projects sales and use taxes—see Local taxes

Vessels
. property tax
. . exemption 1504

Vessels—continued
. property tax—continued
. . prepayment by dealers 1506

Veterans
. property tax
. . exemption 1504

W

Wages
. administration and procedure
. . refund, employees receiving financial assistance 2002
. franchise tax
. . compensation deduction 204
. labor costs for cost of goods sold deduction 205
. franchise tax, credits
. . employees receiving financial assistance 404
. unemployment compensation 1603

Waivers
. estate tax 1411
. property tax 1508

Waste removal
. environmental taxes and fees
. . disposal fees 1710
. franchise tax
. . exemptions 104
. sales and use taxes
. . exemptions 1002

Water services
. utilities taxes 1708

Watercraft
. property tax
. . exemption 1504

WebFile
. sales and use tax return filing 1102

Wind-powered energy devices
. property tax
. . exemption 1504

Wrapping, packing, and packaging supplies
. sales and use taxes
. . exemptions 1002

Y

Youth
. sales and use taxes
. . exemptions, specific organizations 1004

UNC